State *vs.* Defense

ALSO BY STEPHEN GLAIN

Mullahs, Merchants, and Militants:
The Economic Collapse of the Arab World

STATE *vs.* DEFENSE

*The Battle to Define
America's Empire*

STEPHEN GLAIN

Crown Publishers

NEW YORK

Library of Congress Cataloging-in-Publication Data

Glain, Stephen.
State vs. Defense: the battle to define America's empire / Stephen Glain.—1st ed.
p. cm.
Includes bibliographical references.
1. United States—Military policy—20th century.   2. United States—Military
policy—21st century.   3. United States—Foreign relations—1945–   4. Cold
War.   5. Radicalism—Religious aspects—Islam.   6. United States—Economic
conditions—21st century.   I. Title.
UA23.G634 2011
355'.033573—dc22   2010053206

ISBN 978-0-307-40841-9
eISBN 978-0-307-88898-3

Printed in the United States of America

Book design by Lauren Dong
Jacket design by Pete Garceau
Jacket and title page illustration: Granger Collection

10 9 8 7 6 5 4 3 2 1

First Edition

For Atticus and his extraordinary mother

CONTENTS

Preface

I grew up in a small Southern California town near Camp Pendleton, the world's largest U.S. Marine base. Many of my friends were the children of active-duty officers, and over Sunday dinner in the Seventeen Area, where the camp's flag billets were clustered, I would listen to their parents' talk of adventures in exotic lands. They were good storytellers, which stoked my wanderlust, and soon after graduating from college in 1985 I lit out on my own. For the next fourteen years, as a foreign correspondent in Asia and the Middle East, I would often find myself living and working in the countries that once hosted my friends and their families. Although the regions had changed dramatically, America's military presence had remained more or less intact. The Eighth Army, the Second Infantry Division, and the Seventh Air Force were still based in South Korea, defending what was by then one of the world's most prosperous countries from its famine-stricken neighbor. Japan, the world's third-largest economy, still played host to the Seventh Fleet, the Fifth Air Force, and the Marines' Third Expeditionary Force. In the Middle East, U.S. forces patrolled Egypt's Sinai Desert as they had since 1982 as part of a multinational peacekeeping force. The U.S. Central Command, the first of America's enormous combatant commands, operated throughout the Persian Gulf and the Gulf Cooperation Council, launched in 1981, had mushroomed into a sprawling network of U.S. bases and naval port facilities. The North Atlantic Treaty Organization, a Cold War alliance established to prevent the Soviet Union from overrunning Western Europe, was seeking new adversaries and manufacturing new missions to sustain itself.

The longer I lived overseas, the more it became apparent that America was increasingly represented abroad not by teachers, doctors, engineers, or even diplomats but by men and women in military uniform. And although I liked and respected the soldiers, airmen, sailors, and Marines I so frequently encountered, it struck me that their growing prevalence relative to their civilian counterparts was more consistent with an empire than a republic. Having seen the long-term consequences of imperialism in countries as varied as Vietnam and Iraq, I was disturbed by this. At the same time, there was an obvious divergence between the expansion of the nation's imperial writ and its necessity. The Cold War was over, Russia and its former satellites had withdrawn into a postimperial introspection, and China, well into what would be an irreversible modernization drive, showed no signs of coveting anything beyond its historical sphere of influence that dated back thousands of years. North Korea, Iraq, and Iran, identified during the Clinton administration as primary security threats, seemed from the inside to be of greater menace to themselves than they would ever be to the United States. By the time I came home, in summer 2001, I worried that Washington not only sought dominion, it did so for its own sake.

America's militant response to the September 11 attacks—the wrongheaded evaluation of radical Islam's composition and motives; the decision to wage a world war against what is, at heart, a political movement; the invasion of Iraq—confirmed my worst fears. To much of humanity, America was changing from a de facto to a de jure empire. The militarist instinct to embellish threats, to overreach, to smother allies as well as antagonists in the relentless need for control, to resist the possibility that there may be *less* to things than meets the eye, has done more to subvert the framers' republican vision than any external threat that confronts the United States today. Worse, despite the enormous damage caused by American militarists over the last decade, to say nothing of the last century, their influence is still potent enough to delude politicians and perhaps even presidents into believing that America has an interest in going to war with China. Nothing could be further from the truth, particularly among those who respect it. It is in that spirit that I wrote this book.

INTRODUCTION

If you believe the doctors, nothing is wholesome;
if you believe the theologians, nothing is innocent;
if you believe the military, nothing is safe.
—LORD SALISBURY

NEWS TRAVELS FAST ACROSS THE RED DESERT BUSH OF REMOTE Djibouti. Even as U.S. military reservists hurry to erect a small field hospital around a cluster of tents and vacant blockhouses near a desolate watering hole, dozens of tribespeople are waiting for treatment in orderly rows. They arrive with maladies of every sort—bad teeth, diarrhea, fevers, colds, arthritis. At the triage center, a middle-aged tribesman has had a thorn removed from the instep of his foot, a wound that had been infected for months. At the dental surgery station, Navy lieutenant Bill Anderson, an orthodontist from Northfield, New Jersey, will over the next few hours extract a dozen rotting or impacted teeth using instruments that sparkle in the late-morning sun. His patients endure their operations without so much as a wince or low groan, and he gives each one an antibiotic rinse to prevent infection.

It is 2008, and this Medical Civil Action Program, as it is known, is provided courtesy of Combined Joint Task Force–Horn of Africa, an 1,800-man deployment of soldiers, sailors, airmen, and Marines. The base was established in Djibouti, an enclave of calm in an unstable area, immediately after the September 11 attacks. Al Qaeda units, it was feared, would take advantage of the chaos in neighboring Somalia and nest there. When no terrorists turned up, the task force was assigned to perform humanitarian initiatives with the guidance of the United States Agency for International Development, the State Department's foreign-assistance arm.

Embedded in the operation is a lone USAID official. Her minority status is symptomatic of a new age in U.S. foreign policy, one in which America, in peacetime as well as in war, is represented abroad more by warriors than by civilians.

Quietly, gradually—and inevitably, given the weight of its colossal budget and imperial writ—the Pentagon has all but eclipsed the State Department at the center of U.S. foreign policy. The process began just over a century ago, gathered pace with World War II, and hit its stride during the Cold War with a global empire that not only survived the collapse of the Soviet Union but was greatly enhanced by it. Even before terrorists struck the nation on September 11, America was spring-loaded for conflict on many fronts. A decade later, U.S. troops are engaged in the country's longest war in addition to counterinsurgency and developmental assistance work throughout the world. At the same time, the capability of the nation's diplomatic and foreign aid agencies has dramatically diminished. While four-star generals wield enormous influence among U.S. allies, ambassadors and senior USAID officials are regarded more and more as functionaries and contractors. They are saddled with chronic staff shortages, eroded language skills, and low morale. In an era of endless war, a growing share of diplomats and aid workers are assigned to missions in areas so hazardous they require armed escorts when traveling. And unlike their uniformed counterparts, they lack replacement staff for regular rotations. In the increasingly tight competition for humanitarian and development funds, they are losing out to the Pentagon, now the federal government's fastest-growing source of foreign aid.

Even Robert Gates, the former CIA director and the defense secretary to both presidents George W. Bush and Barack Obama, has lamented the militarization of America's presence overseas. He has called for a significant boost in the State Department–USAID budgets, so that diplomats and development experts can bring more to the evolving partnership between civilian agencies and the military in the battle for hearts and minds. This implies, of course, that military might is key to the resolution of America's global challenges, when in fact it creates more problems than it solves. Twenty years after the end of the Cold War, political leaders in

Washington and their proconsuls abroad continue to behave as if U.S. hegemony is not only inevitable and necessary but sustainable and desired. It is a costly misperception that led, at least in part, to the September 11 attacks and America's ruinous involvement in Iraq and Afghanistan. With the geopolitical map shifting from a U.S.-centric world back to a Victorian-era cluster of competing regional powers, the myth of American exceptionalism has been dispelled nearly everywhere but in Washington.

American militarism is unique for its civilian provenance. It did not follow a barracks coup or a popular call for a man on horseback to impose order on an unraveling republic. No martial law was declared and there is no military cabal pulling the strings of a nominal civilian authority. In fact, it is largely civilians who have played the dominant role in weaponizing foreign policy abroad and security policy at home. Of the militarists profiled in these pages, only two of them—Generals Douglas MacArthur and Curtis LeMay—were military men. The balance consists mostly of legislators and civil servants who for myriad reasons primed the nation for needless war and manipulated presidents into waging them. It is an ecumenical order, ranging from the liberal President Woodrow Wilson, who in mistaking Russia's communist revolution for a German cat's-paw launched Washington's first adventure in regime change, to George W. Bush and his neoconservative cadres, who consecrated global hegemony as an American entitlement and maneuvered the nation into Iraq.

However diverse in temperament and background, American militarists throughout the last century share common values and proclivities: In the algorithms of global affairs they see a simple contest between good and evil, and in engagement they see a graveyard filled with grand, game-changing initiatives. Their reality is selective, a buffet rather than a set-course meal, from which convenient facts may be selected and neatly presented. Their impulse is not to reason but to alarm, and they freely concoct dangers when real ones are unavailable. For much of the Cold War, they believed in a communist monolith that never existed. Until the day the Berlin Wall fell, they promoted Pentagon exaggerations of Soviet power abroad while overlooking its crippling weaknesses at home.

Today, they counsel an armed onslaught against an Islamist movement that cannot be subdued by force, and they agitate for a militarized response to a resurgent China, which, if pursued as effectively as their other star-crossed enterprises, will make a war between the United States and the world's most populous nation all but inevitable. They have disparaged not only the agents of diplomacy but diplomacy itself, impoverishing the State Department and USAID and compelling the military to fill a growing share of what were once the roles and responsibilities of civilians. The Pentagon, wisely identifying such missions as a growth industry in the absence of a clear and present military threat, is very much along for the ride. A half century after Dwight Eisenhower's historic warning about an aggrandizing "military-industrial complex," American militarization is an established and probably immutable fact. It is a manifestation of the founders' deepest fears and the worst betrayal of the nation's republican ideals.

The lawyers, farmers, and merchants who shaped late-eighteenth-century America were preoccupied not with military adventures but with commerce. They had seen how permanent military bureaucracies in Europe had routinely eroded civilian authority and they emphatically rejected a standing army for their infant republic. In 1796 the outgoing President George Washington spoke for a nation of citizen-soldiers when he said that unity and neutrality would safeguard American interests far more efficiently than "overgrown military establishments which . . . are to be regarded as particularly hostile to republican liberty."

If the founders were suspicious of standing armies led by Prussian-style general staffs, they held the European tradition of diplomacy in similarly low esteem—to the point of ambivalence about whether the United States should have a diplomatic corps. Serving President Washington as America's first secretary of state, Thomas Jefferson led a department with three clerks, two ambassadors, and ten counselors posted abroad. Even then, lawmakers considered high diplomacy a luxury and would deny the nation's envoys the resources enjoyed by their counterparts across the Atlantic. There would be no European-style academies for the study of languages, culture, history, and protocol. Jefferson's budget, at $56,000, was so tight he was forced to sell a horse and some of his furniture to keep America's overseas missions adequately funded.

For much of the nineteenth century, it was diplomats, more often than not men in morning suits and top hats, who represented the United States as it extended its sovereign frontier westward and beyond. William Henry Seward, secretary of state to presidents Abraham Lincoln and Andrew Johnson, famously negotiated the purchase of Alaska from Russia for the equivalent today of $95 million. John Hay, statesman, author, journalist, and one of the most agile and renowned American minds of his era, began his career in government at the age of twenty-two as Lincoln's assistant private secretary. In 1898, as President William McKinley's secretary of state, he negotiated the Treaty of Paris that ended the Spanish-American War on terms favorable to Washington. In the early 1900s, he was an influential promoter of the Open Door Policy toward China, which gave Washington pole position in the extraterritorial rush among Western powers and Japan to colonize the coastal rim of China. Hay also shepherded the transfer of U.S. authority over what would become the Panama Canal from its French concessionaire.

Throughout his prolific career, Hay presided over some fifty bilateral and multilateral treaties. It was the high renaissance of American diplomacy and it succeeded too well. On behalf of a republic, Hay had negotiated the foundations of empire. It now required a military to build one.

Like so many of its recent wars, imperial America was itself a needless extravagance. The country is not an island nation like Britain or Japan, critically dependent on outside sources for raw materials and energy supplies. Nor was it forced to punch above its weight like tiny Belgium or Holland, wedged between rival and often hostile powers. The United States enjoyed a huge domestic market, was rich in natural resources, and was safely distant from potential aggressors. Instead of managing costly armies and imperial projects that had defined and debilitated Europe, America had wisely invested in the sinew and gray matter of a modern, self-reliant, and prosperous state: education, a transparent judicial system, railroads, seaports, agriculture, and industry.

The more America prospered, however, the greater its hunger for expansionism became. By the end of the nineteenth century, militarists in Washington and the media were angling for war with Spain and, sotto voce, its stable of dependencies. Bourgeois evangelicals who were already building churches and universities in Latin America, Asia, and the Middle East knew that a colonial system meant whole new tributaries of redeemable souls for the netting. American industry, most prominently tropical food processors such as United Fruit Company and the Hawaiian Pineapple Company (later known as the Dole Food Company), together with their financiers, similarly craved new markets and suppliers.*

Opponents, meanwhile, argued that empire was antithetical to American ideals. In 1898 former president Grover Cleveland warned that expansionism was a "perversion of our national mission . . . to build up and make a greater country out of what we have instead of annexing islands." A year later, the sociologist William Graham Sumner warned that Americans "cannot govern dependencies with our political system, and . . . if we try it, the state which our fathers founded will suffer a reaction that will transform it into another empire just after the fashion of the old ones. That is what imperialism means."

To this, hegemonists had a ready answer: the nation's colonial mission was a righteous enterprise, divinely inspired. Accepting his Republican Party's nomination for governor of New York in October 1898, Theodore

---

* Smedley Butler, a Marine major general who at the time of his death in 1940 was the most decorated Marine in U.S. history, served on nearly every front where U.S. troops were engaged, from the Philippines in 1899 to World War I to China in the late 1920s. In his book *War Is a Racket,* he cites the close link between corporate America and military interventions abroad:

> I spent 33 years and four months in active military service and during that period I spent most of my time as a high class muscle man for Big Business, for Wall Street and the bankers. In short, I was a racketeer, a gangster for capitalism. I helped make Mexico and especially Tampico safe for American oil interests in 1914. I helped make Haiti and Cuba a decent place for the National City Bank boys to collect revenues in. I helped in the raping of half a dozen Central American republics for the benefit of Wall Street. I helped purify Nicaragua for the International Banking House of Brown Brothers in 1902–1912. I brought light to the Dominican Republic for the American sugar interests in 1916. I helped make Honduras right for the American fruit companies in 1903. In China in 1927 I helped see to it that Standard Oil went on its way unmolested. Looking back on it, I might have given Al Capone a few hints. The best he could do was to operate his racket in three districts. I operated on three continents.

Roosevelt delivered a soaring, chauvinist oration. Admonishing a packed crowd at Carnegie Hall against "a life of fossilized isolation," and with U.S. troops mopping up resistance in Cuba and the Philippines, Roosevelt played the White Messiah card. The American flag, he said, "stands for liberty and civilization. Where it has once floated, there must and shall be no return to tyranny or savagery." It is no wonder that, while Franklin D. Roosevelt is the darling of the American left, militarists on the right are besotted with his excitable uncle.

Americans would have their empire, an enterprise rooted in the belief system of American exceptionalism that dates back to the seventeenth century, when religious exiles fancied the colonies a new Jerusalem ordained to Christianize a pagan land. Like the ideological impulse that drove it, American empire would differ from its European counterparts. There would be no colonial office, for example, no large administrative bureaucracies in villas and bungalows led by citizens from the mother stem and staffed by the foreign unfortunates. American empire would come in a carapace of large-scale military deployments and bases to accommodate them, together with pre-positioned arms depots and commissaries stocked with material goods from home. In concert with allied armies, key constituents in U.S. foreign relations, it would flex its expeditionary muscle through joint exercises with such code names as Cobra Gold and Team Spirit.

Geography, which made American empire unnecessary in the first place, now perversely accounts for its resilience. The United States, corseted as it is by two vast oceans, is the only country rich enough to afford the modern warships needed to patrol them. Most Americans, meanwhile, wrongly credit the warships, rather than the oceans, as the reason they can take security for granted. When the United States makes war, it does so in obscure, distant lands, and a vast majority of Americans are happily estranged from the conflicts waged in their name. For the 99.5 percent of the population that constitutes the civilian demographic, war is something experienced as a video game or an HBO miniseries, if at all.

Decades ago, when military service in America was compulsory, U.S. Army Chief of Staff General Fred C. Weyand wrote that "the American

Army really is a people's Army in the sense that it belongs to the American people, who take a jealous and propriety interest in its involvement. . . . The Army, therefore, cannot be committed lightly." Weyand's remarks are as dated as conscription. Since the collapse of the Soviet Union, Washington has waged war eight more times than it did during its sixty-year confrontation with Moscow. Precisely because the U.S. military is professional and largely segregated from civilian society, it is deployed not only lightly but promiscuously, often out of domestic political imperatives rather than national security interests and in ways that evade public knowledge altogether.

As of 2007, the Pentagon acknowledged the concentration of 190,000 troops and 115,000 civilian employees inside 909 military facilities in forty-six countries and territories. They included, for example, Balad Air Base in Iraq, which covers sixteen square miles, with an additional twelve-square-mile "security perimeter" large enough to be seen from outer space. In August 2010, President Barack Obama declared that America's major combat mission in Iraq was over. Balad Air Base, however, like Pentagon installations that have been around since the early years of the Cold War, is going nowhere.

The price of America's military base network overseas, along with the expense of its national security state at home, is enormous. There is the Defense Department's budget of more than $700 billion, of course, but beyond that is a host of related outlays that get little attention. There is the Department of Energy's $20 billion expense for nuclear weapons research and storage. The country's intelligence community, a subculture of sixteen agencies that engage in everything from satellite reconnaissance to cloak-and-dagger espionage, is funded from a "black" budget estimated conservatively at about $75 billion. The Department of Veterans Affairs is the federal government's third-richest agency, with a funding mandate of over $120 billion, while the Department of Homeland Security draws nearly $45 billion. The Department of the Treasury spends another $25 billion or so underwriting veterans' retirement plans. Add to all this the interest owed on the money Washington borrows to pay for national security—America is a net debtor, after all—and the bill comes in at well over $1 trillion. That is equal to nearly 8 percent of gross domestic product and more than 20 percent of the federal budget. (By comparison, China, Russia, Iran, and North Korea, the four countries Pentagon planners routinely trot out as conventional threats to the general welfare, have cumulative defense expenditures of less than $200 billion.) These are only the known costs of hegemony. In July 2010, the *Washington Post* published a three-part exposé of a post–September 11 "top-secret world," a counterinsurgency network that had become "so large, so unwieldy and so secretive that no one knows how much money it costs, how many people it employs, how many programs exist within it or exactly how many agencies do the same work."

In February 2011, facing trillion-dollar budget deficits for the next decade, President Barack Obama called for a five-year freeze on all domestic discretionary spending. But he exempted Medicare, Medicaid, and Social Security, the entitlement programs that consume nearly two-thirds of the federal budget, as well as funding for the Pentagon, the Veterans Administration, and homeland security, which accounts for nearly everything else. In late 2010, a presidential debt-reduction commission called for a 15 percent cut in the Pentagon's procurement budget, a three-year freeze in noncombatant military pay, and a reduction in its overseas deployments by a third. This met with howls of opposition, from the halls of Congress to the respected *Small Wars Journal,* an electronic journal focused on the culture and mechanics of counterinsurgency. Deep cuts in weapons procurement and research, argued its managing editor in a November 11 post, amounted to an unacceptable concession to "emerging peer competitors like China" while posing "higher risks to [U.S.] alliances in East Asia and around the Persian Gulf." The federal budget, it seems, has become a $3.8 trillion perpetual trust—rolled over annually by America's foreign creditors—for the armed services and their contractors, the elderly, and the infirm.

As of this writing, lawmakers from both sides of the legislative aisle are talking seriously about cutting defense outlays, a measure of how advanced is the nation's fiscal decay. Unveiling the Defense Department's 2012 budget, Secretary Gates placed several costly weapons programs on the chopping block and called for a "culture of savings" to replace the Pentagon's "culture of spending." Inevitably, that will put him on a collision course with politicians who cling to armaments projects for the employment opportunities they offer constituents back home. For them, the dividing line between national security and job security is all but invisible, and as a result even obsolete weapons have survived sustained attempts by Gates and his predecessors to have them killed. Moreover, long after the current budget debate is resolved, the State Department will still be struggling to make do with a fraction of the resources enjoyed by the Pentagon. Until that imbalance is reconciled, the militarization of U.S. foreign policy will only proliferate.

It is unusual, perhaps unprecedented, for a government to wage simultaneous wars while sparing all but a fraction of its citizens from their human costs. This creates its own kind of vulnerability. As the soldier-historian John McAuley Palmer noted between the world wars, professional armies subvert democracy because they "relieve the people themselves of the duty of self-defense. . . . An enduring government by the people must include an army of the people among its vital institutions." Elaborating on this, Boston University professor and Vietnam veteran Andrew Bacevich has written that "the ideal relationship between the armed forces and democratic society is a symbiotic one, in which each draws nourishment from the other. Symbiosis implies intimacy. . . . Whatever its other merits, the present-day professionalized force is not conducive to civil-military intimacy."

State vs. Defense, the century-old competition between those who would confront America's overseas challenges through diplomatic means and those who would subdue them by force of arms, is all but decided. The economic and political resources commanded by the latter group are vast and powerful, while the former has been reduced to a cadre of supplicants forced to beg before the lavish table of the national security state. Such a lopsided state of affairs has been abetted by a citizenry generally uninterested in the policies carried out in its name and unwilling to share in the burden of their prosecution. Only now, with the specter of bankruptcy looming over the national accounts, are some in Washington daring to contest the bill for, if not the value of, unchecked global hegemony.*

At the close of the Constitutional Convention in 1787, Benjamin Franklin was asked if the delegates had adopted a monarchy or a republic. "A Republic," Franklin famously replied, "if you can keep it." Franklin and his contemporaries worried that the democracy they inspired would, like republican Rome, which Palladian Washington so closely resembles, be enveloped by militarism and empire. Today, the United States is struggling under the weight of both. Nor has the nation evolved much beyond its regard of diplomacy as a mistress who, for the sake of irregular service, is kept on a miserly retainer.

This book examines how and why American leaders realized their founders' dread by succumbing to the sirens of militarism and the costs of their rapture. It considers the uniquely American impulse to choose force over statesmanship when inconvenienced abroad. It weighs the hazards of exempting all but a tiny share of the public from the human costs of empire, and it offers a frank appraisal of the financial burden. It begins in early 1947, when America was reborn as a global powerhouse and steered by a handful of men who, for their modesty and judiciousness, had more in common with their eighteenth-century predecessors than with the political elites who came after them. If truth is the first casualty of war, the unkindest cut of global imperium may well be to measured restraint.

---

* In January 2010, with the budget process revving to life, a confederation of deficit hawks and libertarians formed around the need to cut defense spending by as much as one-fifth of the Pentagon's overall outlay over a ten-year period. On neither side of the legislative aisle, however, was there a willingness to simultaneously increase funding for America's diplomatic and aid agencies.

1

ARCHETYPE

This was the noblest Roman of them all.
—William Shakespeare, *Julius Caesar*

George Catlett Marshall had been Harry Truman's
new secretary of state for sixteen days when his train pulled
into Washington, D.C.'s Union Station on January 21, 1947. He
had arrived tanned and rested after spending a two-week holiday with
his wife in Hawaii, though now he was wrapped in the beaver-trimmed
camel hair coat he had worn two years earlier at the Yalta Conference,
where the postwar world had been struck. It was cold—the temperature
was in the mid-30s and the forecast was for subfreezing weather—and
Marshall was blasted by powerful gales as he stepped onto the station platform. The elements, it seemed, were colluding with the cold peace that
was growing increasingly bitter between the world's capitalist and communist realms.

The confidence inspired at Yalta—that the United States and the Soviet Union could coexist peacefully within agreed-upon spheres of
influence—had quickly evaporated. In spring 1946, Moscow refused to
withdraw its forces from Iran despite stern warnings from Washington,
fueling a crisis that peaked only after Russia was guaranteed a twenty-
five-year oil concession in the country. In August, Truman ordered a
naval task force to enter the Turkish Straits, where the USS *Missouri* had
already been deployed, in response to Soviet demands for basing rights
there. Earlier, on March 5, Winston Churchill had declared at Westminster College in Fulton, Missouri, that the Soviet Union had incarcerated
half of Europe behind an "iron curtain." A year later, American financier
and presidential adviser Bernard Baruch coined a new phrase to describe
the escalating tensions. "Let us not be deceived," he told an audience in

South Carolina. "We are today in the midst of a cold war." The term was seized upon by journalists and pundits, particularly their high priest, Walter Lippmann.

Yet battle-weary Americans wore their superpower mantle uneasily and they were conflicted over how to move forward. Was confrontation or accommodation the best way to handle an expansionist Moscow? The division extended to Truman's own cabinet. On September 12, 1946, Commerce Secretary Henry Wallace addressed a rally at Madison Square Garden held in opposition to Republican Thomas E. Dewey's bid for reelection as New York governor. A dove by contemporary standards, Wallace had already sent Truman a long memo criticizing the White House for provoking the Soviets, and his speech at the Garden blasted what he characterized as an overly aggressive U.S. foreign policy. Secretary of State James Byrnes, who was in Paris negotiating peace treaties with the former Axis allies and who counseled a tougher line with Moscow, threatened to resign after learning of Wallace's oration. When Truman tried to distance himself from the dispute by telling reporters he had not been given an advance copy of Wallace's speech—in fact, Wallace had given the president a line-by-line brief of what he was going to deliver and said so at the Garden—*Time* magazine condemned the president's "clumsy lie." The affair convulsed Truman's presidency. Wallace resigned within days and Byrnes, whom Truman respected but never trusted—"able and conniving" was how the president referred to him in his diary—would be out by the end of the year.

Ironically—and illustrative of an entrenched paradox of U.S. foreign policy—George Marshall was in China at the time, negotiating with the same communist menace that hard-liners like Byrnes were trying to isolate. A year earlier, and within hours after Marshall retired as Army chief of staff, Truman had named the general his special envoy to China, where he was to mediate a truce between Mao Zedong's Red Army and Chiang Kai-shek's Nationalists. (Truman had announced his decision on the radio without notifying Marshall, knowing it would corner the general into accepting what he knew would be a thankless job.) Now, with the future of the free world seemingly in the balance, Truman abandoned China to its fate. He recruited Dwight Eisenhower, who was en route to Asia on an inspection tour, to recruit Marshall to replace Byrnes.

Marshall's appointment would force him to postpone his retirement for the second time in twelve months. His wife, Katherine, despaired of the burden such a commitment would have on her aging husband's health. Dean Acheson, Byrne's undersecretary and not one inclined to hyperbole, described Marshall's return to Washington as "an act of God."

Marshall was met at Union Station by his liaison officer with the State Department and the military, who delivered to the new secretary of state what would be one of his first communiqués as America's top diplomat. Marshall read the note as he approached a covey of shivering reporters. It was from James Shepley, a journalist with *Time-Life,* who warned the new secretary that his name was being circulated as a possible presidential contender. Left unchecked, such talk could jeopardize Marshall's position with congressional Republicans, who would be reluctant to support the policies of a potential Democratic candidate for president. It could also strain his relations with Truman, who was vying for the 1948 nomination. Marshall parried with the reporters for several minutes and then, fielding no questions about his presidential ambitions, he struck preemptively. It was a good time, he announced, to neutralize any speculation about his political future beyond his current assignment. "I am being explicit and emphatic in order to terminate once and for all any discussion of my name with regard to political office," he declared. The centripetal pull of the White House, irresistible to other men, had no purchase on George Marshall.

Attributed to anyone else, even a conclusive statement like that could be interpreted as pretense. But in Marshall there was no such guile. His strength of character and sureness in command were as cherished and as vital a national asset as Franklin Roosevelt's abundant, occasionally devious charm. In January 1944, with history's most lethal slaughter coming to a close, *Time* magazine named Marshall its "Man of the Year," lauding him as "the closest thing to the 'indispensable man'" and a "trustee for the nation" for his lack of political ambition. "In a general's uniform," the magazine decreed, "he stood for the civilian substance of this democratic society."

It was a fair—if gushing—tribute, and one that ages well. For Marshall, the covenant of a civilian-controlled military was as sacred as any religion. While testifying on Capitol Hill with his civilian counterparts, he would insist they precede him into hearing rooms in a show of deference to their authority. To Sam Rayburn, the most powerful lawmaker of the last century and another giant of his age, Marshall had "the presence of a great man. . . . He laid it on the line. He would tell the truth even if it hurt his cause. Congress respected him." Marshall succeeded in a city where candor and integrity were (and remain) an unheard-of state of affairs. For his refusal to support the creation of Israel, which he believed would envelop the Middle East in endless conflict and harm U.S. interests there, an exasperated lawmaker paid him this uniquely Washingtonian compliment: "All he can see is the point."

Few Americans have made decisions of such seismic and transcendent importance with so light a touch. No one did more to project U.S. military might worldwide, nor has anyone understood better its power to corrupt republican ideals. In 1943, with Eisenhower's armies having cleared enemy troops from North Africa and Italy, a fierce debate erupted in Washington over whether civilian or military agencies should administer subdued Axis countries. Roosevelt, sympathetic to Eisenhower's complaints of inadequate civilian management in Africa, instructed Marshall, his chief of staff, to set up military governments. Marshall did as he was told, though it was the most delicate and unappetizing of assignments. For him, the journey from liberator to occupier was swift and perilous, one that would test the U.S. military's greatest and most vulnerable asset: restraint. Having formed a civil affairs unit of military governors, Marshall assigned General John Hilldring to lead it. Then, in a hasty transfer-of-command ceremony, he issued a statement that resonates today.

> We are completely devoted, we are members of a priesthood really, the sole purpose of which is to defend the republic. . . . This is the sacred trust that I am turning over to you today. . . . And I don't want you to . . . permit the enormous corps of military governors that you are in the process of training and that you are going to dispatch all over the world, to damage this high regard in which

the professional soldiers in the Army are held by our people. . . .
This is my principal charge to you, this is the thing I never want you
to forget in the dust of battle and when the pressures will be on you.

George Marshall was first among equals in a fraternity of civilian and
military elites who, though not above petty rivalry, charted a prudent
course throughout the often harrowing early years of the Cold War.
For the next four decades, storm-tossed by Red Scares, nuclear show-
downs, proxy wars, and an at-times imperious Pentagon, it was Marshall's
America—modest in appetites, pious but not messianic in faith, respectful
and nurturing of its allies, wary of militarism, and judicious in its use of
force—that prevailed. More than anyone else, George Marshall made the
last century a uniquely American one.

He was born in 1880 in Uniontown, Pennsylvania, the son of an independent businessman and the product of a blue-blood lineage that
included, remotely at least, the great Supreme Court justice John Marshall. It was the twilight of the Victorian era and the dawning of America's
imperialist identity. In declaring war against Spain in 1898, Washington
sided with Old Europe in the global divide between occupiers and occupied, rulers and ruled. When Commodore George Dewey, commanding the U.S. Navy's Asiatic Squadron aboard the USS *Olympia,* attacked
Spain's forlorn fleet in the Philippines' Manila Bay ("You may fire when
you are ready, Gridley," he had calmly said to *Olympia*'s captain), he was
announcing America's arrival as a colonial power and an industrial leviathan.

It would be a rude introduction, however. What had begun as a "splendid little war," as the future secretary of state John Hay would call it, had
become a costly adventure. After easily ejecting the Spanish from the
Philippines, U.S. forces were soon faced with an insurgency that would
take a decade to subdue and consume much of Washington's military resources. Among the thousands of American troops who were churned
through what quickly became known as the Philippine-American War
was a twenty-two-year-old George Marshall, fresh from the Virginia Military Institute with the rank of second lieutenant. He graduated in 1902,
just in time to ship out with Company G of the Thirtieth Infantry.

By the time Marshall arrived in Manila, it was clear the U.S. commander there, Major General Arthur MacArthur, was failing to subdue the insurrection by cracking down on every shadow of subversion. He was replaced by a civilian commission led by William Howard Taft, all 326 pounds of him, who complained in a letter to Secretary of War Elihu Root that his predecessor trusted only "the strong hand of the military." This was quickly understood by Marshall, who had already developed an instinct that would serve him well throughout his career: empathy. He had studied official reports of maladministration under MacArthur and concluded that restoring civilian authority was the best way to gain the support of the local population and starve the insurgency. Anticipating by nearly a century the use of public affairs officers in U.S. counterinsurgency operations today, Marshall suggested turning the Army's most gifted young leaders into civil affairs specialists who, he said, "would have a much better understanding of the point of view of these fellows who suffered the torture of the damned, as it were, than would the man who had just come from the States." Marshall opposed the interrogation technique dubbed "the water cure," known today as waterboarding, used on captured *insurrectos* to make them talk. The process was primitive and brutish, he said, and the results were unreliable.

Prior to becoming a staff officer, Marshall distinguished himself as a master logistician, trainer, and planner. While battling Philippine insurgents in 1913, Lieutenant Henry H. Arnold remembered watching Marshall lying against a thicket of bamboo and glancing at a map while coolly giving orders for the advance. Arnold, who would be named commander of the U.S. Army Air Forces in World War II, would later write his wife that Marshall's performance was no doubt that of a future chief of staff. During World War I, Marshall excelled not on the battlefield—in fact, he would never see extensive combat up close—but as director of training and planning under General John Pershing. In 1918, during the last two months of the war, he so impressed the French with his logistical work that he earned the nickname "Wizard."

Throughout his career, Marshall was defined less by class or social rank in an America still defined by Victorian hierarchy than by a cool professionalism that alternated between gruff and graceful. As Roosevelt's Army chief of staff, he could be ruthless with unprepared subordinates during briefings but rewarded independent and enterprising thinkers.

One of those men, Omar Bradley, was an assistant secretary on Marshall's general staff from 1939 to 1942. After his first week on the job, he remembered his boss convening a meeting in his office and complaining that not one staff member had disagreed with him on a single issue. "Unless I hear all the arguments against something," he told them, "I am not sure whether I have made the right decision or not." In conferences, Marshall signaled his opinions only by the questions he put to his staff officers. He would shape written proposals through endless revisions, usually with margin notes or through casual discussions with aides and division heads, then consecrate them with a brusque "Do it" to a staff member or "Send this out" scrawled on the top of a memo.

Marshall was sworn in as Army chief of staff on September 1, 1939, the day Germany invaded Poland, and it was at Roosevelt's side where his storied candor would fully assert itself. During Marshall's first cabinet meeting, on November 14, 1939, the president outlined a plan to build 10,000 military aircraft for England and France as a deterrent against the Nazis. Roosevelt did most of the talking, a virtual monologue, with cabinet members nodding their heads in solemn agreement. Marshall, now a full general but ever the canny logistician, sat quietly as he listened to what he knew was a half-baked scheme. Finally, FDR turned to Marshall—"George," as the president referred to his new chief of staff, who responded to his first name only with his most intimate friends and family members—and asked him if he agreed.

"I am sorry, Mr. President," Marshall replied, "but I don't agree with that at all."

That ended the meeting. The president, startled, ushered away his aides, several of whom intimated to Marshall later that he was damaged goods and not long for his tour in Washington. Roosevelt, however, having met the limits of his legendary charm, happily kept Marshall on. Over the course of their six-year partnership, Roosevelt would tell close aides that he couldn't sleep on the rare occasions his chief of staff was out of Washington. And he never again referred to him by his first name.

It is easy to forget, given the extent of American militarization today, how pacifist the nation was less than a century ago. If Washington's imperial overreach following the collapse of the Soviet Union and the September 11 terrorist attacks led to foreign policy disasters and the erosion of America's image abroad, its post–World War I retreat into isolationism was just as foolhardy. Reversing that parochial bias and the way he went about it remains one of Marshall's most important achievements.

Though the nation was a minor imperial power by the late nineteenth century, most Americans were opposed to foreign adventures and the means of entering into them. In this way, they were merely keeping faith with the founding fathers' suspicions of large standing armies and foreign alliances. Throughout the first 150 years of its history, what stood for an armed force in the United States was a loose array of scattered bases and poorly trained and underpaid personnel. Like an accordion, stagnant defense budgets would expand in wartime and then contract again once the fighting ended. American participation in World War I was motivated less by a desire to help the Allies than as a prophylactic measure against the kind of creeping militarization George Washington had warned against in his farewell speech. "Many Americans," wrote Walter Lippmann, who served in the Wilson administration as an adviser, "saw in 1917 that if Germany won, the United States would have to face a new and aggressively expanding German empire [which] would require immense armaments . . . and a perpetual state of high and alert military preparedness." In the closing days of the war, Marshall warned his superiors against a march on Berlin because it would delay demobilization beyond the point where Germany's forces had been neutralized. Instead—and here we have a glimpse of the mind that would later inspire the greatest postwar rebuilding plan in history—he recommended the Allies invest their energies in German reconstruction. Tragically, his advice was ignored.

In the immediate aftermath of World War I, in which 170,000 U.S. troops perished in a war that presumed to have abolished conflict, an alliance of religious groups, labor unions, and intellectuals opposed a War Department request for a standing army of half a million men, forcing Congress to back down. A year later, the Senate considered legislation that would provide four months of military training for all able-bodied men between the ages of nineteen and twenty-one. A grassroots campaign forced its Republican sponsors to withdraw the bill. In 1921 Congress slashed the defense budget. In 1922, at the Washington Naval Disarmament Conference, the United States entered into a treaty with its World War I allies, including Japan, to limit their naval power. Over the years, a pacifist America would allow its naval capability to slip below treaty thresholds.

Almost alone in an isolationist wilderness, Marshall, as Army chief of staff, toiled for congressional funding to expand and modernize the armed forces. At the time, compulsory military service was limited to one year, which was hardly enough time to hew draftees into a competent fighting force. Underfunded, unpopular, and badly equipped, the military suffered from low morale as well as poor readiness. To make matters worse, Roosevelt and his social welfare programs had become deeply unpopular—so much so that many Americans feared his call for military mobilization was a Trojan horse for dictatorship. In February 1940, Marshall appeared before Congress—in civilian clothes, so as to quell popular suspicion of his motives—to equip a regular army of 227,000 men, a 235,000-man National Guard, and a 500,000-man emergency reserve. For this he submitted a budget request of $850 million. On April 3, lawmakers cut that budget in half. A week later, Nazi forces invaded Denmark and Norway.

As late as summer 1941, Marshall was fighting for an extension of the Selective Service Act just so he could retain existing troop strength. On August 14, with Nazi troops nearing the Black Sea—a strategic pivot from which they could defeat Russia and outflank the British in the Middle East—and with isolationists fuming against White House efforts to drag America into another European war, Congress approved his request by a single vote.

Marshall had taken a lethargic nation and rallied it for a second war in Europe, one he had anticipated two years earlier. In September 1939, a week after he was appointed chief of staff, Marshall returned to his native Uniontown, where he delivered a speech to four hundred guests of the White Swan Hotel, beginning with an oral history of the region. As a boy, he told the audience, he hunted pheasant along the trail where General Edward Braddock, Great Britain's commander in chief for North America during the French and Indian Wars, had campaigned. Not far from where they were standing, he said, George Washington was forced to surrender Fort Necessity, his first command, to a superior Franco-Indian force. He reminded his listeners how fortunate they had been for America's long heritage of secure borders and relative peace. Then he calmly prepared them for war. "I will not trouble you with the perplexities, the problems, and requirements for the defense of this country," he said, "except to say that the importance of this matter is so great and the cost, unfortunately, is bound to be so high, that all that we do should be planned and executed in a businesslike manner, without emotional hysteria, demagogic speeches, or other unfortunate methods which will befog the issue and mislead our efforts."

By today's standard, Marshall's address was refreshingly understated. It was no herald of conflict between darkness and light but an honest assessment from a man confident in his understanding of the coming storm and his ability to navigate through it. It was, in short, the kind of spare, honest meditation that went down well in Marshall's America.

Despite Marshall's efforts to stiffen America's defenses, Washington was ill prepared to fight a transatlantic war, let alone a two-ocean one, when Japan struck U.S. bases in Hawaii and the Philippines in December 1941. Even when Germany allied itself with Japan after the United States declared war on Tokyo, Washington subordinated its Asian operations to the demands of the European theater. That decision, arrived at by Roosevelt, Marshall, and their British counterparts, would place the chief of staff at odds with his most famous general officer, a passionate militarist, a hero of the China lobby, and one of the nation's greatest megalomaniacs. He also happened to be the son of the military governor with whom Marshall had found so much to fault in the Philippines four decades earlier: Douglas MacArthur.*

If Marshall was the archetypical American statesman, Douglas MacArthur was a khaki-clad, pipe-smoking patriarch of American militarism.

---

* "Arthur MacArthur was the most flamboyantly egotistical man I had ever seen," said MacArthur aide Colonel Enoch H. Crowder, who served as MacArthur's secretary in the Philippines. "Until I met the son."

While Marshall revered the tradition of civilian authority over the military, MacArthur openly defied it. Where Marshall was conciliatory, MacArthur was imperious. Eventually, in the final struggle of their respective careers, the two men would clash over the very foundation of republican governance.

In Senate hearings after he was relieved of his post in Korea in 1951, MacArthur ruled that civilian authority over the military ceased "the minute you reached the killing stage." He told lawmakers that "a theater commander in any campaign is not merely limited to the handling of his troops; he commands the whole area politically, economically, and militarily." For Marshall, who had managed dozens of armies in a global conflict, this notion was not only contemptuous of the founders' legacy, it was dangerously simplistic. He told Congress:

> The fundamental divergence is one of judgment as to the proposed course of action to be followed by the United States. This divergence arises from the inherent difference between the positions of field commanders, whose mission is limited to a particular area and a particular antagonist, and the position of the Joint Chiefs of Staff, the Secretary of Defense, and the President, who are responsible for the total security of the United States, and who . . . must weigh our interests and objectives in one part of the globe with those in other areas of the world so as to attain the best overall balance.

It was a sober exposition of why war-making is best left to a well-defined chain of command under civilian control. But it did little to stop MacArthur's rhetoric, evocative and absolute, from resonating with a growing corps of American militarists even as he had come to the end of a brilliant and controversial career.

Douglas MacArthur was born in 1880 in what was then Fort Dodge on the outskirts of Little Rock, Arkansas. His father, Arthur, was a Civil War hero on the Union side who eventually rose to the rank of lieutenant general. His mother, Pinky, was of such maternal devotion that she moved into Craney's Hotel at West Point so she could keep an eye on her son during his four-year enrollment at the U.S. Military Academy there. To this day, MacArthur is regarded as the second most successful cadet in West Point history, behind Robert E. Lee. Athletic, charming, and fiercely intelligent, he was the number one student and First Captain in his ninety-three-man senior class and voted most likely to succeed by his classmates. Graduating with the rank of second lieutenant with the Army Corps of Engineers, he was quickly posted to the Philippines. His father, struggling in Manila as military proconsul, appointed Douglas his aide-de-camp. In 1905 the two men embarked on a grand tour of the Orient, with stops in Japan, China, Java, Southeast Asia, and India, almost all of which were the colonial possessions of either Britain, France, or the Netherlands. While inspecting Japanese military bases at Nagasaki, Kobe, and Kyoto, the MacArthurs were welcomed as dignitaries and feted by officers of the Imperial Army and Navy. The encounter convinced the elder MacArthur that Washington needed to bolster Philippine defenses "to prevent the archipelago's strategic position from becoming a liability rather than an asset."

Much later, Douglas MacArthur would recount how the trip "was without question the most important factor of preparation in my entire life. . . . It was clear to me that the future and the very existence of America were irrevocably entwined with Asia and its island outposts." Indeed, one envies the young Army officer for his privileged tour of the region at such a pivotal time in its history. Japan, which only a half century earlier had been forced by the Perry expedition to open its ports to trade, had just defeated the Russians in a war for control of Manchuria. It was the first time in modern history that an Asian army had beaten a Western one, and the implications for global commerce and multipolar rivalry were vast. Only five years earlier, Senator Albert J. Beveridge had declared in a speech that "whoever rules the Pacific . . . is the power that rules the world." MacArthur carried a copy of Beveridge's address during his East Asian tour and it would define his worldview for the rest of his life.

Back in Washington a year later, MacArthur worked as an aide to President Theodore Roosevelt and was later assigned to the Army General Staff. In 1917 he shipped out to France as chief of staff of the famous

Forty-second "Rainbow" Division, so named—by MacArthur, according to military lore—because it comprised troops from twenty-six states. It was there that he established his reputation as a maverick if somewhat foppish field commander. Inordinately self-possessed, MacArthur raised eyebrows with his unorthodox interpretation of military attire. Not long after his arrival in Europe, he began sporting a flowing raccoon coat and a vivid purple scarf. He removed the steel-wire lining of his officer's cap, allowing its peak to collapse rakishly. (It was an early iteration of the "fifty-mission crush" cap that he would make famous in World War II.) He was known by his charges as the "Beau Brummel" of the American Expeditionary Force, or simply as the "Fighting Dude."

So it was that on the night of November 4, 1918, having pitched camp within striking distance of the French city of Sedan in the Meuse heights, a retired MacArthur was awakened by elements of the First Infantry Division making their own bid for the city through his sector. In the chaos and confusion that followed, MacArthur, who emerged to calm the situation in a floppy hat, muffler, riding breeches, and polished boots, was mistaken as a German officer and arrested. He was released with an apology and, for his role in capturing the Meuse heights, was awarded the Silver Star. It would be his seventh Silver Star of the war, along with two Distinguished Service Crosses, a Distinguished Service Medal, and two Purple Hearts. But the incident at Sedan and the recriminations that followed incubated in MacArthur a persecution complex that would plague him for the rest of his career. In this case, it was Pershing and his staff, including the young Marshall, who were out to get him. Later, his "tormentors" would include Marshall and the Joint Chiefs, Marshall and Roosevelt, and Marshall and the U.S. Navy.

MacArthur returned to America as the most decorated officer of the war and one of the youngest brigadier generals in U.S. history. He was also a pop-culture phenomenon, the debut of the American celebrity-soldier. Things were changing from the days when military men kept a low profile and avoided politics. (The one major exception, General George McClellan's challenge of Abraham Lincoln in the 1864 presidential election, not only failed but scandalized many of his brother officers who saw it as impudent.) MacArthur's notoriety surged following the Depression-era Red Scares, stoked as they were by growing social and economic unrest. One incident in particular entrenched him as a divisive figure in an increasingly turbulent era.

In May 1932, while MacArthur served as President Herbert Hoover's chief of staff, some 12,000 jobless veterans of World War I marched on Washington, D.C., and demanded immediate unemployment relief. According to a study done later by the Veterans Administration, 94 percent of the men in the so-called Bonus Expeditionary Force, or BEF, had Army or Navy records, 67 percent had served overseas, and 20 percent had been disabled. MacArthur, however, perceived it as the vanguard of a communist insurrection. Deploying his talent for alarmist cant, he denounced the BEF as a Red conspiracy "far deeper and more dangerous than an effort to secure funds from a nearly depleted federal treasury." In fact, MacArthur's own intelligence unit reported that only three of the twenty-six leaders of the veterans were communists, and that most of the men seemed to be vehemently anticommunist, if anything.

MacArthur would not listen. Tasked by Hoover to clear the National Mall of demonstrators, he sent an orderly for his uniform at Fort Meyer and, freshly appointed in riding breeches and a field tunic layered with ribbons and medals, warned of an "incipient revolution in the air." Twice advised by Secretary of War Patrick Hurley to let the movement burn itself out, he responded by ordering Major General George S. Patton to form a perimeter of tanks, infantry, and cavalrymen around the Washington Monument. (Before the confrontation was over, Patton would roughly eject from the camp an ex-sergeant who had saved his life in France.) The crowds refused to disperse, so in July, MacArthur, violating a direct order from President Hoover, led a phalanx of troops through the BEF's encampment along the Anacostia River. The raid killed four people, including two babies who died from tear gas, while dozens were injured, among them a seven-year-old boy who was bayoneted in the leg while trying to rescue his pet rabbit. It was the first—though sadly not the last—time MacArthur would exceed his orders to calamitous effect.

Reactions to the incident were mixed. Eisenhower, then MacArthur's second in command, was appalled at his boss's conduct and apprehensive of the impact it would have on the War Department's upcoming budget requests. James Gavin, a lieutenant at Fort Benning at the time and a future lieutenant general and ambassador to France, applauded

MacArthur for leading from the front in the crisis rather than delegating the job to a subordinate. Hoover, validating his caricature as a Hamlet-like ditherer, was savaged by opposition Democrats on the eve of a presidential campaign. Popular opinion was generally sympathetic to the veterans; particularly shocking was the specter of tear gas being used against men who a generation earlier had been subjected to gas attacks on the killing fields of Europe.

If Hoover had any intention of disciplining his insubordinate chief of staff, he was preempted by a midnight press conference MacArthur staged after the Anacostia raid. The president had acted decisively and admirably, he told reporters. Otherwise, he said, "I believe the institutions of our government would have been threatened." Secretary of War Hurley praised the action as a great victory. "Mac did a great job," he said. "He's the man of the hour."

Years after the BEF was crushed, MacArthur ally General Courtney Whitney circulated a secret document allegedly captured among the marchers. The memo was proof, Whitney told anyone who would listen, that the BEF was part of a communist conspiracy to hold public trials and hangings of senior government officials on the steps of the Capitol. Heading the list, he said, was Army chief of staff MacArthur. The plot existed only in Whitney's head—an early example of the alacrity with which American militarists have made fraudulent claims to vindicate their actions—and the violent eviction of starving war veterans in the nation's capital remains one of the most shameful civil-rights abuses in U.S. history.

There is more to it than that, however. Assuming MacArthur actually believed the Bonus March was inspired by a worldwide communist movement, his response to it showed how excessive force against an alleged threat, despite considerable evidence to the contrary, could be carried out and even praised if done so in a fortified climate of fear. If, on the other hand, the politically ambitious field marshal was playing to certain galleries—Wall Street capitalists and law-and-order Republicans, for example—then the violence he committed on that humid summer's day could be interpreted as an early skirmish in what is known today as the culture wars, in which bold conservatives routinely trump squeamish liberals.

Weeks after the Bonus March killings, Franklin Roosevelt was at Hyde Park preserving his strength for the upcoming presidential campaign when he took a call from Louisiana governor Huey Long. When the conversation ended and Roosevelt hung up the phone, he told an adviser that Long "was one of the two most dangerous men in the country." The other, he said, was Douglas MacArthur. Indeed, MacArthur has often been cited as "America's Boulanger," a reference to Georges Ernest Jean Marie Boulanger, a late-nineteenth-century French general and equestrian whose political ambitions fueled the expression "man on horseback" as the harbinger of a coup. Roosevelt must have reasoned, however, that MacArthur was more of a menace outside the White House than in it. Having ejected Hoover from the Oval Office as conclusively as MacArthur scattered the Bonus Marchers, Roosevelt asked MacArthur to stay on as chief of staff. MacArthur, despite his conservative instincts and aversion to New Deal–like social programs, agreed. He even led Roosevelt's Inauguration Day parade, Boulanger-like, astride a huge stallion.

MacArthur spoke the language of fear with native fluency. Hyperbole, which served to heighten the contrasts of his defiantly monochromatic world, came naturally to him. Though he rarely went to church, he spoke often of God and Providence and Divinity. His clarion call—"in war there is no substitute for victory"—betrays a whiff of subversion, as it is civilian leaders who define America's wartime objectives, which may include a negotiated peace. Such rhetoric, he knew, has a powerfully parochial appeal, especially when projected in the reassuringly baritone voice of a tall, patrician war hero. By 1942 the MacArthur legend had grown to leviathan proportions. His retreat from Manila to the island of Corregidor was a textbook execution of war's most difficult and most distasteful maneuver. (Pershing called it "a masterpiece, one of the greatest moves in all military history.") His escape to Australia—he and his retinue slipped past a Japanese blockade via PT boat to Mindanao, where they were whisked to Melbourne by two B-17s—shocked the world. His epic vow to "return" victoriously to the Philippines captured the imagination of a home front demoralized by one disaster after the other.

By the fall of 1943, the Republican presidential nomination appeared to be MacArthur's for the taking. Party leader Wendell Willkie demanded the general be brought home and "given the responsibility and the power of coordinating all the armed forces of the nation to their most effective use." Senator Robert La Follette Jr. submitted a resolution to Congress that would set aside a "Douglas MacArthur Day." Bob Considine, a reporter for the conservative Hearst newspaper chain, published the hagiographic *MacArthur the Magnificent,* a copy of which Michigan senator Arthur Vandenberg displayed prominently on his desk. It was Vandenberg who first recognized MacArthur as the only person who could beat Roosevelt in the 1944 election. After speaking out against a War Department rule that prohibited Army officers from running for public office (which Roosevelt would soon abolish), Vandenberg received a letter from MacArthur thanking him for his "complete attitude of friendship," appealing to his "wise mentorship," and regretting how "there is much more that I would like to say to you which circumstances prevent." With that, the train had left the station.

Vandenberg was a rank-and-file Republican. Though an isolationist until the attack on Pearl Harbor, he was a respected, sincere conservative who was once a viable presidential candidate in his own right. Several of MacArthur's aides and many of his key supporters, however, were products of an emerging extreme right. There was General George Van Horn Moseley, for example, who warned MacArthur in a letter how the American people, appalled at the "mongrelization" of the nation by "low bred" immigrants, blacks, New Dealers, and Jews, would overthrow the government and recall him as dictator. (Moseley was eventually eased into retirement by Roosevelt for his anti-Semitic views.) MacArthur was a favorite of Father Edward Coughlin, a Canadian-born Catholic priest whose weekly radio broadcasts included anti-Semitic commentary as well as apologia for Hitler and Mussolini. General Charles Willoughby, MacArthur's intelligence expert throughout World War II and the Korean conflict, was awarded the Order of Saints Maurizio and Lazzaro from Mussolini's government and during the postwar occupation of Japan greatly exaggerated the scope of communist activity there, fueling Tokyo's own anticommunist witch hunt. He later became an adviser to Spanish dictator Francisco Franco.

By mid-1944, *Newsweek* magazine was reporting how "MacArthur has become the rallying point for extreme reactionary and isolationist or su-pernationalist leaders in the Republican party." The *American Mercury* remarked that "it may not be his fault but it is surely his misfortune that the worst elements on the political right, including its most blatant lunatic fringe, are whooping it up for MacArthur." Informed that the *Mercury* story was being circulated in the Army's library service, Vandenberg con-demned the War Department, while MacArthur himself ordered the magazine banned from Army ranks. Taking no chances, Army librarians also suspended copies of *Harper's* magazine and the London *Daily Express,* with commentary on the MacArthur candidacy, on the grounds of "security."

Through it all, there were no public signs of rancor between Mac-Arthur and the administration, and both Roosevelt and Marshall were careful to praise the general for his leadership during the darkest passage of the war. Eventually, however, MacArthur's star would burn out. As vain as he was autocratic, he surrounded himself with adoring aides who tried to shape his public image with ham-fisted censorship of correspondents' reports from the field, a tactic that naturally antagonized the press. In 1944 inexperienced handlers submitted MacArthur's name for the Wis-consin primary ballot before his campaign had had a chance to mature, and the general came in third behind Thomas Dewey and Harold Stassen.

MacArthur's candidacy may have survived that primary outcome had it not been for a Nebraskan legislator named A. L. Miller, who, like most MacArthur advocates, harbored a near-pathological hatred of Roo-sevelt. "Unless this New Deal can be stopped, our American way of life is forever doomed," Miller wrote the general in one of several communi-qués. In another, he referred to Roosevelt as "a monstrosity . . . which is engulfing the nation" and must be destroyed. Displaying his fecundity as a correspondent as well as his tin ear as an aspiring politician, Mac-Arthur not only replied to the obscure congressman's letters but emphat-ically agreed with him. "Your description of conditions in the United States is a sober one indeed and is calculated to arouse the thoughtful consideration of every true patriot," he wrote Miller. Then, in a clear gibe at a wartime president, he added: "Out here we are doing what we can with what we have. I will be glad, however, when more substantial forces are placed at my disposition."

Miller, apparently seeking to leaven his hero's political prospects, released the entire correspondence to the press. From Australia, MacArthur issued a statement that his letters to the legislator were not intended for publication and "were neither politically inspired nor intended to convey blanket support for the congressman's views." Vandenberg, who knew political gangrene when he smelled it, grimly advised the general to fall on his sword. On April 30, from Hollandia, New Guinea, where he had moved his headquarters from Brisbane, MacArthur requested "that no action be taken that would link my name in any way with the nomination. I do not covet it nor would I accept it."

One senses that Roosevelt instinctively knew that MacArthur, if given enough rope from sycophants and hangers-on in Washington, would eventually hang himself. The president alluded as much to MacArthur himself not long after his 1933 inaugural. "Douglas," Roosevelt told his then chief of staff, "I think you are our best general, but I believe you would be our worst politician."

In his oral memoirs, Marshall avoided discussing his contemporaries in detail, though in MacArthur's case he made an exception:

> He was of a very independent nature and he made himself a political factor from the start. . . . And the President was very careful in handling him because of that. . . . Over there [in Australia], he made beautiful use of what he got, but he spent so much time scrapping with the Navy. [Commander of the U.S. Third Fleet William] Halsey tried his best to please MacArthur. He tried to cooperate all the way through [but MacArthur] was . . . supersensitive about everything. He was conspicuous in the matter of temperament.

Such was the soft-spoken way in which Marshall described a headstrong officer who flirted heavily with insubordination. MacArthur would consummate the affair less than a decade later.

2

—

THE WAGES OF FEAR

More important than the observable nature of external reality,
when it comes to the determination of Washington's view of the
world, is the subjective state of readiness on the part of Washington
officialdom to recognize this or that feature of it.
—GEORGE F. KENNAN, *Memoirs, 1925–1950*

NONE OF HIS MYRIAD VOCATIONS, NOT AS A FAILED FARMER
or haberdasher, nor as a U.S. senator or vice president, had pre-
pared Harry Truman for the challenges that awaited him after
Roosevelt's death. The late president had treated him like a squatter, con-
fiding nothing, not even details of the atomic bomb. So on the evening of
April 12, 1945, when Truman took the oath of office in the White House
Cabinet Room surrounded by what had been Roosevelt's inner circle—
Secretary of War Henry Stimson, Vice President Henry Wallace, Interior
Secretary Harold Ickes, Secretary of the Navy James Forrestal, Attorney
General Francis Biddle, and others—he was the least-informed man in
the room at the most critical period in the history of the republic he was
being sworn in to lead.

His first order of business was a fateful message from his ambassador
to Moscow: it was time to get tough with the Soviets.

Averell Harriman, who had long endorsed rapprochement with Soviet
Russia, was having second thoughts. Moscow was reneging on commitments made at the Yalta Conference, where Stalin humored Roosevelt's
vision for a U.S.-Soviet "Grand Alliance," to allow free elections in the
Eastern European countries it now occupied. Clearly, Harriman argued,
the Soviets were turning their new possessions, particularly Poland, into

puppet states arrayed against the West. In the zero-sum calculus of the Kremlin, he concluded, "friendly" relations with its neighbors meant absolute Soviet control. He returned to Washington on April 18—the anniversary of Paul Revere's historic nighttime ride—and met Forrestal that evening for dinner. "We might well have to face an ideological warfare just as vigorous and dangerous as Fascism or Nazism," Forrestal recorded Harriman as saying. On April 23, Truman gathered his cabinet members to discuss the visiting ambassador's views prior to his scheduled meeting with the Soviet foreign minister, the pince-nez'd and mustachioed V. M. Molotov. Stimson and Marshall urged caution; America needed Soviet help in the Far East, where the Pacific war raged. The others, particularly Forrestal and Charles "Chip" Bohlen, an ally of Harriman's deputy George Kennan and a fellow Kremlinologist, disagreed. An independent Poland, they said, was a red line worth defending.

Truman went with the majority. After receiving Molotov and the Soviet ambassador, Andrei Gromyko, he quickly went about upbraiding his visitors for what he described as the one-way street of U.S.-Soviet relations. America would not recognize any Polish government that was not freely elected by its people. When Molotov protested that the Poles were working against the Red Army, Truman cut him short, dangling over his head a cut in Lend-Lease aid unless Stalin lived up to his commitments at Yalta.

"I have never been talked to like that in my life," said Molotov.

"Carry out your agreements," Truman responded, "and you won't get talked to like that."*

Later, Harriman would admit to being "taken aback" by the intensity of Truman's rebuke and regarded it as a mistake. A month later, Truman himself would come to regret what he called the "get tough" policy promoted by Harriman and other hard-liners.

Germany surrendered to the Allies in May. Washington, as per the limited terms of the Lend-Lease agreement, then discontinued aid to both London and Moscow. It was done so brusquely, however—even ships that were midway to Soviet ports were turned around—that it was received in

---

* This is how Truman remembered it. According to Bohlen, Truman dismissed Molotov with a simple, if curt, "That will be all, Mr. Molotov. I would appreciate it if you would transmit my views to Marshal Stalin." One can imagine a wide-eyed Molotov losing his pince-nez, though there is no record of this.

Moscow as a provocation. (The Brits, needless to say, were not very happy about it either.) At the recently established United Nations, there were ominous suggestions that another war was all but unavoidable. "That there were those who looked upon war between the democratic-capitalistic U.S. and authoritarian Communist Russia as 'inevitable' was no longer news," *Time* magazine reported from UN headquarters in San Francisco. "Last week the possibility of World War III was more and more in the horrified world's public eye."

It was the Americans who blinked. Harriman, along with Bohlen and former Roosevelt adviser Harry Hopkins, flew to Moscow to hammer out a compromise with Stalin on the future of Poland. Over the course of six meetings that would extend to June, Stalin offered hollow gestures of self-determination for what would eventually be known as the Soviet bloc. Conceding to Russia a buffer state against the West, it seemed, was preferable to war. The fault lines for the Cold War, which Truman would all but declare less than two years later, had been drawn.

Tensions between Washington and Moscow, which had their origins in the Russian Revolution, were not inevitable. In 1918, when newly communist Russia withdrew its forces from World War I after toppling the tsar—consistent with Bolshevik leader Vladimir Lenin's rejection of capitalist wars—President Woodrow Wilson assumed the communists were stooges of imperial Germany. He rejected those who advised engagement with the new regime in Moscow and set in motion America's first attempt at regime change.* When covert operations failed, Wilson released

---

*Among those who recommended that Washington recognize Lenin as Russia's legitimate leader—and thus give him incentive to remain in the war—was William V. Judson, the U.S. military attaché in Moscow. Alone among most U.S. officials in Russia, Judson actually knew the country, having observed firsthand the Russo-Japanese War. Businessman and philanthropist Robert Boyce Thompson, who spearheaded a vital food-distribution plan in famine-stricken revolutionary Russia, also urged the Allies to reach out to Lenin. So did Raymond Robins, a Chicago social reformer with socialist sympathies who managed a rare and intimate relationship with Trotsky. Recruited by Thompson to be part of his Red Cross mission, the indefatigable Robins pulled off what no one else could achieve: a written commitment from both Lenin and Trotsky to stay in the war in return for Allied protection from a Japanese invasion of the Russian Far East and against German encroachments on its northern port cities. In signing the documents, Lenin was taking

a trove of documents that allegedly proved the Bolsheviks were paid agents of Berlin. Publication of the Semenev papers, so named for the journalist who uncovered them, outraged Americans, providing Wilson with a public mandate for war. Soon thousands of troops were landing on Russia's northern coast, part of a U.S.-led coalition called the Polar Bear Expedition. Years later, U.S. Sovietologist George Kennan would expose the Semenev papers as forgeries.

The Polar Bear Expedition remains one of the most disastrous campaigns in U.S. military history. A year of skirmishing with irregular Red Army elements had cost the Americans 600 dead and thousands wounded, plus $30 million in war-related expenditures. By April 1919, the last U.S. troops had evacuated from a country that, due largely to the invasion, was far more unified and nationalistic than they had found it. Not only did Wilson's debacle vindicate Marx's most vituperative writings about the motives and weaknesses of the capitalist state, it ignited an anti-Soviet frenzy in the United States that made some future conflict all but inevitable.

With Germany made prostrate by the draconian terms of Versailles, Russia became for Washington the command post of a global movement to subvert America's ideals. A postwar plague of anarchist bombings on U.S. soil was perceived as the vanguard of a Moscow-inspired proletarian revolt. The movement was real enough, though utterly out of proportion to the hysteria it provoked; out of a total population of 125 million, only 34,000 Americans identified themselves as communists. Not since the Civil War had habeas corpus been so compromised, however, and citizens were cavalierly stripped of due process. In 1920, a year after his house was firebombed by an Italian radical, Attorney General A. Mitchell Palmer authorized raids on some 10,000 suspected communists in dozens of cities. A year later, in a speech to the American Legion, Judge

---

an extraordinary step, placing the revolution's fate, and his own, in the hands of the very powers he knew were conspiring against him. Fortunately for the anti-Bolshevik hawks in Wilson's circle, the president was unaware of the Lenin-Trotsky commitments until it was too late. Evidently, U.S. officials who resented Robins's freelance diplomacy delayed cabling the details of the Soviet offer for two weeks. Despite stalling by Trotsky while awaiting a response from Washington, an All-Soviet Congress ratified a peace deal with Berlin.

Kenesaw Mountain Landis argued for a looser definition of treason and for vigilante executions "for those who would destroy our government." The first Red Scare would last only a year or so, but it burned hot enough to ensure U.S.-Soviet estrangement for more than a decade.

In 1933 Roosevelt decided to normalize relations with the Soviet Union, a move supported by most of his foreign policy advisers. With the outbreak of World War II, the Soviet Union became an important ally, if only because it was locked with much of the German army in a lethal intercourse that claimed more than 20 million Soviet men and women, or 14 percent of its population.* However, mutual suspicion, the germ of Wilson's ill-starred intervention, stalked the relationship. It was only natural that Washington would regard postwar Soviet Russia, though its devastation nearly matched that of Nazi Germany's, as a treacherous, even offensive threat. Having defined Moscow as a major adversary, America needed a doctrine to go with it. It would soon have one, thanks to the least doctrinaire of men.

In 1959 revisionist historian William Appleman Williams offered a courageously empathic account of the Soviet condition and warned that Washington's policy to "contain" communism would only humor a national paranoia bred from centuries of foreign aggression. With rational minds still flinching from the jabs and haymakers of McCarthyism, Williams wrote,

> The central fact confronting any past or present Russian leader is the imbalance of the economic and political development of the nation. Czarist and Soviet history is the record of a continuous, all-pervading struggle to reach a minimum level of material well-being, let alone relative prosperity or actual wealth. . . . At the same time, moreover, it has been necessary for Russia to maintain strong armed forces, urgently needed to defend open borders against the continuous threat and recurring actuality of foreign attack. . . .

---

* By contrast, America's war dead, nearly all of the toll comprising military men, accounted for 0.32 percent of its total population.

The present actuality of nuclear bases around its borders feeds back into, and reinforces, the historical memory of the Tatars, of Napoleon, of World War I, of the intervention against the revolution itself, and of Japan and Germany from the 1930s on through World War II.

Perhaps the only Truman adviser subversive enough in his way to appreciate Williams's point was the same man who, however unintentionally, aroused Moscow's "historical memory" of the predations of foreign powers. George Kennan—diffident, thoughtful, soft-spoken—was a human Rorschach test. The man who proved the Semenev papers were counterfeit was so highly evolved intellectually that he seemed to be of at least two minds about everything, and Washington elites often exploited his genius to give their divergent biases and presumptions respectability. He is popularly known as the man who counseled a hard, even militant position against Soviet expansionism but then spent the rest of his career arguing that Russia was in fact non-hegemonic. He was adopted by hawks in the Truman administration but considered himself a sober-minded realist who counseled a static confrontation between capitalists and communists in their respective spheres of influence. He bitterly opposed American meddling in places such as Indochina and Latin America, which he considered distractions from the far more important job of balancing Western power and resources against that of its Eastern rival. According to Karl Marx, a communist victory was inevitable because capitalism would succumb to its own class divisions and corruption; early in his career, Kennan predicted, rightly, that just the opposite was true.

Kennan was a profoundly conflicted and solitary creature. Socially awkward and shy, he nonetheless craved affection and approval. That paradox—being in the world but not of it—was a source of both personal melancholy and professional empowerment. As he was always the outsider, his views were uncluttered by emotional or ideological commitment. He basked in the fame of being containment's creator but later, horrified at its abuse in the hands of Washington alarmists and demagogues, withdrew into the wilderness. A prolific reader—not surprisingly, he was fascinated with the doomed and darkly enigmatic heroes of

F. Scott Fitzgerald's novels—and with a passion for history, Kennan was everywhere during the Cold War but left behind little trace of himself. He sums up his undergraduate studies at Princeton with a simple elegy that might well apply to his life generally: "I left college as obscurely as I entered it."

Kennan was born in Milwaukee on February 16, 1904, the only son of Scots-Irish Presbyterian parents whose forebearers had migrated to New England in the late eighteenth century. His mother died suddenly two months after his birth, and he was raised by an aloof, austere father. He arrived at Princeton directly from St. John's Military Academy, a terrified Midwestern hayseed in the bosom of East Coast swells. When a group of fellow freshmen invited him to join their club, he joyfully agreed. But a few hours later, spooked by the prospect of human intimacy, he resigned, exiling himself to the dining tables of the un-clubbed. Having survived to his eighteenth year, he contracted scarlet fever on the first day of his summer job as a mail delivery boy—he worked the whole day in a torrential downpour—and nearly died from it.

Kennan decided to join the Foreign Service in part because of his facility for languages. (At the age of eight, he picked up German while spending a summer with his stepmother in Kassel. Eventually, he would also master Russian, French, Polish, Czech, Portuguese, and Norwegian.) He passed the exam in 1925 and began work in the old State, War, and Navy Building overlooking the White House grounds, followed by enjoyable postings to Geneva and Hamburg. The glamour of embassy dinners and receptions was obscuring his inhibitions and he was having fun. In 1928 he decided some postgraduate study would enhance his career prospects, and after returning to Washington he prepared to submit his resignation. Fate intervened when a State Department mentor explained to him that he could qualify for three years of graduate work in Europe once he signed up as a specialist in either Chinese, Japanese, Arabic, or Russian. Kennan shrewdly opted for the latter; Washington had yet to establish diplomatic relations with Moscow and when it did, he reasoned, there would be a great need for Russian hands.

For five and a half years, starting in 1929, Kennan rotated from Berlin to the Baltic capitals of Tallinn and Riga, which served as listening posts for Washington's Russia desk. It was there that he developed his talent for Sovietology. Where Russophobes and Red-baiters saw an aggressive hegemon, Kennan saw a nation trapped in its own self-destructive Marxist cant. In 1932 he was tasked by the chief of mission to analyze Moscow's most recent Five-Year Plan and how it would affect Soviet opinion. The memo that followed revealed the young diplomat's gift for synthesis and extrapolation.

Life in Soviet Russia, Kennan wrote, orbits around a doctrine rooted in the inevitability of communist revolution in all countries and an endless class struggle in every phase of human conduct. "This doctrine has created and necessitated the continued hostility between Russia and the rest of the world. It has necessitated the maintenance of the Red Army and the entire industrial military development known as the Five-Year Plan." This garrison state was unsustainable, Kennan argued. A successful Five-Year Plan would attenuate the Russians' revolutionary zeal, particularly among its youth. However, he went on:

> The rate of construction cannot be maintained. Collectivized agriculture cannot reabsorb the masses of transient labor released from construction projects, nor do these masses, uprooted and inspired with vague political hopes, wish to be reabsorbed by the countryside. They pile into the big cities. Discontent and increasing government expenses do their work. Foreign credit breaks down. Depreciation gains the upper hand over production. The system falls to pieces.

At the age of twenty-eight, Kennan was a half century ahead of his time.

Kennan toiled as a gnome in the boiler rooms of American diplomacy, a respected but obscure specialist. He consulted to the first U.S. ambassador to Moscow, William C. Bullitt, and was a senior policy planner in the American embassy in Berlin. From June 1944 to April 1946 he served as the deputy chief of mission in Moscow, which he often ran in the absence of Ambassador Harriman. It was a cold and dismal posting. While Washington allowed a generous number of Russian diplomats into the nation's fold after the two sides normalized relations, their American counterparts were few in number and closely monitored—just as Kennan had predicted. For much of his assignment as Harriman's number two, Kennan wrote carefully worded cables to Washington that were received, as he put it, with an "unechoing silence." Then, in 1946, while bedridden with a host of ailments no doubt brought on by a typically arctic Moscow winter, he wrote a 5,300-word memo that would largely define the course of the Cold War.

The so-called Long Telegram, the most famous diplomatic cable in U.S. history, was inspired by the White House's response to a February 9 speech Joseph Stalin delivered during an election rally at the Bolshoi Theater. In it, Stalin condemned an American-led "capitalist encirclement" of Russia and its allies and implied that war was inevitable. The speech emboldened hard-liners like Forrestal, while obligating Undersecretary of State Dean Acheson to reconsider his goal of some kind of postwar collaboration with Moscow. He appealed to his subordinates for fresh thinking and suggested they survey State Department experts such as Kennan. The forty-two-year-old sage was more than ready to oblige, despite his interminable *douleurs,* as he called his relentless maladies.

With his personal secretary taking notes, Kennan composed a five-part lecture on Soviet motives and mores. Russian expansion, he argued, was the inevitable consequence of foreign aggression, be it from sixteenth-century Poland, Napoleonic France, or the U.S. invasion only three decades earlier. At the same time, Kennan explained, this fear of foreign meddling served to justify the Kremlin's long history of dictatorship, of which Marxism was only the latest incarnation. An important difference, however, was that communism's "honeyed promises" appealed to the worst of Russian instincts and made Moscow "more dangerous and insidious" than ever before. Only if confronted with a strong deterrent, preferably one supported by alliances with Britain and other Western nations, would the Soviets back down. Checking the Soviet threat would be "undoubtedly the greatest task our diplomacy has ever faced and probably the greatest it will ever have to face."

This was strong stuff—and red meat for people like Forrestal, who made copies of Kennan's telegram and eagerly circulated them. Before becoming secretary of the Navy under Roosevelt, Forrestal was a flinty, tightly wound U.S. Navy aviator who conquered Wall Street as a bond trader at Dillon, Read & Co., then a finishing school for some of America's most influential minds. Kennan's stature as America's top Sovietologist lent his own hard-line views intellectual credibility. Lost on Forrestal, however, was Kennan's emphasis on Russian history and internal politics as the cipher by which Moscow's intentions should be decoded. A month before Kennan sent his long cable, Forrestal told columnist Walter Lippmann that communism was more a cult than a form of governance, and like any fanatical religious movement could not be reasoned or negotiated with. Convinced of the inevitability of war with the Soviet empire, Forrestal interpreted the Long Telegram as reassurance from the country's top Russian hand of the need for a military response to what he regarded as a clear military threat. It was also perhaps no coincidence that an expansionist interpretation of the threat suited the parochial ambitions of the secretary of the Navy, to say nothing of his brother service heads, who during World War II had pioneered the art of strategic warfare. Aircraft carriers and long-range bombers enabled Washington to attack not only an enemy's frontline forces but its home front as well. No other country had such capability, and men like Forrestal would make certain the United States preserved its ability to attack its adversaries wherever they lurked. Forrestal wanted whole fleets of carrier battle groups, just as his Air Force counterpart wanted new air wings of B-29s.

Others around Truman, the so-called Wise Men, read the memo differently. Acheson, who believed that America's offensive military capacity, including its arsenal of atomic weaponry, would for many years be vastly superior to Russia's, was not impressed. Kennan's recommendations, he would later write, "were of no help." Harriman and Chip Bohlen, though not afraid to get tough with Stalin, never believed war with the Kremlin was unavoidable. Instead, they used Kennan's arguments as the basis for a policy of checking, with military force, if necessary, Soviet hegemony where it threatened U.S. interests. In a word, they favored "containment."

It was Truman, however, who seized on Kennan's telegram as an excuse to stiffen his Russian policy. As he prepared to deliver a speech on the matter in mid-1946, Truman tasked his speechwriter, a shrewd and slick lawyer named Clark Clifford, to gather a top-secret report of Soviet violations of international agreements, one that Clifford argued successfully should focus on all manner of Russian misconduct. Editing together reams of diplomatic cables, many of them written by Kennan, Bohlen, and Harriman, Clifford produced a document that went well beyond Kennan's worst characterization of the Kremlin's intentions. It recommended that the United States prepare itself to "wage atomic and biological warfare . . . and support and assist all democratic countries which are in any way menaced or endangered by the USSR."* Truman, struck by the dossier, demanded all ten copies be collected for safekeeping. "If this got out it would blow the roof off the White House," he told Clifford. Thus did an obscure White House aide produce the anvil on which the Long Telegram was beaten into the Truman Doctrine. Kennan, perhaps seduced by his proximity to power, signed off on the report.

In early 1947, Kennan was tapped by Secretary Marshall to lead his planning staff in Washington. By then Forrestal was already courting Kennan for his views. He arranged a position for him at the War College at Fort McNair and invited him to Pentagon lunches as well as dinner parties at his Georgetown home. It was an odd pairing. At one point, Kennan, not unlike the class nerd tutoring a somewhat excitable high-school football star, offered to write Forrestal a paper that laid out the motives behind Soviet aggression and Russia's communist ideology, which he held was informed largely by Moscow's bitter experience with outsiders. It would be, as he later described it, "a literary extrapolation of the thoughts that had been maturing in my mind" about postwar Russia's foreign policy. Today, "Psychological Background of Soviet Foreign Policy," as Kennan's paper was titled, is better known as "The Sources of Soviet Conduct," which appeared in the summer 1947 edition of *Foreign Affairs,* the nation's foremost journal of international affairs. It was published anonymously—by "X," as Kennan requested—to avoid drawing attention to himself as he prepared for his new position under Marshall. Famously known as the "X-article," it would play into the hands of Beltway militarists and haunt Kennan for the rest of his life.

---

* Moscow, of course, had its own share of alarmists and mischief-makers. Pandering to Stalin's paranoia, Russian linguists in their translation of Kennan's Long Telegram rendered "containment" not as the appropriate *sderzhivanie* but as *udushenie*—strangulation.

It proved all too easy for one of Washington's top pundits to identify the X-man. As it turned out, Arthur Krock, a columnist for the *New York Times,* had read a position paper in Forrestal's office that he quickly recognized was the genesis of Kennan's article. Within days the article, with all its "serious deficiencies," as Kennan refers to them in his memoirs, had upended America's policy universe. Most notably, it had attracted the attention of Walter Lippmann, perhaps America's most influential and respected pundit. In a series of columns, he attacked Kennan's article and the White House policy he believed it represented as a recklessly expansionist and wholly unsustainable attempt to go toe-to-toe with the Russian bear wherever he may lie. Containment as it was laid out by Kennan's article, he argued, committed the United States to Cold War sideshows such as Turkey, Greece, and China. It implied there was no room for neutrality in an us-versus-them world, even for countries in particularly complex situations such as West Germany. If anything, Lippmann wrote, the United States should scale back its military commitments in a dangerous world, not add to them.

In his memoirs, Kennan laments Lippmann's interpretation of containment "in just the military sense I had not meant to give it." But he acknowledges that the article's most forceful passages could be construed as the language of conflict. It recommends, for example, "a long-term, patient but firm and vigilant containment of Russian expansive tendencies," and asserts that "the Soviet pressures against the free institutions of the Western world can be contained by the adroit and vigilant application of counterforce at a series of constantly shifting geographical and political points." Ironically for the Russia hand who anticipated the collapse of the Soviet Union a half century in advance, the memoirist Kennan searches in vain for reasons why he omitted or glazed over sources of Soviet vulnerability, such as the enormous burden Russia's satellites were placing on Moscow, which would hasten the country's undoing. Tellingly, however, Kennan suggests he may have been trying to please his hawkish patron. "It had something to do, I suspect, with what I felt to be Mr. Forrestal's needs at the time when I prepared the original paper for him."

———

Roosevelt's dream of a Grand Alliance with Moscow shuffled along for another eighteen months or so, with the United States battling Stalin on one
diplomatic flank and backing down on another. Then, at a White House
meeting hosted by President Truman, the Cold War was finally joined—
along with a ruinous American commitment to fight it on every front.

It was February 27, 1947. A week earlier, the British ambassador to
Washington, Lord Inverness, had sent by courier to Undersecretary of
State Dean Acheson "a blue piece of paper"—foreign office parlance for
high-level communiqués. It turned out to be two letters, delivered by Loy
Henderson, the head of the State Department's Near East and African Affairs desk. (Secretary of State Marshall, the designated recipient of the
message, was at Princeton University delivering his first address since assuming the office.) The letters were, Acheson would later recall, "shockers." The first declared that Britain could no longer afford to subsidize the
Greek government, which was facing a foreign exchange shortage of an
estimated $250 million along with a communist uprising. The second
carried the same message about Turkey, which was forced by Soviet pressure to spend a fortune modernizing its army. The implication was clear:
unless the United States assumed Britain's burden, neither Greece nor
Turkey could sustain its independence. Two strategically vital allies would
become Russian proxies, and with viral effect. The Mediterranean would go
first, followed by Central Asia. Not even the Himalayan range could stem
the tide, particularly if Mao's People's Army prevailed in China. Eventually two-thirds of the world's humanity and three-quarters of its surface
would be under Moscow's bullwhip.

At least that's how Acheson put it that cold winter day to a delegation
of senior lawmakers the president had gathered in the Oval Office for a
briefing. They included such Capitol Hill heavyweights as Representative Sam Rayburn and Senator Arthur Vandenberg, chairman of the
Foreign Relations Committee. The son of an Episcopal bishop, Acheson
made his case with evangelical zeal, summoning allusions between the
Soviet-U.S. divide and the Hellenistic rivalries of Athens and Sparta and
the imperial wars between Rome and Carthage. Nothing less than the
fate of Western civilization was at stake, Acheson declared. "This was
my crisis," he later recalled in his memoirs. "For a week I had nurtured
it. These congressmen had no conception of what challenged them;

it was my task to bring it home. . . . No time was left for measured approach."

Interestingly, it was up to Acheson to rouse the delegation only after Marshall failed to summon a sufficiently alarmist register. "My most distinguished chief," the undersecretary writes, "most unusually and unhappily, flubbed his opening statement." In fact, Marshall would rise to the occasion with uncharacteristically shrill commentary when he was lobbying for an even larger commitment than what the White House was now preparing to assume: the reconstruction plan for Europe that bears his name. He was generally uncomfortable with hyperbole, however, particularly in the foreign policy realm and especially if it lacked adequate military muscle to back it up. "When you don't pack a punch," Marshall often said, "you don't hit a man across the face and call him names." Very likely the old logistician, who understood what eluded so many others—that only a foreign policy that matches commitments with resources is sustainable—was uneasy about where all this was heading.

Acheson spoke for a full ten minutes. A long pause followed, then Vandenberg rose. "Mr. President," he said, "if you will say that to Congress and the country, I will support you and I believe that most of its members will do the same." At least that is how the courtly Acheson records it in his memoirs. Loy Henderson remembers a less solemn response: "Mr. President, the only way you are ever going to get this is to make a speech and scare the hell out of the country."

Unlike Woodrow Wilson's armed intervention in Russia, which is unfamiliar to most Americans despite its bitter and enduring consequences, Truman's decision to spare Greece and Turkey from the communist yoke is required reading in high-school history books. The image of the president drawing a line against Soviet expansion in Europe, and, in doing so, shouldering Britain's imperial obligation, makes for a crisp starting point for a Cold War rivalry that ended just as neatly. It also established the root cause of confrontation: a hungry Soviet predator, roaming the frontier in search of isolated calves for the taking. Both countries were strategically significant—Greece as a maritime shipping power and Turkey for its Bosporus Strait, one of Europe's most strategic natural waterways.

However unpopular the decision was politically, Britain had to be relieved. The future of Europe was at stake.

That, at least, is how the White House saw things. For war-weary London, neither Turkey nor Greece was worth the candle. Obscured by the gravity of its urgent communiqués to the White House was a more pedestrian British urge to rid itself of a needless imposition. In November 1946, Chancellor of the Exchequer Hugh Dalton wrote to Clement Attlee, Churchill's successor as prime minister, that "I am very doubtful indeed about this policy of propping up, even with American aid, weak states in the Eastern Mediterranean against Russia." Two months later, facing an economic and political crisis, Dalton overcame resistance from the Foreign Office and persuaded his colleagues to "put an end to our endless dribble of British taxpayers' money to the Greeks." In its appeal to the Americans for help, however, London cast the imperatives of Greco-Turkish subsidies in such a breathless manner as to force an accommodating hand. The blue cables were composed and delivered and, as Dalton noted in March 1947, "the Americans took fright lest Russia should overrun the whole of the Balkans and Eastern Mediterranean. The Treasury officials told me afterwards that they never thought the effect would be so quick and so volcanic."

However perfidious were the Brits in transferring their obligations to Washington, were not Truman and his aides correct to confront Soviet aggression? Only a year earlier, after all, Washington had been forced to pressure Moscow to honor its postwar commitment to withdraw from Iran. Was there not ample reason to fear Soviet intrigue in Greece or Turkey?

Actually, no. Although communist movements existed in both countries, their leaders were as independent of Moscow as was Yugoslavia's Marshal Tito. Not until it faced the threat of eradication following "the White Terror," a dirty war waged by right-wing forces and their supporters in which thousands of communists were killed and tortured, did the Greek communist party turn to Moscow for help. Even then, assistance was not forthcoming. In early 1946, having journeyed to Moscow with cap in hand, party leader Nikos Zachariades was told by Soviet foreign minister Molotov to defer an armed response and participate in upcoming elections. Stalin, it turned out, was in no mood to beard the

West over Greece. The Turkish insurrection, meanwhile, was centered less around a communist insurgency and was more about ethnic tensions involving disputed territory claimed by both Ankara and Moscow. As with the Soviet revolution itself, communist movements in Greece and Turkey were inspired by indigenous factors, only to be wrongly identified by Washington as part of a broad international conspiracy. Leading with its chin, the White House was suckered by its closest ally into assuming the role of bulwark against a Soviet aggressor that did not exist.

The policy of containment, however dubious in conception, was born. It had taken a while to gestate after it was conceived unwittingly by one of America's most brilliant diplomats in one of its most forsaken diplomatic outposts. Fertilized for months in arcane position papers and policy shops, it was delivered in a speech Truman gave only a few weeks after Acheson mounted his spirited pitch at the White House. Not long after that, "containment" as a strategic response to a global threat would take on a life of its own.

In the strange communion between George Kennan and James Forrestal, nuance had succumbed to militarism without putting up a fight. The die cast, Truman on March 12, 1947, injected the molten ore that would anneal into his doctrine of containment. In a speech to Congress, he warned that if Greece fell, Turkey would wobble and the entire Middle East might be consumed by "confusion and disorder." The world had entered a crucial juncture, he said, "when nearly every nation must choose between alternative ways of life. . . . If we falter in our leadership, we may endanger the peace of the world—and we shall surely endanger the welfare of our own nation."

Truman asked Congress to support a bill to provide $400 million to Greece and Turkey. Vandenberg was on board but other lawmakers were less enthusiastic. While testifying in support of the proposal, Acheson was asked by Representative Karl Mundt of South Dakota whether the Truman Doctrine was "the first step in a consistent and complete American policy to stop the expansion of communism." Representative Christian Herter, a moderate Republican from Massachusetts, wondered if

U.S. officials had the "extraordinary skill" needed to intervene successfully. Walter Judd of Minnesota, an outspoken anticommunist and a supporter of the Nationalist Chinese leader Chiang Kai-shek, asked why the administration was drawing the line at the eastern Mediterranean when Chiang's forces were battling communists head-on. The unkindest cut, however, and the most difficult to ignore, came from a thrusting Walter Lippmann, who in one column after another attacked the Truman Doctrine as unfocused and extravagant. Once, after a day of grueling testimony, Acheson ran into Lippmann at a dinner party and accused him of trying to "sabotage" U.S. foreign policy. Lippmann hit back, and the two lions of Georgetown's salon society nearly came to blows. It was a foretaste of far more vicious battles to come.

Even among Truman's inner circle of advisers, there were concerns that the doctrine was being oversold. White House aide George Elsey, for one, noted how "there has been no overt action in the immediate past by the USSR" relating to the Greek crisis. Kennan believed containment should not be applied unless there were clear vested interests at stake and expressed as much in a report to Marshall. "The notion should be dispelled that the Truman Doctrine was a blank check to be used for economic and military aid anywhere in the world where the Communists show signs of being successful," he wrote. George Marshall and Chip Bohlen, meanwhile, en route to Moscow for a council of foreign ministers, wired back concerns that there was "a little too much flamboyant anticommunism in Truman's speech." In response, the White House explained that the aid package would have been an impossible sell without the emphasis on the communist danger.

In April, the Greek-Turkish aid package passed Congress. Not long after that, with Marshall on point, the White House successfully lobbied Capitol Hill to endorse the European Recovery Program, which Marshall had outlined in his June speech at Harvard University. For the time being at least, Western civilization was safe. Things looked differently from Moscow, however. Having been strong-armed by Washington into quitting Iran, only to watch the Americans erect military bases in Turkey and Greece, it perceived itself as being enveloped in a cordon sanitaire.

———

Over the next four decades, American presidents and politicians would cite the containment doctrine to justify U.S. military intervention worldwide, most tragically of course in Indochina. Despite his anguish at being associated with what he thought was a flawed policy, Kennan would distinguish himself with a prophet's eye on the U.S.-Soviet rivalry. He accurately predicted that the unacceptable cost of total war between the two great powers would lead to smaller conflicts of limited political ends. He was an early critic of America's intervention in Vietnam, and he correctly diagnosed Khrushchev's decision to build the Berlin Wall as a way of avoiding a third world war, not starting one. It was Kennan who warned that the Chinese would intervene militarily against the United States in North Korea, just as he foresaw the Sino-Soviet split. With his death in 2005 at the age of 101, Kennan was widely hailed as one of the country's most able foreign-policy experts, though his warnings were routinely ignored. Forrestal, meanwhile, died violently in a suspected suicide in March 1949 at Bethesda Naval Hospital. To the end, he failed to appreciate the subtlety in Kennan's writings and speeches, explaining to an old Wall Street associate that "nothing about Russia can be understood without understanding the implacable and unchanging direction of Lenin's religion-philosophy."

In many ways, the Hamlet-like agony of George Kennan is the lot of the postwar American diplomat generally. The United States entered World War II as a wealthy, regional power. With the war's conclusion, it was one of two superpowers and one of the few combatant states that had fought the war from a distance. Europe and Russia were devastated. Most of Japan's major cities had been incinerated, first by incendiary bombs dropped by B-29s and then by two solitary nuclear strikes. The industrial mobilization that built America's powerful arsenal had accelerated the country's shift from a largely agrarian economy to a heavily industrialized and affluent one. Gradually, the isolationist Midwest conceded much of its influence with Washington to urban districts, which with their immigrant communities and educated elites tended to be internationalist in worldview. While Marshall's postwar plan for the recovery of Europe and a less rapid demobilization of U.S. troops abroad was a tough sell in a country weary of foreign wars, such policies would have been inconceivable in prewar America, when even the notion of a standing army was regarded with suspicion.

If, as the journalist Edward R. Murrow frequently pointed out, Americans never sought global hegemony, neither did they decline the prize once it presented itself. Gradually, as its prerogatives and privileges manifested themselves, a once insular nation grew comfortable in the mantle of global leadership. The most provincial farmer could appreciate the benefits of selling his surplus grain to the U.S. government for distribution as food aid overseas. Line workers in factory plants found steady work driving rivets in next-generation weaponry. Their employers' influence would expand exponentially as part of what an outgoing President Dwight Eisenhower would famously describe as the "military-industrial complex." As the armed forces became professionalized and their wages and benefits more generous, legislative districts with large military bases became important constituencies that lawmakers assiduously courted by endorsing ever-larger defense budgets and muscular foreign policies to go with them. These converging interests transformed Washington from a sleepy southern town into a New Rome. By the war's end, the old State, War, and Navy Building had been broken up into separate departments like a generous inheritance divided among siblings. (In a blow to official candor, the War Office in 1949 was renamed the Department of Defense.) America's war-fighting and foreign policy agencies now had their own dedicated compounds and a global preeminence that dare not speak its name: empire.

Yet budgets were still finite. Although State and Defense were the stars of the country's postwar bureaucracies, they were increasingly reliant for funding on legislative committees and the lawmakers who chaired them, men who delighted in their close proximity to the nation's vast diplomatic and military resources. High-profile tours by congressional delegations—"codels" in Beltway jargon—to overseas military bases made for compelling political theater for lawmakers eager to establish their national security credentials. With America now at the center of the world, and with all the power, prestige, and influence such a location confers, U.S. foreign policy was captured by local politics, with Congress demanding a preponderant say in how the country's overseas interests were defined. Suddenly men like Kennan, steeped through firsthand experience in the arcana of foreign lands and cultures, found themselves discussing policy on equal terms with men and women whose understanding of international affairs began and ended with the demands of Beltway politics.

As we have already seen, the strongest of these two competing realities is often the one that can scare the most people. In the aftermath of World War II, a small group of American experts on China would bear witness to the corrosive effect of this myopia on the world beyond the Beltway, where reality is nonnegotiable.

3

SEEING REDS

The nation which indulges toward another an habitual hatred or
an habitual fondness is in some degree a slave.
—GEORGE WASHINGTON, FROM HIS FAREWELL ADDRESS

IN THE HISTORY OF COLD WAR CONFLICT, THERE WAS PERHAPS NO
greater mismatch of forces than in the clash between Joseph Mc-
Carthy and John Stewart Service.

McCarthy, of course, needs no introduction. Even in his own time,
as he thrashed about congressional hearing rooms with feral intensity,
laying waste to the careers of civil servants, scientists, actors, academics,
and writers, his name had became an epithet for guilt by association and
the tyranny of the mind. As a political phenomenon, he burned hot and
fast; his journey from notorious Red-baiter, an identity forged for him
by colleagues one January night at a Georgetown eatery—an eerie derivative of Hitler's beer-hall putsch—to his death in 1957 took a mere
seven years. (When McCarthy's star finally crested, wags referred sardonically to McCarthy*was*ism.) In his infamy he is more metaphor than
man, a parody of the oafish, bullying alarmist. But he played a key role
in the perversion of U.S. foreign policy, a legacy that, like his signature
tactics, survives to this day.

John Stewart Service never sought notoriety. A model diplomat and
one of the country's greatest Sinologists, he was happiest in some remote
part of China, conversing with village elders about the events that were
then capsizing the nation. By refusing to bend his conclusions to match
the political fashions of Washington, Service put himself on a collision
course with McCarthy. The soft-spoken diplomat was as admired,
thoughtful, and worldly as the abusive Wisconsin senator was detested,
parochial, and intolerant. As was common among many of the State

Department's "China Hands" during World War II and its aftermath, Service's life is resonant of a hero's tale in Greek tragedy.* In diplomatic cables and congressional testimony, he accurately predicted that America's China policy, the cornerstone of which was unconditional support for Chiang Kai-shek, was leading to disaster. He worked intimately with both sides in the country's civil war and won the respect—grudgingly so, in the case of Chiang—for his deep knowledge of that ancient and most complex land. He served with distinction under some of America's finest statesmen, including George Marshall.

In 1949 Mao Zedong and his forces triumphed over Chiang's Kuomintang, or Nationalist, government, an outcome foretold years earlier by Service and his colleagues. Yet their prophecies were ignored at home and many of them were destroyed professionally amid allegations, nearly all of them bogus, of having communist sympathies. Richard Johnson, who was head of the department's Office of Chinese Affairs during the worst of the second Red Scare, remembered watching with dread as McCarthy claimed one Sinologist after another. "McCarthy had succeeded in creating a good deal of fear in the ranks," Johnson said years later. "You never knew when you were going to show up on some list for some crime you really didn't commit."

It was Service, however, who bore the full punitive wrath of McCarthy and his supporters. One of them, Richard Nixon, would vindicate the China Hands two decades later by restoring relations with China, a policy they had prescribed all along. But the damage to the State Department was deep and long-lasting. Had President Truman tapped the wiser, more mature heads under his employ, had he listened to his Sinologists unbowed by politics, the Cold War may have been shortened by decades. As historian Barbara Tuchman wrote in 1972, on the eve of Nixon's groundbreaking visit to Beijing:

> Three years of civil war in a country desperately weary of war and
> misgovernment might have been, if not entirely averted, certainly

---

* Service and his colleagues objected to being referred to as China Hands, a term they employed pejoratively to describe the often overindulged and underachieving career expatriates common to the bars and clubs of Shanghai, Hong Kong, and Singapore. It is used here for the sake of expediency.

curtailed. The United States, guiltless of prolonging the civil war by consistently aiding the certain loser, would not have aroused the profound antagonism of the ultimate winner. . . . If, in the absence of ill-feeling, we had established relations on some level with the People's Republic . . . and if the Chinese had not been moved by hate and suspicion of us to make common cause with the Soviet Union, it is conceivable that there might have been no Korean War with all its evil consequences. From that war rose the twin specters of an expansionist Chinese communism and an indivisible Sino-Soviet partnership. Without these concepts to addle statesmen and nourish demagogues, our history, our present, and our future would have been different. We may not have come to Vietnam.

Instead, politics prevailed. McCarthy, the demon seed of a nation's fears and prejudices, would become an important midwife to a new wave of American militarism.

There was, in fact, one issue on which both McCarthy and Service were in agreement: they both thought the accords reached at the Yalta Conference were flawed. Code-named Argonaut, the conference of the Allied powers held at the Black Sea resort in February 1945 committed the United States, Britain, and Russia on the eve of victory in Europe to the restructuring of the postwar world. Partition of Germany was discussed, as was the fate of Eastern European countries occupied by Soviet forces having been "liberated" from Nazi aggression. Among the meeting's landmark achievements was Stalin's promise to Roosevelt of Russian participation in the newly formed United Nations and an assurance, which he had no intention of honoring, of free elections in Poland. Roosevelt also got out of Stalin two other commitments the Americans badly wanted: Russian participation in the Pacific war, where Japan was still holding out, and support of a unity government in China. Should the atomic bomb program fail, worried Marshall and Secretary of War Henry Stimson, Washington would need Russian help in the invasion of Japan. At the same time, it was thought, Stalin's blessing of Nationalist-Communist rapprochement would guarantee postwar stability in China, given Stalin's presumed influence over Mao.

In 1951 McCarthy would attack the Yalta accords in general and Marshall in particular for their "craven appeasement" of Russian hegemony in Eastern Europe while at the same time allowing Moscow entrée to the Far East. Marshall's goal, McCarthy thundered, was to "diminish the United States in world affairs and . . . to impair our will to resist evil." McCarthy was not alone. Months earlier, the conservative but more respectable Robert Taft had blamed the war in Korea on Marshall's failure to negotiate an end to China's civil war in a manner favorable to Chiang.

Service, of course, had a different interpretation of Yalta and its failings. The problem, he told an interviewer years later, was the American assumption that China was subordinate to Russia in an indivisible communist bloc. The Yalta agreement, Service said, "was based on the idea that if we made a deal with Stalin, the Chinese Communists would very nicely and quietly go along with what Stalin had told them to do, which was the exact opposite of what all of us in the field were bitterly reporting." It was a specialist's bias: nuanced, sophisticated, and, at least in this case, wholly accurate. Just as Woodrow Wilson erred in 1918 by dismissing the Bolsheviks as German stooges, so did Roosevelt and his circle of advisers—and for that matter, many of his political enemies—create in their minds a Sino-Soviet monolith that did not exist. And just as Wilson ignored informed advice from Moscow about the authenticity of the communist revolt against the tsar, so did Roosevelt discount intelligence he was getting from his own experts at the very epicenter of China's convulsions.

The result was no mean diplomatic feat: twice in thirty years, a myopic Washington managed to antagonize the legitimate governments of two of the world's most important geopolitical powers. These blunders—costly in both blood and coin—may have been prevented but for a deeply ingrained American contempt for diplomats and diplomacy that prevailed throughout much of the country's first two centuries and that lingers to this day. During the Victorian era, when antipathy for Old World intrigue and equipoise was at its peak, diplomats were considered exotic and somewhat malign confections. Their frequency of international travel and fluency in languages implied wealth and levels of education well beyond the national average. In an electorate with a finely tuned ear for snobbery, ambitious politicians associated with diplomatic elites at their peril.

No one understood this better than Roosevelt, who himself had descended to the White House from the upper echelons of American aristocracy. Just prior to the nation's entry into the war, he is said to have remarked that the State Department was neutral on the question of war and he hoped it would remain so. He considered career diplomats as out of touch with the country politically, and he treated key diplomatic posts, as did so many presidents before and after him, as a currency of political patronage. The estrangement between Roosevelt and his diplomatic corps was particularly pronounced as it related to China, a country with which he had a filial bond: Russell & Company, which plied the opium trade that linked South Asia with Shanghai and Hong Kong, did a lucrative business with the Delano family. The connection to such renegade commerce gave the blue-blood Roosevelts a hint of menace that the president relished. It also imbued him with that most dangerous of presidential conceits: a belief that he possessed an "instinct" for a country or region that, though lacking in quantifiable value, somehow transcended the real-world expertise of his Foreign Service officers. Taken together, Roosevelt's self-delusion, the caricature of the diplomat as an effete other, and a parochial Congress, would seal the fate of the China Hands and guarantee a series of U.S. foreign policy disasters in East Asia.

John Service—throughout his life he went by the nickname "Jack"— was born on August 3, 1909, in the Sichuan provincial city of Chengdu. His parents, who graduated together from the University of California at Berkeley, were missionaries who had come to China four years earlier. Jack's father, Robert, was a disciplined man who enjoyed running and horseback riding and had a fondness for Tibetan art. Grace Boggs, his wife, was a small but resilient Presbyterian (Robert was a Baptist) who despite an abundance of servants rose every morning at six thirty to ensure her husband's collars were suitably starched.

Service was fluent in the Sichuan provincial dialect by the age of eleven. He attended high schools in Shanghai and later at Berkeley, where the family had returned for a second home leave in 1924. Three years later he entered Oberlin College, where he majored in both art history and economics. Like his father, Service was an avid runner and distinguished himself as a cross-country and track-and-field star. (Years later, in wartime China, he would operate under the code name Hare.) He joined the Foreign Service immediately after graduation and in 1933 was assigned as a clerk to the U.S. consulate in Kunming, the capital of Yunnan province. He received a full commission as a Foreign Service officer and two years later was rotated to the U.S. embassy in Chungking, the capital of Nationalist China. There he served under Ambassador Clarence E. Gauss, a seasoned China expert. A native of Washington, D.C., Gauss tutored Service as to the capricious ways of America's capital and quickly elevated his new charge to second secretary.

In 1950, when Service's patriotism and character were under assault, Gauss testified on his behalf in response to a State Department Loyalty Security Board inquiry:

> I don't know of any officer in my whole thirty-nine years of service who impressed me more favorably than Jack Service. . . . He was objective in his approach to all the political problems we had. . . . In his political information and everything else, he thought as an American. And to me, that was the most refreshing thing I could have had in my whole service. For instance, in Chungking I had an officer who was so pro–Chiang Kai-shek that he would go red in the face when anybody said anything in criticism of the existing government. You couldn't deal—you couldn't use an officer like that. But Jack Service impressed me . . . as one of that type of American that could go right down the middle of the road as an American who recognized that he was abroad to recognize American interests at things from the American standpoint. There was no suggestion in any case of pro or anti anybody.

Here, by projecting Service's nonpartisan analysis as being authentically and extraordinarily "American," Gauss implies conflict between the nation's foreign policy interests as they are and the way politicians in Washington often make them out to be. If Service did write critically of the Nationalist government, and he was one of many who expressed doubt about the Generalissimo's staying power, it was because there was much to be critical about.

Mao Zedong and Chiang Kai-shek differed from each other in nearly every way. Mao was a revolutionary hero from Hunan province, having left his father's farm to join the rebellion against the Qing dynasty when he was eighteen years old. He embraced communism in his mid-twenties and he dedicated his life to ridding China of foreign influence. Chiang, in contrast, was born to upper-middle-class parents in Zhejiang province along China's eastern coast. He chose a military career early in life, and the eclectic nature of his education reflects in many ways the complexity of interests vying for control of China in the early twentieth century. Chiang attended several Japanese military academies, and in the 1920s he worked closely with Bolshevik military instructors in the Whampoa Military Academy in Canton. He fought alongside Soviet officers in skirmishes with warlords, and he negotiated with advisers from the Third Communist International. In the early 1930s he retained a cadre of German officers, veterans of World War I, as technical advisers and trainers. Later, in the war with Japan, he would work closely with the Americans.

While Chiang, a committed Christian after converting to the faith for the sake of his marriage, labored to modernize China under Western tutelage, the atheist Mao sought to industrialize the country alone and under a Marxist rubric. Although Chiang's vision was ultimately vindicated by the economic miracle he helped engineer in Taiwan, he could never outgrow his association with criminal elements and the perception of him as a Western stooge. While Mao was taking the fight to the Japanese during World War II, for example, Chiang clung to power by cutting deals with warlords and gangsters. Chiang rarely campaigned in any meaningful way, seeking instead to husband his resources for the civil war he knew would come once the Americans defeated Japan.

———

Impressed by the communists' resistance against the Japanese, the U.S. Army investigated whether it might be in Washington's interests to open relations with Mao and develop him into a useful postwar ally. It launched an observation group, known as the Dixie Mission, which would liaise with Mao and his second in command, Zhou Enlai, at their headquarters and Communist Party capital in Yan'an. John Paton Davies Jr., a Foreign Service officer and diplomatic attaché to Lieutenant General Joseph Stilwell, arranged to have his childhood friend and colleague Jack Service assigned to the mission as its State Department representative. Chiang, still recognized by the United States as China's legitimate head of state, resisted the Dixie Mission but relented under pressure from Roosevelt.

Service, now attached to Stilwell's China-Burma-India command, flew to Yan'an on July 22, 1944, along with his nine military counterparts. They were treated amiably but austerely, living alongside their hosts in mud structures carved from beneath cliffs along the Yen River. ("The Allies should be received warmly and modestly," according to a stiffly worded directive of the Central Committee of the Communist Party. "It is necessary to refrain from excessive luxury while avoiding indifference.") They would organize baseball games and, together with the Chinese, hunt pheasant. During the warm spring and summer months, they would gather for Saturday-night parties in a nearby pear orchard.

Until his departure from Yan'an in April 1945, Service filed a trove of reports to Stilwell about the communists' vision for China, based on personal interviews with the leadership from Mao on down. He recommended that a request from Mao and Zhou for an audience with Roosevelt, forwarded by him to Patrick Hurley, the new U.S. ambassador to the Nationalists' capital city of Nanjing, should be given serious consideration. The Nationalists, he wrote Stilwell on October 10, 1944, from his chilly, dried-mud dormitory in Yan'an, were in disarray. The esteem in which the Generalissimo was once held had crumbled. His inner circle was corrupt and inept, and he had refused to engage the Japanese until prodded by his own people. The notion of Nationalist "authority" over a unified China, according to Service, was a canard that only Washington believed in.

"Our policy toward China should be guided by two facts," he wrote. "First, we cannot hope to deal successfully with Chiang without being hard-boiled. *Second, we cannot hope to solve China's problems (which are now our problems) without consideration of the opposition [communist] forces."* [Service's emphasis.] Service then suggested Tito's Yugoslavia—communist, but independent of Moscow—as a useful model on which to base U.S. relations with a postwar Communist China. "We should end the hollow pretense that China is unified and that we can talk only to Chiang. This puts the trump card in Chiang's hands."

Service's was no lone voice in the wilderness. Albert C. Wedemeyer, the U.S. Army lieutenant general who succeeded Stilwell as Marshall's liaison to Chiang, filed reports throughout 1944–1945 that were consistent with those written by Service and his colleagues. Though he would later line up behind McCarthy against Marshall for "losing" China, Wedemeyer wrote that Chiang was "impotent and confounded," while Chiang's staff hid their incompetence and cravenness behind incomplete and inaccurate reporting. The bankruptcy of Nationalist credibility relative to the communists was intuitively summed up by John Melby, the political officer at the U.S. embassy in Nanjing. "It was easier to talk with [the communists] than with the Nationalists," he told an interviewer. "You knew the Nationalists were lying most of the time. The communists never lied." The subtext is obvious: Mao and his advisers could of course be expert liars if their needs required it. But in this case they had no reason to lie. They were winning.

Such assessments echoed those cabled to Washington by Stilwell, who despised Chiang and who was replaced at the Generalissimo's urging with the help of the virulently anticommunist Hurley. Stilwell aide John Davies told the White House that civil war was inevitable after Japan's defeat and that Chiang would in all likelihood lose. Edward Rice, who served throughout China in the Foreign Service from 1935 until the defeat of Japan, predicted during his home leave in 1945 that the communists would be in control of mainland China "within four years," a forecast that would prove remarkably accurate. There was even a perception circulating among the China Hands of a likely Sino-Soviet split. Certainly the communists were signaling such an outcome as early as 1945, when Zhou told Marshall that "prosperity and peace of China could only be promoted by the introduction of the American political system, science, industrialization, and of agrarian reform in a program of free individual enterprise." When Marshall, in China at Truman's request to jump-start efforts for a unity government, asked Zhou about reports that Mao would soon be traveling to Moscow, Zhou scoffed in reply. "On the contrary," he said. "He would very much like to go [to] the United States, where he believes he would be able to learn much."

Were the communists indulging in what would become a familiar Cold War stratagem—playing Washington and Moscow against one another? Marshall reported that his staff was divided over "whether or not [Zhou] was implying that his party would cooperate with the United States rather than Russia." But only four years later, a majority of China experts were counting on it. Ralph Clough, who spent his entire career as a U.S. diplomat in China and Taiwan, said in an interview that in mid-1949 he and his colleagues cabled Washington "to the effect that the Nationalists were losing the civil war, that it was important for us to maintain some connection [with Mao]. We expressed the view that, in time, strains would develop between the Soviet Union and China . . . that we should wait for that time, take advantage of what we felt then would be a growing division between the Soviet Union and China."

All these things would come to pass. In 1946 Chiang declared he would attack Mao directly at Yan'an despite advice against such a strike by Marshall. Northern China was too big for the Nationalists to operate effectively, he told Chiang. The communists controlled the countryside and would cut his supply lines to ribbons. Predictably, Chiang's offensive failed. By spring 1947, it was clear even Marshall could not engineer a communist-Nationalist entente, and by March the last of the Dixie Mission's delegates had gone home. It was the beginning of the end of a briefly lived Chinese republicanism. "We could see it coming," Clough remembered. "We'd go into our embassies and our military attaché would put up a map and give us a briefing on the latest military situation. Any layman could see it was going badly for the Nationalists."

By May 1950, China's civil war had been reduced to communist harassment of Chiang's disheveled troops as they scrambled aboard ships and ferries bound for the island of Taiwan, the final seat of republican

China. The battles for China were over, but the war on the China Hands was just revving up.

The October 10, 1944, cable Service wrote for Stilwell, in which he foreshadowed a Nationalist defeat and encouraged entente with the communists, never reached the general. Having been recalled from China, Stilwell had been tethered to a desk in Washington when Service filed copies of his memo, as he did with all his communications, at the U.S. embassy in Chungking, then serving as the Nationalists' provisional capital. Upon receipt of Service's plea to dump the Generalissimo, U.S. ambassador Hurley seized the memo as evidence of insubordination and demanded its author be returned to Washington, though in fact Service was working for Stilwell, not Hurley. Secretary of State James Byrnes defended his officer's reporting procedures as entirely appropriate, though this would be of little help. The consequences of Service's last-ditch effort to salvage America's China policy would refract through the network of Chiang's allies in Washington and, over time, redound to his destruction.

Ambassador Hurley—the same man who, as secretary of war, applauded Douglas MacArthur's attack on the Bonus Army in 1932—was another Roosevelt envoy chosen more for his charisma and political connections than for his expertise. Born in Indian territory in 1883, he would regularly punctuate somber diplomatic meetings and ceremonies with Choctaw war whoops and snake dances. A successful energy lawyer from Tulsa, Hurley was known in Chungking as the "Big Wind" for his gaseous volubility. So unschooled was he in Chinese tradition and culture that he once referred to Chiang's wife as "Madame Shek." Ignorant American envoys, however, were valuable assets to the Nationalist cause; the less they knew about China's true circumstances, the more pliant they would be in the mother-of-pearl clutches of Madame Chiang. Inevitably, Hurley would become an important node in the nebula of hard-line conservative interests that made up the China lobby.

Throughout his posting to Chungking, the ambassador happily subverted Roosevelt's goal of a unity government. With Wedemeyer's help, Hurley intercepted Service's relay of Mao's desire for a meeting with

Roosevelt. The White House was unaware of the request, as were Marshall and his staff as they considered the sincerity and significance of Zhou's entreaties for warmer ties with Washington. In jamming the gears of U.S. foreign policy, Hurley, like so many members of the China lobby in their myriad vocations, was effectively acting as a double agent. Because he regarded the interests of the United States as seamlessly and sacredly one with those of Nationalist China, however, he saw no conflict in his actions. This presumption, uncompromised by doubt and combined with a profound disinterest in China for its own sake, was the fuel of the lobby's power and the ducts for its venom. Like other alliances built on ideology rather than self-interest, the China lobby prevailed less as a means to an end than as an end in itself.

At the vortex of the lobby was the Soong clan. Its patriarch was a Hakka Chinese runaway who was scooped up in the spiritual embrace of a Methodist minister and who chose for himself the name Charlie Soong. He attended Trinity College and Vanderbilt University and, upon his return to China, married the third daughter of a venerable Christian family, who bore him three sons and three daughters. Charlie's eldest daughter, Ai-ling, married into one of China's richest banking families. Ch'ing-ling, the middle daughter, eloped with the revolutionary Sun Yat-sen. The third daughter, Mei-ling, married Chiang Kai-shek. As a Wellesley graduate, Mei-ling would dazzle Christian America as Madame Chiang.

Charlie's eldest son—Tse-Ven, who quickly became known as "T.V."—was a prominent banker in his own right. In the early 1930s, T.V. found his niche in the family business as the fund-raiser for Chiang's wars on the communists, which Chiang called "bandit suppression campaigns." As China's central bank governor and finance minister, he caught the eye of Henry Luce, the legendary media mogul. In Luce, the Soong clan had found another American benefactor, albeit this time a Presbyterian. Luce was born a son of missionaries in Penglai City, China, and attended several Chinese and British boarding schools before he was sent to the United States. By the 1940s, the archconservative Luce was among the most influential men in America. In addition to *Time* magazine, which he launched in 1923, he controlled such properties as *Fortune, Life,* and *Sports Illus-*

trated. Together with his wife, Clare Boothe, a congresswomen, playwright, editor, and writer who would serve as America's ambassador to Italy, the two were a powerful force in the emerging postwar conservative movement.

Prior to the war, Luce rejected his fellow conservatives' hidebound isolationism in a landmark editorial penned less than a year before the attack on Pearl Harbor. "The American Century," as Luce's column was headlined, appeared in the February 17, 1941, edition of *Life*. In the archaeology of U.S. militarization, "The American Century" is the equivalent of a Paleolithic cave drawing of things to come, embroidered as it is with the messianism that informs U.S. foreign policy today. With Britain savaged by the blitz, Luce argues, America was already at war as its values, if not its homeland, were under attack. Luce concedes as justifiable popular fears that joining the war with Nazi Germany "will be the end of our constitutional democracy . . . that some form of dictatorship is required to fight a modern war, that we will certainly go bankrupt, that in the process of war and its aftermath our economy will largely be socialized." Nevertheless, he implores his readers to discard their overabundance of humility and restraint and "accept wholeheartedly our duty and opportunity as the most powerful and vital nation in the world and in consequence to exert upon the world the full impact of our influence, for such purposes as we see fit and by such means as we see fit."

What distinguishes "The American Century" is Luce's avuncular optimism forty years before Ronald Reagan made it an art form. No other country, he writes, has so "teemed with manifold projects and magnificent purposes . . . weaving them all together into the most exciting flag of all." Furthermore, if Americans would only accept their destiny as a world leader, "we can drive confidently towards a victorious conclusion and, what's more, have at least an even chance of establishing a workable peace." Luce makes no mention of empire. There is no urgent call for a massive mobilization of men and arms to meet the horror to come. Instead, he calls for a robust "internationalism" over "old, old . . . battered isolationism." Luce the missionary's son insists that America be the "Good Samaritan" of the world and set aside "at least a dime" for every dollar spent on national defense "in a gigantic effort to feed the world."

In being responsible to itself, according to Luce, America was being responsible to the world it was destined to lead.

In this American idyll, Luce guaranteed the Chiangs and Nationalist China pride of place. During the war, *Time*'s famed China correspondent Theodore White hung a sign on the wall of his bureau in Chungking that read: "Any resemblance to what is written here and what is printed in *Time* magazine is purely coincidental." Luce fumed whenever White's reports were not sufficiently laudatory of the Nationalists and White often pushed back, most notably over his frank account of Stilwell's dismissal. The story, he wrote to Luce in a stinging forty-five-page rebuke, was "edited into a lie" by foreign editor Whittaker Chambers, who recast the piece to reflect the biases of Chiang and Chiang ally General Claire Chennault, commander of the U.S. Fourteenth Air Force. In response, Luce countered that backing Chiang was no different from supporting Winston Churchill.

The legendary clashes between the Yankee curmudgeon Stilwell and the flamboyant Texan Chennault yielded Chiang another powerful friend in Captain Joseph Alsop, a Chennault staff officer. At the center of their ongoing dispute was Chennault's conviction that the Japanese could be defeated with American bombing strikes in coordination with Nationalist forces. (A misguided faith in airpower would become a costly factor in the militarization of U.S. foreign policy generally, though particularly in Vietnam.) Alsop, himself a zealous anticommunist, considered Stilwell an obstacle to victory who, he once told Service, "should be drawn and quartered." Through his A-list connections in Washington—he was a friend of Harry Hopkins's and a distant relative of Eleanor Roosevelt's—Alsop played a pivotal role in Stilwell's removal. A half decade later, Alsop would agitate shamelessly but effectively against the China Hands. But for Service, the storm arrived almost immediately upon his return to the United States following his confrontation with Hurley. After so many years of living a stranger-than-fiction life of high adventure in an exotic land, the missionary's son was about to slip into the dark labyrinth of a Kafka novel.

On April 19, 1949, less than a week after his return to Washington, Service met with Philip Jaffe, the editor of an obscure fortnightly journal called *Amerasia*. It was their first meeting, though Jaffe was known among China specialists and journalists as a left-wing greeting-card mogul with a passionate interest in the Far East. He had met Mao in Yan'an and was a supporter of the *Voice of China*, an English-language, pro-communist journal published in Shanghai. So when FBI agents learned that an article published in a January 1945 edition of *Amerasia* contained information that had been classified by the U.S. government, they figured Jaffe for a spy and placed him under round-the-clock surveillance.

Service was unaware Jaffe was being staked out, so he saw no reason why he should not continue to meet with him, as he did seven times in the six weeks that followed their first encounter. Jaffe was hungry for news from China, and Service, who considered helping the media to understand U.S. foreign policy as part of his job as a diplomat, shared with him copies of reports he had filed from China. Several were marked confidential, but mostly by Service himself. On May 8, Service visited Jaffe at his office at the Statler Hotel in Washington, unaware the premises had been bugged. Four weeks later, on June 5, Service was arrested at his home by special agents and charged with violating the Espionage Act. (Upon hearing of his arrest, the Nationalist press reported that Service was a Japanese spy.) Jaffe and four others were arrested as part of a sweep. In early August, Jaffe and two of the alleged conspirators were indicted by a federal grand jury and given modest fines, while the charges against Service and the two other suspects were dismissed. (In Service's case, the jurors had voted 20–0 against indictment.) On August 12, Service was restored to active duty after being cleared by a Foreign Service Personnel Board. He was sent to Tokyo to work briefly on Douglas MacArthur's occupation administration and over the next five years would serve U.S. missions in New Zealand and India. Subsequent personnel hearings would clear him of any wrongdoing. But his nightmare had just begun.

Soviet espionage in Cold War America was a fact, and some alleged spies—most famously Alger Hiss, though he was convicted of perjury, not spying—were prominent government officials. The great political events of the last century were driven by an intense ideological struggle that was often waged in the shadows by both sides. But was there any substance at all to the wild claims that fanned the postwar Red Scare?

It is important to place McCarthyism within the context of American communism's rise and fall. Throughout much of the 1930s, America, like Europe, was home to a vigorous communist movement. The Great Depression and the ascent of fascism across the Atlantic elevated the Communist Party in America from a loose association of "parlor Bolsheviks," as they were once dismissed, to a fiercely motivated and highly disciplined political force. Membership in the CPA and its affiliate groups contested elections on the national, state, and local levels. In 1932, the CPA ticket (it included the first black vice presidential nominee in U.S. history) won 102,785 votes, compared with the Socialist candidate's 884,000 and Roosevelt's 22.8 million. In 1938 three-quarters of Americans supported the Moscow-backed Spanish Republicans in their war against the Nazi-supported monarchists and the fascist Falange. Soviet Russia was a potential ally against fascism, not an enemy. Until the Foreign Agents Registration Act became law in 1938, the KGB's activities in America were not considered illegal. Nor, of course, was Communist Party membership.

The decision by Roosevelt to restore diplomatic ties with Moscow uncorked a torrent of Russian spies and other shadowy figures into U.S. cities, and by 1936 he was compelled to give the FBI a green light to track subversives on both ends of the ideological spectrum. Not surprisingly, Stalin's agents exploited the asymmetrical nature of the espionage war—it is by definition easier to infiltrate a free society than an authoritarian one—with alacrity. Their operations were as much tragicomic as they were pernicious, however, and most of them were intercepted and rolled up by U.S. agents. Party membership, which had been dwindling throughout the 1930s, plunged after Stalin signed his 1939 nonaggression pact with Hitler, a stunning betrayal of the communists' struggle against fascism. By 1945, with the Depression over and Nazi Germany destroyed, the communist movement in America had lost its raison d'être, reducing the pool of Stalin's spy rings into a puddle.*

---

* One of the most successful counterespionage efforts in U.S. history was Operation Venona, a highly secretive cryptanalysis network managed largely by the U.S. Army's

McCarthy, wielding his list of high-level traitors like a barbed mace, was flailing at an empty threat. That did little to stop him, of course, and it would be cold comfort for men such as Jack Service. Even before McCarthy's notorious debut on the national political stage, the State Department and its East Asia desk were drifting squarely into the China lobby's crosshairs. In the fall of 1949, with the Nationalists licked and the communists erecting a bamboo curtain around China, Service's treachery against the Generalissimo was dredged up on the floor of Congress. On October 19, 1949, Minnesota representative Walter Judd, who years earlier had toured China as a medical missionary, read Service's October 1944 cable to Stilwell into the *Congressional Record*. A member of the Council Against Communist Aggression, Judd characterized Service's memo as a smoking gun of complicity with Chinese communism.

By early 1950, the Nationalists' defeat had rendered the Truman administration vulnerable to a Republican Party eager to regain the White House after seventeen years in the political wilderness. The offensive began in January with a three-part series of columns by Joe Alsop, in the *Saturday Evening Post*. Entitled "Why We Lost China," the articles resurrected the China lobby's familiar dirge about how the Chiangs were sold out by a faction—Alsop stopped just short of calling it a conspiracy—of State Department and Pentagon officials with clear communist sympathies.

The *Post* series was not only an important milestone in the China Hands' forced march into disgrace. It was also a manifesto for an imperial vision of American foreign policy that has survived to this day. At a time when most colonial powers were disgorging their possessions, either willingly or in response to national liberation movements, the Alsop articles lent intellectual credibility to the notion that the world was divided between "our" dominions and "theirs." Nationalist China was Washington's

---

Signals Intelligence Service. Launched in 1943, Venona exposed 349 citizens as Soviet operatives, including New York congressman Samuel Dickstein, the only federal legislator known to have been in Moscow's employ. Perhaps the most significant achievement of Soviet espionage in the United States was its infiltration of the Los Alamos National Laboratory, site of the Manhattan Project, which historians estimate accelerated the development of a Russian bomb by about a year.

to lose, and the men who "lost" it were, if not actual traitors, then certainly too naive to be entrusted with affairs of state. Alsop's barrage assumed even greater resonance with the conviction in January of Alger Hiss and the bombshell revelation that same month that top nuclear physicist Klaus Fuchs had passed sensitive information and data to the Soviets while working on the Manhattan Project. Clearly, Truman and his inner circle couldn't recognize a communist conspiracy even as it enveloped half the planet. Republican leaders had found a weakness in the White House's defenses. All they needed was a battering ram.

On February 9, 1950, the city of Wheeling, West Virginia, became to twentieth-century demagoguery what Dallas is to political assassination. The obscure forty-one-year-old Joe McCarthy, who had recently been voted the worst member of the Senate in a poll of Capitol Hill correspondents, was expected to give a speech to the Women's Republican Club in favor of "adequate old age and other pensions," according to the *Wheeling News-Register*. Instead, McCarthy unveiled what he said was a list of pro-communist diplomats "known to the Secretary of State and who are nevertheless still working and shaping the policy of the State Department." McCarthyism was born. In a Senate speech, McCarthy spoke of "individuals who are loyal to the ideals and designs of communism rather than those of the free, God-fearing half of the world." The State Department's Far East desk was, according to McCarthy, honeycombed with "Communists and queers who have sold 400,000,000 Asiatic people into atheistic slavery." As historian Bruce Cumings put it, "For Americans who had to be told what a communist looked like, McCarthy supplied plausible models: mainly Eastern establishment blue bloods, but also Foggy Bottom scribblers, tweedy professors, closet-bound homosexuals, and China experts who had been abroad too long—anyone who might be identified as an internal foreigner, alien to the American heartland." On February 12, at a celebration of Lincoln's 141st birthday, McCarthy fingered the forty-year-old John Service along with three other people by name as "specific cases of people with communist connections." He slammed Dean Acheson, the new secretary of state, who refused to repudiate his old friend and aide Hiss, as a "pompous diplomat in striped pants, with the phony British accent [who] proclaimed to the American people that Christ on the Mount endorsed communism, high treason, and betrayal of sacred trust."

Pressured by McCarthy's rants, Congress convened in March an investigative committee led by Senator Millard Tydings. One by one, the Tydings Committee interrogated the most prominent men named on McCarthy's ever-evolving lists. John Carter Vincent, a former director of the State Department's Office of Far Eastern Affairs who was ambassador to Switzerland at the time, was accused of links to Red groups based on a copy of a telegram sent to him by a Swiss communist named Emile Stampfli. Another Asia scholar and writer, Owen Lattimore, was singled out by McCarthy as "a top Soviet agent" and "the architect of our Far Eastern policy," even though he did not work for the State Department and was unknown to Acheson. Lattimore returned to the United States from Afghanistan to defend himself before the committee. His testimony is as relevant today as it was then:

I say to you, gentlemen, that the sure way to destroy freedom of speech and the free expression of ideas and views is to attach to that freedom the penalty of abuse and vilification. If the people of this country can differ with the so-called China Lobby or with Senator McCarthy only at the risk of the abuse to which I have been subjected, freedom will not long survive. If officials of our government cannot consult people of diverse views without exposing themselves to the kind of attack that Senator McCarthy has visited upon officers of the State Department, our government policy will necessarily be sterile. It is only from a diversity of views fully expressed and strongly advocated that sound policy is distilled. He who contributes to the destruction of this process is either a fool or an enemy of this country.

While the Tydings Committee sifted through McCarthy's charges, Service was on a freighter with his wife, three children, and household belongings en route to India for his next posting. He would not reach Calcutta, however. Unbeknownst to Service, the Loyalty Review Board, which Truman had established in 1947 to protect his flank from Red-baiters, was recommending that the State Department's Loyalty Security Board summon him home for an interview. McCarthy, meanwhile, working from information supplied by Patrick Hurley and other Nationalist allies, was telling the Tydings Committee that Service was "a known associate and collaborator with communists" and espionage agents. He also charged that J. Edgar Hoover had a bulletproof case against Service for his role in the *Amerasia* affair, though this was denied in writing by the Department of Justice.

On March 15, Service was ordered via telegram to return to Washington by airplane the moment his ship reached the Japanese port city of Yokohama. He arrived in Washington on March 27 and was hosted by fellow Foreign Service officer and China specialist Fulton Freeman and his wife. ("We'll take our chances," Freeman replied when reminded by his guest that associating with someone on McCarthy's list could be hazardous to his career.) Service would hang his hat at the Freemans' Georgetown home for the next six months while he defended himself before the State Department committee.

The panel convened on May 26. Among those who testified on Service's behalf was George Kennan, then counselor to the State Department and still the undisputed expert on foreign affairs, particularly as it related to communism. Kennan praised memorandums written by Service that warned how America's support of Chiang Kai-shek and his ruinous policies was only rewarding Moscow by discounting China as a possible counterweight to the Soviets. The adamant tenor of Service's cables could be explained, Kennan said, drawing from his own experience living and working abroad, "by the natural tendency of all official observers . . . to try to debunk the official propaganda of a foreign government which you feel is trying to put something over on your own government."

The board found nothing sinister in Service's record. The papers he had passed on to Jaffe were dismissed as nonsensitive, and the microphones at the Statler had picked up nothing but harmless banter during his visit there. On October 9 he was cleared. In June, the Tydings Committee had concluded its hearings with no evidence of wrongdoing by any of McCarthy's targets, including Service. (The Stampfli telegram to Vincent turned out to be a forgery concocted by a murky figure named

Charles Davis in the pay of John Farrand, a McCarthy agent.) Tydings, a Democrat, condemned McCarthy's charges as "a fraud and a hoax." Republicans gave as good as they got, with California's William Jenner lashing out at Tydings's findings as "the most brazen whitewash of treasonable conspiracy in our history." The Senate voted to endorse the committee's finding, albeit along party lines.*

The war for America's soul was just beginning. If McCarthy was on a fishing expedition, Republican elites were right behind him, eagerly chopping bait. With an eye on his reelection that year and sensing a potential presidential bid two years later, Republican Robert Taft allegedly told McCarthy to "keep talking and if one case doesn't work out, proceed with another."

The fallout from McCarthy's charges was as real as their substance was baseless, particularly for Acheson. A year after he succeeded George Marshall as secretary of state on January 1, 1949, the same day Chiang Kai-shek resigned as president of republican China, Acheson was one of the most reviled men in government. So many threatening letters had cluttered his inbox he was forced to post guards at his Georgetown manor house day and night.

In June 1950, when North Korea invaded its southern neighbor only six months after Acheson appeared to have excluded it from America's Asia-defense perimeter, the attacks against him intensified. On August 7, Senator Kenneth Wherry of Nebraska called for Acheson's dismissal and a week later he declared that "the blood of our boys in Korea is on [his] shoulders, and no one else." When Wherry resumed his badgering of Acheson at a Senate committee hearing, the secretary of state rose and shouted, "Don't you dare shake your dirty little finger in my face!" When

---

* A notable exception was Margaret Chase Smith, a Republican senator from Maine, along with a half-dozen senators who signed her "Declaration of Conscience" on June 2, 1950. Smith criticized her own party for allowing the Senate to have been "too often . . . debased to the level of a forum of hate and character assassination sheltered by the shield of Congressional immunity. The nation sorely needs a Republican victory. But I do not want to see the Republican Party ride to victory on the Four Horsemen of Calumny— fear, ignorance, bigotry and smear."

Wherry, a former mortician from Pawnee City, persisted with his digit-wagging, the blue-blooded Acheson took what he later described as a "rather inexpertly aimed and executed swing" at Wherry's offending mouth. Fortunately for the dignity of the Senate, Adrian Fisher, the legal adviser to the State Department and a former guard on the Princeton football team, caught the arm of America's top diplomat before it could deliver its awful fury.*

Dean Acheson and his contemporaries lived in a crucible of global tension the likes of which the world has not known since. A superpower rivalry, catalyzed by a nuclear arms race, made war possible on several fronts at once—in Asia, in Berlin, in Iran, in Central Asia. His job was made more difficult by the war within, led by McCarthy, which made respectable the deranged notion that negotiation is appeasement.

Perhaps because of the McCarthy attacks, Acheson is commonly remembered as a soft-liner. He was not. In later years, as éminence grise to the Kennedy and Johnson administrations, he positioned himself on the hawkish side on the debates over Berlin in 1961 and the Cuban missile crisis a year later. In the late 1960s, he was among the last of Johnson's circle of advisers to conclude that the United States could not prevail in Vietnam. Resonant in his soaring appeals for the nation to confront a Soviet-inspired, if not Soviet-controlled, communist challenge to American ideals is the Reformed Protestantism he learned from his father. At heart a liberal interventionist with a Wilsonian worldview, Acheson saw the Cold War in terms as Manichaean as the Puritans saw their own righteous struggle against the evil "other." In some ways, he was more rigid in outlook than John Foster Dulles, Acheson's alter ego and successor as secretary of state, who despite his hard-line rubric was not averse to cutting the occasional backroom deal.

Acheson was no Marshall, however. He could not, as his former boss

---

* The next day, Acheson phoned the committee chairman, Tennessee senator Kenneth McKellar, to apologize for the incident. McKellar replied by telling Acheson he had phoned Truman after the meeting and suggested the president pay down the federal deficit "by putting you two on the vaudeville circuit." Acheson later wrote that his relations with Wherry improved considerably after his failed roundhouse attempt.

did in February 1948, admonish Congress against "a tendency to feel that wherever communist influence is brought to bear, we should immediately meet it." It was Acheson who as secretary of state was bound by both honor and duty to protect his Foreign Service officers from "the attack of the primitives," as he called the cabal of right-wing politicians and pundits, and it was Acheson who failed them. A Europeanist with little interest in China, Acheson felt no obligation to Chiang and the Nationalists; indeed both he and Truman were prepared to recognize Red China after the Nationalists fled. By mid-1949, however—four years after Mao's request for an audience with Roosevelt was stifled by Hurley and Wedemeyer—the communists began their "lean to one side" campaign in favor of Moscow. In Washington, of course, few outside the China Hands would make any distinction between the cause and the effect.

In August 1949, Acheson attempted to defuse the controversy over China with the release of a 1,054-page white paper. *United States Relations with China: With Special Reference to the Period 1944–1949* was compiled from more than a hundred thousand cables and transcribed interviews with officials from different agencies. Its goal was to reveal, through a meticulous, detailed, and transparent accounting, the corruption and ineptitude that did in the Nationalist government despite some $2 billion in U.S. aid. George Kennan, hospitalized with another one of his many ailments, read the document prior to its publication and proclaimed it one of the finest such reports he had ever seen. In *The Best and the Brightest*, David Halberstam's classic account of the American descent into Vietnam, the author praises the paper for "the intelligence and quality of the reporting. It was written by very bright young men putting their assessments on the line; in that sense it would be a high water mark for the Department."

As a political tool, however, it was a disaster. Declaring the paper "a sorry record of well-meaning mistakes," the *New York Times* admonished Acheson for holding Chiang responsible for the chaos in China rather than "the foreign-inspired dynamism of the Chinese Communist party." It went on:

What must stand out in any honest approach to the China problem is the fact that there has been a change of attitude on the part of the

United States toward the aims and the objectives of the Chinese Communists and the Soviet Union. What is now quite clear is that President Chiang's estimate of those aims was right and that the State Department's estimate was wrong.

Lest there be any doubt the Chinese communists were taking their orders from Moscow, the *Times* also ran a five-column analysis of the situation in Asia that began, "The state of the world-wide struggle between the United States and Soviet Russia seems to be this: We are winning in Europe; they are winning in the Far East."

For Hurley, the report was "a smooth alibi for the pro-communists in the State Department who had engineered the overthrow of our ally." William Knowland—"the senator from Formosa," as he was known to the press—condemned it as a "whitewash of a wishful, do-nothing policy which has succeeded only in placing Asia in danger of Soviet conquest." Even Mao Zedong got into the act. Though the white paper buttressed his own criticism of the Nationalists as void of public support, he dashed off five editorials in the communist press about how the document unmasked America's imperialist agenda. Acheson made things worse with the white paper's letter of transmittal. In it, he stated that the Chinese communist leaders "have publicly announced their subservience to a foreign power, Russia." Not only did such a statement undermine his own China experts, who had spent years trying to dispel the notion of a Sino-Soviet monolith, it played into the hands of the very China lobby his language was meant to appease. For that, Acheson provoked a drubbing from his rival, the shrewd Walter Lippmann. In a series of articles, the *New York Times* columnist attacked the white paper as an attempt by the administration to absolve itself of a crisis it lacked the courage to resolve. If Chiang was as corrupt and incapable as the White House claimed, he argued, why had the United States bankrolled him with a fortune in taxpayer funds? Why had it fully invested itself in a leader it knew was "hopelessly incompetent"? To imply that the State Department was not responsible for the China debacle because of the sheer inevitability of war, as the white paper seemed to do, is "tantamount to saying that there was no such thing as a sound or an unsound, a right or a wrong, a wise or an unwise policy toward the Chinese civil war." Lippmann demanded a full inquiry.

In his memoirs, Acheson lamented how the white paper was "unpalatable to believers in American omnipotence, to whom every goal unattained is explicable only by incompetence or treason." Outrage over the document, Acheson goes on, inspired Supreme Court justice Felix Frankfurter, Acheson's good friend and morning walking partner, to describe him as "a frustrated schoolteacher, persisting against overwhelming evidence to the contrary in the belief that the human mind can be moved by fact and reason."

Battered, Acheson effectively left his specialists to their fate. During a visit to Washington, Jerome Holloway, the U.S. consul general in Shanghai, found the nation's huddled diplomats in a funereal state. "They just didn't know what to do," he recalled later. "The amount of guidance they were getting was minimal, because the administration was under fairly heavy fire from the China lobby." In late 1949, Undersecretary of State Robert Lovett telegrammed the department's Chinese consulates and urged officers there to stand by while the White House charted a new China policy. The cable raised hopes that Washington was poised to offer the communist leadership normal relations. Those hopes were dashed a few weeks later with the arrival of a second cable ordering them to bug out.

"We got another telegram to all the China posts saying, 'Get out and get out immediately,'" remembered Philip Manhard, the vice counsel in Tianjin. "So evidently, . . . [by] January 1950, policy had been decided that we were not going to recognize Communist China."

As a political tactic, McCarthyism was a success. Truman, having been successfully portrayed as soft on communism, was handily defeated in the 1952 election by Republican candidate Dwight Eisenhower. Service would lose more than an election. In 1951 he was summoned before the Loyalty Review Board, which, based on a revised interpretation of his role in the *Amerasia* affair, concluded there was "reasonable doubt" as to his loyalty. Accordingly, it reversed the favorable finding handed down a year earlier by the State Department's Loyalty Security Board. Acheson, worn down by the constant jousting with McCarthy and his cabalists, dismissed Service immediately after learning of the decision.

Years later, the Supreme Court would vindicate Service by upholding the original findings of the Loyalty Security Board. But the damage was done—to Service, certainly, and many other China Hands who were emasculated by the China lobby. So great was the emotional stress on Fulton Freeman, it was said, that he had to have two-thirds of his stomach removed due to bleeding ulcers. Davies, Vincent, and a half-dozen others were either dismissed or exiled to obscure diplomatic outposts, a fellowship of martyrs who, as Senator J. William Fulbright put it, served their country well but were not served well by their country.* While many of them were vindicated in a variety of small ways, they were denied the hero's redemption they deserved.

In many ways, the damage done to the State Department by McCarthy's attacks was irreparable. Two years after John Foster Dulles assumed the reins at State, with his insistence on an Orwellian "positive loyalty" within his ranks, the number of applications for the Foreign Service examination had fallen from 2,710 to 1,261. Henceforth, it would be much harder for the department to recruit from among the nation's best-educated young people. Those who did pursue diplomatic careers would find a culture of caution that impaired lateral thinking. Apologists for Joe McCarthy may celebrate him for dispatching security risks where none existed, but his real legacy is the diminution of the Department of State into the intellectually inert and politically impotent agency that it is today. As historian Cumings writes, "Tailgunner Joe was a good marksman: he left a generation of liberals looking over their shoulders to the right, fearing another case of mistaken identity. . . . In foreign policy, the effect was to tie off and cauterize any thought of internationalist accommodation, and to push through to acceptability the rollback alternative."

---

* Vincent would be pink-slipped personally, if cordially, by Secretary of State John Dulles. He was given the choice between being fired and forfeiting his pension or quietly resigning and receiving $6,200 a year; Vincent chose the latter. The next Saturday, as instructed, he presented himself along with his lawyer, Walter Surrey, at Dulles's home with a letter of resignation. The secretary of state warmly invited his guests to sit down for a drink and talk about China. "After all," said Dulles without a trace of irony, "[Vincent] knows the situation there better than just about anybody."

The consequences of McCarthy's work would be reflected years later, in the February 1964 appointment of William Bundy as the assistant secretary of state for Far Eastern affairs. The elevation of a man like Bundy, a Washington insider with no East Asian experience, to such a job would come at a high price. By the time America's leaders were wading deeper into their country's greatest quagmire, there was no one with the experience, candor, authority, and thoughtfulness to lead them away.

4

INSIDE JOB

The integrity and vitality of our system is in greater
jeopardy than ever before in our history.
—NSC 68, APRIL 14, 1950

HENRY STIMSON WAS THE PRODUCT OF AN EARLIER AGE. HE
was born in 1867 to a wealthy New York family and attended
the Ivy League academies requisite for the political and financial elites of the day—Andover, Yale (where he was initiated into Skull &
Bones), and Harvard Law School. After joining the prestigious Wall
Street law firm Root & Clark in 1891, he became a protégé of Elihu Root,
the great American statesman who for his work as secretary of state to
William McKinley and Theodore Roosevelt would receive the Nobel
Peace Prize.

Stimson was a conservative Republican in an era when conservatism
stood for moderation and, at least among some wealthy families, a tradition of noblesse oblige. During World War I he helped raise an infantry
division of American volunteers that was sent to France, and he finished
the war as a colonel after serving in the regular Army as an artilleryman.
He was governor-general of the Philippines under Calvin Coolidge and
served as secretary of state under Herbert Hoover, when he famously
shut down the department's intelligence-gathering agency because, in
his words, "gentlemen don't read other gentlemen's mail." Joe Alsop, the
conservative columnist, referred to Stimson as "that granitic statue to
the ancient virtues."

Stimson was Roosevelt's secretary of war and he remained at his post
during the first year of the Truman administration. He was an early
critic of the Nazis and alongside George Marshall worked tirelessly to
prepare the country for war. He understood clearly what it would cost

and he was profoundly aware of his role in the prosecution of the deadliest conflict in human history. Like Marshall, he was a product of the kind of Victorian values, particularly humility and restraint, that would not age well in the postwar era. Intellectually and spiritually, he straddled an old world and a new one as distinct from one another as kerosene lamps and neon lighting.

By the summer of 1945, Stimson had already expressed his revulsion at the firebombing of Japanese cities by long-range B-29s. Though he had helped compile the list of Japanese cities earmarked for nuclear annihilation, he lamented the destruction of Hiroshima and Nagasaki as the only means of avoiding a long and costly ground attack on Japan— "the least abhorrent choice," as he put it. Within a month after Japan's surrender, he launched a rearguard action against a growing movement within the Truman White House to adopt an expanded atomic arsenal as both enforcer and talisman of American power.

On September 11, 1945, four years to the day after workers broke ground on the Pentagon construction site, Stimson made a formal case for relinquishing America's nuclear monopoly. In a memorandum he delivered personally to the president, Stimson argued that the atomic bomb "constitutes merely a first step in a new control by man over the forces of nature too revolutionary and dangerous to fit into the old concepts." Rejecting claims by some in the administration—disputed vigorously by the scientists who had built the bomb—that it would take decades for the Soviets to develop a nuclear device of their own, Stimson warned that relations between Washington and Moscow would be "virtually dominated by the problem of the atomic bomb." To preempt the weaponization of U.S.-Russian relations, he said, Washington must offer to "impound what bombs we now have in the United States, provided the Russian and the British would agree with us that in no event will they or we use a bomb as an instrument of war." On the eve of retirement after a lifetime of service in the military and the government, the seventy-seven-year-old Stimson was advising Truman to share the nation's nuclear technology with Stalin, and to do so urgently. He had no illusions about the dangers of entering into such a covenant with the likes of Joseph Stalin. But the price of a war waged with nuclear weapons, he reasoned, was greater than the risk of negotiating for their removal with someone whose interests in avoiding such a conflict were equal to his own. "The chief lesson I have learned in a long life," he wrote in the memo, "is that the only way you can make a man trustworthy is to trust him; and the surest way to make him untrustworthy is to distrust him and show your distrust."

The Stimson memo was endorsed by Secretary of Labor Lewis Schwellenbach, Postmaster General Robert Hannegan, and Dean Acheson, then acting secretary of state while Secretary James Byrnes was in London for a summit meeting of foreign ministers. Henry A. Wallace, secretary of commerce and a former vice president, fulsomely praised Stimson's proposal. Even the Joint Chiefs of Staff initially supported Stimson, in part because of their suspicion that a nuclear-armed Stalin would be far more likely than Washington to launch a preemptive strike.

Not everyone was so agreeable. At a September 21 cabinet meeting—it would be Stimson's last; immediately afterward he would say goodbye to the president and head for National Airport, where he was met by dozens of general officers in double rows, singing "Auld Lang Syne"—Stimson's proposal was condemned by Secretary of the Navy James Forrestal. To Stimson's case that "we do not have a secret to give away—the secret will give itself away," Forrestal declared that the bomb was "the property of the American people" and not for barter. The Soviets, he said, were so "Oriental in their thinking" they could not be trusted. Foreshadowing the demagoguery to come, Forrestal would deride any attempt to defuse an inevitable arms race as capitulation. "We tried that once with Hitler," he said. "There are no returns on appeasement." Secretary of State James Byrnes was no less adamant. At the summit meeting in London, he used the specter of America's nuclear monopoly like a truncheon to beat concessions out of Soviet foreign minister Molotov, but the talks ended inconclusively. Upon his return to Washington, Byrnes made it clear there could be no trusting the Russians.

Absent strong backing from Truman, Stimson's stately appeal for diplomacy never had a chance against Forrestal's jingoism. The president was new to the Oval Office and unsure of himself. The notion that Soviet posturing in Europe and Asia may have been a defensive response to American military might, which was now arrayed along Russia's historical frontiers in both Europe and Asia, sounded dangerous and hinted at apologia. Forced to choose between Stimson's hopeful world and Forrestal's dire one, he chose the latter. Thus orphaned, Stimson's call for direct U.S.-Soviet talks to head off a nuclear arms race "of a rather desperate character," as he had put it to Truman, was left to the very fate he cautioned against: a gradual smothering by low-level deliberation in toothless multilateral rounds.

In his memoirs, Acheson concludes that such an outcome was inevitable, given the depths of Soviet perfidy. James Chace, Acheson's biographer, is not so dismissive. In the January/February 1996 edition of *Foreign Affairs,* he argued that had Truman rejected his cabinet militarists in favor of Stimson's proposal, the Cold War "would have been substantially different. Hiroshima would have produced a balance of power rather than a balance of terror. Soviet behavior would likely have been far less confrontational." It was not to be, however. At an impromptu October press conference in Reelfoot Lake, Tennessee, Truman announced the United States would keep its nuclear secrets to itself. The nation's most valuable resource, he said, was the know-how to put scientific knowledge to work, "just the same as know-how in the construction of the B-29." With regard to the bomb, he said, if the Soviets "catch up with us on that, they will have to do it on their own hook, just as we did."* Secure in his belief that Moscow was decades away from developing its own atomic bomb, Truman withdrew into the security of America's nuclear monopoly.

Four years later, on September 3, 1949, a U.S. Air Force B-29 attached to the 375th Weather Reconnaissance Squadron of the Alaskan Air Command picked up abnormally high levels of atmospheric radiation while patrolling some 18,000 feet over the Bering Sea. Immediately after the plane landed at its base in Fairbanks, Alaska, its filters were packaged and sent to a lab at Berkeley, California, for radiochemical analysis. A team of scientists spent several days analyzing the samples, which contained evidence of fission isotopes of barium and cerium. On Monday, September 19, the scientists rendered their conclusions to David Lilienthal, the chairman

---

* One wonders if Truman appreciated the irony of such a comparison. In 1944 the Soviets rolled out the Tupolev 4, a stunningly accurate, down-to-the-rivet clone of the B-29 based on several of the long-range bombers that had been forced to make emergency landings in Vladivostok. Some three hundred Tu-4s were in operation by the time Moscow tested its first atomic bomb. None ever saw combat, however.

of the U.S. Atomic Energy Commission. That night Lilienthal entered a cryptic note in his diary: "Vermont affair, we are here," referring to the code name for the Russian atomic bomb project.

Truman was incredulous. How could "those Asiatics," as he put it, build something as complicated as a nuclear bomb? Four days later, White House press secretary Charles Ross distributed to reporters mimeographs of a typed statement that acknowledged "evidence that within recent weeks an atomic explosion occurred in the U.S.S.R." The sobriety of the announcement belied a White House in panic. Truman's initial response was to authorize the Atomic Energy Commission to build more atomic warheads—from a stockpile of just 50 in June 1948 to some 300 two years later. He also urged it to develop a hydrogen bomb—the Super-bomb, or simply "the Super," as it was known. Most foreign policy experts and much of the country's scientific community opposed developing such a weapon, which they estimated could be hundreds of times more powerful than the bombs that had obliterated Hiroshima and Nagasaki. Omar Bradley, chairman of the Joint Chiefs of Staff, initially suggested that the only value of such a weapon would be largely psychological, as the radius of its destruction would make it useless against military targets. Lilienthal strongly opposed the H-bomb, as did George Kennan. The General Advisory Committee of the AEC, which was led by Robert Oppenheimer, the "father" of the atomic bomb, issued an appeal to Truman against building a weapon that "would bring about the destruction of innumerable lives."

In support of development was a broad confederation of lawmakers, civil servants, and active-duty and retired military leaders. Defense Secretary Louis Johnson, who was appointed by Truman specifically to reduce the Pentagon's budget, saw the hydrogen bomb as a thrifty way of reducing the size of the standing army and called for its industrialized production. On Capitol Hill, Democratic senator Brien McMahon of Connecticut, chairman of the Joint Committee on Atomic Energy, left no one in doubt of his views. War with the Russians was inevitable, he told Lilienthal, and the United States should "blow them off the face of the earth, quick, before they do the same to us." General Bradley, shaken from his earlier ambivalence about the H-bomb and arguing that immorality lay not in the arsenals of war but in war itself, asked for a crash production program.

The Super's most vocal adherent was Edward Teller, a Hungarian-born nuclear physicist who first began promoting the hydrogen bomb as a leading member of the Manhattan Project. Teller had been overruled by project leader Robert Oppenheimer, who doubted the Super would ever work and considered it a diversion of resources from the ultimate objective of building a fissionable weapon. A keen holder of grudges, Teller would later contribute liberally to Oppenheimer's destruction.*

Teller had a strategic ally in Paul Nitze, whom Acheson had recently elevated as his new chief of the State Department's Policy Planning Staff. A member of the United States Strategic Bombing Survey, which was launched by Stimson during World War II to assess the effectiveness of precision bombing, Nitze was comfortable with the brute logic and power of aerial bombardment. The only difference between the atomic bomb and the Super, he believed, was magnitude of lethality.

Truman had tasked Acheson to deliver a verdict on the H-bomb issue in coordination with Lilienthal and Johnson, the so-called Z Committee. It was a thankless task. Acheson was sympathetic to Lilienthal's opposition to such a dreadful device, but he was also exposed on the right. The Hiss case was reaching its crescendo and Acheson was at least as sensitive to the baying of Capitol Hill reactionaries as he was to the imperatives of foreign policy. Having argued for a strong U.S. military presence in Europe in support of the Marshall Plan, he was now rebuking

---

* Though he was never indicted for illegal activity, Oppenheimer had long been suspected of having communist sympathies. In 1954, during one of several investigations into Oppenheimer's loyalty, Teller labeled his former colleague a security risk. Based largely on Teller's testimony, Oppenheimer was stripped of his security clearance and locked out of the Atomic Energy Commission. It was widely regarded as a maneuver by Teller, who went on to become a darling of the militarist right, to seize Oppenheimer's place at the center of the nuclear physics circle.

talk of disarmament negotiations with Moscow and he warned against the "Trojan doves" of the communist movement. "How do you persuade a paranoid adversary to disarm 'by example'?" he asked Truman aide Gordon Arneson, who told an interviewer that Acheson's "sense of realism prompted him to conclude that even if the Soviet Union refrained from undertaking a thermonuclear program as the result of our refraining . . . the administration would run into a Congressional buzz saw." Similarly, Oppenheimer would recall how the secretary simply could not see "how any President could not survive a policy of not making the H-bomb."

Kennan, who had been made State Department counselor as part of his transition out of government and into academia, had appealed to Acheson to preempt the need for a mega-bomb with a deliberate push for an arms control agreement with the Soviets. In a paper dated January 20, 1950, Kennan argued that Washington should adopt a policy of "no first use" of nuclear weapons and be prepared to "go very far, to show considerable confidence in others, and to accept a certain risk to ourselves, in order to achieve international agreements on their removal from international arsenals." Kennan would later call the paper "one of the most important, if not the most important" of all the documents he had ever written in his career in the Foreign Service. Acheson ignored it, resigning himself to the grim fact that the critical deliberations over which he presided were being swept away in a riptide of domestic politics.

On January 31, the Z Committee convened in Room 216 of the Old State Department building for a final round of deliberation. Louis Johnson, the defense secretary, reiterated his support of the Super. Lilienthal held fast, warning the group how dangerous it was to rely on nuclear weapons as the nation's first line of defense. Acheson responded by citing the "stubborn facts" of grassroots support for the Super. In exchange for Lilienthal's concession, he said he would recommend that Truman authorize the National Security Council to examine America's security interests and how best to protect them in the now-nuclearized Cold War. Agreed, the three men walked to the White House alongside Admiral Sidney W. Souers, the executive secretary of the National Security Council, to meet with the president.

Truman had already made up his mind. His only question—can the Russians build one, too?—was met with grim nods.

"In that case," Truman said, "we have no choice. We'll go ahead."

Not long after Truman made his decision to mass-produce the Super, George Kennan left government. After two decades of distinguished service, the seer who understood Russia and the world around it better than he did his own country was finally out. He was replaced by Paul Nitze, a man whose ambitions and reference points were antithetical to his own. While Kennan at heart loathed the forces of militarization, Nitze was their most public advocate. Nitze the Beltway parochial shared none of the self-doubts of Kennan the worldly philosopher, and he arrived none too soon for the troubled Acheson. Wearied by Kennan's nuanced and politically inconvenient appraisal of Soviet conduct, Acheson saw off the frumpy Sovietologist and turned instead to the more dynamic and artful Beltway manipulator. Nitze would be Acheson's trophy wife, the muse of an emerging national security state.

Nitze was a transitional figure in the Cold War continuum. He was one of Truman's Wise Men, statesmen who plied their trade not unlike John Hay did in the mid-nineteenth century, and he was also a progenitor of the "Whiz Kids" of Kennedy's Camelot, the technocrats who responded to Cold War challenges by collecting data points and plotting them on a graph. He was, first and foremost, a numbers man. As a Wall Street banker, he evaluated companies by delving into ledger books. During the war, as a procurement officer, he executed contracts for minerals—mercury, bauxite, iron ore—that were vital for arms production. As the vice chairman of the Strategic Bombing Survey, he reduced the charnel houses of Dresden, Hamburg, Hiroshima, and Nagasaki into figures on a spreadsheet. (Regarding Hiroshima in particular, Nitze spoke of applying "calipers" to the destruction.) Later in his career, while negotiating landmark reductions of nuclear arms in the 1980s, he became fluent in the arcana of missile ranges, payloads, and throw weight. The Vietnam War policy of measuring success by the number of enemy dead had its antecedent in Nitze's numerology.

Nitze's way of deciphering Moscow was vastly different than that of his predecessor. Kennan had drawn on a long career living in and around Russia. Triangulating from his understanding of Russian history, culture, language, and geography, he had interpreted Soviet conduct as more reactionary than offensive, more episodic probing than strategic. Nitze, in contrast, extrapolated everything he needed to know about the Soviet Union from the size of its military. "Paul loved anything that could be reduced to numbers," Kennan said years later. "He was mesmerized by them. . . . He had no feeling for the intangibles—values, intentions. When there was talk of intentions, as opposed to capabilities, he would say, 'How can you measure intentions? We can't be bothered to get into psychology; we have to face the Russians as competitors, militarily.'" John Kenneth Galbraith, who served under Nitze on the Strategic Bombing Survey, described Nitze as "a Teutonic martinet happiest in a military hierarchy."

Nitze was indeed born of German immigrants who came to America after the Civil War, and he had led a charmed and edifying life. His father was a professor of Romance languages at the University of Chicago, and his mother, a dazzling socialite, doted on him, often appointing him in Buster Brown suits. He was blessed with his parents' fierce intellect and he developed into a competitive athlete. The family name, Nitze would boast, was a derivative of Nike, the name of the Greek goddess of victory, and at eighty he was still winning at tennis. "My body," he would tell friends, "does what I tell it to do."

Inadequately challenged at the University of Chicago High School, Nitze enrolled at Hotchkiss at sixteen. He played football and was popular for his quick wit. At Harvard he milled with the likes of Chip Bohlen and, by his own account, "drank too much, had girls, and a rich, glorious life." Nitze graduated in 1929 and would later joke he was the last man to be hired by Wall Street, having arrived at Dillon, Read two weeks before the October stock market crash. Three years later, he married Phyllis Pratt, daughter of the Standard Oil baron John Teele Pratt. Nitze was twenty-five years old, gainfully employed at a time of global economic disarray, and, between his wife's inheritance and his own wise investments, rich.

In spring 1937, with his family on a rare vacation through Europe—he allowed himself few breaks during his first eight years at Dillon—Nitze made a fateful stop in Germany. Kristallnacht, the explosion of violence against German Jews following years of persecution and torment, was only a year away and the visit allowed Nitze a firsthand glimpse of the fascist ascendancy. It was a searing experience for the young man who for a time had identified with America's isolationist movement. By the time James Forrestal recruited him to come to Washington, the two men were committed adversaries against the twin pillars of tyranny: Nazi Germany and Soviet Russia. They even shared reading lists on the subjects.

Nitze worked as an aide to Forrestal, who was then an administrative assistant to President Roosevelt, and after the war broke out he joined the Metals and Minerals Branch of the Board of Economic Warfare. (Nitze once told an interviewer he deduced the existence of a secret U.S. nuclear program by the huge orders for graphite, zirconium, and beryllium that were landing on his desk.) In 1944 he joined the Strategic Bombing Survey, which served as a seminary for some of the most prominent members of the Cold War priesthood. In addition to Galbraith, who would become a famous economist and U.S. ambassador, there was George Ball, himself a future ambassador and undersecretary of state, along with Robert McNamara, defense secretary during the Kennedy-Johnson years. Although these men sifted through the same data and interviewed the same sources, they emerged with vastly different conclusions about the effectiveness of high-altitude bombing.

Based on interviews with prominent Nazis like Albert Speer, Galbraith and Ball found that American "precision" assaults were ineffectual; indeed, according to Speer, Germany's wartime production rates actually rose during the most intense cycles of bombardment. The survey also concluded that Japan would probably have surrendered "even if the atomic bombs had not been dropped . . . and even if no [U.S.] invasion had been planned or contemplated," as Tokyo had already been bombed into submission by the even more devastating incendiary raids.

Such claims undermined U.S. Air Force requests for expanded strategic bombing capability, and Nitze, sympathetic to Air Force demands, marginalized them. As James Carroll notes in his book *House of War,*

Nitze "epitomized the civilian who, not having been tested or credentialed by combat, rushed to outdo the warriors in bellicosity. . . . Even as
a State Department functionary, he accepted the open-ended necessity of
military dominance." In December 1950, Nitze would lend his support to
a group of distinguished members of America's political-military establishment that would lobby, with varying degrees of success, every president
from Eisenhower to Reagan for ever-larger military spending and asser-
tiveness abroad. The name of the group is a cultural marker for the fe-
tishization of everlasting conflict: the Committee on the Present Danger.

Nitze would serve under six presidents, massaging U.S. policy
rightward during the Cold War's key inflection points. His most singular achievement, however, would come relatively early in his career. To
make good on his promise to David Lilienthal in return for his capitulation on the Z Committee, Acheson would commission a National Security Council report on the nation's security interests and strategic
posture. For this, he turned to Nitze. The result would do little to assuage
the fears of Lilienthal and men like him. NSC 68, as it is known, would
become the manifesto of American militarism.

In choosing Nitze to write NSC 68, Acheson knew what he was getting.*
Nitze made no secret of his concern that Truman's postwar drawdown
for the sake of a balanced budget was leaving Western Europe dangerously exposed to Soviet aggression. During the previous summer, he had
toured the continent as a guest of Allied governments. NATO, his guests
informed him, was an empty shell. The undermanned and outgunned
Western forces were no match for the Red Army, and it would cost $45
billion, three times the budget of the Marshall Plan, to transform them
into a compelling deterrent to a Soviet attack. Nitze knew such an outlay
would never be approved by Congress. The only alternative was a U.S.
arms buildup unprecedented in size and ambition.

---

* The National Security Council was only three years old in 1950 and had a very small
staff. It was created as a cabinet-level committee to advise the president on issues where
foreign policy and defense policy converged. Ordinarily, a paper from the NSC would
come out of a request from the State Department or the Joint Chiefs of Staff. The council's secretariat then assigned it a number as an NSC report.

In his memoirs, Acheson explained that NSC 68 was intended to "bludgeon the mass mind of 'top government' that not only could the President make a decision but that the decision could be carried out." He wrote of the State Department's standard of the "average American citizen" as someone who considers the world beyond his own personal concerns no more than ten minutes a day. "If this were anywhere near right," Acheson wrote, "points to be understandable had to be clear. If we made our points clearer than truth, we did not differ from most other educators and could hardly do otherwise." It is an odd passage in Acheson's otherwise lucid memoir. As a classified document, NSC 68 was not for the eyes of the average American but for foreign policy elites and senior military leaders.* One senses that the author feels uncomfortable with his role as midwife to such a ham-fisted document, and with good reason. Nitze did more than bludgeon. He pandered to America's deepest fears and he did it with Acheson's blessing.

The forty-seven-page NSC 68, titled "United States Objectives and Programs for National Security," is a first-rate specimen of gratuitous, alarmist cant. It begins with an enumeration of freedoms as guaranteed by the Preamble to the United States Constitution. Tranquillity, justice, security, liberty—Nitze gathers them all together like a solicitous mother collecting her children against an oncoming storm. He then engages that tempest in a dreadnought of indictment against Soviet intentions and motives. The Kremlin "design," he opens, is "the complete subversion or forcible destruction of the machinery of government and structure of society in the countries of the non-Soviet world." The destruction of the United States, as the leader of the free world and the only country capable of frustrating that design, is Moscow's most vital and urgent objective. Intrinsic to its dark vision is a moral asymmetry between the two superpowers, in which Moscow was capable of committing dastardly acts that Washington would not contemplate. (As we shall see, exactly the

---

* Though classified, NSC 68 was well circulated within the foreign policy and defense establishment, and senior officials, beginning with Acheson, openly referred to it in briefings with journalists. It was declassified in 1975.

opposite was the case.) Nitze twins the Soviet Union and venality as rue-
fully as Saint Augustine does man and original sin. "No other value system," he writes, "is so wholly irreconcilable with ours, so implacable in its
purpose to destroy ours, so capable of turning to its own uses the most
dangerous and divisive trends in our society." Nothing less than democratic civilization—the text is studded with references to Western
"values"—is at stake. "The integrity and vitality of our system," he warns,
"is in greater jeopardy than ever before in our history." The Soviets were
capable of waging a multifront war for world domination, beginning with
an invasion of Western Europe, followed by a second blitz against the
British Isles, albeit this time by both air and sea, and then atomic bomb
attacks on North America. Once the Kremlin had consolidated control
over Europe, it would attack Iberia and Scandinavia, then extend its
reach to the Near and Middle East.

Nitze acknowledges a gap between the rich West and impoverished
Russia, which was still recovering from its crippling war with Germany,
but he argues this plays to the Kremlin's strengths. "The Soviet world
can do more with less," he writes. "It has a lower standard of living, its
economy requires less to keep it functioning, and its military machine
operates effectively with less elaborate equipment and organization."
Only a few paragraphs later, he pivots, arguing that Moscow is chipping
away at America's margin of military superiority "by continuing to de-
vote proportionally more to capital investment than the U.S." The Soviet nuclear arsenal, he estimated, would grow exponentially, from 10
warheads in early 1950 to 200 by 1955. He also warned it was just a matter of time before Moscow would find a way to deliver them to targets in
the United States. NSC 68 warned that the Soviet Union already had
long-range bombers that could reach America and by mid-1954 would
be able to drop 100 atomic bombs on the United States, enough to "strike
swiftly and with steel" and "seriously damage this country."

These estimates were wildly exaggerated. The Tu-4, the replicated B-29
that in the early 1950s served as the Soviet's frontline bomber, could indeed reach the United States, but it certainly could not have made it back
to a friendly base, as the communist takeover of Cuba was a full six years
away. The same is true of the Tu-4's successor, the Tu-16. By Nitze's calculations, the Soviets would have stockpiled some 200 warheads within four

years, which was not too far off the mark. But he ignored the rapid pace of U.S. bomb production. By 1954 the United States had deployed more than 1,400 strategic weapons with a total yield of more than 300 megatons, certainly enough to dissuade Moscow from launching a first strike. Having omitted this fact, and concluding that the U.S. military at current levels "is becoming dangerously inadequate," Nitze then lays out his argument for a sweeping mobilization of all war-related resources, including a massive stockpiling of nuclear warheads and delivery systems. Significantly, he calls for an end to America's defensive posture in the Cold War, urging instead offensive operations to destroy vital elements of the Soviet war-making capacity . . . until the full offensive strength of the United States can be brought to bear. Nitze estimated the costs of such a mobilization at $40 billion to $50 billion, which he believed would pay for itself: "The economic effects of the program might be to increase the gross national product by more than the amount being absorbed for additional military and foreign assistance purposes."

If there is reason in Nitze's world for negotiations between Washington and Moscow, it is not as a means for peaceful coexistence but as a tool for subduing the Soviets. Any settlement with the Russians, he writes, "can only record the progress which the free world will have made in creating a political and economic system in the world so successful that the frustration of the Kremlin's design for world domination will be complete." In the end, however, the war is eternal. "Even if there were no Soviet Union," Nitze allows cryptically, "we would face the great problem of the free society, accentuated many fold in this industrial age, of reconciling order, security, the need for participation, with the requirement of freedom. We would face the fact that in a shrinking world the absence of order among nations is becoming less and less tolerable."

NSC 68 landed on Truman's desk on April 7, 1950, and it both surprised and disappointed him. Despite the document's bold appeal for an urgent military buildup, Truman still wanted to balance the budget largely by spending less on national defense. Even as he was telling reporters about the need for fiscal discipline, however, he was noticing press reports about the Soviet's aggressive military modernization program. In the May 15 edition of *Newsweek*, for example, an article featured language that could have been lifted directly from NSC 68. In leak-prone Washington, it is unlikely Truman could have opposed NSC 68 without Congress finding out. Caught between his desire for a balanced budget and his fear of being tarred by the right as an appeaser, Truman endorsed it in principle but called for a study of its costs. The outbreak of the Korean War in June forced his hand, however, and on September 30, 1950, he ordered that NSC 68 be taken "as a statement of policy to be followed over the next four or five years and . . . that implementing programs . . . be put into effect as rapidly as possible." One of the programs was a tripling in defense spending for 1951, and over the next forty years the Pentagon's budget would remain two to three times higher as a percentage of the U.S. economy than during any previous peacetime period. Nitze's brainchild, concludes Ernest May's *American Cold War Strategy: Interpreting NSC 68,* a retrospective published in 1993, "provides an example of how officialdom can force a president to follow policies that are against his own inclinations."

Some insider. Nitze had even outflanked the president.

Nitze once called NSC 68 "a product of its times," as if his assessment of the Soviet threat was appropriate to the reality of the world in January 1950. In fact, the document is exclusively Nitze, a vivid reflection of the author's biases and the peculiar parochialism of the insider. Kennan saw through it immediately. In a February 17 memo to Acheson, he opposed Nitze's call for a military buildup and rejected the argument that the United States was in danger of forfeiting its advantages, either economic or military, to Moscow. "There is little justification for the impression that the 'cold war,' by virtue of events beyond our control, has suddenly taken a drastic turn to our disadvantage," he wrote. By assuming the worst of worst-case hypotheticals and by placing too much emphasis on Soviet intentions rather than capabilities, Kennan suggested, Nitze had succumbed to the temptations of military planning, to the "planner's dummy." A decade after NSC 68 was circulated, Kennan wrote he was "disgusted by [its] assumptions concerning Soviet intentions."

In April, having seen a draft copy of Nitze's work, Chip Bohlen challenged his old Harvard classmate's assumption that the domination of the world was the Kremlin's fundamental design: "It tends to oversimplify the problem and, in my opinion, leads inevitably to the conclusion that war is inevitable. I think that the thought would be more accurate if it were to the effect that the fundamental design of those who control the USSR is (a) the maintenance of the regime in the Soviet Union and (b) its extension throughout the world to the degree that is possible without serious risk to the internal regime." Bohlen believed Nitze had exaggerated Soviet capability as well as Soviet intentions; he dismissed his estimates that Moscow was dramatically expanding its arsenal and he regarded global hegemony a tertiary Soviet concern. Such remarks, needless to say, are not reflected in the final version of NSC 68. To acknowledge that the Kremlin was first and foremost concerned with its own survival would have subverted the very essence of the document.

Historians have not been kind to NSC 68. In *The United States and the Origins of the Cold War, 1941–1947*, John Lewis Gaddis, like Kennan, rejects NSC 68's dystopic vision of a superpower clash over every tributary and client state, no matter how meager. Assigning to Moscow a hunger for world domination for its own sake, he suggests, is a straw man for militarism, its ultimate destination the kind of garrison state against which men like Marshall and Stimson were constantly on the alert. According to Gaddis, "Frustrating the Kremlin design, as the document so frequently put it, became an end in itself, not a means to a larger end. . . . NSC 68 was then, a flawed document in the sense that the measures it recommended undercut the goals it was trying to achieve." Henry Kissinger, though generally supportive of the strategy of containment, agreed. NSC 68, he wrote, was "based on a flawed premise; that we were weaker than the Soviets and had to build from positions of strength. In fact, we were stronger than they were."

The final nail in the coffin of NSC 68's credibility was driven home by Georgi M. Kornienko, an American expert in the Russian foreign ministry who worked both in Moscow and as a Soviet diplomat in Washington. In 1990 Kornienko dismissed NSC 68 as the fabulist musings of a man whose understanding of the Cold War and its foundations was informed by a few visits to Europe and a deluded inflation of what James Forrestal might have called "Asiatic" treachery. NSC 68, Kornienko wrote, "not only simply exaggerated. It did not correspond at all with reality. When I acquainted the leaders of the General Staff of the armed forces of the USSR with NSC 68's estimates of Soviet military capabilities in 1950, they termed it deliberately false and risible. They could not believe that such an estimate was seriously adhered to by their counterparts from the U.S."

For all its notoriety, the legacy of NSC 68 is mixed. In one sense, it did not survive the Truman administration. Eisenhower would effectively jettison Nitze's absolutism for a less provocative approach to Moscow, while Kennedy would do away with broad, doctrinal pronouncements altogether, choosing instead to tailor policy papers to the circumstances unique to each Cold War confrontation. Still, NSC 68 is a critical part of America's Cold War archive. It made respectable demands by American militants, most notably Douglas MacArthur and Air Force general Curtis LeMay, for tactical use of atomic weaponry. It is significant not for what it tells us about the world in 1950—quite the contrary—but for what it says about Washington. As Kornienko implies, it is more papal bull than clearheaded analysis, based as it is on a foundation of ideological extrapolation rather than empirical fact. As a work of scholarly research, NSC 68 would not pass muster as a graduate-school thesis. Nitze's grave assertions are backed up by no more than two footnotes, and the document's sourcing on the Soviet military's consumption of raw materials is scandalously vague. Even Nitze would later acknowledge, for example, that of the 175 Red Army divisions cited in NSC 68 as an offensive threat, only a third were at full strength. The rest either were undermanned or consisted of ill-equipped militia. For this oversight, Nitze blamed poor intelligence.

That such a sloppily composed document could become the touchstone of U.S. defense policy speaks volumes about the force of Nitze's personality and his skill at working the gears and pulleys of Washington. The logic and language of NSC 68, leaked most certainly by Nitze and his allies, was designed to arouse rather than inform. Its herald of a strategic imbalance between the United States and the USSR set the stage for subsequent debates in Washington about America's bomber and missile "gaps" that never existed. As Assistant Secretary of the Army Karl R. Bendetsen explained, once President Truman approved NSC 68, he "laid the foundation for U.S. rearmament, for the reestablishment of an industrial base, for the generation of new, modern weapon systems, and for NATO and the several follow-on mutual security pacts."

At its core, NSC 68 is a classic example of threat inflation. Indirectly at least, it paved the way for runaway defense spending by ushering in the bottom-up way in which the Pentagon's annual outlays are budgeted. Prior to 1950, the White House would determine the size of the federal budget and allocate part of that total to the Defense Department. Against the dire projections of NSC 68, however, it was decided that the White House, in consultation with the military, would first decide how much money was needed to defend U.S. interests and adjust the rest of the federal budget to suit those needs. This was precisely how the Soviet Union determined its national security outlays, and as a result Moscow's military-industrial complex grew so large it ingested the entire economy. Today, sixty years after NSC 68's adoption by President Truman, it remains to be seen whether the United States can avoid the same fate.

Nitze's alchemizing of fact from fiction, strategic misuse of context, admonition against negotiating with adversaries, and dismissal of anyone who might reject his notion of permanent war as defeatist would be employed with great effect generations later. Just as the September 11 terrorist attacks animated neoconservative plans to topple Iraqi dictator Saddam Hussein, so too did the Korean War give NSC 68 an impetus it wouldn't have otherwise had. Stunned at what was received as a Soviet-ordained strike at a U.S. ally—the opening salvo in the "Kremlin design" for East Asia—Truman dusted off Nitze's clarion call and mobilized the nation for war. Not to be outdone, Nitze in the twilight of the Truman administration produced and submitted NSC 141, which called for an aggressive increase in U.S. conventional military forces in the Middle East and East Asia as well as in Europe. Short of a massive buildup, it argued, the likelihood of a Soviet attack on the United States would reach "critical proportions" by 1954, which NSC 68 had cited as the "year of maximum danger."

Without the Korean War as validation, NSC 68 would have been mere grist for the policymaking paper mill. Instead, as Acheson said at a Princeton seminar in 1954, "Korea saved us."

5

ROGUE ORIENTALISTS

Humankind cannot stand very much reality.
—T. S. ELIOT

THE KOREAN WAR SEEMED TO VINDICATE NOT ONLY THE ANAL-yses of NSC 68 but also its subtext: the enemy is monolithic, in-tractable, and untrustworthy. War is therefore unavoidable, so better to invest in the soldier rather than the diplomat. In this, Nitze and Douglas MacArthur were ideally matched. Both men were Manichaeans with an evangelical's faith in their own presumptions and unburdened by doubt. Each believed that Joseph Stalin was the puppet master of the communist world and that a victory for a nonaligned leader, to say noth-ing of a communist one, was a victory for the Kremlin. Neither man had any use for subtlety and nuance. If Nitze was the brains of NSC 68, Mac-Arthur, the living caricature of an addled American militarist abroad, was its heart and sinew.

As we have seen, MacArthur's militarism was reflected in the com-pany he kept. There was the gauleiter to his army of followers, the anti-Semitic and crypto-fascist Father Coughlin, as well as his friend and confidant General George Van Horn Moseley, who was cashiered for his racist views. As Supreme Commander of the Allied Powers, both during the war and throughout the postwar occupation of Japan, MacArthur surrounded himself with a cabal of intensely loyal men known collo-quially as the Bataan Gang, named after the Philippine city where MacArthur's outnumbered forces held out for three months before sur-rendering to Japanese invaders in 1941. First and foremost was the com-mand's intelligence chief, the aforementioned General Charles Willoughby, an uninhibited racist and anti-Semite. MacArthur referred to Willoughby as "my little fascist" and he relied upon him as his eyes and ears. A "clinical paranoiac," according to Korea historian Bruce Cumings, Willoughby was the only senior officer who enjoyed unfettered access to MacArthur. The two men discussed intelligence issues frequently and in complete privacy, so there is every reason to assume MacArthur was aware of Willoughby's operations in postwar Japan. In the summer of 1948, Willoughby directed an anticommunist purge that a British liaison officer to U.S. general headquarters, the conspicuously named Ivan Pink, characterized as "almost hysterical." According to Pink, the "communist menace" had replaced "fascism and militarism" as "enemies of the Occupation." Willoughby, Pink reported to London, engineered the Red Scare with such "Teutonic rigidity" that rightists under his authority were scrambling to "collect every scrap of information they could find [or invent] on this subject."

In an attempt to protect Emperor Hirohito from prosecution, Willoughby apparently concealed troves of documents provided to him by the royal court. He also sheltered Class A war criminals from prosecution by an international team of investigators. In particular, he abetted the concealment of the notorious and much wanted Masanobu Tsuji, a ruthless former colonel implicated in massacres in Singapore and the Philippines (including, ironically, the "death march" of American troops captured on the Bataan Peninsula near Manila Bay to POW camps), and the bacteriological warfare specialist Shiro Ishii. Tsuji was given refuge by a fraternity of like-minded former Japanese officers whom Willoughby had stood up as the leaders of an anticipated new anticommunist Japanese army. Both Tsuji and Ishii died free men.

MacArthur's chief of staff, Lieutenant Colonel Richard K. Sutherland, was a bloodless martinet who once held forth at a dinner with MacArthur and his aides about how Washington should suspend democracy in wartime and replace its president with a dictator. To his credit, MacArthur defended American democracy while scolding Sutherland as "a natural-born autocrat." When it came to autocracy, however, MacArthur was preternatural, no more so than as America's viceroy in Japan.

MacArthur's general headquarters, or GHQ, in Tokyo assumed all the pomp, intrigue, and paranoia of St. Petersburg during the twilight of the Romanovs. (When George Marshall visited MacArthur in the Pacific in December 1943, he remarked to his old rival: "General, you don't have a

staff; you have a court.") He and his circle insulated themselves in the
Dai Ichi Building in Tokyo's Chiyoda district and regarded outsiders,
particularly those from the State Department, with suspicion and dis-
dain. After interviewing MacArthur at GHQ during the Korean War,
columnist Joe Alsop remembered the general and his retinue as

> proof of the basic rule for armies at war: the farther one gets from
> the front, the more laggards, toadies, and fools one encounters. The
> great general had chosen his subordinates in the main from . . . his
> Philippine days. For the most part, they were insipid men, arrogant
> with the press, wary of each other, and generally incompetent.
> Their tone toward MacArthur was almost wholly simpering and
> reverential, and I have always held the view that this sycophancy
> was what tripped him up so badly.

When Nitze was doing fieldwork in Japan for the U.S. Strategic Bombing Survey, he accepted an offer from MacArthur to join his staff in
Tokyo as an economics adviser. His only condition was that he appoint
an East Asia specialist in Washington to coordinate with White House
policy, but MacArthur would have none of it. According to Nitze, the
general roared back: "I have absolutely no use for Washington at all, including the President. Nobody in my command is going to have any relationships between anybody in Washington."

Eventually, MacArthur did allow for a small diplomatic section at
GHQ. It was staffed by a skilled career diplomat named George Atcheson
Jr., a China expert who had spent several years in Chungking. Tragically,
the young Atcheson was killed in a plane crash two years into his assignment, but he had been marginalized well before then. In a November
1945 letter to then Undersecretary of State Acheson, Atcheson wrote that
MacArthur refused to acknowledge that "the making of foreign policy is
centered in the State Department" and wished to keep diplomats out of
all matters of substance.

Even Nitze remarked disparagingly about the "right-wing sycophant
colonels" in MacArthur's office, the most senior of whom were far more
faithful to their boss's career interests and reputation than they were to

civilian authority in Washington. When facts subverted the MacArthur myth, they debunked the facts or ignored them altogether. That is what happened in Korea, and thousands died as a result. Only now, with hindsight clarified by the release of declassified Soviet archives, is it clear just how badly MacArthur and his staff misdiagnosed the sources and motivations of communist aggression. Ordained by NSC 68, MacArthur engaged in what he believed was America's reckoning with godless communism, a delusion that brought the world to the brink of nuclear war before he and the Bataan Gang were finally swept away.

The Korean peninsula is a craggy extrusion into the Yellow Sea, as rugged and uncompromising in landscape as its people are in spirit. It is blessed with an austere aesthetic beauty and some mineral resources but little else. In its more than four millennia of recorded history, it has endured foreign occupation, warlordism, vassalage, despotism, civil war, and, most recently, a cruel division between an impoverished authoritarian North and a prosperous democratic South. The peninsula occupies one of the most geostrategically important locations in Asia, a political fault line where empires, like tectonic plates, regularly collide. It is a staging ground for invasions north into China and the Russian Far East and south toward Japan, and it is the latchkey to fertile, mineral-rich Manchuria, the "cockpit of Asia." To Koreans, their country is a "shrimp" between neighboring whales China and Japan, while the Japanese regard it as a dagger aimed at their bosom.

Despite its tortured past, or perhaps because of it, Koreans are fiercely nationalistic, as learned well by both their occupiers and their patrons. Japan, which ruled the peninsula as an imperial fiefdom from 1910 until the end of World War II, tried to break Korean will by driving spikes into the peaks of the country's highest mountains, for centuries a source of national pride and spiritual serenity. For Joseph Stalin, the need to maintain North Korea as a buffer state against foreign meddling was a Cold War imperative, so it was natural that one of the many wartime commitments he would violate was the Allied agreement for a unified peninsula. The promised Pan-Korean elections never took place and the two Koreas hardened into superpower proxies. Skirmishing from both sides became increasingly regular, and on June 25, 1950, a Sunday, Pyongyang unleashed a massive air and ground assault on South Korea.

The attack caught Washington completely by surprise. Early in the year, Acheson had essentially written off the strategic importance of the peninsula while addressing reporters at an impromptu press briefing. In congressional testimony, Assistant Secretary of State for Far Eastern Affairs Dean Rusk had discounted the possibility of war in Korea. (It was Rusk, as part of a postwar interagency committee, who in August 1945 established the 38th parallel as the dividing line between North and South Korea.) In Tokyo, intelligence chief Willoughby agreed. Among the first of what would be a series of costly mistakes, he cabled the Pentagon in March that "there will be no civil war in Korea." Now, with unification of the Korean peninsula under a Soviet ally a clear possibility, the White House mobilized for what President Truman mused to his daughter could be the opening salvo of World War III. The invasion abbreviated a Truman family vacation in Kansas City, Missouri, and that evening the president was back in Washington for dinner with his war counselors.

The meeting was scheduled for 7:30 p.m. at Blair House, the presidential guesthouse that accommodated the first family while the executive mansion was being renovated. With the meal over and the table cleared, Acheson gave a briefing on the increasingly dire situation in Korea. Attendees included Defense Secretary Johnson, Rusk, General Omar Bradley (the chairman of the Joint Chiefs of Staff), the chiefs of staff of the Army, Navy, and Air Force, and about a half-dozen other senior officials. Truman solicited their views, and one by one the argument for war was made. There was no doubt that the attack on South Korea was the brainchild and handiwork of Moscow. As Bradley would later write, "Underlying these discussions was an intense moral outrage, even more than we felt over the Czechoslovakia coup in 1948."

Earlier in the day, Bradley had been contacted by Lieutenant General Matthew Ridgway, an adviser to Army chief of staff Joseph Collins and the former commander of the Eighteenth Airborne Corps during the Normandy landings. One of the country's most respected general officers at the time, Ridgway was certain the Korea crisis was the first strike, or perhaps a tactical feint, in a Soviet bid for world dominance. He urged

Bradley to recommend to Truman that the nation go on "immediate partial mobilization." From his office in the Pentagon, he instructed his aides to monitor Soviet military positions in Western Europe and the Middle East. Ridgway, who developed a jaundiced view of the Soviets during his two-year tour as Eisenhower's personal representative to the United Nations, believed the invasion of South Korea might be "the beginning of World War III . . . Armageddon, the last great battle between East and West."

However astute Matt Ridgway was—and his finest hour as a field marshal was still to come—the Korean War was no harbinger of the apocalypse. It was an isolated turf fight leveraged by a Kremlin angling for strategic depth on its eastern flank. The wager carried limited downside risk for Moscow, and it would have the added benefit of miring China, its historic rival, in a costly war. Neither Ridgway nor his comrades in Washington, to say nothing of MacArthur in Tokyo, understood this, and their response to the North Korean invasion threatened to precipitate the very world war they feared they were joining.

The facts are these: Pyongyang's invasion of its southern rival was the exclusive inspiration of Kim Il Sung, a Soviet-trained guerrilla fighter who had led raids on the Japanese during World War II and who emerged after Japan's defeat as the undisputed leader of the Democratic People's Republic of Korea, as North Korea is officially known. It was Kim who, through equal parts pandering and manipulation, persuaded an initially reluctant Stalin to support him in his quest to reunite the peninsula by force. Had Kim not attacked when he did, it is entirely possible South Korea would have struck first.

Stalin had no military designs on Korea. In 1948 he pulled his two remaining Red Army divisions out of the peninsula. With no Soviet forces left in North Korea, some 20,000 U.S. troops still in the South, and Manchuria firmly in Chinese hands, Soviet influence in East Asia was reduced to a shadow. Exactly why Stalin was so willing to relinquish a military presence in Northeast Asia is unclear. It may be a measure of the limits of Soviet power in East Asia at a time when the main Cold War front was in Europe. Or perhaps he knew that Kim, with China triumphant but exhausted after its war with Chiang Kai-shek, would eventually have to turn to the Kremlin for massive amounts of economic assistance. If so, it wouldn't have been the first time Stalin's instincts served him well.*

As late as fall 1949, Moscow remained cool to Kim's desire for an assault on the South, which Terenty Fomich Shtykov, the Soviet ambassador to Pyongyang, and officials in the Kremlin feared would engender a U.S. response. It was a telegram from Shtykov a few months later, the archives suggest, that in the end compelled Stalin to turn Kim loose. According to the ambassador's memo of January 19, 1950, at a luncheon hosted two days earlier for a small circle of Chinese officials and diplomats at the Ministry of Foreign Affairs, Kim had lavished upon his Chinese guests a demonstrable friendliness, bantering in Mandarin and Korean and praising Mao Zedong. After the meal, "in a mood of some intoxication," he declared it was time to prepare the "liberation" of the Korean people from foreign domination just as China had done for its own citizenry. By then the atavistic Stalin must have understood, given the depths of Korean obstinacy, that if Kim wanted a war it would happen sooner or later and as Kim's consigliere he could modulate its tempo. But Stalin may have had another motive for unleashing Kim: fearful of an ascendant China, he wanted to bleed Mao white in what he rightly surmised would be a protracted conflict.

Stalin feared a strong, independent China, a fact known among the State Department's Asia specialists but largely ignored by establishment Washington until the 1960s, as centuries-old tensions between the two sides erupted into a series of fierce border clashes. Stalin also understood that Beijing had a clear interest in rapprochement with the United States,

---

* On March 5, 1949, Stalin received Kim and a delegation of his senior aides at the Kremlin. Notes from the encounter reveal Stalin as deliberate and concise, with a masterful grasp of economic development and material supply. By the end of the meeting, Stalin had committed the USSR to provide Kim with tens of millions of dollars in credit for programs that guaranteed North Korean dependence on Moscow for its most basic economic needs. Just as significant, however, was what the two men did not discuss. At no time during this, the only official meeting allowed the delegation during its visit to Russia, did Kim mention his desire to reunite Korea by force. When Kim broached the subject with Stalin informally, he was rebuffed.

an idea that was gaining currency in Washington. What better way to pre-empt Sino-U.S. conjugation than to goad Mao into a debilitating war with the Americans over Korea? As Kathryn Weathersby, an expert on the trove of Soviet documents released by Moscow in the early 1990s, put it,

> Stalin's concerns about the new communist regime in Beijing must have figured prominently in his decision to approve a military campaign against South Korea. . . . It may well be that Stalin calcu-lated that a war in Korea would be beneficial to the Soviet Union because it would tie the PRC more firmly to Moscow by making it less likely that the Chinese communists would be able to turn to the United States for the economic support they so badly needed.

On January 30, 1950, the day before Truman issued his directive for NSC 68 and less than two weeks after Shtykov wired his account of Kim's boozy lunch, Stalin replied with an assurance that he was "ready to help" Kim realize his ambitions for a unified Korean peninsula. Five months later, Kim unleashed the assault that would bring the U.S.-Soviet rivalry perilously close to a third world war.

None of this was known to the Truman White House at the time of that fateful Sunday dinner meeting at Blair House in June 1950. The decision was made to draw the line "most emphatically" against what was unani-mously interpreted as an act of centralized Soviet aggression. It was agreed that Truman would order General MacArthur to arm and supply South Korean forces as soon as possible, and U.S. civilians on the peninsula would be evacuated. The Seventh Fleet would sail to the Philippines and patrol the Formosa Strait to deter Communist China from taking advan-tage of the situation by mounting an attack on Taiwan (and vice versa, as Acheson stressed).

As the meeting was winding down, Defense Secretary Johnson sug-gested that MacArthur's orders be clearly cut, "so as not to give him too much discretion." It was a judicious but already belated observation. Un-beknownst to the president or even the defense secretary, who had just met with MacArthur in Tokyo, GHQ had already responded positively to a request from John J. Muccio, the U.S. ambassador in Seoul, for a ten-day supply of ammunition for the South Korean military. MacArthur ordered that the ammunition be delivered immediately aboard two supply ships under U.S. naval escort and air cover. In so doing, he had introduced American forces into a war zone without presidential authority, effectively assuming command over the Korean conflict with an act of insubordination. It would not be his last.

MacArthur delivered the first shot in his historic confrontation with the White House a few weeks before his successful landing at the central Korean port city of Inchon. Having promised Averell Harriman during a meeting in Tokyo that he would keep his opinions to himself—Truman had made Harriman a kind of special envoy for wartime emergencies—MacArthur accepted an invitation from Clyde Lewis, the head of the Veterans of Foreign Wars, to write a message to be read at the VFW's upcoming annual encampment. Seizing upon what he told aide Courtney Whitney would be "an excellent opportunity to place himself on record as being squarely behind the President," MacArthur did just the opposite by implying a White House betrayal of the Nationalist cause.

"Nothing," MacArthur wrote, "could be more fallacious than the threadbare argument by those who advocate appeasement and defeatism in the Pacific that if we defend Formosa we alienate continental Asia. Those who speak thus do not understand the Orient. They do not grant that it is in the pattern of Oriental psychology to respect and follow aggressive, resolute, and dynamic leadership—to turn quickly from a leadership characterized by timidity or vacillation—and they underestimate the Oriental mentality."

MacArthur's impassioned appeal was a clear repudiation of the administration's July assurance to Congress and the United Nations that it would do nothing to provoke a conflict between China and Taiwan. The morning after the Associated Press picked up MacArthur's remarks, Acheson met with Rusk and Harriman at the State Department. "We agreed that this insubordination could not be tolerated," Acheson wrote in his memoirs. "MacArthur had to be forced publicly to retract his statement." That morning, Truman convened a previously scheduled meeting in the

Oval Office with the secretaries of state, treasury, and defense, Harriman, and the Joint Chiefs of Staff. Outraged, "with lips white and compressed," as Acheson recalls, Truman directed Johnson, serving out his last days as defense secretary, to order MacArthur to withdraw the message. Johnson demurred. Later that day he telephoned Acheson and advised against ordering MacArthur to recant, suggesting it could become an embarrassment for the administration and mumbling something about the general's right to free speech. Then Johnson asked Acheson, plaintively, one senses from Acheson's account, whether they should "dare" send MacArthur such a directive.

Ultimately, Truman dictated to Johnson the message he wanted sent to MacArthur:

> The President of the United States directs that you withdraw your
> message for National Encampment of Veterans of Foreign Wars
> because various features with regard to Formosa are in conflict with
> the policy of the United States and its position in the United Nations.

The directive given and received, MacArthur duly withdrew. By then, of course, it was too late. Within days, MacArthur's VFW greeting would find its way into *Life* (as a lead editorial), *U.S. News & World Report,* and Britain's *Guardian, Observer,* and the *Times of London.* Much later, after his departure from office, Truman wrote that he seriously considered relieving MacArthur because of his VFW statement and replacing him with Omar Bradley. (Bradley, for his part, subsequently wrote that Truman "would have saved himself a lot of grief" had he removed both MacArthur and Johnson at the outset of the war.) In his memoirs, Acheson disagrees with Truman. "To do so did not occur to me at the time to be appropriate to the offense," he wrote, "although if the future had been revealed, I should have advised it at considerable cost."

If the administration's patience with MacArthur was running thin in the summer of 1950, the fate of his boss at the Pentagon had already been sealed. A holdover from the Roosevelt administration, Johnson was given the Defense portfolio on the strength of his fund-raising abilities, a decision Truman soon regretted. His ambitions for higher office—he had his sights on the presidency—were exceeded only by his malevolence. He managed to antagonize every cabinet member, according to Truman's diary entries, as well as a majority of civilian and uniformed officials at the Pentagon. Within a month after the Korean crisis began, the president decided Johnson had to go. He would be replaced by George Marshall.

It was the third time the president would recall Marshall for active duty since his retirement as Army chief of staff five years earlier. His two previous assignments—the China mission and his tenure as secretary of state—had taken a demanding physical toll. Only a few months away from his seventieth birthday, Marshall was ailing, in part because of the stress and frustrations of the China mission, but also because of the long hours he invested in his signature achievement as secretary of state, the European Recovery Program, or the Marshall Plan, as it is known today. The president considered dumping Johnson for Marshall as early as July 4, when he and his daughter, Margaret, drove out to see the Marshalls at their farm in Leesburg, Virginia. Ostensibly, it was a pleasant, spontaneous visit; in reality, Truman wanted to probe the old general's acuity and his grasp of the situation in Korea. In August, while Marshall and his wife were vacationing at Huron Mountain in Michigan, Truman reached him via a telephone at a country store and asked him to come by the White House when he was next in Washington.

Marshall met with Truman at the White House on September 8. By then the president's intentions were obvious. Among Johnson's many transgressions was his contemptuous disregard for the State Department in general and for Acheson in particular. In his memoirs, Acheson refers archly to the "acerbity" of Johnson's nature and suggests he was clinically insane; Joe Alsop, in his autobiography, describes Johnson as "luridly close to being a truly evil man." The breach in relations between the Pentagon and the State Department was enfeebling Truman's administration at a precarious time, both Truman and Marshall knew, so it came as no surprise when the president asked Marshall if he would "act as Secretary of Defense through the crisis if I can get Congressional approval."

Despite partisan accusations that he had abandoned Chiang Kai-shek and the Nationalists, Marshall's nomination sailed through the Senate Armed Services Committee, and foreign policy experts celebrated his return to public service. By the establishment's measure, Marshall's

appointment was an inspired move. But then, as now, there lurked a na-
tivist subculture that was powerful enough to subvert the White House in
its battle of wills with MacArthur. In less than a year, the United States
would confront two of its greatest crises of the Cold War—a constitutional one at home and a geopolitical one in Asia.

Unlike Stalin, Mao did not believe Kim's assault on South Korea would
draw in the Americans. According to Ambassador Shtykov, he had told
Kim in a meeting in Beijing that the United States "will not enter a third
world war for such a small territory" as the Korean peninsula. By early
June, however, Mao and Zhou Enlai would have fully understood the
magnitude of their error about Truman's willingness to fight and perhaps even suspected Stalinist treachery. For at least two months leading
to the Inchon landing, which cut the North Korean invasion force in
half and allowed the U.S. Eighth Army to break out of its tiny defensive
perimeter around the southern city of Pusan, the Chinese sought through
diplomatic channels to avoid a military confrontation with the Americans. On July 10, the White House had been approached by the Indian
government with news that Beijing would agree to support a settlement on
two conditions: restoration of the status quo ante and China's admission
into the United Nations. Tantalizingly, Moscow had also reviewed the
proposal and found the terms unacceptable. Rather than exploit this most
generous opportunity to split the Sino-Soviet bloc, the White House
backed away.

In his diary, George Kennan noted at the time that Moscow's opposition to the Indian proposal indicated that "here was indeed a serious
difference of policy between the Soviet and Chinese governments." But
negotiating with either Moscow or Beijing, Kennan wrote sardonically,
"would be a 'reward to the aggressor' and therefore unthinkable." A
week later, on July 17, Kennan met with senior State Department officials to discuss the Indian initiative. He appealed for serious consideration of the proposal as well as the normalization of Sino-U.S. relations,
though the White House summarily quashed the suggestion. By mid-
August, an invasion of North Korea had assumed an inertial thrust of its

own. Truman's ambassador to the United Nations, Warren Austin, was talking about the impossibility of leaving Korea "half slave and half free," and negotiations for a UN sanction of an allied advance beyond the 38th parallel were under way. An unlikely coalition had congealed between right-wing Republicans aching for a reprisal raid against the communist bloc and "wide-eyed enthusiasts for the UN," as Kennan referred to them, "who, like so many idealists, often promoted with the best of motives causes which ultimately only added to . . . the total volume of violence taking place in the affairs of nations." MacArthur biographer William Manchester agrees. In *American Caesar,* he writes, "the diplomats saw the peninsular war as an excellent chance to affirm the moral authority of the United Nations."

As early as August 20, Zhou declared to the United Nations that "the Chinese people cannot but be most concerned about the solution of the Korean question." After Chinese antiaircraft batteries fired several rounds at U.S. bombers over Korea, Truman was compelled to declare publicly that there was no need for Beijing to enter the war. A month later, Zhou broadcast a warning that Chinese troops would not "supinely tolerate" a crossing of the 38th parallel by UN forces and that Mao's armies would "not stand aside" in response to an attack on North Korea. Days later, Zhou asked the Indian ambassador to Beijing, K. M. Panikkar, to alert the West that China would deploy troops in defense of North Korea should the allies march north of the parallel.

From the U.S. embassy in London, China Hand Arthur Ringwalt alerted Washington that Zhou's warnings should be taken seriously. Between July and October, Edmund Chubb, director of the Office of Chinese Affairs, had cautioned three times that China was likely to enter the war if UN forces pushed too far north. "The theoretical alternative," Chubb wrote in a memorandum dated July 14, "of the Chinese communists' remaining passive may be arbitrarily ruled out." There was the sage Kennan, who advised Acheson that "we should make it an objective of policy to terminate our involvements on the mainland of Asia as rapidly as possible," particularly the U.S. role in the "hopeless" mess France had made for itself in Indochina as well as America's own quagmire in Korea. The entry of China into the war inspired calls for restraint from fairly hawkish corners. Deputy Defense Secretary Robert Lovett believed that Korea was peripheral to Washington's primary interests in Europe and could be left to its fate, while CIA director Bedell Smith warned that Moscow could "bleed us to death in Asia." (In this, Smith was in faith with the Joint Chiefs of Staff, who in a September 25, 1947, memo concluded that the United States had "little strategic interest in maintaining [its] present troops and bases" in South Korea.) Even Paul Nitze understood the United States could not afford a prolonged and distant war. With Nitze's help, Kennan wrote a memo to the secretary of state advising against pushing any farther north than was necessary to cleanse South Korea of North Korean forces. He also recommended admitting China to the United Nations.

Acheson was sympathetic to such an entreaty. In July, the secretary of state had told Nitze that America's objective in Korea was to drive the North Koreans out of the South and restore the prewar status quo. By fall, however, it was clear to him that such a measured policy was politically impossible. Members of Congress had charged him with "selling out" the Nationalist Chinese, a betrayal they said had led directly to the war in Korea. The blood "of our boys in Korea" was on his hands, they said. Pennsylvania congressman Hugh Scott accused the State Department of urging capitulation from behind the 38th parallel. In August, Acheson worried in a memo to his deputy, Jim Webb, that anything short of reunification would be received by Republicans as "giving the Communists the green light for aggression."

John Foster Dulles, the patriarch of Republican hard-liners and an informal adviser to the State Department, had written to Nitze that the United States should "obliterate" the 38th parallel. Dean Rusk, like Kim Il Sung the son of a pious Presbyterian, pushed for an invasion of North Korea in part to show hawkish Republicans that the Truman White House knew how to confront Soviet adventurism. His deputy, John Allison, prepared a secret memo on July 13, 1950, that characterized the 38th parallel as a postwar expediency for the surrender of Japanese troops, and as such, "the United States had made no commitments with regard to the continuing validity of the line for any other purpose." In other words, as the historian Bruce Cumings has tartly observed, "the parallel bisecting

Korea was an internationally recognized boundary if Koreans cross it but not when Americans do." Allison's memo is flush with the hubristic militarism of NSC 68. "Since a basic policy of the United States is to check and reduce the preponderant power of the USSR in Asia and elsewhere," it declares, "then UN operations in Korea can set the stage for the non-communist penetration into an area under Soviet control." Here was a perfect opportunity to transform the concept of "rolling back" communist hegemony, as it was enshrined in NSC 68, from theory into practice. As author James Carroll notes, "the crisis in Korea was merely the occasion for learning what NSC 68 looked like in reality."

The White House was hardly clear on where it stood on the policy of rollback, at least as it related to Korea. When hostilities first broke out, Truman stated that his objective was "to restore peace there and to restore the border." Acheson had opposed an invasion of North Korea, though he allowed that it was unreasonable to expect advancing troops to "march up to a surveyor's line and stop," particularly at one with "no political validity." With the success at Inchon, however, the Joint Chiefs pushed for rollback and the White House reluctantly went along. On September 27, MacArthur was directed to cross the 38th parallel and destroy the North Korean army. The orders were heavily conditioned, however. Air and naval actions against Manchurian or Soviet territory in support of U.S. operations were prohibited. No U.S. troops were to converge on any Korean province that bordered China. If Chinese or Soviet forces announced plans to enter the war should he advance into North Korea, MacArthur was to report to Washington. Once inside North Korean territory, South Korean troops, not American GIs, were to disarm the enemy and lead guerrilla operations against them.

Advised of Eighth Army commander General Walton Walker's stated intention to stop at the 38th parallel to await UN approval to pursue the enemy in its homeland, Marshall surmised that such a move might inconvenience UN delegates reluctant to vote on the matter at that time. He radioed MacArthur the Joint Chiefs' sentiment, and his own, that "we want you to feel unhampered tactically and strategically to proceed north." Defenders of Marshall interpret this communiqué as a morale booster from one old soldier to another. Its recipient saw things differently. "I regard all of Korea open for our military operations" was Mac-Arthur's response. He was off to the races.

On September 28, MacArthur wired the Joint Chiefs that he was ordering the Eighth Army to capture Pyongyang and prepare for an amphibious landing at North Korea's eastern port at Wonsan. He waived off warnings from Beijing that this new campaign would have consequences. If the Chinese were serious, MacArthur said, they would not reveal their intentions.

Mao was now forced to commit his country to Kim's survival. On October 9, 1950, Zhou Enlai led a small Chinese delegation in a meeting with Stalin at his dacha on the Black Sea to finalize the details of this new phase of the war. Zhou arrived expecting a briefing of how many fighters and bombers the Soviets would deploy, and he was staggered when Stalin declared he could send military equipment for only twenty infantry divisions. His air forces, he explained, needed more time to ready for combat. Zhou spent the rest of the meeting, which began at 7:00 p.m. and went on until 5:00 a.m. the next morning, fruitlessly trying to persuade Stalin to change his mind. Informed by Zhou via telegram of Stalin's decision, Mao ordered the Thirteenth Army Corps, the lead assault unit that was poised just across the Yalu River, to stand down. On October 13, following an emergency meeting of the Politburo that lasted the entire night, Mao decided to go ahead with the attack.

On October 15, Truman met MacArthur, for the first and only time, at Wake Island, a tiny, isolated atoll in the southwest Pacific and the site of a heroic but doomed stand by U.S. Marines in the first few weeks of World War II. The purpose of the meeting was to discuss what was widely believed would be the final thrust of the war. Exactly what was discussed has been greatly disputed, as no notes were kept while the two men conferred alone for thirty minutes in an immense Quonset hut. In his memoirs, Truman said he was assured by MacArthur that victory in Korea was at hand and that China would not enter the war. MacArthur, in his *Reminiscences*, corroborates this account, but with qualifications:

My views were asked as to the chance of Red China's intervention in Korea. I replied that the answer could only be speculative; that neither the State Department through its diplomatic listening stations abroad, nor the Central Intelligence Agency, to whom a field commander must look for guidance as to a foreign nation's intention to move from peace to war, reported any evidence of intent by the Peking government to intervene with major forces. My own military estimate was that with our largely unopposed air force, with its potential capable of destroying at will bases of attack and lines of supply north as well as south of the Yalu River, no Chinese military commander would hazard the commitment of large forces upon the devastated Korean peninsula.

Later, during a longer meeting with aides present, MacArthur said most hostilities in Korea would be over by Thanksgiving. By the first of the year, he said, the United Nations would be holding elections in a unified Korea, and the Eighth Army would be back in Japan. Residual U.S. forces would be withdrawn completely not long after that. "Nothing is gained by military occupation," MacArthur said. "All occupations are failures."

On October 26, with the comedian Bob Hope performing in freshly captured Pyongyang, a South Korean regiment patrolling the Yalu River was overwhelmed by a large concentration of Chinese troops. Its commanding officer, General Paik San Yup, managed to salvage most of his unit and even captured some of the attackers. Interrogations revealed them to be members of China's Thirty-ninth Army, the vanguard of tens of thousands of regular Chinese forces in the mountains nearby.

This information was relayed to Willoughby, MacArthur's intelligence chief, who concluded that the prisoners were ethnic Korean residents of China who had volunteered to fight on North Korea's behalf. This would be Willoughby's first act in a command performance of denial. With hard evidence that Chinese units were forming in Korea, he told the Pentagon that "the most auspicious time" for Chinese intervention in the war had long since passed. By early November, with thirty Chinese infantry divisions on the peninsula, a force of hundreds of thousands of men, Willoughby reported there were no more than 30,000 Chinese troops in theater. On November 24, with bizarre exactitude, he pronounced Chinese troop strength at 82,799 men. On the basis of Willoughby's reports, General Walker calculated that his forces enjoyed numerical superiority over the enemy of slightly over 2 to 1. The true ratio was just the reverse. A more realistic accounting of combined Chinese–North Korean forces was about 250,000 and growing. Not only were the GIs dramatically outnumbered, they were exhausted by the march north, their supply lines were badly overstretched, and their South Korean comrades in arms had performed abysmally in battle.

On November 5, MacArthur unleashed a punishing air campaign on a series of Yalu River bridges, a clear violation of his JCS directive to stay "well clear" of the Manchurian border. Truman, furious, rebuked him, and the JCS ordered the suspension of all bombing within five miles of the river and demanded an explanation for the campaign. It was the first time during the war that Washington had countermanded a MacArthur field order. Later, however, MacArthur would bully Truman and the Joint Chiefs into lifting the suspension on "the Korean ends" of the bridges. Two weeks later, the day after U.S. troops celebrated Thanksgiving with shrimp cocktails, stuffed olives, and roast turkey with gravy and mashed potatoes, MacArthur arrived from Tokyo for a tour of the front. From Sinuiju, the North Korean city perched on the banks of the Yalu, he flew over the region and saw nothing in the way of a sizable Chinese force on either side of the river. Back in Tokyo, he issued a statement that his recent air offensive had "markedly limited" the flow of men and matériel from China into North Korea. He declared that his troops were poised for a major offensive against the enemy that "could for all practical purposes end the war."

On Sunday, November 26, GHQ announced that the allied advance was encountering little resistance. On Monday, its tone changed ominously. A "strong enemy counterattack," it reported, had "stalled the United Nations general offensive." Some 300,000 Chinese regular soldiers, steeled by a generation of war at home and soon to double in number, had cascaded down the nape of the Manchurian ridgeline in a much larger offensive of their own. MacArthur's forces were in disarray. On November 30, with the United Nations in near panic, Truman gave a press conference in which he declared the United States would do whatever was needed to prevail in Korea, including, he implied, using atomic weapons.

———

Early on in the war, during a briefing on U.S. military actions, Mao was delighted to learn of MacArthur's vainglory. "Fine, fine," he said. "An arrogant enemy is easy to defeat." America's overlord in Asia was undone by the same "Orientals" who, according to his rubric, understood nothing but force. Over the next few months he would make a series of statements that diminished his credibility as a leader and reduced his stature as a man. In late December, the Joint Chiefs gave him a new set of directives that essentially redefined U.S. objectives in Korea to the status quo ante, the same recommendation Kennan and Nitze had made six months and many thousands of lives earlier. MacArthur responded by proposing the very opposite course—namely, extending the war into China. Among other things, he suggested blockading the Chinese coastline, destroying the country's industrial base, and reinforcing UN troops in Korea with Nationalist forces from Taiwan.

On March 15, 1951, after General Ridgway had managed to stabilize the situation on the peninsula and mount a counterattack, MacArthur spoke critically to a reporter about how the war was conducted, a violation of the president's December 6 order to military commanders forbidding them from making unauthorized statements to the press. A week later, with Seoul back in UN hands and with the White House preparing to announce it was ready to open peace negotiations, MacArthur poisoned the well by publicly implying that an expansion of the war to China's coastal regions was imminent. Truman denounced MacArthur's statement as an ill-timed ultimatum. On April 5, Joseph W. Martin, the minority leader of the House of Representatives, read in Congress a March 20 letter he had received from MacArthur. In it, the general had agreed with Martin that the UN command should deploy Nationalist Chinese forces to Korea. "It seems strangely difficult for some to realize," MacArthur wrote, "that here in Asia is where the communist conspirators have elected to make their play for global conquest and we have joined the issue thus raised on the battlefield . . . while the diplomats there still fight it with words." On that same day, the London *Daily Telegraph* published a story about remarks MacArthur had allegedly made to a British army general. UN forces in Korea, he was quoted as saying, were "circumscribed by a web of conditions" and that the situation would be "ludicrous if men's lives were not involved."

MacArthur was now finished. "This looks like the last straw," Truman wrote in his diary the following night. "I've come to the conclusion that our Big General in the Far East must be recalled." The day after Martin revealed his letter, Truman gathered with Marshall, Acheson, Harriman, and Bradley. While Harriman advocated MacArthur's recall, Marshall and Bradley advised caution. On Sunday, April 8, after having consulted with the Joint Chiefs, Chief Justice Fred Vinson, and Sam Rayburn, among others, the four men met again with the president and unanimously agreed MacArthur should be relieved. As usual, it was Marshall's voice that commanded the most authority. Having spent much of the weekend poring over the cable traffic between GHQ and Washington, he rendered his final verdict: "We should have fired him two years before," he told Truman.

Marshall's role in MacArthur's recall was one of his last acts of public service. He left government for good in September 1951, an infirm old man forced to spend lengthy spells at Walter Reed Army Hospital. In 1953, as the architect of the European Recovery Program, he was awarded the Nobel Peace Prize. In his acceptance speech, he meditated on the futility of military power. "The cost of war is constantly spread before me, written neatly in many ledgers whose columns are gravestones," he said. "The maintenance of large armies for an indefinite period is not practical or a promising basis for power." As he did while promoting the European Recovery Program, Marshall extolled the virtue of democracy but warned it could not survive in a vacuum. He warned that "democratic principles do not flourish on empty stomachs, and that people turn to false promises of dictators because they are hopeless for anything that promises something better than the miserable existence they endure."

Marshall died on October 16, 1959, just two months before his seventy-ninth birthday. It was a difficult and prolonged death from a variety of ailments, not unlike the demise of George Washington, the man with whom Marshall is most frequently compared. He had ruled out a state funeral and wanted no eulogy. Interment was private and the list of honorary pallbearers was brief. They included Admiral Harold R. Stark, General Bradley, former CIA director Bedell Smith, and Sergeant Richard Wing, Marshall's Chinese American orderly.

Wing, who had been with Marshall in China and Moscow, had arrived at the Pentagon office where the pallbearers had gathered prior to the ceremony and asked if he could be at the general's side one last time. He was seated just behind Acheson.

6

TREATY-PORT YANKS

*A nation can act in many ways and yet become neither
a satellite nor a dupe of the Soviet Union.*
—HISTORIAN WILLIAM APPLEMAN WILLIAMS

O NE LATE SUMMER DAY, MIDWAY THROUGH PRESIDENT DWIGHT
Eisenhower's second term, speechwriter Malcolm Moos was
lounging in his White House office when Pete Aurand, Ike's naval
attaché, dropped by for a chat. As he often did, Aurand left behind a few
copies of his aerospace journals, which Moos would occasionally browse.
On this day, however, Moos was struck by something in the magazines
he hadn't noticed before: an abundance of advertisements from what
seemed to be hundreds of defense companies. As it happened, one of his
interns was working on a study about the rising number of retired military officers who were launching lucrative careers in the defense industry. And Moos himself, who taught political science at Johns
Hopkins University, had been thinking a lot about the Pentagon's growing role as a patron of scientific research. "It wasn't just the solitary investigator tinkering in his laboratory," Moos said years later, "but these
huge grants and research teams . . . [this is] a significant kind of combination."

Moos, who had joined the White House speechwriting team in mid-
1958, had been kicking around ideas for Eisenhower's final speech as
president. In a meeting with Moos on May 20, 1959, Eisenhower proposed
an idea for "one speech I would very much like to make. . . . A ten-minute
farewell address to Congress and the American people." Moos liked the
idea and set about making notes. Ike had made it clear he was not interested in a canned reiteration of his achievements, but in something of

substance that might survive the night of the broadcast. It is possible that Eisenhower, who revered George Washington as a boy, saw an opportunity to deliver the kind of profound yet hard-boiled appeal to Americans that Washington had done in his farewell address, when he had warned the nation against the hazards of a large standing army. Moos teamed up with staff writer Ralph Williams, an expert on national security and military matters. In a brainstorming session on October 31, 1960, they raised several possible themes for the speech, and the one that stood out was, as Williams put it, the "problem of militarism."

In a memo Williams wrote that day, he noted how

> . . . for the first time in its history, the United States has a
> permanent war-based economy. . . . Not only that, but flag and
> general officers retiring at an early age take positions in [a]
> war-based industrial complex shaping its decisions and guiding
> the direction of its tremendous thrust. This creates a danger
> that what the Communists have always said about us is true.
> We must be careful to ensure that the "merchants of death"
> do not come to dictate policy.

In early December, Moos and Williams had a completed draft of the speech ready for the president's review. Ike liked it. "I think you've got something there," he told Moos.

Like so many members of his generation of military leaders, Dwight D. Eisenhower feared an overweening military and its corrosive effects on civilian authority. As his administration progressed, he wrote in his White House memoir, *Waging Peace,* he felt "more and more uneasiness about the effect on the nation of tremendous peacetime military expenditure" and "the almost overpowering influence" of the nation's defense contractors. He was appalled at how Pentagon leaders were not above exaggerating the Soviet threat to leverage congressional support for ever-expanding budget requests. His parting shot at the "military-industrial complex," as it emerged in the final version of his farewell speech, echoed the anxieties of his former commander George Marshall, who was himself mindful of the concerns expressed nearly two centuries earlier by Washington about the hazards posed by a large standing army.

As the hero of Normandy, Eisenhower was one of the most trusted and respected men in America. As president, however, he was no less vulnerable to cheap shots and score-settling than any other Washington pol. His attempts to de-escalate tensions with Moscow and his refusal to attack China with nuclear bombs were condemned by conservative Republicans such as Senators Joseph McCarthy and William Knowland, and he was attacked by both left and right for not doing enough to protect America from Soviet aggression. Certain in its nuclear supremacy, Washington's security establishment was prepared to launch first-strike assaults on its communist rivals with an eager willingness that today seems nothing short of grotesque. Eisenhower emphatically rejected such schemes, and at a high political price. Like his most hawkish critics, he was committed to the Kremlin's defeat, but not at the moral cost of an unprovoked attack. Instead, he would bedevil the communist bloc on its frontiers with a cordon of client states.

At times during the Eisenhower years, it seemed the only man in America who understood the true nature of the Soviet "threat" and how best to contain it was Ike himself. He even found himself at odds with his own secretary of state, John Foster Dulles. Together, Ike and Dulles—"the only bull I know who carries his own china shop with him," as Winston Churchill described him—were perhaps the most cohesive foreign-policy team in U.S. Cold War history. Yet ironically—and blessedly—Ike spent as much time resisting his top diplomat's advice as he did taking it.

They were a defiantly implausible pair: the affable war hero with a home-spun smile and a dour, half-blind Manichaean with ashtray breath and tobacco-stained teeth. Ike arrived in the nation's capital by way of Abilene, Kansas, where he was raised, West Point, and the blood-drenched beaches of France. Dulles was the progeny of Beltway nobility that included two secretaries of state—his grandfather and namesake, John W. Foster, and his uncle Robert Lansing. During World War II, Eisenhower had deftly negotiated with allies as distinct in temperament and ideology as Churchill and Stalin. Dulles believed the only good communist was a dead one and he publicly condemned the agreements at Yalta as a betrayal of Europe. He was even a charter member of the China lobby, his paternal grandfather having served as a Presbyterian minister in Asia. In "War or Peace," a paper he wrote in 1950, Dulles called for an end to the policy of containment in favor of a crusade to "liberate" subject Soviet peoples. One of his first acts as secretary of state was to fire George Kennan.

Eisenhower had originally wanted John McCloy, the Wall Street banker who under Truman had served as assistant secretary of war, to run the State Department. Ike's political advisers, however, had warned him that such a choice would antagonize prominent isolationist Republicans such as Robert Taft, who insisted on a complete break from Truman and his internationalist associations. Dulles, who had developed a tight relationship with Douglas MacArthur while negotiating the peace treaty with Japan, was considered a suitable compromise. Ike's choice demoralized the Foreign Service, given Dulles's ties to McCarthy, yet he never looked back. He knew Dulles, he said, "until I thought I understood the inside of that man's mind as I knew my own."

The two men brought out the best and the worst in each other. As the president had some moderating influence on Dulles—there would be no attempt to forcibly relieve Moscow of its European satellites, for example—so too did Dulles's militant-Christian worldview influence Eisenhower. Together, they would dramatically extend the nation's ability to project military power anywhere in the world. They often dealt brusquely with allies and they allowed no elasticity among proxy regimes. Both men regarded the Third World as a chessboard inhabited by American clients on one side and Soviet ones on the other. There was no room for "nonaligned" leaders in Eisenhower's Cold War. You were either with the United States or against it. "I can assure you," Dulles said in congressional testimony in 1957, "that the leaders of International communism will take every risk that they dare in order to win." Dulles was referring specifically to the Middle East, a region where the Soviet Union would never establish a significant presence, though he could have been talking about East Asia, Latin America, or Africa.

America had become a new kind of empire, imposed to control not just the world's vital commodities and sea-lanes but also its "hearts and minds" in an existential struggle with communism. No longer could military officers from the New World sniff at their imperious English counterparts as "treaty-port Brits," as Marshall and his staff referred to Churchill and his generals during the war. By the late 1950s, U.S. forces garrisoned much of the world, their status as "guests" in host countries negotiated in signed agreements with pliant and often authoritarian regimes. Over time, these installations would assume a life of their own. With the collapse of the Soviet Union in the early 1990s, they would become ends in themselves.

At home, an iron triangle linking the Pentagon, America's defense contractors, and legislators was closing in on the republic like a noose. Yet in his efforts to contain that triad, Eisenhower kindled a new kind of militarism. Ever the fiscal conservative, he rejected costly and needless weapons systems as "nothing more than a distorted use of the nation's resources." In a bid to purchase security on the cheap, he expanded America's strategic deterrence—its stockpile of atomic warheads and the means to deliver them—while rejecting Pentagon requests for the latest tanks, bombers, and battleships. At the same time, he unleashed the CIA against foreign leaders he considered to be inimical to U.S. interests, though many of them were freely elected and their only vice was choosing neutrality in the superpower standoff.

In pursuing the low-cost antipodes of unconventional warfare—nuclear bombs on the one hand, covert operations on the other—Eisenhower gave life to what would become a shadowy subculture in America's security realm. Romanced by the promise of ever more destructive bombs and clever coups, and galvanized by the illusion of a communist monolith, the Pentagon and the CIA became handmaidens to what journalist Daniel Yergin called the "national security state." By the end of his second term, Eisenhower was struggling to account for, let alone contain, the monsters he had created. Reflecting on the unanticipated consequences of his two terms, Ike lamented his failure to control the half-mad spooks and nuclear fetishists he had unleashed—what he called his "eight-year defeat." To CIA director Allen Dulles, Foster's brother, he bemoaned how he was leaving his successor "a legacy of ashes."

In taking on the military establishment, Eisenhower greatly diminished the prospect of nuclear war. But in sustaining containment's extravagantly broad definition of U.S. interests, he committed the nation to needless and costly peripheral wars against governments that had little to do with a fractured and impoverished communist bloc and even less relevance to national security.

Eisenhower's biggest foreign policy challenge was not a hegemonic communist bloc but an outmatched, fractured, and timid one. A generation since the collapse of the Soviet Union, Americans are still willing hostages to a Cold War narrative that allows for a balance of military and economic resources between Washington and Moscow. The Russians, so this tale goes, had their long-range bombers and missiles and we had ours. They maintained client states in their hemisphere just as we cultivated a buffer zone of allies around North America, at least until Moscow broke the rules by provocatively installing missiles in Cuba. The United States enjoyed plentiful annual grain yields and built huge automobiles with tailfins; Soviet farm cooperatives produced bumper cabbage harvests and its factories churned out austere but doughty ZILs and Trabants. Americans and Soviets shared the anxieties of life under the shadow of a possible nuclear strike launched at them from ground, sea, and air. Both sides were suspended, as Canadian scholar and statesman Lester B. Pearson put it, by "a balance of terror."

It is a historical accounting that rests on two flawed presumptions: that Soviet military and economic might was as abundant as Moscow wanted the world to think, thus the Potemkin May Day parades and "model" farm co-ops, whereas the United States was as exposed to Soviet aggression as militarists in Washington wanted Americans to believe. In fact, there was nothing even remotely equitable about the U.S.-Soviet rivalry in the 1950s and much of the 1960s. So conclusive was U.S. dominance at this time that some Pentagon insiders were arguing that Washington should demand Moscow's capitulation on all fronts or else face annihilation. Fearing that such talk might create centripetal tensions over Berlin, the one place on the globe where the Red Army had quantitative, if not qualitative, superiority, Eisenhower and Foster Dulles talked up the Soviet threat in an attempt to appease Beltway hawks. In November 1954, Dulles argued that "the increased destructiveness of nuclear weapons and the approach of effective atomic parity are creating a situation in which general war would threaten the destruction of Western civilization." In fact, such parity was at least a decade away, and the White House knew it. In 1952, not long after his inauguration, Eisenhower remarked that Kremlin leaders "must be scared as hell" given their vulnerability to the full spectrum of American armed might. In July 1958, while the United States was toppling or menacing potential Soviet allies in the Middle East, Ike dismissed the likelihood of a reprisal attack because Moscow was "far inferior [to the United States] in long-range aircraft." As late as 1963, Assistant Secretary of Defense William P. Bundy would tell a Pentagon strategy seminar that Moscow was facing "a very drastic resource pinch" and was thus unable to compete with the United States in the arms race without collapsing its economy.

Stalin died in 1953, leaving behind a bleak inheritance of his own to Nikita Khrushchev, who would emerge from a power struggle as the general secretary of the Communist Party. While Americans were discovering the joys of consumer durables and subdividing the nation into an infinite suburban landscape of ranch houses and cul-de-sacs, the Russians were still digging out from the rubble of their war with Nazi Germany. In 1953 the U.S. gross national product was 2.6 times that of the USSR, and it was nearly 2.2 times larger a decade later. Soviet productivity was estimated at only 20 percent of U.S. output when measured in rubles and 45 percent when exchanged into dollars. Across all sectors of technology, the Soviets were thought to be about a quarter century behind the United States. Far from a global hegemon, Moscow did not even try to match U.S. military spending levels. While Washington's defense budget rose steadily from 1945 to 1960, Soviet defense spending actually contracted in the first few years of Khrushchev's rule.

Throughout the Eisenhower years, relative to its closest rival the United States was the most powerful of any superpower since the dawn of the nation-state more than four centuries earlier. According to a 1984 study by M. D. Ward, Washington's war-making capability in 1955 was some forty times greater than Moscow's. Nearly a decade later, the United States was still nine times more powerful militarily. Its dominance of land and sea more than made up for the large Soviet ground force in Eastern Europe. American B-47 Stratojets could bomb Soviet targets with nuclear weapons on two-way missions from bases in Europe and Japan without refueling. The B-47's successor, the B-52, could strike anywhere in the world operating from bases in the continental United States by refueling in midflight. Washington had a worldwide network of 3,000 military facilities and dozens of bases from which it could launch a preemptive attack against the Soviet Union at a time when Moscow had little in the way of airborne or ground alert systems. Soviet bombers, missiles, and warships—the Kremlin had no aircraft carriers and most of its submarines were powered by noisy diesel engines—were either too few in quantity or of inadequate range to offer a credible second-strike, let alone a first-strike, option. Not until the Cuban missile crisis in 1962, Khrushchev's desperate gambit for deterrence, would Moscow achieve a semblance of strategic parity with Washington.

Such disequilibrium was impossible to ignore, despite a Cold War fog thickened by Soviet propaganda and cooked economic data. A National Intelligence Estimate in late 1955 concluded that the conciliatory posture assumed by Khrushchev during his first years in power was motivated by "the realization of . . . the fact that at present U.S. nuclear capabilities greatly exceed those of the USSR." The report concluded that "as long as this gap exists the Soviet leaders will almost certainly wish to minimize the risk of general war." In the late 1950s, Willard Mathias of the Office of National Estimates forecast that a growing divide between the Soviet proletariat and an emerging class of technocrats and white-collar workers would tear the USSR apart. (For that, Mathias was told by a U.S. Army general that he was "suspected of being a Communist because [he had] not been tough enough on the Russians.") Eisenhower surmised a power imbalance well before airborne surveillance confirmed his suspicions. The Joint Chiefs of Staff certainly knew of Moscow's vulnerability, which is why some general officers, beginning with Curtis LeMay, wanted to strike Soviet Russia preemptively. On July 13, 1954, the *Washington Post* reported that "certain Air Force Generals were advocating a preemptive strike that would destroy or at least permanently cripple Russian war-making centers." LeMay had boasted at the time that he could destroy Moscow's war-making capacity "without losing a man to their defenses."

It was a fair, if chilling, assessment, one that failed to account for the Western Europeans who would be killed as a result of a likely retaliatory Soviet ground attack, and it precipitated a cycle of alarmist one-upmanship between the Joint Chiefs and the White House. As Cold War scholar Gareth Porter notes, the asymmetry of power was a strong incentive for Washington to pressure Moscow, particularly in areas of conflict along the periphery of the Soviet Union and China. But while Ike favored exploiting U.S. supremacy for political and diplomatic gains, he resisted pressure from the Joint Chiefs and others to present ultimatums to Moscow and Beijing. To keep men like LeMay in check, the president and his aides publicly attributed to the Kremlin a destructive capacity that leaders in both hemispheres knew existed only in the minds of Soviet propagandists. The Joint Chiefs, who favored a preemptive nuclear attack along with bigger defense budgets to sustain such capability, had to raise the stakes even higher. They had to persuade the country that Moscow was working overtime to develop a first-strike option.

One can imagine what the Russians thought of such nonsense. Khrushchev, who long feared a war with the Americans, once referred to the Soviet Union as "a great big target range for American bombers operating from airfields in Norway, Germany, Italy, South Korea, and Japan." Taking in the view from his vacation home in the Crimea, he would offer his visitors a pair of binoculars and ask them what they saw. When they replied there was nothing there but the Black Sea, Khrushchev would answer back: "I see U.S. missiles in Turkey aimed at my dacha." Though he engaged in bombastic saber-rattling and extreme brinkmanship, Khrushchev stressed how neither he nor his predecessor wanted to provoke a war with the United States. "Stalin," he said, "trembled with fear" at such a prospect. "How he quivered! He was afraid of war. He knew his weakness."

Washington, on the other hand, was chock-full of militarists aching to sock it to the new Soviet leader before he had the chance to carry out his diabolical plan for world domination. They had invested their hopes in Dulles, who, when asked to write the Republican Party's foreign policy platform in 1952, laid down a barrage of rollback rhetoric. The GOP, he wrote, would "repudiate all commitments contained in secret understandings such as Yalta which aid communist enslavement. . . . [It] shall again make liberty into a beacon of hope that will penetrate the dark places. . . . It will mark the end of the negative, futile and immoral policy of 'containment' which abandons countless human beings to despotism and godless terrorism." Years later, this would be known as "red meat for the base."

Only four months into his first term, however, Eisenhower signaled he would appeal to a different set of angels, both at home and abroad. Stalin was dead, after all, and while his successor did not impress Western diplomats—Khrushchev, according to U.S. ambassador to Moscow Chip Bohlen, "wasn't especially bright"—it was an opportunity to ease Cold War tensions. In early 1953, with Dulles reminding his boss that "time was America's enemy" and nudging him to "draw a line" against Soviet hegemony, Eisenhower coolly launched a policy shop to examine competing ideas for how best to deal with Moscow. It was called the Solarium Project after the White House room in which the inspiration came to the president and it included three teams: a pro-containment Team A, a Team B that recognized containment as a guiding principle but that endorsed immediate retaliation against any act of Soviet aggression anywhere in the world, and Team C, which argued for the "overthrow of the communist regime in China" and the "reduction of Soviet power . . . and the elimination of the communist conspiracy." Ike made sure the odds favored the diplomatists. When the project secretly convened in June 1953 at the National War College, any uncertainty about its outcome dissolved as none other than George Kennan, rehabilitated once again and warmly praised by the president himself, arrived as the leader of Team A. When Solarium wrapped up five weeks later, Ike listened to the conclusions of the three groups, then spoke for forty-five minutes about the futility of armed might absent a robust diplomatic channel. He chose Team A's recommendation to "wage peace," said Colonel Andrew Goodpaster, a Kennan ally on the project, because "he wanted to reduce the militarization of the U.S.-Soviet Cold War confrontation."

The work of the Solarium Project crystallized into National Security Policy NSC-162/2. This would become the basis for the New Look doctrine, Eisenhower's response to the Truman administration's runaway defense spending impelled by NSC 68 and the Korean War. Ike feared that the Pentagon's relentless drive for costly new weapons would plunder the treasury and he wanted to avoid "an unbearable security burden leading to economic disaster." With the New Look the president would save money by expanding the strategic air force while reducing conventional ground and sea forces. He laid it out in November 1954, days after the Democrats won control over both houses of Congress. "We cannot defend the nation in a way which will exhaust our economy," he said during a cabinet meeting.

The New Look, then, was enameled with a threat of "massive retaliation"—an option Eisenhower would be loath to even consider. Budget hawks may have welcomed the doctrine, but the old-school military warned it was dangerously inflexible. Army chief of staff Matthew Ridgway said it cornered the United States into two policy options—all or nothing. Of what use, critics wondered, was the New Look against insurgencies and proxy wars of limited scope, such as the one the French were then waging against communist guerrillas in Vietnam? The answer, though never explicitly made, was obvious to anyone who understood Eisenhower and his generation's aversion to protracted conflicts in places of dubious relation to core U.S. interests. He was downsizing the military—in 1954 the Army would decline from 1.4 million men to 1 million and its budget would be slashed to $8.8 billion from $12.9 billion—precisely to starve the United States of the resources it would need to intervene in places such as Vietnam. "Our most valued . . . asset is our young men," he told a reporter from the *Washington Post*. "Let's don't [*sic*] use them any more than we have to."

In opposing Ike's spending cuts, the Joint Chiefs supplied his critics with data and anecdotal evidence to suggest the White House was neglecting national security. Ridgway was the most outspoken, declaring he would not be held responsible for the security of U.S. troops in Europe, South Korea, and elsewhere with such a diminished force. But no one was better at gaming the system than Curtis LeMay, who as chief of Strategic Air Command had the most to gain from the New Look. He shrewdly peddled to Capitol Hill a counterfeit gulf between U.S. and Soviet strategic power, a "bomber gap" as it was called, and in so doing he sired the Pentagon's lucrative tradition of threat inflation.

LeMay also deployed the help of Arthur Godfrey, an airpower advocate and television host. In an article that appeared in the December 4, 1955, edition of the *Saturday Evening Post,* Godfrey warned Americans about a "desperate need for airpower—now!" and he disparaged the "pathetic" number of deployable B-52s relative to their Soviet counterparts. Meanwhile, Senator Stuart Symington solicited testimony from senior Air Force generals on what they described as America's comparative decline vis-à-vis the Soviets. They were led by LeMay, who was angling for a significant increase in SAC's budget. Twice in spring 1956, LeMay told Congress that the United States would prevail in a nuclear exchange with Moscow only after "receiving very serious damage." He said the Soviets were building their M-4 and Tu-95 bombers "at a combined rate substantially higher" than production in the United States of the B-52, so that by 1960, "they will have a greater striking power than we will have."

It was a gymnastic display of dissembling. At the time of LeMay's testimony, the USSR's estimated fleet of 150 intercontinental bombers was dwarfed by hundreds of U.S. B-36 bombers, well over a thousand B-47s, and dozens of B-52s fresh off the production line. Crucially, LeMay declined to mention that Russia's slow and lumbering M-4 would have been easy prey for U.S. air defenses and, in any case, lacked the range to manage a round-trip strike on North America.* The Tu-95, though of suitable range for a returned mission against the continental United States, was a turboprop that would have been chopped to pieces by U.S. interceptors. Even if the Soviet Union had a numerical edge in bombers—and one wonders, given the state of its economy, how many of them were airworthy at any one time and how many hours of in-flight training

---

* In his memoirs, Khrushchev remembers an aircraft designer suggesting in the early 1950s that the M-4 could "bomb the United States and then land in Mexico." The Soviet leader responded tartly: "What do you think Mexico is—our mother-in-law? You think we can go calling anytime we want?"

their pilots had—LeMay knew better than anyone else that the balance in war swings less on numbers than on the quality of weaponry and equipment, training, intelligence, morale, mobility, availability of spare parts, and resupply channels—all of which favored the United States. Needless to say, LeMay did not volunteer this information to the committee, nor was he encouraged by Symington, an airpower ally, to do so.

LeMay's testimony, a direct challenge to Eisenhower's skimpy defense budgets, prompted a swift White House response. Defense Secretary Charlie Wilson told reporters that the rate of long-term bomber production on both sides of the Cold War divide was modest. He then implied that LeMay's remarks were the by-product of willful myopia, a common Pentagon affliction. "A dedicated specialist usually gets pretty well sold on his particular part of the business," Wilson said. "In my experience, if you add up the desires and all the stated needs and ambitions of your specialists, you would have an impossible total on your hands." What Wilson did not say was that the president had just authorized the first U-2 reconnaissance flights through Soviet airspace to investigate LeMay's claims.

Eisenhower had approved the U-2 missions reluctantly. Nothing, he told Richard Bissell, Allen Dulles's number two at the CIA, which controlled the U-2s, would make him "request authority to declare war more quickly than violation of our airspace by Soviet aircraft." The president personally authorized each flight, and he was deeply involved in the planning of them, sometimes to the point of altering their flight paths to reduce the likelihood of Soviet detection. Though Soviet fighter jets and ground-to-air missiles lacked the range to disrupt the overflights, Ike did not want to antagonize Moscow. He was hoping to engage Khrushchev in a nuclear test ban treaty as a prelude to a disarmament agreement, and the last thing he wanted was for the Kremlin leader to discover the routine U.S. violation of Soviet airspace. In fact, Moscow did detect the U-2s and twice lodged protests. Beyond that, however, the Soviet government resigned itself to the situation rather than draw attention to its weak air defenses.

Within months, the CIA had collected enough evidence to prove conclusively that a bomber deficit did indeed exist, but on Russia's side of the ledger. The president kept the data secret, however, lest the Kremlin learn how effective the U-2s were. Ike's restraint played into the hands of LeMay, who managed to pry an additional $1 billion out of Congress for that year's SAC budget, the envy of the other branch services amid Eisenhower-era austerity. The public would pay the bill, both as taxpayers and as citizens unnerved by LeMay's untruths.

For LeMay and his allies, however, this wasn't enough. In the wake of Soviet advances in rocket technology and persistent criticism of the New Look, Eisenhower in May 1957 convened a blue-ribbon commission to investigate whether the United States should embark on a national bomb-shelter program. It was chaired by H. Rowan Gaither of the Ford Foundation and included among its many consultants none other than Paul Nitze, the architect of the fire-breathing, fabulist NSC 68. Not surprisingly, Nitze believed that America's strategic deterrent was inadequate and he opposed the New Look. He intrigued to do for the Gaither Committee what he had done for NSC 68: finesse it into a clarion call for a lethargic nation.

Part of the committee's brief was to probe the effectiveness of SAC. After several appeals, LeMay finally agreed to sit for an interview with committee members at the Pentagon. With the general and a host of senior Air Force officers planted stiffly on one side of the table and the civilian delegation seated on the other, the meeting began. One of the committee members gamed out a worst-case scenario: a Soviet bomber wing has just tripped the Distant Early Warning Line in Canada. How many of LeMay's SAC bombers would be gassed up and ready for a counterattack?

None, LeMay answered.

The committee member rephrased the question and put it again to LeMay, who gave the same reply.

While there is nothing in the record to confirm LeMay was puffing on his trademark cigar during the meeting, it is easy to imagine him blowing mushroom clouds of gray smoke into the faces of his inquisitors as he explained how Strategic Air Command did not "do" retaliation. He had no intention of waiting on the Distant Early Warning Line. Instead, he would launch his bombers preemptively at his own discretion based on his own reconnaissance.

"If I see that the Russians are amassing their planes for an attack," he said during a later meeting with Robert C. Sprague, who replaced Gaither as committee chairman after Gaither took ill, "I am going to knock the shit out of them before they take off the ground."

"But, General LeMay," Sprague objected, "that is not national policy."

"I don't care," LeMay replied. "It's my policy. That's what I'm going to do."

Thus did the Gaither Committee unearth its first significant finding: the bold-faced insubordination of a four-star Air Force general.

It is true that U.S. theater commanders at this time were allowed considerable authority to launch a nuclear strike under certain circumstances—if the Soviets suddenly attacked Western Europe, say, or if the president could not be reached during a crisis. It is also the case that four-star generals who had this limited autonomy would often delegate it to subordinates, which increased the prospect for tragic mistakes or abuse. Eisenhower sought to reduce that margin for error by confining a commander's "pre-delegation" authority to a "major assault" by the Soviet bloc on U.S. territory or U.S. forces overseas. The authority would be "effective only until it is possible . . . to communicate with the President or other person empowered to work in his stead." However, there was nothing in Eisenhower's instructions to suggest commanders could launch unilateral nuclear strikes based on their own intelligence, as LeMay indicated he would do in his remarks to Sprague. In his remaining months in office, as we shall see, Eisenhower would try to make sense of America's nuclear policy by centralizing control of its nuclear stockpile under a single command.

If LeMay and other military preemption enthusiasts represented a minority within Washington's national security establishment, that changed on October 4, 1957, with the success of the Earth-orbiting Soviet satellite *Sputnik*. Though the launch was of largely symbolic significance, nuclear physicist Edward Teller declared the challenge from the basketball-sized craft as "worse than Pearl Harbor" and the trigger for "a race that is not so much a race for arms or even prestige, but a race for survival."* (Clare Boothe Luce called the launch "a space-age raspberry to the American way of life.") With *Sputnik*-inspired hysteria gripping much of the nation, Eisenhower met with reporters on October 9 for a scheduled press call. Though he generally enjoyed good relations with the media, the questions on this day were unusually pointed. "Russia has launched an Earth satellite," the first questioner began. "They also claim to have had a successful firing of an intercontinental ballistic missile, none of which this country has done. I ask you, sir, what are you going to do about it?"

Eisenhower played down the *Sputnik* launch as more of a psychological success than a strategic one. He said it proved the Soviets "can hurl an object a considerable distance," but could they hit anything with it?

More questions: Was the B-52 "outmoded," as Khrushchev said it was? *Absolutely not.* Could the Russians use satellites as platforms from which to launch missiles at America? *Not at this time.* Are you, Mr. President, not more concerned about our national security with that Russian thing spinning around the Earth? *Not one iota.*

Just as the Korean War had given thrust to Nitze's militarist appeals in NSC 68, so did *Sputnik*'s success provide him and other hawks on the Gaither panel with the opportunity to extend their writ beyond the question of bomb shelters. With Gaither dying of cancer, the job of writing the report fell to Nitze—three years after the "year of maximum danger" he heralded in NSC 68 had come and gone. "Deterrence and Survival in the Nuclear Age," as the Gaither Report is titled, sizzles with Nitze's signature alarmism. "We have found no evidence in Russian foreign and military policy since 1945," the report declared, "to refute the conclusion that [Soviet] intentions are expansionist and that [Russia's] great efforts to use military power go beyond any concepts of Soviet defense." Moscow, it stated, had processed enough material for at least 1,500 nuclear weapons and it would have 12 ICBMs ready for use within a year.

Nitze even provided a new year of maximum danger. By 1959, the report stated, the Soviet lead in ICBM production would become all but

---

* The governor of Michigan marked the occasion of *Sputnik*'s success with an ode: "Oh little *Sputnik,* flying high / With made-in-Moscow beep / You tell the world it's a Commie sky / And Uncle Sam's asleep."

irreversible. It warned of SAC vulnerability to a Pearl Harbor–like "bolt from the blue" and recommended improvements to the nation's radar system; construction of widely dispersed, hardened hangars for SAC aircraft; better aerial reconnaissance; and a network of shelters for civilian defense. (In West Virginia, work would soon begin on a vast underground bunker complex for government officials.)

Predictably, Nitze gave only perfunctory consideration of America's deterrent capacity. He made little mention of the Air Force's new Titan ICBM as a replacement for the aged Atlas, and the Navy's soon-to-be-proven Polaris, which could be launched from submarines lurking just off Soviet waters. The report overlooked recent advances in U.S. guidance technology and new warhead designs. Instead, it emphasized the Kremlin's unquenchable hegemonic ambition. Once again, Nitze had stacked the deck in favor of a massive military buildup. Its price tag, an estimated $44 billion, was about equal to the Defense Department's entire budget during the Korean War. "The American people have always been ready to shoulder heavy costs for their defense when convinced of their necessity," the report averred.

Eisenhower was having none of it. He took receipt of the report on November 7, 1957, and, having read its recommendations, dismissed them just as Truman had shelved NSC 68 seven years earlier. The Gaither Report, he told its chairman, was the foundation stone for "a garrison state." He was particularly opposed to the fallout shelter program. Even if such an underground network could save 30 to 40 million people during a nuclear war, he said, "there still wouldn't be enough bulldozers to scrape the dead off the pavement."

But if Ike thought he could bury the Gaither study, he underestimated the low cunning of Paul Nitze. In December, Gaither Committee deputy head William Foster held a dinner party at his Georgetown manor for frustrated members and their hawkish friends. Nitze seized on the dinner as an opportunity to persuade Sprague to go public with Eisenhower's rejection of their findings. Sprague demurred, but two days later, on December 11, the *New York Times* carried a story about the dinner and what was discussed. Later that month, the *Washington Post* showcased the Gaither recommendations with a front-page article. Under the headline ENORMOUS ARMS OUTLAY IS HELD VITAL TO SURVIVAL, the story reported that the still-confidential report "portrays a United States in the gravest danger in its history" from a "missile-bristling Soviet Union." For the second time in less than a decade, Nitze had left his calling card with a U.S. president who stood in his way. The "missile gap" was born.

Politicians seized on the *Post* story. Presidential hopeful Symington announced that the USSR would soon have 3,000 intercontinental ballistic missiles at its disposal, dwarfing the U.S. arsenal. He was basing his estimates on an Air Force intelligence report that was later revealed to be faulty. But the political points had been made and Ike was once again on the defensive on matters of national security. Subsequent U-2 flights disproved the existence of a missile gap as handily as they had discounted the bomber gap. The Russian ICBM force, it turned out, consisted of exactly four missiles and two launchpads. Once again, Eisenhower refused to go public with the truth, though this time at considerable cost to his vice president, Richard Nixon, who was cranking up his own presidential bid in the face of charges that the current White House occupants had been too easy on the Russians. The truth would come out within days after the inauguration of Eisenhower's successor, John F. Kennedy.

Eisenhower successfully challenged the military-industrial complex and he had the courage to expose it as a threat to republican democracy. But he could not shut it down. Even in his time, it had grown too large and feathered too many political and corporate nests for one man, even a great one, to dissolve. The demands of containment created an ever-growing and predatory web of shared interests that, as Eisenhower made clear in his farewell address, was "not productive of itself [and] necessarily must feed on the energy, productivity, and brainpower of the country." At the center of this complex was a sinecure of scientists and mathematicians who came to define the deranged pursuit of new and more destructive ways to expand the precincts of American power.

The characters in *Dr. Strangelove,* Stanley Kubrick's rapier assault on the military planners who made thermonuclear war respectable, are all the more unsettling because they were based on living creatures. In Jack D. Ripper, the paranoid, cigar-smoking U.S. Air Force general who orders his strategic air wing to bomb the Soviet Union, is Kubrick's dark homage to

Curtis LeMay. The title role, played with savage dexterity by Peter Sellers, is a montage of what author and historian P. D. Smith calls "the four horsemen of the apocalypse": Edward Teller, the father of the H-bomb; Wernher von Braun, the captured Nazi inventor of the first ballistic missile; John von Neumann, who pioneered the computer; and Herman Kahn, author, nuclear physicist, and promoter of the so-called Doomsday Bomb, a device that would asphyxiate every living thing on Earth by releasing a deadly radioactive cloud into the atmosphere. These men and others like them had in common a close association with the RAND Corporation, which LeMay established as the contingency planning and research arm of the Air Force. (The acronym derives from Research ANd Development.) In a rare commingling between Moscow's state-run media and truthfulness, the daily organ *Pravda* called it "the academy of science and death."

Look under any Cold War rock and you're liable to find a RAND member or the handiwork of one. What Dillon, Read & Co., the Wall Street investment bank, was to hawkish policy circles in the 1930s and 1940s, and what the American Enterprise Institute would be in the 1990s, RAND was in much of the interim. Many of the recommendations of the Gaither Committee, for example, had been hatched in RAND incubators. It was RAND policy analyst and University of Chicago professor Albert Wohlstetter who argued that Soviet Russia, like imperial Japan in December 1941, was intent on delivering a preemptive attack against the United States. Rowan Gaither himself helped establish RAND in the late 1940s. Kahn, the inspiration behind Gaither's civil defense program, was a RAND adviser. His defining book, *On Thermonuclear War,* assured readers that nuclear war could be won and offered a somewhat hopeful vision for post-apocalyptia. It dismissed the effects of radioactive fallout as highly exaggerated and suggested that food be labeled according to its contamination level, with the least toxic supplies reserved for children and pregnant women and the worst of the lot distributed to survivors over forty or fifty since "most of these people would die of other causes before they got cancer."

RANDites, as they were known, worked in the corporation's neo-Bauhaus offices in Santa Monica, California, just a few blocks from the sparkling Pacific Ocean, to excogitate upon defense policy. In this way, LeMay and his eggheads forged a common understanding on a single idea: that nuclear war was both inevitable and winnable. Their influence on U.S. nuclear policy in the mid-twentieth century was inordinate, though they could not have been more remote from the Cold War's frontiers. Weekends were spent on the golf links and tennis courts, racing catamarans and indulging in a RANDite's revival of Kriegspiel, a kind of three-dimensional chess popular among Prussian military planners of the nineteenth century. Some of them, particularly Wohlstetter, an ex-Trotskyite who would become a patron saint of the neoconservative movement, considered themselves to be world-class gourmands. Their wives even formed cooking clubs.

It was an Eisenhower-era suburban idyll queered by a cultic faith in the Kremlin's desire to dominate the world. In "The Delicate Balance of Terror," an article published in 1959 by *Foreign Affairs* and frequently compared in Cold War eschatology to Kennan's X-article, Wohlstetter dismissed orthodox theories of containment and deterrence. He warned readers they "must expect a vast increase in the weight of attack which the Soviets can deliver with little warning." The United States could win a nuclear war at an acceptable cost, he wrote, if it had the resources to mount a compelling second strike. After all, he argued, "Russian fatalities in World War II were more than 20,000,000. Yet Russia recovered extremely well from this catastrophe." Under what circumstances might Moscow unleash Armageddon? According to Wohlstetter, "the risks of *not* striking might at some juncture appear very great to the Soviets involving, for example, disastrous defeat in a peripheral war, loss of key satellites with danger of revolt spreading—possibly to Russia itself—or fear of an attack by ourselves. Then, striking first would be the sensible choice for them, and from their point of view the smaller risk."

Here was the highest expression of RANDism: an influential defense strategist seriously suggesting that Moscow might respond to an internal rebellion by launching an unprovoked thermonuclear attack against a foreign power. Wohlstetter and his fellow RANDites employed game theory, "rational choice" paradigms, and arcane systems of numerology to divine Kremlin motives until "the human factor was a mere adjutant to the empirical," as RAND historian Alex Abella puts it. However rarefied in mind and taste, they were ignorant not only of Soviet Russia but of human nature. Like LeMay, with whom they shared little but a single-minded militarism, they lacked an asset that was far more profound than their advanced degrees and faculty for Kriegspiel: curiosity.

They were not alone. By the mid-1950s, the CIA was conducting regular U-2 spy plane missions over the USSR, offering a wealth of forensic snapshots of the Soviet economy—what raw materials were going in and what finished goods were coming out, whether factories were operating at full capacity or if laborers were spending a surplus of idle hours on park benches. Were stores stocked with goods or were shoppers lined up for such staples as meat and flour? Were city streets illuminated at night or was there evidence of fuel rationing? It was the Defense Department that determined the U-2's target set, however, and it focused exclusively on the Soviet armory: how many missiles, bombers, and tanks Moscow had and how and where they were deployed. Had the CIA been allowed to expand its scope of inquiry and present the data in a broader context, argues CIA historian Tim Weiner, "it would have learned that the Soviets were putting little money into the resources that truly made a nation strong. They might have seen that Russians were unable to produce the necessities of life. They were a weak enemy. The idea that the final battles of the Cold War would be economic instead of military was beyond [the Pentagon's] imagination." It may have redeemed George Kennan's prophecy made decades earlier about the USSR's mortal contradictions. Instead, blind to Soviet fears and weaknesses, the Pentagon went about expanding America's strategic deterrent until it all but dominated national security policy.

Eisenhower knew more about the bomb than any U.S. president. As Army chief of staff in 1946, he had worked closely with Congress on strategic issues. He was the leading advocate for the Joint Chiefs' nuclear war plan of 1947, and two years later, as temporary chairman of the JCS, he called for increased warhead production. As the first NATO Supreme Allied Commander, from 1950 to 1952, he was well acquainted with the JCS targeting categories and priorities and he encouraged the use of tactical nukes in the defense of Europe. As president, however, Eisenhower was concerned about the rapid proliferation of warheads among the four branch services and the wasteful duplications among their separate war plans. Miniaturization had made possible megaton weapons that could be delivered by fighter-bombers, so the tactical air forces, the Navy, and the Army had developed their own nuclear capability. While Strategic Air Command accounted for about half the U.S. nuclear arsenal, commanders in Europe, the Atlantic, and the Pacific controlled the rest. By 1959, of the estimated 2,400 Soviet sites earmarked for destruction, 300 were redundancies. Joint-operation war games conducted from 1958 to 1960 revealed 200 "time-over-target" conflicts—Pentagon-speak for two or more missiles colliding over the same site. Ike also worried that, given the ever-compartmentalized and secretive nature of the bureaucracy responsible for the country's nuclear stockpile, there were a dwindling number of people with overall control of it.

In 1958, on the advice of White House science adviser George Kistiakowsky, Eisenhower requested the JCS to pull together the Pentagon's myriad nuclear war plans under one command. The result was the Single Integrated Operational Plan, or SIOP, and it remains the most devastating war plan ever devised. Under SIOP 62 (for fiscal year 1962, the year the plan would become fully operational), a full nuclear strike launched on a preemptive basis would have delivered 3,200 nuclear weapons on 1,060 targets both military and civilian, in China and the Soviet Union. Moscow itself was targeted by some 400 weapons. A retaliatory strike would have included 1,706 bombs against 725 sites.

Though four-fifths of SIOP targets were military, the projected magnitude of fallout, in addition to the close proximity between military and civilian areas, rendered such distinctions meaningless. In addition, damage calculations considered only the destructive impact of the initial blast and ignored the consequences of subsequent heat, fire, and radioactivity. Casualty estimates ranged between 175 million and 285 million Russian and Chinese dead, *regardless of whether or not China was party to a Soviet attack,* in addition to millions more dead in Eastern Europe. Had the resulting mass fires been taken into account, the projected death rate would have surpassed 1 billion. The monolithic Sino-Soviet bloc remained a Pentagon idée fixe, despite the fact that by 1960, when Eisenhower signed off on SIOP, the split in the alliance was clear for all to see.

From the start, Eisenhower suspected that the Pentagon's war plans employed far more throw weight than was needed. At a November 20, 1958, National Security Council meeting, it was concluded that a U.S. response to a Soviet first strike should target every city in the USSR with a population of over 25,000. The minutes of the session suggest Ike was shocked at such a barrage. "One could not go on to argue that we must require a 100 percent pulverization of the Soviet Union," he is recorded as saying. "There was obviously a limit, a human limit, to the devastation which human beings could endure."

An integrated list of targets had been compiled and was presented at a National Security Council meeting on February 12, 1960. Kistiakowsky was appalled. In his diary, he wrote that the target set as submitted would lead "to unnecessary and undesirable overkill." By the fall, representatives of both the Army and the Navy were also expressing concerns about the lack of constraints on surface-burst detonations that created an "excessive and intolerable radioactive hazard." Chief of naval operations Admiral Arleigh Burke was the most vocal critic of the plan. In a November 20, 1960, cable, he warned that the radioactive fallout from a U.S. first strike, either preemptive or retaliatory, would threaten U.S. allies in Asia, particularly South Korea, and he advised eliminating "unneeded weapons" from the plan. In a cable dated January 18, 1961, Burke advised that he was "more concerned about residual radiation damage resulting from our own weapons than from those of the enemy." Others criticized the plan for not taking into account the cumulative impact of a U.S. strike, which militated in favor of overkill. As an example, Rear Admiral Paul Blackburn noted how the destruction of the pumping stations at the Moscow water reservoir would deprive the city of the means to extinguish the fires that would most surely erupt from an attack.

Blackburn also asked if SIOP would come with "a cut-off point." Was it wise, he implied, to reflexively presume Chinese complicity in an attack from Moscow? In a February 11, 1961, memo to the Joint Chiefs, Marine Corps commandant David Shoup makes the point more explicit. Shoup takes the JCS to task for the inflexibility of SIOP, pointing out its lack of distinction between the USSR, China, and other communist bloc countries as it instead "dictates that [the plan] provide for a single list of Sino-Soviet countries." During the Pentagon's initial review of SIOP in 1960,

Shoup asked Lieutenant General Thomas Power, the commander in chief of SAC, whether or not there was an option to leave the Chinese targets out of the attack profile. Power responded that he hoped no one would think of that because "it would really screw up the plan." Later, Shoup would formally condemn SIOP. "Sir," he told a senior Pentagon official, "any plan that kills millions of Chinese when it isn't even their war is not a good plan. This is not the American way."

With only a month left in office, Eisenhower had become "shocked and angered" at SIOP's gargantuan scope, according to Cold War historian Norman Graebner, and he ordered the JCS to ratchet "this thing right down to deterrence." But by then it was too late. When Eisenhower read the completed SIOP 62, he told Aurand, his naval aide, that it "frighten[ed] the devil out of me." Responsibility for SIOP would be concentrated at SAC headquarters in Omaha, where it would proliferate in a culture of overkill nurtured by LeMay. Far from correcting the problems associated with target planning, SAC amplified them by demanding unreasonably high damage thresholds, which required multiple strikes on more targets—30 percent more than Eisenhower had initially thought necessary. Few if any of the concerns expressed about the plan by the other branch services—its arbitrary target priorities, its failure to take into account the combined destructive potential of each nuclear strike, and the fact that radioactive fallout does not respect international boundaries—were addressed in SIOP's final version.

SIOP 62 would become operational on April 1, 1961. Kennedy was sickened by the plan, and his national security adviser called it "dangerously rigid." Nixon and Kissinger called it a "horror strategy." Jimmy Carter revised it slightly to make it more flexible. But in general SIOP proved impervious to change. Even the collapse of the Soviet Union could not kill it. SIOP lingered until March 2003, when it was folded into a new top-secret war plan.

If Eisenhower could not control the Pentagon's plans for the total destruction of the communist world, he could at least resist its manic push for nuclear strikes on its eastern flank. In May 1954, the French, fearing Chinese intervention in Vietnam in support of communist rebels there, appealed for a security guarantee from Washington. In response, both the Joint Chiefs and the National Security Council urged the president to forgo any "defense" of Southeast Asia and instead take the fight directly to China with a thermonuclear assault. Secretary of States Dulles agreed. He told the president that Chinese intervention in Vietnam would be the "equivalent of a declaration of war against the United States," and he counseled the president to request a congressional resolution that would authorize him to use lethal force against Beijing whenever and however he saw fit. This was the equivalent of Andrei A. Gromyko, Khrushchev's foreign minister, declaring that active U.S. support of a libertarian insurgency in the Dominican Republic was a mortal threat to the Soviet way of life.

In response, Eisenhower pointed out that a U.S. declaration of war against China would inevitably drag in the Russians. Were Dulles, the NSC, and the Joint Chiefs prepared to start World War III to vouchsafe France's colonial ambitions in Vietnam? What if it was possible to destroy Russia? Eisenhower asked the Joint Chiefs. "Gain such a victory, and what do you do with it? Here would be a great area from the Elbe to Vladivostok . . . torn up and destroyed, without government, without its communications, just an area of starvation and disaster. I ask you, what would the civilized world do about it? I repeat, there is no victory except through our imaginations."

To reporters asking about the viability of preventive war, Eisenhower questioned the very logic of the term. "I don't believe there is such a thing," he said, "and frankly, I wouldn't even listen to anyone seriously who came in and talked about it." When South Korean leader Syngman Rhee told Eisenhower during a summit meeting in Washington that it was time to get tough with the communists, the president replied that "if war comes it will be horrible. Atomic war will destroy civilization. If the Kremlin and Washington ever lock up in a war, the results will be too horrible to contemplate. I can't even imagine them."

Calls for a nuclear strike on China erupted again in the fall when Beijing shelled the disputed islands of Quemoy and Matsu in the Formosa Strait after Taiwan deployed troops there in a clear provocation of Beijing. Once again, the Joint Chiefs recommended retaliatory action, first by putting U.S. troops on the islands and then by dropping atomic bombs on Chinese targets. Once again, Eisenhower reminded them that a war with China might well mean war with the Soviet Union, which would require congressional approval. Would the American people support such an authorization? The Joint Chiefs demurred. Should the Chinese attack Taiwan, Ike assured them, they would be met defensively by elements of the Seventh Fleet. The White House, he said, was not about to debut its doctrine of massive retaliation over two small islands in the South China Sea.

On January 28, 1955, the Senate approved a resolution at Eisenhower's request that authorized him to use military force in the defense of Taiwan and the Pescadores islands off the nation's southwest coast, but not Quemoy and Matsu. It was a decidedly vague resolution, which is what Eisenhower wanted. Its constructive ambiguity allowed both sides to climb down from the brink, and the crisis cooled by the spring. Mao was taking no chances, however. Fearful of the kind of preemptive assault that some of Eisenhower's advisers were prescribing for the Soviets, he ordered an ambitious civil defense program. By July 1955, Marshal Ye Jianying was warning the nation to be prepared for a devastating nuclear strike by "the imperialists." The phrase "sudden atomic attack" began to appear in Chinese military training exercises. In mid-1957, the chief of the general staff of the People's Liberation Army argued that factories and machinery, as well as entire populations of people, should be dispersed to lessen the destruction of an attack. In an October 1959 conversation with S. F. Antonov, the Soviet ambassador to Beijing, Mao said that he considered everything from Taiwan to Turkey to be an American domain and that Washington would relinquish control over nothing, "not even our Chinese island Quemoy." So as not to arouse the Americans, Mao told Antonov, he would not "touch them, even where they are weak."

Khrushchev was similarly keen to avoid confrontation with Washington. Despite the popular impression of him as a shoe-banging recalcitrant, by 1958 he had taken calculated risks to open the USSR to the West. He publicly rejected Stalin's notion that a third world war was inevitable. He had made deep unilateral cuts in the Soviet armed forces and he had softened his position on disarmament. He pulled troops out of Austria and Finland and encouraged reform among Soviet satellites. Yet each gesture was ignored by Washington. The U.S. ambassador to Moscow, Llewellyn Thompson, noted in a March 1959 cable that the White House "refused these overtures or made their acceptance subject to conditions he as a communist considers impossible. We are in the process of rearming Germany and strengthening our bases surrounding Soviet territory. Our proposals for settling the German problem would in his opinion end in dissolution of the communist bloc and threaten the regime in the Soviet Union itself. He has offered a European settlement based on the status quo. This we have also rejected."

Though Khrushchev suffered many slights at the hands of the Americans, nothing angered him more than the U-2 overflights. There they were, those ungainly black birds hurtling above Mother Russia at 60,000 feet, mocking his air interceptors and antiaircraft batteries, their cameras whirring away intrusively. The humiliation was so great that Khrushchev unburdened himself only to his son, Sergei. "The way to teach smart alecks a lesson," he said, "is with a fist. Our fist will look impressive enough. Just let them poke their nose in here again."

Then, on May 1, 1960, the Soviets downed a U-2 as it headed for Sverdlovsk, where the first operational Soviet ICBMs were supposedly located, and captured its pilot, Francis Gary Powers. The incident, which occurred just weeks before Eisenhower was to meet with Khrushchev for a summit in Paris, vindicated the Soviets' new ground-to-air missile system and was a source of great pride and cause for celebration throughout the USSR. (It also torpedoed Eisenhower's hopes of obtaining some kind of arms-control agreement at Paris.)

Triumph turned to despair, however, after analyses of the U-2's photos revealed the extraordinary quality of intelligence Washington was getting out of the flights. The Americans, it was now clear, knew not only what the Soviets had but also what they did not have, particularly in the way of long-range delivery systems for nuclear warheads and early-warning capability. A month later, Khrushchev received a report confirming that the United States had the ability to destroy Soviet strategic forces several times over in a preemptive nuclear strike. Ominously, it concluded that the Pentagon believed that the window of opportunity for such an attack was rapidly closing. (It wasn't, but that is what the Joint Chiefs were telling the White House and their friends in Congress.)

Nearly two years later, in April 1962, Khrushchev decided to install intermediate-range missiles in Cuba. He expected little in the way of reaction from Washington. Moscow, after all, had filed only minor protests when the Americans installed their missiles in Italy and Turkey a few years earlier. Why would they deny the Soviets parity?

Having revealed Russia's critical weaknesses from the air, Washington moved to exploit them on the ground. The perfect man for the job was John Foster Dulles, a fundamentalist Christian who, like the atheist Khrushchev, beheld the world and saw nothing but existential threats. Unlike those facing Moscow, however, the dangers Dulles perceived were either imagined or self-created, a fact lost not only on him but also on his brother and the nascent intelligence agency he chaired. The consequences of their malpractice haunt the United States to this day.

Dulles would often spend late evenings in his wood-paneled office at his home. There, he would sip from a glass of Old Overholt rye in his armchair, peer into the fireplace, and consider the evil that his Old Testament faith assured him lurked within the communist fold. As a child he attended three church services on Sunday and several others on weekdays, and he could effortlessly recite prayer hymns and verses from the Psalms. Dulles's grandfather was a missionary and his father was pastor of the First Presbyterian Church in Watertown, New York, and until he began undergraduate study at Princeton it was presumed he would continue their spiritual quest. Though he ultimately chose law and international affairs over the clergy, he preserved his doctrinal rigidity. He opposed the idea of cultural exchanges between the United States and the communist world—he even prohibited American journalists from traveling to China—and he counseled against U.S.-Soviet summits as gestures of appeasement to a venal, relentless foe. "Dulles," historian John Lewis Gaddis has written, "scarcely knew the meaning of compromise."

Like many evangelicals, Dulles believed faith and foreign policy should be harnessed in tandem with each other. "Those who found a good way of life," he wrote, "had a duty to help others to find the same way." According to Gaddis, Dulles was receptive to Arnold Toynbee's notion that civilizations require an external threat to refresh themselves. Stiff and charmless, Dulles was easy to dislike. He was among the few informed Americans who was unimpressed with George Marshall, thinking him naive in his dealings with the Russians. As secretary of state, he had little sympathy for his foreign service professionals and wasted no time tossing them into McCarthy's lair. He eased out George Kennan without a word or note of thanks for his public service, and he refused to ride in the same car or be photographed with Charles Bohlen when McCarthy was railing against him during the Senate review of his nomination as ambassador to Moscow. (Both Kennan and Bohlen, it so happens, had complained publicly about Dulles's habit of leaking government secrets to the media.)

In an effort to woo the support of China lobby hawks such as William Knowland, Dulles coaxed Eisenhower into suggesting publicly that it was time to turn Chiang loose on Communist China. Most notoriously, he hired as a kind of security officer one Scott McLeod, "an overtly McCarthyite goon," according to columnist Joseph Alsop, who went about purging the department of anyone who failed to meet Dulles's ecclesiastic standards of virtue. Dulles biographer Leonard Mosley described McLeod as "a sort of Pavlovian dog who salivated over certain trigger words like 'Communist,' 'liberal,' 'freethinker,' 'homosexual,' and 'nymphomaniac' and he organized a squad of goons to root all such elements out of the State Department. His operatives broke open desks, read private letters, listened in on private conversations and telephones, and tailed employees for hours."

Within a few weeks of Dulles's arrival at Foggy Bottom, he succeeded in demoralizing an already enfeebled diplomatic corps. Averell Harriman characterized him as "an outsider . . . sacrificing Foreign Service officers who had any connection [to], or were accused of having anything to do with communism. He was throwing them to the wolves. Why he did this I don't know. I always thought that his mistake about Alger Hiss made him feel that in order to protect himself he had to sacrifice others."*

Allen Dulles, meanwhile, was his elder brother's mirror image, possessing the charm Foster lacked but little of his discipline. If young Foster was a "paragon" of a boy, studious and upright, Allen indulged in the privileges of his youth while flouting its strictures. Whereas Foster drank prudently, Allen imbibed liberally. While Foster was loyal to his wife, Janet, throughout their forty-seven-year marriage, Allen was a serial philanderer. Foster opposed his sister Eleanor's marriage to a Jew, while Allen lent his passive support.†

An adventurer at heart, Allen thrilled to the tales of Victorian Britain's colonial wars and as a child was an ardent supporter of the Boers. As an adult, Allen would fight America's colonial wars, albeit from the shadows. Like Foster, he was also a lawyer who spent considerable time in prewar Europe. During the war he was lured into the spy trade by William "Wild Bill" Donovan, the godfather of the CIA's precursor, the Office of Strategic Services. Following Germany's surrender, Dulles was promoted by Donovan to run the Berlin office of the OSS.

Within four months after he'd settled in, military police discovered his operatives were running a $1 million trade in black-market currency, gold, and artwork. General Lucius Clay, the U.S. military governor in Berlin, was not impressed. "How the hell can you expect those guys to catch spies," he asked, "when they can't smell the stink under their noses?" In response to congressional outrage over his "New Deal Gestapo," President Truman disbanded the OSS in the fall of 1945, only to revive it as the Cen-

---

* Dulles held Hiss in high regard and after World War II recommended him to head the Carnegie Foundation. But when Hiss was accused of having communist links, Dulles refused to testify on his behalf.

† In many ways, Eleanor Dulles was the most exceptional of the five Dulles siblings. An author, teacher, and diplomat, she became a German specialist and was instrumental in that country's postwar economic revival. She is widely regarded as the architect of the postwar Deutschemark and was remembered fondly by Germans as the "mother of Berlin." In 1932 Eleanor married David Simon Blondheim, whose Orthodox Jewish family cast him out in response. A brilliant linguist and a professor at Johns Hopkins University, Blondheim committed suicide in 1934.

tral Intelligence Agency under the National Security Act of 1947. For Dean Acheson, who would soon become secretary of state, the CIA was antithetical to America's republican ideals. "I had the gravest forebodings about this organization," he wrote in his memoirs, "and warned the president that as set up neither he nor anyone else would be in a position to know what it was doing or control it."

Within a decade, Acheson's fears were vindicated. By the time Ike appointed Allen Dulles as CIA director, the agency had racked up an impressive list of failed missions written in the blood of its agents. They were called "Roll Back" operations and they were the inspiration of Frank Wisner, the head of the planning directorate. A typical Roll Back mission was launched in September 1949, when an element of green Hungarian operatives were parachute-dropped into the Ukraine as the nucleus of a spy ring. The operation was quickly blown and all the agents were eliminated. For years, James Angleton, the agency's dipsomaniacal counterintelligence chief, provided the exact coordinates and drop zones for Roll Back missions to Kim Philby, his British counterpart and Moscow's double agent in London. The missions continued for several years despite the deaths of some 200 agents. In Asia, the CIA recruited hundreds of ethnic Korean and Chinese agents for paramilitary operations in North Korea and the PRC. None survived, yet those missions would continue for years.

During the Truman administration, John Melby, a State Department China Hand, was asked to look into rumors that the CIA was processing a covert army of spies into a slaughterhouse. In an eyes-only report, Melby wrote that "our intelligence is so bad it approaches malfeasance in office." A copy of the report was leaked to then CIA director Bedell Smith, who after reading it summoned Melby to his office and gave him a tonguelashing while Deputy Director Allen Dulles silently looked on.

Now at the agency's helm, Allen was directing the covert side of U.S. foreign policy while Foster led the overt one. They were blood brothers, Christian soldiers marching onto war.

From 1953 to 1960, the CIA, often with the support of the State Department, conducted 170 secret operations in forty-eight countries. It overthrew heads of state on four continents, and its plans for regime change in Cuba were in an advanced stage by the time Eisenhower left office. It conspired to install pro-Western governments in Egypt and Laos, and it plotted to assassinate such leaders as Gamal Abdel Nasser of Egypt, China's Zhou Enlai, Patrice Lumumba of the Congo, Fidel Castro in Cuba, and Rafael Trujillo of the Dominican Republic. Many of its targets were popular leaders who were swept to power on a surge of nationalist ferment that ushered out the colonial era. Some were inspired by socialism, which is not surprising given how wars of national liberation were often waged against Western-capitalist proxies. Few, if any, were Soviet clients in situ, though some sought Moscow's support in response to CIA plots against them. They had provoked Washington's ire not because they were ostensibly pro-Soviet but because they were not demonstrably pro-American.

Certainly that was the case with Iranian prime minister Mohammad Mossadegh. His March 1951 decision to nationalize the British-controlled Anglo-Iranian Oil made him a celebrated revolutionary and an international symbol of anti-imperialism. Clearly, he would have to go. At a March 4, 1953, meeting of the National Security Council, Allen Dulles told the president that Iran was ripe for revolution and spoke darkly of the "consequences of a Soviet takeover." Eisenhower gave the Dulles brothers a green light to take Mossadegh out, but on the condition that the plot not betray a trace of U.S. involvement. By August Iran's freely elected leader was overthrown in a bungled operation that left no doubt as to its authorship. The consequences of Operation Ajax, as it was known, resonate still.

Facts, "stubborn things," as John Adams, America's second president, called them, meant little in Washington's war on neutrality. Immediately after Indonesian leader Sukarno hosted the first Non-Aligned Movement conference at Bandung in 1955, the CIA was well into a plot to remove him despite Vice President Nixon's conviction, expressed during a January 1954 CIA briefing after meeting the Indonesian leader, that he "is completely noncommunist." Following his first meeting with Guatemalan president Jacobo Arbenz Guzmán, Jack Peurifoy, the new U.S. ambassador to Guatemala City, cabled Washington: "I am definitely convinced that if the President is not a communist, he will certainly do until one comes along." In December 1953, Allen Dulles formally approved a plot to oust the Guatemalan leader, who had been elected president three years earlier in the country's first free and fair election. By late summer, Arbenz had been chased into exile and replaced by a military junta funded by the CIA and led by Castillo Armas, a cashiered army colonel described by his agency handler as "bold but incompetent."

Often, plots against uncooperative heads of state were mooted by Foster Dulles over cocktails with the president in the Oval Office, then mapped out between Foster, Allen, and Eleanor by the family swimming pool that Sunday. The process was not always so genteel, however. In 1960, when Congolese prime minister Lumumba accepted Soviet offers of help in his revolt against Belgian colonial rule, Foster Dulles presented Eisenhower with a steamy cable from the CIA's station chief in Brussels. It recommended urgent action against a "classic communist takeover . . . another Cuba." There was no time for highballs with a warning like that. In early October, the CIA added strongman Joseph Mobutu to its payroll with an allotment of $250,000, followed by shipments of arms and ammunition. A month later, Mobutu captured Lumumba and deposited him into the custody of a Belgian officer, who had him executed by firing squad. Mobutu would remain a staunch anticommunist and U.S. ally throughout his thirty-two years as president of Congo, which he renamed Zaire. In his horn-rim glasses and leopard-skin fez, he ruled as a caricature of a megalomaniacal Third World despot.

On January 5, 1961, the President's Board of Consultants on Foreign Intelligence Activities issued a review of the CIA's record of covert operations. It found that the programs were unworthy of "the great expenditure of manpower, money and other resources involved," and it called for "a total reassessment" of covert operations. It warned that the "CIA's concentration on political, psychological and related covert action activities [has] tended to distract substantially from the execution of its primary intelligence-gathering mission." Pointedly, the board recommended the "complete separation" of the director of central intelligence from the CIA and it decreed that Allen Dulles was incapable of running the agency.

Despite this, John Kennedy, Eisenhower's successor, would ask Dulles to remain at his post. He did so on the advice of his father, Joe Kennedy, who, as one of Eisenhower's foreign intelligence consultants, was keenly aware that Dulles knew what FBI director J. Edgar Hoover knew about the Kennedy family's trove of dark secrets. It would take one of the greatest debacles in the history of U.S. foreign policy to finally overthrow Allen Dulles.

7

WAR FOR PEACE

First starving Chinese coolie: Where are all those soldiers going?
Second starving Chinese coolie: They say there's a revolution coming.
First coolie: What is revolution?
Second coolie: I don't know, but it has something to do with food.
—FROM THE 1937 SCREEN ADAPTATION OF *The Good Earth*

IN FEBRUARY 1972, A MONTH BEFORE RICHARD NIXON WENT TO China and with U.S. forces still mired in Vietnam, the martyred Sinologist John Service was asked to testify before the Senate Foreign Relations Committee. Service had just returned from a six-and-a-half-week tour of China, where he had been given a rare audience with Premier Zhou Enlai. His remarks were as profound in retrospect as they had been prophetic decades earlier.

"Our involvement in Vietnam," Service told the committee, "our insistence on the need to contain China and to prevent what we thought was the spread of communist influence in Southeast Asia, was based very largely on our misunderstanding and our lack of knowledge of the Chinese, the nature of the Chinese communist movement, and the intention of their leaders. We assumed that they were an aggressive country, and I don't believe that they really have been, and, therefore, I think we got into Vietnam largely, as I say, through the misinterpretation and . . . fear of China."

Fear and its enabler, ignorance, have cost Americans dearly over the years, and Vietnam was a particularly stiff bill. The war was said to be a key battleground against an alleged Soviet hegemony, though Vietnam was the kind of place George Kennan, the architect of containment, had dismissed as unworthy of U.S. blood and treasure. Official lies about Vietnam and Washington's objectives there grew in proportion to the widening gap between the cost of the conflict and its remoteness from

Washington's core interests. Americans were told they were fighting in Southeast Asia to aid a loyal democratic ally in the fight against communism; by 1964, with nearly a decade of fighting to go and the government of Saigon exposed as dysfunctional and corrupt, the White House concluded that its real goal was to avoid the specter of retreat. Even as the White House was showcasing metrics of success in the fight against North Vietnam and its Vietcong allies, National Security Adviser McGeorge "Mac" Bundy was privately placing odds for a U.S. victory at 25 percent. He counseled the president to keep fighting, however, to preserve U.S. credibility.

The war was, as Robert McNamara put it, employing his gift for rendering human slaughter into something antiseptic and data-driven, a "laboratory" for studying counterinsurgency and a way of "communicating" with China and Russia. It rested on a scaffolding of flawed presumptions informed by the weaponized rubric of NSC 68 and the Gaither Report. As with North Korea's Kim Il Sung, the United States identified in North Vietnamese leader Ho Chi Minh a Sino-Soviet drone, when in fact the Moscow-Beijing-Hanoi triad was tactical, defensive, and, as it turned out, highly fissionable. With Richard Nixon's strategy of "triangulation," playing Beijing and Moscow against each other, in true Metternichian fashion, the communist front in Southeast Asia unraveled as nastily as did the Sino-Soviet bloc.

No one ever wanted Vietnam. Truman was happy to leave the French to their postcolonial fate until the hysteria that followed the Korean War transformed Paris's *mission civilisatrice* into a key front in the battle against communism. Eisenhower and his generation of pragmatists had little appetite for Asian conflicts and they managed to limit the U.S. role in South Vietnam to an advisory one.* Kennedy, rattled by the Bay of

---

* In spring 1954, with Eisenhower under pressure to help French forces trapped by North Vietnam's proxy armies at Dienbienphu, US. Army chief of staff Matthew Ridgway submitted a report to the president that estimated it would take ten divisions to defeat the communists (compared with the six divisions that had battled North Korea to a stalemate) and fifty-five engineering battalions. With that, Ridgway would later write, "the idea of intervening was abandoned."

Pigs debacle and spooked by Khrushchev at a stormy summit meeting in Vienna, escalated Washington's commitment only to regret it with no time left to reverse course. Johnson, who was as fearless pushing domestic initiatives such as civil rights as he was leery of foreign entanglements, was destroyed by his inability to understand what motivated men like Ho Chi Minh.

The Vietnam entanglement was the bastard creation of a parochial, militarized, and divisive policymaking establishment. The administration "principals," the leaders of the government's civilian and military agencies, beginning with a drifting State Department and an aggrandizing Pentagon, were divided from both within and without. Infighting and a bloated bureaucracy distorted the spare but relatively efficient policymaking apparatus that had subdued the Nazis and Imperial Japan and kept America out of extraneous wars. Scientists, statisticians, and engineers were seconded to the Pentagon, where they draped militarist conceit in academic finery. An increasingly cavalier approach to war—both conventional and thermonuclear—and its consequences fueled ever-larger defense budgets that elevated "the military option" in Cold War confrontations from a last resort to a reflexive first response.

When the novice president enters the realm of foreign policy, remarked Chester Bowles, an aide to Truman and Kennedy and one in a group of specialists who foresaw the Sino-Soviet split, "he becomes an easy target for military-CIA-paramilitary type answers which can be added, subtracted, multiplied or divided." So it was during the worst of the Vietnam years. If John Kennedy and Lyndon Johnson were openly wary of militarists in their ranks, they occasionally engaged them in tactical alliances. Kennedy in particular owed his presidency in no small part to that militarists' fantasy, the "missile gap."

Despite their vast differences in generation and background, Eisenhower and the man destined to succeed him had much in common. The two men had an easy, restrained manner and were uncomfortable with ideologues. Both were war heroes with distinct views about the military's proper function in a democracy. Kennedy shared Eisenhower's desire to keep defense budgets low while embracing nonconventional means, such as coups and insurgencies, in defense of U.S. interests. Ike read paperback Westerns; Kennedy enjoyed Ian Fleming's James Bond thrillers.

Both men were also politicians, a vocation that requires even war heroes to check their principles like greatcoats at the foyers of power. Campaigning for his first term as president in 1952 against Adlai Stevenson, Eisenhower notoriously declined to distance himself from Joe McCarthy and his attacks on George Marshall. That same year, Kennedy praised the Wisconsin senator as a great American patriot. (In reciprocation, McCarthy appointed Kennedy's brother Bobby as assistant counsel on his investigative committees and was godfather to his first child.) During his 1960 campaign for president against Richard Nixon, the favored incumbent vice president, Kennedy leveraged the charge that Eisenhower had allowed Moscow to open a decisive lead in ballistic capability by failing to keep up with Soviet missile production. Kennedy also blamed Ike for skimping on defense—placing "fiscal security ahead of national security," as he put it—and he warned of a looming "dangerous period . . . in which our own offensive and defensive missile capabilities will lag so far behind those of the Soviets as to place us in a position of grave peril." It was a nice riff, whether intentional or not, off NSC 68's "year of maximum danger," and just as duplicitous. As with the earlier "bomber gap," U-2 spy flights exposed the Russian lead in ballistic missiles as imaginary. One wonders if Kennedy, whose experience as a naval officer in World War II left him deeply skeptical about the military, was taking the Pentagon's missile-gap nonsense at face value. If he had doubts about the Air Force's claims, however, he kept them to himself as he rode the controversy straight to the White House.

Within weeks after Kennedy's inauguration, his new defense secretary, Robert McNamara, let slip in a press conference what the CIA had told him only a few days earlier: U-2 surveillance had confirmed there *was* a missile gap, though one that favored the United States. Pundits bayed for McNamara's resignation, while leading Republicans demanded that new elections be held. Kennedy rejected McNamara's offer to resign, and the missile-gap scandal was finally laid to rest by the man who had done so much to exploit it. Now the young president, having been elected with the help of alarmist warnings, would spend the last few years of his life battling militarists over crises that were very real indeed. The Zeus among them, hurling napalm bombs like lightning bolts at enemies both real and imagined, was Curtis LeMay.

"Iron Ass" LeMay, as he was called by his men (though never to his face), was one of the most successful officers in U.S. military history. His career spanned the evolution of the United States Air Force from its genesis as a U.S. Army orphan to the creation of the Strategic Air Command. Along with Admiral Hyman Rickover, the father of the U.S. Navy's nuclear fleet, he did more than anyone to endow the United States with the power to strike militarily anywhere in the world within hours, if not minutes. As SAC commander, LeMay presided over the most lethal concentration of weaponry ever known. As Air Force chief of staff during the Vietnam War, he watched helplessly as the immense power at his disposal failed to subdue a communist insurrection waged by scrawny guerrilla fighters armed with machine guns and grenade launchers.

There was nothing flamboyant about Curtis LeMay. Even his signature cigar was something of a prop to hide a mild case of Bell's palsy that caused his mouth to tighten into a snarl. Husky, with a full head of black hair, he could be brusque in conversation but listened more than he talked. When he did speak, he did so in a low, muffled voice that attendants often struggled to hear clearly. In that sense at least, LeMay the man was very different from Jack D. Ripper, the psychotic Air Force general and LeMay caricature from the film *Dr. Strangelove.* Yet he did as much to weaponize the Cold War as anyone. His appeals to widen the conflict in Vietnam—to stop swatting at "flies" in the south and bomb "the manure pile" up north, as he earthily put it—nearly tipped the world down the thermonuclear abyss. He was both angel of death and a stunning anachronism, the lord of the world's largest arsenal of nuclear weaponry with no morally defensible cause to use it. LeMay knew that Soviet bombers were fewer in number and inferior in quality to America's B-52, the B-29's ferocious successor, but he also understood, according to biographer Thomas M. Coffey, "that fear was a powerful tool in getting money out of Congress." LeMay used that money and the force of his personality to turn the Air Force, with SAC as its turbine, into the most powerful of the branch services. The authority from that franchise mingled chillingly with LeMay's theology that nuclear war was winnable. As his authority expanded along with the range and payloads of the bombers under his command, so too did his hair-trigger imperiousness, and he ardently pushed for a preemptive attack on Soviet military and industrial targets.

With the close of the Eisenhower administration, LeMay had managed to estrange himself from the White House with his implicit criticism of its budget priorities, as well as from the other service chiefs, who believed their budget requests were being short-changed for the sake of SAC. Even within the Air Force, LeMay's emphasis on long-range bombing alienated the missile command as well as the tactical, or fighter, wings. He even antagonized the CIA by demanding authority over its U-2 reconnaissance fleet. According to General Frederic Smith, a LeMay ally, in a 1976 interview, "Curt became more dictatorial and more and more insistent on SAC being *it*. Anything else was purely secondary." By 1960 LeMay's descent into self-parody was complete. He was no longer one in a larger command of general officers committed to defending the nation against hostile intent. He was probing for an opportunity to launch a preemptive strike against the Soviet Union before it was strong enough to stage one of its own. He was a lone wolf, obsessive. He was Jack D. Ripper.

The Kennedy administration, beginning with the president himself, had little use for men like Curtis LeMay and his hawkish allies in Congress. Throughout his political career, Kennedy struggled to reconcile his desire to ease America's severe Cold War posture with the political imperative of talking tough to communists. He blamed the Truman administration for the "loss" of China. While running for president, Kennedy portrayed Eisenhower as napping in the crosshairs of a vast Soviet missile fleet that did not exist, and he made the clatter of falling dominoes the chin music of his campaign. Such alarmism from a fellow Harvard man disappointed John Kenneth Galbraith, who would serve as Kennedy's ambassador to India. "JFK has made the point that he isn't soft," he told a friend at the time. "Henceforth he can only frighten."

Yet Kennedy, a self-described realist, also understood and remarked openly upon the limits of military might. Following a tour of Asia and the Middle East during his 1952 campaign for the Senate, he criticized the

Eisenhower administration for funding an arms bazaar in both regions with weaponry. "Communism," he declared in a radio address, "cannot be met effectively by merely the force of arms. The central core of our Middle East policy [should not be] the export of arms or the show of armed might but the export of ideas, of techniques, and rebirth of our traditional sympathy for and understanding of the desires of men to be free." As a senator he rejected French neocolonialism, urging against U.S. intervention in Vietnam and supporting a free and independent Algeria. In June 1958, he spoke from the Senate floor of the need to preserve the State Department's primacy over the country's foreign policy, and he opposed a bill that would give the Pentagon control over foreign economic assistance. As a presidential candidate, he called for "a new foreign policy that will break out of the confines of the Cold War. Then . . . we can stop the vicious cycle of the arms race and promote diversity and peaceful change within the Soviet bloc."

Once elected, Kennedy made clear his desire to reach out to Moscow and to make arms control the cornerstone of his first term. Meeting with a group of Soviet experts on February 11, 1961, he displayed, according to Charles Bohlen, "a mentality extraordinarily free of preconceived prejudices, inherited or otherwise . . . almost as though he had thrown aside the normal prejudices that beset human mentality." He responded warmly to a suggestion from a friend, the British economist Lady Barbara Ward Jackson, to deliver a speech to the UN General Assembly inspired by the poetry of W. H. Auden. "We must love each other or / We must die," Lady Jackson offered. It was a charming entreaty. But if Kennedy ever intended to give such a speech, he was mugged on his way to the dais by Fidel Castro, Nikita Khrushchev, the CIA, the Joint Chiefs of Staff, and civilian militarists in his own administration.

The famously harebrained CIA plan to overthrow Fidel Castro by turning loose a brigade of Cuban exiles at La Batalla de Girón—the Bay of Pigs—had been hatched during the Eisenhower administration. It might have been unleashed under Ike's watch had not Vice President Richard Nixon, campaigning against Kennedy in 1960 and well aware the plot was nowhere near ready for launch, insisted the operation be delayed until after the election. In fact, there would never be an ideal time to invade Cuba, because there was never compelling opposition to Castro's rule. Prior to the election, Tracy Barnes, a senior CIA official, commissioned a private survey that revealed that a great majority of Cubans supported their new leader. As the results were not to his liking, Barnes buried them. Castro no doubt knew of the American plot to destroy him before Kennedy did, owing to the CIA's fruitless efforts to undermine him. (In fall 1960, the CIA staged thirty airborne drops of firearms for resistance groups throughout Cuba, no more than three of which succeeded.) What stood for a resistance movement in Cuba was eradicated in the waning months of the Eisenhower administration.

The invasion of the Bay of Pigs in April 1961 stands as one of the greatest disasters in covert U.S. military operations and an abject failure of the interagency process. Absent air support and denied the element of surprise, the rebels were slaughtered on the beach or knee-deep in the surf. In the waning hours of the assault, Kennedy requested Admiral Arleigh Burke, the commander of the U.S. Navy, to salvage the operation. Burke replied, "Nobody knew what to do, nor did the CIA, who were running the operation and who were wholly responsible for the operation, know what to do, or what was happening. We have been kept pretty ignorant of this and have just been told partial truths."

The Joint Chiefs would later claim the White House did not consult them in any meaningful way until after the operation had been approved. LeMay, who was Air Force vice chief of staff at the time, said he knew nothing of the operation until March and protested vigorously when informed of Kennedy's proscription against U.S. air cover. Kennedy took responsibility for the disaster but also blamed his military and intelligence leaders for poor advice. The Bay of Pigs and its bloody aftermath created an irredeemable rift between Kennedy on one side and his generals and spies on the other. In his first confrontation with the national security state, it was the war-hero president who blinked.

The Bay of Pigs debacle was followed by an interlude of calm before the deluge: Berlin, Laos, Cuba again, Vietnam. It was an opportunity for Americans to reflect on the nature and motives of their adversaries, the

moral and strategic hazards of preemptive war, and the realities of cause
and effect in foreign affairs. The point could have been made that Fidel
Castro's popularity among his people was the consequence of U.S. support of Fulgencio Batista, the ruthless and corrupt dictator who aroused
nationalist passions and built constituencies for revolt. It may have been
argued that successful revolutions are virtuous in youth but devour their
own as they mature. It may also have been argued that the threat posed
by a communist Cuba was nothing compared with the perils of the arms
race that was now consuming U.S.-Soviet relations and that the United
States, with its preponderant advantage in military might, did so much
to fuel.

Instead, Washington dug in—and would have done so literally, had
Edward Teller gotten his way. The physicist-hawk stunned Kennedy with
a plan for a nationwide honeycomb of bomb shelters that could easily
have been interpreted by Moscow as the prelude to a prophylactic assault.
The Joint Chiefs and their friends in Congress rose to the bait of Castro's
survival by ordering up a dramatic expansion of America's intercontinental ballistic missile fleet. They wanted 3,000 of them at a time when
America's "missile gap" had long since been exposed as a lie. Kennedy
and his circle held the line at 950. This is what passed for restraint and
self-reflection in the New Frontier.

Within months of his arrival, Kennedy found himself struggling with
the Joint Chiefs and Congress on an array of foreign policy and security
issues. His desire to sign a nuclear test ban treaty with Moscow was frustrated by what Deputy Defense Secretary Roswell Gilpatric called Washington's "built-in, knee-jerk reaction to anything like . . . arms control."
Briefed on the Strategic Air Command's decentralized command and
control procedures, the new president was shocked to learn how vulnerable
the system was to an isolated or rogue officer launching an inadvertent or
unprovoked U.S. nuclear attack. The new administration was equally appalled by the Single Integrated Operational Plan, the cornerstone of Eisenhower's doctrine of "massive retaliation" that Pentagon planners discussed
with an appalling insouciance.* Walt Rostow, the hardly dovish State

---

* While briefing the new defense secretary and his aides on SIOP, Strategic Air Commander General Tommy Power turned to McNamara and joked, "Mr. Secretary, I hope

Department policy planner, called SIOP "an orgiastic, Wagnerian plan" and said that Kennedy "was determined . . . to get the plan changed so he would have total control of it."

Massive retaliation, however, was a systematized madness that Kennedy in the few years allotted him could do little to deprogram. In a February 4, 1963, meeting of the National Security Council, Bundy said there was "no logic whatever to nuclear policy," according to a staff member present, and disparaged "the military planners who calculate that we will win if only we can kill 100 million Russians while they are killing 30 million Americans." Years later, Gilpatric would remark how "horrified" he and other Kennedy allies were "over how little positive control the President really had over the use of this great arsenal."

That was just fine with the brass. Asked in January 1961 whether he feared the destructive power under his authority, General Tommy Power replied he was "more worried by the civilian control over him and equally frightened by both." To LeMay, first among equals within the fraternity of service heads, the New Frontiersmen were not "Whiz Kids" as they were popularly known but "happy little hotdogs." The two sides clashed over everything, from nuclear doctrine, beginning with the "no-first-use" policy—which McNamara wanted to state publicly and LeMay believed should remain confidential—to the defense budget. When McNamara refused to earmark additional funds for the Air Force's cherished but costly and accident-prone B-70 bomber, LeMay appealed directly to Congress. With the help of Carl Vinson, the chairman of the House Armed Services Committee, he secured a funding mandate of nearly $500 million. In sidestepping the White House in such a manner, LeMay was flirting yet again with insubordination, though not even McNamara was prepared to take on LeMay and his hawkish supporters in Congress.

LeMay once suggested to a fellow airman that Khrushchev would make just as damaging a secretary of defense as McNamara. For him, it was Kennedy and his "egotistical" patrician aides who were abusing the

---

you don't have any friends or relations in Albania because we're just going to have to wipe it out." McNamara was stunned. "We essentially blasted our way through the Warsaw Pact countries in order to get to the Soviet Union," he told an interviewer many years later, "and I was thinking, 'My God, what are we going to do to Poland.'"

military, not the other way around. "They had no faith in the military," he said. "They were better than all the rest of us, otherwise they wouldn't have gotten their superior education, as they saw it." The president's inner circle, by and large, took an equally dim view of the brass. Immediately after settling in, Kennedy reduced the Joint Chiefs' influence by eliminating two prominent White House committees, the Operations Coordinating Board and the Planning Board, through which they had enjoyed regular access to Eisenhower. After the Bay of Pigs fiasco, Kennedy, McNamara, and the others had come to believe LeMay and his counterparts were literally mad. Participating in the Kennedy Oral History Program in June 1970, Gilpatric revealed that "every time the President had to see LeMay, he ended up in sort of a fit. I mean, he would just be frantic at the end of a session with LeMay because, you know, LeMay couldn't listen or wouldn't take in, and he would make what Kennedy considered . . . outrageous proposals that bore no relation to the state of affairs in the 1960s."

The Joint Chiefs were pointedly excluded from the White House executive committee, the so-called ExComm, convened during the Cuban missile crisis of mid-October 1962. They were represented by General Maxwell Taylor, a Kennedy favorite and the sole military officer seated at the ExComm table, and they resented having to express their views by proxy. (Congressional leaders felt the same way about their own exclusion from the deliberations.) When ExComm members rallied around McNamara's suggestion of a naval blockade of Cuba as a first step in a graduated response to the crisis, LeMay argued in a face-to-face meeting with Kennedy that there "was no other solution than military action." Anything less than a full-scale air-and-ground assault, he said, would be "almost as bad as the appeasement [of Hitler] at Munich" and would encourage the Soviets to try the depths of U.S. commitments elsewhere. The other chiefs agreed, arguing that a surprise air strike and invasion would be the "lowest-risk course of action." Later, Kennedy told White House troubleshooter Kenneth O'Donnell that "these brass hats have one great advantage in their favor. If we listen to them, and do what they want us to do, none of us will be alive later to tell them they were wrong."

Even the prosecution of the embargo revealed the conflicting sensibilities between the men in Kennedy's world and the ones in LeMay's. Navy

secretary Admiral George Anderson chafed at McNamara's microman-
agement of the operation, particularly his resistance to the use of force.
When Anderson curtly explained that the Navy had been conducting
blockades since the American Revolution and suggested the secretary
stick to administrative affairs, McNamara rose from his chair and tersely
explained that the operation "was not a blockade but a means of communication between Kennedy and Khrushchev." Even after the two-week-
long confrontation ended peacefully with Kennedy's concession to remove
Jupiter missiles from Turkey in exchange for the withdrawal of the Soviet
missiles in Cuba, the Joint Chiefs were not satisfied. Meeting with the
president in the Oval Office a few days after the crisis was defused, Anderson declared that the compromise agreement had swindled the nation of
credibility. LeMay called it "the greatest defeat in our history" and counseled an immediate invasion. Kennedy, according to McNamara, was "absolutely shocked" and "stuttering in reply."

Kennedy wanted to sack both LeMay and Anderson during the crisis
but feared Republican reprisals from Congress. Two weeks after the showdown concluded, in a postmortem with journalist and future *Washington
Post* editor Benjamin Bradlee, Kennedy revealed that "the first advice I'm
going to give my successor is to watch the generals and . . . avoid the feeling that just because they were military men their opinions on military
matters were worth a damn."

If anyone was going to avoid the mistake of rushing blindly into another conflict, particularly in Asia, it was Kennedy. So it was no surprise
when, four months after the Vienna summit, in October 1961, he named
Harriman assistant secretary of state for Far Eastern affairs. The interagency battles to come would be as intense as their consequences were
sustained.

The appointment signaled Kennedy's seriousness about his hard-line
commitment to South Vietnam. Harriman was the oldest and in many
ways the most prominent member of the foreign policy priesthood that
had guided Truman through the immediate postwar years. A hugely successful financier by his early thirties, he went on to establish an empire
that included such assets as the Southern Pacific Railroad and the Union

Pacific Steamship Co., as well as banks such as Wells Fargo & Co. With war approaching, Roosevelt had dispatched Harriman to Europe as his special envoy. Over the next two decades, he would serve as ambassador to both Moscow and London, deploying his negotiating skills in the service of high diplomacy. Seventy years old and with the country mobilizing for a very different kind of war, Harriman was back in the arena. His first task was to recultivate the State Department's Bureau for Far Eastern Affairs, which was still fallow a decade after it had been steeped in the brine of McCarthyism. What was once a wellspring of Sinology, a convergence of supple minds like those of Service, Davies, Chubb, and Vincent, was now a "wasteland" of demoralized desk officers, according to Harriman.

The new assistant secretary arrived at a time of subtle, though potentially significant shifts in U.S. Asian policy. In 1961 the East Asia desk opened the Office of Asian Communist Affairs, a gesture of de facto recognition of the People's Republic of China. It did not go unnoticed at the State Department, even depleted of Asian expertise, that the global communist movement, at least in Asia, was splintering. Skirmishes along China's border with Russia betrayed the myth of Sino-Soviet harmony, and Mao's failed "Great Leap Forward" had plunged the country into chaos. (As late as 1960, a clueless CIA was forecasting a robust Chinese grain harvest.) Quietly, the nation's remaining Far East specialists were probing ways to draw a weakened China toward Washington and away from Moscow. They were discussing ways to ease the embargo on Chinese-made goods as well as the ban on travel to China, beginning with journalists and doctors. The China lobby was on to them, however, and did what it could to frustrate their efforts. Early in 1961, it blocked State Department attempts to normalize relations with Soviet-dominated Outer Mongolia, which the Nationalists considered part of China, laying a marker down on how far the new administration could go in its first term.

Harriman strongly favored rapprochement. Closer relations with Beijing, he believed, would give the United States leverage over the problems in Indochina and against Moscow on such issues as Berlin and arms control. But it would also antagonize Taipei, the seat of the Nationalists' government in exile in Taiwan. This was strongly opposed by Harriman's boss, Secretary of State Dean Rusk, a supporter of Chiang Kai-shek since his days as a staff officer in China during World War II. While Harriman was in Geneva negotiating the Laotian accords, the secretary infuriated him by denying his request to meet with the Chinese delegation. In 1951 Rusk had called China a "colonial Russian government, a Slavic [Manchuria] on a larger scale." As the head of the Far East bureau after the communist takeover, Rusk would display his outdated notions of the country by remarking on the prospect of a return to warlordism. He was, his colleagues said, a "real Grandma Moses on China."

Under Rusk, the barricade of Foreign Service officers who had resisted militarist hokum about monolithic communism sweeping Southeast Asia was thinned out and finally overwhelmed. What McCarthy had begun in the 1950s, Rusk finished less than a decade later, removing what was left of the department's Asia-hand stalwarts. Roger Hilsman, a veteran Vietnam expert who had warned Rusk in a December 1962 memo that the Vietcong would likely prevail over the regime of Ngo Dinh Diem, was replaced by McNamara acolyte Bill Bundy. Michael Forrestal, son of James Forrestal and a Harriman aide who shared none of his father's militarist fantasies, was reassigned to a State Department boiler room and left government not long afterward. William Trueheart, chargé d'affaires at the U.S. embassy in Saigon, who earned the hostility of Maxwell Taylor and his allies by openly opposing their indulgence of Diem, was ordered by Rusk to return to Washington at McNamara's request. He was made desk officer of all of Southeast Asia, though his new brief excluded Vietnam.

Gentlemanly and loyal, Dean Rusk was perfectly content to be a lamb among wolves. Nicknamed "Buddha" for his passivity at high-level meetings, he presided over the near-total eclipse of the State Department from the epicenter of foreign policy making. As Rusk plodded about Foggy Bottom's seventh floor, groping his way through the twentieth century with nineteenth-century coordinates, National Security Adviser Mac Bundy was busy setting up an elite staff at the White House that gradually absorbed what should have been State's responsibility. Defense Secretary McNamara, meanwhile, was broadly identifying U.S. objectives in Vietnam in a way that previously would have been unthinkable for a defense official.

Upon his return from Geneva, Harriman began nurturing his own direct lines to the White House as he maneuvered to fill the vacuum at the State Department created by Rusk's failure of leadership. Others would beat him to it, however.

As early as September 1960, with presidential candidates Nixon and Kennedy both stumping in support of the South Vietnamese regime as the campaign entered its home stretch, the U.S. ambassador to Saigon, Elbridge Durbrow, filed home a warning about Ngo Dinh Diem's staying power and suggested Washington consider "[an] alternative course of actions and leaders in order to achieve our objective" in Southeast Asia. A year later, with his credibility diminished further by a series of Vietcong victories over his units, Diem was begging Washington for a mutual defense treaty. Previously, he had told his U.S. allies he could handle the insurgency on his own. The presence of foreign troops on Vietnamese soil, he feared, might spark a backlash from a people still haunted by memories of the French occupation. Kennedy interpreted Diem's reversal as a sign that the situation was deteriorating, and on October 13, 1961, he announced he was dispatching General Maxwell Taylor on a tour of South Vietnam alongside Walt Rostow, assistant to National Security Adviser Bundy. Rather than take Durbrow's advice, the White House was poised to deepen its investment in a doomed autocrat.

The president's announcement alarmed and demoralized an already diminished State Department. Rostow was the most hawkish of Kennedy's civilian advisers. He believed the United States should have rushed to France's aid after its defeat at Dien Bien Phu in 1954, and he had an abiding faith that Hanoi could be bombed into submission. "The inclusion of Rostow [on Taylor's mission] worried me," reflected George Ball, who in his memoirs describes Rostow as "an articulate amateur tactician . . . unduly fascinated by the then faddish theories about counter-insurgency." For his part, Secretary Rusk did nothing to protest what was a clear snub of his authority and the value of his department. He believed Vietnam was a military problem that demanded a military solution and he left it up to McNamara and Taylor. His top diplomats disagreed, however. For Chester

Bowles, undersecretary of state at the time, assigning Rostow to colead the Taylor mission "indicated that the State Department had either abdicated its responsibility or that the President, with no confidence in the State Department, had decided to make it that way."

The Taylor mission was thoroughly militarized, with its Pentagon officers outnumbering civilians by a ratio of 3 to 1. Rostow had taken along with him to Saigon a bundle of reports that all validated his desire to not only assist Diem but to "liberate" the North Vietnamese. By the time the mission had made a brief stop in Hawaii, Rostow had convinced Taylor of the need to bomb North Vietnam. On October 23, the two men cabled Kennedy that "NVN is extremely vulnerable to conventional bombing, a weakness that should be exploited diplomatically in convincing Hanoi to lay off SVN."

Arriving in Saigon for its one-week tour, the mission was told by a besieged Diem that President Kennedy should be eager to confront "with American forces" a communist assault on Vietnam that was, after all, "an international problem." Judging by the high number of military men among the visitors, it seemed that such a decision had already been made. (Certainly Hanoi and Moscow thought so; they jointly condemned the mission, correctly, as it turned out, as a precipitous step toward the Americanization of the war.) The South Vietnamese army was clearly in need of help. Informed in interviews with U.S. and South Vietnamese officials that the country's border was "like a sieve," Taylor and Rostow assured Diem they would recommend he be provided with immediate direct assistance, including the introduction of combat troops.

Back in Washington, the two men prepared a laundry list for Diem that included attack helicopters and B-26 light bombers, military advisers, and training experts. Most significantly, they would call for an expeditionary force of some 8,000 GIs, with a mandate for significant increases in force strength if circumstances demanded it. Rostow framed the urgency of the situation in the report's cover letter, declaring "our common sense of outrage at the burden which this kind of aggression imposes on a new country. . . . It is easy and cheap to destroy such a country whereas it is difficult undisturbed to build a nation coming out of a complex past without carrying the burden of guerrilla war." Significantly, the report advocated that the United States make clear its intention to "attack the source of guerrilla aggression in North Vietnam" in order to combat "Khrushchev's 'wars of liberation.'"

Here was an authentic call to the ramparts of containment, and administrative doves, led by George Ball, raged against it. In a Saturday meeting with McNamara and Gilpatric on November 4, 1961, Ball warned that expanding the Vietnam conflict risked provoking a Chinese response, just as MacArthur's push to the Yalu River had in Korea. "Moreover," he argued, "the Vietnam problem was not one of repelling armed invasion but of mixing ourselves up in a revolutionary situation with strong anti-colonialist overtones." Neither McNamara nor Gilpatric shared Ball's concerns. Indeed, McNamara said he would be prepared to deploy as many as 250,000 troops to South Vietnam in support of the Diem government. "The 'falling domino' theory," Ball writes, "was a brooding omnipresence." On November 7, Ball told Kennedy that if he adopted the Taylor-Rostow recommendations, "within five years we'll have three hundred thousand men in the paddies and jungles and never find them again." To which Kennedy responded: "George, you're just crazier than hell. That just isn't going to happen." As it would turn out, Ball's estimate was about 200,000 men light.

Chester Bowles, realizing the futility of waging asymmetrical war of any kind, let alone an Asian one on behalf of a fragile dictatorship, warned that "a direct military response to increased Communist pressure has the supreme disadvantage of involving our prestige and power in a remote area under the most adverse circumstances." Both Bowles and Harriman suggested that the guarantee of neutralization negotiated for Laos be extended to all of Southeast Asia. Kennedy found the idea admirable but impossible to sell politically, given the lingering specter of McCarthyism on Capitol Hill. "The time is not yet ripe," he told Bowles.

Kenneth Galbraith also advised against the Taylor-Rostow line, writing in his diary that both "are advocating exceedingly half-baked intervention." Even Dean Rusk piped up against sending troops. While loath to allow a shaft of light between him and McNamara, he questioned whether Diem was committed to "the kind of reforms that would validate direct U.S. intervention on his behalf." Otherwise, the secretary argued, it would be "difficult to see how [a] handful of American troops can have [a] decisive influence."

In the end, Rusk and McNamara split the difference. On November 11, they submitted to Kennedy a joint recommendation that the White House assist the Diem government "as speedily as possible" with communications equipment, helicopters, reconnaissance aircraft, naval patrols, and intelligence teams, while holding in abeyance any decision to deploy a large combat force to South Vietnam. The president approved the request, setting in motion the gears of militarization. Even the world-weary Kennedy, in authorizing more military aid and advisers to Saigon as recommended by the Taylor-Rostow study, underestimated the addicting quality of military commitments abroad and the powerful interests they create. As David Halberstam explains:

> For many reasons the Taylor-Rostow report was far more decisive than anyone realized, not because Kennedy did what they recommended but because in doing less than what it called for, he felt he was being moderate, cautious. There had been an illusion that he was holding the line, whereas in reality he was steering us far deeper into the quagmire. . . . Where there had been relatively low levels of verbal commitment—speeches, press conferences, slogans, fine words—his Administration would now have to escalate the rhetoric considerably to justify the increased . . . commitment. He was expanding the cycle of American interest and involvement in ways he did not know.

The additional advisers would more than double the 1,200-strong cadre already in Saigon. They would accompany South Vietnamese troops on missions and they would inevitably get drawn into the fight. The White House assiduously played this down. At a press conference on January 15, 1962, Kennedy denied U.S. troops were in combat in Vietnam even as he abetted restrictions on reporters working there to conceal the truth of the matter. In mid-February, the State Department's public affairs officer warned that "we seem headed for a major domestic furor over the 'undeclared' war in South Vietnam and U.S.-imposed 'secrecy regulations' that prevent American newsmen from telling our people the truth about our involvement in that war."

At a February 14 press briefing, a reporter asked Kennedy to respond to Republican charges that he had been less than candid with the American people about the depths of America's commitment to Vietnam. The president replied: "We have not sent combat troops in the generally understood sense of the word. We have increased our training mission and we've increased our logistic support. . . . I feel that we are being as frank as we can be." It was an early specimen of Vietnam War doublespeak, the kind that would serve as the U.S. government's principal means of communication throughout the conflict.

A favorite amusement among Cold War salonists is to ponder the unanswerable question: Would Kennedy, had he survived to contest and win a second term, have withdrawn the United States from Vietnam? Not surprisingly, his enthusiasts think so. Ted Sorenson, Kennedy's speechwriter, counselor, and confidant, cites the numerous occasions the president resisted pressure from both his civilian and his military advisers to dispatch thousands of troops to Vietnam and Laos. "He was determined not to precipitate a general land war in Asia," Sorenson writes in his memoirs. "He never reversed Eisenhower's commitment, but neither did he escalate the conflict to a level anything like that reached under LBJ."

Sorenson's bias notwithstanding, the record strongly suggests that Kennedy was keen on ending the U.S. role in Vietnam. In his tragically abbreviated first term, he made no secret of his wish not only to end the U.S. commitment in Southeast Asia but to demilitarize U.S.-Soviet relations altogether. His hand was stayed, however, for fear of another Red Scare. In April 1963, with some 16,000 U.S. troops in Vietnam, he told journalist Charles Bartlett that "we don't have a prayer" of remaining in Indochina. "Those people hate us. They are going to throw our asses out at any point." Kennedy went on to lament how "I can't give up a piece of territory like that to the communists and get the people to re-elect me." In May, the president told Senator Mike Mansfield that he concurred with the legislator's position on the need for a complete withdrawal from Vietnam, but that any such disassociation would have to await his reelection. After Mansfield's departure, Kennedy bemoaned to Kenneth O'Donnell how, in response to a preelection withdrawal, "we would have another Joe McCarthy scare on our hands."

A month later, on June 10, 1963, Kennedy delivered his landmark address at the American University commencement. It was, his defenders say, a herald for his second term, tempered as he was by three turbulent and often harrowing years as president. It was also an act of statesmanship by itself. Advised by Norman Cousins, the peace activist and editor of the *Saturday Review*, that Khrushchev was still smarting after caving to the United States in the Cuban missile crisis, Kennedy and his advisers agreed to provide the Soviet leader with an opening. The result was one of the most memorable of presidential speeches. For the first time during the Cold War, a U.S. president spoke more about the power and potential of peace than about the likelihood of war:

> What kind of peace do I mean and what kind of a peace do we seek? Not a Pax Americana enforced on the world by American weapons of war. Not the peace of the grave or the security of the slave. I am talking about genuine peace, the kind of peace that makes life on Earth worth living, and the kind that enables men and nations to grow, and to hope, and build a better life for their children—not merely peace for Americans but peace for all men and women, not merely peace in our time but peace in all time.

To Khrushchev's delight, Kennedy acknowledged Russia as a great power and he expressed empathy for the enormous losses Russia suffered during World War II, which Russians had long believed had been overlooked by the West. Kennedy also announced a unilateral moratorium on nuclear testing in the atmosphere, which led to negotiations with Moscow for a nuclear test ban treaty. Tellingly, Khrushchev allowed the speech to be rebroadcast throughout Russia and to be published in full in the state-run press.

On November 21, 1963, just prior to his fateful trip to Dallas, Kennedy told an aide to McGeorge Bundy that upon his return he wanted to "start a complete and very profound review of how we got into [Vietnam], and what we thought we were doing, and what we think we can do. I even want to think about whether or not we should be there."

It is fair to say, then, that a reelected Kennedy might well have redefined the contours of the Cold War. Significantly, he might have begun that process during his first term but for militarist reactionaries in Congress and the media. And that begs another question: Like Eisenhower, John Kennedy was a war hero who fully appreciated the offensive presumptions of a standing army. He enjoyed the bedrock credibility of someone who had stared down the Russians on the brink of Armageddon and prevailed. If a man like that could not resist the gravitational pull of militarization, no one could—certainly not the man destined to succeed him.

8

LOOKING-GLASS WAR

People who shut their eyes to reality simply invite
their own destruction.
—JAMES BALDWIN

LYNDON B. JOHNSON WAS FAMOUSLY UNSCHOOLED IN INTERNA-
tional affairs. In 1961, on a goodwill tour of South Vietnam as
Kennedy's vice president, he made foreign policy elites cringe by
hailing Ngo Dinh Diem, Saigon's authoritarian president, as "the Winston Churchill of Asia" and handing out official White House cigarette
lighters to bewildered villagers. Even so, upon his return he delivered a
sharp and prescient warning to Kennedy about the dangers of wading
deeper into Vietnam. "We should make clear," he wrote in a report to the
president, that "we have no intention of employing ground troops in Vietnam . . . or even using naval or air support which is but the first step in
that direction. If the Vietnamese government, backed by a three-year liberal aid program, cannot do this job, then we had better remember the
French who wound up with several hundred thousand men in Vietnam
and were still unable to do it." Johnson was even blunter in an aside to
National Security Adviser Mac Bundy. Vietnam, he said, "was the biggest
damn mess that I ever saw."

Now as president, Johnson was loath to expand the U.S. commitment to Saigon lest such a move divert resources from his cherished domestic policy agenda. He once told White House speechwriter Bill Moyers
that he wanted the South Vietnamese government to "leave me alone because I've got bigger things to do right here at home." But the president
was no match for the Brahmin counselors he had asked to stay on after
Kennedy's passing, nor could he entirely control the Joint Chiefs of Staff,
all of whom were calling for a wider war. As the situation in Indochina

unraveled, and with Johnson in deference to his civilian and military advisers, there was no one to block the rush to militarization. The checks and balances within the interagency process that usually conspire, however ungainly, in favor of restraint had collapsed. In Washington, the State Department abdicated its authority to the Pentagon, while Congress, still in thrall to, or in fear of, the China lobby, conceded its war-making authority to the White House. In Saigon, regional experts were sidelined by their own chiefs of mission. Within two years of Kennedy's assassination, a reluctant Johnson ordered the first major contingent of American warfighters into South Vietnam. Though his political instincts about the war were rock-solid, they were betrayed by his insecurities. Largely as a result, the nation was plunged irrevocably into an unwinnable conflict.

The war in Vietnam was the last one Americans waged under one roof. Among its many casualties would be national conscription, the way in which the country had raised its armies since World War II. Henceforth, professional soldiers, sailors, airmen, and Marines would assume responsibility for fighting America's wars, creating a separate "warrior" class largely segregated from civilian America. During the Vietnam era, however, the cold clutch of the draft on an entire generation of young men made the conflict an irresistible part of daily life. It balkanized Americans by race, class, age, and gender, and it launched the culture wars that roil us still. Its tremors destroyed what could have been one of the most historic presidencies of the last century, and it transformed the Republican Party from a buttoned-down enclave for Wall Street lawyers and bankers into the avenging angel of the desegregated South. The Democrats, meanwhile, by their association with Johnson's failure in Vietnam and increasingly violent and lawless antiwar protests, would be tarred for years as the party of appeasement, fellow travelers, and moral decay. The lessons of Vietnam would resonate with military elites, who learned from their mistakes, but they were lost on a political leadership that came of age watching grainy, monochromatic images of war on the evening news. For all the carnage it left behind, America departed from Vietnam almost as if it had never set foot there, just another aggressor among many that failed to impress its hosts.

If the war had proved anything, it is that "saving face" is not a preoc-cupation unique to inscrutable Asians. For more than a decade, over the course of four presidential administrations, the United States waged a costly war for the sake of not losing it. Its commitment to South Vietnam had little to do with the South Vietnamese and everything to do with cred-ibility, that most expensive of foreign policy commodities, denominated as it is in the blood of America's youth and local innocents. In a July 1964 briefing, General Maxwell Taylor explained that a U.S. failure in Southeast Asia "would destroy and severely damage our standing elsewhere in the world." For Dean Rusk, America's objective in Vietnam was to preserve its image as "the pillar of peace throughout the world." Once America became militarily involved, the war became largely about avoiding a humiliating U.S. defeat, as well as about political cover. Arguing in a March 21, 1965, memo for a major American escalation of the war, Bundy asked rhetori-cally whether "in terms of U.S. politics" would it be better to " 'lose' now or to 'lose' after committing 100,000 men? Tentative answer: the latter."

At no point was there any serious talk of an exit strategy. A succes-sion of corrupt regimes in Saigon—they would rise and fall in a carousel of assassinations and coups—offered the White House little in the way of a strategic partner, though the illusion of one was created through press releases about "joint" operations conducted by a "combined" U.S.–South Vietnamese military command. "Vietnamization," Richard Nixon's way of obliging the host government to assume greater responsibility for the war, was years away. Throughout the 1960s, it was Lyndon Johnson's war. He was forced to sustain an armed presence in the south large enough to appease Republican hawks and to keep the Joint Chiefs in line, but not so large or so aggressively deployed as to provoke China.

Less than a year after beating Republican senator Barry Goldwater in the 1964 presidential election, Johnson was indulging in the most tawdry of stump-speech hyperbole to justify a wartime mobilization he knew had nothing to do with national security. Announcing an increase in the number of U.S. troops in South Vietnam from 75,000 to 125,000, he declared that the "lesson of history" was to stand firm against Hanoi. "We learned from Hitler at Munich," the president said, "that success only feeds the appetite of aggression." George Kennan, who from the start had warned against U.S. involvement in Southeast Asia, complained in a letter to former Eisenhower aide Emmet John Hughes how the president was "doing all in [his] power to stimulate the most violent sort of American patriotic emotionalism."

Tragically, no one understood this better than Johnson. Had he served in peacetime, he may have been one of the most successful of U.S. presidents. Yet here he now was, his vision of a nation free of poverty and discrimination obscured by an unwanted war, the demon seed of ignorance and untruths.

The stated U.S. mission was to maintain a "free and independent" South Vietnam, though even the South Vietnamese weren't particularly interested. A 1965 study done by the U.S. Information Agency found that "the population is largely apathetic and is primarily interested in ending the twenty years of war; they care less as to which side will win, although there appears to be a substantial degree of support for the Viet Cong." These findings were consistent with the conclusions of a RAND study commissioned by McNamara's office to examine what was driving the insurgency. For months beginning in late 1964, RAND analysts interviewed captured guerrilla fighters with the help of University of Saigon scholars and translators. They found that Vietcong militia members considered themselves to be nationalists first, freedom fighters second, and communists third.

Indeed, far from a militia-drone assembled, trained, armed, and operated exclusively by Hanoi, as it was assumed to be by official Washington, the Vietcong was very much indigenous to South Vietnam. Saigon's Chinese merchants—they were concentrated in their own quarter called Cholon—were also well aware of the Vietcong's domestic character and how well it had insinuated itself in the higher echelons of local politics. The Cholon Chinese, like their ethnic counterparts throughout Southeast Asia, controlled the South Vietnamese economy through a host of family-run business empires, and they knew well the balance of power in the country. They represented a rich source of intelligence that was freely available and largely wasted because the State Department's stock of Chinese speakers had been so drastically winnowed by the Red Scare.

The senior officials who ran the U.S. embassy in Saigon were Francophile holdovers from the colonial days, or Europeanists such as Frederick

E. Nolting Jr., a senior NATO official who was named ambassador to Saigon in 1961 despite his lack of Asian experience. Nolting was a favorite of the hard-liners, and Chester Bowles had tried unsuccessfully to interdict his appointment and reroute him to Bangkok. For Nolting and Foreign Service elites like him, Chinese experts were either irrelevant or uninteresting. Recalled Herbert Levin, who taught Chinese for the State Department and served as assistant national intelligence officer for East Asia during the Reagan administration: "They gradually pushed these officers into the consular and administrative sections and decided that they really didn't need them all."

However damaging the marginalization of the State Department during the Kennedy-Johnson era was, its exile from the policymaking process was largely irrelevant because Secretary of State Dean Rusk was as hawkish as his counterparts at the National Security Council and the Pentagon. They were "with-us-or-against us" militarists, as intolerant of foreign national liberation movements as their stodgy Republican predecessors. Despite conclusive military superiority over Russia and China, they refused to concede any of its client states, no matter how corrupt, incompetent, or strategically insignificant. Like Eisenhower and Dulles before them, they dismissed any possibility of coexistence with "neutralist" or nonaligned regimes. Nor did they question the solidarity of the Sino-Soviet alliance, a blind spot that denied them the advantage of peeling Beijing from Moscow as relations between the two sides deteriorated. Kennedy had signaled he would work to improve relations with Moscow, just as he vowed to reopen the case of disgraced China Hand John Paton Davies Jr. in a second term that would remain sadly hypothetical.

Instead, America's Asia policy would be administered by men such as Walter Robertson, Harriman's successor as assistant secretary of state for Far Eastern affairs, who dismissed signs of strained relations between China and the Soviet Union as a conspiracy. Like Rusk, Robertson believed talk of estrangement between Moscow and Beijing was a feint to lull Washington into a false sense of security, despite the daily exchanges of vitriol in the pages of *Pravda* and the *People's Daily*. So relentless were the editorial broadsides from the Chinese side that translators at the U.S. consulate in Hong Kong were running out of English matches for the scatological epithets intrinsic to Mandarin Chinese.

With the exception of Undersecretary of State George Ball, the only senior official who vigorously questioned the value of Vietnam was the president himself. In a May 1964 telephone conversation with Bundy, Johnson plaintively asked, "What the hell is Vietnam to me? And what the hell is Vietnam to the country?" Faced with an onslaught of recommendations to begin bombing North Vietnam, Johnson lamented how "if I don't go in now and they show later I should have gone, then they'll be all over me in Congress. They won't be talking about my civil rights bill, or education or beautification. No sir, they'll push Vietnam up my ass every time. Vietnam. Vietnam. Vietnam. Right up my ass." (One wonders if those Chinese language translators in Hong Kong could have done with a little Texan vernacular.)

So reluctant was Johnson to escalate the war, it appears, he was hoping for a deus ex machina in the form of a putsch that would result in a neutral government in Saigon and a request that the United States withdraw its troops. When Bundy voiced concern in 1964 that the Americans may get "invited out" of Vietnam in the event of a coup, Johnson expressed a conspicuous indifference. "I don't know what we can do if there is," he said. "What alternative do we have then?" In May, Johnson told Senator Richard Russell that the only politically acceptable way for him to extricate the country from Vietnam was if Saigon showed him the door. Even as the president's top aides took it for granted they would oppose any coup leader who offered to negotiate peace with Hanoi, a November 29 policy paper drafted by Bundy had been approved by the president only after the removal of a line that would have committed the United States to do just that.

Fearful that his boss was getting soft, Bundy authored something of a coup himself. With McNamara's help, he admonished Johnson in a memo that staying "the enormous power of the United States" was the "worst course of action" that "would only lead to defeat and an invitation to get out in humiliating circumstances." The Pentagon's National Security paper 288, signed by Johnson on March 17 , warned that unless the United States succeeded in its objective of establishing a free and independent South Vietnam, "all of Southeast Asia will probably fall under Communist dominance." The State Department's Vietnam Working Group, meanwhile, had mapped out a contingency plan for the use of

U.S. force, if necessary, to reverse any seizure of power by a "neutralist coup." In a December 31 telegram to the State Department, Ambassador Maxwell Taylor in Saigon recommended an immediate air assault on North Vietnam as a way to preempt negotiations for a peaceful settlement between Saigon and Hanoi. As Vice President Hubert Humphrey would later observe, Johnson was pinned down by events and bureaucracies that, when working in lockstep, represented a power and authority that could overwhelm the presidency itself.

The foreign policy establishment had transformed Vietnam—war-torn, feudal, and of little strategic value—into a vital coordinate along the East-West divide, a testing ground for American resolve and a worthy flash point for a third world war. "We believed in it because that's what the establishment in Washington believed," said Leslie Gelb, who served as director of policy planning at the Pentagon from 1967 to 1969. "Everyone said the stakes were too high to fail. And we knew nothing about Vietnam. The people who did know about [Southeast Asia] did not participate in the process and as a result we didn't know what we could and couldn't do."

As the White House raised the pitch of its anti-Soviet cant, hawks in Congress sharpened theirs. So by the mid-1960s, with the situation in South Vietnam worsening, Johnson was unable to unwind a Cold War commitment that had become larger than the country it was made to protect. The only available direction was forward—bombing North Vietnam, deploying ground troops in the south, doubling and tripling aid to feckless leaders in Saigon. The most powerful nation in history was lashing about, grasping for one ad hoc solution after another like blades of elephant grass.

America's intervention in Vietnam was militarized less than a year into Johnson's presidency on the strength of an incident off the North Vietnamese coast that in all likelihood never happened. The Gulf of Tonkin incident of August 2, 1964, served as justification for America's massive retaliatory response against what the president assured his fellow citizens was an unprovoked attack. In fact, by the time of the Tonkin Gulf incident, the U.S. government was seven months into a secret war against

North Vietnam that Johnson had acquiesced to within a month after assuming office. Part of the campaign was a maritime surveillance operation that involved raids by South Vietnamese commandos on the radar stations of enemy surface-to-air missile batteries. The patrols were conducted alongside another far more ambitious covert operation, in which U.S. swift boats and airborne South Vietnamese commandos would infiltrate North Vietnam to interdict Vietcong patrols maneuvering south, disrupt supply chains, and capture fishermen for interrogation. The U.S. plan was to gather intelligence and soften the ground for an amphibious invasion of the north promoted by Johnson's more hawkish civilian and military advisers.

McNamara was among the few senior White House officials who supported covert operations in North Vietnam. He pressured reluctant admirals into ramping up the coastal harassment missions, many of which were focused on the Tonkin Gulf—the preferred attack corridor, it is worth noting, for the legions of armies that have invaded Vietnam over the course of many centuries. The North Vietnamese, predictably enough, responded by augmenting their gunboat squadrons in the region. On July 31, the Joint Chiefs of Staff authorized a mission to appraise North Vietnamese naval capability. The first attack on the U.S. Navy destroyer *Maddox* occurred two days later—by any measure a defensive response by Hanoi against a hostile vessel operating within the murkily defined limits of its territorial waters.

Unaware that Washington was running a covert military campaign in Southeast Asia, Congress was easily manipulated into passing a resolution that would give Johnson unlimited war powers. The Gulf of Tonkin Resolution, as it would be forever known, passed with only two dissenting votes in the Senate. The House of Representatives passed the resolution unanimously. Years later, Johnson would rue how "those dumb, stupid sailors" that fateful stormy night "were probably just shooting at flying fish." But the Tonkin Gulf incident and the resolution it enabled was a huge victory for those in the White House who wanted to take the fight to North Vietnam. The most energized White House hawk was Walter Rostow, Paul Nitze's successor as the director of the State Department's Policy Planning Division and the most ardent civilian supporter of intensified aerial and maritime attacks on the north. "You know," he told his State

Department colleagues, "the wonderful thing is we don't even know if this thing happened at all. . . . It gives us the chance to really go for broke on the bombing. The evidence is unclear, but our golden opportunity is at hand."

Hanoi and Beijing, tactical Cold War allies but strategic adversaries since before the first century BC, reacted to the Tonkin Gulf affair by closing ranks. Beijing placed its ground, sea, and air forces based along China's southern rim on high alert and mobilized four air divisions and one anti-aircraft unit along its border with North Vietnam. It dispatched more than a dozen Soviet-made MiG-15 and MiG-17 jets and trainers to Hanoi along with engineers to build new airfields. In short, China was manning the parapet of its ancient 'sphere of influence. By June 1965, it was providing North Vietnam with ground-to-air missiles, antiaircraft artillery, and railroad, engineering, and minesweeping units, as well as sizable troop deployments. By 1967, at the height of the Cultural Revolution, Hanoi would play host to some 170,000 PLA soldiers.

Mao would never deviate from his desire to avoid open conflict with the United States. Though he lifted restrictions against surface-to-air missile attacks on U.S. aircraft passing over Hainan Island, for example, any aerial "victories" were downplayed by China's state-run media. Nevertheless, a U.S. invasion of North Vietnam was a red line that Mao—or any other Chinese leader, for that matter—would not hesitate to contest with the full force of the abundant human resources under his command. Beijing made this clear to Washington, far more emphatically than it had under similar circumstances in Korea. Beijing worked the Sino-American ambassadorial talks in Warsaw, as well as third-party leaders and British diplomats in Beijing, to deliver a simple but stern warning: limit your offensive on North Vietnam to air assaults. Otherwise, you'll have a full-scale war in Asia on your hands with the most populated nation on Earth.

The White House got the message, and the specter of a Korea-style Chinese intervention in Vietnam was a major factor in Johnson's insistence that the military confine its attacks north of the 17th parallel to air strikes. Washington's war would be restricted to the south, a generally tedious, occasionally harrowing and grisly struggle waged across rice paddies, under thick jungle canopies, and from thousands of feet over North Vietnam in a failed and unconscionable bombing campaign. Confining the war to modulated cycles of aerial bombardment would do little to move a country that knew conflict more than it did peace, whether in medieval struggles against the Chinese or modern ones against the French and Japanese.

Under Kennedy, the rejection of Eisenhower's doctrine of "massive retaliation" and a commitment to parry Moscow's thrusts in low-intensity conflict would become known as "flexible response," and it would serve as a basis for the strategy of gradualism that extended into the Johnson administration. It is a controversial doctrine to this day, with holdouts on the right condemning it as a series of inconclusive half measures—"tying one hand behind our backs"—while war critics characterize it as the descent by drip-feed into a needless war that should have been avoided altogether.

The war in Vietnam was a classic asymmetrical conflict, pitting as it did a global power boxed into a strategy of attrition against a small country possessed of few resources other than a highly motivated and fervently nationalist population. While the military injudiciously applied the strictures of a conventional war to a counterinsurgency struggle, Johnson's civilian advisers employed "systems analysis," the discipline of breaking down the components of a problem to identify the most efficient way of resolving it. The architects of gradualism—Rostow, McNamara, Bundy— believed that with each more intensified round of bombing they could "communicate" to Hanoi their awesome capacity to inflict harm. It was a strategy inspired by Thomas Schelling, a Nobel Prize–winning economist and RAND fellow who wrote that a rationed application of force would result in opposing sides "simultaneously [reaching] a judgment about what is the most reasonable choice for us to make and what is a reasonable choice for him to be making."

This inductive approach, also known as "mirror imaging," has been criticized by some military historians, who suggest that Ho Chi Minh's revolutionary zeal unmoored him from the kind of rational calculation implied in the theory of gradualism. In fact, just the opposite was the case. It was not the method of divining Hanoi's intentions that failed the Americans in Vietnam. It was the flawed assumption, bred by a crisis of imagination and common sense, that the North Vietnamese would behave any differently than would anyone else when subjected to a protracted bombing campaign from a foreign aggressor. The engineers of the nation's greatest foreign policy disaster ignored the lesson of the U.S. Strategic Bombing Survey—that aerial bombardment can fortify an enemy as much as degrade it—in favor of the flawed presumptions of "the language of force." To the highly destructive but ultimately failed bombing campaigns of World War II—the Nazi blitz of London, the Allied assault on Hamburg, LeMay's nonnuclear devastation of Japan—would be added Lyndon Johnson's attempt to "communicate" with North Vietnam via sustained aerial bombardment.

Years later, McNamara acknowledged his failure to interpret Hanoi's motivations. "We totally underestimated the nationalist aspect of Ho Chi Minh's movement," he wrote in his 1996 memoir. "We saw him first as a communist and only second as a Vietnamese nationalist. . . . The foundations of our decision making were gravely flawed." McNamara's mea culpa is rendered all the more tragic when compared with remarks made by a member of Bundy's staff in response to White House plans for a spring 1965 bombing offensive. "The thing that bothers me," said the aide, "is that no matter what we do to them, they live there and we don't, and they know that someday we'll have to go away and thus they know they can outlast us."

Bundy mulled this over. "That's a good point," he finally replied.

By then, however, Bundy and most of his colleagues had reached the point of no return. In February 1965, while visiting a U.S. air base in Pleiku in Vietnam's central highland region, he and his retinue were caught in a Vietcong attack that killed eight GIs and wounded hundreds of others. Clearly shaken, Bundy immediately called Johnson with his aides assembled in the Cabinet Room and declared that Hanoi had "thrown down the gauntlet" in collusion with the USSR to press such an attack to coincide with his tour. This was nonsense; as Cold War historian Gareth Porter points out, the operation would have been planned

long before Bundy's arrival was announced. There was no evidence of
Soviet complicity and certainly no need of any. But it provided Bundy
with enough leverage to shame the president into retaliation. Johnson
immediately approved air strikes on three targets in the north. The White
House announced the assaults were "appropriate and fitting . . . as in the
case of the North Vietnamese attacks in the Gulf of Tonkin last August."

Maxwell Taylor, who had so much invested in the prospect of a successful bombing campaign, withheld from the White House a CIA report that cast doubt on its effectiveness. The die was cast. After months
of resistance, Johnson had finally submitted to his advisers. With boots
on the ground and bombers screaming down the tarmac, Major General
Arthur Collins of the Army's operations staff was reminded "of the story
of not letting the camel get its nose in the tent" before it eats everything
before it.

Operation Rolling Thunder, a JCS plan for an eight-week-long, staged
bombing campaign against North Vietnam, commenced on March 2,
1965. In April 1967, Earle Wheeler, an early proponent of the campaign,
decided it had "struck all worthwhile fixed targets except the ports."
Despite that, Rolling Thunder achieved none of its objectives and was
declared a strategic failure. By November 1968, U.S. warplanes had dropped
860,000 tons of bombs on North Vietnam, more than the United States
had dropped either on North Korea during the Korean War or on Japan
during World War II. Some 90,000 North Vietnamese are thought to have
been bombed to death and nearly all of North Vietnam's industrial and
communications facilities were destroyed. The guerrilla campaign against
the south, waged as it was by small, decentralized militias in need of few
external supplies, proved resistant to one of the largest air interdiction efforts in history.

None of this should have come as a surprise. In September 1964, six
months before Rolling Thunder was unleashed, the Defense Department
and RAND held a simulation game to analyze the likely outcome of a
staged bombing campaign against North Vietnam. It was called SIGMA
II-64 and was engineered specifically to test a version of gradualism
promoted by White House aide Walt Rostow. The conclusions of SIGMA
II totally debunked Rostow's thesis. Far from retarding the enemy's
capacity to fight, sustained aerial bombardment actually strengthened

it. Not only that, the SIGMA II results were consistent with those yielded by a similar war game, SIGMA I-64, which had been held in April.

With Rolling Thunder failing to achieve its desired ends, outgoing CIA director John McCone conveyed to the White House what it did not want to hear: anything less than either a negotiated settlement with Hanoi or a dramatic expansion of the war would lead to an "ever-increasing commitment of U.S. personnel without materially improving the chance of victory." In a May 8, 1965, memo to Johnson, McCone's successor, Vice Admiral William Raborn, delivered a similarly grim appraisal. As with the French, he predicted, "we will find ourselves pinned down, with little choice left among possible subsequent courses of action: i.e. disengagement at very high cost or broadening the conflict in quantum jumps."

How, after failing such a battery of tests and analyses conducted by such senior officials, was the Rostow thesis allowed to become fact in the terrible form of Rolling Thunder? Why did White House planners not take the SIGMA results into account? For one thing, the sessions were just games, while gradualism had been tested and proven in that most chilling of Cold War crucibles, the Cuban missile crisis. Plus, a managed escalation of pressure was politically expedient. As military historian H. R. McMaster writes, "The growing consensus behind the strategic concept of graduated pressure overpowered SIGMA II's unpromising conclusions because the president and his advisers were unwilling to risk either disengagement or escalation" and instead chose the politically safe middle ground.

In other words, when the facts do not support the policy, keep the policy and assemble new facts. The Rostow thesis would weather SIGMA's burden of proof, just as its author would prevail by distilling his myriad theories into politically palatable snake oil.

Walt Whitman Rostow may not have been a direct antecedent of the neoconservative movement, but he certainly shared its faculty for crackpot theories. He was born to Jewish refugees from tsarist Russia in Flatbush, a working-class neighborhood in Brooklyn, New York. His parents were arch-socialists, and their three sons were weaned on vigorous political discussion and polemics at the family dinner table, where fellow Bolshevik émigrés were often featured guests. Such leftist leanings would find no purchase with the Rostow boys, who pioneered an ardent and scholarly anticommunism that would do much to inspire neoconservatives years later. Eugene, Walt's older brother, would serve as a foreign policy adviser in the Truman and Johnson administrations and together they would join Paul Nitze in founding the Committee on the Present Danger, the militant Cold War policy shop that survives to this day.

Walt Rostow was blessed with a brilliant mind, particularly when it came to theory and other intellectual abstractions. After graduating from Yale at the age of nineteen, he was awarded a Rhodes Scholarship to study at Oxford in the late 1930s. He completed a Ph.D. degree in economics two years later, and in fall 1940 he was appointed a professor of economics at Columbia University. When war broke out, he joined the Office of Strategic Services, where he developed targeting strategies for Anglo-American bombing campaigns. The lessons and legacies of the war, particularly the consequences of appeasement and the potential of airpower, did much to shape Rostow's worldview. (Three prominent members of the United States Strategic Bombing Survey, John Kenneth Galbraith, George Ball, and Arthur Schlesinger Jr., all opposed the U.S. bombing campaign against North Vietnam.)

In 1950 Rostow joined the faculty at the Massachusetts Institute of Technology, where he would evolve fully into an anticommunist hawk. The outbreak of the Korean War convinced him that there could be no negotiating with the communist bloc, and he disparaged what he perceived was American abandonment of noncommunist leaders in Laos and France's abdication of Vietnam to China. As a member of MIT's Center for International Studies, a RAND precursor funded overtly by groups such as the Ford Foundation and covertly by the CIA, he wrote prodigiously about the geopolitics of foreign aid.

A decade later, Rostow published his influential *Stages of Economic Growth: A Non-Communist Manifesto* as a riposte to the Marxist theories he had come to despise and a nonlethal war plan for wooing newly independent Third World states into the capitalist fold. In it, he unveils an American rubric for phased development based on five stages of evolution that would raise living standards at a time when Moscow and Beijing were seemingly winning over the nonaligned movement. Over a prolonged period of independence, according to Rostow, decolonized states would voluntarily choose the invisible hand of free markets over the ham-fisted one of the state. The process cuts two ways, however. As states industrialize, their evolving infrastructure becomes vulnerable to aggression. Thus Hanoi, Rostow would point out in his interminable arguments for air strikes against North Vietnam, "has an industrial complex to protect; [Ho Chi Minh] is no longer a guerrilla fighter with nothing to lose."

Stages has not aged well for its contradictions and facile characterization of Marxism and the developing world, with which Rostow had no firsthand knowledge. Its author commits the error typical of so many Cold Warriors: the assumption that communism represents an offensive threat to capitalism, when in fact, according to Marxist theory, capitalism will collapse from the rot of its own corruption and inadequacy. Where Marx saw in capitalism a tumor of contradictions, Rostow and his Manichaean soul mates saw a duel to the death with monolithic, global communism. They reflexively interpreted Khrushchev's vow to "bury" the West as a rhetorical dagger at the heart of capitalism; they failed to understand how the Soviet chairman's remarks, uttered as Moscow and Beijing were entering their long, public breach, were delivered as much to intimidate Beijing as the West. Indeed, they failed to notice the breach.

The thesis of *Stages*—"culturally presumptuous and excessively hopeful," rules Rostow biographer David Milne—was also conspicuously at odds with U.S. policy. While Rostow condemns the communist bloc for its attempt to manipulate and control the decolonized world, he makes no mention of Washington's own handiwork in that area. When measured against the Eisenhower-Dulles war on neutrality, which survived through much of the Nixon administration, it is hard to see how *Stages of Economic Growth* could be anything more than a liberal's fantasy. Like most hawks in and out of government, Rostow urged the United States to assist national movements in the Eastern bloc opposed to Soviet autocracy while neglecting a fundamental question: Will communism prevail absent active U.S. support of its enemies, or will it suffocate under the burden of its own dead hand? And if the latter, why invest immense resources in fighting it?

Aid and arms. Independence and intervention. It was Rostow's ability to reconcile mutually exclusive properties that sustained him in the looking-glass world that was Lyndon Johnson's White House.

By the time he joined the Kennedy administration as Bundy's deputy at the NSC and then as Nitze's successor at the State Department's newly named Policy Planning Council, Rostow had established himself as one of Kennedy's most hawkish foreign policy intellectuals. Rostow recommended special operations against Castro, criticized the State Department for its "pure diplomacy" approach to diplomatic challenges, and endorsed nuclear brinkmanship during the 1961 Berlin crisis. In Asia, he recommended the deployment of U.S. forces to Thailand, Laos, and Vietnam's Mekong Delta region, and he supported Eisenhower's policy to block national elections in Vietnam as called for in the 1954 Geneva Accords because, like the CIA, he knew Ho Chi Minh would win.

To the Air Force, Rostow was a rainmaker. Undersecretary of the Air Force Townsend Hoopes called him the "closest thing we had near the top of the U.S. government to a genuine, all-wool anti-communist ideologue and true believer." In a June 28, 1961, speech, Rostow identified Hanoi as the source of communist aggression in Vietnam and suggested the White House might target the north with reprisal attacks, making him the first Kennedy administration official to urge such a move.

The prolix Rostow wearied Kennedy, however, and as part of a November 1961 cabinet reshuffle he was transferred from the National Security Council to the State Department's Policy Planning Council. Ironically, it was early into this exile that Rostow produced his first truly influential policy initiative. In his final memo of the year, he argued that General Lionel McGarr, the head of the Military Assistance Advisory Group in Saigon, was spending too much energy trying to pacify the south and reform its government and not enough time molding the South Vietnamese army into an effective Vietcong killer. McGarr was removed and, more significantly, the MAAG was transformed into Military Assistance Command, Vietnam. What was a seemingly minor bureaucratic transition had far-reaching consequences. The launch of MACV on February 8,

1962, effectively transformed the mission of U.S. advisers in Saigon from the subordinate role of training local soldiers and personnel in the counterinsurgency effort into a leading one. McGarr's departure was followed by a significant increase in American advisers, military wares, and weaponry. On the strength of a single memo, Walt Rostow had Americanized the Vietnam War, a fact that would not escape notice in Hanoi and Beijing.

Rostow would have remained a marginal White House player, just as Lyndon Johnson would have remained an obscure vice president, had it not been for Kennedy's assassination. As the new president struggled to find his footing with congressional hawks bellowing for a get-tough approach to Vietnam, he increasingly turned to Rostow for support and reassurance. Ironically, being on the periphery may have helped Rostow. Johnson was painfully aware of his own inexperience in foreign affairs and he was never comfortable with the Kennedy clique. A hillbilly from Texas's Hill Country, he may have seen in Rostow, a bookish Brooklyn Jew, the kindred spirit of a fellow outsider. Rostow's growing influence was first detectable in Johnson's debut State of the Union address, in which the new president declared America was ready to "defend the cause of freedom, whether it is threatened by outright aggression or by the infiltration practiced by those in Hanoi and Havana." The Rostovian embellishments were hard to miss.

As tensions in Vietnam rose, so too did Rostow's credibility. In January 1964, Robert Komer, a National Security Council stalwart, wrote Bundy that Rostow's hard-line rhetoric "seems to make more sense now than it did previously." Rostow was tasked to write the administration's first public response to the Tonkin Gulf incident, as well as Johnson's speech the next day at Syracuse University, titled "The Communist Challenge in Southeast Asia." His National Security Action Memorandum, which called for "graduated, overt military pressure" on North Vietnam, was approved by Johnson on March 17, 1964, and would serve as the foundation stone for Rolling Thunder. By late 1964, Johnson was lauding Rostow's policy shop as "the only place in the State Department where I get any new ideas."

Those ideas yielded few results, however, particularly when it came to Rolling Thunder. Contrary to Rostow's assurances, North Vietnam offered little in the way of vital industrial infrastructure for American bombs to destroy. Despite a modest Soviet-style plan to centralize its economy in the 1950s, the country remained largely agrarian and feudal, with energy grids limited to a handful of urban areas. In 1966 a joint CIA-Defense Information Agency study concluded that North Vietnam "demonstrated excellent ability to improvise transportation and because the primitive nature of their economy is such that Rolling Thunder can affect only a small fraction of the population. There is very little hope that [the] Ho Chi Minh Government will lose control of the population because of Rolling Thunder. The lessons of the Korean War are very relevant in these respects." With airpower alone exhausted as an option, Johnson increased U.S. ground forces in South Vietnam to 82,000 men, with orders to clear Vietcong enclaves in the Da Nang area. It was hoped the anvil of increased pressure on the ground together with the hammer of intensified aerial strikes would force Hanoi to the negotiating table. This escalation failed, however.

To make matters worse, the reality of the U.S. intervention in South Vietnam was suddenly made public on June 8, 1965, when State Department spokesman Robert McCloskey, in response to a reporter's question, acknowledged that American troops were engaged in combat missions in Da Nang in addition to protecting facilities there. When the New York Times expressed outrage that such a significant change in the U.S. mission was revealed not by the president but by a State Department functionary, the White House issued a statement that repudiated McCloskey's remarks. Lies, like the marching brooms of The Sorcerer's Apprentice, begat more lies. On July 27, Johnson and McNamara briefed senior members of Congress on a request from General William Westmoreland, commander of U.S. forces in Vietnam, for additional resources. They understated Westmoreland's appeal for new funding by about $10 billion and for another 100,000 troops by half. McNamara told the lawmakers that no U.S. troops were involved in combat operations in South Vietnam and stated that South

Vietnamese soldiers had demonstrated a "willingness to fight" despite suffering heavy casualties.

The politicians ate it up. Speaker of the House John McCormack in particular assured the president he would "have the support of all true Americans." Besides Johnson and McNamara, the only man in the room who understood the level to which senior U.S. legislators were being deceived was Earle Wheeler, who had recently replaced Taylor as chairman of the Joint Chiefs of Staff. He sat through the meeting in stony silence.

The reality of the war, however, was impervious to all the half-truths and falsehoods told about it in Washington. At one point, in April 1965, the Joint Chiefs urged a massive use of airpower to kill Vietcong in the south, though such a strategy failed to account for how well the enemy had insinuated itself within the civilian population. As one escalation after the other failed to stem U.S. losses, Johnson was reduced to ranting at his advisers. "Bomb, bomb, bomb, that's all you know," he complained several times in frustration. In 1965, with the inadequacy of Rolling Thunder slowly revealing itself, Johnson told McNamara that he saw "no program from either State or Defense that gives us much hope of doing anything, except for praying [that] they'll quit. I don't believe they're ever going to quit. And I don't see any plan for victory—militarily or diplomatically." Even Rostow was feeling the heat, though that did not discourage him from writing sunny memos to steel the embattled president the way a cloying mother inserts handwritten notes in her child's lunch pail. "It is time for a war-leader speech and not a peace-keeper speech," Rostow wrote in an attachment to an address he had drafted for the president. "It is time to slay the credibility dragon with one blow." He kept it up until Johnson's last day in office.

Since the dawn of containment, security alliances have both intoxicated and incarcerated U.S. foreign policy makers. Ordained in signing ceremonies and reaffirmed at elaborate summits, they suggest a concert of interests and ideals between nations that are larger than the sum of their parts. But they also play host to corruption, codependency, and abuse of all kinds.

By declaring a Cold War on multiple fronts, America required a network of allies and treaty organizations with which to wage it. In addition to NATO, there were the South East Asian Treaty Organization, the Baghdad Pact, the Alliance for Progress, and a thicket of bilateral treaties in Asia and the Persian Gulf, plus overflight agreements, basing rights, and armament coproduction deals. Not only have some of these commitments survived the Cold War, Washington has aggressively expanded its web of regional commands and security guarantees since the Soviet Union's collapse in 1991. It is the largest alliance system in history, and it is all held together by a huge line of credit in the form of U.S. finance, matériel, and war-fighters.

To ensure the purity of America's cause—first during the Cold War and later in its war against radical Islam—Washington's allies needed to be pure, too. They were moral and indispensable, however despotic and inept. If one was to backslide, if it refused to cooperate in America's periphery wars or open its skies to U.S. warplanes, the United States would cajole it into line by raising its credit limit. The greater Washington's stake in a client, the greater the cost in U.S. credibility should it collapse or go "neutralist," and the more pressing the need to keep it afloat.

This was the situation the U.S. government faced in Saigon in the summer of 1965.

George Ball was among the very few White House advisers who understood that in South Vietnam, Washington had become "a puppet of a puppet." With the situation in Saigon deteriorating by the day, he argued Americans should "free ourselves from subservience to whatever regime might at the time be in power." He wrote in his memoirs that "we could never achieve terms which would satisfy the Saigon government; its war aims were rigidly defined by the desire of those in power to keep their jobs. [It] was corrupt and without national roots." In his June 18, 1965, memo to the president, which he wrote after the Vietcong had launched a massive spring offensive in retaliation for the Rolling Thunder assaults, Ball urged against a further escalation of the war until "we . . . have more evidence than we now have that our troops will not bog down in the jungles and rice paddies—while we slowly blow the country to pieces." Ten days later, in a paper titled "Cutting Our Losses in South Vietnam," Ball advised disengagement from the war if the military junta led by air force general Nguyen Cao Ky did not agree to step down in favor of a civilian government, a condition General Ky would certainly have rejected.

Such arguments appealed to Johnson, and within hours after reading Ball's paper he asked his political aide, Jack Valenti, to request a CIA study on how Hanoi and Beijing might respond to peace overtures. But the very idea of disengagement scandalized the rump of the policy priesthood. McNamara at Defense said the Ball plan offered the United States "no good way out," while Rusk at State declared that abandoning an ally to Soviet hegemony would "lead to our ruin and almost certainly to catastrophic war." After sharing the Ball paper with the Joint Chiefs, a strategic deviation from his usual practice of locking them out of important policy matters, McNamara submitted to Johnson their emphatic opposition to withdrawal. Fearful of a public revolt by the JCS, the president shelved the Ball memorandum. For good measure, National Security Adviser Bundy told Johnson in a July 2 memo that "the paper should not be argued with you in any audience larger than Rusk, McNamara, Ball, and me. . . . It is exceedingly dangerous to have this possibility reported in a wide circle."

Ball would never back down from his belief, informed by his experience on the Strategic Bombing Survey, that "bombing never wins a war." But for Walt Rostow, possessed as he was of a transmogrifying optimism, there was nothing wrong with Rolling Thunder that a little escalation couldn't fix. The philosophies of the two men occupied opposite ends of the policy spectrum, with Rostow's increasingly hawkish views prevailing as Ball's dovish—and prophetic—warnings were tossed overboard.

McNamara, however, was at last beginning to share Ball's doubts. In summer 1965, he questioned in a memo to Johnson whether it was possible to arrest North Vietnamese infiltration no matter how many U.S. troops were positioned in the south, and he expressed concern that sustained deployments of GIs in South Vietnam might spark a backlash among their hosts. In November 1965, upon his return from a tour of Vietnam, the secretary informed Johnson that his recommendation that U.S. forces in Vietnam be topped up to 400,000 "will not guarantee success" and he projected troop fatality rates of a thousand per month. In a January 1966 memo, he wrote to Westmoreland that "the odds are about even that, even with the recommended deployments, we will be faced in early 1967 with a military standoff at a much higher level, with pacification hardly under way, and with requirements for the deployment of still more U.S. forces." McNamara, it seemed, had finally met with the realization that the war was unwinnable. No one in Johnson's war council, he said in an aside to the British ambassador, was talking about "winning a victory" in Vietnam. No one, that is, except for Walt Rostow, whom Johnson appointed as Bundy's successor as national security adviser on April 1, 1966—April Fool's Day.

Within a year or so after Rostow's appointment, the White House was all but vacant of dissenting voices. Ball was at the United Nations, serving as the U.S. ambassador there, and Komer was doing fieldwork in Vietnam. Bundy, who was appalled at Johnson's choice of Rostow as his successor and who by the 1968 Tet Offensive may have also adjusted his views to fit reality, was running the Ford Foundation.* Only the increasingly doubt-ridden McNamara was left.

As national security adviser, Rostow immediately extended Rolling Thunder's target list to include oil refineries and electrical grids in Hanoi and Haiphong harbor, though he had argued earlier that his thesis of gradual response would obviate the need for all-out destruction. Rusk and McNamara were now deferring to Rostow regarding target selection, effectively making him solely responsible for a disastrous failure. By the fall, with Vietcong attacks continuing unabated and with the partition line as porous as ever, he was desperate for something to show for the most destructive bombing campaign ever. He infuriated the CIA by dismissing or cherry-picking from the agency's negative reports, an eerie preview of how neoconservatives in the George W. Bush administration would reject or distort CIA findings in the run-up to the American invasion of Iraq. In December 1967, when Rostow asked John Paul Vann, the

---

* It wasn't until 1995, when he began writing his memoirs in collaboration with foreign affairs scholar Gordon Goldstein, that Bundy acknowledged his complicity in it all. "The doves were right," he would reveal in his notes. "A war we should not have fought. . . . I had a part in a great failure. I made mistakes of perception, recommendation, and execution." Bundy died a year later.

U.S. Army's legendary counterinsurgency specialist, whether he believed the worst of the war would be over in six months, Vann replied: "Oh hell no, Mr. Rostow. I'm a born optimist. Think we can hold on for longer than that." A miffed Rostow later remarked that there was no room for such defeatism in the government's Vietnam policy. Only a month earlier, Rostow had given his infamous assurance about rays of "light at the end of the tunnel." On January 30, 1968, some 84,000 communist insurgents launched attacks throughout South Vietnam, the so-called Tet Offensive. Even then, Rostow told Johnson that "the net effect of Tet could be the shortening of the war." He urged the president to approve Westmoreland's proposal for 206,000 more troops and an extension of Rolling Thunder over McNamara's protests that the bombing be terminated.

On February 27, 1968, Johnson convened his war cabinet to consider Westmoreland's request. McNamara spoke first. It was his last day in office—he would soon become president of the World Bank—and his report was pointedly negative. Accommodating Westmoreland's proposal, he said, would require the mobilization of 150,000 reservists, an extension of the draft, a vast increase in defense spending, and costly tax increases that would come at the expense of the president's Great Society programs. For the first and last time as secretary of defense, McNamara was drawing the line and Rostow, predictably, rebuked him. Like a boxing coach urging on his punch-drunk charge, he assured the council that Tet had been a defeat for the communists. Westmoreland should have his reinforcements and bombing should be intensified. Victory was just around the corner.

Then, as Rostow biographer David Milne recounts, "something snapped" in McNamara:

"What then?" the defense secretary demanded of Rostow's plan. "This goddamned bombing campaign, it's been worth nothing, it's done nothing, they've dropped more bombs than in all of Europe in all of World War II and it hasn't done a fucking thing." Speaking with the intensity of a tortured soul who had helped create an unnecessary war, the defense secretary finished his sentence, broke down, and wept. Rostow could only look on, stunned, as Robert McNamara . . . melted down in a room filled with Washington's most powerful men.

By the end of 1968, more than 36,000 U.S. troops had been killed fighting in Vietnam. There were still more than 22,000 lives to go.

Walt Rostow was a superb example of the upwardly bound failure, a species that is not unique to Washington but is certainly overrepresented in it. No single individual did more to Americanize and militarize the U.S. role in Vietnam, and to the end he refused to acknowledge the disastrous consequences of his counsel. Throughout his career, Rostow misread the nature of postwar nationalist movements, and he invested heavily in the idea of a Sino-Soviet bloc long after its dissolution. The most prominent of his writings, a study of the political economy of nonaligned states, reveals a shallow understanding of communism in both theory and practice, as well as of the realities of the developing world. He kept faith with his theory of graduated warfare even as the Vietcong was keeping a half-million GIs bottled up in a misbegotten war. He was, like his mentor Paul Nitze, optimistic, comfortable with power, and self-delusional. Carl Kaysen, who succeeded Rostow as Bundy's number two, referred to Rostow's disquisitions as Manichaean "nonsense" and Henry Kissinger remembered him as "a fool." Yet he outlasted them all.

By the late 1960s, with Bundy and McNamara gone and men like George Ball turfed out to distant outposts, Rostow would be the last person left for Johnson to cling to as the dire prophecies of the SIGMA sessions cruelly came to life and claimed his legacy. "Walt Rostow was a believer to the end," says Leslie Gelb, the former Defense Department policy planner who now heads the Council on Foreign Relations. "He continued to believe the war was right and could have been won. Even years later, we'd argue the same points that we did years before."

Today, Rostovian casuistry has been resurrected for the sake of a revisionist interpretation of the Vietnam War in which civilian leaders chose defeat by not listening to their generals. Rostow's conceit echoes in contemporary counterinsurgency doctrine, which confuses popular resistance to foreign invasion and occupation with illiberal forces of darkness that can be pacified with economic and social works. In the insurgencies that bedevil U.S. forces in Afghanistan, major setbacks are portrayed as tactical in nature rather than strategic; if foreign policy militarization has yet to achieve stated objectives, so the narrative goes, it is the fault of flawed execution rather than militarization itself. Blame for the current generation of quagmires may then be reapportioned from the militarists who conceived them to unbelievers who managed them. Given the cluster of interests at stake and civilian America's short attention span, this is not nearly as difficult a transfer as it might seem.

One of Rostow's last acts as a member of the Johnson cabinet was to conspire in Richard Nixon's favor in the 1968 presidential election. In doing so, he helped to prolong the U.S. role in Vietnam by nearly five years.

While negotiating for peace with their North Vietnamese counterparts in Paris, Averell Harriman and Cyrus Vance in mid-September 1968 had persuaded Hanoi to commit to substantive talks in return for the suspension of Rolling Thunder, terms to which Lyndon Johnson agreed. It was an eleventh-hour break for Democratic Party contender and underdog Hubert Humphrey, and it was just the kind of October surprise his Republican opponent had feared. Informed of the breakthrough via a spy in Paris, Nixon immediately conspired to undermine it. Working through Anna Chennault, the wife of the legendary Flying Tigers commander and China lobby veteran Claire Chennault, he conveyed to South Vietnamese president Nguyen Van Thieu that he should shun the talks as he was certain to get a better deal after the election with Nixon in the White House. Otherwise, Harriman would most certainly undercut Saigon in a reckless pursuit of peace.

Word of the Nixon-Chennault channel, which Rostow was alerted to by his brother Eugene, the then undersecretary of state, was a bombshell for the Democrats. Nixon's overtures to Thieu were a clear violation of the Logan Act, which strictly prohibits independent American citizens from negotiating with foreign governments. Had Johnson leaked the news, he could have easily subverted Nixon's campaign. "Can you imagine," Johnson said, "what people would say if it were to be known that Hanoi has met all these conditions and then Nixon's conniving with them kept us from getting it?" Rostow, however, urged Johnson against taking the matter public. The matter was so sensitive, he reasoned, it could lead to a constitutional crisis should Nixon prevail. Better to warn the challenger confidentially that his plot to sandbag the peace talks was blown.

Johnson followed Rostow's advice, even though it all but guaranteed the Republicans would reclaim control of the White House. In part, the president was motivated by his outrage with Humphrey, who a month earlier had tried to salvage his campaign by declaring that the United States was losing the war and that he would support an unconditional bombing halt. But Johnson was also trying to protect his own goal, one passionately shared by Rostow, of sustaining a U.S. ally in the war against communism. Nixon's transgression was thus concealed, and he swept to victory with a narrow majority in the popular ballot of a mere half-million votes. Within weeks, the Paris peace talks had all but collapsed.

The age of Nixon had begun.

9
MADMEN

If I had to choose between justice and disorder on the one hand and injustice and order on the other, I would always choose the latter.
—HENRY KISSINGER

Now is the time to thank God Richard Nixon is President.
—RICHARD NIXON

IN SPRING 1969 THE WORLD WAS SKIRTING PERILOUSLY CLOSE TO A third world war. The principal antagonists were not Washington and Moscow but Moscow and Beijing, and the flash point was not Berlin or Cuba but an island in the Ussuri River near the northeastern rim of Asia. Both countries laid claim to the island—called Zhenbao by the Chinese, Damansky by the Russians—and in March a Chinese unit had ambushed a Russian patrol there. Over the next six months, hundreds of similar clashes followed as the two sides coiled for a war that would have pitted the western and eastern communist worlds against each other. From London, Paris, New York, and Geneva, Soviet diplomats condemned a "most bellicose" China as the greatest threat to peace. In Washington, Soviet ambassador Anatoly Dobrynin was reported to have asked the U.S. government for "cooperation" in restraining Beijing, an appeal that included a proposed joint attack on China's nuclear sites.

In China, meanwhile, Mao Zedong approved a 30 percent increase in military spending and deployed millions of Chinese to dig air-raid shelters in anticipation of a Soviet nuclear strike. During Beijing's Ninth Congress that April, some 400 million Chinese, or half the population, staged protests against "the new tsars." The Kremlin, in turn, launched a massive buildup of military force in Mongolia. In September, the two sides pulled back from the brink. Mao agreed to a meeting between Zhou

Enlai and Soviet premier Andrei Kosygin at the Beijing airport, a venue suited to keep the barbarians safely distant from the Middle Kingdom's gates, and an accommodation was reached. Yet the Sino-Soviet alliance, crudely tactical during the best of times, had been irretrievably breached. Each side now openly regarded the other as a graver threat than the United States. Of the two communist giants, it would be China—its industry devastated by the Cultural Revolution, its army short of assault rifles as well as ammunition—that would outflank the plodding Russian bear by reaching out to Washington.

As tensions between the two communist giants began to simmer much the way Khrushchev had predicted they would, Beijing was pushing through back channels for a resumption of the Sino-U.S. ambassadorial talks in Warsaw, an ongoing if fitful diplomatic round that had been established in the mid-1950s. In September 1969, four senior Chinese cadres led by Chen Yi, China's cancer-ridden foreign minister, concluded in a report that a thaw in Sino-U.S. relations would be desirable for its "strategic effects." In December, Beijing signaled as much to Washington by releasing two American yachtsmen held in custody since they had strayed into Chinese waters several months earlier.

After a twenty-two-year estrangement, China was knocking on Washington's door. And it was President Nixon—Nixon the arch anticommunist, who had shocked friend and foe alike two years earlier by advocating Sino-American rapprochement—who was poised to open it. His overture to Beijing would do more to lessen global tensions than any diplomatic initiative of the Cold War. By warming relations with China and establishing détente with the Soviet Union, Nixon secured an orderly, if painful, U.S. withdrawal from Vietnam. He also made possible a landmark nuclear arms control deal with Moscow and laid the rails for commercial and cultural exchanges with Beijing that would be the foundation of the world's most vital economic relationship.

For Nixon, it was as much a triumph of political brinksmanship as it was a breakthrough in international affairs, requiring as it did the betrayal of his Republican Party's increasingly conservative base. Besides the Watergate scandal that led to his resignation in 1973, Nixon will always be associated with the China card, his summitry with the Russians, and his sometimes creative, sometimes futile back-channel deals. This same geopolitical visionary, however, suffered from a crisis of imagination. However bold his embrace of triangulation—playing Beijing off against Moscow and vice versa—the thought of deviating from the rubric of containment never occurred to him. Though he clearly perceived the tensions between Moscow and Beijing, Nixon was, like John Foster Dulles and other staunch conservatives, blind to the essentially parochial character and aspirations of communist movements elsewhere. His preoccupation with "credibility" as the linchpin of power and security impelled his ruinous expansion of the Vietnam War into Cambodia and Laos. The Nixon Doctrine, under which responsibility for regional security would migrate from the United States to its allies, was an empty slogan that did nothing to reduce the country's global network of military bases, the manifolds of foreign policy militarization.

Having created a landmark opportunity to revolutionize America's relations abroad, Nixon proved himself unwilling or unable to exploit it, a strategic failure as significant as the China mission was a success. In this sense, the Nixon-Kissinger projection of foreign policy realism, implying a sense of proportion, consistency, and discretion, was a mirage.

At home, Nixon's paranoid obsessions and vindictiveness corrupted the interagency process in ways that would take years to repair. The Department of State, already neglected under Kennedy and Johnson, was diminished nearly into oblivion during the Nixon years. His use of the CIA and FBI to discredit and harass war critics damaged the integrity and morale of those agencies and revived the specters of the Red Scares. With the help of his like-minded foreign policy maestro, the equally paranoid and imperious Henry Kissinger, Nixon concentrated executive authority into what Arthur Schlesinger would call "the imperial presidency." Nixon not only ignored his top diplomats and intelligence agents, depriving himself of their expertise on crucial issues in the process, he kept them ignorant of his most important initiatives.

To the success of triangulation and détente as Nixon's legacy must be added low cunning and deceit on an extravagant scale. No other U.S. president has more deftly plotted and executed such bold foreign policy maneuvers only to darken them under the shadow of his own venality.

As Ivo Daalder and I. M. Destler write of Nixon and Kissinger in their account of America's national security advisers, "If . . . secrecy undeniably facilitated some of their achievements, it limited their reach within the U.S. government and motivated other senior players to work against rather than with them. . . . They would also make [Nixon's] substantial foreign policy achievements more limited and less durable than they ought to have been."

Such was the coarse and ephemeral quality of Richard Nixon and his works.

Nixon entered the 1968 presidential race with one of the most impressive résumés of any candidate in history. The son of a Quaker and pacifist mother, he had enlisted in the U.S. Navy during World War II and rose to the rank of lieutenant commander. As a young legislator he established himself as a relentless investigator in the Alger Hiss case, which ended with Hiss's conviction on perjury charges. As vice president under Eisenhower he traveled frequently, developing a familiarity with foreign lands and their leaders that was rare among previous holders of the office. During his wilderness years after his failed 1960 presidential bid, Nixon remained active in Republican Party affairs and his memoirs, *Six Crises,* was a bestseller. After waging a disastrous campaign for the office of California governor in 1962, he moved his family to New York City, where he salved his wounds working as a senior partner for the law firm Nixon, Mudge, Rose, Guthrie & Alexander. The essay he had written for admission to the New York bar was the best that body had received in nearly three decades, according to the chairman of the bar's Committee on Character and Fitness. It was a response to the question "What do you believe the principles underlying the form of government of the United States should be?"

As a highly paid and prominent corporate lawyer, Nixon continued to travel extensively and dazzled elites on both the left and the right with his penetrating grasp of international affairs. In an article he wrote for the October 1967 edition of *Foreign Affairs* magazine, he established himself as a strategic visionary who correctly anticipated the rise of a powerful, prosperous Asia. The economic success of postwar Japan, he

wrote, presaging the rise of the region's "tiger economies" decades before the term was coined, would be followed by that of South Korea,
Taiwan, Southeast Asia, Australia, and New Zealand. He affirmed the
United States as a "Pacific power" but cautioned that the ability of Washington to assert itself militarily in Asia would be limited. "One of the legacies of Vietnam," he wrote, foreshadowing the eponymous doctrine he
would unveil years later, "almost certainly will be deep reluctance on the
part of the United States to become involved once again in a similar intervention on a similar basis." The heart of the piece, and a prologue to how
Nixon would soon invert the geopolitical world, was his assertion that
"any American policy toward Asia must come urgently to grips with the
reality of China." While cautioning against a pell-mell rush to normalize relations with Beijing, he made clear that "we simply cannot afford to
leave China forever outside the family of nations, there to nurture its
fantasies, cherish its hates and threaten its neighbors."

The *Foreign Affairs* article was circulated widely among liberal elites,
historically a target of Nixonian attacks. Just two years earlier, he had
condemned as "appeasement and retreat" Democratic senator J. William Fulbright's suggestion that the United States should review its
China policy to exploit the schism between Moscow and Beijing. Now, it
seemed, there was a new Nixon, a man willing to dispense with alarmist
caricature and accept Asia, perhaps even China, on its terms. Nixon's de-
tractors, meanwhile, dismissed the *Foreign Affairs* piece as a cynical attempt to broaden his appeal among moderate voters.

Most likely, neither side was correct. Nixon was as much a pragmatist
as he was an opportunist. Though he gives no hint in his memoirs about
exactly how his thoughts on U.S.-Chinese relations evolved, he does note
that he had given up on the notion of a Nationalist conquest of the mainland as early as 1953 and said as much to Chiang Kai-shek. The *Foreign
Affairs* article, it could be argued, was Nixon's first honest public meditation on the American century. It was not the expression of a "new" Nixon
but the unburdening of one who had been posturing, cruelly and cyni-
cally, inside the old Nixon of the McCarthy years. The *Foreign Affairs* article was Nixon's striptease, the calibrated exposure of a refined worldview
that may well have been incubating inside him for years. It was, as presidential historian Robert Dallek writes, "an astonishing shift away from

the anti-communist rhetoric that Nixon had previously used to advance his political career. It was also a demonstration of how pragmatic he could be to achieve something he believed would establish him as a great president."

In his memoirs, Leonard Garment, a Nixon confidant and legal adviser, recounts a rare Nixon confessional. It was 1965 and Garment was accompanying Nixon in Miami, where he was to give a speech to the directors of an investment firm. On the eve of his engagement, Garment wrote, Nixon spent half the night revealing how "he felt his life had to be dedicated to great foreign policy purposes. This man, fiercely determined to stay in the political life for which he was in many ways so ill-suited, told me he felt driven to do so not by the rivalries or ideological commitments or domestic politics but by his pacifist mother's idealism and the profound importance of foreign affairs." It was for Nixon an uncommon display of intimacy and introspection and it revealed a very different politician than the Republican agitator of a generation earlier.

By 1967, with the Sino-Soviet alliance clearly unraveling, Nixon was well ahead of the foreign policy curve. Yet for him to secure a second and no doubt final bid for the White House, he would have to navigate carefully past the coastal batteries of the very militarist camp for which he had been a cadre. His most powerful enemies were no longer liberal Democrats but members of the "New Right," the acolytes of Barry Goldwater and William Buckley, two men who equated containment with appeasement. (In his book *The Conscience of a Conservative*, which was ghostwritten by Brent Bozell, Buckley's brother-in-law and debating partner at Yale, Goldwater dismissed calls for negotiation with Moscow and Beijing and confined the word itself in quotation marks to highlight his contempt for it.) The New Rightists were slowly gaining control over the Republican Party, and they had their suspicions about Nixon's commitment to the anticommunist cause. He had been, after all, a servant to Eisenhower, the appeaser and staunch internationalist who had pointedly refused to embrace McCarthy. In the 1968 presidential stakes, they were plumping for California governor Ronald Reagan, not the former vice president who had tried and failed twice for executive office.

Undaunted, Nixon worked his reputation as a foreign policy savant to the hilt in his quest for the hawks' favor. In summer 1966, after returning from a round-the-world tour that included a stop in Saigon, he hosted twenty or so hard-line conservatives at the Shoreham Hotel in Washington. Included at the meeting was the publisher of William Buckley's *National Review,* house organ of the New Right, and a covey of prominent Goldwater backers. Nixon was faced with a contortionist's challenge: he could not at once be faithful to the realities of the world while at the same time indulge the fantasies of the power brokers who held his political fate in their grip. They were expecting the old Nixon, the China lobby Nixon—not, as he would soon become, the *Foreign Affairs* Nixon—and they got a little of both. Nixon made clear to his guests that it was not the time to consider direct contact with Beijing, but he also made reference to the Sino-Soviet split as an opportunity to exploit in the future. One of those in attendance, a member of Young Americans for Freedom, described Nixon's performance as an improvisational tour de force. "No notes," the YAF member recalled. "He goes around the world. Rattling off names, connections, 'this is what we have to look for here.' . . . Russia and China . . . and he starts mentioning *names,* and names below names, and names below names below names, and 'here is what France is saying,' and de Gaulle is saying this, and whoever was the British prime minister, and the prime minister of Japan. . . . I mean, he was *rattling* off all these names."

The Shoreham crowd loved it. Two years later, having seduced his skeptics on the right, Nixon tacked back again in an exclusive interview with journalist Theodore White that built on the foundation of his *Foreign Affairs* essay. According to White, Nixon said that "if he were elected president, the first thing he'd do would be to try to get in touch with Red China."

On February 1, 1969, in his preliminary instructions to Kissinger after his inauguration as president, Nixon did just that.

It is fitting, given the grim morality play that was the Nixon White House, that one of the most effective foreign policy teams in U.S. history evolved out of an act of espionage. As it turns out, candidate Nixon's mole at the Paris peace talks—the spy who sabotaged Averell Harriman's bid for a deal that would have saved an untold number of lives—was none other than Henry Kissinger.

Like the Beatles, Nixon and Kissinger were worth more in collaboration than as solo acts. Together they leveraged what made them both petty and great, so that their finest achievements were equal in magnitude to their most execrable intrigues. Both men were intruders upon Washington's elite foreign policy establishment—Nixon as an émigré from a desolate California burg, Kissinger as a Jewish refugee from the Nazi terror—and both shared a similar checklist of hates and fears. There was Nixon, an awkward but ruthless misfit who at Whittier College formed a social club of less privileged students, the "Orthogonians" ("straight shooters"), and who got elected student body president by harnessing popular resentment of campus elites. And there was Kissinger, the brilliant mind with the courtier's instinct, the exile of elastic loyalty who ditched the cloisters of academia for the corridors of secular power.

A native of Bavaria, Kissinger fled to New York with his family at the age of fifteen in 1938, a year before the Nazi invasion of Poland. He graduated from Harvard College summa cum laude in 1950 and two years later entered Harvard's Government Ph.D. program. He was also made executive director of its University Summer International Seminar, which offered paid fellowships to some of the world's most powerful thinkers and statesmen. Their adventures in high diplomacy made university life seem wretchedly dull—its turf battles are so fierce, Kissinger once remarked of academia, because the stakes are so low—and he drifted toward the policymaking realm.

In 1955, after *Foreign Affairs* had published an article by Kissinger about nuclear weapons and defense policy, the Council on Foreign Affairs in New York asked him to lead a related study group. Its members included the nation's top policy elites, and he worked their connections for entrée into the Kennedy White House, where he worked for a year as a consultant before he was let go for making unauthorized statements to the press. Kissinger spent the next few years writing critically about transatlantic relations while carving out an influential role for himself on the staff of Nelson Rockefeller, the moderate Republican and governor of New York who planned to challenge Kennedy in 1964.

It was Rockefeller's close ties to the Johnson White House that gave Kissinger access to the Paris peace talks, where even as he was feeding candidate Nixon intelligence on Harriman's negotiations, he was dismissing his coconspirator to Humphrey's advisers as "unfit to be president" and a potential "disaster" for the country. Even after the election, as Nixon's national security adviser, Kissinger would accent his independence by referring to the president as "our drunken friend" and "that madman."

The one fixed coordinate to Kissinger's identity was his devotion to realpolitik, or at least his interpretation of it. As a sophomore at Harvard in 1947, he stunned his Jewish classmates by opposing U.S. recognition of Israel because it would antagonize Arab regimes and threaten American interests in the Middle East.* (Years later, while negotiating a truce to the 1973 Arab-Israeli war, Kissinger would be criticized for an alleged pro-Israel bias.) Kissinger's Ph.D. dissertation, *A World Restored: Metternich, Castlereagh, and the Problems of Peace, 1812–22,* is a panegyric to enlightened self-interest in defense of global stability. Just as Austrian statesman Klemens Wenzel von Metternich employed dispassionate, balance-of-power diplomacy to keep the French at bay, it implies, so too should the United States adopt a clearheaded, idealism-free foreign policy when confronting the Soviets. "Napoleon's defeat in Russia made clear that Europe could no longer be governed by force, that the man of will would have to find safety in recognition of limits," Kissinger wrote. The destruction of Napoleon's army "obliged the European nations to . . . create a balance of forces to discourage future aggression." Written in 1954 and published in book form three years later, *A World Restored* emphasizes restraint and equilibrium as the foundation of a sustainable peace. One of its most memorable lines, that "moral claims involve a quest for absolutes, a denial of nuance, a rejection of history," would serve as Kissinger's leitmotif throughout much of his career, particularly in his dealings with Moscow and Beijing. His celebration of an understated foreign

---

* In this regard, Kissinger was in good company. Nearly all of Truman's foreign policy specialists, including George Marshall, Robert Lovett, Dean Acheson, George Kennan, Loy Henderson, Charles Bohlen, Dean Rusk, and James Forrestal, advised the president against supporting the State of Israel for the harm it would do to America's image and interests in the Arab world. In favor of recognition was Clark Clifford, the president's domestic political adviser.

policy unburdened by ideology dovetailed with Nixon's vision for rapprochement with America's Cold War antagonists. Their collaboration would yield historic results, but at a price: working in lockstep, they would so thoroughly trample the Department of State as to make it barely recognizable.

If, under Johnson, the war in Vietnam was conducted by militarists in the shadows, Johnson's successor would remove it from the temporal world altogether, subsuming foreign policy generally into the dimly lit bunker of his mind. Not only would Richard Nixon deepen the State Department's exile from the policymaking process, he would also marginalize or subdue the Pentagon, the National Security Council, the U.S. Treasury, Congress, and the media from any meaningful participation in or examination of exactly what he had in store for America's relations abroad. So exclusively did Nixon and Kissinger connive, senior government officials learned about seismic policy shifts by reading about them in newspapers or by watching the nightly newscasts.

Nixon's behavior was as much punitive as it was strategic. He habitually slighted veteran diplomats and security experts as payback for perceived wrongs done to him earlier in his career. He was very much the Orthogonian, the lone sentinel exposing hypocrisies and subversives among the nation's elites. Foreign Service officers were "jerks" and "faggots." Members of Congress were "midgets." Pundits and academics were "bastards." He frequently spoke of the need to undermine popular faith in "the American establishment," code for a honeycomb of liberal media, legislators, and intellectuals. For Nixon, diplomatic breakthroughs were as much cudgels for use against his enemies as they were positive ends in themselves. Even the outreach to China, his signature diplomatic achievement, was as much about "destroying" establishment liberals as it was about neutralizing a Cold War flank.

In his memoirs, Kissinger recounts his first postelection meeting with Nixon at New York's Pierre Hotel on Fifth Avenue, where the president-elect was charting his transition to the White House. Nixon, according to Kissinger, declared how "he had little confidence in the State Department. Its personnel had no loyalty to him; the Foreign Service had disdained him when he was vice president and ignored him the moment he was out of office. He was determined to run foreign policy from the White House. . . . He felt it imperative to exclude the CIA from the formulation of policy; it was staffed by Ivy League liberals who behind the façade of analytical objectivity were usually pushing their own preferences. They had always opposed him politically."

Nixon was staging a coup against his own administration, a resource that was not without its store of useful expertise. With the help of his "Berlin Wall"—Chief of Staff H. R. Haldeman and assistant for domestic affairs John Ehrlichman—Nixon saw to it that presidential access was rationed for even the most senior administration officials. Early on in the administration, having concluded a meeting with the president, Federal Reserve chairman Arthur Burns doubled back after remembering an outstanding item he should have raised. Returning to the Oval Office, Burns found himself blocked bodily at the door by Haldeman, who informed the world's most important central banker that his appointment was over and anything else he had to tell the president should be conveyed by memo. Such treatment was ordained by Nixon's credo of total secrecy. "Whenever there's anything important, you don't tell anybody," the president once told Haldeman. "We don't tell Rogers, Laird, anybody. We just don't tell any son-of-a-bitch at all."

That would be William Rogers and Melvin Laird, the president's secretaries of state and defense.

Nixon filled what are traditionally the nation's most important presidential posts with a duet of contrasting personalities. William Rogers was a respected New York lawyer who counseled Nixon during the Hiss trials and who served as attorney general to President Eisenhower. He was a trusted Republican Party member and, given his lack of experience in global affairs, was just the man Nixon was looking for as a rubber-stamp secretary of state. Chas Freeman, a Sinologist and retired Foreign Service officer who served as Nixon's translator during his historic visit to China, remembers Rogers as "a very nice man [whose] proudest achievement was some product-liability suits that he'd engaged in to defend Bayer Aspirin and other miscreants of great renown, and who was intensely loyal to the president on a personal level. He . . . could not engage intellectually with Nixon and Kissinger on grand strategy and didn't attempt to do so." In other words, he was a worthy heir to the inert Dean Rusk.

Laird was of a different cast entirely. A former U.S. Navy ensign who served with distinction in the Pacific, Laird was a nine-term Wisconsin congressman, an expert on defense appropriations, and a formidable Republican Party leader and political insider. In 1967, when Nixon was mulling a second bid for the presidency, he mentioned Laird in a conversation with Eisenhower about who might be his rivals for the Republican nomination. The president shook his head. Laird, he said, was "the smartest of the lot, but he is too devious." Laird as secretary of defense, however, was something else again. "Of course Laird is devious," Ike acknowledged to Nixon months later when the president-elect was forming his cabinet, "but for anyone who has to run the Pentagon and get along with Congress, that is a valuable asset." Balding, with an enormous cranium that was shaped like an artillery round, Laird by one reporter's account was the "cheese country Richelieu." Vice President Spiro Agnew called Laird "pragmatic, evasive, with ice water in his veins."

Significantly, Laird was an early advocate for American troop withdrawals from Vietnam. As a member of what he called the "loyal opposition," Laird would challenge the Johnson administration's habit of financing the war through supplemental funding requests rather than as budget items, which Laird condemned as a "fight now, pay later" policy designed to wage war "on the installment plan."* His verbal jousts with McNamara during hearings over the defense budget were popular grist for journalists and Georgetown salonists.

In July 1967, addressing the Lions International Convention in Chicago, Laird declared himself to be "neither a 'hawk' nor a 'dove,' but a pessimist" on the war. "Precisely what is the end result we are striving to attain?" he asked rhetorically. "What is the shooting all about? What is it in Southeast Asia that justifies a kill rate of ten thousand Americans annually and possibly fifty thousand wounded?" Two months later, Laird issued a more explicit call for a U.S. withdrawal from Vietnam in a speech

---

* Decades later, President George W. Bush would pay for the wars in Iraq and Afghanistan in much the same manner.

to the American Mining Convention in Denver. "If the choice is between turning South Vietnam over to the communists in 1969 or right
now in 1967, we might as well do it now and prevent further American
casualties."

One might wonder why Nixon, who during the election offered only
that he had "a secret plan" for ending the war in Vietnam, would box himself in by choosing as his defense secretary someone so clearly identified
with the option of withdrawal. The answer is simple: no one else wanted
the job. Nixon demanded Laird take the post after he failed to persuade
Senator Henry Jackson, a Democrat who wisely chose not to associate his
party with the politics of a failed military enterprise, to do so. Laird
agreed, but only on the condition that he could appoint his staff members
with no interference from Nixon. To Laird's surprise, Nixon acquiesced.
Laird then asked Nixon to put their agreement in writing on a cocktail
napkin, which Nixon did, signing the napkin.

Nixon would keep his promise, and Laird surrounded himself with
competent Democrats as well as Republicans. He restored trust between
his office and the Joint Chiefs of Staff and established a working relationship strong enough to prevent Nixon and Kissinger from co-opting
individual members into supporting policies Laird opposed, such as the
secret bombing of Cambodia. With the JCS and senior legislators as his
power base, Laird would play a forceful role in the downsizing of U.S.
forces in Vietnam. He called his plan "Vietnamization" and Kissinger
was very much opposed to it. In a memo to Nixon, Kissinger said troop
withdrawals as called for by the defense secretary would become like
"salted peanuts to the American public: the more U.S. troops come
home, the more will be demanded" and the weaker Washington's negotiating leverage with Hanoi would become.

Nixon, on the other hand, saw in Laird a tough operator who could
sell troop reductions that were, if nothing else, politically popular. In
spring 1969, Laird dodged queries from Congress and the press about a
drawdown, preferring instead to let Nixon announce the first round of
reductions. But as a guest on NBC's *Meet the Press,* he referred to the
process of *Vietnamizing* the war, effectively unveiling his program for

training and equipping the South Vietnamese military to make possible a deliberate departure of U.S. forces from Indochina. He then went a step further, leaking to columnists Rowland Evans and Robert Novak his policy that South Vietnamese soldiers should be trained to combat not only Vietcong guerrillas but also North Vietnamese regulars, "thus creating the proper psychological climate for the start of U.S. troop withdrawals."

In June, Nixon would announce the first round of troop reductions in a speech on Midway Island alongside South Vietnamese president Nguyen Van Thieu. In his memoirs, Nixon would write that it was "largely on the basis of Laird's enthusiastic advocacy that we undertook the policy of Vietnamization." At the time, however, Laird was skewered by the left for dragging out the troop withdrawals and by the right for undermining what it believed was a just and necessary war. Agnew, for one, lamented the "sad thing . . . to see Nixon at the National Security Sessions, seated across the massive conference table with a dove at each elbow—Bill Rogers on the right hand and Mel Laird on the left."

Proximity to the president during cabinet meetings, however, did not necessarily imply power. Immediately after his inauguration, Nixon set about concentrating executive authority in the White House with a directive that subordinated the State Department's top regional officials to the national security adviser. Entitled "Reorganization of the National Security Council System," it declared that the NSC "shall be the principal forum for consideration of policy issues" and it established a nest of interagency committees to support the NSC's work. At the center was Kissinger, who would examine all policy memos prior to their submission to the council. Nixon's edict was followed by a cascade of memorandums that entrenched Kissinger's position at the administrative helm. In restructuring the interagency process, Nixon said he was only restoring the NSC's traditional role after its neglect during the Kennedy and Johnson years. In fact, he expanded and installed it as the central policymaking agency. The NSC would now have an independently recruited staff and a situation room that would be used not only to monitor intragovernmental communications but also to create back channels that enabled Nixon and Kissinger to deal directly with foreign governments without the knowledge of the State Department, or anyone else for that matter. The new structure placed Kissinger, alongside the president, at the vortex of the foreign policy process.

Not surprisingly, Kissinger was the architect of the plan, having worked it out a month earlier at a transition-team meeting at Key Biscayne, Florida, with the help of General Andrew J. Goodpaster, national security adviser under Eisenhower. Kissinger would always assert that it was Goodpaster and Eisenhower himself who first urged that he and Nixon rebuild the NSC as the helm of foreign policy. In his memoirs, Kissinger notes how his plan removed the Senior Interdepartmental Group (SIG), composed of senior officials from the Departments of State, Defense, and the Treasury as well as the CIA and the Joint Chiefs of Staff, as the pivotal policymaking body. "Needless to say," he writes, "the State Department considered this structure to be a major bureaucratic triumph because it formally enshrined the Department's preeminence in foreign policy." Such prestige was illusory, according to Kissinger, because for the last six years the real foreign policy decisions had been made during the regular Tuesday lunches President Johnson had with McNamara, Rusk, and Rostow.

Kissinger says he was "agnostic" about whether or not to preserve the SIG until the ailing Eisenhower, whom Kissinger called upon at Walter Reed Army Hospital, strongly advised he eliminate it. "Eisenhower insisted that the SIG structure had to be ended because the Pentagon would never willingly accept State Department domination of the national security process," Kissinger writes. "It would either attempt end runs or counterattack by leaking." Ultimately, according to Kissinger, the SIG was swept away because Nixon himself wanted it destroyed. "Firmly persuaded of the Foreign Service's ineradicable hostility toward him," Kissinger writes, "Nixon flatly refused to consider preserving the SIG. My notes after a meeting reflect this instruction: 'Influence of State Department establishment must be reduced.'"

And reduced it was. As Chas Freeman put it, the Nixon era was "an odd period in American foreign policy, because, in effect, the National Security Council became the bureau of great power affairs, and the State Department became the bureau for details, relations with lesser states, administrivia, and support of grand enterprises launched out of [the] NSC." Eventually, even the NSC, with the exception of Kissinger and a handful of his aides, would be sidestepped. He and Nixon would conduct foreign policy via elaborate networks of secret channels that freed them from accountability but were frequently more trouble than they were worth. Managing often conflicting agreements, said Winston Lord, one of Kissinger's top China aides, "was like juggling a double or triple booking system," with separate memos compiled for different stations in the bureaucracy. Anthony Lake, who worked for Kissinger during the peace talks with Hanoi, likened "the levels of knowledge and duplicity [to] a Mozart opera in complexity. One reason I quit was because I kept finding myself writing misleading memos." According to Lawrence Eagleburger, Kissinger's principal aide, the White House objective was to allow subordinates no more than a compartmentalized view of policy "even if it meant deceiving them."

Laird no less than Rogers was also neutralized by the turf-conscious Kissinger. With his office in the West Wing basement, Kissinger became one of the few White House aides who would see the president repeatedly every day. The secretaries of state and defense, however, together managed only thirty meetings during Nixon's first one hundred days. Even then, Kissinger jealously guarded his access to the president. When William Bundy, the assistant secretary of state for Asian affairs, told CIA director Richard Helms that he would organize a Saturday briefing on Vietnam, Kissinger snapped at Helms: "This is not a State Department show and Bundy is not in charge." Later, when the State Department's Middle East division sent a policy paper directly to the president, Kissinger declared that if he wasn't sent a copy, he would cancel its scheduled meeting with the president.

Even the frequency of NSC meetings declined dramatically—from twenty-seven in the first six months of the administration to ten in the following six months. In late April 1970, Nixon convened two NSC meetings ahead of his decision to attack North Vietnamese enclaves in Cambodia. But the second was scripted to reduce input from Rogers and Laird, both of whom Nixon knew were opposed to a widening of the war. In 1972, the most eventful year of his presidency, Nixon held a total of three meetings of the very council he had asserted at the advent of his term that he was restoring. Five months into the administration, Dick Sneider, Kissinger's East Asia specialist, declared that "the NSC system is dead."

The infrequency of high-level meetings was due in part to the famously misanthropic Nixon's inability to deal with people in a frank and candid way. ("It would be goddamn easy to run this office if you didn't have to deal with people," he once told his press secretary.) For all his tough-mindedness, the president had an almost pathological dread of being challenged by strong-willed advisers, as Laird often did. Exasperated with his boss, the ever-loyal Haldeman once noted in his diary that "problem is that P is not willing to stand tight on unpleasant personnel situations and won't back us if we do." Whether by instinct or design, Nixon's demons and Kissinger's paranoia compelled both men to retreat into themselves, an act of insularity that led to several grave miscalculations.

In February 1969, Kissinger accompanied the president on his first overseas tour, a series of state visits throughout Europe. The most enlightening of their summit encounters, according to Kissinger, was with French president Charles de Gaulle, who in the twilight of a thirty-year career in politics and international affairs was the preeminent elder statesman of his time. Over the course of several meetings, de Gaulle and Nixon discussed the Soviet Union, transatlantic issues, NATO, and Indochina. Officially, de Gaulle said little that deviated from what other European leaders were telling the new U.S. president and his closest adviser. According to Kissinger's memoirs, however, de Gaulle was considerably more frank at the end of a formal dinner at the Elysée Palace.

"Why don't you get out of Vietnam?" the general asked Kissinger privately.

Kissinger, startled by such candor, muttered something about the perils withdrawal would pose to U.S. credibility, particularly in the Middle East.

"How very odd," replied de Gaulle. "It is precisely in the Middle East that I thought your enemies had the credibility problem."

Kissinger's account is revealing for what it omits. De Gaulle's inference that it was Moscow that was held in low regard in the Middle East and not Washington suggests a firmer grasp of the region's power balance than Kissinger's, coming as it did three years before Soviet military advisers were kicked out of Egypt. However awkward the exchange may have been for Kissinger, for de Gaulle it must have triggered a measure of déjà vu. In June 1966, having been informed by presidential envoy Arthur Goldberg about U.S. objectives in Vietnam, de Gaulle offered some unsolicited advice to President Johnson: pull out.

"But won't it go communist?" stuttered an astonished Goldberg.

"Yes it will go communist," de Gaulle replied.

"But isn't that against us?" Goldberg pressed.

"Yes," said de Gaulle. "But it will be a messy kind of communism. . . . It will be more of a problem for them than for us."

In this context, Kissinger, the hard-minded realist and scholar of multipolar diplomacy, had more in common with Goldberg, a former secretary of labor, than he did with the truly worldly de Gaulle. To the French president, there was nothing "realistic" about adhering to a security commitment after it had become a costly disaster. He had, after all, survived summary exits from France's own fiascos in Indochina and Algeria. For de Gaulle, as for other European leaders who had seen total war not only on their doorsteps but in their living rooms, the costs of "credibility" would never be equal to its returns. The same could not be said of Nixon and Kissinger and their derivative species of realpolitik.

If a heavyweight like de Gaulle could not sway Nixon and Kissinger on Indochina, they were not about to listen to what their own Asia experts had to say about it. Upon his return from Europe, Nixon submitted to Congress the administration's annual report on U.S. foreign policy. This was unusual, as the report was customarily produced by the State Department. To mark the event, the president gathered senior policymakers from various agencies in the Cabinet Room and belittled them. "He gave us a little harangue about what our jobs were and how, by God, he was going to run foreign policy," remembered veteran diplomat and Asia specialist John Holdridge. "In the course of this he said, 'If the Department of State has had a new idea in the last twenty-five years, it is not known to me.'"

It was a startling rebuke to a department that had issued one warning after another about the rise of Communist China and the need to engage rather than isolate it. Even then, had Nixon listened to what his diplomats were telling him about Indochina, it might have saved him from one of the biggest missteps of his presidency. In Paris, the peace talks with North Vietnam had snagged on Hanoi's demand for a U.S. withdrawal from South Vietnam as a precondition for negotiations. Fluent as he was in the language of force, Nixon decided he would coerce Ho Chi Minh back to the table by bombing North Vietnamese sanctuaries along the border with neighboring Cambodia. This would be the first application of what he called the "Madman theory." As Nixon explained it to Haldeman, if Hanoi and its allies believed that he was borderline psychotic, they might sue for peace. "We'll just slip the word to them that, 'for God's sake, you know Nixon is obsessed about communism. We can't restrain him when he is angry—and he has his hand on the nuclear button'—and Ho Chi Minh himself will be in Paris in two days begging for peace."

The irony of Nixon's Madman theory was that by expanding an unpopular and, for a growing share of the population, unnecessary war, voters might become convinced that their commander in chief was indeed lunatic, or at least a dangerous militarist unfit for office. Nixon seemed to grasp this, so he instructed his generals to conduct the bombings in secret, an edict Strangelovian in its delusion. The Joint Chiefs were behind the plan. Laird was opposed, though he reluctantly backed the chiefs in the hope of winning their support later on for a full withdrawal from Vietnam. In February 1969, in retaliation for a Vietcong offensive, the president ordered contingency plans be drawn up for strikes on targets in Cambodia along its hilly border frontier with southwestern Vietnam. Secrecy was critical to the mission—dubbed Operation Menu—for several reasons. Should news of the raids leak to the press, it would embarrass the ostensibly neutral Cambodian government in Phnom Penh, which the White House was hoping to befriend, and China might abandon efforts for a Sino-U.S. convergence. It would also provoke a firestorm of opposition in America against a war Nixon had promised to end.

Prior to the bombardment, Nixon staged a last-minute attempt to lure Hanoi back to the table by enlisting pressure from Moscow. On February 17, he and Kissinger had suggested to Ambassador Dobrynin that

Washington might engage in arms control talks in return for Russian assistance in Indochina and elsewhere, particularly with Arab governments. (By then the range, accuracy, and destructive power of missiles such as the SS-9 had finally given the Soviets strategic parity with the United States.) Dobrynin appeared to be receptive. But Malcolm Toon, the State Department's director of Soviet affairs and a future U.S. ambassador to Moscow, protested that the Soviets lacked real influence, not only with North Vietnam but also with Russia's "allies" in the Middle East. Ignoring Toon's dissent, Nixon and Kissinger set about opening a subterranean channel with Dobrynin, which unlike their secret dealings with China would lead to more headaches than headway.

The bombing of Cambodia continued until May 1970. Some 2.8 million tons of bombs were dropped and tens of thousands of civilians are thought to have been killed. Throughout the Nixon administration, Cambodia would be targeted by covert bombings and joint U.S.–South Vietnamese incursions of negligible military value, and its government would receive a fortune in military and economic assistance from Washington. By 1972 North Vietnam had conceded control of the communist movement in Cambodia to the genocidal Khmer Rouge. In spring 1973, the White House ordered another bombing campaign, with equally meager results, and soon thereafter Congress banned all future American military action in Southeast Asia. For nearly two decades, Cambodia lay prostrate under the purges of the murderous Khmer, who turned the nation into a medieval feudal state and eliminated an eighth of its population. As William Bundy points out, "The policy behind these . . . decisions produced extraordinarily tragic consequences in human terms, with no remotely offsetting strategic benefits." The long-suffering Cambodian people, Bundy argues, could have done no worse had they been taken over by North Vietnam or had their government become a geopolitical football between Beijing and Hanoi.

More than three years later, the White House was still working its back channel with Soviet ambassador Dobrynin. During one of his regular luncheons with the ambassador, Kissinger raised the matter of Hanoi's violation of a cease-fire agreement. The Russians had failed to deliver anything in the way of concessions from North Vietnam, he said. If anything, Moscow and Hanoi appeared to be getting cozier as U.S.

relations with Beijing warmed. "There should be no illusion that we will forget who put us in this uncomfortable position," Kissinger warned. A put-upon Dobrynin responded by scolding Kissinger for allowing the U.S. Congress to prohibit further bombing missions in the region. "In that case, you should go after Fulbright," snarled Dobrynin, referring to the chairman of the Senate Committee on Foreign Relations, "not us."

One of the many paradoxes of the Nixon presidency is how the secretaries of state and defense, habitually at odds in previous administrations, were about the only ones who got along in the Nixon White House. Although of vastly different temperaments, both Rogers and Laird were gentlemen who respected the traditions, protocols, and perils of national politics. Prior to assuming office, the presumptive defense secretary was given a briefing by Lyndon Johnson at the White House. Johnson, having informed Laird that he fully expected to keep the valet and cook that had been assigned to him from the Pentagon—permanently, and on the taxpayer's dime—then offered some useful advice: cultivate good relations with Rogers, otherwise predators within the administration would conspire to divide and rule them. Johnson suggested the two play golf occasionally, and Laird and Rogers would develop an easy relationship during their regular rounds on the links at Burning Tree.

Working for a man like Nixon, the two men quickly learned, it was preferable to hang together rather than hang separately. In the annals of American militarization, Laird's service during the stormy Nixon years represents an important, underappreciated, and tragically belated triumph of sanity and restraint. On January 23, 1973, Nixon was scheduled to give a televised address to the nation to announce the Paris peace accord that ended America's role in the Vietnam War. Prior to delivering it, Nixon held a cabinet meeting in which he praised Laird for his enormous contribution to the agreement. "Without Vietnamization," he said, "there would have been no settlement, and this night would not have been possible." It was, for Nixon, a rare gesture of graciousness and generosity.

There would be no such vindication for Rogers. Until his resignation in September 1973, the forlorn secretary of state endured Kissinger's intrigues with little to show for it. He was kept ignorant of Operation

Menu and the other furtive initiatives—such as a prolonged coup against a freely and fairly elected government in Chile—until it was too late to mount a compelling dissent. His promising plan for a resolution of the Arab-Israeli dispute was abandoned after Golda Meir, the Israeli prime minister, signaled she would mobilize America's Jewish community against Nixon unless he dropped the proposal. During the Strategic Arms Limitation Talks in 1971, Rogers, along with Laird and senior U.S. nuclear arms specialists, was locked out of side deliberations between Kissinger and Dobrynin, with disastrous results. Kissinger had told Moscow in May that submarine-launched ballistic missiles would not need to be part of an overall agreement, even as Nixon himself was insisting publicly that such weapons must be included. An uproar ensued and Kissinger withdrew his concession, though it took another year for the talks to recover. It was, in Bundy's view, a "sloppy negotiating performance" that revealed "how risky it was to have any one man, especially one as pressed as Kissinger, handle a complex matter without full expert support."

Rogers was particularly outraged at the manner in which Kissinger had snatched authority over a process he was clearly not qualified to lead. Haldeman, after taking the brunt of Rogers's fury, recorded how "both K and P had promised him that they would not have any other further meetings with any Ambassadors, and particularly Dobrynin, without letting him know. He said he would bet a large amount that all the magazines would have a full report on . . . the meetings. This would make him a laughingstock again; it destroys his effectiveness and credibility." Nixon was sympathetic and forbade Kissinger from regaling reporters about his preeminent role in the negotiations. Kissinger, however, hailed the SALT I agreement as "a milestone in confirming White House dominance of foreign affairs. For the first two years White House control had been confined to the formulation of policy; now it extended to its execution."

For Kissinger's staff, however, his unchecked authority was taking an exceptional toll on the interagency process. In "Relations with the State Department," a carefully worded memo dated November 14, 1969, White House aide Anthony Lake quantified the damage:

- Relations between the NSC staff and the State Department are at their lowest ebb in years;

- The State Department sees the NSC now in an adversary role in a way that it has not before;
- Some comments attributed to you denigrating the State Department have been given fairly wide circulation in some Bureaus . . . ;
- All of these factors have contributed to a vicious circle of reactions and counter-reactions between the staff and the State Department;
- The major consequences [include] the serious inconsistencies we have displayed to foreigners with regard to critically important substantive issues and the impression of indiscipline and lack of coherence we have displayed to the press.

The most extravagant of White House deceptions, Kissinger's secret trip to Beijing, was yet to come. It would be the first face-to-face round in the China initiative and it would salvage a Nixon presidency weakened politically by its expansion of the war in Vietnam. Talk in Washington about a U.S. overture to Beijing, Nixon knew, was not helpful. Sino-American rapprochement, Nixon told an aide, "doesn't help us with folks." It was helpful "with intellectuals, but people are against Communist China, period." Nevertheless, by the end of Nixon's first year in office, the question was not whether Sino-American accommodation would happen on his watch, but when. On October 1, 1970, Mao publicly signaled for the first time his desire for a thaw in relations when journalist Edgar Snow appeared by his side on the reviewing stand at Tiananmen Square during the National Day celebration. In December, Nixon told reporters there were no plans to reverse policy regarding "Red China," but that he would not rule out the prospect of improved ties with Beijing in the future. In February 1971, when the United States directed and supported a South Vietnamese attack on Vietcong positions in Laos, Beijing issued a conspicuously mild rebuke. In April, China and the United States hosted each other's national table-tennis teams, the famous "Ping-Pong" diplomacy tour, and while receiving the Chinese team Nixon remarked how he would like to one day visit China. On April 27, Kissinger received the message he and

Nixon had been waiting for. It was from Zhou Enlai via Yahya Khan, the president of Pakistan, and it read in part:

> The Chinese government reaffirms its willingness to receive
> publicly in Peking a special envoy of the President of the United
> States . . . or the U.S. Secretary of State or even the President of the
> United States himself for direct discussions.

Three months later, Kissinger and a small group of aides secretly arrived in Beijing, the first Americans in an official capacity to do so in twenty-two years. After several days of negotiation, they produced a working draft of the Shanghai Communiqué, the joint statement that laid out both nations' shared interest in full diplomatic relations. At Zhou's insistence, the document made no effort to reconcile their myriad differences, particularly over the issue of Taiwan. After nearly a quarter-century estrangement, Zhou told the Americans, it would be "absurd" to suggest there were no significant divisions between the two sides. The Shanghai Communiqué remains unique among such documents for its candor.

The Mao-Nixon summit followed seven months later, on February 21, 1972. It consecrated one of the most important of U.S. diplomatic initiatives, something four presidents prior to Nixon either would not or could not do. In political terms it is a tale of redemption, with Statesman Nixon vanquishing Demagogue Nixon to the delight of voters transfixed by television images of him shaking hands with the leaders of a forbidden and mysterious land. Diplomatically it was a masterstroke, and it was Nixon's to celebrate. For all Kissinger's legwork, triangulation was the president's inspiration, simmering as it had been since at least the publication of the *Foreign Affairs* article. Owing to a conspiracy of factors—Nixon's vision, Zhou's daring, Soviet lethargy—what had been a circling of wary rivals had become a waltz. The jilted Russians, meanwhile, having resisted Washington's appeals for a summit, could only look on. When they finally grasped the significance of Nixon's gambit, they scrambled for a summit meeting and were politely told to wait their turn.

Nixon was fortunate in having adroit negotiating partners in Beijing. For him, a Sino-American summit meant the pelting of criticism from a handful of Republican hawks ahead of a reelection campaign he was now sure to win. For Mao and Zhou the process was far more complex and precarious. There was the Gang of Four, leftist reactionaries responsible for the worst crimes of the Cultural Revolution, who worked to undermine accommodation with the West. Mao and Zhou also knew that, in exchange for better ties, the United States would expect China's help in negotiating an end to the war in Vietnam. Any attempt to strong-arm Hanoi, however, would create a breach between the two allies that Moscow could easily manipulate. The last thing Beijing wanted was a unified, Moscow-backed Vietnam, and Hanoi, sensing an opening, wasted no time driving a wedge between the two communist giants. It condemned Nixon's China mission as a "perfidious maneuver" and a "false peace offensive" designed to split the socialist world. In early February, when the Chinese had asked permission to officially discuss Indochinese affairs at the summit, the North Vietnamese not only rejected the idea, they duly reported the matter to Moscow. During Hanoi's spring offensive, Moscow offered to neutralize the mining of Haiphong Harbor by shipping weapons and supplies overland through China, knowing Beijing would reject such a proposal even as Hanoi supported it.

The North Vietnamese were responding bitterly to what they must have suspected all along: that Beijing was concerned less with the global communist movement than with the pursuit of its own best interests. Mao said as much in his one and only meeting with Nixon. "People like me sound like a lot of big cannons," he said. "For example, [we say] things like 'the whole world should unite and defeat imperialism, revisionism, and all reactionaries, and establish socialism . . .'"—at which point he and Zhou slipped into sardonic laughter. Ultimately, relations between Hanoi and Beijing would collapse in the wake of North Vietnam's 1979 invasion of Cambodia, a Chinese ally, and China's retaliatory war on Vietnam. Kissinger put it best. "The leaders of China were beyond ideology in their dealings with us," he wrote in his memoirs. "Their peril had established the absolute primacy of geopolitics."

Most historians and foreign policy experts agree that the China mission would have failed had it not been done covertly. The State Department, like most government bureaucracies, is packed with vested interests that could have subverted the negotiations through leaks and soft-stalling. In addition, countries with an interest in the status quo, such as Japan, might have maneuvered to disrupt the process. There was, however, characteristic perfidy and base motives in the way Nixon and Kissinger locked out even the most senior State Department officials. By early 1971, with the indirect exchanges between Beijing and the White House intensifying, Nixon and Kissinger were already scheming to ensure historians gave them their due. "If we succeed in . . . the Communist China thing," Nixon told Kissinger, "if it goes and the Soviet thing goes, we're not going to let those bastards take the credit for it. We've got to take credit every time we turn around." Kissinger, of course, concurred with his boss. According to Haldeman's diary, Kissinger told him that "the big thing now is to get the credit for all the shifts in China policy, rather than letting it go to the State Department, which of course had nothing to do with it—in fact opposed every step the P took because they were afraid any moves toward China would offend Russia." Even by the low standards of the Nixon White House, Kissinger's remark is appallingly dishonest and mean-spirited. It was the State Department's China specialists who for decades not only counseled engagement with Beijing but were destroyed politically for doing so, in no small part by Nixon himself.

From the start, Nixon and Kissinger insisted through their interlocutors with Beijing that all negotiations must be held in private.* During

---

* Nixon claimed that he kept the China channel secret at Beijing's insistence. This is not true. Zhou's April 21 message to Kissinger makes clear that he and Mao would publicly welcome a U.S. envoy to Beijing. A year earlier, when U.S. ambassador to Poland Walter Stoessel was invited to the Chinese embassy in Warsaw to resume talks, he offered to sneak in through the back door. The Chinese chargé, a man named Lei Yang, countered that he would like to come over and discuss the matter, as his ambassador had been called away. A few days later, Lei arrived at the U.S. embassy gates in his limousine, a pair of China's red national flags fluttering from the hood, to the great excitement of the press.

the Warsaw talks, the State Department's team asked for an assurance from Kissinger that the discussions would be allowed to evolve into high-level negotiations and would not get snuffed out for political reasons. "Nothing would be worse than to go out there and then get slapped in the face," said Marshall Green, State's assistant secretary for East Asian affairs. "It would be the end of all that we hoped to achieve in our U.S.-China relations. [Kissinger] implies that we were throwing cold water. It was not true at all. All we were saying is that we didn't know all of the pieces in the puzzle. We weren't in communication with each other. It created distrust." Green remembers how, when it was announced that Kissinger was laid low with stomach flu in Islamabad, Pakistan, as cover for his July journey to Beijing, he speculated aloud among his staff that "he's probably gone to China." Such asides are the stuff of leaks in Washington, and Green had the presence of mind to swear his staff to secrecy. Nevertheless, he said, "not to inform me about Henry's trip was almost disastrous." Green and other diplomats acknowledged that back channels were critical to the success of the initiative. But they argued that keeping assistant secretaries in the dark, to say nothing of the secretary of state himself, was as irresponsible as it was petty. In late April, the oblivious Rogers commented in London on China's "rather paranoic" policies, obliging Kissinger to tell the Chinese that the U.S. secretary of state was not to be taken seriously. Rogers would not be informed of Kissinger's trip to Beijing until the last moment. Even Winston Lord, the aide who accompanied Kissinger on the first mission to Beijing, disparaged the degree of secrecy under which U.S.-China policy was administered. "We couldn't fully take advantage of the people in the State Department on the China desk," said Lord. "We didn't have the intimate, day-to-day exchanges that some of these people might have provided had they been included."

In his memoirs, Kissinger gives a startlingly candid and self-serving explanation for his monopolization of foreign policy, which he implies was a burden imposed on him by Rogers's personal limitations as secretary of state.

It was painful enough [for Rogers] to see me and the NSC staff dominate the policy process in Washington; it was harder still to accept the proposition that I might begin to intrude on the conduct of foreign policy overseas. The objection was, in fact, well taken. The State Department should be the visible focus of our foreign policy; if the President has no confidence in his Secretary of State he should replace him, not substitute the security adviser for him. If he does not trust the State Department, the President should enforce compliance with his directive, not circumvent it with the NSC machinery. Yet, while these postulates are beyond argument as a matter of theory, they are not easy to carry out. To achieve the essential coherence of policy there is need for a strong Secretary of State who is at the same time quite prepared to carry out Presidential wishes not only formally but in all nuances. The combination has been a historical rarity; in recent times, one or the other quality has, alas, often been missing.

The elephant in the room here is, of course, Kissinger's voracious ego and ambition. In the end, the further coarsening of relations between the White House and the State Department would be a mere backstory to what Nixon called "the most significant foreign policy achievement in this century." To their credit, none of the snubbed senior diplomats leaked to the press about their treatment or condemned the sellout of Taiwan. Nixon's China triumph was followed by his summit with Leonid Brezhnev in Moscow in May 1972, where the two leaders signed the largely symbolic but groundbreaking SALT I agreement along with protocols for expanding two-way commerce and trade. Nixon, with Kissinger's help, had delivered détente to a world exhausted by Cold War confrontation. Criticism from the right was predictable and largely irrelevant. In the summer of 1971, prominent conservatives led by Bill Buckley met at his Upper East Side Manhattan townhouse to announce their "suspension of support" for Nixon. Following the China summit, the "Manhattan Twelve" declared themselves to be Republican renegades who would contest the president's nomination for reelection. Among the group's most outspoken members was an unknown Ohio congressman named John Ashbrook, who declared Nixon's opening to the communist world as an "apostasy" and the SALT agreement as "close to clinical lunacy." The Manhattan Twelve were throwing rocks at a passing train, however, and

Nixon would be reelected in a landslide. Dissenting voices such as Ashbrook's were obscured by the overwhelmingly positive response to détente. The public, at least, understood what militarists like Ashbrook refused to believe and what Zhou Enlai had known all along.

"There is no monolithism," Zhou told Nixon and Kissinger in Beijing, "neither in western nor in socialist countries."

10

INTERREGNUM

Our army when it arrives in Afghanistan, will be the aggressor.
Against whom shall we fight? Against the Afghan people first of all,
and [we] will have to shoot them. . . . And what would we gain?
Afghanistan with its present government, with a backward
economy, with inconsequential weight in international affairs.
—SOVIET FOREIGN MINISTER ANDREI GROMYKO
DURING A MEETING OF THE CENTRAL COMMITTEE OF
THE COMMUNIST PARTY OF THE SOVIET UNION, MARCH 17, 1979

T HE TWO VIETNAMS WERE NOT THE ONLY COLD WAR PROXIES
in Asia unnerved by Sino-American rapprochement. Implicit in
the Shanghai Communiqué was a message to regimes throughout the communist and capitalist realms, from Thailand to the Korean
peninsula: neither Washington nor Beijing would imperil détente with
"entangling alliances," as Thomas Jefferson called them.*

Nixon had put America's Asian allies on notice as early as August
1969. While inspecting the U.S. protectorate of Guam as part of a round-
the-world tour, he gathered reporters at an officers' club and told them
that the United States "must avoid that kind of policy that will make
countries in Asia so dependent upon us that we are dragged into conflicts such as the one that we have in Vietnam." To be sure, he told the
newsmen, Washington would support its allies struggling with communist insurgencies. It would increase the volume of their cash and in-kind
assistance programs and it would help them modernize their armed
forces, but it would also reduce its forward deployments in the region. The
days of U.S. troops fighting and dying on behalf of Asian governments

---

* The term is often wrongfully attributed to George Washington.

were over. There would be "no more Vietnams," he said. The president formally unveiled the Nixon Doctrine in an evening address to the country on November 3, 1969, declaring that "we shall look to the nation directly threatened to assume the primary responsibility of providing the manpower necessary for its defense."

Along with détente and triangulation, the Nixon Doctrine could have been one of its architect's most thoughtful contributions to U.S. foreign policy. In practice, however, the doctrine failed to deliver. Long after the president was forced from the White House, U.S. troops were still deployed on behalf of complacent Asian allies, particularly Japan, South Korea, and the Philippines. Even Vietnamization, hailed by the president as the cornerstone of the Nixon Doctrine, was a strategic failure. True, it provided the administration with the cover it needed to withdraw from the war "with honor." But the steamrolling of Saigon under a North Vietnamese onslaught three years later revealed fundamental weaknesses in the program, including, first and foremost, South Vietnam's sclerotic leadership. Vietnamization was the last in a series of failed counterinsurgency efforts to save Saigon and the prelude to similar U.S. campaigns in Iraq and Afghanistan.

In war there is symmetrical conflict—a clash of combatants with roughly equal resources at their command—and there is the asymmetrical kind, a war of attrition between a conventional army on one side and a lightly armed but agile militia on the other. The Philippine-American war of 1889, for example, began with a set-piece victory by U.S. warships over the Spanish fleet in Manila Bay, followed by a decade or so of guerrilla warfare pitting American forces against Philippine freedom fighters. Today, with the age of symmetrical conflict a distant memory, counterinsurgency is the U.S. military's stock-in-trade. (As will be seen, the Pentagon now interprets the principles of counterinsurgency quite broadly, from digging wells on behalf of host nations to developing capitalist economies and independent legal systems.) One of the many lessons learned from Vietnam is that armed insurgency is typically the most forceful expression of a political movement that can rarely be subdued by armed might alone. If, to paraphrase the Prussian military philosopher Carl von Clausewitz, guerrilla war is politics by other means, robust civilian aid is a vital component in gaining the trust of indigenous populations and establishing a sustainable peace.

The United States had waged pacification campaigns in Vietnam long before Washington militarized the war. In the 1950s, the Eisenhower administration introduced land reform and the Agroville Plan, in which thousands of villagers were quarantined from the Vietcong through forced relocation. During the Kennedy years, the United States introduced "strategic hamlets," in which entire populations of South Vietnamese were installed in fortified communities. Neither plan lasted very long, however, as each succeeded only in alienating the very people it was devised to win over. In April 1965, Lyndon Johnson pledged to build a Tennessee Valley Authority–type regional development project for the Mekong River valley that North Vietnam could share with the south. Though Hanoi rejected the offer, Johnson would not relinquish the idea of overwhelming communism with American "smart" power, rather than the exclusive wielding of its traditional "hard" military power. A year later, he named Robert Komer, a senior National Security Council member and former CIA officer, to head up a new, broad-based pacification program. Johnson called it "the other war," and its objective was to beat the Vietcong at its own game, providing villagers with the kind of goods and services the communists were so skilled at distributing in the vacuum of Saigon's neglect.

Komer set up shop at the U.S. embassy in Saigon in 1967, the most senior civilian official below the ambassador, Ellsworth Bunker. He was soon followed by an army of civilian advisers to the recently created United States Agency for International Development, or USAID, with expertise in agriculture, medicine, engineering, management, and economics. They improved irrigation methods, developed the world's most durable varieties of rice, built roads, and introduced modern pharmaceuticals and health care. But they did not work alone. In a unique occasion of multiagency collaboration, civilian officials labored alongside U.S. military personnel, propaganda specialists, and CIA agents in an attempt both to improve the living standards of ordinary South Vietnamese and to gain intelligence for counterinsurgency purposes. It was known as Civil Operations and Revolutionary Development Support, or CORDS, and it is cited by some senior military leaders today as a model for ground-up pacification campaigns. In fact, the conflicts between CORDS's civilian and military participants, with the former routinely conceding to the latter, and the Saigon government's refusal to work constructively with either side, would in the end militarize CORDS along with the rest of America's efforts in Vietnam. Even Komer would later admit the program was "a small tail to the very large conventional military dog."

The centerpiece of CORDS was USAID, Washington's main distributor of foreign aid. USAID was conceived as part of the Foreign Assistance Act of 1961 and it was orphaned at birth. Unlike other federal bureaucracies—the Department of Agriculture, say, with its trough of farm subsidies, or the Department of Defense, with its huge procurement budget—there is no political constituency in support of foreign assistance programs. Even at the peak of the Cold War, when the battle for "hearts and minds" was at full pitch, USAID directors had to beg for expanded budgets to finance new programs and to sustain existing ones. In retrospect, however, the war years in Vietnam were USAID's golden era. The multiagency CORDS mission was very much consistent with Lyndon Johnson's faith in government as an agent for positive change, which ensured it ample funding.

On paper at least, CORDS was an elegantly designed interagency program. In practice, it fell victim to the natural tendency of bureaucracies to problem-solve with "supply side" solutions. While civilians saw in South Vietnam socioeconomic problems in need of nonmilitary solutions, its military and intelligence cadres saw a security crisis that demanded the destruction of the Vietcong and its network. Not surprisingly in a war zone, military priorities and prescriptions prevailed. "From the outset," noted Komer in a 1972 report he wrote for the RAND Corporation on the failings of U.S. pacification efforts in Vietnam, "the preponderant weight of the U.S. and [South Vietnamese] military . . . tended to dictate an overly militarized response. The institutional background of U.S. and [South Vietnamese] military leaders helped shape the nature of that response." In other words, despite ardent support for pacification initiatives in Washington, they were ultimately sidelined by military imperatives in Vietnam.

What Komer did not reveal, at least not in his RAND paper, is that he was as responsible as anyone for the militarization of U.S. pacification efforts. Impatient with CORDS's early results, he appealed to the CIA to assume a more assertive role in the program. In his hunger for data points, he insisted on at least 3,000 Vietcong killed or captured each month, all but guaranteeing systemic abuses. William Colby, a senior CIA official who served as the Saigon station chief in the early 1960s and who would play a key role in CORDS, mapped out something called "infrastructure coordination and exploitation," in which CIA officers would help South Vietnamese paramilitaries ferret out suspected Vietcong cadres. In December 1967, under heavy pressure from Washington, Prime Minister Nguyen Van Loc instructed his ministers to go after the insurgents and their network. The assignment was not popular among Loc's advisers, given the considerable mistrust between the military and the police, which would hamper communication. Also, not a few generals and gendarmes were loathe to take on the mission due to family connections they had with prominent Vietcong operatives.

The government called the plan Phung Hoang, or "all-seeing bird." The closest thing to an English-language equivalent was "Phoenix." The name stuck, and for all the wrong reasons. As Colby himself would acknowledge in his 1978 memoir, "the word 'Phoenix' became a shorthand for all the negative aspects of the war."

Colby would run the Phoenix program as the U.S. ambassador to South Vietnam from 1968 to 1971. It evolved into a counterinsurgency campaign of arrest, assassination, and, allegedly at least, torture, and it killed or captured an estimated 80,000 Vietcong members. Most certainly, a considerable number of those killed were unfairly charged, victims of tribal feuds that had nothing to do with the Vietcong or communism. Sensing a lucrative opportunity for extortion, South Vietnamese military and security officials threatened to arrest innocent citizens unless they were offered bribes while at the same time setting loose genuine Vietcong sympathizers from captivity. As one adviser put it, "All the way up the chain of custody there was ample opportunity for an individual to buy his way out." Over time, Phoenix took on a life of its own. Kangaroo courts were set up and detention centers were established, though not nearly enough to keep up with demand. Less than two years after Phoenix was up and running, some 20,000 suspected Vietcong members were being held in a prison system designed to contain no more than 16,000.

In 1968, as part of a Komer-inspired "accelerated pacification plan" aimed at bringing the Mekong Delta under Saigon's control as peace talks convened in Paris, the U.S. Ninth Infantry Division unleashed a large-scale operation with the support of helicopter gunships and B-52s. Known as "Speedy Express," the operation was carried out from December 1968 to May 1969 and left 10,883 enemy troops dead—more combatants than the Saigon press estimated were in the entire area. What was meant to be a coordinated civilian-military pacification campaign became a fury of violence visited upon innocents largely from the air. Eyewitness reports of civilian deaths quickly proliferated—of U.S. snipers killing dozens of noncombatants per day with early versions of night-vision goggles; of "express raids" that "mopped up many thousands, slaughtering 3,000 people, mostly old folks, women and children"; of U.S. F-4 Phantom fighter jets strafing a herd of water buffalo and a half dozen or so children tending them, according to a 1971 *Washington Monthly* article, leaving behind "a bloody ooze littered with bits of mangled flesh."

Even before the Delta massacres, Komer was losing faith in the very program he had pioneered. In 1970 he wrote a tightly held memo for CIA director William Colby and Defense Secretary Melvin Laird in which he called Phoenix a "fiasco." Coordination among South Vietnamese intelligence and security divisions was inadequate, he wrote, and as a result Phoenix's successes were not worth the bad press they were generating. Allegations of Phoenix-related torture and assassination surfaced in congressional hearings in 1971. Though the CORDS leadership adamantly denied abetting such conduct and repeatedly admonished Phoenix interrogators to obey international laws of warfare, it acknowledged that it had little control over CORDS's South Vietnamese counterparts.*

---

* Needless to say, this was before torture was known in America as "forceful interrogation" and practiced openly under both Republican and Democratic presidents. In *Pacification,* published in 1995, author Richard Hunt makes a point rendered quaint by today's standards: "The CORDS leadership had other reasons to prohibit torture and assassination. It was an axiom of professional American intelligence agencies that coercion elicited

In his 1972 RAND study, Komer scolds U.S. diplomats for not doing enough to prevent the militarization of Washington's pacification efforts. "The State Department," he wrote, "did not often deviate from its concept of normal diplomatic dealings with [Saigon], not even when the government was falling apart. Similarly, State . . . made little effort to assert control over our military effort on political grounds. . . . State's concept of institution-building in Vietnam turned largely on encouragement of American democratic forms, a kind of mirror-imaging which proved hard to apply to the conditions of Vietnam."

This is unfair. To blame civilian agencies for not halting the centripetal forces of militarism in a war zone is to allow them a level of power and authority they clearly lacked, particularly when compared with the awesome resources available to the Pentagon. The implication that diplomatic sensitivities denied Washington a serious partner in its counterinsurgency effort ignores how civilian and military hawks such as Walt Rostow and William Westmoreland overindulged Saigon well before the arrival of Komer in Saigon. Komer's frustration with intractable bureaucracies and their inability to respond to extraordinary situations with enterprising solutions reduces a dilemma such as South Vietnam, in defiance of its long, complex, and violent history, into a mathematical equation that begs only the proper set of variables to resolve.

It is a RANDite's conceit, one that intuits the price of everything and the value of nothing. It ignores the most inconvenient fact of counterinsurgency operations, the one that explains why they are so rarely successful.* To engage in counterinsurgency on behalf of an ally implies recognition that he is unable to defend himself. To compensate for his weakness with money and matériel only exposes his deficiencies to both his enemies and his own people. In South Vietnam, continued U.S. support bred an unhealthy codependence between benefactor and beneficiary—the latter for his survival, the former for a yield on his investment. As returns diminished, the benefactor began searching for an exit. Diplomats were deployed and retreat was improvised into something honorable.

---

little useful information, and it was the American way to try persuading the South Vietnamese that humane treatment was more likely to produce reliable information."
* Notable failures include the counterinsurgency campaign waged by Great Britain in late-eighteenth-century North America.

———

Which brings us back to Vietnamization and the failure of the Nixon Doctrine.

Because of Nixon's unwillingness to confront the Joint Chiefs and Congress, America's military footprint worldwide would be more or less unchanged by the time of his ignominious departure from the White House. The Nixon Doctrine was a well-intentioned but naive attempt to demilitarize containment, the demands of which threatened to turn the United States into "an elective dictatorship," as Senator William Fulbright put it. Nixon may have surmised that the Pentagon's chain of forward deployments, as well as the ballooning budgets that funded them, was itself a perpetual-motion machine for military intervention and escalation. He may have understood that only base reductions and defense spending cuts could reduce what Arthur Schlesinger Jr. called the "imperial heat" that so arouses Washington's security cadres. Yet he failed to exploit the opening created by U.S.-Sino reconciliation and the resolution of the war in Vietnam. No single president, to say nothing of one crippled by a massive scandal, could have prevailed against a cluster of hawkish legislators, ambitious military officers, and defense contractors so deeply invested in the status quo.

The depths of American militarization would be revealed in 1971, ironically out of an act of catharsis by Robert McNamara for his role in expanding the war in Vietnam. Having concluded that the United States could not prevail militarily in Indochina, McNamara in 1967 commissioned RAND to compile a report on the war for the lessons it might provide. The project was entrusted to a junior RAND researcher named Daniel Ellsberg, a former Marine lieutenant who served in Vietnam as a civilian Pentagon military analyst. By then Ellsberg had become disillusioned with the war. Two years into his research, in October 1969, he smuggled out from the RAND building a voluminous compilation of top-secret Pentagon documents chronicling a quarter century of U.S. involvement in Southeast Asia. With the help of Anthony Russo, a RAND researcher, he photocopied the documents and leaked them to the press. The disclosure of the Pentagon Papers, as they would be known, and the story they told of high-level, institutionalized treachery would scandalize the nation. Even McNamara, by then out of government, was stunned. "You know," he told a friend, "you could hang people for what's in there."

Publication of the papers, writes historian George Herring, "challenged the myth of America as a reluctant participant in the war, added to an already large credibility gap between public and government, and gave legitimacy to some of the key arguments of the antiwar opposition." For Neil Sheehan, the *New York Times* reporter who trolled through the archive in its entirety, the documents provided a "step through the looking glass into a new and different world . . . a centralized state, far more powerful than anything else, for whom the enemy is not simply the communists but . . . its own press, its own judiciary, its own Congress, foreign and friendly governments—all these are potentially antagonistic."

The withdrawal from Vietnam, the corrosive effect of the war on the armed forces, and the release of the Pentagon Papers plunged the American military into an existential crisis and delivered a near-death blow to the U.S. Army in particular. It would achieve a Lazarus-like resurrection in less than a decade, however, thanks to a generation of officers who managed to replenish the "hollow Army" of the 1970s.

Whatever tensions the war in Vietnam may have generated between civilians and the military in America, they paled in significance compared with the damage the war did to the military itself. It left the uniformed services with high rates of chronic alcohol and drug addiction, which, together with racial tensions, plagued operations. By the late 1970s, the number of high-school graduates recruited into the all-volunteer force was so low there was talk of reviving the draft.

No one understood this better than Melvin Laird. As Nixon's secretary of defense, Laird lamented the toll multiple tours in Vietnam were having on active-duty troops deployed overseas. Johnson had refused to mobilize the reserves lest it trigger a voter backlash, and as a result America's overseas bases were burdened by chronic shortages of manpower and equipment, while reserve units were in a derelict state. For Laird, the primary goal of Vietnamization was less to prepare South Vietnam for its ultimate fate than it was to extricate the U.S. Army from Indochina so it could be rebuilt. To get the job done, he turned to General Creighton Abrams, the Army chief of staff. For the next two years, Abrams would do as much as anyone to reassemble the U.S. military into the kind of robust expeditionary force that could manage the enormous burdens it shoulders today.

Abrams was a skilled tank commander—it was his column that relieved the besieged 101st Airborne Division at Bastogne during World War II—and he was an agile combatant in Pentagon turf wars. In 1964, three years after earning his first general's star, he was made deputy to William Westmoreland, by then the top commander of U.S. forces in Vietnam. Promoted to commander in 1968 when Westmoreland became Army chief of staff, Abrams quickly set about reforming the Army's tactical approach to the war. Unlike his predecessor, the cigar-puffing Abrams actively supported the Johnson administration's pacification programs, though he was under no illusions about the Thieu government's commitment to the effort. "They've got to shape up," he told his regional commanders in 1968. "They are letting days slide by—very important days—while they fool around with secondary matters."

With the approach of Westmoreland's retirement in June 1972, a political squall gathered over his likely successor. Abrams was widely regarded as the finest strategic thinker in the military—the best, some argued, since Ulysses S. Grant. But he was not favored by Nixon, who wanted Alexander Haig, a Kissinger aide, to fill Westmoreland's spot. Laird insisted on Abrams, however. The two men had formed a solid friendship during the secretary's first visit to Saigon in February 1969, when they were forced to spend several hours together in an underground shelter waiting out an enemy attack. Plus, Abrams was one of few flag officers to support Vietnamization even as the Joint Chiefs of Staff opposed it. In March 1972, while in Brussels for a NATO function, Laird phoned Nixon and redeemed his special authority as defense secretary—that presidential guarantee, written and signed by Nixon himself on a cocktail napkin, that he could appoint whomever he wanted if he took the cabinet job. After a thirty-six-year career in the U.S. Army, Abrams was now in charge of fixing it.

Once confirmed, Abrams mounted a fact-finding tour of U.S. bases abroad, first in Vietnam and then on to Europe, where the conditions appalled him. After nearly a decade of war in Indochina with no slack in rotation schedules, "the proud, well-trained, and combat-ready Seventh Army in Germany was in effect . . . destroyed as a fighting force," concluded General Bruce Palmer, acting Army chief of staff. Only four of the Army's thirteen divisions were combat worthy, and troop morale was abysmally low. The Army's standard performance-evaluation system, Abrams found, was prone to chronic ratings inflation that compromised the way in which officers were promoted, educated, and assigned. Young officers complained about a culture they said forced them to violate ethical standards in order to get by. Clearly, the war in Vietnam had taken its toll on the Army's values as well as its readiness.

Abrams tasked a committee of unorthodox thinkers to redefine the Army's proper role in the post-Vietnam nuclear age. The group was named after its chairman, Colonel Edward F. Astarita, and it crafted a spare new mission statement: the Army exists, it concluded, "to serve just two ends. First is the defense of our land. . . . Second is the preservation of freedom of action, which might be defined as immunity from coercion." It was an elegantly devised, deceptively simple declaration. The term "immunity from coercion" could be defined as the protection of strategic assets in America's historical sphere of influence—the Panama Canal, say—from the clutches of hostile powers that would deprive it of commerce and vital resources. But it could also validate U.S. hegemony over the sea-lanes of the Persian Gulf or the Malacca Strait, through which so much of the world's petroleum reserves are transported. In January 1980, President Jimmy Carter would invoke the spirit of the Astarita manifesto with his own doctrine when he announced that any move by a foreign power to seize control of the Persian Gulf region would be repelled as a threat to vital U.S. interests.

A year later, General John W. Vessey Jr., the then Army vice chief of staff and a future chairman of the Joint Chiefs, concluded that the Astarita Group and its findings marked a turning point in the military's post-Vietnam malaise. It also reoriented the Pentagon's focus away from Indochina, a region tough-minded realists such as George Kennan had long believed was a strategic irrelevancy, and back to the major Cold War fronts of Europe and northeast Asia. Despite the harm done to America's reputation by the loss of Vietnam, it noted, the United States and its alliance network remained the world's dominant power. The onus was on Washington to preserve its comparative advantage, and that would require a larger army. Abrams called for a reversal of proposed force reductions and, in what would be known as the "round-out" program, ordered the formation of an additional three Army divisions. At the core of his expansion plan was the return to prominence of the Army Reserve and the National Guard, the key to U.S. tactical success in World War I, World War II, and the Korean War. Not only did Abrams seek to expand the number of Army divisions, he wanted each one rendered battle worthy, an audacious undertaking that was met with incredulity when he announced his new policy during a March 1974 congressional hearing.

In ramping up the Army's capacity, Abrams hoped to achieve several things at once. He wanted to restore its deterrent capability, particularly in Europe and East Asia, and critical to that effort was the seamless integration of reserve and active-duty forces. Not only would it provide the manpower for the three extra divisions, it would make it all but impossible for a president to commit the active-duty Army to battle without mobilizing the reserves as well. A blended force structure would also be difficult to whittle down to nine or ten divisions, as the Office of Management and Budget was recommending. Such a reduced force, Abrams and his aides feared, not only would be stretched thin by the demands of the Cold War, it would engender a rigid dependency on nuclear weapons similar to the one that plagued Eisenhower's New Look.

By January 1974, Abrams's plan to field sixteen battle-ready divisions was taking shape, though he would not live to see their elements parade and drill. On September 4, after a prolonged struggle, he succumbed to complications from cancer. The restoration he set in motion would survive him, however. The post-Vietnam U.S. Army was on its way to becoming the most powerful armed force ever—militarily, and over the course of a generation, politically.*

---

* So trusted was Abrams that at one point during the Watergate hearings, amid concerns that President Nixon might try to distract the public with some kind of surprise military

It would take the better part of the decade, however, for Abrams's work to bear fruit. The twenty-nine-month-long administration of Nixon's vice president and successor, Gerald Ford, was consumed with the business of healing a nation stricken by war and the Watergate scandal, with little time or resources to build on the foundation Abrams left behind. The legacy of Jimmy Carter, who defeated Ford in the 1976 national elections, is more complex. Though critics claim he starved the military of everything from manpower to spare parts, leaving the country exposed to Soviet adventurism in the Persian Gulf, defense spending during Carter's single term actually rose at an average annualized rate of 13 percent. Under ordinary standards, that would be a respectable clip. But the economy inherited by the new president—plagued as it was by virulent inflation, record high interest rates, and sluggish growth—was hardly accommodating of a decisive arms buildup.

Lyndon Johnson, as we have seen, waged the Vietnam War on the political cheap. There would be no deploying of reserves or even a request from Congress for a declaration of war. With far-reaching consequences for the economy, Johnson chose to finance the conflict with borrowed money rather than raised taxes. Beginning in 1965, as budget deficits swelled, the dollar's purchasing power waned. Inflation intensified after 1972, when a powerful Arkansas congressman named Wilbur Mills decided he would ride to the presidency on the gratitude of senior citizens by fixing Social Security payments to the Consumer Price Index.* Introduced in 1975, the Cost of Living Adjustment represents a huge budget burden by driving up the costs of entitlements, particularly during periods of slow growth. American income was further eroded by

---

operation, judge advocates of the 82nd and 101st Airborne Divisions advised their commanders to respond to such orders only if General Abrams himself declared—in person, if possible—that it was all right to do so.

* Mills finished a miserable fourth in New Hampshire's Democratic primary and his presidential bid quickly collapsed. Two years later he was picked up by U.S. Park Police in Washington as he tried to prevent his girlfriend, a nightclub stripper named Fanne Fox, aka "the Argentine firecracker," from flinging herself into the Tidal Basin. Exposed as an alcoholic, Mills lost his seat in Congress and prospered as a lobbyist.

an extraordinary rise in oil prices. In 1973, during their war with Israel, the petroleum-producing Arab states imposed an embargo on shipments to the West in retaliation for U.S. support of Tel Aviv. By 1980, the price of a gallon of gas had risen to $1.60, up from $0.37 a decade earlier. Gas rationing was imposed, the first time since World War II, and lines of automobiles snaked out from filling stations nationwide.

Though these events predated Carter's election, the Great Inflation, as historian Theodore H. White put it, would supply the political, economic, and cultural reference point of his presidency. (It was also a burden on Ford, whose rallying cry of "Whip Inflation Now" did little to inspire voters ahead of the 1976 presidential race.) By 1980 inflation rates had reached the 18 percent level, among the highest in modern American history, while banks were charging 15 to 16 percent interest on prime loans. The specter of an America laid low militarily by a primitive militia in an obscure land, together with symptoms of deterioration at home—gas stations with no fuel to sell, storefronts boarded up, rising crime, the near bankruptcy of New York City—defined the era. As White writes, "The quality of American talk began to resemble what must have been that of the Gauls, the Dacians, the Britons, as they realized that the might of Rome could no longer safely insure them against the future."

Such were the cards dealt Jimmy Carter as he settled into the White House. It was a poor hand and it would only get worse, due to external factors as much as his own missteps. So bleak and blighted was Carter's term that his most important address, the famous "malaise speech" in which he sermonized against wasteful self-indulgence, never contained the word for which it is known. The singular achievements of his administration—a landmark arms-control treaty with Moscow and a brokered peace between Egypt and Israel—were obscured by the Soviet invasion of Afghanistan and the arrival of radical Islam as a political force in the Middle East. A dove by instinct, Carter left Washington a reluctant hawk. Having condemned the USSR as "the most serious threat to peace since the Second World War," he launched a massive military buildup that is commonly and wrongly believed to have been exclusive to his successor. His failed reelection bid was all but preordained, so indelibly was his presidency associated with the dissolution of his times.

While campaigning for the White House, Carter promised to reduce defense spending, promote human rights as a key U.S. foreign policy issue, and negotiate reciprocal cuts in strategic weapons with Moscow. While he redeemed part of that pledge by delivering SALT II, a refinement of the Nixon-era arms control treaty that was augmented by Ford, Carter's military budgets actually grew modestly during his first three years in office. The rate of growth was not nearly enough to keep up with inflation, however, or to offset the declining value of the dollar against the currencies of the nations that hosted U.S. bases. According to Army chief of staff General Edward Meyer during a presidential briefing, only four U.S. Army divisions were capable of deploying overseas in an emergency and the reserves were still undermanned. During the same briefing, Admiral Thomas Hayward, chief of naval operations, told the president that the troops not only were demoralized but were ill-trained to the point of being a menace to themselves. In early 1979, the captain of the USS *Canisteo*, a frontline support ship, was forced to cancel a scheduled deployment because the vessel was critically short of experienced crew members. Bases and ships were neglected, Hayward told the president, and it was generally believed that at any one time half the people in the Navy were high on drugs. It would take some of the most seismic events in Cold War history to shock Carter into a major investment in national defense and a massive military commitment to Persian Gulf stability, one that would expand dramatically over the following three decades.

On November 4, 1979, eight months after the popular overthrow of Iran's Shah Mohammad Reza Pahlavi, hundreds of students stormed the U.S. embassy in Tehran and took the staff hostage. Inspired by radical clerics, they demanded the return for trial of the shah, who was in America undergoing medical treatment; the release of Iran's overseas assets frozen by Washington since the revolution; and a U.S. apology for its past meddling in Iranian affairs, beginning with the CIA's 1953 coup against Mohammad Mossadegh, the country's freely elected prime minister.* An April 1980 attempt to rescue the sixty hostages failed with the deaths of eight servicemen when two of the mission's aircraft, evacuating a rendezvous site in a remote strip of Iranian desert, collided in a sandstorm. The 444-day crisis ended only after Carter stepped down.

Just sixteen days after the embassy siege, unrest among religious radicals in Saudi Arabia angry at reforms promoted by King Fahd bin Abdul Aziz Al Saud climaxed with an assault on the Grand Mosque in Mecca, the holiest shrine in Islam. Royal troops cleared the site two weeks later and the surviving insurgents were publicly beheaded, but the incident broke Fahd's nerve. To pacify conservatives, the king pledged a "Fundamental Law" that enshrined much of the extremists' agenda. Hairdressing salons were closed, female broadcasters were removed from television broadcasts, and girls were banned from attending schools outside the kingdom. Though largely overlooked in the United States, the Grand Mosque crisis led to Saudi Arabia's self-imposed exile from modernity, the implications of which would reveal themselves with staggering effect two decades later.

On December 27, having already dispatched two airborne battalions to Afghanistan to repel an Islamist rebellion waged against its erstwhile ally in Kabul, the Soviet Union unleashed a massive invasion of the country. It was widely perceived as a show of contempt in Moscow for détente, which was already under attack in Washington as a one-way street, and as the debut of a new, more provocative USSR with obvious designs on the Persian Gulf. Deciphering the attack as a consequence of American weakness, Zbigniew Brzezinski, Carter's hawkish national security adviser, wrote in his journal: "Had we been tougher sooner, had we drawn the line more clearly . . . maybe the Soviets would not have engaged in this kind of miscalculation."

The Soviets indeed miscalculated, though not for want of U.S. resolve. According to declassified Russian documents, the Soviet occupation of Afghanistan was a purely defensive response to an Islamic insurgency and an imagined CIA plot against its most vulnerable flank.† For Moscow, a stable,

---

* This was a disingenuous demand if ever there was one; Iran's Islamists despised the secular and aristocratic Mossadegh almost as much as they did the CIA.
† Collections are available at the Cold War International History Project at the Woodrow Wilson Center in Washington, D.C., as well as materials from the National Security Archive, also in Washington, D.C. For individual citations, see source notes.

nonhostile Afghanistan was a vital cushion against the tremors of a radical Islam radiating from the Middle East. The Soviet empire, after all, numbered among its subjects some 40 million Muslims in the central Asian republics, many of whom had separatist inclinations. The declassified archive makes clear that Moscow had no designs on the Persian Gulf, a misperception that motivated Carter's militarist claim on the region, which unlike the Nixon Doctrine not only survived but has been greatly embellished upon. Nor was the invasion a Soviet bid to exploit post-Vietnam American insecurities, as claimed by Brzezinski, or a move on the Indian Ocean in pursuit of a warm-water port, as has also been suggested.

Brzezinski and other senior U.S. officials may be forgiven their misreading of Soviet intentions, however, for the poor and incomplete information they were getting from Kabul. American agents took Soviet influence in Afghanistan for granted and, having expended little energy recruiting Afghan sources, knew little of the evolving Islamist movement there. A top-secret memo prepared for Brzezinski in September 1979—drawn from all available intelligence sources and titled "What are the Soviets doing in Afghanistan?"—began with the forlorn conclusion "Simply, we don't know." Indeed, the most favorable thing one might say about the CIA's record in the run-up to the Soviet invasion of Afghanistan is that the KGB's performance was even worse.

Throughout much of the nineteenth century, Afghanistan was the chessboard in the imperial rivalry between Russia and Great Britain, the "Great Game" of Victorian superpower intrigue. By the dawn of the next century, however, the country had dwindled in strategic importance. Landlocked and poor, without easy access to either the Persian Gulf or the Indian Ocean, Afghanistan was largely ignored by both sides during the Cold War. Though Moscow suspected the United States might covet bases there as part of its containment strategy, no such plans existed. In 1954 CIA director Allen Dulles even shrugged that the USSR was "inclined to look on Afghanistan much as the United States did Guatemala." In the words of historian David Gibbs, "A more accurate comparison might be the way the United States viewed Mexico, i.e., as a country on its immediate border and therefore a security concern of special importance."

By the 1950s, Moscow had become Afghanistan's primary patron for economic and military aid, a fact that barely registered in Washington. In 1954, the National Security Council determined that the U.S. response to a hypothetical Soviet attack on Afghanistan should be limited to "diplomatic measures . . . to obtain prompt withdrawal of Soviet forces" while leaving any further action to the United Nations.

It was the shah of Iran who, as part of his ambitions to make his country a regional power, sought to lure Afghanistan away from the Soviet sphere of influence. In 1973, with U.S. support, he offered to outbid Moscow for the loyalties of then Afghan prime minister Mohammed Daud. A deal was struck, and Daud quickly set about repressing local communist groups until he provoked a backlash. In April 1978, putschists deposed and killed Daud and set up a Marxist government. Within months, it too was targeted by a revolt, this time from Islamists opposed to the communists' godless credo. On March 17, 1979, senior Soviet leaders convened to discuss the deteriorating conditions in Kabul and how to respond to them. According to transcripts of the meeting, KGB chief Yuri Andropov strongly opposed armed intervention, declaring that "in such a situation, tanks and armored cars cannot save anything." Foreign Minister Andrei Gromyko agreed, warning his counterparts that the invasion would devastate U.S.-Soviet rapprochement. "All that we have done in recent years with such effort in terms of détente, arms control, and much more—all that would be thrown back . . . and what would we gain?" Gromyko noted that Afghanistan had little to offer Moscow with its "inconsequential weight in international affairs," and he admonished his comrades to "keep in mind that from a legal point of view too we would not be justified in sending troops."

For much of 1979, Moscow rejected requests from the Afghan government for direct Soviet assistance against the mujahideen forces. This was despite the fact that Carter in July had ordered the CIA to support the Islamic insurgency with medicine, money, and propaganda, which the Soviet media naturally trumpeted as a bid by Washington to destabilize Moscow's southern frontier. (Robert Gates, who worked for Brzezinski during the Carter years, cites the order in his memoirs to rebut charges that the administration was late in responding to what he described, wrongfully, as Soviet designs on its neighbor.)

The Kremlin was even beginning to doubt the legitimacy of Afghanistan's national leader, an architect of the 1978 coup named Hafizullah Amin. Moscow took an even dimmer view of Amin after he consolidated power by killing a close rival in defiance of Soviet appeals against such a move. In an attempt to undermine him, the KGB began spreading rumors that Amin, who briefly attended Columbia University in New York, was on the CIA's payroll. Amin was subsequently reported to have met on several occasions with American diplomats in Kabul, prompting Russian agents to conclude that the U.S. government was trying to recruit him.

Not only did Amin have no relations with the CIA, at least according to the Kabul station chief when asked by American diplomats about the KGB's gossip campaign, embassy officials regarded him as a thug complicit in the recent kidnapping and murder of U.S. ambassador Adolph Dubs. What limited contact U.S. officials did have with the putative Afghan leader revealed little beyond his loathing for the United States—informed, apparently, by his two failed attempts to earn a Ph.D. at Columbia University.

None of this, however, was filtering back to Moscow, which was now reconsidering its earlier opposition to armed intervention in Afghanistan. In early December 1979, Andropov warned Soviet premier Leonid Brezhnev in a personal memorandum that Amin was an American agent, the trump card in a grand conspiracy "to create a 'New Great Ottoman Empire' including the southern republics of the Soviet Union." Concerns about Amin's loyalty, according to author Steve Coll, "accelerated the timetable for decision making, encouraged the Politburo's inner circle to think they faced devious CIA intrigues in Kabul, and helped encourage them that only drastic measures could succeed." In a typically too-weird-to-make-up moment so common to Cold War espionage, the USSR launched one of the era's greatest provocations over a paranoid delusion.

The invasion transformed the Carter presidency, which was already toughening its relations with Moscow under pressure from hard-liners in Congress. Earlier in the year, largely to generate support for SALT II, the administration had authorized production of 200 MX missiles and had deployed ground-launched cruise missiles and medium-range Pershing IIs in Europe. Now, with Soviet troops poised on the rim of the Persian Gulf, Carter intensified the process with a 10 percent increase in the Pentagon's 1980 budget and a five-year arms buildup program. He initiated a sweeping defense organization study that recommended strengthening the role of the Joint Chiefs and upgrading the management responsibilities of the service secretaries. He cut grain shipments to Moscow—against the advice of his vice president, Walter Mondale, who warned that such a move would cost him votes in the Midwest—and he announced that the United States would boycott the 1980 Winter Olympics, to be held in Moscow. He also declared, without referring to the USSR by name, that a Soviet march on the Persian Gulf would mean a third world war. The Carter Doctrine, as it became known, included the creation of a rapid deployment force, the genesis of what is now Central Command, or CENTCOM, one of the Pentagon's most powerful combatant commands.

Finally, Carter promulgated a new presidential directive, PD-59, which endorsed the prospect of waging an extended nuclear war, rather than the kind of all-out onslaught as laid out in SIOP. "If deterrence fails," according to the directive, "we must be capable of fighting successfully so that the adversary would not achieve his war aims and would suffer costs that are unacceptable, or in any event greater than his gains, from having initiated an attack." The concept of prolonged nuclear war implied a shift away from the strategy of mutual assured destruction (MAD), under which both Washington and Moscow targeted population centers rather than military installations, and called instead for an attack on the Soviet leadership, or, in the ghoulish parlance of the time, "decapitation." Thanks to one of the more bizarre of Cold War conversions, Jimmy Carter the dove would leave the White House primed for his successor to launch a massive military buildup that would take American militarization to a new level. As Robert Gates writes in his memoirs, "Carter laid down the foundations for much of what Ronald Reagan would undertake in the defense area, albeit with a vastly increased budget and genuine presidential enthusiasm. That's a fact, despite how distasteful partisans on both sides of the political fence might find it."

In March 1980, Brzezinski asked CIA director Stansfield Turner to evaluate whether Moscow's occupation of Afghanistan was an aberration in Soviet behavior or a glimpse of a more aggressive Moscow that might upend the global power balance. The assessment, prepared by mid-April, concluded that "the possibility that Afghanistan represents a qualitative turn in Soviet foreign policy in the region and toward the third world should be taken seriously." In his cover letter to Brzezinski, Turner suggested that détente was all but dead, though "how assertive the Soviets will be in the future will very likely depend upon how 'successful' the Soviet leadership views their intervention in Afghanistan to have been." Seemingly alone in clearheaded analysis among Carter's top aides was Secretary of State Cyrus Vance. In his memoirs, published in 1983, Vance argues that Moscow's move on Afghanistan was a bid to preempt a potentially destabilizing power vacuum that might well have followed Amin's demise. "They feared that the regime would be replaced by a fundamentalist Islamic government and that this would, in turn, be followed by a spread of 'Khomeini fever' to other nations along Russia's southern border." Vance also reasoned that Moscow may have acted out of frustration with legislative foot-dragging on the SALT accords. "If, as is likely," he wrote, "Moscow had decided by late December that the SALT Treaty was in deep trouble, that access to American trade and technology was drying up . . . , it probably concluded that there was little reason to show restraint in dealing with a dangerous problem on its border."

Within a few years, it was obvious that Moscow had committed a titanic blunder. The Soviet army was bogged down in its own Vietnam: an insurgency waged by mujahideen fighters and covertly supported by Washington that bled the empire white. By the time Soviet forces withdrew from Afghanistan in February 1989, the Soviet system was on the brink of collapse.

All of this, however, would be revealed long after Moscow's invasion had seemingly vindicated the Committee on the Present Danger, the public lobby group led by anticommunist hawks who had attacked Carter from the start of his administration for not being tough enough with the Russians. They were mostly Democrats, a tightly knit and intellectually inbred group of agitators who spent much of their careers on the margins of policymaking. Their benefactor at the time was a powerful senator named Henry "Scoop" Jackson and their apostle was the inimitable Paul Nitze, pied piper to the many ghosts and goblins that transfixed American militarists throughout the Cold War.

The neoconservative movement in America—the name was coined by Michael Harrington in a 1973 article he wrote for *Dissent* magazine about welfare policy—began largely as a reaction against the Democratic Party's lurch against the war in Vietnam. In 1972 policymakers and intellectuals such as Eugene Rostow, the former undersecretary of state for political affairs, Georgetown University professor Jeane Kirkpatrick, and Harvard Russian studies expert Richard Pipes formed the Coalition for a Democratic Majority in an effort to revive the Democrats' anticommunist vigor as embodied by party standard-bearer Harry Truman. They saw themselves as the vanguard of an existential conflict with the Soviet Union, a Wagnerian struggle with no shades of gray. Talk of arms reduction, they argued, was code for disarmament. Détente was a Trojan horse for Soviet expansion. Containment was capitulation. There could be no coexistence with the communist evil, they argued. One way or another, it had to be destroyed.

Angered by the way Richard Nixon abandoned the global struggle for détente and arms control negotiations, they turned instead to men such as Nitze, who undermined Nixon's arms-reduction efforts for fear he would barter away national security as a way to salvage his scandal-ridden presidency. In a January 1976 article in *Foreign Affairs,* Nitze warned that the Soviets would betray their commitments under the Strategic Arms Limitation Talks and scheme "to produce a theoretical war-winning capability." He urged the discarding of MAD—which because of the higher stakes involved was a more compelling deterrent against a nuclear exchange—for the more offensive "counterforce" posture of targeting Soviet military sites. Moscow, he argued, regarded nuclear war as just another military option against its Cold War rival and Americans were naive not to do the same.

As we will see, what Nitze had to say about Soviet motives and capabilities in the 1970s and 1980s was as much alarmist nonsense as it was in the 1950s and 1960s. He had, however, a powerful ally in senior RAND fellow Albert Wohlstetter. Wohlstetter's charges that the CIA had grossly underestimated the number of Soviet ICBMs so electrified Republican hard-liners that President Gerald Ford, under fire by fellow Republican Ronald Reagan, his conservative challenger in the 1976 presidential campaign, allowed Nitze and his acolytes to cross-examine CIA analysts.

Nitze formed a panel that would become known as Team B. It enjoyed the support of White House chief of staff Dick Cheney, while William Colby, the CIA's outgoing director, opposed the very notion of an ad hoc group second-guessing his experts. Colby's successor, George H. W. Bush, reluctantly went ahead with the exercise as a bone for the Republican Party's increasingly assertive conservative wing. In addition to Nitze, Team B was led by Wohlstetter and Nitze's protégé Richard Perle, as well as a young aide to Senator Jackson named Paul Wolfowitz. Other team members included General Daniel Graham, the chief of defense intelligence who would become a prime advocate for the Pentagon's strategic missile defense system, and Richard Pipes, who in addition to his work at Harvard also advised Senator Jackson. For the men of Team B, there was no such thing as "overkill" within the context of nuclear warfare. In an article for *Commentary*, Pipes scorned the U.S. intelligence community for being "no more prepared to take seriously the proposition that nuclear weapons might be effective instruments of warfare than to waste time proving the world is not flat."

It was clear upon their first meeting with their CIA counterparts, dubbed Team A, that there would be no convivial exchange of views. The CIA had put up a group of guileless midlevel officials, none of whom expected the mauling they received from Nitze, the sharp-elbowed insider, and the evangelical mad-genius Wohlstetter. Asked by a reporter for comment on Team B's performance, an account of which had been leaked to the *Boston Globe*, former CIA deputy director Ray Cline lamented how "the process of making national security estimates [had] been subverted by . . . a kangaroo court of outside critics all picked from one point of view." Not surprisingly, the two teams submitted entirely different reports. While Team A acknowledged an aggressive Soviet game of catch-up and offered estimates of when Moscow might achieve parity with Washington, Team B stressed the relentless threat of Soviet hegemony and the increasing accuracy of its missiles, an assessment rejected by the Air Force chief of intelligence. Its final report was embroidered with Nitze's trademark alarmism. "While hoping to crush the capitalist realm by other than military means," it warned, "the Soviet Union is nevertheless preparing for a Third World War as if it were unavoidable." Within ten years, Moscow would command "a degree of military superiority which would permit a dramatically more aggressive pursuit of their hegemonial objectives . . . in the belief that such superior military force can pressure the West to acquiesce or, if not, can be used to win a military contest at any level."

Though Bush was dismissive of the interlopers' conclusions, Team B's dire warnings were echoed in the CIA's National Intelligence Estimate for 1976, which the *New York Times* reported "flatly states that the Soviet Union is seeking superiority over United States forces." The *Times* account, which featured no voices critical of Team B, was emblematic of a growing rightward trend in the established media in its coverage of national security affairs. An October 29, 1979, *Time* cover story, for example, concluded that "the nation's most fundamental social-welfare obligation to its citizen is to defend them against attack . . . [but] the U.S. military has been denied sufficient resources to fulfill its responsibility." Earlier, in its April 3, 1978, edition, *Time* had asked a panel of experts that included three hawks and one centrist whether the United States could defend itself against Soviet aggression. The answer, not surprisingly, was negative. One of the participants, Edward Luttwak, even sketched his version of what arch neoconservative Norman Podhoretz in his 1980 tract *The Present Danger* called "the Finlandization of America, the political and economic subordination of the United States to superior Soviet power." Luttwak went on:

> The Soviet Union's continuing nuclear and conventional military buildup is increasingly ominous and may jeopardize the delicate balance of power that has deterred nuclear war. . . . Moscow could . . . say to the west, "Gentlemen, we are superior in ground forces, we can take most of West Germany in 48 hours, you cannot checkmate that by strategic nuclear forces, for you no longer have superiority. Now we want to collect."

New York Times defense correspondent Drew Middleton habitually conveyed the Soviet threat in alarmist terms. In a February 1979 story headlined SOVIETS SAID TO WIDEN ARMS-SPENDING GAP, he reported that the decade ending 1978 was marked by a "pattern . . . of continuous growth" in Soviet military spending versus a "downward trend" in U.S. defense outlays. On October 14, Middleton colleague Richard Burt wrote that many experts believed the United States did not "possess sufficient military power to discharge the commitments it is taking on" and compared the U.S. military's lot to Britain's after World War II. In the aftermath of the Soviet invasion of Afghanistan, Middleton's stories led a pack of overwrought reportage that was redolent of Team B's throaty predictions. "The conventional wisdom in the Pentagon," he reported in January 1980, "is that in purely military terms, the Russians are in a far better position vis-à-vis the United States than Hitler was against Britain and France in 1939." *Newsweek*'s Tom Matthews, meanwhile, declared that the "Soviet thrust" represented a "severe threat" to U.S. interests. Under a story headlined THE CHILL OF A NEW COLD WAR, Matthews wrote that Soviet control of Afghanistan "would put the Russians within 350 miles of the Arabian Sea, the oil lifeline of the West and Japan."

Team B effectively folded itself into the Committee on the Present Danger, the revival of which was inspired by Eugene Rostow over several rounds of Bloody Marys on Thanksgiving Day 1975. The CPD's mission statement—*The principal threat to our nation, to world peace, and to the cause of human freedom is the Soviet drive for world dominance*—was a concise summation of its Hobbesian worldview. Its founding members included prominent conservatives such as Ronald Reagan, but it was run largely by Nitze from offices overlooking the Potomac River that were donated by the Systems Planning Corporation, an Arlington-based defense contracting firm. From there, Nitze and his allies prepared to do battle with the Carter administration and its menacing emphasis on human rights and arms reduction.

Nitze would strike a lucrative alliance with "Scoop" Jackson, the hawkish senator from Washington State. The two men had known each other since the Truman years, and Jackson would prove a loyal friend to Nitze for much of his career. Though a Democrat, Jackson was among the most hard-line adversaries against arms control negotiations. In a bid to gain Jackson's support for, or at least neutralize his opposition to, the next SALT round, Richard Nixon had purged the independent Arms Control and Disarmament Agency of anyone objectionable to the senator. Richard Perle was particularly effective in sullying ACDA members with what he called "knee-jerk arms-controlitis." Among the new guard installed at the ACDA was Wolfowitz, a close Perle associate and a Wohlstetter protégé.

Nixon's attempt to pacify Jackson and like-minded hawks, however, only emboldened them in their assault on arms reduction talks of any kind. The Committee on the Present Danger declared that the United States should muster both the capacity and the will to launch a first-strike response to the USSR's nuclear buildup, which it said was "reminiscent of Nazi Germany's rearmament in the 1930s." As author Peter Scoblic writes, "The CPD saw itself as a collection of Churchills facing a country of Chamberlains." When Carter and Brezhnev signed SALT II in Vienna on June 18, 1979, after two years of negotiations, Jackson attacked it as "appeasement in its purest form" and pledged to work against its confirmation. Joining in the attack was Donald Rumsfeld, Ford's defense secretary, who called instead for a $44 billion increase in defense spending and warned that "our nation's situation is much more dangerous today than it has been at any time since Neville Chamberlain left Munich, setting the stage for World War II."

SALT II allowed for slightly larger arms reductions than those provided under the framework agreement left behind by the Ford administration. It was opposed by the defense establishment, not only by Rumsfeld but also by General Edward Rowny, the Joint Chiefs of Staff representative to the SALT II delegation and a mole for Jackson and Perle. For the first time in its fifteen-year history, ACDA aligned itself with the Pentagon and against the State Department in its opposition to arms control. Ronald Reagan, his eye on the White House, blamed SALT II's architects for having presided over the "neglect" of American defenses.

In his memoirs, Cyrus Vance, Carter's secretary of state, acknowledged that "the president was probably right when he told me that many Republicans, as well as Democratic Senator Henry Jackson, were going to oppose the treaty no matter what was in it." In the end, however, the furor over SALT II was engulfed by the storm created by the Soviet invasion of Afghanistan. In the panic that followed, Carter jettisoned his own treaty rather than risk its rejection by the Senate. Though he would spend the rest of his crippled presidency edging ever closer to the world as the CPD beheld it, nothing would help him come election time, particularly with hard-liners in his own party. With the exception of Henry Jackson, no one was more closely associated with the neoconservative vision than the Republican Ronald Reagan, who swept to the White House in 1980 on the promise of rebuilding America's enfeebled defenses against the pernicious Russian bear.

Détente was now dead. The militarists had prevailed. Their messiah had come.

11
―
1983

Fear is a very dangerous thing. . . . It may act as a deterrent in
people's minds against war, but it is much more likely to make them
want to increase armaments.
—British prime minister Stanley Baldwin in a speech to the
House of Commons, November 10, 1932

I N May 1981, Yuri Andropov, the then head of the Soviet
KGB, informed his subordinates at a conference in Moscow that
America was readying a preemptive nuclear strike on the Soviet
Union. The situation was so grave, he said, that for the first time in So-
viet history the KGB and its military counterpart, the GRU, would work
jointly in the largest intelligence-gathering mission Moscow had ever
conducted in peacetime. Andropov dubbed the operation RYAN, the
Russian acronym for "Surprise Nuclear Missile Attack."

It would be a classic gumshoe job. With the help of electronic listening devices, agents attached to Soviet embassies in NATO countries and
Japan were to engage in "close observation of all political, military, and
intelligence activities that might indicate preparation for mobilization."
Were senior Defense Ministry officials keeping unusually late hours?
Had cable traffic from Foreign Ministries to their embassies abroad intensified? Were medical centers stocking up on blood supplies? Were
weekend passes at military outposts abruptly canceled and were troops
shipping out on unscheduled deployments? Agents were to keep an especially tight watch on bankers, as "they would have some kind of advance
warning because the nature of the capitalist system was such that the leading capitalists would be commissioned to try to keep some kind of credit
system going after the battle of Armageddon."

Soviet officials with experience in the West believed Andropov's scheme was an overreaction to the results of the U.S. presidential election the previous fall. True, the new president, Ronald Reagan, was by any measure an iron-clad Cold Warrior. He had campaigned against what he called Jimmy Carter's sluggish response to Soviet advances on Afghanistan, Latin America, and parts of Africa. He had accused his predecessor of disarming the United States in the face of a massive Soviet buildup in strategic weaponry, and he disdained arms control agreements. In a spring 1981 address at the University of Notre Dame, he declared that the West "will not contain Communism, it will transcend Communism. We'll dismiss it as a sad, bizarre chapter in human history whose last pages are even now being written." But such rhetoric, assured Kremlin Occidentalists, was surely a kabuki dance to pacify extremists in the Republican Party. Nixon had charted the same course en route to the White House, they reasoned, and he rode it all the way to Beijing. Though a true conservative and no fan of détente, Ronald Reagan was not so crazy as to unleash a third world war, at least not without provocation.

In fact, soon after settling into the Oval Office, Reagan promulgated a series of operations and directives that gave the Soviets every reason to believe he was preparing a military assault on the communist world. Within days of his inauguration, he green-lighted an operation hatched by the new CIA director, William Casey, that would needle the Soviets on all fronts. Under the plan, which was so secret it had no code name, U.S. bombers would head deliberately for Soviet airspace over the North Pole, only to reverse course once they had triggered enemy alert systems. Fighter-bombers would taunt Soviet pilots over Asia and Europe from the limits of international airspace. Allied maneuvers would suddenly increase in intensity and at irregular intervals, only to return to normal tempo. The plan was designed to have a domesticating effect on Moscow, to make it "less prone to take risks," according to Reagan hagiographer Peter Schweizer. Not surprisingly for anyone who understands human nature, it had the opposite effect, placing Soviet radar operators and trip-wire forces on knife-edge. Andropov, once dismissed by Kremlin elites as paranoid, was looking prophetic.

Moscow had other reasons to believe the Reagan administration was serious about "rolling back" communism, a significantly more aggressive Cold War posture than the containment doctrine on which U.S. policy had long been predicated. The Soviets were already unnerved by PD-59, the presidential directive signed by President Carter in response to the Soviet invasion of Afghanistan, which called for the capacity to fight prolonged nuclear conflicts and to "decapitate" the USSR leadership in the process. The concept of protracted nuclear war, in which major cities on both sides would be held hostage to the next cycle of attacks, was eagerly adopted by the Reagan White House. In a 1980 essay they had written titled "Victory is Possible," defense strategists Colin Gray and Keith Payne argued that a key Soviet weakness, and thus a prime target in a nuclear exchange, was Moscow's centralized command chain and highly concentrated security apparatus. "If the Moscow bureaucracy could be eliminated, damaged, or isolated," the authors explained, "the USSR might disintegrate into anarchy."

Nor did Reagan's peacetime military buildup, the largest in U.S. history, inspire much confidence within the Kremlin. He would raise defense spending to $265 billion by 1986, up 72 percent from Carter's own aggressive increase in fiscal year 1981. In his first five years in office, he would shower nearly as much money on the Pentagon as had Ford, Nixon, and Carter combined. He ordered dramatic increases in the production of conventional weapons—tanks, attack helicopters, battleships, fighter jets—together with a massive increase in the number of nuclear warheads and delivery systems. He reactivated the B-1 bomber and the neutron bomb programs, both canceled by Carter, and he authorized the deployment of 3,000 cruise missiles and aircraft to deliver them.* He also accelerated production of the submarine-based Trident II nuclear missile as well as the B-2 bomber.

It was not just the size of Reagan's budget that aroused Andropov and other Kremlin hawks. Parsing through the outlays, they would have noted a $20 billion expenditure for the upgrade of the Pentagon's command, control, communications, and intelligence nodes, or C3I, for years the most vulnerable component of both American and Soviet nuclear arsenals. By modernizing the vast network of satellites, telecommunications

---

* The neutron bomb was a fission-fusion tactical weapon designed to destroy its target by releasing neutron radiation rather than an explosive force typical of a fission-type atomic bomb. Simply put, it was built to kill people while preserving buildings and infrastructure.

systems, and radars that served as the nerve center for America's nuclear force, according to strategic analyst John D. Steinbruner, the United States was erecting a command structure that would have been perceived by Moscow "as a sign of increased willingness to initiate war."

Lest anyone dare think the Reagan buildup was a feint, an opening gambit in a bid to open arms-reduction talks from a position of strength, Secretary of Defense Caspar Weinberger told the press soon after his confirmation that such negotiations would have to wait until after the C3I modernization plan was completed and the United States had deployed its neutron bomb in Europe. Though Weinberger was speaking somewhat out of turn, he was only reflecting his boss's lack of faith in arms control agreements. As early as September 1979, Reagan asked rhetorically in a radio address whether "arms limitation agreements, even good ones, really bring or preserve peace? History would seem to say 'No.'" His knowledge of arms control negotiations was limited to what he read in *The Treaty Trap: A History of the Performance of Political Treaties by the United States and European Nations,* an obscure 1969 tract written by the ex-actor's old Hollywood pal, a lawyer named Laurence Beilenson. According to Beilenson, states respect treaty obligations only when it is in their interests to do so and inevitably abrogate them. Reagan hailed the book as "the best book written on defense" and cited it during his 1981 commencement address at West Point. The *Treaty Trap,* he declared, "makes plain that no nation that placed its faith in parchment or paper, while at the same time it gave up on its protective hardware, ever lasted long enough to write many pages of history." It was in this spirit that his nuclear experts would stall talks with Moscow aimed at eliminating intermediate-range missiles in Europe, a negotiating round they inherited from the Carter administration. Later, they would sabotage the talks altogether.

The Reagan military buildup was necessary, according to its architects, to check what they said was Soviet parity on some fronts in the superpower confrontation and a mushrooming superiority on others— what the neoconservative Committee on the Present Danger had called America's "window of vulnerability." In a speech delivered on October 31, 1983, Deputy Secretary of State Kenneth Dam declared that the United States and the Soviet Union were locked in a decisive confrontation for control of such strategically important regions as Latin America and the Middle East. This superpower duel would continue, he said, until the Kremlin relinquished its "quest for absolute security," and he warned that relations would be strained for some time. "We should be wary of illusions about the possibility of quick or dramatic breakthroughs," he said.

Secretary of State Alexander Haig was even harsher. "Moscow," he said shortly after taking office, "is the greatest source of international insecurity today. Soviet promotion of violence as the instrument of change constitutes the greatest danger to world peace." In April 1981 he said there was "no useful purpose" in engaging in arms talks with Moscow so long as the Soviets continued their "imperialist activities abroad." To Undersecretary of State for Political Affairs Lawrence Eagleburger, the USSR was "not only our rival, but the rival of a humane world order," he said in February 1983. "We will not see the day of days with the Soviet Union. Our rivalry will, I fear, outlive everyone in this room."

Few senior officials in the new administration, particularly members of Team B, the neoconservative panel set up to bird-dog the CIA, would allow that the Soviet system might be crumbling under its own weight. Those who did, including the president himself, suggested economic debility made the Soviet threat more, not less, pernicious, which rendered the need for the USSR's removal all the more urgent. Reagan had said as much in a speech to the British Parliament at Westminster on June 8, 1982. He characterized the Soviet Union as an empire "that runs against the tide of history by denying human freedom and human dignity to its citizens" and pledged "open assistance . . . to foster democratic change" in Eastern Europe and in the Soviet Union itself. The Kremlin, not irrationally, perceived this as a declaration of war against communism. As it turned out, Reagan's speech to Parliament was a public projection of National Security Decision Directive 32, which according to White House Soviet expert Thomas Reed advocated "the dissolution of the Soviet empire."

There were other signs of a growing U.S. militarism. The Kremlin would have duly noted Reagan's appointment of Richard Pipes as National Security Council adviser, a leader of Team B and a Russian specialist who believed that "all the evidence points to an undeviating

Soviet commitment to what is euphemistically called the 'worldwide triumph of socialism' but in fact connotes global Soviet hegemony." Moscow would have seized upon an August 1982 story in the *Los Angeles
Times* about National Security Decision Directive 13, signed by Reagan in
late 1981, which was the first executive document to declare that a nuclear
war could be won. Politburo members would have pored over the trans-
lated testimony given by Reagan aides during their Senate confirmation
hearings, talking blithely about the prospects for fighting and winning
nuclear wars. Among them was Eugene Rostow, who, ironically enough,
was appointed the director of the White House Arms Control and Disarmament Agency. When asked whether he believed the United States
could survive a nuclear attack, Rostow noted cheerfully that Japan "not
only survived but flourished" after it endured the two atomic blasts that
leveled Hiroshima and Nagasaki. Pushed further to consider the devastation that would follow an all-out nuclear strike, Rostow replied that
"the human race is very resilient. . . . Depending upon certain assumptions, some estimates predict that there would be ten million casualties
on one side and one hundred million on another. But that is not the
whole of the population." If that wasn't enough to rattle Kremlin octoge-
narians, imagine their reaction to remarks made to the *Los Angeles Times*
by Thomas K. Jones, Reagan's deputy undersecretary of defense, about
the survivability of a thermonuclear war: "Dig a hole, cover it with a couple
of doors, and then throw three feet of dirt on top. Everyone's going to
make it if there are enough shovels to go around."

Summing up the first several months of the new administration's Soviet policy, *Foreign Policy* editor Charles William Maynes rued how the
president "has publicly blamed the Soviet Union for all events abroad
adverse to U.S. interests [and] he has asserted that Soviet leaders will
resort to any tactics to achieve their revolutionary goals." Senior administration officials, Maynes wrote, have declared that "war is inevitable,"
while their Soviet counterparts "contend privately that the United States is
increasing arms expenditure at the worst possible moment. They argue
that having achieved nuclear parity, [Moscow] was ready to level off its
strategic programs but that the Reagan administration is now reopening
the arms race with its massive defense programs."

To make matters more precarious, the Kremlin was entering a fragile leadership transition. Leonid Brezhnev, the aging general secretary, died in November 1982. He was succeeded by Andropov, whose brainchild, Operation RYAN, was expanded in scope and intensity. That summer, Nikolai Ogarkov, the Soviet chief of staff and deputy defense minister, told a gathering of Warsaw Pact leaders in Minsk that the United States was openly preparing for war on a range of fronts—political, economic, diplomatic, as well as military. "In several fields, the battle is already going on," Ogarkov said. "The risk of war is as high as ever."

Such was the state of superpower relations on the eve of 1983, the year Washington and Moscow came closer to waging nuclear war than they had in twenty years.

On the seismograph of Cold War confrontation, there was the occasional spike of a near miss, an isolated event when, for a few terrifying moments, the fate of humanity was in play. We now know, for example, that at the peak of the Cuban missile crisis, a sabotage alarm sounded at a military base in Minnesota was mistaken at Wisconsin's Volk Field for the signal to "scramble all jets." As the pilots fired up their aircraft, no doubt presuming a Soviet attack was under way, the base commander finally identified the error and intercepted the lead jet with his jeep just as it was pivoting on the runway to begin takeoff. In another close call during the crisis, on October 27, a U-2 spy plane had mistakenly flown deep into Russian airspace for about ten hours, an incursion that could have been interpreted as the vanguard of a U.S. attack. The pilot managed to guide his craft back to a friendly base in Alaska, ending what is still known as "Black Saturday."

At least three times in 1980, the U.S. early-warning computer system failed, signaling combat-alert orders to American strategic forces. During one such mishap, President Carter's national security adviser, Zbigniew Brzezinski, was rattled awake at 3:00 a.m. by his military assistant, Colonel William Odom, who informed his boss that Moscow had launched some 220 missiles against the United States. Brzezinski told Odom that he wanted confirmation before awakening the president, who would have less than seven minutes to decide whether or not to retaliate. A few minutes later, Odom phoned Brzezinski and told him there had been a mistake; the early-warning system was now reporting the launch of *2,200* missiles, a full Soviet strike only minutes away from its targets.

Then, seconds before Brzezinski was to phone President Carter, Odom called a third time. The Soviet "attack," he informed Brzezinski, had not been detected by any other radar systems. It was just a glitch in the early-warning grid.

"Sitting alone in the middle of the night," Robert Gates, who worked in the Carter White House as well as successive Republican administrations, writes in his memoirs, "Brzezinski had not awakened his wife, reckoning that everyone would be dead in half an hour." According to Gates, the CIA learned that the Soviets interpreted these events not as failures but as a deliberate plan to ease Moscow into "a false sense of security by giving the impression that such errors were possible, and thereby diminish Soviet concerns over future alerts—thus providing a cover for possible surprise attack."*

Though it did not seem quite so dire at the time, 1983 ranks alongside 1962 as a defining moment of "high" Cold War. It began with the Reagan administration's declaration that it would deploy intermediate-range Pershing II missiles as a counterweight to Soviet SS-20s. The introduction of the Pershings effectively gave NATO a nuclear deterrent independent of Washington's and a first-strike capability that could destroy numerous Soviet cities within four to six minutes after launch. Moscow interpreted the Pershing deployment as a mirror image of the Cuban missile crisis. In January, Andropov warned a gathering of the Warsaw Pact's Political Consultative Committee of a "new round of the arms race, imposed by the USA, [which] has major, qualitative differences." Whereas Washington once spoke of strategic forces as a tool of deterrence and intimidation, Andropov said, "now . . . they do not hide the fact that they are really intended for a future war. From here spring the doctrines of 'rational' and 'limited' nuclear war; from here spring the statements

---

* Such miscues continued well into the post–Cold War era. On January 25, 1995, Russian president Boris Yeltsin was notified that radar systems had picked up a missile launch that may well have been from a U.S. nuclear submarine ordered to destroy the Russian leadership. Yeltsin gathered his senior defense officials in a teleconference to discuss whether or not to respond in kind. Minutes later, it was revealed that the "missile" was in reality a rocket launched by Norwegian scientists.

about the possibility of surviving and winning a protracted nuclear conflict. It is hard to say what is blackmail and what is genuine readiness to take the fatal step."

Not to be outdone, Reagan delivered what would be the peroration of his ongoing herald against communist villainy. On March 8, at the annual convention of the National Association of Evangelicals in Orlando, he called the Soviet Union "an evil empire" and "the focus of evil in the modern world." The speech, among the most memorable of the Cold War and a prelude to the wrathful Pentecostalism that fuels the conservative movement today, was an appeal for the rejection of the nuclear freeze movement. "We know that living in this world means dealing with . . . evil or, as theologians would put it, the doctrine of sin," said Reagan. "There is sin and there is evil in the world, and we're enjoined to oppose it with all our might." For militants in the Kremlin, godless apparatchiks all, this was the highest form of redemption. According to Vladimir Slipchenko, a member of the Soviet general staff, Reagan's "evil empire" speech was seized upon "as a reason to begin a very intense preparation inside the military for a state of war. . . . For the military, the period when we were called the evil empire was actually very good and useful, because we achieved a very high military readiness."

Throughout the spring, the U.S. Pacific Fleet was maneuvering within a few hundred miles of Soviet waters, part of the CIA's cat-and-mouse game that had been authorized by the White House. The deployment included three aircraft carrier battle groups at sea as well as Air Force B-52s soaring aloft, plus antisubmarine aircraft and attack submarines. For the first time, they were operating in the same waters where Soviet subs routinely patrolled. It would have been impossible for the Soviets to have missed the U.S. operation, so close was it to their intelligence hub on the Kamchatka Peninsula on Russia's east coast. Nearly a month after Reagan's speech in Orlando, the USS *Midway* peeled away from its battle group, shut down its electronic systems, and sailed straight for the Kuril Islands, which Moscow had snatched from Japan during the closing days of World War II. It then "popped up" southeast of Kamchatka, switching its electronics back on for the Soviets to see. As if that was not provocative enough, on April 4, several Navy planes from the *Midway* and the *Enterprise* violated Soviet airspace.

"Within hours of the overflight," according to journalist Seymour Hersh, "the Soviet Air Defense Forces in the Far East were put on alert. They would stay that way through much of the spring and summer. The stakes, already high, had become higher."

Among the exaggerated claims by Reagan hawks about the USSR's military might was its supposedly impenetrable air-defense systems. That assertion was tragically dispelled on September 1, 1983, when Korean Airlines Flight 007, en route to Seoul from New York, crossed into Soviet airspace and proceeded for two hours before it was finally detected by radar operators. Fighter jets were scrambled and within minutes they had intercepted the airliner, a Boeing 747. After firing a burst of warning shots across the intruder's bow, which the captain and crew failed to notice, the order was given to destroy the aircraft. Two missiles were fired, and the civilian jetliner tumbled into the Sea of Okhotsk, killing all 269 people aboard.

In his book *Arsenals of Folly,* the third installment in his definitive account of the nuclear age, author Richard Rhodes attributes much of the blame for the tragedy of KAL 007 to Andropov and his draconian airspace-security regime, which made no distinction between civilian intruders and military ones. Nevertheless, he points out, "since the laws, however cruel, had responded to [the U.S. Navy's] belligerent policies of . . . threat display, of showing the Soviets who was boss, some share of blame for the loss of innocent life surely belongs as well to the Reagan administration." Of course, the White House reaction to the tragedy included no reference to the fact that Soviet frontier units had for the better part of two years been on hair-trigger alert in response to aggressive U.S. maneuvers throughout the Russian Far East. Nor did it mention a crucial piece of information: shortly before detecting KAL 007, Soviet radar had picked up a U.S. Air Force RC-135 reconnaissance aircraft, a converted Boeing 707, east of Kamchatka, which was snooping about in anticipation of a Soviet missile test. Reagan was informed in his daily briefing by CIA director Casey that "confusion between the U.S. reconnaissance plane and the KAL plane could . . . have developed as the [reconnaissance] plane departed and the Korean airliner approached the area northeast of the Kamchatka Peninsula."

In his memoirs, published in 1996, Robert Gates makes clear that a majority of CIA and Defense Intelligence Agency analysts believed that the Soviets on the ground misidentified the plane. (That conclusion was confirmed a decade after the attack, when then Russian prime minister Boris Yeltsin handed over transcriptions of KAL 007's black box recordings, which the Soviets had recovered soon after the craft was shot down, to the United Nations' International Civil Aviation Organization.) Despite this, as Gates continues, "the administration's rhetoric outran the facts that were known to it." On September 5, Reagan declared in an Oval Office speech, "There is no way a pilot could mistake this for anything other than a civilian airliner." The president called the tragedy a "crime against humanity," consistent with the Kremlin's past acts of aggression.

Two days later, Jeane Kirkpatrick, the U.S. ambassador to the United Nations and a charter member of the Committee on the Present Danger, told the General Assembly that "the Soviets decided to shoot down a civilian airliner, shot it down, murdering two hundred and sixty-nine people on board, and then lied about it." Jesse Helms, the archconservative senator, who had been scheduled to fly on KAL 007 but changed planes at the last minute, demanded that sanctions be imposed on Moscow and that Soviet diplomats be expelled from the United States. He led a Senate resolution in solidarity with the families of the disaster's victims and called for "real action" against this "criminal, brutal, premeditated, cowardly act."

It would not be the last time American political and diplomatic elites would obscure the motivation behind a tragic assault on innocents. Though a story in the October 7 edition of the *New York Times* revealed the extent of Soviet confusion about KAL 007's identity, the already corrupted well of U.S.-Soviet relations had been thoroughly poisoned.

The year brought other convulsions and defining events for Washington. In April, a suicide bomber had destroyed the U.S. embassy in Beirut, Lebanon, killing 63 people. In October, 241 American Marines were killed in their Beirut barracks in a similar attack. That same month, U.S. forces launched an assault on the Caribbean island of Grenada, where Cuban-backed revolutionaries were consolidating their grip after staging a coup, ostensibly to free a handful of American students there.

Finally, in early November, NATO began nine days of scheduled military maneuvers known as Able Archer 83. It was a combined simulated-combat operation and command-post exercise, involving senior military and civilian officials who would participate in the consultation process that would precede a nuclear strike. Originally, Reagan himself was to take part as well as his vice president, George H. W. Bush, Defense Secretary Caspar Weinberger, and the chairman of the Joint Chiefs of Staff. Their participation was scrubbed in favor of more junior officials, however, due to CIA reports that the Kremlin was taking "very seriously" the prospect that Able Archer was in fact a preemptive first strike against the Soviet Union concealed as a training exercise. That was largely because Able Archer provided Andropov's spies working the RYAN operation with exactly the kind of activity they had been ordered to monitor.

Able Archer was particularly disconcerting to Moscow because its procedures and the communication channels used in the transition from conventional to nuclear war were different from those used in previous training sessions. The operation was conspicuously comprehensive, as participants shuffled through all the alert phases from normal readiness to general alert. Exaggerated reporting by the KGB, no doubt stoked by alarmism from the upper reaches of the Soviet hierarchy, beginning with Andropov, persuaded the Kremlin that Able Archer was a "real alert involving real troops," according to Robert Gates. Combined with the scurrying of activity on and around U.S. bases in Europe and irregular patterns of officer movement, Gates writes, "the KGB concluded that American forces had been placed on alert—and might even have begun the countdown to nuclear war." Throughout the NATO maneuvers, Soviet and other Warsaw Pact forces in the Baltic States went to peak readiness, as did Soviet air force units. In early November, Moscow elevated the alert status of twelve of its nuclear-capable fighter wings. Significantly, Warsaw Pact television and radio stations canceled weather reports—a way to frustrate NATO attempts to gauge from which direction the winds might carry radioactive fallout.

The insularity of senior Moscow leaders, Gates concludes, and the inordinate tension in superpower relations "makes me think that they really felt a NATO attack was at least possible. . . . They did seem to believe that the situation was very dangerous. And U.S. intelligence had failed to grasp the true extent of their anxiety." Ironically, that may have been a blessing. Had the Americans picked up on the Soviets' heightened alert status, they may have gone on counteralert, which could have triggered a chain of fail-safe mechanisms that might have brought both sides to the precipice of war. French president François Mitterrand remarked in reflection that the encounter was as perilous as the Cuban missile crisis, an assessment with which KGB historian Christopher Andrew concurred. Not long after Mikhail Gorbachev was appointed the Soviet leader, he remarked how "never, perhaps, in the postwar decades was the situation in the world as explosive, and hence more difficult and unfavorable, as in the first half of the 1980s."*

Weeks after the crisis passed, CIA director Casey gave the president a full briefing about Operation RYAN and the Soviets' panicked response to Able Archer. Most of Reagan's aides were dismissive of reports that the Soviets had interpreted the exercise as the first step in an all-out attack against them. Robert McFarlane, Reagan's national security adviser, argued that Soviet foreign minister Andrei Gromyko "knew us well enough to know that there was no way the U.S. could launch a first strike." Reagan, on the other hand, was not so sure. "Do you think they really believe that?" he asked McFarlane. "I don't see how they could believe that—but it's something to think about."

Ronald Reagan, an "amiable dunce" as the Washington fixer Clark Clifford once called him, could have easily ranked among the greatest of Cold War presidents. For much of his second term, he and his Soviet counterpart, Mikhail Gorbachev, parried and thrust their way through

---

* Able Archer was only one of two nuclear "near misses" that haunted 1983. On September 26, 1983, just weeks after the downing of KAL 007, a lieutenant colonel of the Soviet Air Defense Forces named Stanislav Yevgrafovich Petrov was monitoring the Soviet early-warning system from its command center in the Serpukhov-15 bunker near Moscow. Shortly after midnight, the computer detected several U.S. intercontinental ballistic missiles bound for the Soviet Union. With a lack of faith in Soviet technology not uncommon among citizens of the USSR, Petrov correctly diagnosed the report as a glitch in the system. Though this was a deviation from Soviet doctrine, he was praised for his action by his superiors. The incident was kept a secret until the 1990s. In January 2006, Petrov was honored in New York City, first during a ceremony at the United Nations and again by the Association of World Citizens.

two historic summit meetings and a cascade of written correspondence. Their work at arms reduction was an unprecedented bid to demilitarize the Cold War and it defined their relationship. At Reykjavik, Iceland, they stunned their own aides by setting aggressive reduction targets and at one point even agreed in principle to eliminate all nuclear weapons. The promise of a nuclear-free world was shattered, however, by Reagan's refusal to barter away his Strategic Defense Initiative, a missile shield that he believed would render nuclear warfare obsolete. The opportunity lost to Reagan's obduracy is by far his most expensive legacy. As of this writing, with the Cold War a dim memory, Washington has invested some $44 billion for the sake of a viable missile-defense system with little to show for it. Meanwhile, there remain enough U.S. and Russian nuclear warheads to destroy civilization several times over.

That is not to say, however, that Reagan's second term was without historic achievement. He would subdue his instinctive hatred for communism and the Soviet Union and negotiate in good faith with Gorbachev, netting significant reductions in nuclear stockpiles, including the withdrawal of intermediate-range missiles from Europe. Having assumed the presidency as Caesar to American militarism, Reagan left it as the standard-bearer of neo-détente. Having tacked to the center, he distanced himself from a new generation of Beltway primitives who would have otherwise plunged the world in an unprovoked war that would have been its last. And by investing so much authority in his top diplomat, Secretary of State George Shultz, he revived the Department of State as the locus of foreign policy making.

It is said that John F. Kennedy, America's youngest president when he was elected in 1960, learned from his early mistakes and "grew" in stature during the time allotted him. The same could be said about the nation's oldest leader, who evolved with the help of his Soviet counterpart to set the stage for the Cold War's peaceful conclusion. Rare is the politician, particularly one in his seventies, as Reagan was during his eight years as president, who is capable of adjusting his reference points so deliberately in response to a shifting political landscape. As Henry Kissinger notes in his memoirs, the statesman is a "prisoner of necessity . . . confronted with an environment he did not create, and is shaped by a personal history he can no longer change. It is an illusion to believe that

leaders gain in profundity while they gain in experience." By that definition, Ronald Reagan was a transcendent president. Not only did this
most doctrinaire of men reverse his policies with the Soviet Union, he
completely reformed his ideas about superpower relations.

Ronald Reagan's journey from B-level film star to president of the United
States was a matter of exchanging one dream factory for another. If he
made the transition look so easy, it is because Washington and Hollywood have so much in common.

Both are capital cities—one of power, the other of celebrity—and their
inhabitants are shameless in pursuit of both. To advance professionally,
politicians and actors must know how to seduce, finesse, and bamboozle
in a variety of media. In both towns there is little room for modesty or
restraint; the camera is king and there is no such thing as overexposure.
They make laws in Washington and in Hollywood they make films, pro-
cesses that are both collaborative and at times unsightly. In the competition for votes and eyeballs, lawmakers and filmmakers often pander to
their audience's fears and ignorance.

There is, however, a fundamental difference between the two company towns: in Hollywood, people freely acknowledge they make things
up for a living; in Washington, they often become captives of their own
embellished narrative. Reagan did, and it was a source of both weakness
and strength. Often confusing form for substance, he displayed a stunning lack of interest in the details of governance, though he could woo a
packed convention hall with his soaring rhetoric and pitch-perfect delivery. He would frequently embroider speeches with snippets of dialogue
from some of his films and he would refer to them in press conferences
and meetings, almost as if they were real events. The inspiration for his
Strategic Defense Initiative is thought to have been *Murder in the Air,* a
1940 film in which he played a double agent who protects an airborne
death-ray that could destroy enemy aircraft in midflight, as was *Torn
Curtain,* the 1966 Alfred Hitchcock movie in which the Pentagon tries to
develop a system of "antimissile missiles." On the other hand, it was a
postapocalyptic drama called *The Day After* that would do much to focus
Ronald Reagan's view of nuclear war.

Since he first entered politics, as president of the Screen Actors Guild in the late 1940s, Ronald Reagan was obsessed with communism. His 1965 memoir is a postmortem of Red Scare America as told by Hollywood's leading anticommunist. Between amusing anecdotes featuring the likes of Dick Powell, Jack Warner, and William Holden, Reagan cites the California state legislature's reports on "Un-American Activities" as proof that Bolsheviks were infiltrating the nation's film industry. During the run-up to the 1976 presidential election, he lost an aggressive primary campaign to unseat the incumbent Gerald Ford, but only after Ford was forced to shift right under assault from Reagan as well as members of his own cabinet, particularly his hawkish defense secretary, Donald Rumsfeld, and his chief of staff, Dick Cheney. Squaring off against Jimmy Carter in 1980, Reagan pledged to liberate America from its 1970s-era malaise. By most accounts, the seemingly Hamlet-like Carter had failed to restore America's military readiness following the trauma of Vietnam, an impression Reagan shrewdly leveraged to his advantage. He called the war in Vietnam a "noble cause" and endorsed the militarist view that politicians in Washington had tied the hands of America's fighting men there.

Reagan also pioneered the use of servicemen and servicewomen as campaign props, not unlike the way in which he introduced Army Air Corps training films during World War II. Far from distancing himself from the military, as did so many of his successors, Reagan hailed them as keepers of the nation's virtue. As the neoconservative Norman Podhoretz has written, Reagan "made free and frequent use of patriotic language and engaged in an unembarrassed manipulation of patriotic symbols; he lost no opportunity to restore confidence in the utility of military force as an instrument of worthy political purposes." By exorcising the nation of its Vietnam War guilt, Reagan prepared the ground for a military buildup that led to what historian and author Andrew Bacevich has called the "reflexive militarization of U.S. policy."

During his two terms in office, Reagan devoted $2.7 trillion to defense spending. To be sure, it was not all $640 toilet seats and $7,622 coffeemakers, cost overruns that achieved notoriety in the press. The enlarged expenditures, building on reforms pioneered a decade earlier by General Creighton Abrams, greatly enhanced readiness and morale. The number and quality of recruiting increased dramatically, as did retention rates. In 1980, for example, slightly more than half of U.S. Army enlistees were high-school graduates and 57 percent scored in the lowest percentile, known as Category IV, on their aptitude tests. By 1986, 91 percent of new Army recruits had graduated from high school and the ratio of Category IVs was only 4 percent. By 1983, Reagan could boast, as he did to a meeting of newspaper editors, that "we have a waiting line of people who want to enlist."

By elevating the military as a totem of American values, however, Reagan implicitly challenged the nation's tradition of civilian-led policymaking. In October 1983, defending his decision to deploy U.S. Marines to Lebanon, he quoted at length from a letter he had received from a corporal serving there. "It is our duty as Americans," Reagan read aloud, "to stop the cancerous spread of Soviet influence wherever it may be because someday we or some future generation will wake up and find the USA to be the only free state left, with communism upon our doorstep. And then it will be too late."

As will be made clear later in this chapter, Soviet influence worldwide, to say nothing in the Middle East, where it was all but nonexistent, had diminished into irrelevance by the time Reagan was elected president. Not only that, Reagan would withdraw the Marines from Lebanon after the terrorist bombing of their barracks and the U.S. embassy in Beirut, a move later condemned by conservatives as an act of appeasement. In citing the corporal's moving appeal, however, the president signaled that the military's interpretation of U.S. interests abroad was a decisive element in the foreign policy–making process. This would have appalled an older generation of soldier-statesmen, men such as Henry Stimson, George Marshall, and Dwight Eisenhower, who would have recognized it as an ominous step toward a weaponized foreign policy. For the young hawks who now occupied prominent positions in the Reagan White House, however, it was a long time coming.

"What exactly is a neoconservative?" Irving Kristol asked retrospectively in an August 2003 column in the rightist *Weekly Standard*. "Those of us who are designated as 'neocons' are amused, flattered, or dismissive, depending on the context. . . . Even I, frequently referred to as the 'godfather' of all those neocons, have had moments of wonderment."

One can forgive Kristol for appearing to downplay the movement he did so much to advance, which by the time his column appeared was on its way to becoming thoroughly discredited. At the dawn of Reagan's first term, however, the joystick of presidential power was finally within its grasp. Represented in the White House were 31 appointees (out of 182 in total) who were members of the Committee on the Present Danger. It was vindication of a movement that had its roots in the bruising intellectual slugfests waged by a klatch of students at City College of New York in the 1930s. Like Kristol, most of them were the children of Eastern European Jewish immigrants. Adherents of the non-Stalinist left, they were inspired by the teachings of Leo Strauss, the political philosopher who argued that moral relativism, the notion that there is no absolute truth and that values differ from one culture to the next, was a gateway drug for "permissive egalitarianism." From there come hedonism, nihilism, and, ultimately, various forms of tyranny. As they evolved from the coffeehouses and alcoves of CCNY and the University of Chicago, where Strauss spent most of his career (though an atheist, he was also a committed Zionist and was once considered for a post at Hebrew University in Jerusalem), these same leftists transformed themselves into a new breed of virulently anticommunist conservatives.

During the counterculture 1960s and 1970s, neoconservatives resisted the student youth movement and its protests against the war in Vietnam, the rise of affirmative action and the death of meritocracy, the race riots that immolated the nation's urban centers, and what they perceived as a near breakdown in Judeo-Christian values. They were, as Kristol famously described his journey from the Trotskyite left to the neocon right, liberals who were "mugged by reality." Like the Counter-Enlightenment of the late eighteenth century, theirs is less a proactive political movement than a reactive one against perceived threats, most of which have been revealed as bogus. As Columbia University professor Mark Lilla has written, its leaders neither possess nor desire a popular constituency. Instead, they nurture "a network of think tanks and study groups that began as a counter-establishment of Washington intellectuals and became a Washington establishment of counter-intellectuals. Its task is two-fold: to keep the home fires burning with shocking revelations about the disintegration of American culture and society . . . and to provide comforting Team-B analysis for whatever Republican policy contributes to the counter-revolutionary struggle."

The neoconservative movement also has explicit ties to the defense industry. Under Reagan's first term, the military-industrial complex Eisenhower had done so much to resist moved squarely into the West Wing. Committee on the Present Danger member and Navy Secretary John Lehman, for example, owned the Abington Corporation, a consulting firm where Richard Perle also worked and which represented such clients as Northrop, Boeing, TRW, the Finnish arms firm Tampella, and Salgad, the marketing firm for the Israeli arms producer Soltam. RAND, meanwhile, was in many ways a neocon incubator. RAND patriarch Al Wohlstetter was a comrade of Irving Kristol's who shed his Bolshevik sympathies—he was briefly a member of the League for a Revolutionary Workers Party, a communist splinter group—long before his alarmist "The Delicate Balance of Terror" appeared in the 1959 edition of *Foreign Affairs.* Among Wohlstetter's admirers was Perle, who was born in New York City but grew up in Southern California. The two had met at a pool party hosted by Wohlstetter's daughter for her Hollywood High schoolmates one spring day. Impressed by his young visitor's inquisitiveness about global affairs and nuclear disarmament, Wohlstetter gave Perle a copy of his signature disquisition. It must have had an indelible impact on the young man, who as an adult would build his career undermining arms reduction talks. Perle's assault on détente would exceed even Paul Nitze's, and his agitation for foreign policy militarization would survive the Cold War. His subversion of efforts to remove medium-range missiles from Europe was a major factor in the war scare of 1983. If Irving Kristol was the godfather of neoconservatism, Richard Perle was its *shtarker,* its street fighter.

For Perle, reducing the number of nuclear warheads "does violence to our ability to maintain adequate defenses." He was fiercely opposed to anyone who believed otherwise, and he was skilled at attaching himself to powerful hosts. As Senator Henry Jackson's eyes and ears on Capitol Hill during the SALT negotiations, he rallied the anti–arms control forces in Congress and the country's security establishment to wring from Henry Kissinger concessions that seriously weakened the agreement. During the Ford administration, Perle joked to an interviewer that the president will be "more careful with foreigners who drink vodka" after he hears the "likely congressional reaction to his initiatives." When Ford, an enlightened moderate, called Jackson to express his strong objections to Perle's attack—this was when Washington operated under a code of civility that was prim by today's standards—Jackson defended his aide, taking full responsibility for his remarks.

Perle and his allies habitually overstated both the frequency and the nature of Moscow's treaty violations. As foreign policy expert Strobe Talbott writes, "The Soviet record was one of chiseling at the margins, taking advantage of loopholes and imprecisions, rarely of outright violations." Soviet diplomats and military officers, according to Talbott, "held their own" against U.S. accusations of cheating at the Standing Consultative Commission, the deliberative body established as part of SALT to address such disputes. When he was not alleging Kremlin violations of the SALT accords, Perle was making unreasonable demands such as his insistence on equal throw weight between U.S. and Soviet missiles. Because American missiles were generally smaller but more accurate, the only way such an objective could have been achieved was if the United States tripled its arsenal or if the Soviets cut theirs by a third. Gradually, writes Kissinger, it became clear that the tactics employed by Jackson and Perle "were designed to gut rather than improve our East-West policy." Perle, Kissinger writes, "was far too intelligent not to have realized that some of the charges he was making were more cynical than substantive."

Both Perle and Jackson mired arms negotiations by holding them hostage to issues such as Russia's poor human rights record and its restrictions on Jewish emigration, provocative issues that, though unrelated to national security, could easily arouse Congress. So effective was Perle at frustrating the SALT negotiations that Kissinger once blurted, "You just wait and see! If that son of a bitch Richard Perle ever gets into an administration, after six months he'll be pursuing exactly the same policies I've been attempting and that he's been sabotaging."

In fact, Perle would prove a remarkably consistent saboteur, at least when it came to the matter of arms reduction. Of course, when he joined the Reagan White House in 1981, there was little reason to believe he would have much in the way of negotiations to sabotage. The president had, after all, campaigned on a pledge to expand America's nuclear arsenal, not reduce it. As the assistant secretary of defense for international affairs, Perle had a new patron in Defense Secretary Weinberger, who, as a Reagan ally from California, was at least as influential as Jackson and just as hawkish. He had known Reagan since 1965, when he supported him in his gubernatorial campaign, and he served as California's director of finance throughout Governor Reagan's term. Having served on the winning side of the 1980 presidential campaign, Weinberger was hoping to garner the post of secretary of state. Offered the Defense Department instead, he took the job on the not unfair assumption that he would enjoy greater influence as the civilian leader of the world's largest military than as the headmaster of the nation's diplomatic corps.

A lawyer by training and inexperienced in military and foreign affairs, Weinberger interpreted the world through an ideologically hawkish lens that left little room for doubt or thoughtful examination. In several interviews, he said it would be disastrous for the Soviets to develop an antimissile system like the one the Reagan administration was demanding as a guarantor of peace and stability. Asked why this was so, he asserted that the Soviets were aggressive and America was not. "Bear in mind," he told NBC's *Meet the Press* on March 27, 1983, "that we had . . . a monopoly on nuclear weapons for some years and we never used them. . . . The other reason why they have no need to worry [about a U.S. antimissile system] is that they know perfectly well that we will never launch a first strike on the Soviet Union. And all of their . . . preparations [and] acquisitions in the military field in the last few years have been offensive in nature." Declassified information would later prove most of these claims highly misleading or patently false.

Unfortunately for the Weinberger-Perle axis, there was the inconvenient matter of the people's will. Despite growing disillusionment with détente, most Americans thought limitations on nuclear weapons was a good idea. In 1980 MIT graduate student Randall Forsberg wrote "A Call to Halt the Nuclear Arms Race," a manifesto that served as the genesis of a national nuclear freeze campaign. In 1982 a million people gathered in New York's Central Park to protest the Reagan military buildup. That same year, *New Yorker* journalist Jonathan Schell wrote "The Fate of the Earth," an award-winning series of articles about nuclear war that catalyzed the nuclear freeze movement. Professional associations formed in opposition to the arms race. It was, as author James Carroll puts it, "a forthright popular act of moral reckoning with the truth of what society has become."

Even a president as contemptuous of arms reduction as Ronald Reagan could not ignore such a movement. Something, even a perfunctory gesture that would at least give the appearance of action, needed to be done. An opportunity emerged with the help of the SS-20, the USSR's new, highly accurate and multiple-warhead missile. Because the Americans had not deployed a suitable deterrent to the SS-20, there evolved what West German chancellor Helmut Schmidt described in October 1977 as "disparities of military power in Europe." In December 1979, the Carter administration responded by pledging to NATO deliveries of Tomahawk cruise missiles and the Pershing II intermediate-range missile, which were more than a match for the SS-20. At the same time, it declared it would negotiate with Moscow for reductions in intermediate-range weapons.

The debate over what to do with the Carter initiative posed one of the first major schisms within the Reagan administration. Hawks, with Perle in the lead, insisted it should be abandoned. Moderates disagreed and, arguing for the importance of continuity in transatlantic relations, prevailed. They included, of all people, Paul Nitze, who had worked so ardently to scupper SALT and its pale derivative, SALT II. Welshing on Carter's pledge, he told his colleagues, "would appall the Europeans and confirm the impression that the United States couldn't be counted on for anything." Eugene Rostow, Reagan's director of the Arms Control and Disarmament Agency, nominated Nitze to head the U.S. delegation to the intermediate-range missile talks. When Nixon holdovers on the Reagan team such as former Kissinger aides Lawrence Eagleburger and Alexander Haig expressed concerns about Nitze's "notorious hawkishness," Rostow countered that the appointment would be "the best possible signal to the Europeans and the Russians that we take these negotiations seriously." If only Nixon could go to China, it seemed, only Nitze could negotiate meaningful arms reduction.

At the age of seventy-four, Nitze, soul of the Committee on the Present Danger, author of NSC 68 and the Gaither Report, was back in the arena working for a president whose low regard for arms control seemed to be in concert with his own. This time, he would be working with Perle, his protégé and comrade in the war against SALT II, as well as Kenneth Adelman, a Perle confederate and fellow neoconservative. Perle had already fired an opening shot in the conservatives' plan to soft-stall an arms deal to death. Under his so-called zero option, the United States would cancel deployment of its intermediate-range missiles if Moscow withdrew its SS-20s. It was offered as a prelude to U.S.-Soviet negotiations but was in fact nonnegotiable. On December 1, 1981, as Nitze was packing his bags for Geneva, Perle told the Senate Armed Services Committee that there was no alternative to the zero option. He then read from the memoirs of Sir Samuel Hoare, a British statesman, who reflected with regret on his role in Neville Chamberlain's failed attempts to appease Adolf Hitler in Munich in 1938.

As Perle no doubt understood, it is one thing to insist your opponent concede to an unreasonable demand; it is quite another to imply he is Nazi Germany. Needless to say, prospects for a breakthrough appeared bleak even before Nitze's departure. It would be a mistake, however, to assume Nitze had been scrambled merely to browbeat the Soviets. He had, after all, negotiated much of the SALT I accord and, unlike Perle, he believed in the doctrine of mutual assured destruction, which required rough parity in force strength between the two superpowers. With the introduction of SS-20s in Europe, the Soviets had established a strategic advantage. Because of that alone, Nitze wanted to cut an agreement on intermediate-range missiles. This put him on a collision course with Perle, who had once disparaged Nitze revealingly as "an inveterate problem-solver . . . result-oriented to a fault." Not long after his arrival in Geneva, he found his requests for flexibility countermanded by Perle. Soon he was grumbling about Perle's "obstructionism." In a meeting in

January 1982, he accused Perle of "talking rubbish," making fraudulent claims and trying to "torpedo" the negotiations.

By summer, in a bid to undercut Perle's meddling, Nitze invited Yuli Kvitsinsky, his counterpart on the Soviet delegation, to several one-on-one talks. The most significant, later known as the "walk in the woods," occurred in the Jura Mountains on July 16, 1982, when the two men agreed on a comprehensive plan to establish a strategic balance of power in Europe while also freezing the levels of SS-20s in Asia. The plan provoked furious debate in the White House, with Perle, who condemned Nitze's side channel as "an act of intellectual and political cowardice," leading the opposition. During a September 1 meeting, in response to a participant's appeal to give Nitze at least some benefit of the doubt, Perle snapped that his mentor "doesn't deserve a damned thing." When the Joint Chiefs of Staff concluded in a paper that the reductions of SS-20s as outlined in the Nitze-Kvitsinsky plan were worth the concessions demanded from the Soviet side, their memo was intercepted by Perle and Weinberger and swapped with one that counseled Perle's hard line.

With the deadline approaching for the deployment of American Pershing II and cruise missiles in Europe, and with NATO members clamoring for a compromise deal, Nitze redoubled his efforts to win Reagan's support for his deal with Kvitsinsky. In a meeting with Reagan on September 13, Nitze tried to explain to the president why it was unreasonable to expect the Soviets to furlough their deadliest missiles in exchange for a U.S. pledge to do nothing. The president, who had been greatly influenced by Perle's arguments for deployment, overruled Nitze. "Well, Paul," Reagan said, "you just tell the Soviets that you're working for one tough son-of-a-bitch." With that, the negotiations were dissolved and American Tomahawk and Pershing II missiles were fanned out across Europe, pointing east at a time when the Kremlin believed Washington was actively preparing for a first strike. The prospect of arms reduction, at least during Reagan's first term, had been extinguished.

Could the militarists in President Reagan's first-term inner circle be forgiven for believing that the Soviet Union by the mid-1980s posed an existential threat to the United States? Moscow had, after all, achieved rough parity with the United States in strategic forces and it was meddling in proxy wars with U.S. allies in Africa and Central America. Given what was known at the time, could it be argued that men such as Perle and Weinberger were any less reckless in resisting détente than those who embraced it? Would a "fog-of-war handicap" redeem the hawks as more judicious than the diplomatists?

The answer is no. The more one trolls through the documents and memorandums available during the Reagan years, to say nothing of archives that have been declassified since the Cold War ended, the more irresponsible their conduct is revealed to be.

In 1966 a report from Congress concluded that "both official Soviet data and Western estimates show a marked decline in the rate of growth of industrial production in the USSR." It noted falling birthrates and fuel shortages due to diminished oil production. Massive Soviet grain purchases revealed critical weaknesses in its agriculture sector for all to see. Melvin Laird, Nixon's defense secretary, remarked in 1974 that "the Soviet economy is in trouble. The growth rate of Soviet productivity has been declining. [The USSR's] technological industries . . . have shown marked incapacity to come up with economical, efficient and innovative products. . . . The availability of consumer goods in the Soviet Union is still among the lowest of developing nations."

In a series of widely circulated letters between 1968 and 1972, Andrei Sakharov, a nuclear physicist and dissident, lamented to Leonid Brezhnev how "the total capacity of our computers is hundreds of times less than the USA, and as for the use of electronic computers in the national economy, here the rift is so enormous that it is impossible to measure. We are simply living in a different era." He also focused on the militarization of the state—Moscow's defense industry accounted for an estimated 40 percent of the Soviet budget and 15 to 20 percent of its GDP—as a massive burden. "In no country," he wrote, "does the share of military expenditure with relation to national income reach such proportions as in the USSR."

At its all-time peak, in 1970, the Soviet economy accounted for less · than 60 percent of U.S. gross domestic product. An onerous share of

Soviet output went to subsidizing its economically enfeebled satellite governments in Eastern Europe. In exchange for the energy and raw materials Moscow exported to its European proxies—at a time when the easily exploitable reserves had already been exhausted—it received shoddily manufactured goods. By the 1980s, Eastern Europe had fallen irreparably behind its Western rivals in both technological competitiveness and economic growth, its average rate of real GDP growth having declined from 3.2 percent in 1971–1980 to 0.9 percent in 1981–1985.

In 1979 an English translation of a book titled *The Final Fall: An Essay on the Decomposition of the Soviet Sphere* percolated among Sovietologists. It was written by a French demographer named Emmanuel Todd while he was still a graduate student, and it stated flatly that within "ten, twenty, or thirty years, an astonished world will be witness to the dissolution or the collapse of this, the first of the communist systems." Mining through arcane statistics, Todd concluded that the Soviet system was sclerotic and incapable of healing itself. "How is it possible," he wrote, "for a central organization to coordinate the activity of 250 million Soviet inhabitants, distributed over 22 million square kilometers, by arbitrarily fixing prices and wages?" Like Sakharov, Todd warned that Soviet defense spending was both unsustainable and a pillar of the centrally planned economy, which was locked in a losing competition with the unofficial consumer sector. The high ratio of defense spending relative to economic output, he argued, "is necessary to prevent the transfer of productive forces to the consumer sector. Arms expenses serve, among other things, to maintain the preeminence of the centralized sector of the economy." Moscow's obsessive desire to control everything from coal production to the minds of its people, Todd projected, would eventually undo the USSR.*

Not surprisingly, the decaying Soviet economy greatly impaired the Kremlin's ability to project force, even in areas not actively contested by its American rival. In 1980, the independent Center for Defense Information claimed that Moscow's economic, political, and military influence worldwide had peaked in the 1950s and had been declining ever since.

---

* In 2001, Todd published *After the Empire: The Breakdown of the American Order*, in which he forecast the fall of the United States as the sole superpower and the emergence of a multipolar world, with the rise of Europe, Asia, and Russia.

The study, titled "Soviet Geopolitical Momentum: Myth or Menace?" noted that the Kremlin was forced to concentrate a quarter of its armed forces along its border with its former ally, China. Beyond its imperial possessions in Eastern Europe, it enjoyed meaningful influence over countries with a mere 6 percent of the world's population, down from its peak of 31 percent in 1958, and 5 percent of global economic output.

An updated version of the CDI report, issued in 1986, took an even dimmer view of Soviet hegemony. "It would be very difficult," it concluded, "to find any country outside Eastern Europe and Mongolia over which the Soviet Union has exercised a measure of influence which approaches control." For the Kremlin's investment overseas, few of the nations over which it held sway had much to offer in return. "Nearly half of the 18 countries . . . where the Soviet Union has significant influence today are poverty-stricken countries at the bottom of the development ladder and in dire need of foreign assistance." Soviet prestige in Latin America and Africa, seized by the Reagan administration as definitive examples of Kremlin ambitions to take over the world, was diminishing, according to the study. Though Cuba remained a loyal ally, Moscow had little to show for its bankrolling of Marxist insurgencies in countries such as Nicaragua, where its influence was limited. Congo, Mozambique, Angola, Madagascar, and the Seychelles had defied Soviet efforts to gather them into the USSR's orbit. In the Middle East, most Arab states gestured toward the Soviets, particularly for weapons sales, while turning to Washington for political and economic assistance.

The CDI dispelled Soviet armed might as leverage in Moscow's quest for global influence. "Apocalyptic predictions about the relationship between Soviet power and Soviet adventurism have been made repeatedly over the past 35 years," its report stated, but "there is little evidence in the Soviet case that military power produces effective or enduring influence."

The caricature of the Soviet Union as perennial loser in its Cold War rivalry with America was best summed up in a joke in which Reagan and Brezhnev are trying to woo a generic Third World potentate.

"Turn left," Brezhnev advises the leader while the three men are seated in his official limousine.

"No, turn right," implores Reagan.

With that, their host leans forward and commands the driver to "signal left but turn right."

If the prodigious Committee on the Present Danger had either ignored or missed such clear evidence of Soviet decline—neither the Sakharov letters nor *The Final Fall* made any impression on Kremlin-watcher Richard Pipes, for example—they were not alone. The U.S. media also hyped the threat from Moscow. The *New York Times* was breathless in its accounts of a looming Soviet supremacy and its consequences. In addition to overstating the expertise of Team B members, it reported in the prelude to Reagan's election a "pattern . . . of continuous growth" in Kremlin military spending compared with a "downward trend" in U.S. defense outlays. In the event of war in Europe, it stated, the U.S. side would be compromised by "tanks and infantry vehicles designed in the 1950s, helicopters designed in the 1940s, and artillery that is basically no better than the guns used in World War II." Such reporting became powerful grist for Reagan's campaign mill. In speeches, he would warn how the Soviets could just "take us with a phone call" in the form of an ultimatum: "Look at the difference in our relative strengths. Now, here's what we want. . . . Surrender or die."

Time magazine endorsed the Pentagon's request for "billions and billions," concluding that a "nation's most fundamental social welfare obligation to its citizens is to defend them against attack. The responsibility for this is entrusted to the armed forces, but the U.S. military has been denied sufficient resources to fulfill the responsibility." In a fall 1980 cover story, *Newsweek* reported that U.S. readiness had eroded "so badly that the nation may no longer be capable of protecting its interests abroad, or of containing Soviet expansionism." Advances in Soviet arms technology threatened "to subject the United States to nuclear blackmail, if not a Soviet first strike, by as early as 1982."

In *The Myth of Soviet Supremacy,* a landmark but largely overlooked work published in 1986, author Tom Gervasi revealed in clinical detail how the Reagan White House grossly inflated the Soviet military threat and how media elites were complicit in the deception. "In most news organizations," Gervasi wrote, "the response to [White House] pressure, as well as growing internal pressure from ownership and management that increasingly favored the administration's views, was simply to report whatever the administration said or did without commentary or challenge. This meant suppressing a considerable amount of information." In one example among many, Gervasi notes the *Washington Post*'s publication in late 1982 of a White House chart that attributed the United States with 7,100 warheads and the Soviets with 7,500. The chart included the number of strategic bombers in the U.S. arsenal, but it failed to quantify the multiple nuclear weapons each bomber carried. "Its implication," the study reported, "was either that the Soviets held the lead in deliverable strategic warheads, or that even if we had enough bomber weapons to surpass their total, the Soviets still had the lead in the most important *category* of strategic missiles. Neither implication was true." (According to the Center for Defense Information, the United States during the Reagan years had a stockpile of 12,000 warheads, compared with the Soviets' 8,000.)

Routinely, the Reagan administration also excluded from its own force estimates America's inventory of submarine-launched missiles, which represented a crucial edge over Moscow as they could not be targeted. In a March 1983 edition, *Newsweek* published a chart that purported to show the competing orders of battle in Europe while making no reference to America's stealthy nuclear-powered *Poseidon* subs, its frontline strategic deterrent in Europe. "It was as though our missiles at sea did not exist," Gervasi wrote.

Gervasi also revealed how the White House created the myth of Soviet superiority in conventional force strength in Europe. For starters, it omitted the 504,650 troops in the French army, which was withdrawn from NATO's multinational command in 1966 but which remained staunchly committed to the defense of Europe. It also left out 342,000 troops from Spain, which joined NATO in May 1982. Taking into account these and other sleights of hand, Gervasi confirmed conclusions by London's International Institute for Strategic Studies that NATO had some 5,275,889 troops under its command, while the Warsaw Pact countries had 4,788,000. The Reagan administration, meanwhile, maintained a balance of 2,578,155 and 4,000,000, respectively.

———

If the White House was able to exaggerate the Soviet threat with the help of the pliant media, it also had a powerful accomplice in the Pentagon. In congressional hearings and in interviews on the Sunday-morning news shows, the uniformed services unfurled their wish list of new machinery they said was vital to keep the Soviets at bay. It included B-2 "stealth" bombers to penetrate the Soviet Union's improved air defense systems and replace aging B-52s, costly upgrades to the nuclear submarine fleet to evade enhanced Soviet detection grids, and better ballistic missiles such as the rail-based Peacekeeper and the Minuteman III. By the mid-1980s, the U.S. government had spent up to $350 billion on new strategic systems alone, including the B-1B and B-2 bombers, cruise missiles, and the MX intercontinental ballistic missiles.

In April 1990, the House Committee on Foreign Affairs asked the General Accounting Office to evaluate the strengths and weaknesses of Reagan-era weapons programs and identify which were the most cost-effective. This required an examination of the Pentagon's triad of sea, air, and land operations, "taking into account the threat they were intended to address and the arms control agreements that would likely constrain or curtail them," according to GAO investigators. They would have little in the way of benchmarks for their work, as the Department of Defense had not conducted its own such evaluation since the Eisenhower administration.

The GAO findings were summarized in testimony delivered before the U.S. Senate three years later. Titled "The U.S. Nuclear Triad: GAO's Evaluation of the Strategic Modernization Program," it reads like a rap sheet against a military establishment that misled Congress about the capability and necessity of its proposed new weapons while exaggerating the capacity of Soviet forces and U.S. vulnerabilities. Of the B-2, for example, investigators found not only that defense planners had vastly overstated the effectiveness of Soviet air defenses but that an upgraded system the bomber was designed to overcome was never deployed. Regarding the Soviet sea leg of the triad, Pentagon officials inflated the threat using "unsubstantiated allegations" about the prospect of new Russian submarine-detection technologies while understating the quality of their own subs. With respect to land defenses, the GAO found that the "window of vulnerability" caused by improved Soviet missile capability against America's ground-based missile fleet was flawed on several counts: it presumed Moscow would be reckless enough to launch an all-out attack on U.S. silos despite its inability to target enemy submarines and bombers, which could easily mount a retaliatory strike; it assumed inordinately high accuracy, yield, and reliability rates for Soviet missiles while discounting their known uncertainties; and it factored out U.S. early-warning systems and the advantages they would provide Washington in planning a counterattack. Overall, the GAO concluded that Pentagon procurement requests often exaggerated the performance of new systems and muted the capability of mature ones while making "inappropriate claims of obsolescence."

In 2009 the Pentagon's Office of Net Assessments declassified its *Soviet Intentions, 1965–1985*. First published in 1994, the two-volume study reveals a Kremlin in a defensive crouch under the shadow of U.S. strategic supremacy. According to interviews with nearly two dozen former Soviet military officers, analysts, technicians, industrialists, and scientists, at no time did Moscow consider a strategic first strike against the United States, nor did it ever contemplate how it might "win" a nuclear war. "The Soviet nuclear strategy relied heavily on deterrence," the report states. It "did not subscribe to the concept of nuclear warfighting as conceived by U.S. strategists [and it] neither embraced nor really accepted the possibility of fighting a limited nuclear war . . . or of managing a nuclear war by climbing a ladder of escalation."

At the same time, according to the study, the Soviet high command believed a preemptive U.S. strike was all but inevitable. This was in part because of Washington's refusal to reject a nuclear policy of "no first use," unlike Moscow, which officially adopted such a doctrine in 1982, as well as a host of other factors. They included the production by the mid-1960s of highly accurate, multiwarhead MX missiles, followed by MIRVed warheads for existing and new delivery systems, which put Soviet land-based ICBMs and control nodes at risk;* the dense manner in

---

* The acronym MIRV stands for multiple independently targetable reentry vehicle. A U.S. MIRVed missile can carry as many as a dozen warheads, each programmed to hit a different target or the same target several times.

which U.S. missile silos and control centers were clustered, which theoretically made them vulnerable and suggested they were built to wage a preemptive strike rather than to deter one; the large and varied arsenal of tactical nuclear weapons fielded by NATO forces in Europe; and the Reagan administration's deployment in and around Europe of mid-range missiles capable of destroying command and control targets deep inside Soviet territory with little warning time. *Soviet Intentions* also notes how the Kremlin interpreted the Carter administration's PD-59 as a deliberate policy for launching a surprise, decapitating blow against the Soviet leadership. "The Soviets found this policy, backed up in the early 1980s by the technical capability to execute it, extremely threatening," the report states.

The Soviet quest for a quantitative edge over the United States in ICBM stockpiles was fueled by an acute awareness of the technological shortcomings of the USSR's strategic arsenal. This was corroborated by former Soviet foreign minister Sergei Tarasenko, who said at the Carter-Brezhnev Project, a May 1994 conference of U.S. and Russian policy-makers and scholars, that "all the talk about the Soviet desire to achieve military superiority had no grounds." The Soviet high command, he stated, "deeply felt that the Soviet Union was substantially inferior in strategic weapons . . . and the best they could hope for was to preserve the status quo and not fall behind any more." A year earlier, Tarasenko shared an anecdote that underlined how committed the Soviets were to avoid a nuclear exchange with America. During the Able Archer exercises in November 1983, he was shown a top-secret KGB paper that warned that the United States was preparing a first strike, possibly a surgical attack against command centers in the Soviet Union. "We were given the task of preparing a paper for the Politburo and putting forward some suggestions on how to counter this threat *not physically but politically*," Tarasenko told the conference. (Italics added.) "So we prepared a paper [suggesting] that we should leak some information that we know about these capabilities and contingency plans, and that we are not afraid of these plans because we have taken the necessary measures."

With striking consistency, former Soviet officials emphasized that America's qualitative lead in strategic weaponry, particularly submarine-deployed missiles, rendered the prospect of a first strike unthinkable. In his interview for *Soviet Intentions,* Vitalii Leonidovich Kataev, a senior adviser to the chairman of the Central Committee of the Defense Industry Department, said: "We assumed that the U.S. would launch first, and given your focus on accuracy and relatively smaller yields per warhead, that you intended to strike our weapons and control systems in an attempt to disarm us." General Makhmut A. Gareev, deputy chief of the General Staff for Scientific Work and Operational Readiness, told Pentagon interviewers: "The Soviet Armed Forces did not plan to use nuclear weapons first and were forbidden to exercise initiation of nuclear use." (Though the issue of U.S. tactical doctrine was not raised in the study, one can imagine the Russians would have been shocked by the wide discretion American flag officers were given over the use of nuclear weapons under their command.)

Even in the face of a massive invasion of Eastern Europe by NATO conventional forces, Moscow would not be the first to go nuclear. "We always planned to destroy all our silos, rather than use them to launch missiles," said retired general Varfolomei Vladimirovich Korobushin, the former deputy chief of staff of Strategic Rocket Forces. "This was standard operating procedure." The Soviets were even leery of establishing a "launch-under-attack" policy, in which Moscow would authorize retaliation once it was confirmed that a U.S. first strike had been launched. In a session of the Carter-Brezhnev Project, Tarasenko relayed a story about how Soviet premier Alexsei Kosygin "very categorically prohibited even discussing the question" of a launch-under-attack doctrine. "He said that by saying such certain things, it would make it more likely that we would be put in a situation where it would be necessary to use such weapons."

During the Carter-Brezhnev Project talks, former Soviet ambassador to the United States Anatoly Dobrynin asks his American counterparts whether or not they ever had plans for a nuclear first strike. The question is taken by Harold Brown, Jimmy Carter's secretary of defense, who fidgets:

BROWN: Well, the U.S. certainly had no first strike *intentions.* There was—and there is, I suppose, still now; but there certainly was then—a so-called "strategic integrated operational plan" that included a very large number of targets in the Soviet Union. Periodically the Joint Chiefs of Staff would go through an exercise: a command post exercise, or a study of what an exchange would look like. Those exchanges always began with a Soviet strike on the United States. . . . We always evaluated our forces in a retaliatory mode, so there was a strike plan, but . . .

DOBRYNIN: Was it a first strike?

BROWN: We never did exercises with the U.S. striking first, although we did calculations as to how the exchange would come out if the U.S. struck first and the Soviet Union retaliated, and *vice versa*. And what we always found was that it didn't really matter who began the war: both sides ended up being destroyed. Our operational planning always assumed that the war would begin with a Soviet strike. . . .

DOBRYNIN: You've heard what the military just said: that they did not have a first-strike capability, or first-strike intentions. So, Harold: did you have them or not? I am not speaking about how you evaluated *our* intentions. Did you have plans for a first strike against the Soviet Union under certain circumstances or not? Yes or no?

BROWN: We never had any intentions of a first strike.

Another participant, Viktor Starodubov, a former lieutenant general in the Soviet army and an adviser to the Kremlin's arms-control negotiating team, was not willing to let Brown off the hook. He pointed out that the United States was accumulating a huge stockpile of weapons during the infant years of the Cold War, when Moscow had no strategic arsenal of its own. "To say that in 1947, or 1948 or 1949, the U.S. was developing its nuclear strategy on the basis of expecting a Soviet attack requiring a U.S. response—this is groundless." Brown responded with an anecdote about a meeting he attended during the Kennedy administration in which the president was informed by Curtis LeMay that 60 million

Americans would die if the Soviets launched a preemptive nuclear strike against the United States.

> And the president asked me what would be the number if the U.S. struck first. I said, "Probably 20 million to 30 million." And General LeMay had to agree. And President Kennedy said, "I don't see that there is very much difference. The answer is the same: there must never be a thermonuclear war." And that, I think, has been the attitude of every president since.

However inspiring, there is something hollow in Brown's account. It makes no mention of the enormous pressure Cold War presidents were under, from generals such as LeMay as well as militarists in Congress and civilians in the national security establishment, to exploit Soviet weakness with a preemptive attack. Nor does he elaborate on the Single Integrated Operational Plan, the Pentagon's ghastly playbook for the destruction of the communist bloc with thousands of warheads. Had the Russians who participated in the Carter-Brezhnev Project known about the enormity of SIOP—which even then, with the Warsaw Pact dead and buried, listed 1,100 nuclear, 500 conventional military, 500 industrial, and 500 leadership targets—could they have been persuaded that it was an innocent means of deterrence? The United States may not have had the intention of waging a preemptive war against the Soviet Union, but it certainly had invested heavily in the means. Military planners often cite the imperative of war-gaming against capacity rather than intentions, as a restrained adversary today may be replaced by a reckless one tomorrow. Small wonder, then, that the Soviets had no choice but to assume a worst-case scenario when plumbing the motives behind U.S. policy, however powerless they were to do anything about it.

The transcripts of the Carter-Brezhnev Project and the interviews from *Soviet Intentions* evoke a breezy symposium, a collegial, sometimes jocular, exchange between former archrivals. Both sides in the discussions are respectful of each other's views and sensibilities. They are distinguished by their commentary as sober-minded men, professional and intellectually curious. The inclusion in such an ensemble of an Alfred Wohlstetter or a Richard Perle would be as harmonious as an air-raid siren in a string quartet. The spiritual conceits of such men, that their own cultural tradition is intrinsically more virtuous and its intention less threatening than another, is both racist in implication and violent in application. Russian specialist and Team B leader Richard Pipes frequently criticized CIA analysts for "mirror-imaging" the communist threat, the presumption among analysts that both sides shared the same ambition, fears, and reference points. It was the operative form of empathy, and as a policy tool it usually worked.

For Team B, this was the apostate mingling of analytical methodology with moral relativism. As Pipes put it, "Because the Soviet Union ultimately wishes to destroy not merely its opponents' fighting capacity but their very capacity to function as organized political, social, and economic entities, its strategic arsenal includes a great choice of political, social, and economic weapons besides the obvious military ones. For this reason, Soviet strategic objectives cannot be accurately ascertained and appreciated by an examination of the USSR's strategic nuclear or general purpose forces alone." Such an assessment inverted traditional doctrine by emphasizing intentions over capabilities. Because it imposed on the Kremlin an irredeemable venality, détente betrayed weakness, which equaled death.

Ronald Reagan, who had done so much to enable the neocons' parochial rubric, may have gone on believing in it right into his second term had he not been mugged by the near-apocalyptic reality of 1983.

12

—

ENDGAME

Now I become death, the destroyer of worlds.
—ROBERT OPPENHEIMER, QUOTING HINDU SCRIPTURE,
AFTER WATCHING THE FIRST SUCCESSFUL TEST BLAST OF
A NUCLEAR DEVICE AT LOS ALAMOS NATIONAL LABORATORY,
NEW MEXICO, ON JULY 16, 1945

*The worst thing in the world would be to eliminate
nuclear weapons.*
—RICHARD PERLE

EN ROUTE TO THE 1980 REPUBLICAN NATIONAL CONVENTION IN Detroit, Ronald Reagan's campaign manager asked him why, for heaven's sake, he wanted to be president.

"To end the Cold War," Reagan replied without hesitation. He then explained how he believed the Soviet system was not only authoritarian but nearly bankrupt, and how he dreaded the prospect of nuclear war, which he equated with Armageddon as related in the Book of Revelations. Somehow, Reagan maintained, the United States must leverage its power to "end this thing" peacefully, without either side firing a shot.

"There has to be a way," he said, "and it's time."

It was a breathtaking admission. Every other president had been content to simply coexist peacefully, however uneasily, with the Soviet empire. For Reagan, ending the Cold War was a moral necessity, even if it meant cheating the Holy Scripture of its pyrotechnic finale. For those who asserted that nuclear war was winnable, this would ultimately expose Reagan as a false messiah. Neoconservatives felt particularly betrayed. Norman Podhoretz would bewail how Reagan appeared "ready to embrace the course of détente wholeheartedly." Richard Pipes, who advised Reagan on national security matters, once sniffed that "for all his toughness, [the president] was terribly afraid of nuclear war," as if likening Reagan to a bull elephant cowering before the church mouse of a nuclear holocaust.

Though a founding member of the Committee on the Present Danger, Reagan never believed, as did his neoconservative advisers, that the Soviet threat was worthy of a preemptive nuclear strike. His anxiety about the prospect of nuclear war intensified after he survived a nearly successful assassination attempt in the spring of 1981, which obliged him, he wrote in his memoirs, to "do whatever I could in the years God had given me to reduce the threat of nuclear war." Jack Matlock, a career diplomat who served as Reagan's top adviser on Soviet affairs, theorized that the president would have been unable to launch a nuclear attack even in response to a Soviet first strike. Far from a sign of weakness, Reagan's fear of nuclear weapons and his resolve to eliminate them suggests a measure of humanity alien to the Washington gestalt. For insiders such as Paul Nitze and Richard Perle, nuclear war was a cold calculus of vectors and target sets, launch trajectories and throw weight. For everyone else, it was a thing to be avoided. Reagan may have frequently conflated real life with Hollywood plotlines, but he had no illusions when it came to the consequences of a nuclear exchange. At least twice during his first term in office, he tasked his aides to produce a blueprint for the elimination of all nuclear warheads and their delivery systems. The bureaucracy yielded nothing.

Even before Able Archer, Reagan had been rattled emotionally by two isolated but sobering events that made the removal of nuclear arms, or at least their neutralization, the central goal of his presidency. On October 10, 1983, Reagan was given a special preview of *The Day After*, a made-for-television movie that portrayed Lawrence, Kansas, as ground zero for a nuclear war between the United States and the Soviet Union. The film generated the kind of media clamor that occurred every so often in the analogue age, when a major offering from one of the country's three television networks could galvanize the entire nation. Health experts warned that the movie's vivid depictions of nuclear war might cause emotional distress for viewers, particularly young children. Churches and civic organizations staged group viewings of the film, and special phone lines were set up to help people process what they had seen. For the first time in its history, the National Education Association released a national alert ahead of the movie's November 20 broadcast date. Among other things, it suggested children under the age of twelve should not be allowed to watch the film.

Given the technology of its time, *The Day After* is indeed a chilling account of a nuclear exchange and its aftermath, with humans turned to ashes and one survivor after another culled by radiation disease and famine. Its stark imagery triggered a popular reappraisal of the Cold War rivalry and revived the appeal of détente. Among viewers deeply touched by the film was the president himself, who described it in his diary: "very effective and left me greatly depressed. . . . My own reaction is that we must do all we can . . . to see that there is never a nuclear war." A short time later, in late October, Reagan received the Pentagon's briefing on its plans for nuclear war. This was Reagan's first encounter with the Single Integrated Operational Plan, the Cold War golem that had survived more or less intact throughout the years despite efforts by several presidents to domesticate it. Defense Secretary Caspar Weinberger had tried several times to persuade Reagan to sit in on the briefing, but the president, no doubt fearful of what he might learn, begged off. Now nearly three years into his first term, Reagan's ordination was unavoidable.

The meeting was led by Weinberger and Army general John Vessey, the chairman of the Joint Chiefs of Staff, and held in the White House Situation Room. There, Reagan was introduced to the magnitude of America's nuclear might, the destructive power of which had been animated with such raw detail in *The Day After*. SIOP had recently been updated with a new emphasis on the "decapitation" of Soviet officialdom as part of a nuclear strike. Just prior to the departure of outgoing president Jimmy Carter, Defense Secretary Harold Brown had testified to Congress that "the Soviet leadership clearly places a high value on preservation of the regime and on the survival and continued effectiveness of the instruments of state power and control," and that "a clear U.S. ability to destroy [Soviet officials and control centers] poses a marked challenge to the essence of the Soviet system and thus contributes to deterrence."

Pentagon analysts estimated the number of targeted Kremlin leaders at 100,000 individuals. According to scholar and author Beth Fischer,

> Weinberger and Vessey explained to the president that the U.S. nuclear arsenal was targeting over fifty thousand sites in the Soviet Union. Only half of these targets were military sites. The rest consisted of economic and industrial locations, as well as concentrations of human beings. The United States was now targeting the Soviet leadership to a greater extent than it had in the past, in the belief that this increased threat would make the Kremlin less inclined to launch a first strike. The officials also explained that if the United States were to carry out this plan, Soviet nuclear retaliation was almost certain. Such retaliatory strikes, they cautioned, would destroy Washington, if not the entire country.

Reagan later described the briefing as "a most sobering experience." Like his predecessors, he was appalled at the bloodless way in which the presenters discussed target selections and the human toll of a "successful" attack. "There are still some people at the Pentagon who claim nuclear war is 'winnable,'" Reagan complained after the briefing. "I thought they were crazy."

Was this the same man who electrified the crowds at the Republican National Convention in 1964 when he compared Lyndon Johnson's refusal to confront Moscow to the specter of "the patriots at Concord Bridge [throwing] down their guns and [refusing] to fire the shot heard 'round the world"? Had Reagan, on the strength of a made-for-TV movie and a single Pentagon briefing, reversed his perceptions of the Soviet menace? Or had he been playing his supporters—first the Goldwater brigades, then the neocons—for chumps all along, much the way Nixon did the China lobby?

If Reagan was not a hard-boiled realist like Nixon, neither was he an inflexible ideologue. Though a founding father of modern conservatism, as a negotiator he was a pragmatist with an instinct for common ground. When Reagan's initial round of tax cuts proved to be excessive, for example, he repealed many of them. In 1983, when Social Security was heading for bankruptcy, he worked with congressional Democrats for entitlement reform. Under his watch, the Federal Reserve intervened aggressively in foreign exchange markets for the sake of currency stability. Once it was clear the costs of maintaining U.S. troops in Lebanon outweighed the benefits, he withdrew them. When militarists in Congress and right-wing think tanks demanded he send U.S. ground troops to prevent Soviet subversion of Central America, he settled for providing friendly regimes with advisers and caches of relatively modest weaponry. (Of his neoconservative critics, Reagan once complained to his chief of staff, "Those sons-of-bitches won't be happy until we have 25,000 troops in Managua, and I'm not going to do it.")

In his approach to policymaking, Reagan was less Goldwater or Nixon and more John Maynard Keynes, the liberal economist who once declared drily, "When the facts change, I change my mind." What Reagan lacked in strategic thinking, at least when it came to foreign affairs, he compensated with that rarest of political qualities: a faculty for self-examination. Responding to the events of 1983, he wrote in his memoirs that his first three years in office

> ... taught me something surprising about the Russians: Many people at the top of the Soviet hierarchy were genuinely afraid of America and Americans. ... I had difficulty accepting my own conclusions at first. I'd always felt that from our deeds it must be clear to anyone that Americans were a moral people who starting at the birth of our nation had always used our power only as a force of good in the world. ... But the more experience I had with Soviet leaders and [those] who knew them, the more I began to realize that many Soviet officials feared us not only as adversaries, but as potential aggressors. ... Well, if that was the case, I was even more anxious to get a top leader in a room alone and try to convince him we had no designs on the Soviet Union and the Russians had nothing to fear from us.

Jimmy Carter's ideas about the Soviet Union underwent a very different conversion. The Soviet invasion of Afghanistan revealed to him the pernicious quality of Moscow's intentions, an epiphany that, as it turned out, evolved from a gross misreading of Kremlin motives. The Reagan awakening, in contrast, was based on truer perceptions. It evolved from an empathic reading of events that not only allowed for a measure of vulnerability in his adversaries but accepted that America might be perceived as malign. This was a rare kind of courage, and it changed everything.

A day after the conclusion of Able Archer, Reagan gave a speech in Tokyo that contrasted profoundly with the bellicose address he had delivered at Westminster Abbey in June 1982, in which he pledged support for democratic change in Eastern Europe. Speaking to the Japanese parliament, he made his first appeal for a world free of nuclear weapons. "I believe there can only be one policy for preserving our precious civilization in this modern age: a nuclear war can never be won and must never be fought." On January 16, 1984, Reagan delivered a speech that was inspired in part by John F. Kennedy's June 1963 speech at the American University, which helped calm U.S.-Soviet relations following the Cuban missile crisis. "So let us not be blind to our differences," Reagan said, "but let us also direct attention to our common interests and to the means by which those differences can be resolved." Reagan was now speaking the language of détente, stirred by written appeals he was receiving from new Soviet leader Konstantin Chernenko for "a complete ban . . . and liquidation of nuclear arms." Rifts within the White House between moderates and militarists, however, and lingering Soviet suspicions over U.S. motives limited both sides' room to maneuver.

In March 1985, after Chernenko died and was succeeded by Mikhail Gorbachev, Reagan sent Vice President George H. W. Bush and George Shultz, who had replaced the unruly Alexander Haig as Reagan's secretary of state, to the funeral and to extend an invitation to the new Soviet leader for a summit meeting. Gorbachev received the U.S. delegation at the Kremlin flanked by Foreign Minister Andrei Gromyko, a foreign policy adviser, and a translator. He thanked his guests for paying their respects to Chernenko and, as Shultz writes in his memoirs, "launched into the most far-ranging statement on foreign policy that I had heard from a Soviet leader." At first Gorbachev spoke from a bundle of typed notes, but he soon set them aside. He assured his visitors continuity in Soviet policy but scolded the Americans for characterizing global events as "simply the result of Moscow's mischief making." Leavening the mood,

Gorbachev gave the assurance that "we have no territorial claims against the United States, not even in respect to Alaska or Russian Hill in San Francisco." Then, looking straight at Vice President Bush, Gorbachev stated plainly: "The USSR has never intended to fight the United States and does not have any such intentions now. There have never been such madmen within the Soviet Union and there are none now."

Afterward, a buoyant Shultz told the others in his delegation that Gorbachev's arrival could mean a tectonic shift in Cold War relations. "He performs like a man who has been in charge for a while," he said, "not like a man who is just taking charge." Shultz praised Gorbachev at a March 15 press briefing as "totally different than any Soviet leader I've met." Not all of Reagan's aides were won over, however. Weinberger in particular would resist any meaningful high-level contact with Moscow, from Paul Nitze's July 1982 "walk in the woods" with his Soviet counterpart at arms reduction talks in Geneva, to Shultz's proposal for a Reagan-Andropov summit in 1982 and his meeting with Gromyko at the United Nations later that year, to the 1985 Reagan-Gorbachev summit in Geneva and the second one in Reykjavik a year later. It could be argued, given how defense spending had grown more or less in tandem with the levels of Cold War tension, that Weinberger had a professional stake in the status quo. This overlooks Weinberger's visceral loathing for communism, however, and the fact that he still coveted the job held by Shultz, for whom he would always play bridesmaid.

Shultz and Weinberger were fierce competitors going back to their days as senior aides in the Nixon administration—Shultz as treasury secretary, Weinberger as director of the Office of Management and Budget—and as top executives of Bechtel Corporation, a multinational engineering company. As the two most powerful members of Reagan's cabinet, they were correct in their dealings with each other, breakfasting together once a week, alternating as hosts, and conferring regularly by phone. As they were old-school types, their memoirs betray not a hint of mutual animosity and they would dismiss reports of friction, to say nothing of outright feuding, between them in the Reagan White House.

There were clashes, however, both of personality and over policy.

Throughout their careers, Weinberger was junior to Shultz—at Bechtel, where Shultz was president, as well as under Nixon and Reagan—and he resented what he regarded as his rival's high-handed manner. It was said that the low-profile Shultz, known among diplomats as the "Phantom of the Seventh Floor," would stay on as secretary of state "till hell freezes over" rather than leave a vacuum for Weinberger to fill. On the other hand, Weinberger had known Reagan since their years together in California, a connection he and Perle would exploit while attempting to outmaneuver Shultz during arms reduction talks with Moscow. By the end of Reagan's first term, the UN ambassador at the time, Jeane Kirkpatrick, was telling friends that tension between the two men had become "palpable," while a Pentagon insider told *Time* magazine that their mutual dislike "is only thinly disguised when they meet publicly."

There was a convergence of views, though, at least on some issues. Both men initially opposed Reagan's proposal to build a space-based antimissile system, only to support it later on—Shultz out of loyalty to the president, Weinberger as a way to scupper rapprochement with the Soviets—and both resisted the ill-advised covert attempt to swap arms with Iran for the release of American hostages in Lebanon.* Fundamentally, they were both hawks, though in conflicting ways when it came to the use of diplomacy and arms as alternative means of achieving policy ends. Although fiercely opposed to détente, Weinberger resisted agitation from the right for direct U.S. involvement in peripheral conflicts in Central America and the Middle East. He ruled out intervention in Nicaragua, for example, and he insisted on withdrawing U.S. Marines from Lebanon in 1983 after their barracks were destroyed in a terrorist attack. Responses to acts of terrorism, he said, "should be decided on a

---

* The Iran-Contra Affair nearly derailed the Reagan administration when it was discovered in November 1986 that White House aides had secretly sold weapons to U.S.-embargoed Iran in an attempt to free American hostages held by extremist groups close to Tehran. Money from the deal was then diverted to help fund guerrilla forces fighting the communist government in Nicaragua. Though Weinberger, along with Shultz, opposed the operation, he in fact participated in the sale of TOW missiles to Iran, the revelation of which was a likely factor in his resignation as defense secretary in late 1987. In June 1992, a federal grand jury indicted Weinberger on two counts of perjury and one count of obstruction of justice. That November, he received a full pardon from outgoing president George H. W. Bush.

case-to-case basis" and even then action should be taken only when the responsible group could be clearly identified.

In December 1984, Weinberger unveiled in an address at the National Press Club six conditions for taking the nation to war. They included clearly defined political and military objectives, an overwhelming commitment of force, and a "reasonable assurance" of popular support for the mission. The Weinberger Doctrine, as it would be known, was clearly informed by the lessons the military had learned from Vietnam, memories of which were still fresh among the Joint Chiefs at the time. (Its essence would be appropriated and expanded upon by Colin Powell when he served as JCS chairman in the George H. W. Bush administration.) While former senator William Fulbright, in an opinion column he co-wrote for the *New York Times,* dismissed Weinberger's conditions as too "broad and subjective" to preclude another Vietnam-like quagmire, Shultz derides them in his memoirs as "the Vietnam syndrome in spades, carried to an absurd level, and a complete abdication of leadership."

Weinberger's speech was, in fact, a direct challenge to Shultz's public campaign for a more aggressive response to terrorism. Shultz believed the United States should act preemptively against terrorism, in what he called "active defense," and he rebuked the adage "One man's terrorist is another man's freedom fighter" as subversive relativism. "If we got ourselves in the frame of mind that these terrorist acts could be justified and legitimized," Shultz writes in his memoirs, "and that somehow we were to blame, then we would have lost the battle." He condemned as "an erosion of control of foreign policy" the War Powers Resolution Act of 1973, which restricted the president's ability to take the nation to war, because "we need the capability to act on a moment's notice." He insisted on a mailed fist inside the velvet glove of engagement for his diplomats overseas lest Washington's credibility be "frittered away." An ex-Marine and World War II veteran, he grumbled that yanking the Marines from Lebanon "undercut prospects for successful negotiation" between Israel and Syria.

Shultz the diplomatist could be just as hawkish as Weinberger the militarist, and vice versa. Weinberger refused appeals by Alexander Haig, Shultz's predecessor, for direct attacks in Cuba and Central America but ended up supporting military aid to the government of El Salvador. In March 1986, with Shultz pushing for air strikes on targets in Libya for Libya's meddling with U.S. Navy exercises in the Gulf of Sidra, Weinberger successfully opposed such action in favor of looser rules for engagement. When Kuwait requested protection for its oil tankers in the Persian Gulf during the Iran-Iraq War, Weinberger readily agreed to "re-flag" its vessels under the Stars and Stripes and provide them with U.S. Navy escorts. His willingness to help the emirate was more about limiting Soviet influence in the region than it was about freedom of the seas, however, as the Kuwaitis had also asked Moscow for help. Shultz demurred; allowing some Soviet presence, he argued, would spread the risk. Weinberger took the matter to the president, and Shultz was overruled.

When it came to the singular issue that defined Reagan's foreign policy, however, it was all Shultz. By emphatically supporting Reagan's desire to sharply reduce the world's strategic arsenals and end three decades of superpower confrontation, Shultz would rank among the most powerful of Cold War secretaries of state, albeit with Weinberger and Perle waging a guerrilla war against him. For their efforts, the president and his top diplomat would be rewarded with a key arms reduction deal signed just as the Soviet Union was on the verge of collapse, an epochal event rooted in factors that preceded the Reagan presidency by generations.

The peaceful and conclusive way in which the Cold War ended—with the sudden collapse of the Soviet Union and the apparent triumph of democratic capitalism over communism—has engendered the myth that an uncompromising Reagan administration broke Moscow by engaging it in a withering arms race. Such a narrative, clutched like a life raft by American militarists and defense industrialists, ignores the fact that the Soviet empire had pauperized itself decades earlier. Reagan and his moderate advisers did play an important role in the Cold War's passing—but as diplomatists rather than militarists. It was not the relentless output of American tanks, missiles, and bombers that drove the USSR to its knees. Rather, it was the Soviet Union's own voracious arms industry.

Recall how George Kennan, as a young Sovietologist working at the American consulate in Riga, Latvia, wrote in an August 1932 cable that the USSR would ultimately collapse. Soviet communism, he knew, was intrinsically violent, predicated as it was on an endless class struggle that required a huge military bureaucracy and a domestic intelligence apparatus to sustain itself. Inevitably, Kennan argued, this national security state would dominate the economy and strangle it. He was exactly right. The VPK—the acronym is derived from the Russian for "industrial-military commission"—eventually became a perpetual motion machine that accounted for nearly half the USSR's budget and a quarter of its gross domestic product. Effectively the Soviet Union's largest employer in an economy bloated by subsidies, the VPK built weapons as much to create jobs and enhance its economic influence as for military purposes. Its overlords instructed the Red Army what weapons it would build, rather than the other way around. Sources interviewed for *Soviet Intentions, 1965–1985,* the Pentagon's post–Cold War debriefing project, emphasized that the defense industry had dominated the weapons-procurement process to the detriment of Soviet war-fighting capability. Manufacturers favored proven but obsolete weapons systems over investment in new technology and innovation. The Red Army's General Staff, according to *Soviet Intentions,* "exerted relatively little control over the R&D and production process while promotion of the VPK's interests became an end in itself."

With the Defense Ministry at its vortex, the VPK was a nebula of eight to ten industrial ministries that channeled their demands through the Defense Council, a key decision-making body within the Politburo. It became the ultimate supply-side-driven growth machine, an oligopoly with hordes of captive suppliers prone to overengineering and cost-plus pricing. In some regions of the Soviet Union, it was responsible for as much as 70 percent of industrial output, and it ingested most, if not all, of the empire's raw materials. The VPK was also an enormous patronage system, an enclave for cronies of Soviet general secretary Leonid Brezhnev, himself a product of the defense industry. Rather than favor one ally over another in procurement battles, Brezhnev tended to appease all sides, which, according to *Soviet Intentions,* "led to situations where the USSR was developing twelve ICBM programs simultaneously or continuing to produce outdated or low-quality versions of a tank at the same time that more modern, effective variants were coming on line. Production lines were kept open to satisfy the producers without consideration of the economic consequences or the true needs of the military customer."

The Soviets would reflexively, and usually with crude result, follow America's lead in new weapons development. When the United States introduced MIRV missile systems in the early 1970s, so did the Soviets. When Washington launched its Space Shuttle program, Moscow responded with its own system on the assumption that the U.S. version was to be used for military purposes. On the basis of collaborative testimony from dozens of senior Soviet leaders, *Soviet Intentions* concludes that the Soviet military expansion was more Sisyphean than Herculean, an attempt to keep the gears turning in a massive jobs mill and hideously corrupt bureaucracy. Whistle-blowing was frowned upon; when a senior official in the Defense Industrial Department submitted evidence of waste to department leaders, he was told to mind his own business.

To subsidize demand for VPK output among its occupied possessions in Eastern Europe and Central Asia, Moscow was forced to extend a thicket of credit lines to economies that were as supine as Russia's. Rather than diversify its industrial base away from the defense sector after it had achieved rough parity with the United States in conventional and nonconventional weaponry, the Soviet Union defied the law of diminishing returns by building more arms. Eventually the law won. By 1985, the year Gorbachev was elected general secretary, the Soviet economy had become little more than a host for a predatory defense-industrial establishment. "For the first time in the Cold War era," according to economists Stephen G. Brooks and William C. Wohlforth, "it was clear that barring some dramatic turnaround the Soviet Union would never close the gap in brute economic output with the United States, to say nothing of closing the gap in technology."

A CIA report circulated in September 1985 summarized the Soviet Union as "a technologically backward economy that had experienced decades of slowing growth punctuated by harvest failures, industrial bottlenecks, labor and energy shortages, low productivity, and declining efficiency." Its energy-production capacity was stagnant, its farm sector lacked adequate storage and transportation facilities, and its aging stock of industrial equipment was badly in need of replacement. Without mentioning the VPK by name, the report notes how the defense industry assumed a preponderant share of output. Gorbachev could, it suggested, "attempt to reallocate resources away from defense allocations," though at the political cost of antagonizing entrenched elites. It acknowledges that weapons-makers could be retrofitted for civilian production, but only after "extensive, time-consuming re-tooling." The report credited Gorbachev as "the most aggressive and activist Soviet leader since Khrushchev," though it implied that the political and economic imperatives of the defense industry would be too strong for even him to resist. Significantly, the report cited Reagan's Strategic Defense Initiative as a tonic for VPK budget requests, noting how "U.S. defense modernization and the long-term implications of the Strategic Defense Initiative probably are being cited by Soviet military leaders as justification of higher growth rates for defense spending."

Gorbachev's solution to thwart such demands was simple: end the arms race.*

It took him less than a year to acknowledge the systemic failures of Soviet communism and the triumph of free enterprise. "There is something deeply wrong in our evaluation of the American administration and the American life," he told a senior aide. "Our class analysis is failing and does not give us an answer that would provide a good basis for any kind of realistic politics." For a loyal Communist Party member, this was a revelation akin to a pious man's conclusion that God is dead. Like Reagan, Gorbachev would challenge and conquer cherished presumptions to historic and in many ways unintended effect.

The first of their two summits was held on November 19, 1985, in Geneva. At stake were the restoration of détente and the promise of substantial

---

* As General William Odom, who chaired the National Security Agency under Reagan, wrote in *The Collapse of the Soviet Military*, "A surprisingly broad consensus existed among most of the Soviet elite that the Soviet economy was in serious trouble and that the burden of military expenditure was to blame. To reduce it, Gorbachev turned to disarmament through arms control."

arms reduction. Failure meant a return to hair-trigger confrontation. Compared with the choreographed summits of today, with their prenegotiated treaties, tightly orchestrated ceremonies, and canned speeches, the meeting in Geneva was a high-wire act with no net. Its fortunes would turn on the Anti-Ballistic Missile Treaty, the 1972 accord that restricted development of weapons that could destroy incoming missiles because of the destabilizing effect they might have on the strategic balance. Technical difficulties in developing a missile that could strike another in midflight—the equivalent, it is often said, of a bullet hitting a bullet—together with the deployment of missiles with multiple warheads that could overwhelm defensive systems, made the question of antimissile systems moot until Reagan unleashed SDI. Proponents of Reagan's vision called for the United States to withdraw from the ABM Treaty, citing Defense Secretary Weinberger's warnings that the Soviets were poised to field an antimissile system "relatively quickly." This was nonsense. The chairman of Reagan's own Defensive Technologies Study Team concluded that the battle-management technologies for a viable ABM system were beyond the reach of scientists on both sides of the superpower divide.

No one had to convince the Soviets of the prohibitive challenges and ruinous costs of such a weapon. After struggling to match U.S. efforts to develop a deployable system in the 1960s, Moscow all but gave up on antiballistic defense beyond a relatively primitive network it built at the Siberian city of Krasnoyarsk, which Gorbachev would ultimately order scrapped. Such a thin reed was strong enough leverage for Perle and Weinberger, however. On the eve of Reagan's departure for Geneva, the *New York Times* and the *Washington Post* carried page-one stories about a letter, drafted by Perle and delivered to the president under Weinberger's imprimatur, that advised against agreeing to any limits on a robust SDI research program. Reagan, according to the memo, should resist opposition not only from the Soviets but also from their enablers at the State Department and in Congress. "You will almost certainly come under great pressure," according to the Perle memo as it appeared in the press, "to agree formally to limit SDI research, development and testing to only that research allowed under the most restrictive interpretation of the ABM treaty, even though you have determined that a less restrictive interpretation is justified legally."

In newspaper reports the next day, Perle was accused by unnamed White House officials of attempting to "sabotage" the Geneva summit by leaking the Pentagon letter. Perle denied the charge, though it was clear he was pushing the centrality of SDI research not as the germ of a viable defensive shield but as a way to scupper arms reductions. Arrayed against him were Secretary of State Shultz, National Security Adviser McFarlane, and Nitze, who regarded Star Wars as a potentially decisive bargaining chip in exchange for deep cuts in nuclear stockpiles.

The initial round at Geneva's Fleur d'Eau, the stately château where the summit took place, did little to inspire confidence on either side. Huddling with their advisers after the first session, Gorbachev dismissed the American president as "a caveman," a living relic of McCarthy-era thinking, while Reagan described his counterpart as "a die-hard Bolshevik." The exchanges during the afternoon plenary session were civil, if frank and sometimes pointed. When Reagan cited Moscow's invasion of Afghanistan as proof of its designs on the Persian Gulf, Gorbachev called the assertion baseless and implied the United States was trying to bleed the Soviet army there with its support of mujahideen rebels. (Several years later, Gorbachev would announce the withdrawal of Soviet forces from Afghanistan.) When Reagan blamed the Soviets for launching a dangerous arms race with their relentless production of nuclear weapons, Gorbachev turned the argument on its head. Two decades ago, he said, when the Soviets had no nuclear arsenal worth deterring, the United States deployed four times as many strategic delivery systems as the USSR, along with forward-based weapons for good measure. If the Soviets were working overtime to produce their own nuclear arsenal, he said, it was only to achieve parity with the Americans.

Whenever Reagan tried to divert the conversation away from arms reduction, accusing the Soviets of expansionism in places such as Afghanistan, Nicaragua, and Ethiopia, for example, Gorbachev wrestled it back to the need for weapons reduction. At one point, the Soviet leader proposed the two sides cut their nuclear arsenals in half, an offer that was endorsed by Reagan and that later became the foundation of even bolder proposals. Gorbachev insisted, however, that there could be no ending the arms race while the Americans were resolved to develop SDI, which would only catapult that race to a new dimension with the weaponization of space. Since any such network could be overwhelmed with enough missiles, Gorbachev argued, it would be of use only against a Soviet Union whose retaliatory capability had been weakened by a U.S. first strike. That would force Moscow to escalate, not reduce, its offensive arsenal, which would only engender mistrust, waste resources, and destabilize relations. And who would ultimately control such a weapon? The level of automation would be so great that a computer, perhaps aroused by a meteor shower, might trigger itself.

Reagan, however, was sticking to his extraterrestrial, if very much theoretical, antimissile guns. Later, the two men ambled over to the Fleur d'Eau pool house, where the president promoted SDI as a purely defensive system, something to be held in reserve even if nuclear arms were abolished, the same way the European powers kept their protective masks ready after agreeing to ban poison gas as a weapon of war. The American people wanted SDI, he told Gorbachev, if not as a deterrent against Soviet missiles, then as insurance against the impulse of a madman. Washington would share the technology, he pledged, as a kind of neighborhood watch against non-status-quo actors such as Libya's Muammar Gadhafi, who loomed as the Osama bin Laden of his time.

The impasse over Star Wars was irreconcilable, with Gorbachev holding fast to a strict interpretation of the ABM Treaty and Reagan insisting that the United States would continue SDI research. Neither the Americans nor the Soviets left Geneva empty-handed, however. Gorbachev had readily accepted Reagan's suggestion for reciprocal summit meetings in Washington and Moscow, and the U.S. side reversed its earlier opposition to a joint communiqué and worked with the Soviets to produce a statement that established as a bilateral goal a 50 percent reduction in strategic arms. What made the document truly historic, Gorbachev would later note, was its declaration that "a nuclear war cannot be won and must never be fought." Gorbachev also recounted how "[White House chief of staff Donald] Regan came to our [delegation] and shared his delight with [our] actions, and asked [us] to 'keep going in this way, to put pressure on the President, cajole him, melt him down . . . for his own benefit.'"

For every moderate in Reagan's cabinet who opposed militarizing the heavens, however, there were others who were banking on SDI to destroy what could have been sweeping cuts in nuclear weapons with the ultimate goal of full eradication. It would be the system's first and, as of this writing, only conclusive kill.

It should come as no surprise that the inspiration behind SDI can be traced back to Edward Teller, the RAND Corporation fountainhead for ever-more addled ways of making war. In 1967 Reagan visited the Lawrence Livermore National Laboratory, where Teller seized the California governor's imagination with tales of a purely defensive contraption that would make nuclear missiles obsolete. (Later, Teller would testify to Congress that the system represented "a third-generation nuclear weapon.") Reagan also fell in with a like-minded group of millionaire conservatives known as High Frontier, founded by Karl R. Bendetsen, a charter member of the Committee on the Present Danger and an assistant secretary of the Army who, as head of the Wartime Civil Control Association during World War II, directed the concentration of Japanese Americans into internment camps. For men like Teller and Bendetsen, weaponizing space was just the thing America needed to revive its first-strike capability, which was gradually eroding in the face of accelerated Soviet missile production.

For his part, Reagan regarded a space-based missile system as a defensive shield, an integral part of his plan to preempt Armageddon. Toward that goal, however, he was happy to leverage Teller's resources. As president, he appointed as his science adviser Teller protégé George Keyworth, a nuclear physicist from the Los Alamos National Laboratory who in January 1983 declared the "bomb-pumped X-ray laser" as "one of the most important programs that may seriously influence the nation's defense posture in the next decades." Keyworth also put forth an alternative system: a ground-based laser grid that would bounce deadly rays off mirrors orbiting in space.

In February 1983, with the Carter-era debate about how to deploy the MX missile raging well into the Reagan administration, some strategic planners began questioning the morality of so-called mutual assured destruction, in which both nuclear powers targeted civilians as a way of holding them hostage for the sake of deterrence. For Reagan, this was just the quandary a viable antimissile network could resolve. During one of his regular meetings with the Joint Chiefs of Staff, the president asked whether it was "worthwhile to see if we could not develop a weapon that could perhaps take out, as they left their silos, those nuclear missiles?" When none of the chiefs replied that the technology was beyond the ken of America's best scientists, engineers, and missile experts, or that the funds that would be wasted on such a futile enterprise could be more profitably invested elsewhere, Reagan ordered them to delve into it. The chiefs agreed to seek funding for such a defense system, a process that would require months of staff meetings, interagency policy reviews, and congressional testimony.

On March 23, Reagan was scheduled to deliver a televised speech to pitch his latest increase in defense spending while promoting the beleaguered MX missile. The conclusion of his draft speech, which was circulated to the heads of the foreign policy and defense agencies, included a blank space, a placeholder in which, according to the White House, "something of substance" was to be inserted. When word leaked out that the president was set to unveil his vision to provide the free world with a nuke-proof prophylactic, the president's national security and foreign policy teams panicked. Both Secretary of State Shultz and General John Vessey, the chairman of the Joint Chiefs of Staff, recommended the speech be scotched, and Defense Secretary Weinberger refused to endorse the plan. Reagan ignored all of them. After delivering the rump of a speech devoted largely to quantifying Moscow's increasingly menacing posture worldwide, Reagan dared viewers to imagine a world in which "free people could live secure in the knowledge that their security did not rest upon the threat of instant U.S. retaliation to deter a Soviet attack; that we could intercept and destroy strategic ballistic missiles before they reached our own soil or that of our allies." While allowing that a defensive shield in space posed monumental technical challenges, the president appealed to Americans' romance with the possible. "Isn't it worth every investment necessary to free the world from the threat of nuclear war?" he asked. "We know it is!"

The speech was widely panned. Intoned the New York Times's editorial page: "President Reagan's desire for a missile-proof shield around

America and its allies expresses the deepest longing of the nuclear age—for a place to hide. But it remains a pipe dream, a projection of fantasy into policy." Kosta Tsipis, an MIT scientist, called the speech "a cruel hoax," while former White House science adviser Jerome Wiesner said it was "a declaration of a new arms race." *Time* magazine that week rendered on its cover a stern-looking Reagan with missiles roaring skyward and satellites hovering about his head like a nimbus. The subtext—science fiction on the brain—was obvious. Suddenly, "Star Wars" was no longer just a successful motion picture. It was sardonic shorthand for the military-industrial complex's latest boondoggle.

Reagan ignored the critics just as he did his advisers. For him, the idea of antimissile defense, rather than the fact of a proven system, was suitable foundation for a bold new strategic doctrine. Everything else could be willed into place, and if the Soviets could be brought on board with promises of technology sharing, perhaps even codevelopment partnerships, so much the better. It was the purest expression of Reagan's America—industrious, bold, beneficent—and his biggest blind spot. The same Reagan who could discursively concede Russian anxiety over U.S. strategic intentions failed to understand how militarizing space would deepen those anxieties. Just as he pitched products for General Electric on television and radio in the 1950s, Reagan would spend the rest of his presidency relentlessly selling an anti-weapon system that only the defense industry and its patrons in Washington could love, all the while reconciling it with his stated goal to eliminate nuclear weapons.

Just how far along the Soviets were in embracing Reagan's vision of a demilitarized world would be made startlingly clear not long after the president's reelection. For years, Reagan and other Cold Warriors had warned that one day Moscow would contact the White House and demand America's capitulation on Soviet terms. The Kremlin was now serving notice all right, but with a very different message. On January 15, 1986, Soviet ambassador Anatoly Dobrynin presented Secretary of State Shultz with a letter from Gorbachev and announced that it would be made public in a few hours. After looking it over, Shultz phoned National Security Adviser John Poindexter and asked that it be given the highest priority. The letter was on the president's desk within minutes of its delivery to the White House.

In his letter, one of the most historic transmissions of the Cold War, Gorbachev offered what he called "a concrete program . . . for the complete liquidation of nuclear weapons throughout the world" within the next fifteen years. The letter came as a shock to the president's advisers, many of whom believed Gorbachev had yet to secure his authority and was having difficulty controlling his generals. Reagan welcomed the proposal, however. "Gorbachev surprisingly is calling for an arms reduction plan which will rid the world of nuclear weapons," he wrote in his diary that day. "We'd be hard put to explain how we could turn it down." For Gorbachev, frustrated at what he regarded as the White House's failure to build on the goodwill fostered at their Geneva summit two months earlier, it was a direct appeal to Reagan the nuclear abolitionist, a key step in his efforts to demilitarize the Soviet economy. But would the president's hard-line advisers allow it?

In mid-January, Richard Perle had told the Senior Arms Control Group that the president's dream of a world without nuclear weapons was "a disaster, a total delusion," Shultz writes in his memoirs. Now, in the wake of Gorbachev's bombshell, Perle was warning the National Security Council it should not take up the matter "because then the president would direct his arms controllers to come up with a program to achieve that result." According to Shultz, "the naysayers were hard at work." Even the Joint Chiefs "feared the institutionalization and acceptance of the idea as our policy." On January 18, Shultz met with Perle and Paul Nitze. According to Shultz, "Perle insisted that Gorbachev's letter was not serious, just propaganda. 'We must not discuss it as though it were serious,' he said. 'The worst thing in the world would be to eliminate nuclear weapons.'"

To which Shultz replied, laughing: "You've got a problem. The president thinks it is a *good* idea." Not only did Reagan embrace Gorbachev's offer, he wanted to improve on it. The Soviet leader had proposed a three-stage process for ridding the world of nuclear bombs by 2000. Reagan saw no reason why the two sides should wait so long.

———

Strongly implied in Gorbachev's letter was that the zero option he was offering, the most daring arms-reduction proposal in history, was valid only if Reagan would relinquish SDI. No one knew that better than the now-estranged Perle and Nitze. Though neither man had much faith in the feasibility of a space-based missile system—Perle dismissed the concept as "the product of millions of American teenagers putting quarters into video machines"—each claimed it as the trump card in their rival gambits. For Nitze, SDI was barter for a landmark weapons-reduction deal, and his greatest fear was that "we'll give it up and we won't get a goddamn thing for it." Careful not to overtly suggest the president's cherished shield was negotiable, he earmarked the whole spectrum of nuclear systems, both offensive and defensive, for elimination over a ten-year period while holding the deployment of SDI in abeyance for at least several years. It was a thinly veiled gesture to the Soviets, but Nitze worked behind the scenes to line up support from powerful constituencies on the U.S. side. Just as he did while incubating NSC 68 a quarter century earlier, Nitze shopped his idea to various officials in isolation of each other, dazzling each with an exclusive pitch. He also imposed a particularly high performance standard on SDI. In a speech before the World Affairs Council of Philadelphia, he outlined rates of effectiveness, survivability, and affordability that were so onerous that proponents of Star Wars scorned the "Nitze criteria" for what they were: the slaying of SDI in exchange for significant bilateral reductions in offensive strategic weapons.

Perle, in his ambition to subvert the abolitionist goals of both U.S. and Soviet leaders, had the president's unwitting assistance working for him. All he had to do was play the Reagan loyalist by exposing the Nitze criteria, which he referred to as "the killer criteria," as a stalking horse. He also argued for an early introduction of the system, in contrast to Nitze's efforts to strangle it softly through a protracted deployment schedule. In November 1985, in closed-door testimony to a subcommittee of the Senate Armed Services Committee, Perle said $100 billion for a working antimissile shield was a bargain, particularly given how unlikely it was that the Soviets would follow through with threats to build their own system. When Senator Albert Gore Jr. asked why this was so, Perle replied that the Soviets knew the United States would never launch a first strike.

It was a theme echoed consistently by Weinberger. On March 27, 1983, for example, Weinberger said on NBC's *Meet the Press* that it was "widely known to the Soviets that we would never launch a first strike," while "all of their preparations—I should say, and all of their acquisitions in the military field in the last few years—have been offensive in nature."

In fact, exactly the opposite was true. The prospect of a U.S. preemptive attack not only was anticipated by Moscow, it was the defining element of its strategic doctrine. Just as the Soviet Union responded in kind to America's MIRV missiles and the Space Shuttle, it would most certainly have embarked on its own antimissile system had perestroika, Gorbachev's attempt to liberalize the Soviet political system, not resulted instead in its liquidation. Not only that, the presumption among White House hawks in both the fact and the perception of American restraint jarred with statements from a succession of U.S. security experts that a "limited" or "protracted" nuclear war was winnable. (That included the unreformed Paul Nitze, who had argued in a 1956 *Foreign Affairs* article that America could prevail in a nuclear conflict.) At the same time, the mischaracterization of the USSR as unrelentingly aggressive was a source of provocation in itself. One can imagine the Soviet response to Weinberger's warning in a *Wall Street Journal* opinion piece, for example, that there could be no "more debilitating factor for the world than if the Soviets should acquire a thoroughly reliable defense against these missiles before we did."

Working through Weinberger, Perle had managed to persuade the president to end American compliance with the SALT II accord while assuming a broad interpretation of the ABM Treaty to enable the militarization of space. As with the "zero option," his proposal to offer the Soviets nothing in return for their unilateral withdrawal of intermediate-range missiles in Europe, he circulated an equally unrealistic counteroffer to Gorbachev's plan for nuclear eradication: the United States would remove all ground-based ballistic missiles but maintain its sea-launched missiles, ground-based cruise missiles, and bombers. Though Weinberger supported the idea, it was dismissed by others on Reagan's arms control team. Michael Guhin, a counselor to the Arms Control and Disarmament Agency, called it "a propaganda ploy," while Nitze, the master of soft-stall tactics, said it was "ridiculous." Perle would hold this poison pill in reserve, however, and slip it to Reagan at a key juncture in negotiations with Gorbachev.

On July 18, 1986, during a visit to Moscow, Richard Nixon met with Gorbachev and confirmed what the Soviet leader already suspected: that militarists within the Reagan administration were trying to derail his plans for vast cuts in nuclear stockpiles. "They believe that if they can isolate the Soviet Union diplomatically, apply economic pressure on it, achieve military superiority, then the Soviet order would collapse," Nixon told him. Gorbachev's challenge, said the former president, was to sidestep Reagan's deeply divided inner circle and appeal to him directly.

By now, Gorbachev had lashed himself to the mast of a ship entering unknown waters. In May 1986, before an extraordinary meeting of ambassadors and other members of the foreign policy elite, he introduced his "new thinking" about how Moscow must engage an increasingly interconnected world on its terms. "In today's world of mutual interdependence," he declared, "progress is unthinkable for any society which is fenced off from the world by impenetrable frontiers and ideological barriers. . . . We [cannot] ensure our country's security without reckoning with the interests of other countries, and . . . in our nuclear age, you [cannot] build a safe security system based on solely military means." A year earlier, Gorbachev had put his plans for nuclear disarmament, the so-called Gorbachev initiative, before the Big Five commission, a complex of military, diplomatic, intelligence, and defense industry officials. The commission approved it without serious objection largely because its members, like Richard Perle, believed it was a confidence game.

In September 1986, impatient with what he called the Reagan administration's "pretense of a continuing dialogue," Gorbachev acted on Nixon's advice and proposed a snap summit. "In almost a year since Geneva, there has been no movement on these issues," he wrote the president in a letter hand-delivered by his foreign minister, Eduard Shevardnadze. "I have come to the conclusion that the negotiations need a major impulse. . . . They will lead nowhere unless you and I intervene personally." Reagan accepted the invitation. In two weeks, on October 10, the two men would meet for their second summit meeting, held in the small Icelandic capital of Reykjavik.

The city was, to say the least, far removed from the traditional summit circuit. Upon their arrival, the Americans set up offices in a school building identified by a crudely made sign, probably erected by a U.S. embassy wag, as the ICELANDIC EXECUTIVE OFFICE BUILDING. There would be little in the way of light humor to come, however. The Americans had expected a series of planning sessions for a larger summit to be announced. Instead, they soon found themselves locked with the Soviets in the most intense arms-reduction talks of the Cold War.

The Soviets proposed Reykjavik as their preferred venue precisely because a more conventional site such as London, the alternative choice, would have required the participation in some form of the host nation and NATO. Instead, the Russians had the Americans right where they wanted them: on a remote island nation, insulated from the intrusive protocols of alliance diplomacy. The summit's main venue, Hofdi House, was a twin-gabled clapboard manor perched austerely on the edge of the North Atlantic. A former ambassador's residence, it was said to be haunted, though any specters who may have inhabited it wisely chose to lie low for this particular event. There would be nothing scripted about the meetings at Reykjavik, which was less a summit than an intellectual and emotional slugfest between two global leaders who shared the same objectives but who insisted on irreconcilable ways of reaching them.

There was a strict news blackout and there were no ceremonies. The summit convened under gunmetal gray skies and a bitter cold, pelting rain. At 10:30 a.m., as host of the first meeting, Reagan invited Gorbachev to speak first. The Soviet leader responded with a three-point plan for the reduction by half of all strategic weapons on both sides, from cruise missiles to long-range ICBMs. He proposed the total elimination of all U.S. and Soviet missiles in Europe, and he dropped a previous demand that the British and French nuclear arsenals be included in any arms reduction agreements. Reagan and his Soviet counterpart confirmed their mutual commitment to abolish all nuclear weapons. Then came the matter of the ABM Treaty and SDI. Gorbachev suggested the two sides agree to a nuclear test ban and a ten-year extension of the treaty, followed by a period of negotiations over several years. Under the Soviets' narrow interpretation of the treaty, development of SDI would be confined to the laboratory.

Reagan demurred. Apparently, he suggested, Gorbachev still perceived his vision for an antiballistic shield as somehow threatening. Since it would be deployed only after all nuclear weapons had been eliminated, it could play no role in a preemptive strike. The president argued that either side should be permitted to deploy such a system at the end of a five-year period of research, development, and testing. He then repeated his offer to share with Moscow the technology behind a proven system.

Despite the impasse over SDI, Shultz believed Gorbachev's plan was "new and highly significant." Nitze declared it "the best Soviet proposal we have received in twenty-five years." Perle, however, complained that the Soviet position would leave intermediate-range missiles in Asia, which could be easily dispatched to Europe. When Reagan pointed out in the next session that the United States had no ballistic missiles in the Far East, Gorbachev countered that the United States had nuclear stockpiles in South Korea and other bases throughout Asia. (That included Japan, which, despite a government ban on nuclear weapons from its territory, secretly allowed U.S. warships with "special weapons" to enter its waters.) Nevertheless, Gorbachev reluctantly agreed to include Soviet Asia–based missiles in any reduction agreement. When the U.S. side objected that Gorbachev's offer for a 50 percent cut in nuclear forces would leave the Soviets with a numerical edge in most classes of missiles, he conceded that point as well, agreeing on dramatic cuts that would produce equal outcomes of 6,000 warheads and 1,600 delivery vehicles.

On and on the negotiations went. At 7:10 a.m. the next day, with the conclusion of all-night deliberations, an elated Shultz remarked to Nitze that both sides had achieved "a terrific night's work." All that was left was SDI. Relations between the delegations were now brittle. Shultz found Soviet foreign minister Eduard Shevardnadze "cold, almost taunting. The Soviets had made all the concessions, he said. Now it was our turn. . . . Everything depended on how to handle SDI: a ten-year period of nonwithdrawal and strict adherence to the terms of the ABM Treaty during that period. That was their bottom line."

The verbatim transcript of the final meeting between Reagan and Gorbachev reveals men from starkly different places informed by vastly divergent pasts. Both sides wanted a world free of the deadliest weapons ever devised and the end of a forty-year feud that made cannon fodder of their civilian populations. The commonality ended there, however. For Gorbachev, Reykjavik was about more than nuclear abolition. It was a gateway for the deliverance of his people from a thousand-year inheritance of war, famine, pogroms, empire, and autocracy. Gorbachev, whose generation of Kremlin leaders was the first to openly acknowledge the depths of Soviet sclerosis—and, as it would turn out, the last to endure it—had no use for hegemonism. To save the communist ideal meant slaying the empire and its predatory embrace of Mother Russia. To do that, he needed to neutralize the Soviet military-industrial complex, which meant eliminating the eternal state of war that was nourishing it. With the Reykjavik summit entering its final hours, the only thing frustrating his ambition was the mating call of a science fantasy and its mesmerizing claim on the leader of the free world.

Ronald Reagan was in no such hurry. Empire had come relatively cheap to America. At the cost of a mere 6 percent of its GDP, its armies and navies had encircled the Soviet Union with an array of forward-deployed bases and battle fleets. For Reagan, ridding the world of nuclear weapons was a moral imperative that, however profound, was never a matter of national survival. America was a rich nation insulated by two oceans laterally and two undefended borders longitudinally. With a margin for error like that, he could afford, if he so chose, to scuttle sweeping arms reduction for the sake of an unproven weapons system of dubious viability. Several times during the deliberations, Reagan asked his Soviet counterpart why he objected so strongly to the concept of SDI. It was not a question he had to ask the American people, who had a comparatively minor stake in the matter. This made his bargaining position all but impregnable.

There would be no deal, in no small part because of the guileful Richard Perle. During a break in the final session, Perle strongly advised Reagan against any compromise that would restrict SDI development to theoretical research, according to author Jay Winik. Such a concession, he said, would "effectively kill" the system. In this account, Reagan sided with Perle over conciliators Shultz and Nitze. Author Richard Rhodes, citing several sources, including an interview with Perle himself, makes it clear that Perle played a definitive role in Reykjavik's collapse. Perle implied his was the deciding voice as Reagan caucused with his advisers about the system's sustainability if confined to the lab. As the recess concluded, Reagan directed Perle to update the U.S. position on the ABM Treaty by striking from it the word "laboratory." With that, the fate of Reykjavik was sealed.

According to Thomas Graham Jr., who was general counsel to the Arms Control and Disarmament Agency at the time of the summit, "Perle regarded his successful frustration of an agreement at Reykjavik as one of his most important achievements." It was also a seminal moment in the history of American militarism.

News footage of Reagan and Gorbachev departing Hofdi House for the last time on that cold October evening reveals two emotionally vacant men seemingly held together only by their overcoats against the weight of their failure and disappointment. Not since a quarter century earlier, when Kennedy and Khrushchev had parried so acrimoniously at Vienna, had superpower relations been so viscerally probed. Once again it seemed, it would be a cold winter.

The collapse of the Soviet Union, a process that began in 1989 and continued until 1991, was triggered by endemic corruption and inefficiency that prevailed well before the Reagan era. The Soviet economic system, in which the state rather than the marketplace determined the price and availability of goods and services, was no more sustainable at the end of the twentieth century than it was at its beginning. Gorbachev understood this even before his elevation to power, and the way he went about defusing the Cold War was as inspirational as it was unilateral.

In March 1985, on the day he was elected general secretary of the Soviet Communist Party, Gorbachev convened a special meeting of the Warsaw Pact nations and announced the separation of their political bonds. "You are independent," he said. "You are responsible for your policies, we are responsible for ours. We will not intervene in your affairs, I promise you." At the Twenty-ninth Party Congress in June 1988, he admonished his predecessors for giving in to the sirens of militarism. "As a result," he said, "we let ourselves be drawn into the arms race, which was bound to affect the socio-economic development of the country and our international position." Several months later, in October, Gorbachev ordered his Defense Ministry to prepare for the withdrawal of Soviet forces from Eastern Europe. Announcing his plans to the Politburo, he declared the 6-million-man Soviet army bloated and technically obsolete. "Our announced military doctrine contradicts our actual military programs," he said. "Our military expenses are 2.5 times larger than those of the United States. . . . What do we need such an army for?"

Even for the general secretary, this was a brazen proposal. Fortunately for Gorbachev, once-recalcitrant Politburo members had been replaced with loyal functionaries, the legacy of a bizarre incident that had occurred a year earlier. On May 13, 1987, a nineteen-year-old German student and aviator named Mathias Rust rented a Cessna single-engine airplane and began a multistop journey that began in Hamburg and ended with a three-point landing in a parking lot behind St. Basil's Cathedral in Moscow. From there Rust, who said he "hoped to build an imaginary bridge between East and West," taxied to Red Square and emerged from his cockpit with a twenty-two-page plan for nuclear disarmament he had prepared for Gorbachev.

Having dramatically revealed the porous nature of Soviet air defenses, the very system Richard Perle had said was impenetrable, Rust would spend thirty-six months in prison at KGB headquarters. But he provided Gorbachev with just the opportunity he needed to purge what was left of the Kremlin's old-guard leadership, including senior cadres in the VPK. With a friendly Politburo behind him, Gorbachev was dissolving the Soviet empire, diminishing the Red Army, and dismantling the defense industry. A few months later, in a speech at the United Nations, he unveiled his plans for massive and unilateral cuts in Soviet assault divisions in Eastern Europe—the withdrawal and eventual liquidation of 10,000 tanks, 8,500 artillery systems, 800 combat aircraft, and 500,000 troops. Soviet units remaining in Eastern Europe would retrench into an "unambiguously defensive" posture, he said.

Gorbachev then turned to the challenge that had so thoroughly preoccupied him since he assumed the Kremlin helm:

By this act, just as by all our actions aimed at the demilitarization of international relations, we would also like to draw the attention of the world community to another topical problem, the problem of changing over from an economy of armament to an economy of disarmament. Is the conversion of military production realistic? We believe that it is, indeed, realistic. For its part, the Soviet Union is ready to do the following. Within the framework of the economic reform we are ready to draw up and submit our internal plan for conversion, to prepare in the course of 1989, as an experiment, the plans for the conversion of two or three defense enterprises, to publish our experience of job relocation of specialists from the military industry, and also of using its equipment, buildings, and works in civilian industry. It is desirable that all states, primarily the major military powers, submit their national plans on this issue to the United Nations.

This was an authentic "swords into plowshares" moment, and a packed General Assembly responded with a standing ovation. As usual, the mainstream American press smelled a rat. Gorbachev's "gambit," as *Time* magazine described the Soviet leader's force-reduction plan, was "substantive enough to lure the West toward complacency, yet . . . too small to dent significantly the advantages of men, material and geography the Soviet bloc has over NATO." If not careful, warned *Time,* Western Europe might allow itself to be seduced by the Soviet leader into a "neutered neutralism."

Within a year, however, even the late Henry Luce's publishing empire had to acknowledge what the world was witnessing in real time: the implosion of that enduring Soviet "bloc." In December 1989, at a summit in Malta, Gorbachev and Reagan's successor, George H. W. Bush, declared that Moscow and Washington were no longer enemies or adversaries. With that, history's largest and most costly strategic confrontation came to an end. Like the collapse of the Sino-Soviet alliance, the fall of the Iron Curtain was anticipated by no one among the Beltway cognoscenti; the CIA missed it, as did established pundits and Sovietologists. The Committee on the Present Danger, which believed the Cold War would

end with an epic military conflict that was not only inevitable but preferable, had no clue.

For Mikhail Gorbachev and his allies in the Kremlin, unilateral withdrawal from the USSR's confrontation with the West was as natural and
logical as it was liberating. Among his former Cold War rivals, however,
demilitarization would never be seriously considered as an option. The
collapse of Soviet Russia would confront America's militarists with what
Chas Freeman, the outspoken former U.S. ambassador, called "enemy deprivation syndrome." Fortunately for them, it would be only a temporary
condition.

13

REFORMATION

*The question is, can we, as a country, any longer afford a 207-year-
old concept that in military matters the civilian is supreme?*
—U.S. SENATOR BARRY GOLDWATER

IN A 2009 INTERVIEW WITH *THE NATION* MAGAZINE, MIKHAIL
Gorbachev insisted it was perestroika that felled the Soviet Union,
not the Reagan military buildup, and he worried that the restraint
that had served Washington so well during the Cold War had been replaced by a reckless triumphalism. "When people came to the conclusion that they had won the Cold War," Gorbachev said, "they concluded
that they didn't need to change. That point of view is mistaken, and
it undermined what we had envisaged for Europe—mutual collective
security for everyone and a new world order. All of that was lost. . . .
Instead, it was proposed that NATO's jurisdiction be extended to the
whole world. . . . World leadership is now understood to mean that America gives the orders."

These were not the bitter reflections of a man who had labored to
reform a bankrupt economy only to lose an empire. A year later, Jack
Matlock, a top State Department Soviet expert who served as the U.S.
ambassador to Moscow from 1987 to 1991, echoed Gorbachev's lament
of Washington's post–Cold War expansionism. In *Superpower Illusions,*
Matlock argued that the end of the bipolar world was "a negotiated outcome that benefited both sides" and he rejected the militarists' account
that the Soviet Union was brought down by record-high U.S. defense
spending and the hard-line policies of Ronald Reagan's first few years in
office. Such claims, he wrote, "are all distortions, all incorrect, all misleading, and all dangerous to the safety and future prosperity of the American people."

The Soviet collapse was followed not by the unwinding of America's Cold War alliances and commitments but by the mushrooming of its hegemony worldwide—to Eastern Europe, despite U.S. assurance that it would not enlarge NATO authority; to Central Asia, where Washington negotiated security agreements with oil-rich and strategically important former Soviet satellites; to the Balkans, on Russia's postimperial doorstep; to Asia and the Persian Gulf, where the Pentagon expanded its military presence and basing rights; and to Latin America, where the Pentagon was called upon by Congress to wage a war on drugs in defiance of a century-old proscription against making law enforcement officers out of U.S. military personnel. At the same time, lawmakers starved the State Department of its diplomatic and humanitarian aid resources, creating a vacuum for the Pentagon to fill. Throughout the 1990s, American soldiers and Marines would engage in everything from disaster-relief and counternarcotics operations to democracy and human rights promotion—work that was once the preserve of civilians. By the end of the decade, the Pentagon was involved in so much noncore activity, it even came up with a label for such missions: Military Operations Other Than War.

As the Pentagon's responsibilities proliferated, so too did its authority. A strengthened chairman of the Joint Chiefs of Staff at home and powerful combatant commanders abroad, together with a rapid rebound in defense-spending growth after the Soviet collapse, made the military the most authoritative voice in national security. Having been relegated to the backbenches in policy debates, general and flag officers would in the 1990s achieve parity with their civilian counterparts for power and influence over the interagency mill. For the first time, moreover, Americans would celebrate the Pentagon's growing clout and dominion. Once disdained as a federal intrusion, the U.S. military would emerge as an object of semi-worship, at least for the 99.5 percent of the citizenry that did not serve in it. Having begun the 1980s still flinching from the specters of Vietnam, the all-volunteer force entered the 1990s having evolved into an authentic expression of American values: patriotism, discipline, courage, sacrifice.

To get there, however, the military needed a catalyst, a stunning vindication of the work men such as General Creighton Abrams and

Defense Secretary Mel Laird had done to rebuild it from the ashes of Indochina. That catalyst would arrive courtesy of Saddam Hussein in his first turn as stooge to American militarists.

As we have seen, acts of aggression are rarely unprovoked, a fact that complicates tidy narratives of victimhood and redemption. Tokyo's December 1941 assault on U.S. bases in East Asia and the Pacific, for example, was in retaliation for an Allied oil and steel embargo on Japan designed to thwart its imperial onslaught of China.* In 1950 North Korea invaded its southern neighbor following years of clashes unleashed by both sides across the military demarcation line that divides the Korean peninsula. The Soviet decision in 1962 to erect ballistic missiles in Cuba was a defensive, if dim-witted, maneuver to counter U.S. Jupiter missiles in Turkey and Italy. In 1964 North Vietnamese torpedo boats attacked American Navy vessels in waters claimed by Hanoi several months into covert U.S. operations in the area.

Similarly, Saddam Hussein's 1990 invasion of Kuwait followed a series of provocative actions rooted in the Iran-Iraq War that consumed much of the 1980s. The Arab nation was a bulwark against a Persian-Islamic republic with regional ambitions, and powerful interests ensured that it held—the Americans with weapons and intelligence, including satellite imagery; the Israelis with guns (which they sold to both sides); and the Gulf emirates with money. Though Iran had suffered a quantifiable defeat—its forces were devastated in battle thanks to Iraq's liberal use of chemical weapons—"victory" had left Iraq $90 billion in debt and had laid waste to its once-mighty middle class. With oil prices languishing in the aftermath of the war, the country was starved of the very petrodollars

---

* One could argue that Japan's attack on Pearl Harbor and Clark Field in the Philippines was the final phase in a process that had begun three decades earlier, when U.S. president Theodore Roosevelt was negotiating an end to the Russo-Japanese War. Roosevelt, who greatly admired Japan, believed it was the natural "protector" of "all the Asiatic nations" in their transition to modernity, just as the United States had enriched the Americas under its own imperium. In a secret presidential cable, the president recognized Japanese suzerainty over the Korean peninsula, which it long coveted in its competition with China and Russia. By the end of World War I, having consolidated control over the Korean peninsula, Japan helped itself to large swaths of China.

it needed to rebuild its economy. Iraq was whole but vulnerable, and with Iran extinguished as a regional threat, its wartime benefactors set about diminishing it as well.

For Iraq's hostility toward Israel, the U.S. Senate in August 1988 pressured President George H. W. Bush to deprive Baghdad of key industrial technologies. At the same time, both Kuwait and the United Arab Emirates significantly ramped up oil production despite Iraq's dependence on crude sales to fund its postwar reconstruction. A year later, Baghdad accused Kuwait of siphoning some $2.4 billion in petroleum from the Rumaila oil field on the Iraqi side of its border with the emirate. In May 1990, Congress voted to suspend loans to Iraq, and the emir of Kuwait demanded it repay $8 billion in wartime borrowings. Later that month, at a meeting of the Arab League in Baghdad, Hussein accused Kuwait of waging economic warfare against him by pumping oil in quantities well above its OPEC quota, thus depressing oil prices.

What emboldened tiny Kuwait to taunt the cornered Hussein? According to Middle East historian Said Aburish, "Everyone was telling Kuwait to hold the line—and in this case 'everyone' meant the USA and UK." At the same time, the Iraqi dictator and former U.S. ally had little reason to believe Washington would intervene forcefully to protect Kuwait's interests. On July 25, he had been told by U.S. ambassador April Glaspie that the United States had "no opinion on Arab-Arab conflicts, like your border disagreement with Kuwait."* Only a day before, a State Department spokesman had acknowledged that the United States had no security treaties that would oblige it to involve itself in a confrontation between two Arab states. On July 31, a Saudi-hosted effort to defuse the crisis failed. Two days later, Hussein, clearly convinced that he was under assault by the West via its Gulf proxies and convinced he could lash out at Kuwait with impunity, made his move.

Like the North Korean invasion of its southern neighbor and the Soviet move on Afghanistan, Iraq's blitzkrieg on Kuwait stunned the White House. Having failed to anticipate the assault, the Bush administration set

---

* The only note-takers at the meeting were Hussein's aides, and at least two transcripts of what was discussed have been published. The State Department has made no comment on either version.

about reversing it by marshaling an international coalition of great depth and complexity. It was a diplomatic offensive that proved how a thoughtful U.S. president under the relentless prodding of sage counsel could lead an alliance in the name of collective security. Working with governments whose interests often diverged dramatically from each other, the White House cobbled together a huge multinational force that five months later would eject Iraqi troops from Kuwait in a four-day sweep. In deliberate fashion, peaceful options for a resolution of the crisis were exhausted until only a military one remained. It was, in short, a triumph of coalition diplomacy.

Despite this, the legacy of Operation Desert Storm, as the military phase of the campaign was called, would ultimately prove inimical to U.S. interests. Its chaotic aftermath exposed the perils of using armed might to achieve even limited policy ends, and it manacled the United States to a prolonged mission in Iraq that, together with its support of Israel, assured it the antipathy of the Arab world.

The aides who advised George H. W. Bush during the Kuwait crisis—Secretary of State James Baker, National Security Adviser Brent Scowcroft, Chairman of the Joint Chiefs of Staff Colin Powell, and Deputy National Security Adviser Robert Gates—are widely regarded to be the most accomplished foreign policy specialists since Truman's Wise Men. After a surprisingly sluggish start—the president had initially ruled out a military response to the invasion—the White House declared it would draw the line against Iraqi forces with a troop buildup in Saudi Arabia, an operation that would be known as Desert Shield. It was an appropriately forceful response to a naked act of aggression, but it was also politically expedient. Bush, a former CIA director, U.S. congressman, ambassador to China, and vice president, was the most impressively credentialed American president since Richard Nixon, at least when it came to international affairs. Yet his privileged background as scion to a great American dynasty—his father, Prescott Bush, was a successful Wall Street executive and U.S. senator and his grandfather owned a railroad—tagged him as a preppy dilettante. In 1987 Newsweek magazine featured presidential aspirant Bush on its cover with FIGHTING THE WIMP FACTOR as the headline.

The invasion of Kuwait was a golden opportunity for Bush to show his mettle. Just as Harry Truman in 1950 rallied to South Korea's defense, so too would Bush repel the invaders of the tiny Gulf emirate. He disparaged the likelihood that the embargo imposed on Iraq would work "in an acceptable time frame," no doubt aware that a festering Gulf crisis would damage him politically ahead of the 1992 national elections. Though not given to hyperbole, Bush in public remarks compared Hussein with Adolf Hitler, Iraq's ruling Ba'ath Party with the Nazis, and the invasion of Kuwait with Germany's 1939 assault on Poland. While that may have conditioned the nation for war, it signaled to U.S. allies an intention to topple the regime in Baghdad rather than simply restore the status quo ante. By early November, the president announced that another 200,000 troops were deploying to the Persian Gulf, in addition to the 200,000 already garrisoned in Saudi Arabia to enforce Desert Shield. This gave him the option of going on the offensive against Hussein, which, together with his conflation of Iraq and Nazi Germany, discomfited allied leaders as well some U.S. lawmakers.

At the urging of Scowcroft and Gates, Bush jettisoned the Hussein-as-Hitler talk if only to ease the burden on Secretary of State Baker. It was Baker's job to gather foreign governments into an international framework and keep them there, and by far the most important constituent was Moscow. Without the Kremlin's imprimatur, the coalition would appear to be a U.S.-led grab for Middle East oil, a perception that would make it awkward for Arab leaders to join the alliance. By a stroke of luck, Baker was in the Russian city of Irkutz as a guest of Foreign Minister Eduard Shevardnadze when news of the invasion broke. Despite close Soviet-Iraqi ties that dated back some four decades, Baker urged his host to persuade Soviet leader Mikhail Gorbachev to join a U.S.-led arms embargo on Iraq. Shevardnadze left immediately for Moscow, but not without two close Baker aides on board. By the time they had reached the Russian capital, the foreign minister was prepared to endorse a joint U.S.-Russian statement, written by his American guests, condemning Baghdad's aggression. In the face of stern opposition from the Russian military, the KGB, and his own ministry, Shevardnadze signed the statement with only minor revisions.

Soviet cooperation remained fragile, however, and Bush and Baker worked hard to sustain it. When a U.S. warship enforcing the embargo encountered an Iraqi tanker ship off the coast of Yemen, Bush resisted pressure from his advisers to disable the vessel for fear such a move would weaken Gorbachev's position in the Kremlin. Instead, he gave Baker additional time to work with Shevardnadze for support of a UN resolution that called for international enforcement of the embargo, a gamble that paid off. To enhance Gorbachev's position at home, Bush invited the Soviet leader to a face-to-face meeting in Helsinki on September 8, where he offered him joint sponsorship of a global conference on the Middle East after the Kuwait matter was resolved. On November 8, Shevardnadze assured Baker of Kremlin support for a UN resolution authorizing "all means necessary" to expel Iraq from Kuwait. On January 11, 1991, Bush not only acquiesced to Gorbachev's request for a delay in the unleashing of Desert Storm, he softened the U.S. position against Serbian aggression in the collapsed Yugoslavia, where Russia had sided with its historical Serb ally.

Despite Bush's accommodation of Gorbachev and other foreign leaders—to ensure Israel would not respond to Scud missile attacks from Baghdad, the United States quickly installed Patriot antimissile batteries around its major cities—he continued to push for regime change. Indeed, even after Gorbachev had persuaded Hussein to withdraw his troops from Kuwait in twenty-one days—Baghdad had initially offered a timetable of six weeks—and drop his demands that resolution of the Gulf crisis be linked to other Middle East issues, the White House refused to accept anything short of an unconditional evacuation. The president, according to Gates, was "coldly implacable toward Saddam," a temperament that occasioned one of the few polarizing issues in an otherwise measured policymaking process. "The howling in the Congress was loud," Powell writes in his memoirs. "Was this George Bush, whom some people criticized as a 'wimp,' trying to prove his manhood by starting a war? The debate throughout the country was beginning to take on the acrimony of the hawk-dove controversy of the sixties over Vietnam."

By mid-February, with U.S. troops poised to enter Kuwait, Scowcroft's top Middle East expert concluded in a presidential memo that the war's objectives should be confined to repelling Iraqi troops from the emirate and restoring its monarchy. Marching on Baghdad, he argued, could fracture the coalition, upset the regional balance of power, and saddle the United States with a costly postwar occupation of indeterminate length. After a heated Oval Office debate, a compromise was reached in the form of a vaguely written National Security Directive. The objectives of Desert Storm, it enumerated, were the liberation of Kuwait; the destruction of Iraq's chemical, biological, and nuclear weapons; the elimination of its command and control centers; and the neutralization of the Republican Guard. Military action was to stop short of toppling Hussein unless he were to use weapons of mass destruction or engage in terrorist acts.

Baghdad sealed its fate by rejecting a last-minute White House demand that Iraqi troops withdraw from Kuwait. Desert Storm accomplished its mission in a mere one hundred hours of combat with a loss of 379 allied combatants and 776 wounded. While the retreating remnants of Hussein's forces did indeed set fire to Kuwait's oil fields, Bush resisted the impulse to turn his war machine on Baghdad, his hand stayed by Scowcroft and other cool heads such as Chas Freeman, the U.S. ambassador to Saudi Arabia, who in addition to being a prominent Foreign Service Sinologist also served as an Arabist. "For a range of reasons," Freeman cabled from Riyadh, "we cannot pursue Iraq's unconditional surrender and occupation by us. It is not in our interest to destroy Iraq or weaken it to the point that Iran and/or Syria are not constrained by it."

For once, an American president avoided a foreign policy blunder by listening to his specialists on the ground. Such expert advice, however, was all but absent in the war's aftermath. With victory in hand, the rigorous cabinet-level discussions that had preceded Desert Storm gave way to an ad hoc approach to the post-conflict phase of the war. The cease-fire talks, for example, were led by General Norman Schwarzkopf, the coalition commander, who met his Iraqi counterparts at Safwan Airfield in southeastern Iraq with no guidance from the White House. The Bush team, it seemed, was balancing so many fragile coalitions—with Congress, with the Saudis, with NATO, Russia, and Israel—it was forced to obscure its wartime goals to the point where its own members were unsure of what the terms of surrender should be. "There was no war termination strategy," Freeman said. "I kept arguing for one and I figured they did something about it but they didn't because they were afraid of

leaks. . . . It was a total failure of integration between military and political strategy."

Similarly, the White House was unprepared for the political chaos in
Iraq that followed victory in Kuwait. Bush and his aides had hoped that
the magnitude of Iraq's defeat would inspire an anti-Hussein putsch,
and the president even made public statements suggesting the United
States would support such action. Instead of a barracks coup, however,
Hussein's humiliation triggered popular uprisings in the country's
northern Kurdish regions and in the Shiite-dominated south. Far from
isolating Hussein, the revolts rallied what was left of the Republican
Guard's Sunni leadership behind him. What would become known as
the 1991 intifada, or uprising, was brutally put down with the help of
attack helicopters Iraq was allowed to keep under the terms of the armi-
stice. The White House, now worried the violence might splinter Iraq
into a Kurdish north, a Sunni center, and an Iran-allied Shiite south,
even assisted the Republican Guard in its attacks on the rebels. According to historian Said Aburish, U.S. forces gave air cover for Iraq's ma-
rauding helicopter gunships, stopped rebels from reaching an arms depot
to gather ammunition, and provided Republican Guard forces with safe
passage through their lines. By late March, the revolt had been put down.
In the reprisals that followed, hundreds of thousands of people are
believed to have been killed, many of them executed, tortured to death,
or tossed alive from helicopters. Hospitals in Shiite cities were destroyed
and nurses who had treated intifada members were molested. Those suspected of having participated in the revolt had their foreheads scarred or
had an ear lopped off.

By April, Saddam Hussein had restored himself to power. The status
quo ante had been reclaimed.

George H. W. Bush was a skilled statesman but an unlucky president. It
was his fate to succeed in office a man who had set a standard for likability
few politicians could match, and he had the misfortune to enter a reelection campaign against a weak economy and a political virtuoso. His centerpiece achievement, assembling the grand coalition that had liberated
Kuwait, was similarly compromised. Its limited objectives spared the

United States a drawn-out occupation of Iraq, but the long-term consequences of intervention were profoundly destabilizing. The U.S.-led embargo on Iraq, which would last twelve years over three presidential administrations, gradually impaired the state's ability to provide basic goods and services. In its place emerged a social welfare system administered by religious authorities, particularly in the neglected Shiite regions, which helped to Islamize a once fiercely secular nation.

Perversely, Desert Storm achieved what Iran in its war with Iraq could not do: it enhanced the power of Iraq's Shiite clerics as natural allies for Tehran. The pain of the embargo, endured disproportionately by innocent Iraqis, became a rallying cry for enemies of the United States throughout the Muslim world, including Osama bin Laden. It fostered a parallel economy that enriched Iraq's ruling class but made smugglers, pimps, and prostitutes out of its white-collar professionals. Those with the means to emigrate did so, and their departure hastened the desecularization of the country.

Far more important than the indirect consequences of Desert Storm was the radicalizing impact it had on bin Laden. The decision by the Saudi monarchy—the custodian of Mecca and Medina, the two holiest sites in Islam—to allow the deployment of some 500,000 foreign soldiers in the kingdom was a turning point in bin Laden's life. Following Iraq's invasion of Kuwait, the millionaire jihadist offered to raise an army and repel the secular invaders on behalf of the monarchy, but the Saudi government rebuffed him. The episode triggered "radical changes in his personality," as recounted by Prince Faisal al Turki, the head of the Saudi intelligence agency from 1977 to 1981. According to Abu Mousab al-Suri, a Syrian jihadist who knew bin Laden, the retention of some 5,000 U.S. troops in Saudi Arabia after the Gulf War "convinced [bin Laden] of the necessity of focusing his effort on fighting Jihad against America." Bin Laden himself has made clear the linkage between the U.S. bases in Saudi Arabia and his war on America. In his August 1996 fatwa, first published in the London-based *Al Quds Al Arabi* newspaper under the title "Declaration of War against the Americans Occupying the Land of the Two Holy Places," he condemns the deployment of "crusaders" in the kingdom and laments "the rejection of the idea of replacing the crusader forces by an Islamic force composed of the sons of the country and other Muslim people."

As authors Daalder and Destler conclude, "The open-ended presence of American military forces in Saudi Arabia, which both the Bush administration and the Saudi royal family had sought to avoid, had now become a reality, with consequences that would be felt only many years later."

Finally, the White House's decision to assist the Republican Guard in its crackdown on the intifada was a costly act of betrayal for the people who bore the brunt of Hussein's brutality. It reaffirmed popularly held Arab notions that America's concerns in the region were exclusive to oil and Israel, and it guaranteed that any future U.S. appeals to the Iraqi people, particularly the country's majority Shiites, would be greeted with deep suspicion.

Desert Storm, then, was as much a strategic disaster as it was a tactical success. On behalf of two corrupt oil-rich monarchies, it directly or indirectly brought about the degradation of Iraq's economy and the Islamization of its society, the depletion of its pro-West secular middle class, and the radicalization of bin Laden and Al Qaeda. This was a high price to pay, even for a military operation that was prudential in planning and judicious in execution. The bill would be years in coming, however, and as U.S. troops returned home from the Gulf, there was little reason to regard Desert Storm as anything less than what it appeared to be: America's first conclusive military victory since 1945. In Washington, the outcome of the Gulf War was celebrated as the auger to a new age, the nature and meaning of which was still uncertain. For the Pentagon, though, one thing was clear: the wounds of Vietnam had finally healed, if not disappeared altogether.

Throughout the Kuwait crisis, Bush shrewdly took the lessons of Vietnam to heart. He listened to his regional experts and diplomats, and he made sure he had a broad spectrum of international support behind him. He insisted on getting formal congressional approval for the war, he mobilized the reserves, and, on the Pentagon's advice, he ordered a massive military buildup as a measure of his commitment. With the war successfully concluded, Bush not only could declare the mission accomplished, he could herald the long-awaited dawn of the post-Vietnam era.

When Bush declared in his cease-fire announcement that "we've kicked the Vietnam syndrome once and for all," he received one of the wildest ovations of his presidency. In its March 11 edition, with geysers of flames still erupting from Kuwaiti oil fields, *Time* magazine proclaimed a national catharsis, an end to "self-doubt, fear of power, divisiveness, a fundamental uncertainty about America's purpose in the world." For William Miller, a Detroit advertising executive who initially opposed the war, that meant the deployment, anywhere in the world, of raw military might. "Anyone will have to think twice before messing with the U.S. again," he told *Time*. "Before a dictator attacks another country, he will have to look down the barrel of Uncle Sam's gun."

And what guns! What bombs and missiles, what engines of wrath did America now have at its disposal. Though the Gulf War was waged with ordnance that was decades old, it also marked the debut of precision firepower that would grip the popular imagination. Pentagon officials proudly featured in press briefings video images of "smart" missiles surgically destroying enemy targets with little in the way of allied or civilian casualties. News footage of Patriot air-defense batteries obliterating Iraqi Scuds high above Tel Aviv suggested the American way of war was almost godlike in its authority and clinical in its ability to distinguish friend from foe. Media coverage of the war was as relentless as the war itself. If the conflict in Vietnam was the first "living room war," broadcast in nightly installments on the evening network news, the Gulf War was the first to be chronicled minute by minute, all day and every day, via cable television. Media mogul Ted Turner's Cable News Network was a struggling novelty act before Desert Storm transformed it into a nationwide narcotic. Throughout the four-day conflict, Americans were awed by images of ghostly plumes of smoke erupting under the static crosshairs of a precision bombsight. For the viewers at home it was another miraculously clean kill. (The GIs had another term for it: "pink mist," as in *The targets were pink-misted by a GBU-12*.") Far from *Time* publisher Henry Luce's assertion in "The American Century," his landmark treatise, that "modern man hates war," the triumphant conclusion of Desert Storm had made war a spectator sport, a computer game. "Select enemy. Delete" was how *The Economist* summarized the revolution in precision warfare.

Viewers were also impressed by the cool confidence of the generals as they gave interviews or conducted press briefings. They were poised and articulate, with a language that mingled exotic acronyms with charming, homespun aphorisms. The leading man of CNN's war was Colin Powell, Bush's charismatic chairman of the Joint Chiefs of Staff. The youngest officer ever to chair the Joint Chiefs, Powell not only could lead reporters to water, he could make them drink. In late January, a week after Desert Storm had commenced with an air campaign against targets in Iraq, Powell arranged for a media briefing to quell apprehensions over the looming ground war. In *Soldier*, Powell biographer Karen DeYoung writes:

> He sent back the first delivery of charts and maps for his presentation with instructions to simplify them using only those elements that would show up well on television. His intended audience went far beyond the reporters; he would be speaking directly to the American people and Congress, the troops in the field, foreign capitals and Saddam Hussein himself. . . . The next afternoon, he guided reporters through the 12,000 sorties flown, the hundreds of targets demolished and the coming ground war against Iraqi forces in Kuwait. Then it was time for the money quote: "Our strategy to go after this army is very, very simple. First we're going to cut it off, and then we're going to kill it."

With that concise statement of intent, Powell consummated cable TV's romance with the military and he introduced Americans to a martial ethos they could both love and respect. Whether he liked it or not, Powell became the face of the new American militarism: courageous, self-assured, professional. Pundits began touting him as a presidential candidate in the 1996 election. For an adoring press, it mattered little that Powell had originally opposed an armed response to the invasion of Kuwait, pressing instead for a sustained embargo of Iraq. Nor did the public linger over the fact that many of those "smart-bomb" kills reported by the Pentagon, including the Patriot antimissile strikes over Israel, turned out to have been clean misses. Desert Storm was the closest thing to a crisp victory in a just war most people see in a lifetime. It not only restored Americans' confidence in the Pentagon's ability to accomplish its missions, it engendered a nationwide respect for the military as an institution and an important part of national identity. By the end of the decade, a majority of Americans were prepared to defer to the military on matters of national security; civilians were increasingly seen as extraneous, even obstructive.

In redeeming the U.S. military at home and establishing its uncontested supremacy abroad, the Gulf War relieved the Bush administration of having to answer an important question: With the Cold War over, what should be done with the winning side's enormous political-military apparatus? For all their experience and expertise in superpower affairs, President Bush and his aides failed to anticipate the defining moment of their professional lives: the collapse of the Soviet empire. To be fair, no one else in official Washington had noticed the yawning abyss below their feet. So much had been invested in the nation's Cold War complex that its stakeholders—diplomats, military men, national security experts, intelligence agents, presidents, and politicians, to say nothing of defense contractors—had come to regard it as a perpetual trust.

Compare this with an earlier generation of American leaders who, as early as 1943, with their forces chipping away at Imperial Japan and Nazi Germany, were preparing for global stewardship as well as victory. By 1947, two years after the Malta accords, the Truman administration had sketched the contours of what would become an enduring and vital international architecture: the World Bank, the International Monetary Fund, a convertible exchange rate system, and the Marshall Plan. On the home front, it had created the Department of Defense, the U.S. Air Force, the National Security Council, the Central Intelligence Agency, and the Joint Chiefs of Staff.

A half century later, America's political and military elites were as prepared for a U.S.-led unipolar world as the student whose dog had eaten his homework. President Bush had spoken both vaguely and wanly about a "New World Order" and Colin Powell had joked about the confusion that occurs "when you lose your best enemy," but aside from that, the White House had little to offer in the way of a forward vision. This created the kind of intellectual vacuum that pundits and think-tank specialists were born to fill. A competition of ideas emerged, from neo-isolationists such as former Nixon speechwriter Patrick Buchanan, who suggested the United States dismantle its military bases overseas, to "one-worlders," who favored a federation of nations under a powerful United Nations. There were also realists who believed the United States should liquidate its Cold War alliances and run its international affairs from Washington; liberal internationalists, who called for a global partnership of regional powers, similar in spirit to the "mutual collective security" arrangement Gorbachev had referred to in his UN speech; and liberal interventionists, who believed Washington should aggressively promote U.S.-style economic and political liberalization in troubled or backward regions.

Meanwhile, neoconservatives—close cousins to liberal interventionists, though neither side would ever admit it—called for the United States to jettison restraint in the name of an unprecedented global hegemony. The United States had won the Cold War, they knew, and here was a chance to create an eternal Pax Americana. They urged Washington to rebuild the wreckage of the Soviet bloc into the foundation of a lasting and expanded empire with absolute control over the "global commons," an elegant euphemism for the entire planet and the heavens above it. It was the ultimate expression of foreign policy militarization, and among the rival post–Cold War visions then circulating, it alone prevailed thanks to neoconservative ringers in the White House whom President Bush and his senior aides had rashly dismissed as "the crazies."

If neoconservatives were the Rat Pack, Zalmay Khalilzad would be their Sammy Davis Jr. Like the African American entertainer, who could sing, dance, and play a multitude of instruments, as well as act, Khalilzad is in many ways the most talented of his co-ideologues. He is fluent in Dari and Pashto, the two main languages of his native Afghanistan, as well as English and Arabic. Unlike Richard Perle, he completed his Ph.D., which he earned at the University of Chicago as an acolyte of RAND fellow Albert Wohlstetter. Zhalilzad would ascend to increasingly influential positions in both Democratic and Republican administrations, climaxing with ambassadorial posts at the United Nations and in Afghanistan and Iraq. As a Muslim American, however, Khalilzad always stood apart among the neocon faithful. A senior aide in an administration that waged deeply divisive wars in two Islamic countries, he endured slights from some Islamic quarters as the administration's house Muslim. As ambassador to Iraq, he outraged some of his neoconservative allies by speaking openly about the depths of sectarian violence in that country and the hazardous security environment for U.S. diplomats there.

Perhaps Khalilzad's most consequential assignment, however, was the drafting of the 1992 Defense Planning Guidance, a set of parameters distributed to senior military and civilian officials inside the Pentagon to help them gauge force levels and funding needs. The job of writing it was first tasked by Paul Wolfowitz, the undersecretary of defense for policy, to Lewis I. "Scooter" Libby, his top assistant. Libby in turn delegated it to Khalilzad. Thus did a then obscure functionary, inspired by the neoconservatives' isolated and distorted view of the world, pen the imperialist blueprint that remains official U.S. policy.

In researching the document, Khalilzad solicited the views of both Wolfowitz and Libby, as well as Perle and Wohlstetter. He finished a draft by early March and, with the permission of Libby, who had not read the document, circulated it inside the Pentagon for feedback. Within three days the draft was leaked to the *New York Times,* and its publication ignited a blaze of protest and indignation. Khalilzad had called for nothing short of permanent U.S. hegemony, urging Washington to preempt the emergence of any country that could challenge America's military supremacy. That included close allies such as Japan, perceived in Washington at the time as a threat for its looming financial and economic might. Beltway hawks referred luridly in the press to an ascendant "Japanese militarism." Bestselling books such as Lester Thurow's *Head to Head: The Coming Economic Battle Among Japan, Europe, and America,* and *The Coming War with Japan* by George Friedman and Meredith Lebard, fed the bonfire, as did such neoconservative columnists as Charles Krauthammer, who insisted that the alternative to U.S. hegemony was "Japanese carriers patrolling the Strait of Malacca." Predictably, only a tiny minority of those heralding a recidivist Japan knew much about the

country. Even allowing for Beltway parochialism, the notion of an imperial reawakening in Tokyo was an absurd neocon fantasy.*

The leaked Khalilzad document rightly scandalized political leaders
and pundits in the diplomatic capitals of the world, and it provided fodder for Democratic presidential candidates then stumping on the campaign trail. Bill Clinton called the draft guidance "one more attempt" by
Pentagon officials "to find an excuse for big budgets instead of downsizing." Another candidate, Massachusetts senator Paul Tsongas, called for
"a new internationalism truly based on the principles of collective security." The Khalilzad draft was buried by the Pentagon, only to be resurrected by Defense Secretary Dick Cheney, who shared its author's appetite
for the global commons. "You've discovered a new rationale for our role
in the world," he told Khalilzad.

Libby was not satisfied, however. For the Wolfowitz protégé, Khalilzad's draft did not go far enough. The goal should not be to preserve the
superiority gap the Pentagon enjoyed over the rest of the world, particularly as even the midterm horizon was inconveniently parched of credible
threats. Rather, it should be to open up a lead so vast that no other country would even try to catch up. Simply put, Libby believed Washington
should buy decades' worth of military superiority with defense outlays
that would be prohibitively high for everyone else. He rewrote Khalilzad's
draft, concealing its blunt purpose behind a patina of Beltway jargon.
The result is a masterful deployment of bland arcana in the service of
militarized hegemony. The guidance paper states clearly Washington's
obligation to "preclude any hostile power from dominating a region critical to our interests, and also thereby to strengthen the barriers against
the reemergence of a global threat to the interests of the United States
and our allies." Rather than characterizing American imperium as a zero-
sum game, however, Libby implies that the United States would act as pa-
terfamilias to a great clan of like-minded democracies, a so-called zone
of peace. Within this idyll, America would be first among equals and its
luminescence would obscure the kitchen gods of collective security:

---

* At the time of Krauthammer's writing, Japan was already a year into a withering defla-
tionary cycle that would last two decades after the bursting of record asset bubbles fueled
during the 1980s.

While we favor collective action to respond to threats and challenges in this new era, a collective response will not always be timely and, in the absence of U.S. leadership, may not gel. While the United States cannot become the world's policeman and assume responsibility for solving every international security problem, neither can we allow our critical interests to depend solely on international mechanisms that can be blocked by countries whose interests may be very different from our own.

In Europe, Libby acknowledges an opportunity to rebuild U.S.-Russian relations on the basis of trust and mutual cooperation before making a vaguely worded case for the expansion of NATO, an alliance formed to deter an invasion that never came from an enemy that no longer existed. In Asia and the Middle East, Libby pleads the white man's burden. He insists the United States "must maintain a significant military presence in the area," which he defines broadly as "sufficient forward deployed forces and power projection capability to reassure our regional allies and friends, to preclude destabilizing military rivalries, to secure freedom of the seas, to deter threats to our key political and economic interests, and to preclude any hostile power from attempting to dominate the region." In the Arab world, Libby urges Washington to "help our friends meet their legitimate defensive needs with U.S. foreign military and commercial sales without jeopardizing power balances," by which he means the strategic imbalance of Israel's qualitative edge in military capability and America's dominance of the region. In addition, "we should tailor our security assistance programs to enable our friends to bear better the burden of defense and to facilitate standardization and interoperability of recipient country forces with our own."

As memorandums go, "Defense Strategy for the 1990s: The Regional Defense Strategy," as the 1992 Defense Planning Guidance is called, represents a higher species of Pentagon dissemblance. It implicitly equates anything short of an entrenched and intrusive global military posture with demobilization. It refers to phantom "threats" and "hostile powers," in the face of which "specialized roles" for U.S. forces must be reserved. It cautions against turning the Pentagon into a global gendarme even as it assigns it new responsibilities that would do just that. In making the case for preserving obsolete alliances and base systems, it manufactures new missions such as democracy promotion, human rights awareness, and the creation of free-market capitalism, traditionally the realm of civilian agencies. (Its case for enhanced interoperability between the U.S. military and allied forces, a Pentagon policy orphan if ever there was one, is particularly disingenuous.) It assures allies of Washington's commitment to collective action and cooperation with its allies while gently putting them on notice that in the new unipolar world, they must toe Washington's line.

Most significantly, Libby fails to address (and clearly does not comprehend) the consequences of empire. His planning guidance resonates with the delusion, intrinsic not only to neoconservatives but to militarists of all persuasions, that the world not only tolerates U.S. hegemony but craves it. He asserts that foreign leaders are glad to host large U.S. military bases, lucrative fonts of corruption for ruling elites as well as unhealthy state dependencies on the imperial dole, but he fails to acknowledge how such deployments antagonize the less privileged of their hosts.* He deceptively notes that the United States in 1991 withdrew its forces from the Philippines, "consistent with the desires of the Philippine government," though he omits how the Pentagon had no intention of abandoning its huge installations at Subic Bay and Clark Field until they were rendered inoperable by the volcanic eruption of Mount Pinatubo.

The planning guidance includes no reference to, let alone estimation of, the costs of untrammeled and enduring global hegemony. Though the Pentagon's budget declined modestly in the immediate aftermath of the Soviet collapse, it would soon be restored to its Cold War levels. The proliferation and augmentation of combatant commands overseas and semipermanent naval deployments would take a significant toll on

---

* Over the years, nationalist movements or public campaigns have successfully demanded the liquidation of U.S. bases in Panama, Ecuador, and Puerto Rico and reduced or modified them in dozens of other countries. In other states, including Saudi Arabia, Uzbekistan, and Kyrgyzstan, even autocratic regimes have been forced by public pressure to at least temporarily scale back U.S. military installations.

the U.S. economy, to say nothing of the servicemen and -women who were obliged to shoulder the duty of empire. Throughout the 1990s, during a brief decline in military spending, both officers and enlisted personnel would suffer the grueling operational tempo, or OPTEMPO, of seemingly endless deployments. Mechanics were forced to cannibalize parts from one aircraft or tank to repair another, while personnel cutbacks deprived the ranks of surge capability. An April 1997 report issued by the House Committee on National Security found that "high personnel and operational tempos have all but obscured the reality that the nation's ability to deploy and sustain large military forces during war has been placed in jeopardy, or in some cases, has clearly been lost."

In January 1993, not long after the election of Bill Clinton as America's forty-second president, the Pentagon declassified the first half of the planning guidance. (The second part of the document, which concentrates on new capabilities the Pentagon must develop in the coming years, remains classified.) It was Cheney himself who pushed to make the document, framed by Khalilzad and polished by Libby, public. Years later, Khalilzad told author James Mann that Cheney "wanted to show that he stood for the idea. He took ownership of it." Ironically, it would serve as both his legacy and his inheritance.

In rhetoric, as well as in action, the Clinton administration would not deviate substantially from the neoconservative vision of a preeminent, unilateralist America. There would be interventions in Haiti and Kosovo, as well as inconclusive air attacks on Sudan and Afghanistan (in violation of Pakistan's airspace), and a raid on Iraq with only notional allied support. It also expanded NATO to include Poland, Hungary, and the Czech Republic, sealing an expansionist and provocative foreign policy that Libby could only hint at. While neoconservatives labored for decades to either neutralize or co-opt the Arms Control and Disarmament Agency, Clinton would go one step better by abolishing it outright. Under his watch, the Department of State and the United States Agency for International Development bore drastic budget cuts, and he failed to overcome the Senate's opposition to the Comprehensive Test Ban Treaty.

If the new president wanted to replace American unilateralism with a framework for collective security—an admittedly colossal policy goal, given the poverty of the institutions needed to support it—he lacked either the interest or the capacity to do so. Even as he was settling into the West Wing, the forces behind American foreign policy militarization had become all but irreversible, thanks in part to a landmark piece of legislation that restructured the Pentagon's chain of command in ways that would broaden its reach and proliferate its missions. If the Gulf War proved the U.S. military worthy of a global franchise and the Defense Planning Guidance was its charter, the Goldwater-Nichols Act of 1986 was the flow chart for empire.

A military history of the Cold War might conclude that the biggest threat to U.S. national security was not the communist bloc but the Pentagon's own Joint Chiefs of Staff. Officially an advisory panel to the president, in practice the JCS was an arbitration council for the collection of warring tribes known as the Army, Air Force, Navy, and Marines. Loath to reveal dissent, the chiefs offered nothing but an insipid unanimity on complex issues, and their stubborn advocacy of narrow service interests often led to disaster. Operation Eagle Claw, for example, the Carter administration's doomed attempt to free Americans held hostage in Iran, and Urgent Fury, the ultimately successful but shambolic 1983 invasion of Grenada, were undermined in part by the Joint Chiefs' demands that all four branches be allowed to participate.

If the JCS was indeed divided and weak, however, it was largely because both Congress and the White House wanted it that way. Presidents generally preferred a strong defense secretary as their closest adviser on military matters, a bias carried to extremes during the Vietnam War, when Johnson and McNamara all but ignored input from the service chiefs. Legislators, meanwhile, had no interest in sharing their constitutional powers with a strong, unified caste of officers. Friends of the Navy—meaning lawmakers with naval facilities in their states or districts—vigorously opposed any organizational reform that would compromise that branch's centuries-old tradition of independence. The branch services and their veterans associations wanted brawlers, not ecumenicalists, representing their interests in Washington.

By the mid-1980s, however, tactical breakdowns associated with interservice rivalry and compartmentalization had made it clear the country could no longer afford a balkanized military brass.* Recommendations for reform, first expressed forcefully in 1981 by then JCS chairman General David Jones, caught the attention of Barry Goldwater, the archconservative U.S. senator, who teamed up with House Democrat William Flynt Nichols to hammer out legislation for change.

It was trench warfare all the way. Defense Secretary Caspar Weinberger opposed reorganization, as did Jones's successor, the former Army vice chief of staff General John Vessey. So did Senator John Tower of Texas, a naval reservist who nurtured ambitions of becoming secretary of defense and did not want to antagonize the Joint Chiefs. As the chairman of the Senate Armed Services Committee, Tower vowed to spike any reform bill that reached his desk. His allies on the committee, Senators John Warner of Virginia, Jeremiah Denton of Alabama, and Phil Gramm of Texas, firmly defended the status quo. John Lehman, the hawkish secretary of the Navy, said the Goldwater-Nichols Act slugging its way through Congress would render his post and that of other civilian service secretaries "ceremonial" and "make a hash of our defense structure."

However virulent their opposition to reform and however influential their allies, the Joint Chiefs lacked the support of the one constituent who truly mattered. In July 1985, President Reagan appointed the pro-reform defense industrialist David Packard to head a blue-ribbon commission on defense management. That snuffed out any hope Weinberger may have had of enlisting the president against reorganization, and in May 1986, the Department of Defense Reorganization Act, as the bill was officially known, passed by huge margins in Congress.

The primary objectives of the Goldwater-Nichols Act as laid out by Congress were to improve the quality of advice to civilian decision-makers, ensure that regional commanders in chief had the authority and

---

* In addition to the Vietnam War and Operations Eagle Claw and Urgent Fury, mutual suspicion among the branch services and a mute leadership have been cited as factors in such debacles and disasters as the bombing of Pearl Harbor, the Battle of Leyte Gulf in 1944, the Reagan administration's "arms-for-hostages" deal with Iran, and the 1983 bombing of Marine barracks in Beirut.

resources to meet their objectives, and enhance cohesion and interoperability between the services. Many of these goals have been achieved. By making interservice duty a condition of general-officer rank, for example, the legislation leveled many of the divisions between the branch services. By giving greater control to the Pentagon's field marshals overseas—including authority over their men, which previously lay with their service chiefs and others at the Pentagon—the law resolved the paradox of "generals in the field . . . without armies" and "admirals without fleets," as Goldwater put it.

The most significant legacy of the Goldwater-Nichols Act, however, is the one its supporters either understated or failed to anticipate altogether. Only its primary author, Goldwater himself, candidly addressed the primary objective of reorganization: to empower military men at the expense of civilians in wartime. It not only enhanced the authority of the JCS chairman, it established worldwide commands whose top generals wielded tremendous influence, not only over their own ranks but over the governments of host nations. Between a muscular JCS chairman in Washington and a network of heavily resourced combatant commanders overseas, Goldwater-Nichols all but guaranteed that the Pentagon would become the preeminent player in the execution, and eventually the planning, of national security policy.

As the president's "principal military adviser," the chairman of the Joint Chiefs of Staff is responsible for the most important matters of security policy. He dominates strategy sessions and budget planning, and he leads debate over doctrine, training, education, and roles and missions. He also has under his authority the 1,600-member Joint Staff, which prior to Goldwater-Nichols worked under the service chiefs. Lured by the chairman's augmented power and influence, the Joint Staff attracts the Pentagon's brightest officers, seasoned as they are by duty in joint commands and operations abroad. In his memoirs, Colin Powell, the first of the post–Goldwater-Nichols JCS chairmen, referred to the Joint Staff as "the finest military staff anywhere in the world. . . . I had no trouble recruiting first-rate talent."

Officially, the chairman's policy recommendations are "subject to the authority, direction, and control of the President and the Secretary of Defense." In practice, however, the influence of civilian participants in policy debates pales in comparison to the credibility of the JCS chairman, leavened as it is with expert information from the Joint Staff. In April 1994, recently retired defense secretary Les Aspin spoke of a widening credibility gap between the Joint Staff and its civilian counterparts. "Because of Goldwater-Nichols," Aspin said, "the quality on the military side has gone up tremendously, where the reverse has happened on the civilian side. Revolving-door restrictions have made government service so unattractive that the pool from which you can pick political appointees is not as rich as it once was." Aspin's remarks were corroborated by a May 1995 Pentagon commission that found that "political appointees in [the office of the secretary of defense] and in the military department staffs often lack the experience and expertise in national security and military strategy, operations, budgeting, etc. required by the positions they fill."

Of course, the prerogatives of power are of little value if not harnessed to a personality worthy of them. For Colin Powell, a man steeped in equal measures of principle and cunning, the post–Goldwater-Nichols chairmanship was the perfect mount for his ambitions. One of his first acts as chairman was to replace the old Joint Chiefs of Staff stationery with a new batch that had "Chairman, Joint Chiefs of Staff" embossed across the top. It was a not-so-subtle declaration of his independence from the ancien régime, and he was comfortable asserting it.

In November 1989, convinced that Mikhail Gorbachev's efforts to demilitarize the Cold War were genuine and warranted reciprocal gestures from Washington, Powell composed a memo that called for sizable across-the-board cuts in defense spending. The service chiefs predictably dug in, and while Powell knew he could easily take his proposals straight to the president, "realistically, I knew that we had to shape the new military as a team." Events forced his hand, however. Within days the Berlin Wall was breached and it was clear the Soviet empire was on the verge of collapse. On November 15, without briefing the chiefs, Powell presented his memo to President Bush. The next day, he gathered the service heads in the Tank, the Pentagon's ultrasecure meeting room, and submitted to them the plan he had given the president the day before. "I could see the raised eyebrows," Powell wrote in his memoirs. "I had blindsided them, not a mistake I intended to make again."

In Washington, however, information is a strategic commodity, and Powell could be as proprietary with it as anyone. Charles Boyd, a senior Air Force officer, knew Powell while serving as a top operations officer for the Air Force chief and as deputy chief of the European Command in Stuttgart. The new JCS chairman, he told Powell biographer Karen De-Young, was a "completely different guy" from his predecessors, a new breed of officer who intuitively understood the political dimensions of policy as well as the military ones. "Powell was quite content to go over to the [White House] principals meeting and not ask anybody's opinion before he went, and not necessarily debrief when he came back."

Powell would always insist that his authority ended at the threshold of Defense Secretary Cheney's office, and he dismissed as "revisionist history" the idea that he routinely probed that boundary. "Dick Cheney," he told DeYoung, "was quick to tell me when I was off the farm." Relations between the surly archconservative Cheney and the affable bipartisan Powell were always professional, and between their respective allies and spies in Congress and the military, they made a formidable team. Below the surface, however, there was a steady current of tension between the two men. Whereas Cheney was furtive and tight-lipped, Powell courted reporters and often spoke freely with them on foreign policy issues as well as military matters. When Powell told the *Washington Post* he thought the defense budget could be reduced by 25 percent over the next five years, far more than what Cheney preferred, the secretary personally rebuked him. Though Cheney kept Powell under close scrutiny with the help of aides Wolfowitz and Libby, the general still managed to lobby Congress quietly and effectively for his military restructuring plan. He also struck up a close relationship with Sam Nunn, by then the Senate doyen on military affairs, riling the Cheney clique.

The defining difference between Powell and Cheney, however, was the war in Vietnam. While Powell was serving his two tours there, earning a Purple Heart along the way, Cheney was dodging the draft by claiming five separate student and family deferments. Queried about this during his confirmation hearing, he told the Senate Armed Services Committee that he "had other priorities in the Sixties than military service," a remark that could hardly endear him to an Army careerist like Powell. The Vietnam War also represented a civilian-military divide that would intensify throughout successive post–Cold War administrations. With increasing frequency, civilian officials with no military background would choose war against the advice of generals seared, intellectually as well as emotionally, by their service in Indochina. As JCS chairman, Powell was distinct not only for his age, race, and media savvy, he was the first among the post's occupants who had risen from a corps of officers who knew intimately the perils and futility of waging asymmetrical conflict in faraway places. It was his experience in Vietnam that informed his initial opposition to the invasion of Kuwait, a position repudiated by the dizzying success of Desert Storm but vindicated by its legacy.

As would be made appallingly clear, neither the crucible of Vietnam nor the cauldron of the Iraqi intifada three decades later would serve as useful reference points for Dick Cheney. Despite his enhanced authority under Goldwater-Nichols, Powell failed to talk the first President Bush out of waging a Persian Gulf war just as he would years later while serving the next one as secretary of state. Powell would spend the rest of his public career trying to stay the cavalier impulse among civilian leaders for military solutions to foreign policy challenges. He would not pander to the militarist instincts of civilian leaders, nor would he be seduced by their interventionist muse.

The new combatant commanders, the other beneficiaries of reform, could be another matter.

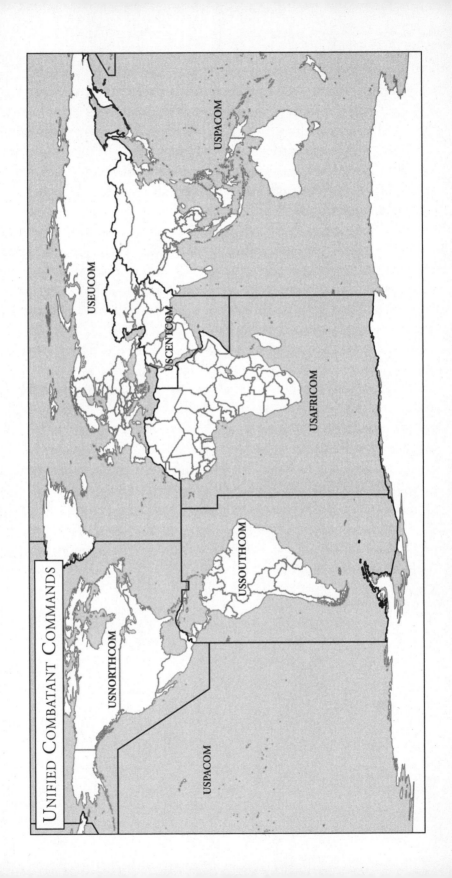

Unified Combatant Commands

14

THE WEIGHT OF PEACE

It's a lousy war, kid . . . but it's the only one we've got.
—JAMES CAGNEY AS CAPTAIN FLAGG IN *What Price Glory*

IN MANY WAYS, THE FOUR-STAR GENERALS AND ADMIRALS WHO lead America's Unified Combatant Commands overseas are the most powerful men on Earth. They are responsible for making war and keeping peace worldwide, and since Goldwater-Nichols they have enjoyed near total control over the human, financial, and material resources under their authority. They are invested with the power of proconsuls, the military governors who ruled the colonial provinces of ancient Rome, and they are commonly referred to as such. They divide the globe into six areas of responsibility—the Middle East and Central Asia, East Asia and Oceania, North America, Central and South America, Europe, and Africa—and their jurisdiction stops just short of the heavens.* Over the years, as Washington expanded its dominions worldwide even as it starved the civilian side of foreign policy making, it encouraged the combatant commanders to assume a range of noncore duties that give them tremendous leverage over the host governments in their regions. In addition to preparing for war, commanders are responsible for what was once civilian work: humanitarian aid, medical care, agricultural development, disaster relief, economic modernization, and more.

By itself, this is nothing new. The U.S. military has been involved in nonlethal operations at least since the Spanish-American War, when soldiers and Marines distributed food and medical supplies, built roads,

---

* The Defense Department also supports three functional commands not defined by geography: Strategic Command, Special Forces Command, and Transportation Command. Joint Forces Command was the fourth functional Unified Combatant Command until its formal disestablishment in August 2011.

dug wells, and enforced curfews in the name of America's new imperium. The postwar restoration of Europe and Japan could not have been
achieved without military governors and army engineers, and the uniformed services were closely involved in pacification programs in Vietnam. What was known to the Pentagon during the 1990s as "Military
Operations Other Than War," and which is now known as "stability operations," has a long tradition in the armed forces.

What has changed, however, is the magnitude of such work and the
pace at which it is becoming a crucial part of the combatant commands'
franchise. With each budget cycle, it seems, the Pentagon appropriates
additional humanitarian aid and funds development projects once run
by civilians. Whereas responsibility for foreign military aid and training
programs used to be concentrated with the State Department, the Defense Department now deals directly with host governments under an
oversight authority that is often less than adequate. This is the legacy of
a policy initiative inspired two decades ago not by the Pentagon but by
the U.S. Congress.

In 1988, with cocaine use racking America's cities and with civilian
agencies powerless to stem the flow of drugs into the United States from
Latin America, Congress passed legislation that ordered the military to
step in. In doing so, it effectively repealed the Posse Comitatus Act of
1878, which prohibits U.S. troops from serving in a law enforcement capacity. Concerned that a war on drugs would distract the military from
its core responsibilities, Secretary of Defense Frank C. Carlucci and the
Joint Chiefs fought the legislation. But the drug epidemic was a powerful
issue in that year's presidential campaign and the White House pressured Carlucci to endorse the bill. (Years later, Carlucci's successor, Dick
Cheney, would back a stronger military role in drug interdiction despite
a GAO report that revealed Pentagon efforts were ineffectual.)

As SOUTHCOM—or Southern Command, as the combatant command responsible for Latin America is known—worked ever closer with
host-government armies to police the narcotics trade, it requested more
money to train and equip them. In 1991—in violation of the 1961 Foreign Assistance Act, which assigns responsibility for military and economic aid programs to the State Department—Congress authorized the
Pentagon to fund allied militaries and police forces in Latin America. It

did so under Section 1004 of the 1991 National Defense Authorization Act, which, though not a permanent authorization, has been extended four times despite limited oversight capability. In early 1999, it was used to finance a 900-man counternarcotics battalion in the Colombian army under a program called "Plan Colombia." The existence of the battalion was unknown to Congress until the following year, when the Defense Department requested funds to more than double its troop strength. In 1997, Congress passed another antidrug-related authorization under Section 1033 of the 1998 National Defense Authorization Act. It too was meant to be temporary and it too is routinely extended.

The war on drugs is the linchpin that binds SOUTHCOM to Latin America, though it is emerging as a springboard for greater ambitions. In *Command Strategy 2016*, released in 2009, SOUTHCOM proposed it be transformed into the nexus for operations "in support of security, stability and prosperity in the Americas," coordinating all relevant U.S. agencies, including nonmilitary ones, working in the region. Pentagon officials have cited *Command Strategy 2016* as a blueprint for all future combatant commands, identifying such "security threats" as corruption, undocumented migration, money laundering, natural and man-made disasters, AIDS, environmental degradation, poverty, and computer hacking in addition to terrorism and drugs. In October 2009, the Colombian government conceded to the Pentagon rights to seven military bases along with an unlimited number of as yet unspecified "facilities and locations." In its 2009 budget request, the Defense Department said it needed funds to upgrade one of its Colombian bases to conduct "full spectrum" operations throughout South America to counter, among other threats, "anti-U.S. governments" and to "expand expeditionary warfare capability."

As Admiral James Stavridis, the then leader of SOUTHCOM, elaborated at the time, "We want to be a big Velcro cube that these other agencies can hook to so we can collectively do what needs to be done in this region." Needless to say, many of those "other agencies," such as USAID and the nongovernmental organizations it contracts with, were reluctant to go along for the ride given the U.S. military's checkered past in Latin America. According to George Withers, a senior fellow at the Washington Office on Latin America, "Southern Command should not be the coordinating agency because then they become the face of U.S. assistance in foreign regions. The agency that coordinates controls the agenda." Nevertheless, *Command Strategy 2016* has been enshrined as the model for how combatant commands will be run in the future, starting with AFRICOM, which was activated in October 2008.

In fact, the combatant commands are already the putative epicenters for security, diplomatic, humanitarian, and commercial affairs in their regions. Commanders travel in a manner appropriate to their rank and authority, with lavish retinues, secure communications sets, and experts on everything from animal husbandry to microlending. They have retainers to manage their schedules, to carry their bags (they travel with several sets of uniforms, from utilities for field inspections to dress whites for state dinners), and to maintain regular communications with Washington. Local leaders receive them as powerful heads of state, with motorcades, honor guards, and ceremonial feasts. Their radiance obscures everything in its midst, including the authority of U.S. ambassadors, who, officially at least, are Washington's most senior representatives in any foreign country with which it has normal relations. This can be a frequent source of interagency tension, in part because the command chain has become so complicated. According to the president's letter of instruction to chiefs of mission, which dates back to the Kennedy administration, ambassadors have "full responsibility for the direction, coordination and supervision of all Executive branch U.S. offices and personnel . . . *except those under the command of a U.S. area military commander.*" (Italics added.) The letter advises the ambassador to communicate closely with his uniformed counterpart and "cooperate on all matters of mutual interest."

The relationship between the two officials, thorny enough during the Cold War, has mushroomed in complexity along with the combatant commanders' responsibilities and prerogatives, particularly their growing intimacy with foreign military elites. According to Edward Gnehm, a career Foreign Service officer who served as ambassador to Yemen and Jordan—both of which fall under the jurisdiction of Central Command, or CENTCOM—Goldwater-Nichols has done as much to marginalize civilian officials in foreign outposts as have depleted civilian aid budgets. "When I was in Yemen in the 1970s and I had a problem with a personality,

I would deal directly with Washington," Gnehm, now retired, said in an interview. Two decades later, "When I had the same problem in Jordan, I had to deal with CENTCOM. Without a doubt, the leadership in the countries I served in sees as the most visible leader of the U.S. someone in uniform." The credibility gap between America's civilian and military representatives abroad would grow exponentially in the post-9/11 era, when the Pentagon obtained its own funding authority as part of its global war on terror.

This yawning asymmetry is fueled by more than budgets and resources, however. Unlike ambassadors, whose responsibility is confined to a single country or city-state, the writ of a combatant commander is hemispheric in scope. His authority covers some of the world's most strategic natural resources and waterways and he has some of the most talented people in the federal government working for him, including the finest special-operations forces on Earth. While his civilian counterpart is mired in such parochial concerns as bilateral trade disputes and visa matters, a combatant commander's horizon is unlimited. The depth of his perspective and the quality of his intelligence, shaped by confidential meetings with heads of state as well as a host of spy agencies, are more than enough to assure him a decisive advantage in interagency deliberations.

"When we spoke, we had more clout," according to Anthony Zinni, the overlord of everything from Egypt to Pakistan when he ran CENTCOM from 1997 to 2000. "There's a mismatch in our stature. Ambassadors don't have regional perspectives. You see the interdependence and interaction in the region when you have a regional responsibility. If you're in a given country, you don't see beyond its borders because that's not your mission. When I viewed the Persian Gulf I saw it in regional terms. I looked at the Gulf Cooperation Council and other groups and how we could use them to get things done collectively and regionally. You have to reach out and think inter-regionally and globally and you're constantly working with everybody else."

Not even a U.S. president can match the broad perspective of his combatant commanders. That was particularly so of George H. W. Bush's successor, whose Achilles' heel, aside from his carnal appetites, was a parochialism hewn from years of dealing with small-bore Arkansas politics. Kindred spirits in their post-presidencies, when they would co-lead vast humanitarian enterprises, Bush and Bill Clinton regarded the world from the Oval Office on vastly different terms. The former invested much of his energy in foreign policy at the expense of bread-and-butter domestic issues; stumping against Clinton at a National Grocers Convention in Orlando during his 1992 reelection bid, Bush was skewered in the press as an elitist when he allegedly expressed a childlike fascination with the store's bar-code scanning system.* Clinton suffered from the opposite myopia. The self-described policy "wonk" who could recite auto-emissions standards on a state-by-state basis showed little interest in international affairs. His unofficial campaign slogan—"It's the economy, stupid"—was a witheringly effective blast at Bush's blind spot as to what truly mattered among post–Cold War Americans.

The transfer of presidential authority from Bush to Clinton represented a sharp break in the continuum of postwar American foreign policy. No longer would a U.S. president work from reference points informed by World War II and its unique, perilous aftermath. Indeed, like so many of his co-generationalists, including Dick Cheney and Bush's own son George W., Clinton avoided the draft during the Vietnam War and was so awkward around his generals that he had to be coached how to salute properly. The top-down, coat-and-tie culture of the Bush White House gave way to the unstructured informality of the incoming team. Under Clinton, every day was casual Friday and it showed in the administration's approach to foreign affairs (particularly when compared with his competent handling of the economy). The hasty withdrawal of U.S. troops in war-torn Somalia, a mission Clinton inherited from his predecessor, only intensified the chaotic violence there and created fertile ground for radical Islamist groups. The feeble response to the genocide in

---

* The scanner affair was fueled by a page-one story in the New York Times that was based on secondhand information. Videotape of Bush's visit later revealed that both orthodox and exotic equipment was on display at the Orlando exhibit and that Bush, according to Newsweek, was "curious and polite, but hardly amused." Bob Graham, the executive who demonstrated the scanner technology for Bush, dismissed the Times report. "It's foolish to think the president doesn't know anything about grocery stores," Graham said. "He knew exactly what I was talking about."

Rwanda was an abdication of American leadership, as Clinton himself would later admit. The restoration of Jean-Bertrand Aristide as president of Haiti after his ouster in a military coup was ham-fisted and ultimately counterproductive given Aristide's corrupt, autocratic, and inept administration. When tensions erupted in East Asia over North Korea's nuclear ambitions, the White House was paralytic; it took former president Jimmy Carter to freelance his way to Pyongyang and defuse the crisis with James Laney, the American ambassador to Seoul, hours away from evacuating nonessential U.S. personnel, a move that Pyongyang might have interpreted as the prelude to a preemptive allied strike against it.

Clinton entered office just as the geopolitical map was being redrawn in unfathomable ways, and his foreign policy team—Warren Christopher as his first secretary of state, Anthony Lake as national security adviser, and Madeleine Albright, UN ambassador before succeeding Christopher at the State Department—failed to adjust to the changing terrain. Nor did the president help matters with his notorious and distracting affair with a White House intern and the impeachment spectacle that followed. Toward the end of Clinton's two-term presidency, the White House lacked the depth and focus needed to adequately address a crisis big enough to topple NATO.

As a presidential candidate, Bill Clinton campaigned against Bush's refusal to intervene militarily in the Balkan crisis, famously expressed by Secretary of State James Baker's assertion that "we don't have a dog in that fight." As president, he found himself pinioned between militarists like Albright on one side and a reluctant Pentagon establishment on the other.

The conflict began in 1991 when Yugoslavia's lesser republics and provinces, held together for nearly four decades by its canny leader, Josip Broz (Tito), declared themselves independent of the Serbian-dominated central government in Belgrade. For much of the decade, Serbian president Slobodan Milošević waged a series of wars, first against Bosnia-Herzegovina and Croatia, then against Kosovo, for the sake of a greater Serbia that resulted in some of the worst human rights abuses of the last half century. At a time when Washington was struggling to find a strategic vision to suit the post–Cold War world, few in the uniformed services believed the Balkans were worth fighting for. When queried about the likely costs of U.S. involvement, they conditioned a successful outcome on excessively high troop estimates and casualty rates.

Interventionists regarded Colin Powell, whom Clinton had asked to stay on as JCS chairman during this transition, as particularly obstructive. With senior White House officials pushing for an armed response to Serbian atrocities, Powell laid out the same set of military options he had outlined for Bush. Yet he also made clear that air assault alone would not resolve the problem, and he argued that a political objective worthy of such action had yet to be articulated. At one point during a senior-level meeting in the Situation Room, Madeleine Albright, Clinton's hawkish UN ambassador, pointedly asked Powell: "What's the point of having this superb military that you're always talking about if we can't use it?" Powell, disturbed by the "wandering deliberations" and "marathon gabfests" that stood for policy debate in the Clinton White House, coolly informed Albright that U.S. forces were not "toy soldiers to be moved around" absent clear commitments in pursuit of well-defined goals.

In September 1995, under growing pressure from NATO members for attacks on Belgrade, the White House ordered a punishing but limited bombardment. Bowed, Milošević in December grudgingly signed a truce brokered by Special Envoy Richard Holbrooke at the Wright-Patterson Air Force Base in Dayton, Ohio. Within a few years, however, another Balkan conflict was brewing, this one between Serbs and ethnic Albanians in the province of Kosovo. By now, the lame-duck Clinton was weary of the crisis and loath to reengage it, particularly after reading *Balkan Ghosts*, Robert Kaplan's travelogue about the region that reportedly intimidated the president from getting too deeply involved in its wars. Reports of systemic Serb attacks on innocent Albanians steeled Albright's hand, however. With the Dayton agreement in ruins and Albright, now America's first female secretary of state, pushing for a strong NATO response, the stage was set for something unprecedented in the alliance's fifty-year history: war.

From beginning to end, the seventy-eight-day air campaign on Serb targets in Kosovo was Madeleine's War, the victory lap for her crossing as a refugee—first from Hitler's terror, then from Stalin's—to salvation, success, and celebrity in America. She distinguished herself as the un-Powell—as well as the un-Kissinger, who despite a similar background operated from a starkly different set of coordinates—insisting the United States had a moral duty to promote the general welfare abroad as it was constitutionally mandated to do so at home. Whereas the thrust of the Powell Doctrine was to wage war only when clear national security interests were at stake, Albright regarded the military as a kind of Swiss Army knife of statecraft: it could be used to punish America's enemies but also to repair societies broken by war or terrorized by oppressive regimes. For the military's new generation of missions, there was a new fashion of code names. In contrast to the austere Husky, Torch, and Overlord of a bygone era, U.S. troops would now Provide Comfort, Restore Hope, and Uphold Democracy. Even trade promotion, once the purview of U.S. chambers of commerce, was added to the Pentagon's expanding business lines. The nation's forward deployments were no longer about checking the Soviet evil but about spreading the gospel of Clinton-era neoliberalism. "Business tends to follow the flag," Defense Secretary William Cohen once assured an audience in Munich. "When [investors] find a secure environment, they will invest."

Robert Jervis, a professor of international affairs at Columbia University, similarly equated American empire with net-sum prosperity in a 1993 article:

The most obvious line of argument is that the United States needs to maintain its dominant position because there are important conflicts of interest between it and other developed countries. But a different chain of reasoning sees the main problem not as others gaining at America's expense, but as the need to provide public or collective goods. In this view, it is still important for the United States to maintain primacy, but doing so is in the interests of other developed countries as well.

In fact, America's far-flung web of garrisons and military alliances would fail to prevent economic meltdowns in Mexico, Russia, and Asia under Clinton's watch, to say nothing of the global financial collapse that occurred a decade after his departure. (Nor would it preempt the

September 11 attacks; on the contrary, the U.S. troop presence in Saudi Arabia, a residual of the 1991 Gulf War, was one of several factors that provoked bin Laden's assault.)

Albright's was an authentic liberal conceit, however, and it would not be deterred. Her declaration of America as "the indispensable nation" was the linear descendant of Woodrow Wilson's assertion that "American principles and policies . . . are the principles and policies of forward-looking men and women everywhere, of every modern nation, of every enlightened community. They are the principles of mankind." Albright conflated "values" with interests as predicates of U.S. foreign policy, an arbitrary marker applied arbitrarily. While she pushed for interventions in the Balkans and Iraq, she precluded operations of similar scope in Haiti, Somalia, and Rwanda. In retaliation for Iraqi artillery fire on U.S. war-planes patrolling that country's no-fly zones, Albright championed a grad-ualist deployment of airpower despite the futility of such tactics when used against Hanoi three decades earlier. She embraced sanctions as a low-cost way to undermine Iraqi leader Saddam Hussein with a stunning callousness as to their consequences for innocent civilians.* (In her mem-oirs, Albright expressed deep regret for her remarks.)

Albright's worldview was informed not by the lessons of Indochina or the Middle East, however, but by the narrative of Munich. As with the neoconservatives who both preceded and succeeded her, Albright re-sponded to foreign aggression against a U.S. ally by flashing the ap-peasement card. To her, the relative motivations of, and the atrocities committed by, a Hitler or a Milošević were indistinguishable against a totalitarian whole that must be subdued, particularly if it loomed over Mother Europe. On the eve of the Kosovo bombing, with an F-16 fighter

---

* On the May 12, 1996, edition of *60 Minutes,* Albright had the following exchange with interviewer Leslie Stahl about the consequences of U.S. sanctions on Iraq:

STAHL: We have heard that a half-million children have died. I mean, that's more children than died in Hiroshima. And—and you know, is the price worth it?

ALBRIGHT: I think this is a very hard choice, but the price—we think the price is worth it.

jet serving as a stage prop behind her, Albright told hundreds of U.S. troops at Spangdahlem Air Base in Germany that "we are reaffirming NATO's core purpose as a defender of democracy, stability, and human decency on European soil."

In fact, NATO was a defensive alliance created to deter a Soviet attack against Western Europe, whereas the war against Serbia would be an offensive war of choice. With Cold War verities scattered like chaff by the Soviet collapse, however, Albright was not above a little retrofitting if it meant reaffirming transatlantic relations as the touchstone of U.S. foreign policy. She was the brains of Washington's liberal internationalist elite and the beating heart of its pro-Atlantic bias. With bombs raining down on Serbian positions in Kosovo, she entreated Viktor Chernomyrdin, a former Russian premier who had been tapped as a mediator by President Boris Yeltsin, to cow Milošević into submission. (They conversed in Russian, one of the six European languages Albright speaks, and at one point she recounted the time she gave flowers to Tito when her father was the U.S. ambassador to Yugoslavia.) Russian support would be as critical to the U.S. mission in the Balkans as it had been in Iraq eight years earlier.

Albright's peremptory expansion of NATO's charter did not go down well with senior diplomats, however. When UN secretary-general Kofi Annan suggested he appoint a group of negotiators to deal with Belgrade, Albright shut him down. "Kofi," she snapped, "we don't need negotiators running all over the place." The United States failed to win approval for war in the UN Security Council, making the enterprise illegal. Nor were America's military elites happy about their emerging role as globo-cops. In early 1999, at the Meridian House mansion in Washington, senior military leaders and diplomats debated the wisdom of going to war for humanitarian reasons. Should the military itself be restructured to take on such missions, they asked themselves, just as neo-imperial Britain and the French did in the nineteenth century? In response, General John Shalikashvili, Powell's successor as JCS chairman, delivered the skunk at the garden party. Rising to speak, he declared it was not the Pentagon's responsibility to address nonmilitary challenges but the nation's near-bankrupt civilian agencies. "What we are doing to our diplomatic capabilities is criminal," he said. "By slashing them, we are less able to avoid disasters such as Somalia and Kosovo, and there we will be obliged to use military force still more often." Several months later, Shalikashvili was succeeded as JCS chairman by General Hugh Shelton, who had his own tart assessment of the looming war for Kosovo: "We're being pressed to become the world's policeman, but we don't have the will or the military structure to do it right. Nor do we have a rational method of picking where we'll get involved. Give us a clear job to do and we can usually do it. . . . But you have to set priorities. China and Russia are Class A priorities. Kosovo would have been a C."

However resourceful Albright may have been as a diplomat, her push for another military intervention in the Balkans failed to resonate with the people who mattered most. The president, mired in scandal over his affair with White House intern Monica Lewinksy, was fighting for his political life, and Pentagon leaders were dead set against a Balkan expedition. There was one exception, however, and he was just guileful and single-minded enough to make all the difference. General Wesley Clark was one of the Pentagon's most powerful and high-profile combatant commanders. As the commander of EUCOM, he was responsible for U.S. interests in Europe, Central Asia, and parts of the Middle East, and it was under his administration that NATO welcomed Poland, Hungary, and the Czech Republic into its ranks, an enlargement that extended its authority all the way to Russia's doorstep.

President Clinton was a big supporter of an expanded NATO and Clark was inclined to use it in the name of the emerging Clinton Doctrine, in which civilian leaders availed themselves of the military to carry out humanitarian and law enforcement missions. That made Clark a solitary and often nettlesome figure in a conservative Pentagon establishment. So he pursued his objective elliptically, bypassing the Pentagon and pleading his case to National Security Adviser and Albright ally Sandy Berger. Clark sweetened the deal by assuring Berger that the mere threat of NATO bombardment would bring Milošević to the negotiating table. In February 1999, Albright led a diplomatic showdown in Rambouillet, France. There she made demands on Belgrade officials—including NATO authority to patrol throughout Yugoslavia—that no Serb leader would ever accept. Writing in London's *Daily Telegraph* after the talks broke down, Henry Kissinger called the U.S. terms drafted at Rambouillet "a provocation, an excuse to start bombing. . . . It was a terrible diplomatic document that should never have been presented in that form."

With the credibility of NATO at stake, the Joint Chiefs had no choice but to fall in line behind Clark and his bold plan to bomb the Serbs into submission. As journalist Dana Priest put it in *The Mission,* the definitive account on the combatant commands and their impact on U.S. foreign policy, "on the scale of just how much responsibility had devolved to the CinCs over the preceding decade, nothing could match the improvised Kosovo operation."*

On the night of March 24, 1999, from his billet—a nineteenth-century château in Mons, Belgium, the most opulent of SACEUR's (Supreme Allied Commander Europe's) perks—Clark gave the order that unleashed a massive American air campaign from both land and sea. Within an hour, forty-five of fifty-two targets had been struck and three Serb fighter jets had been shot down. It was a spectacular performance by America's air armada, though it made little impression on Milošević. Bloodied but not beaten, he held on while a frustrated Clark pushed his bosses for an ever-deeper commitment to the war. He wanted more targets tagged for destruction, and he wanted attack helicopters and infantry readied for action for a possible ground offensive. His constant demands, to say nothing of his frequent media appearances, antagonized the brass at home. In April, he persuaded British prime minister Tony Blair, who favored a much more aggressive prosecution of the war, that the threat of a ground invasion was needed to bring Milošević to heel. His appeal became a point of contention between Blair and Clinton when the two men dined together and the British leader made the case for a ground war. Later that month, he told reporters the Serbs were reinforcing their positions in Kosovo, a remark that was interpreted as tacit admission that the air assault was failing, which further incensed Pentagon officials.

It wasn't until early June, after Chernomyrdin informed Milošević he could no longer bank on Russian protection, that the Serbian leader

---

* The commanders were known colloquially as "CinCs," short for "commanders in chief," until they were busted in 2002 by Defense Secretary Donald Rumsfeld to the more workmanlike title of "combatant commanders." In a memo, Rumsfeld ruled that "there is only one CinC under the Constitution and law," and that is the president of the United States.

finally agreed to withdraw his troops from Kosovo. Within weeks after the war ended, Clark was removed as SACEUR, a martyr for the principle of humanitarian war and for the sake of an alliance that should have been dissolved along with the threat it was established to deter. The Kosovo air assault may have led to thousands of civilian casualties and a massive refugee crisis, but it achieved its primary, if unofficial, mission: to spare NATO, a Cold War relic, from the weight of peace.

During his first meeting with Clark, in mid-1997, NATO secretary-general Javier Solana made clear what was truly at stake in the Balkan wars. "Wes," said the Spanish diplomat, "you've got to make the NATO mission in Bosnia successful. It is the only operation NATO has and it must succeed." Nearly two years later, as the Kosovo air war stripped bare the deep divisions among NATO members, the whiff of panic in Solana's appeal had become a stench. By May, the massive air assault on Kosovo and Belgrade had yet to produce Milošević's surrender. Not only that, several errant NATO warheads had struck civilian targets, including a convoy of Albanian refugees and the Chinese embassy, prompting angry démarches from Beijing. After intense debate, the Clinton administration decided to back Clark's demands for the deployment of Apache attack helicopters, but it refused to use them in battle for fear one might get shot down. Disputes erupted over whether NATO should commit itself to a land war in the face of Serbian defiance, with Germany calling such action "unthinkable" and London urging the rapid deployment of a ground force for a possible march into Kosovo. Italy and Greece, which had blocked proposals for an oil embargo on Belgrade, signaled they might not make their ports available for a ground campaign; the air war alone, after all, had devastated both the Italian tourist sector and Greece's shipping industry. "We have to consider the ecological impact if a tanker gets blown up" was how one diplomat explained the Greco-Italian position.

The political estrangement among NATO members was nothing, however, compared with the alliance's strategic dissonance. More than five decades after NATO was formed, its armies had failed lavishly to establish a minimum level of standardization, whether for transport, communication, ordnance, or air defense. This lack of interoperability vindicated years of American griping about how the Europeans cared more about their domestic defense industries than NATO readiness and cohesion. In response to the civilian deaths by wayward allied missiles, for example, American officials blamed their European partners for not buying a U.S.-built airborne surveillance system that, had it been deployed, might have significantly minimized the number of such incidents. European diplomats and military officials bristled at such comments, which they said reflected America's coarse regard of NATO as a market for its weaponry. Either way, NATO incoherence was now scandalously clear. Aside from a few propeller-driven German transport aircraft, for example, member militaries had no heavy-lift capability beyond what the United States and Britain could bring to bear. Little had changed since the Gulf War, when the Dutch, responding to a request by Turkey for Patriot missiles to protect it from possible attacks from Baghdad, could only deliver by leasing Russian transport aircraft. (Indeed, precisely because of their lack of interoperability, the main armies of the coalition that drove the Iraqis from Kuwait were forced to operate in separate corridors to avoid friendly fire casualties.)

The Defence Capabilities Initiative, launched in April 1999 to resolve NATO's growing technological gap between the United States and its allies—Washington was budgeting 3.5 times more money on research and development than the rest of NATO—was even then dismissed as a hollow gesture that would summon little in the way of real change. The air war on Belgrade exposed just how ineffective was General Klaus Naumann, NATO's lead military officer, in his efforts to restore the alliance's credibility.* While the governments of Europe may have been able to standardize agricultural subsidies for the sake of commercial union, such harmonization eluded them when it came to collective security.† "When it's all said and done," said a director at the U.S. mission

---

* Naumann was resented by many NATO officials as an American stooge for his promotion of a U.S. standard for interoperability. Interestingly, some observers say NATO was at peak readiness in the early postwar years when member states had yet to rebuild their defense industries and were forced to equip their armies with surplus U.S. weapons.

† Problems associated with NATO's lack of interoperability, which hobbled the U.S.-led bombing of Serbian positions in Kosovo in 1999, are even more profound in Afghanistan. The lack of weapons and equipment compatibility is so severe that troops are balkanized from each other to avoid potentially deadly mistakes amid the fog of battle. Radio systems work at the most primitive level, and the alliance suffers from a chronic shortage of

in Brussels, "cooperation is the exception rather than the rule. . . . NATO forces are just not structured properly."

It should be noted, if not for the scandal then for the sheer delicious irony of it all, that NATO was expanded with the help of a massive lobbying campaign by U.S. defense contractors hoping to cash in on an estimated $35 billion market for new weaponry. A pliant Congress eased things along by earmarking billions of dollars in taxpayer funds to cover the arms-modernization needs of new members. The Pentagon did its part, lowballing the estimated cost of NATO expansion at about $30 billion, nearly four times short of what the independent Congressional Budget Office had forecast. Pro-enlargement demagogues in Congress also helped, warning that Russia might go the way of Weimar Germany and produce a new Hitler.

In lobbying their enlargement plan, U.S. defense contractors had a prolific shill in Bruce L. Jackson, who wore two hats—as the president of the U.S. Committee to Expand NATO and as a senior executive at Lockheed Martin, one of the world's largest arms manufacturers. Jackson and his aides met individually with more than thirty senators, testified before Congress, and took out full-page advertisements about the virtues of NATO expansion in *Roll Call*, a digest of legislative affairs. In the summer of 1997, Jackson hosted an elaborate dinner for prominent lawmakers that featured a speech by Secretary of State Madeleine Albright about the need to enlarge and enrich the Atlantic alliance. He and his colleagues also leveraged the political muscle of groups that represented Eastern European ethnic groups in America. Lockheed Martin and Bell Helicopter

air freighters owing in part to the transatlantic rivalry between Boeing and Airbus. To get by, many coalition partners have had to lease cargo plans from Russia—just as they did during the war in Kosovo. As a senior NATO adviser told *Newsweek:* "We're reinventing the situation in Kosovo, where you have coalition troops assigned to certain sectors and they stay there regardless of what's going on in the other sector."

More recently, in 2011, NATO deficiencies were stripped bare as its members struggled to fill a void left by Washington in the Libyan civil war. Committed to the overthrow of Libyan dictator Muammar Gadhafi, Britain and France failed to deliver the kind of sustained aerial support anti-Gadhafi forces demanded after the United States withdrew from its leading role in the campaign.

Textron, for example, endowed a pro-NATO foundation set up by the Romanian embassy in Washington—its ambassador praised the defense corporations and their "direct interest in the issue"—while Boeing, eager to sell its F-18 fighters to Prague, helped finance the American Friends of the Czech Republic. Boeing's bagman at AFoCR was a consultant who worked for Mehl & Associates, which specialized in joint ventures between Czech companies and U.S. defense giants.

Defense contractors also took their campaign across the pond. In April 1997, Lockheed Martin CEO Norman Augustine toured Eastern Europe to generate support for NATO expansion and to showcase Lockheed weaponry. In Romania, he pledged to back Bucharest's bid for NATO membership in exchange for its $82 million purchase of a Lockheed radar system. The company also organized free "defense planning seminars" for government and military officials. These events were less marketing opportunities, assured company representatives, than Lockheed's way of expressing its "personal convictions" about NATO expansion and of familiarizing itself with "who the decision makers are, what their value structures are, and what their needs are."

In the end, all the personal convictions and value structures in the world didn't amount to much. No sooner were the head delegates of Poland, Hungary, and the Czech Republic seated for the first time at the North Atlantic Council, NATO's main deliberative body, than their enthusiasm for American arms diminished. Asked in April 1999 whether Budapest would relent to growing U.S. pressure and purchase F-16 fighters as part of its commitment to NATO air defenses, Hungary's new ambassador to the alliance was defiantly noncommittal. "Their offers have to be better," he said of Lockheed Martin, which produces the F-16. "These big companies are not as scary as they once were. They can be tamed. We're not just a market for them. When NATO is disappointed, I care, but I don't care if Lockheed Martin is disappointed. We will upgrade on our terms—on NATO's terms—not on theirs."

The war in Kosovo was waged for a host of reasons, not the least of which was to protect its ethnic Albanians from Milošević's terror. Because of the willful neglect by European leaders of their obligations as NATO members, only a large-scale deployment of U.S. and British forces could accomplish that mission. Even then, it took a diplomatic offensive from Moscow to finally seal Milošević's surrender. Otherwise, the war may have continued and its awful toll—at least 500 civilians killed and more than 1 million displaced, a foreign mission destroyed, and the devastation of Belgrade's infrastructure—could have been far worse. A UN commission convened after the war concluded that it "was neither a success nor a failure; it was in fact both."

The war claimed not a single U.S. or allied troop death in hostile action. Shortly after the bombing ceased, U.S. forces moved into Kosovo to help rebuild the country. In lieu of adequately resourced civilian agencies, they were called upon to assume roles and duties as varied as law enforcement, refugee assistance and resettlement, road repair, and food and water distribution. In this sense at least, Clark's operational postwar plan was carried out to the letter. More than a decade after the bombing ceased, some 1,500 U.S. troops remain in Kosovo as part of a 10,000-man peacekeeping force. In September 2010, Albanian prime minister Sali Berisha told Bloomberg that U.S. troops were needed in Kosovo to ensure peace in the Balkan Peninsula. "The U.S. military presence is crucial for stability," he said. "The risk from nationalists is still real."

The most obvious legacy of the war is the Republic of Kosovo, a self-declared sovereign state of 1.8 million people with de facto control over most of its territory. Serbia has never recognized the Kosovar republic, which received a strong U.S. endorsement when it announced its independence in 2008.* Russia, however, considers an independent Kosovo to be illegal and it remains a source of friction between Washington and Moscow. The European Union has no official position on Kosovo's status. Notwithstanding its inconclusive outcome, the Kosovo war produced

---

* On December 16, 2010, the Council of Europe published the results of an investigation into senior officers of the Kosovo Liberation Army led by Hashim Thaci, a man celebrated by Albright and Holbrooke as an Albanian patriot. The report concluded that Thaci, now Kosovo's prime minister, enjoyed "violent control" over that nation's heroin trade and accused him of masterminding an organized crime ring in the late 1990s involved in assassinations, beatings, and human organ trafficking.

one clear winner. Despite the obvious and enduring fault lines between members that made a fiction of NATO unity—and in the face of Russian cooperation on critical missions, from the Gulf War to the Balkans crisis—the alliance survived the bombardment not only whole but enlarged. The war may have been ineptly managed and illegal, but it provided Atlanticists in Washington and Europe with enough currency to claim NATO could, and very much should, pursue an array of new missions and operate in new areas of responsibility. Perpetuating NATO after its performance in the Kosovo war was a reward for gross malfeasance—Europe's, for failing to integrate its armies into a true coalition of forces, and America's, for tolerating such a state of affairs to ensure it de facto control of the organization. It was a devil's transaction that would demand a much higher price two years later, when forces from the same counterfeit alliance would meet on a different and far more lethal front.

Bill Clinton would end his presidency with a strong economy to match the nation's military machinery, which was once again running on Cold War–level budgets. Thanks to the outgoing president, however, America would greet the new millennium with its diplomatic resources demoralized and in disarray. Just as the Clinton administration lost control of its Balkans policy to the moralizing Albright and the flighty Clark, so too did it sacrifice the State Department and its related agencies to a legislative assault from which it has yet to recover.

In 1994 the Republican Party captured control of both chambers of Congress. When such a transfer of power occurs, the ranking minority members of legislative committees in most cases become committee chairmen. The 1994 "Republican Revolution," as it became known, was indeed subversive, if only for the fact that it allowed one man to seize inordinate power over U.S. foreign policy. Jesse Helms, the new chairman of the Senate Foreign Relations Committee, was an unreformed segregationist who despised the Department of State. The man who frequently referred to America's diplomats as "compromisers and appeasers" now controlled the State Department's budgets and appointments. In December 1996, when Helms warmly endorsed Madeleine Albright as the first female secretary of state, it was an embrace equal to the seduction in *Richard III* of Anne Neville by the Duke of Gloucester after he had murdered her husband.

Helms served five terms as senator from his native North Carolina, and despite his divisiveness he was widely respected and liked in Washington. Garrett Epps, a columnist for *The Independent,* a liberal Durham newsweekly, found Helms to be "relaxed, friendly, funny, and genuinely curious about ideas and people." John Monk, who covered Helms for the *Charlotte Observer,* called him "gracious, kind and decent." Helms regarded the Senate as a sacred trust and he delighted in showing it off to tourists, whether or not they were from his home state. He particularly enjoyed giving visitors rides on the subway that links both sides of Congress, and he would invariably place a child in the "driver's" seat of the automatic train. This was the avuncular, courtly, patrician Jesse Helms.

The other Jesse Helms, the racist, homophobic unilateralist, drew distinctions between "good" and "bad" blacks, and he dismissed the organizers of the famous Freedom Rides, which challenged the segregated policies of interstate bus companies, as "dangerous, silly groups of people." He complained of "homosexuals and lesbians, disgusting people marching in our streets demanding all sorts of things," and he condemned an "underlying drive to make homosexuality simply an 'alternative lifestyle' rather than the deviant, immoral, perverted behavior it really is." He believed the United States should junk its association with "one world" international bodies such as the United Nations, the World Bank, and arms control panels. Driven by a single-minded hatred for communism, Helms warmly engaged the most odious of dictators and regimes—including Chile's Augusto Pinochet and white minority governments in Africa—as checks on the Soviet-Chinese-Cuban triad.

Helms was the product of a fundamentalist Protestant upbringing in Monroe, a small but prosperous North Carolina town. A Navy recruiter during World War II, where he learned the art of propaganda and discovered the power of radio, he worked as a reporter for the *Raleigh Times* after his decommission and later became a program director and news editor for a radio station in Roanoke Rapids. By the 1950s, he was a well-known radio personality, a godfather to today's right-wing commentators for his anticommunist rants, his support of Joseph McCarthy and J. Edgar Hoover, and his attacks on liberals in Washington. David Brinkley, the NBC radio and television journalist and a native North Carolinian, remembers Helms preceding his nightly coverage of the Eisenhower-era desegregationist movement with his own broadcast to "answer Brinkley's lies." In his memoirs, Brinkley wrote that Helms described him as a "'turncoat southerner turned northern radical,' incapable or unwilling to tell the truth about racial problems in the South, most of the troubles caused by 'outside agitators' like me. He did his job so well he became an admired public figure."

In 1960 Helms joined the Raleigh-based Capitol Broadcast Company, where his strident conservatism was received gratefully throughout northern North Carolina. In 1972, with the help of Richard Nixon's landslide presidential win, he was elected to the U.S. Senate, where he quickly established himself at the vanguard of the burgeoning New Right. One of his first acts in the Senate was to propose a bill that would have authorized the president to grant honorary citizenship to Soviet dissident Aleksandr Solzhenitsyn. He toured Latin America, where he consorted with brutal anti-communist regimes. He railed against international treaties as tentacles in a "death-grip of interdependence." He fought President Jimmy Carter's agreement to hand over the Panama Canal to the Panamanians, and he accused Thomas Pickering, Ronald Reagan's ambassador to El Salvador, of working covertly to deprive Roberto D'Aubuisson, a former general linked to a series of politically motivated killings, of votes in the 1984 presidential election there. When the Reagan administration denied D'Aubuisson a visa to visit the United States, Helms arranged and hosted the visit from San Salvador of five members of his political party.

It was at the dawn of the Reagan era that Helms fired his first shots across the State Department's bow, clashing with the White House about a range of senior appointments. In a sop to the senator, Secretary of State Alexander Haig dismissed Robert White, the U.S. ambassador to El Salvador and a Helms adversary. Helms then trained his sights on Caspar Weinberger, Reagan's nomination as defense secretary, and Frank Carlucci, the president's pick as Weinberger's deputy. In a floor speech, Helms opposed the two men as "unable to break with the very policies" that had precipitated American decline, meaning détente with Moscow, and he doubted Weinberger was strong enough to deal with the Soviets.

Helms also used his Senate prerogative of placing "holds" on several White House appointees, disparaging them as "only nominal Republicans and nominal Reagan supporters as well."

Though Helms lost this round, he would play for much higher stakes in 1986 with a bid for the ranking minority seat on the Senate Foreign Relations Committee. To get it, he would have to outmaneuver Richard Lugar of Indiana, who served as the committee's chairman until Democrats recaptured the Senate in midterm elections in November that year. The Helms-Lugar competition was nothing less than a struggle for the soul of Republican foreign policy. Unlike the hard-line Helms, Lugar was a moderate on policy issues who reached out to Democratic colleagues. Though Lugar had the full support of Republicans on his committee, Helms mounted his challenge on the basis of his seniority, which under Senate rules gave him notional entitlement to the ranking seat. To Lugar's surprise, a plurality of Republican Caucus members agreed, voting in Helms's favor by a margin of 24–17.

Helms wasted no time putting Washington foreign policy elites on notice. A new sheriff was in town, he told the Conservative Political Action Committee, and there would be no more bartering of America's "deepest values" for the sake of "international commitment or interest." He pledged his fierce opposition to the Soviet empire and support of capitalist allies even if they had not "solved all their problems yet." This was strong stuff, even for a Republican administration generally considered among the most conservative in decades. "There's an awful lot of people walking around in shock and horror" was how the New York Times quoted one unnamed White House official. Helms's triumph marked an expansion of the radical right's portfolio from domestic issues to America's relations overseas at a time when neoconservatives were also taking a keener interest in international affairs. Following the 1994 midterm elections and the Republican takeover of Congress, Helms would have nearly as much influence on foreign relations as the president himself.

As the Foreign Relations Committee chairman, Helms moved to halt U.S. dues to the United Nations, which he called "a longtime nemesis of millions of Americans," including funds for U.S. peacekeeping operations. He dismissed U.S. foreign aid programs as money pits for countries that "constantly oppose us in the United Nations and many of which rejected concepts of freedom." A Helms aide predicted "deep, slashing cuts" in foreign assistance levels and in funds for global institutions such as the International Monetary Fund, the World Food Program, and refugee relief work in Somalia, Rwanda, and Sudan. Helms regarded the United States Agency for International Development with particular contempt. The nation's leading foreign-aid agency, he said, had promoted socialism abroad by seeding welfare states in needy countries. Corrupt governments had lined their offshore accounts with USAID funds. According to Helms, the agency had to be "restructured," by which he meant emasculated. In a column published in the *Washington Post*'s February 14, 1995, edition, Helms proposed streamlining USAID's bureaucracy and privatizing assistance programs with the help of nongovernmental organizations, or NGOs. It called for significant cuts in the nation's $21.2 billion international affairs budget, the closure of all USAID missions overseas and the halving of its staff, and sharp cuts in the budgets of the State Department and the U.S. Information Agency, Washington's public-diplomacy arm.

Cleverly, Helms entitled his column "Christopher Is Right," a reference to Secretary of State Warren Christopher's proposal, impelled by post–Cold War budget cuts, to fold USAID, USIA, and the Arms Control and Disarmament Agency into the State Department. The article exploded like a bombshell in front of USAID director Brian Atwood when he was confronted with it during a morning appearance on C-SPAN. In response, Atwood muttered that it did not faithfully represent Christopher's plan and implied it was the kind of political maneuvering that is all too common in Washington. In testimony that day before Helms's committee, Christopher reiterated his position that the three agencies should remain independent. Nearly three weeks later, Vice President Al Gore persuaded Christopher to drop the restructuring plan altogether.

The Helms column placed Atwood squarely on the defensive, however, where he and his allies at the White House would remain for the duration of the Helms onslaught. When Atwood called Helms's ideas "mischievous," the product of a nineteenth-century isolationist sensibility, Helms's staff responded with a media campaign, armed with what it

called "captured enemy documents" that allegedly proved USAID's waste
and inefficiency. When Atwood protested in a letter to Helms that such a
tactic was unworthy of a U.S. senator, he received a "friendly and charming" reply from Helms assuring him that he did not consider the USAID
director an enemy. The offensive on USAID continued, however, albeit in
a less provocative manner.* "It was an effort to cram something down the
administration's throat," said Atwood. "The executive branch has a right
to organize itself the way the president wants and then submit its plan to
the Congress. In this case, Helms was telling the administration how it
should organize itself even before the administration had decided it
should do so. Helms was all-powerful. He was simply telling the White
House what to do."

The dispute over Helms's proposals became mired in stalemate. For
four months, the senator suspended all business meetings of the Foreign
Relations Committee; froze hundreds of State Department promotions,
including ambassadorial postings; and blocked deliberation on a range
of treaties on everything from arms reduction to international conven-
tions on women and the environment. (In 1999, Helms froze Clinton's
nomination of Atwood as the U.S. ambassador to Brazil, forcing the president to withdraw the nomination.) Finally, in December 1995, the White
House offered a compromise: it would impose its own consolidation plan,
much of which was inspired by Helms's proposals, that would save at least
$1.7 billion. Helms accepted the Clinton counteroffer.

By the end of the Clinton presidency, USAID's workforce had been cut
from 11,500 employees to less than the 8,000 it had employed seven years
earlier. The number of countries with USAID programs was slashed from
120 to 70. Helms was not through, however. In 1997 he managed to evis-
cerate a landmark chemical weapons treaty and he persuaded Clinton to
incorporate USIA inside the State Department. USAID, meanwhile, was

---

* The campaign was led with gusto by Marc Thiessen, Helms's press secretary and senior
policy adviser. Thiessen later became President George W. Bush's chief speechwriter and
in January 2010 published *Courting Disaster: How the CIA Kept America Safe and How
Barack Obama Is Inviting the Next Attack*. The book asserts, among other things, that the
torture tactic known as waterboarding is permitted by the doctrines of the Roman Catholic Church.

effectively eliminated as an independent agency when it was made answerable to the secretary of state rather than the president.

This was not all Helms wanted, of course. If it were up to him, he would have dissolved USAID completely and reduced America's diplomatic missions abroad to tiny outposts. But his demolition of America's diplomatic architecture paved the way for the unilateralism and epic militarization that was to come.

15

DENOUEMENT

*Our responsibility to history is clear: to answer these attacks
and rid the world of evil.*
—GEORGE W. BUSH, ADDRESSING MOURNERS AT
THE NATIONAL CATHEDRAL IN WASHINGTON TWO DAYS
AFTER THE SEPTEMBER 11 ATTACKS

Great is the guilt of an unnecessary war.
—JOHN ADAMS

A S THE CLINTON ERA DREW TO A CLOSE, AMERICA WAS LESS A
shining city on a hill than it was a prosperous but listless gated
community. Overseas, it was represented by vast, forbidding
embassy compounds, the imperial redoubts of a superpower estranged
from the world it presumed to lead. At home, it was exhausted by the
Clinton upheavals: the failed battle for health-care reform; the low-
grade, inconclusive wars; the Monica Lewinsky scandal; the high-tech
boom and bust. Anxious in war but unfulfilled in peace, Americans did
not confront the dawn of a new millennium so much as they shuffled
toward it.

The popular TV sitcom *Seinfeld,* proudly declared by its creators to be
"a show about nothing," captured the vacuity of the age. Absent an epic
struggle of their own, Americans embraced World War II, the most destructive conflict in human history, for inspiration and a sense of purpose.
Hollywood, which during the Cold War produced some of the cleverest
and most subversive antiwar films ever made, from *All Quiet on the Western Front* to *Fail-Safe,* now mined the values and ideals of "the greatest
generation," the humble conscripts who defeated the Axis powers. Video
games allowed players to command their own battles for Midway, To-

bruk, and Bastogne. The History Channel, launched during the heart of the Clinton years, became a closed loop of World War II documentaries, many of which focused on Adolf Hitler, the Nazis, and the weaponry of the Wehrmacht. In Clinton-era America, not only had the U.S. military become fetishized, so too had war itself.

Intellectually as well as politically, there were no ideological battles left to fight. In his 1992 treatise *The End of History and the Last Man*, Francis Fukuyama argued that American-style liberal democracy was the fullest and final expression of human values. *New York Times* columnist Thomas L. Friedman promoted a similar theme. With his trademark faculty for reductionism, he unveiled his "Golden Arches Theory of Conflict Prevention," which holds that no two countries with a McDonald's franchise—a symbol of bourgeois affluence that globalization was stimulating worldwide—had ever gone to war with one another. Such a conceit was Clinton's credo as well as his millstone. While it suited his neoliberal bias, an American president needs a war to enter the pantheon of great leaders. Untried by a major conflict, the Clinton administration would instead be judged on its domestic achievements: a healthy economy and a balanced budget, the North American Free Trade Agreement, the Family and Medical Leave Act, welfare reform.

Like many presidents before him, Clinton tried and failed to broker a peace deal between Israel and the Palestinians. He had also struggled with the growing menace of Al Qaeda. In 1998, after the group attacked America's embassies in Kenya and Tanzania, Clinton authorized covert strikes on Osama bin Laden and several of his senior lieutenants in Afghanistan, their base of operations. He ordered attack submarines deployed to within missile range of any target in the country, and he authorized a CIA program to train forces in Pakistan and Uzbekistan to capture or kill bin Laden. On his watch, the CIA had at least once inserted units of its paramilitary forces in Afghanistan to track down and destroy the Al Qaeda leader. Clinton resisted calls for a full-scale invasion of Afghanistan to uproot bin Laden's network, however, angering conservatives who considered the embassy attacks an act of war. In October 2000, after Al Qaeda bombed the U.S. Navy destroyer USS *Cole* in Yemen's Port of Aden, killing seventeen sailors and wounding thirty-nine, moderates as well as conservatives clamored for a ground assault.

Even before the *Cole* bombing, some senior military officers were grumbling that Clinton-era "zero casualty syndrome" was undermining military doctrine and warping foreign policy. (The White House's reluctance to deploy armed force was revealed most appallingly in 1994, when it refused to send U.S. troops to quell mass murder in Rwanda. Clinton officials even avoided using the word "genocide," as acknowledging the enormity of the slaughter would have obliged them to act.) In the summer 2000 edition of *Parameters,* the U.S. Army's top academic journal, Marine Corps colonel Vincent J. Goulding Jr. argued that "reluctance to put the life of U.S. soldiers on the line only exacerbates and accelerates the suffering of those we set out to help."

The *Parameters* article was interpreted by some observers as a sign of panic within the military's ground elements that they would lose out to the Air Force in looming budget battles. If so, they need not have worried.

George W. Bush had campaigned for president in 2000 as a centrist Republican, and for good reason. With his neoliberal economic reforms and interventionist foreign policy, Clinton had left Bush with little room on his right to run on. Clinton, after all, not only restored the nation's defense budget to Cold War levels and abetted the gutting of its foreign aid, he deregulated the banks, cut landmark trade deals, and cozied up to China despite its dismal human rights record. Sensing national exhaustion with Clinton, Bush campaigned more against the incumbent president than against his actual opponent, the sitting vice president, Al Gore. He disparaged nation building for its presumption that Washington alone knew what was best for the world, and he pledged a "compassionate conservatism" to distance himself from his father's perceived elitism. "I think the United States must be humble," Bush said in a debate with Gore.

The tactic worked. After eight years of the voluptuary Clinton, Bush the born-again Christian, reformed alcoholic, and failed oil prospector prevailed over the orotund Gore in one of the most tightly contested and divisive elections in U.S. presidential history. (Only half of eligible voters bothered to go to the polls, the second-lowest voting rate since the end of World War II.) Bush was, as Winston Churchill said of Clement Attlee, a modest man of modest talents. His lack of curiosity seemed appropriate to the age; if the empathic Clinton, who could feel pain across whole spectrums of humanity, was simultaneously America's first black, gay, Jewish, and female president, Bush would be its first titular head of state for an era when the nation's economy was run by Wall Street and its foreign policy by four-star generals.

Despite the low expectations Bush brought with him to Washington, however, there was cause to be hopeful during his dimly remembered pre-9/11 presidency. The new Bush foreign policy team looked very much like the old one, with Don Rumsfeld as defense secretary, Dick Cheney as vice president, and Colin Powell as secretary of state, suggesting continuity with the party's tradition of foreign policy pragmatism. "We thought we were going back to the old days of Bush, so we were not very concerned," remarked Joschka Fischer, who served as German foreign minister and vice chancellor from 1998 to 2005. "Of course, there was this strange thing with these 'neocons,' but every party has its fringes. It was not very alarming."

Such optimism was vindicated by the manner in which Bush resolved his first foreign policy crisis, a standoff with China over the fate of a U.S. EP-3 surveillance aircraft that had collided with a Chinese fighter jet over the South China Sea in April 2001. After a jerky start—the White House was slow to appreciate how seriously Beijing was treating the matter—Secretary of State Powell seized the initiative from an aggrandizing and saber-rattling Rumsfeld and defused the confrontation in workmanlike fashion. The Hainan incident, so named for the island on which the EP-3 was forced to make an emergency landing, stands as a considerable diplomatic achievement and ranks as one of the last occasions when a U.S. secretary of state enjoyed such untrammeled authority in a crisis.

The South China Sea would emerge as a potential flash point for a much more severe confrontation to come, though as of this writing, America is still coming to terms with the long, painful, and costly distraction Bush created for it after the September 11 terrorist attacks.

———

The Al Qaeda assault on America was neither unexpected nor unprovoked. Even before Bush's inauguration, Richard Clarke, the national coordinator for counterterrorism under Clinton, sensed an attack was coming and urged immediate action be taken against Al Qaeda in its lair. Days after the president was sworn in, Clarke sent a memorandum to National Security Adviser Condoleezza Rice "urgently" requesting a meeting of the new team's foreign policy principals for a briefing on bin Laden and his network. Rice ignored the request. Unlike in the Clinton White House, where the leaders of interagency groups such as Clarke's Counterterrorism Security Group could speak directly to the principals, Rice insisted on a far more rigid, top-down structure. Clarke would first have to brief the deputies committee, which was not yet fully staffed. It wasn't until late April that Clarke was able to brief the full committee, which over the course of four meetings throughout the summer mired itself in debate over Clarke's warnings. Representing the State Department, Deputy Secretary of State Richard Armitage urged an expansion of CIA support for Afghanistan's anti-Taliban warlords, whereas Deputy Secretary of Defense Paul Wolfowitz dismissed the focus on Al Qaeda as a deviation from the real threat, Iraq. While the deputies wrangled, the CIA was pulsing with alerts, conveyed to the White House, that Al Qaeda was planning "something spectacular" against the United States. On July 10, CIA director George Tenet reviewed a strategic assessment from his counterterrorism unit that he later recalled "literally made my hair stand on end." Within fifteen minutes, he and a handful of operatives were briefing Rice and her deputy, Stephen Hadley, in her West Wing corner office.

"There will be a significant terrorist attack in the coming weeks or months," said one of Tenet's men. "Attack preparations have been made. Multiple and simultaneous attacks are possible, and they will occur with little warning."

The Tenet delegation pleaded for presidential covert-action authority, a request it first filed in March. Three days later, the deputies committee met to take up the CIA request as well as a presidential directive Clarke had revised from an earlier strategy paper he had drafted in December 2000. On August 6, Tenet had his agents prepare a top-secret briefing for

Bush at his Texas ranch, where he was vacationing for most of August. It was titled "Bin Laden Determined to Strike in U.S.," and it emphasized how relentless were Al Qaeda's efforts to hit targets in America. There was a danger of hijackings, Bush was told, and there was evidence buildings were being cased in New York City.

Bush, apparently, was unimpressed. "All right," he told the assembled spooks. "You've covered your ass now."

The matter of Al Qaeda and the CIA's threat assessments finally percolated to the principals' level in a meeting on September 4. Following a brief discussion, Clarke's proposal for CIA support of anti–Al Qaeda elements in northern Afghanistan was endorsed and a presidential directive was drafted. It was still awaiting Bush's signature when Al Qaeda struck seven days later.

Despite efforts from some quarters in Washington to conceal or distort them, the motivations behind the September 11 attacks are quite clear. In a fatwa, or Islamic religious ruling, released on August 23, 1996, bin Laden lamented how "the people of Islam had suffered from aggression, iniquity and injustice imposed on them by the Zionist-Crusaders alliance," a reference to America's close relations with Israel as well as pliant but oppressive Middle East regimes. He condemned what he said were U.S.-abetted massacres done to Muslim communities from Palestine to Chechnya and the hundreds of thousands of Iraqi children who had died from lack of food and medicine due to the "unjustifiable" U.S.-led sanctions on Iraq during the 1990s. The deployment throughout the Gulf states of U.S. troops, particularly in Saudi Arabia, he said, was "the greatest of . . . aggressions incurred by the Muslims since the death of the Prophet." Over the years, bin Laden had also condemned Arab leaders as corrupt apostates and traitors for bartering away control of their oil fields to Western energy companies, as well as past and current U.S. embargoes on such Muslim countries as Iraq, Syria, Sudan, Afghanistan, Libya, Pakistan, Iran, and Indonesia.

Bin Laden's animus against America was driven largely by secular concerns, not religious ones. While his embrace of violent opposition to U.S. Middle East policy and a fanatical interpretation of Islam were at odds with the Muslim mainstream, his loathing for U.S. Middle East policy was widely shared by a vast majority of Muslims in general and Arab Muslims in particular. The statesmanlike response to the events of September 11, then, would have been a frank acknowledgment of the attacks as the tragic but incidental price of American foreign policy. Bush might have laid out the policies at issue and then, calmly and methodically, explained why they were vital to the national interest, even at so dear a price. Instead, he delivered one of the most dishonest and ruinous speeches a U.S. president has ever given, one that would sow the wind for endless and unnecessary war.

On the night of September 20, at a special joint session of Congress, Bush told a fearful nation that the country had been attacked not as a combatant in the Middle East's sixty-year war but by "enemies of freedom." Al Qaeda, he said, had planned and executed the attacks because "they hate our freedoms: our freedom of religion, our freedom of speech, our freedom to vote and assemble and disagree with each other." Bush then prepared his worldwide audience for the conflict to come. The U.S. response to the attacks, he guaranteed, would be equivalent in scope to total war. Washington would invest the entirety of its diplomatic, intelligence-gathering, law enforcement, financial, and, of course, military resources to keep the enemy at bay. "Americans should not expect one battle," Bush said, "but a lengthy campaign unlike any other we have ever seen." He then outlawed neutrality. Any nation that harbored groups or individuals identified as terrorists by the United States, he said, would be targeted for annihilation. "Every nation in every region now has a decision to make: Either you are with us or you are with the terrorists." It was a masterstroke of dissemblance. By obscuring the real motives behind the attacks, Bush relieved the U.S. government of any responsibility for them. By defining the threat posed by Al Qaeda so broadly and by committing the United States and its allies to "the destruction and to the defeat of the global terror network," he wrote himself an unlimited wartime writ.

Only three weeks earlier, Bush's approval ratings had been hovering at 50 percent after just six months in office. In the immediate aftermath of September 11, they soared above 80 percent. He was now a war president, just like his father, and he was already plotting ways to expand the conflict to include Saddam Hussein as a target. The day after the attacks,

Bush took Richard Clarke aside and told him to "see if Saddam did this. See if he's linked in any way." When Clarke protested that it was obviously the work of Al Qaeda, Bush replied "testily" that he should "look into Iraq, Saddam." Both Donald Rumsfeld and his deputy, Paul Wolfowitz, were convinced of Hussein's complicity, and Wolfowitz pushed the president to make Iraq the first target for retaliation.

That night, remembered Clarke,

> Rumsfeld came over and the others, and the president finally got back, and we had a meeting. And Rumsfeld said, "You know, we've got to do Iraq," and everyone looked at him—at least I looked at him and Powell looked at him. And he said—I'll never forget this—"There just aren't enough targets in Afghanistan. We need to bomb something else to prove that we're, you know, big and strong and not going to be pushed around by these kinds of attacks."
>
> And I made the point certainly that night, and I think Powell acknowledged it, that Iraq had nothing to do with 9/11. That didn't seem to faze Rumsfeld in the least.

By late November, with victory in Afghanistan seemingly assured, Bush privately instructed Rumsfeld to update the military's Iraq invasion plans, a derivative of the 1991 Gulf War. On January 29, 2002, Bush included Iraq, along with Iran and North Korea, as part of an "axis of evil" in his State of the Union address. This triumvirate, he said, posed a "grave and growing danger." Its members coveted weapons of mass destruction, which they could give to terrorists for use against America and its allies. "The price of indifference would be catastrophic," Bush warned.

In Washington, as the president and his advisers no doubt knew, a little fear and demagoguery goes a long way. Speaking at a Nashville convention of the Veterans of Foreign Wars, Cheney averred that there was "no doubt" that Saddam Hussein was stockpiling weapons of mass destruction. Condoleezza Rice, in an interview on *ABC News,* warned that "we don't want the smoking gun to be a mushroom cloud." The trauma and outrage that followed the September 11 attacks, together with a vast public ignorance about the Middle East, was all the leverage Bush needed to aggressively militarize U.S. policy both at home and abroad. In prosecuting their antiterrorism war, the Bush team deliberately and often furtively erected extraordinary executive powers that subverted laws passed in the 1970s in response to the criminality of the Nixon years, which both Cheney and Rumsfeld believed hog-tied the presidency. Nor were Bush and his aides, particularly Karl Rove, his senior adviser, above using popular fears of another attack to put their political opponents on the defensive. "I remember Karl Rove was out there talking at some events about how we'd use 9/11, run on 9/11 in the [midterm] elections, and that it was important to do so," recalled Scott McClellan, Bush's White House deputy press secretary and later press secretary.

Some lonely voices compared Bush's response to the attacks to the Gulf of Tonkin incident, which gave Lyndon Johnson the legal cover to militarize the Vietnam War. There is a key difference between the two events, however. Johnson, like Kennedy before him, wanted to withdraw U.S. troops from Vietnam but ended up vastly increasing their numbers for fear of being tarred as an appeaser at a time when memories of the McCarthy years were still fresh. Bush was under no such pressure. Elected by the slenderest of margins, he emerged from the horror of September 11 as one of the most radically militarist presidents in U.S. history. With the help of his advisers, he restricted the writ of habeas corpus and created the USA Patriot Act, which among other things sanctioned far-reaching government powers of surveillance. He authorized the National Security Agency to conduct warrantless wiretapping of U.S. citizens at home and abroad. He mandated torture as a tool of national security. He had "rendered" thousands of suspected terrorists, arrested on flimsy grounds and mostly without charge, to secret prisons in countries where torture was routine. After promoting democratic elections in the Arab world, he repudiated free and fair ballots in Palestine and Egypt when they yielded results that were unacceptable to Israel. He presided over the exposure of a clandestine CIA agent for partisan political reasons and he took the nation to war on specious grounds.

Under Bush, the Pentagon's budget would swell from $310 billion to nearly $665 billion, an amount equal to the rest of the world's defense outlays. To pay for it, he did not reform the nation's bloated entitlement system, which along with national security–related outlays accounts for more than 80 percent of federal spending, nor did he raise taxes. Instead, he borrowed the money from foreign investors, running up record-high budget shortfalls that would have appalled old-school Republicans such as Dwight Eisenhower or even Ronald Reagan, who restored the taxes he cut early in his first term when federal revenues plummeted to unsustainable levels. For most Americans, what Bush called "the world's fight . . . civilization's fight" would be hassle-free. Speaking from Chicago's O'Hare International Airport two weeks after September 11, Bush advised Americans to "fly and enjoy America's great destination spots. Get down to Disney World in Florida. Take your families and enjoy life, the way we want it to be enjoyed."

Though most heads of state would have responded to a September 11–like assault with massive force against the conspirators and their hosts, as Bush did against Al Qaeda in Afghanistan, it is doubtful they would have expanded it into an asymmetrical world war against a shadowy subculture with no fixed domain. The global war on terror would destabilize the Middle East, undermine U.S. national security, and destroy millions of innocent lives. Within three years after Bush delivered his "axis of evil" speech, Iraq would be torn asunder by the botched aftermath of a U.S.-led invasion, North Korea would have enough enriched plutonium for a small arsenal of nuclear warheads, and Iran, its influence greatly enhanced by the elimination of Iraq as a rival, would be a regional menace with nuclear ambitions of its own.

The story of how the Bush White House blundered from one destructive misstep to another in its Middle East wars is as well told as it is scandalous. It is American militarism in its most unalloyed form, and it came about the same way free societies succumb to authoritarian rule: with a leadership that rewards sycophants and the like-minded, co-opts the ambitious, and punishes those in dissent.

Since the dawn of the nation-state, diplomats have struggled to reconcile the realities of their host countries with political priorities back home. Beyond resolution, however, is the estrangement between the reality of the modern Middle East and Washington's uniquely warped caricature of it. What sabotaged the U.S. position in revolutionary China—namely, a complex of powerful forces unduly devoted to one side in the dispute—similarly undermines America's security interests in the Middle East. Since President Truman defied the advice of his national security experts, from George Marshall on down, and aligned the United States with the interests of a fledgling Israel, America's Middle East policy has been defined by domestic cultural and political concerns rather than geopolitical ones. Largely as a result, the Division of Near Eastern Affairs has been all but emptied of its Middle East expertise. Its desk officers and diplomats have been discredited by allegations of a pro-Arab bias, frustrated with their growing irrelevance to a policymaking process shaped largely by political advisers in the White House, and exhausted by the pressures of living and working in an increasingly violent region.

It is not just diplomats whose Middle East insights are overlooked or ignored, however. Senior U.S. military officers with invaluable experience in the region have also been rebuked for challenging the established political order. In March 2010, CENTCOM commander David Petraeus led his testimony to the Senate Armed Services Committee by characterizing "insufficient progress toward a comprehensive Middle East peace" as inimical to U.S. interests in the region. "The enduring hostilities between Israel and some of its neighbors," Petraeus told Congress, "present distinct challenges to our ability to advance our interests" in the region. "The conflict foments anti-American sentiment, due to a perception of U.S. favoritism for Israel. . . . Meanwhile, Al Qaeda and other militant groups exploit that anger to mobilize support." Though Petraeus's utterances on Capitol Hill are usually regarded as oracular, his thinly veiled appeal for a U.S.-imposed peace settlement in the Middle East was openly scorned by the politicians gathered before him.

Petraeus's predecessor, Anthony Zinni, was even more outspoken about the primacy of a Mideast peace deal to U.S. security interests, a linkage Israel's friends in Washington vehemently deny even exists. "The neocons who wanted to go into Iraq were selling the war as saying 'the road to Jerusalem goes through Baghdad,'" Zinni said. "In fact, the road to everything out there *begins* in Jerusalem. You can't deal with these other problems without dealing with the Middle East peace process."

To be fair, the weight of neoconservative influence on the Bush administration has been exaggerated. Though the neocons were frank in their desire for the use of naked aggression to remake the Middle East as a democratic idyll friendly to Israel's interests, that alone did not impel Bush's assault on the region. As Richard Clarke recounts, Iraq was identified as a target immediately after September 11 not for Israel's sake but as a way to reassert America's credibility as a superpower. A heavy cost of Washington's close alignment with Israel over the years, however, has been the assumption by Washington of its ally's parochial perceptions of the region and the repudiation of those regional experts who would depart from it. This seamless conflation has made Israel's militarism America's militarism. As a result, though much of America's strategic interests diverge dramatically from those of its ally, the two countries perversely share the same enemies. From there, an entire genre of September 11 fiction—that Muslim extremists hate America for its "values" as opposed to its policies, that Saddam Hussein was an Al Qaeda ally, that U.S. troops would be welcomed in Baghdad with flowers and sweets, that democracy can emerge fully formed from societies traumatized by generations of colonial occupation, sanctions, oppression, and war—was made respectable.

Facts are indeed inconvenient things, no more so than in Washington, where Middle Eastern facts are either denied or altered with armed force. In its quest for a new war with Iraq, the Bush administration did both. Iraq experts were shunted aside in favor of political appointees, many of them neoconservatives whose only knowledge of the Middle East was limited to what they knew from Israeli hard-liners. In promoting neocon ringer Ahmed Chalabi as the leader of a free Iraq, Richard Perle, then a senior Pentagon adviser, assured Americans that "the chances for a resolution of the Israeli-Palestinian conflict will improve as soon as Saddam is gone. We will have a good opportunity to persuade Syria to stop supporting [Hezbollah] . . . if we remove Hussein." On July 10, 2002, Perle invited senior Pentagon officials to a meeting with Laurent Murawiec, a RAND defense analyst and member of the Committee on the Present Danger. Among the talking points raised in Murawiec's twenty-four-slide presentation, according to the August 6 edition of the *Washington Post,* was that Saudi Arabia is "the kernel of evil, the prime mover, the most dangerous opponent" in the Middle East. Murawiec also declared that "Palestine is Israel, Jordan is Palestine, and Iraq is the Hashemite Kingdom." Writing for the Israeli daily newspaper *Haaretz,* correspondent Akiva Eldar correctly parsed Murawiec's disquisition as "ethnically cleanse the Palestinians to Jordan, and give Iraq to the Jordanian royal family." In response to the *Post* story, the White House distanced itself from Murawiec, who left RAND not long after he gave his briefing. Still, the *Post* reported, the presentation "represents a point of view that has growing currency within the Bush administration—especially on the staff of Vice President Cheney and in the Pentagon's civilian leadership—and among neoconservative writers and thinkers closely allied with administration policy-makers."

Colin Powell did what he could to dispel such nonsense. Indirectly addressing the "attack Iraq" crowd months after September 11, he told the *New York Times Magazine* that Iraq "isn't going anywhere. It is in a weakened state." (He may have also added that Saddam Hussein had no reason to mess with a good thing, drawing as he was an estimated $2 billion a year as the lord of a black-market economy that had cultured around the embargo on Iraq.) On August 5, 2002, as the momentum for war accelerated, Powell told Bush that invasion would make him "the proud owner of 25 million people. You will own all their hopes, aspirations and problems. You'll own it all." He urged the president to go to the United Nations and build a coalition for action, just as his father had. Bush agreed to submit his quest for war to the United Nations, but as a way to have it sanctioned by the world body, not preempted. By then his decision to invade Iraq was as certain as Madeleine Albright's intention to wage war on Serbia with or without a UN mandate.

Ultimately, Powell was undone by Condoleezza Rice, who as national security adviser was supposed to collate rival policies in the interagency process and submit them to the president. Instead, she was outmaneuvered and bulldozed by old allies Cheney and Rumsfeld. The vice president routinely sat in on principals' meetings, an unusual step for a vice president that had a "chilling effect on the free flow of views," recalled CIA director Tenet. In interagency meetings, State Department officials would be outnumbered 3 to 1, with the Pentagon, Cheney, and the NSC usually aligned against the diplomats' position. When they raised questions, recount scholars Daalder and Destler,

> . . . Rice and [her deputy Stephen] Hadley would make them feel as if "they were not on the team." Often, once the formal meetings were concluded, another separate meeting would take place upstairs, with the president in the Oval Office. Cheney and Rumsfeld would be there, as would Rice and often the JCS chairman and White House chief of staff. But Powell wouldn't be invited.

Rumsfeld, meanwhile, sniffed dismissively at Rice's authority. "I report to the president of the United States," he told her, and he ordered that all communications from the Pentagon to the White House, including the NSC, be approved by him personally. On the few occasions when he would alert Rice of important Pentagon decisions before they were taken to Bush, he would usually send Eric Edelman, a career diplomat who had been seconded to Rumsfeld's office. On one occasion, at the peak of the sectarian violence in Iraq, Rumsfeld tasked Edelman to inform Rice that he would be pulling a U.S. Army brigade from the country. The news enraged Rice, who responded that such a withdrawal would be interpreted as U.S. abandonment of the then-fragile Iraqi government. Edelman would later remark that Rumsfeld "was very amused" that he could, with impunity, dispatch his aide on such unpleasant missions.

If Vietnam was "McNamara's war," Iraq would be Rumsfeld's signature quagmire. The two men had more in common than paternity of needless conflicts, however. They were among the most consequential secretaries of defense since the end of the Cold War. Both men had come to the Pentagon from the private sector and were expert at processing reams of data and analysis. They were ruthless in asserting civilian control over the military and both had distinct ideas about how to improve its responsiveness. Rumsfeld, like McNamara before him, surrounded himself with like-minded civilian aides who struggled against a Pentagon bureaucracy that outlasted his attempts to reform it. There was, however, a singular difference between them: whereas McNamara would concede that the Vietnam War was a tragic mistake and spend the rest of his life in public contrition, Rumsfeld would never renounce the war he did so much to bring about.

Rumsfeld had run the Pentagon before, under President Ford at the age of forty-three, the youngest person ever to hold the job. By the time he returned to the post a quarter century later, he was the oldest secretary of defense and the Pentagon had evolved dramatically. The military was thoroughly professionalized and had long since shed its post-Vietnam psychosis. The combatant commanders, who did not exist during Rumsfeld's first tour, had become power centers in their own right, and the Joint Staff had become a formidable brain trust. For Rumsfeld, the brass had become too powerful, and he quickly set about restoring what he believed was an erosion of civilian control while reshaping the armed forces for a new century.

Like President Bush and National Security Adviser Rice, Rumsfeld believed that the Pentagon had been distracted during the Clinton administration with noncore missions such as drug enforcement and nation building. His first budget request shocked Pentagon functionaries because it did not include a spending increase. He dismissed Cold War–era weaponry—such as the Army's $11 billion Crusader howitzer program, which he had scrapped in May 2002—as costly and obsolete. He wanted to dramatically reduce or concentrate force structures, personnel, and base systems as part of his plan to transform the military into a lighter, more agile expeditionary force. Naturally, this triggered a backlash from the Joint Chiefs. In May 2001, they appealed to their allies on Capitol Hill, which had already rebuked the secretary for his too-modest budget requests and for ending B-1 bomber operations at three bases without first notifying the relevant congressmen. Several times while testifying before the House Armed Services Committee, Rumsfeld so angered his hosts with his dissembling that they would draw his attention to an inscription in the hearing room of their constitutional mandate to fund the military.*

---

* Article I of the Constitution invests Congress with the responsibility "to raise and support Armies," but for a funding cycle of no more than two years.

By August 2001, Rumsfeld was on his heels. Only seven months into his second tour as defense secretary, his reform agenda was blocked by powerful constituencies he had recklessly antagonized. The neoconservative *Weekly Standard* was calling for him and his deputy, Paul Wolfowitz, to resign. The once supple insider whom Henry Kissinger had grudgingly praised as a "skilled full-time politician-bureaucrat in whom ambition, ability, and substance fuse seamlessly" was apparently on his way out. On September 10, a weary Rumsfeld gathered his staff in the Pentagon's inner courtyard and warned them that the most dangerous threat to the security of the United States was not terrorist groups or a resurgent China but "the Pentagon bureaucracy." The military-industrial complex, it seemed, had bent the Brahmin Rumsfeld to its will as easily as an archer strings a bow. Within twenty-four hours, however, redemption would be his.

The September 11 attacks would make Rumsfeld one of the most powerful men in the country, if not the world. The same group of lawmakers who had lectured him about constitutional prerogative responded to one of his briefings with a standing ovation. He would be parodied on *Saturday Night Live.* Pundits celebrated him only half jokingly as a sex symbol. His vengeance would be total.

Rumsfeld gave several press briefings a week. His trademark, if vaguely imperious, candor was welcomed in otherwise prevaricating Washington. "I could answer that. I won't" was one of his stock replies to what stood for a probing press inquiry in September 11's aftermath. Less amusing was his treatment on the dais of General Henry Shelton, the JCS chairman, who like other Clinton appointees was on the secretary's housecleaning list for removal. Rumsfeld crowded the podium, refusing to step back to allow Shelton to comfortably address questions directed to him. Relations between the two men were even worse in private; in panel discussions about his military reform plan and in the run-up to the Iraq war, the secretary often excluded Shelton as well as the service chiefs, and he ignored studies from the Joint Staff.

There was a poignant irony in the way Shelton endured Rumsfeld's slights. In January 1998, three months after he was promoted to the JCS chair, Shelton gathered the service chiefs and combatant commanders in Washington for a breakfast meeting with H. R. McMaster, author of *Dereliction of Duty,* who argued in his book that the Joint Chiefs' passivity during the Johnson administration made them complicit in the tragedy of Vietnam. The meeting concluded, Shelton dismissed everyone but the general officers, and then, slamming his fists on the table, he told them they had a responsibility to the nation to speak their mind. It was an authentic appeal for reason from someone who, like the other men at the table, still bore scars from the Johnson-McNamara years.

A half decade later, however, America's military elites, with Shelton in the lead, were once again herded mutely into a misbegotten adventure by an overbearing civilian leadership. Rumsfeld would make the war in Iraq a showcase for his theory that smart weaponry had rendered large-scale troop deployments obsolete. (Such a strategy would also be a relatively easier sell for an American public that was uneasy about the prospect of simultaneously waging two Middle East wars.) Those who opposed Rumsfeld were cruelly subverted. Less than a month before the war began, Army chief of staff General Eric Shinseki told Congress it would take an invasion force "on the order of several hundred thousand soldiers" to pacify Iraq. For that, Rumsfeld demolished Shinseki's authority by leaking the name of his successor eighteen months ahead of his scheduled retirement. Shelton's successor, General Richard Myers, was all but locked out of the Iraq war–planning sessions, while CENTCOM commander General Tommy Franks was seen as ventriloquist Rumsfeld's four-star dummy. Asked by Bush for his opinion during a meeting at the White House, Franks replied: "Sir, I think exactly what my secretary thinks, what he's ever thought, what he will think, or whatever he thought he might think." Similarly, Generals George Casey and John Abizaid, who, respectively, held the post of commander of allied forces in Iraq and of CENTCOM commander, also agreed with Rumsfeld that the Iraq war could be waged successfully with a relatively light force.

With Powell neutralized and Rice steamrollered, the Joint Chiefs were the last bulwark against the push for war, and their failure to mount a unified challenge to Rumsfeld led to the most costly mistakes of the war. If Franks ever suggested that the White House should postpone an Iraq campaign until after the Taliban in Afghanistan had been defeated, there is no evidence of it. As early as February 2002, after giving a briefing to the Senate Intelligence Committee, Franks took committee chairman Bob Graham aside and explained to him that "we were no longer fighting a war in Afghanistan" and that key personnel were already being redeployed for service in Iraq. It is a measure of Rumsfeld's political finesse that Franks has been assigned at least as much blame for the Iraq debacle as has the secretary of defense; during a June 2006 online discussion of civil-military affairs hosted by *Armed Forces Journal*, military historian Richard Kohn all but absolved Rumsfeld while piling on the hapless Franks. "The charge is that Rumsfeld forced a failed plan on the military—too few troops and a poor [postwar] plan," Kohn said. "But that plan welled up from [CENTCOM]. . . . Wasn't Gen. Franks responsible, ultimately, for a plan that used too few troops to occupy the country, close the borders, maintain order and begin the job of reconstructing Iraq?"

Such criticism, while valid, softpedals Rumsfeldian duplicity. As author and lecturer Charles A. Stevenson summarizes, "Rumsfeld's continuous dialogue with Franks . . . allowed him to deny that he had ever formally rejected military requests for high troop levels. 'I have a feeling that if you ask Gen. Franks . . . about the war plan, he would say that there is nothing he has asked for that he has not gotten,' Rumsfeld declared ten days into the war. 'The plan we have is his.' This was another example of Rumsfeld's skillful application of civilian control." Put another way, Rumsfeld played Franks for a chump.

While Rumsfeld was simultaneously bullying and cajoling his generals into making a doctrinal leap of faith, the nation's intelligence agencies were conspiring to retrofit a case for war. Taking its cue from the White House, the National Intelligence Council, an interagency group that distills analyses from Washington's many spy agencies into executive reports, body-blocked inconvenient truths. Rushing to complete a key report that would sanction the administration's decision to invade Iraq, the council's officers, or NIOs, waged an extensive search for analysts who would back up alarmist White House claims about Iraq. They managed to find, for example, a Department of Energy official willing to reject his agency's consensus position that missile tubes identified in Iraq were not, as the administration insisted, equipment for uranium enrichment. Eager to hype Iraq's primitive fleet of unmanned aerial vehicles into killer drones, they persuaded an Air Force analyst to contradict his own service's position that the UAVs could not be armed.* Crucially, they also succeeded in pressuring the State Department's Bureau of Intelligence and Research, or INR, an agency with no spies or satellites but with analysts steeped in years of regional experience and expertise, to confine its formal doubts that Iraq had weapons of mass destruction to a footnote rather than as an alternative estimate in the main body of its report.

When Fulton Armstrong, an intelligence officer involved in the drafting of the council's paper, openly raised concerns about the quality of its information, he was shouted down. "Who are you to question this paper?" demanded one of his colleagues. "Even the *Washington Post* and the *New York Times* agree with us." For Armstrong, the implication was clear: prowar intelligence agents had been feeding souped-up analyses to the press as a favor to the administration.

As Armstrong would later recall:

The NIOs clearly knew what was going on in that room. Intelligence officers are all trained to remind the recipients of their reports that they are never to take sides in a policy debate. These NIOs, however, said nothing. . . . Instead of allowing INR to develop an alternative analysis in the main text of the [National Intelligence Estimate]—the proper form for a different view when the information is so obviously weak—the [NIO] humiliated the only agency at the table, the State Department's INR, that dared question the administration's preordained conclusions.

---

* Under a headline that read IRAQI DRONES MAY TARGET U.S. CITIES, Fox News warned on its website on February 24, 2003, that "Iraq could be planning a chemical or biological attack on American cities through the use of remote-controlled 'drone' planes equipped with GPS tracking maps, according to U.S. intelligence." In August, nearly six months after the U.S. invasion of Iraq, weapons experts established that the drones were for unarmed reconnaissance work, consistent with the Air Force's official conclusions issued in the run-up to war.

Thus did Rumsfeld, Cheney, and their aides, by harnessing the war wagon of their elephantine egos and delusions to the vast resources at their disposal, plunge America into its greatest foreign policy disaster since Vietnam. While Rumsfeld convened his Office of Special Plans, a boiler room where bogus intelligence data and analyses were cooked in support of war, the State Department hosted its Future of Iraq Project, a workshop attended by hundreds of Iraqi academics, business leaders, and exiled tribal sheikhs whose input would be vital for the postwar reconstruction of the country. Included in its thirteen-volume report is a warning to CENTCOM by State Department officials of "serious planning gaps for post-conflict public security and humanitarian assistance between the end of the war and the beginning of reconstruction." Failure to address such gaps, it warned, "could result in serious human rights abuses which could undermine an otherwise successful military campaign, and our reputation internationally."

Ironically, and unknown to pretty much everyone involved in the buildup, CENTCOM already had a plan for the occupation of Iraq. It had been ordered by General Zinni in 1999 as a contingency plan should the regime in Baghdad suddenly collapse. "Desert Crossing," as the plan was code-named, called for the deployment of 380,000 to 400,000 troops, enough to seal the borders and, with the help of a civilian-led occupation authority, pacify and rebuild the country. As war loomed, Zinni, who retired from the Marine Corps in 2000, contacted CENTCOM headquarters and asked if anyone had dusted off Desert Crossing. No one had heard of the plan. When Zinni warned Lieutenant General James Conway, who would lead the 1st Marine Expeditionary Force in the invasion of Iraq, about the likelihood of a post-invasion civil war, "he looked at me like I had three heads," recalled Zinni. "Conway said they were told not to worry about it."

The Future of Iraq Project completed its study in late 2002 and submitted it to Rumsfeld, who dismissed it along with other reports that anticipated the debacle to follow. In addition to the State Department's challenge to allegations that Iraq was producing weapons of mass destruction, there was also an eight-page memo written for Colin Powell by NEA assistant secretary William Burns and his deputy, Ryan Crocker, about the consequences of invasion. Titled "A Perfect Storm," the report offered a concise overview of Iraq's complex ethnic and religious milieu and warned of sectarian violence should order not be immediately restored after the collapse of the regime. It warned that neighboring countries, in particular Iran, Syria, and Saudi Arabia, would insinuate their way into Iraq's postwar political order. It also emphasized the need for a major commitment to rebuild the Iraqi economy after a generation of devastating UN sanctions. "Nearly everything we said would happen did happen, particularly the insurgency," Crocker, a seasoned Arabist, said in a 2004 interview. "We said you have to take total control, you have to rule with an iron hand. These are Iraqis, after all. They're as tough as they come."

Rumsfeld was having none of this. Pointedly, he ordered General Franks not to plan for post-conflict operations because he wanted no distractions from the war itself. In late March 2003, with the invasion only days away, the Pentagon's civilian leadership administered its coup de grâce against Powell, rejecting a team of Middle East experts the State Department had recommended to assist in the running of post-Hussein Iraq. The group of eight officials was requested by retired general Jay M. Garner, who had been appointed by Rumsfeld to lead the Office of Reconstruction and Humanitarian Assistance, or ORHA, the agency that would become Iraq's postwar authority. The State Department's team, which included several ambassadors to Arab states, had already passed their security checks and were a week away from departing for Kuwait when they were told to "stand down" until further notice. For team member Kenneth Keith, a former U.S. ambassador to Egypt and Qatar, the Pentagon's intervention was nothing less than a neoconservative putsch against the State Department as the lead agency in U.S. foreign policy. "Whether it was in the form of a memo or a phone call from the president, that coup did take place," Keith, who was to administer the Iraqi foreign ministry, said weeks later. "It was part of the struggle led by Wolfowitz and the Secretary of Defense, who convinced the president that postwar Iraq should be in the hands of the Defense Department."

Not only did Rumsfeld bulldoze Powell's constitutional prerogatives as secretary of state, he vigorously, if stealthily, subverted the nation's civilian leaders abroad. Prior to the invasion, for example, he dispatched a three-man team to gather intelligence in several Middle East states without informing the ambassadors of their activities, according to a source with intimate knowledge of the episode. The secret deployment was a direct violation of the executive "Letter of Instruction to Chiefs of Mission," which gives the U.S. ambassador in his or her host country "full responsibility for the direction, coordination, and supervision" of all U.S. government employees, including Department of Defense personnel on official duty.

Having sidelined the diplomats, Rumsfeld turned his sights on NGOs. In the weeks leading up to the invasion, aid groups who were operating in Afghanistan queried the Pentagon about procedures for Iraq, only to find themselves stonewalled. "The plans were classified," said Sandra Mitchell, who was a coordinator for the International Rescue Committee at the time. "We would get answers like 'We're working on it. Don't worry. We'll be handling this.'" When Richard Walden, the head of Los Angeles–based Operation USA, which handles airborne logistics for disaster areas and war zones, began phoning agents to line up charter flights to Iraq, he was shocked to find that the Defense Department had already cornered the market for such excursions. "Every U.S.-flagged air cargo plane [was] soaked up by DOD," according to Walden. The Pentagon, he said, was paying triple the going rate for charters, or up to $500,000 for a flight from LA to Baghdad. Only by appealing for help from the World Economic Forum could Walden secure an affordable charter.

On March 25, Walden and several dozen other NGO members met with USAID administrator Andrew Natsios. The meeting, according to Walden, whose remarks were corroborated by another participant who requested anonymity, "got vicious" after Natsios complained of sloppy reporting standards from USAID-funded programs in Afghanistan. "He was clearly under a lot of pressure," Walden said. "He told us about how some people at the White House didn't like . . . aid people. He implied that it was only him and Colin Powell who stood between the NGOs and the [White House] from going to the private sector for the work they wanted."

On May 1, 2003, two weeks after U.S. and British forces toppled Saddam Hussein, President Bush landed on the deck of the aircraft carrier USS *Abraham Lincoln* in a Navy SB-3 refueling jet. He sprung jauntily from the cockpit, every inch the wartime president in an olive-drab flight suit with a white flight helmet tucked under his arm, and hours later announced from a dais on the carrier deck that major combat operations in Iraq had ended. War advocates celebrated Rumsfeld and disparaged Powell, who for the second time in his career had opposed what would be a triumphant war against evil. The only question was which demon to slay next: Iran or Syria?

However powerful Bush's "Mission Accomplished" moment was as a metaphor for imperial hubris, it was also a graphic measure of Washington's reluctance to acknowledge Middle Eastern reality. Even as Bush touched down on the *Abraham Lincoln,* Iraq was plunging itself into madness. Looters were stripping the country bare and sectarian score-settling had begun. Electricity was rationed—the invaders had smashed the power grids—and there was a shortage of generators. Already there were reports of Saudi and Iranian agents infiltrating the country. Soon, ORHA would have a full-scale Sunni insurgency on its hands.

Rumsfeld's Office of Special Plans clearly had no postwar plan worthy of its name, just a leap of faith that landed far short of the abyss it had created. By late summer, with Bush's reelection bid looming, the very Arabists whom Rumsfeld and his aides had punitively barred from the policy process were giving daily briefings at the White House and leading planning sessions in Hussein's Republican Palace, which now served as ORHA headquarters. "The situation has deteriorated to the point where they're interested in what we have to say," a jaundiced State Department Arab expert said at the time. "They're on their best behavior right now but they're not stating the obvious, which is that this is all about the election."

Restrictions on civilian aid groups were also lifted, though NGOs were obligated to work closely with the U.S. military due to growing security concerns. While operating in Iraq during those first few months of the occupation, Walden of Operation USA ordered his staff to remove the T-shirts they routinely wore when distributing aid because he feared that the group's logo, a twin-engine Dakota dropping humanitarian cargo, might be associated with the American military. It was a sign of things to come.

The depths of Bush administration incompetence in post-invasion Iraq have been well plumbed. Most profoundly, the Pentagon leadership disbanded the Iraqi army, which made legions of suddenly jobless young men armed enemies of the occupation, and it stripped all Ba'ath Party members of government posts, which deprived a fragile, wartorn nation of their technocratic expertise. It also alienated the Sunni tribes, the linchpin of Iraqi society after three decades of war and international isolation, which all but guaranteed a sectarian uprising. Had the White House given its Middle East experts an honest hearing during the war's prelude, Iraq may well have been spared the consequences of its ruinous aftermath.

The Future of Iraq Project has been criticized in thoughtful quarters as not being explicit enough. David Kay, for example, the former chief inspector of the Iraq Survey Group, characterized it as "not a plan to hand to a task force and say 'go implement.'" The goal of the project, however, was to produce a road map, an appraisal of forbidding terrain in the service of what would become a benighted excursion. It was not, nor was it ever meant to be, an instruction manual for neocon misadventures in the Middle East and it remains conspicuous for its honesty. In an administration defined by arrogance and deceit, the Future of Iraq Project was a transparent effort to portray Iraq as it was, for Iraq's sake. It was woven from a diversity of opinions and views, and its conclusions allowed for the unexpected and unwelcome events that can subvert even the most meticulous of war plans. It presumed nothing. It was a line of inquiry with no known destination.

The Office of Special Plans, meanwhile, folded its militaristic agenda in with the data and intelligence it concocted with the help of charlatans and shills. (One of its most prominent sources for information on Iraq and the Middle East was famously code-named "Curveball.") For a presidency that reduced the world's complexities to an eternal conflict between good and evil, the most important morality play in the Bush II era involved the State Department on one side and the Pentagon's civilian leadership on the other.

Friction between diplomats, aid workers, and war-fighters is inevitable, not because they are so different by nature but because they are so similar. All three professions appeal to can-do personalities with an elevated sense of duty and virtue. They are devoted to their institutions and are willing to spend months, if not years, away from their loved ones on behalf of them. They regard themselves as unique and indispensable, which fosters a culture of exceptionalism that can be mistaken for arrogance. They are prepared to risk their lives working in hostile environments and they typically share common objectives, in pursuit of which they employ conflicting methods.

The diplomat's goal is to advance his government's interests by finding areas of agreement and compromise with nations that lay competing claims to those interests. He promotes engagement and negotiation over isolation and estrangement. He favors the distribution of foreign aid as a reward for a friendly government or as a favor to win over a recalcitrant one. For the aid worker, this is politicizing humanitarian assistance, which should be offered not as a means to an end but as a noble end in itself. This is why officials at USAID chafe at their agency's envelopment by the State Department, which controls most of America's $26 billion aid budget. Such fraternization, they and their NGO subcontractors believe, is corrupting.

Foreign aid is also useful to the war-fighter as a means of winning hearts and minds for the purpose of defeating insurgencies. Without it, there is no leverage for hearts and minds. Conquered and secured terrain must be stabilized, which means digging wells for drinking water and irrigation systems; rebuilding and restocking schools and hospitals and hiring and training staff; and repairing roads and railroads, seaports and airports, and energy and communications grids. Refugees must be relocated, elections organized, judicial systems developed, and constabulary forces stood up.

In general, the war-fighter would rather concentrate on what he was trained to do, which is to protect America's interests and punish its enemies, and leave the residuals to civilians. This is no longer an option, however. The Bush administration's militarized response to the September 11 attacks, coming as it did in the wake of Senator Jesse Helms's ransacking of foreign aid, left the nation dangerously exposed on the post-conflict front. Even if USAID had been given the central rebuilding role in Iraq instead of being muscled aside by the Office of Special Plans, its budget, at a mere $13 billion in 2003, was inadequate. Plus, the unilateral manner in which Bush had rushed to war deprived Washington of important allies that might have assisted in addressing postwar needs.

Either way, the question was quickly rendered moot. By the fall of 2003, most NGOs working in Iraq—as well as the United Nations, which suffered a devastating bomb attack on its Baghdad headquarters in August—were forced to flee the country's escalating violence. USAID representation, where it existed, was minimal. Suddenly, the Department of Defense was the single largest humanitarian-aid agency in Iraq and Afghanistan, and it would increasingly assert its nonlethal capacity all over the world. Having established "stability operations" as one of its primary missions—reactively in the cases of Iraq and Afghanistan, and proactively elsewhere—the military was setting the aid agenda. Such broad authority is faithful to the edicts of Directive 3000.5, a Pentagon mission statement that identifies stability operations as "a core U.S. military mission . . . that shall be given priority comparable to combat operations [and] conducted across the spectrum from peace to conflict to establish or maintain order in States and Regions." The directive tasks U.S. forces to develop, among other things, "a viable market economy, rule of law, democratic institutions, and a robust civil society," including "various types of security forces, correctional facilities, and judicial systems."

Directive 3000.5 chilled the foreign aid community when it was unveiled on November 28, 2005, and for good reason. Any mission conducted "from peace to conflict . . . in States and Regions" is by definition everlasting and all-encompassing. The document allows that humanitarian and development work is often best performed by civilian experts and it encourages their input. Lest there be any confusion about who's in charge, however, it affirms that "U.S. forces shall be prepared to perform all tasks necessary to establish or maintain order when civilians cannot do so."

Annoyed at its dependence on civilian agencies for spending money, Rumsfeld demanded, and got, proprietary funding capacity. The State Department's sluggish aid channel, he argued, was unsuited to the fluid demands of postwar reconstruction in Iraq and Afghanistan and the Pentagon's ongoing need to partner with friendly regimes in the war on terror. After then NATO commander James Jones complained in 2005 about the red tape he encountered trying to sell a radar system to Morocco, Rumsfeld secured a broad funding mandate under the 2006 Defense Authorization Act. The allocation was tucked under Section 1206 and gave the Pentagon $200 million to spend on providing lethal and nonlethal equipment, supplies, and training to foreign militaries. For the first time since President Kennedy signed the Foreign Assistance Act of 1961, the U.S. military would fund such activity directly from its own accounts, bypassing the State Department.

Though Section 1206 remains a limited authority, it has been regularly extended and enlarged. In 2008, for example, Congress added maritime security to its list of acceptable activities and topped up its allocation to $350 million. Despite a key condition laid down by Congress for 1206 approval—that the Pentagon submit its programs list to the State Department for "concurrence"—oversight is lax. An April 2010 report by the Government Accountability Office found that "DOD and State have incorporated little monitoring and evaluation into Section 1206 programs. . . . The agencies have not consistently defined performance measures and results reporting has generally been limited to anecdotal information." Invariably, given the unsavory associations that counterterrorism so often demands, 1206 funds have been invested in countries with highly repressive governments, a violation of the Foreign Assistance Act. In August 2009, Senator Russell Feingold responded to the Pentagon's request for additional 1206 funding with a report that $6 million from the program had been given to the government of Chad, which according to a State Department report is "engaging in extra-judicial killing, arbitrary detention and torture." Other recipients of 1206 funding include Algeria, Cameroon, Equatorial Guinea, Gabon, and Tunisia, all of which have abysmal human rights records.

Conspicuously absent from the debate over Section 1206 was Condoleezza Rice, America's secretary of state. To no avail, Senator Patrick

Leahy, a moderate Vermont Democrat, implored Rice in several letters not to relinquish such vital funding authority as requested by the Pentagon. In May 2008, Rice and Robert Gates, Rumsfeld's successor and a passionate supporter of the 1206 channel, testified jointly to the House Armed Services Committee. In addition to their mutual desire for the continuation and augmentation of 1206 funding, Rice also endorsed a new Pentagon-controlled allocation under Section 1207 of the defense bill that could fund State Department projects contingent on the defense secretary's approval. Legislative aides involved in the debate were staggered by Rice's passivity. At one point, Rice was asked whether or not she still believed America's ambassadors should be the most senior representatives of U.S. missions overseas. Rice answered in the affirmative, but her reply was obscured by the fact that the question had to be asked in the first place.

Though the 1206 budget is restricted to a two-year cycle, the Pentagon clearly expects its franchise to be rolled over indefinitely. The Defense Security Cooperation Agency, which controls much of the funding for the military's developmental and disaster relief work, announced in 2009 that it was doubling the size of a chapter on humanitarian affairs in its manual for flag officers advising foreign governments. In January 2009, the Pentagon warned through a leaked document that civilian agencies were too weak to help in "future Iraq-style counterinsurgency operations" and declared the military was prepared to lead such missions absent a "whole-of-government" approach—in other words, unilaterally. In February 2009, an unnamed "senior Defense Department official" told the defense publication *Inside the Pentagon* that the military needed "a great deal of budgetary flexibility . . . to proactively get ahead of problems before they become disasters" and cited Section 1206 as "the gold standard" for future autonomous funding authority. That April, *Inside the Pentagon* reported a growing number of Defense Department officials who believe foreign aid should be regarded as "a vehicle to introduce social reform" within host countries, while a similarly unnamed Pentagon official was quoted saying it would be wrong for the military to transfer its new budgeting power back to civilian agencies before they "acquired the kind of capacity needed to manage very robust aid efforts." A month later, Michael Vickers, assistant secretary of defense for special operations, told Congress it should increase spending "several-fold" for funding under Section 1208, another budget mandate exclusive to the Pentagon, in support of "foreign forces, irregular forces, [and] groups or individuals" engaged in combating terrorism. The oversight mechanism for 1208 programs is considerably less rigorous than those associated with 1206.

What began as a vacuum born of Washington's refusal to sufficiently fund its civilian aid agencies has led to a major Pentagon power grab. From 2006 to 2009, Section 1206 allocations totaled $979.7 million in support of twenty-four bilateral and thirteen multilateral programs. By the end of the Bush administration, the Defense Department claimed a quarter of America's foreign aid budget, up from nearly zero a decade before, while USAID's share had declined to 40 percent from 65 percent during the same period. This makes the U.S. military the federal government's fastest-growing source of overseas assistance programs. Most of its efforts focus on the training and equipping of foreign militaries, and while they fit the broad rubric of stability operations, many are only elliptically related to fighting terrorism. "In the Dominican Republic, the Pentagon is funding anti-drug initiatives," a member of a key Capitol Hill subcommittee said in 2009. "It was funding counterterrorist operations in Sri Lanka to keep an eye on the Tamil Tigers. What does that have to do with us? I'm concerned that a lot of this money is being used to buy new friends."

Predictably, what the Pentagon regards as assets in a dangerous world are often viewed by diplomats as liabilities. Although State Department officials concede that military-to-military contacts can provide useful intelligence about potential threats, as well as diplomatic leverage over authoritarian regimes, the Pentagon's tactical considerations routinely collide with their strategic ones. Aid workers, meanwhile, complain that the military's quest to win hearts and minds frequently ends up in disaster. In a seminal June 2008 study, Reuben Brigety II, a development expert at the Center for American Progress and a former U.S. Navy brigade commander, detailed how the militarization of development assistance "threatens to undermine the moral imperatives of poverty reduction, the neutral provision of emergency relief, and the security of civilian aid workers in the field." Vividly, Brigety shows how U.S. Navy Seabees spent five months and $250,000 drilling two wells for nomadic tribes in Kenya, both of which were eventually abandoned. A civilian agency, he argued, could have done the job far more effectively for about $10,000. Brigety, who has served on research missions in Afghanistan and Iraq for Human Rights Watch, lamented funding cuts in USAID's budget and the dramatic reduction of its cadres available for work overseas.* As a result of such reductions, he writes, "military development activity in the field . . . has not had the benefit of direct and real-time support from civilian development experts on the ground. Further, the relative absence or under-representation of development concerns [has] not been taken into account on important strategic issues."

Even when civilian expertise is available, it is not always warmly shared. Humanitarians are reluctant to be associated with either side in a conflict lest they be targeted as combatants. "To the extent that we become identified with the U.S. military, we become compromised," said George Rupp, president and CEO of the International Rescue Committee. "We're trying to keep it from changing the way we do business but things may be changing whether we like it or not." InterAction, a coalition of American NGOs, has been compelled to issue a code of conduct to its members to lessen the chance for the blowback that often comes from working with the Defense Department. In July 2003, a coalition of local and international NGOs issued a set of recommendations that urged the military to "not engage in assistance work except in those rare circumstances where emergency needs exist and civilian assistance workers are unable to meet those needs due to lack of logistical capacity or levels of insecurity on the ground."

In a 2003 study, Eric James, who served with the U.S. Army in Afghanistan before joining the refugee-focused International Rescue Committee, argues that American troops are not adequately trained to build and manage viable programs and that NGOs increasingly lack the

---

* To be fair, USAID has managed its share of failed programs despite the quality of its expertise. In just one example, the agency's internal inspector found in early 2009 that hundreds of millions of dollars had been wasted on a handful of projects in Afghanistan. Ann Jones, author of a book about her four years as an aid worker in Afghanistan, was quoted in the February 2, 2009, edition of *USA Today* criticizing the aid effort overall in that country as "bedeviled by waste and mismanagement."

resources to advise the Pentagon in any meaningful way. In addition, James writes, formidable cultural conflicts undermine effective collaboration between the two sides. Whereas the military tends to have a rigid, vertical chain of command, for example, that of NGOs tends to be loose and horizontal. Aid workers set a premium on transparency, while warfighters ration information for the sake of operational security. Humanitarians often resent the U.S. military's abundance of resources, which gives it a decisive advantage when bidding for everything from building materials to local staff and relief funds. Citing a report by the Henry L. Stimson Center, a Washington-based think tank, James notes that an aid worker in the field costs a tenth of the $215,000 consumed annually by a U.S. troop. "When both direct and indirect expenses are included," according to James, "the cost of military personnel is vastly more expensive than civilians doing similar jobs."

Despite this, the Pentagon's emphasis on noncore operations has grown steadily alongside its proliferating influence over U.S. security policy. By the end of Bush's second term, senior legislators were expressing concerns that the pendulum of power inside Washington's security establishment had swung too far in the military's favor. While a senator, Vice President Joe Biden led extensive hearings on the matter and lamented the "migration of functions and authorities from the civilian agencies to the Department of Defense." It was not only Democrats who shared Biden's concerns. So did Senator Richard Lugar, the respected Republican moderate who fatefully lost his battle with Jesse Helms for the chairmanship of the Senate Foreign Relations Committee only to mount a successful bid for the seat in 2003. Lugar was concerned enough about the military's growing authority that he dispatched a team of aides worldwide to investigate. The result was two reports—committee "prints," in Capitol Hill parlance—that provide a detailed and alarming account of how the military is aggrandizing key aspects of foreign policy. The first of the two prints, entitled "Embassies as Command Posts in the Anti-Terror Campaign," makes the following conclusion:

> As a result of inadequate funding for civilian programs, U.S. defense agencies are increasingly being granted authority and funding to fill perceived gaps. Such bleeding of civilian responsibilities

overseas from civilian to military agencies risks weakening the Secretary of State's primacy in setting the agenda for U.S. relations and the Secretary of Defense's focus on war fighting.

The report disparages the 12:1 spending ratio between the Pentagon and the State Department, which it says "risks the further encroachment of the military, by default, into areas where civilian leadership is more appropriate because it does not create resistance overseas and is more experienced." Left unchecked, it warns, the proliferation of military personnel and Pentagon activities abroad could lead to "blurred lines of authority between the State Department and the Defense Department [and] interagency turf wars that undermine the effectiveness of the U.S. effort against terrorism." The report also stresses as "imperative" U.S. ambassadors' authority "to challenge and override directives from other government agencies in Washington to their resident or temporary staffs in the embassy."

It is not unusual for ambassadors and combatant commanders to find common ground on many issues. The comity between Ryan Crocker when he was U.S. ambassador to Iraq and General David Petraeus as senior theater commander stands as a model for civilian-military relations. There are plenty of exceptions, however. Feuding between General Stanley McChrystal, the former commander of NATO forces in Afghanistan, and Karl Eikenberry, the U.S. ambassador there, seized headlines in late 2009. The ambassador in Chad several years ago called for a "strategic pause" in military partnership programs, stating "the need to reassess available embassy personnel to support DOD activities in country." Civilian leaders' minimal resources is also a frequent source of conflict. In Niger in 2008, the U.S. ambassador there refused to issue entry visas to U.S. military personnel due to the country's political fragility and because the embassy lacked the billets to accommodate them. In 2003, then CENTCOM commander General John Abizaid wanted to build a $100 million counterterrorist facility in Jordan at the request of Jordanian king Abdullah II. The project was opposed as a needless extravagance by Edward Gnehm, the U.S. ambassador to Jordan. Undaunted, Abizaid went around Gnehm by funding the training facility from his own budget.

On July 16, 2008, Defense Secretary Robert Gates himself warned of the "creeping militarization" of America's profile abroad. That October, at the United States Institute of Peace, he declared "our own national security toolbox must be well-equipped with more than just hammers." In March 2009, he lobbied Congress to sweeten the State Department's diplomatic and foreign assistance budget. While no one doubts Gates's sincerity, he seems less interested in restoring civilian control over U.S. foreign policy than in refreshing civilian agencies as aid vendors for the Pentagon. He and senior military officers speak of a civilian-military "partnership," one in which the Defense Department, by weight of its enormous budget if nothing else, will almost certainly be first among equals and its missions paramount. Secretary of State Hillary Clinton's mantric utterance of the "3Ds"—defense, diplomacy, and development—suggests at least passive acceptance of such a lopsided collusion.

In January 2009, USAID announced it had identified five countries, each within a regional combatant command, where it would set up pilot schemes to enhance civilian-military cooperation. An article in *Inside Defense* quoted a Pentagon official praising the project for "building relationships across the 3Ds." It was a natural next step in a growing collaboration that began in 2004, when USAID opened its Office of Military Affairs, to which the Defense Department seconds officers from each of the four branch services. The debut of such an office was particularly hard on USAID veterans old enough to remember how their work was politicized to suit the military's objectives in Vietnam. There is another cruel irony to this, however: USAID evolved from the Marshall Plan, named after the same man who, as President Roosevelt's Army chief of staff, would testify before Congress in civilian clothes out of respect for a profound grassroots suspicion of standing armies.

Pentagon hegemony over U.S. foreign aid, its growing power to define how it is used and for what purpose, is a crucial but underappreciated Bush legacy, one that has cinched tighter the noose of foreign policy militarization. As the administration drew to a close, America was predominately represented in the developing world not by civilian medics or agrarians or educators but by armed men and women in military fatigues and body armor. Washington was spending more on national security than at any other time since World War II, a core component of a massive and mushrooming federal deficit. It was waging two wars and managing a web of secret detention centers abroad while at home it was harassing its Islamic community in far more pernicious and systemic ways than was ever reported in the mainstream media.

Was there redemption to this? Was there anything quantifiably positive about the political, diplomatic, economic, and cultural militarization Bush engineered? His apologists aver that he "kept us safe," as there were no successful post–September 11 terrorist attacks on his watch. (They forget or ignore the fact that the original attack occurred nine months into the administration's first term despite warnings from numerous sources that an attack was imminent.) The implication is that militarizing foreign policy, however costly in human life and treasure, paid off in the end. Pity Britain and Spain, which despite similarly tough antiterrorist measures endured punishing attacks for, among other things, their participation in the Iraq war.* With their large and increasingly disaffected Muslim communities, European states made for comparably soft targets. The United States was not so vulnerable, or so it appeared, as there is no public evidence of a viable terrorist plot foiled during the Bush years. One could argue that substantial conspiracies were intercepted in the planning stages but kept secret for security reasons. This would be inconsistent, however, with the impudence of a White House that would expose a CIA operative to settle a Beltway political score. It may take decades for the facts to fully reveal themselves.

For those who saw through Bush's alarmist and duplicitous cant about the nature and motives of the September 11 conspirators, the absence of follow-up plots would have come as no surprise. At the time of the assault, Al Qaeda represented a minority of a minority, and its most senior leaders were captured or killed by methods that more closely resembled good police work than world war. (In May 2011, a crack U.S.

---

* Former British prime minister Tony Blair, it is worth noting, allied with Bush in the invasion despite being warned by his intelligence sources that the war would "substantially" raise the terrorist threat to the United Kingdom.

special operations unit finally tracked down and killed Osama bin Laden in a fortified compound in Pakistan, ostensibly America's close ally in the war against radical Islam.) Without Bush militarization, Al Qaeda could never have evolved into a major transnational brand, wielded as a standard in battle by radicals of every sort. No doubt there will be another attack on the United States, and it may even surpass the September 11 assault in terror and lethality. It would be naively arrogant for any nation to presume it could wage a decade-long war against Islam, as it is widely perceived by Muslims and non-Muslims alike, without some kind of reprisal. Though the Bush presidency is behind us, the bill for its malpractice has yet to be served.

CONCLUSION

Of all manifestations of power, restraint impresses men most.
—THUCYDIDES

THE FOUNDING FATHERS FEARED NOTHING MORE THAN THE corrupting influence of a standing army. Even Alexander Hamilton, who for his imperial ambition could be regarded as America's first militarist, warned that a permanent military class "enhances the importance of the soldier, and proportionately degrades the condition of the citizen . . . and by degrees the people are brought to consider the soldiery [*sic*] not only as their protectors but as their superiors."

Hamilton need not have worried. In faith with the founders' vision, the military has kept to the barracks. Its challenges to civilian rule have been rare, isolated, and peacefully reckoned with. There is no popular desire for generals to assume a dominant role in the making of security policy, or for the lifting of constraints on legislators to make it easier for them to declare war. Despite this, U.S. relations with the world, and increasingly America's security policy at home, have become thoroughly and all but irreparably militarized. The culprits are not the nation's military leaders, though they can be aggressive and cunning interagency operators, but civilian elites who have seen to it that the nation is engaged in a self-perpetuating cycle of low-grade conflict. They have been hiding in plain sight, hyping threats and exaggerating the capabilities and resources of adversaries. They have convinced a plurality of citizens that their best guarantee of security is not peace but war, and they did so with the help of a supine or complicit Congress. Since the collapse of the Soviet Union, U.S. presidents have ordered troops into battle twenty-two times, compared with fourteen times during the Cold War. Not once did they appeal to lawmakers for a declaration of war.

The legacy of American militarism is a national security complex that thrives on fraud, falsehood, and deception. In the 1950s, Americans were told the Soviets had not only the means to destroy the United States but the desire to do so. In reality, Moscow lacked the former and so gave little thought to the latter, while Washington squandered billions of dollars on needless weaponry. Time and again, U.S. presidents weaponized their response to challenges overseas to protect them from charges of appeasement from the right, despite informed counsel from diplomats, military officers, and intelligence agents that such policies were at best counterproductive. Habitually, American leaders misinterpreted events—from Russia's Bolshevik revolution to the September 11 attacks—to disastrous effect. In each case, expert advice was overlooked, ignored, or concealed, while in others, threats were manufactured as chips in petty political wagers. The fraudulent bomber and missile gaps and the Gulf of Tonkin incident did as much to injure U.S. interests overseas as did the notion that Saddam Hussein possessed weapons of mass destruction and intended to use them preemptively.

Only a country so rich in resources and blessed by favorable geography could afford such malfeasance. America has been spared foreign invasion for two hundred years and it can expect to remain inviolate for centuries to come. Yet each year, it spends enough money on national security to match the economic output of Indonesia—with money borrowed largely from China, a country with which it is preparing for conflict. It has spent tens of billions of dollars on a hemispheric missile defense system based on unproven technology. More than two decades after the Soviet Union's demise, it maintains a stockpile of some 5,000 nuclear bombs even as it mulls the deployment of a weapon system, known as "Prompt Global Strike," capable of destroying a target anywhere in the world, at any time, using a conventional or nuclear warhead. Washington insists on its right to launch a preemptive nuclear attack against such countries as North Korea and Iran—oafish, bankrupt regimes that seek a complement of atomic bombs because they are surrounded by countries with bunkers full of them. America guarantees its friends and allies a place under its security umbrella even if their interests, particularly in the Middle East, diverge markedly from its own. In Europe, NATO remains a feudal confederation of armed forces with no raison d'être save to lend sanction to America's far-flung military enterprises. In Asia, South Korea, the world's fifteenth-largest economy, remains critically dependent on U.S. forces as a deterrent against its isolated, impoverished northern neighbor, while Japan wallows in a twilight world of middle-class prosperity and political ennui, content to slowly diminish as an American vassal.

In ancient times, empires exacted tribute from their dependencies. In the age of American hegemony, just the opposite is the case. In return for the global commons, the United States bankrolls a geopolitical welfare state that allows some of its largest beneficiaries to neglect their basic responsibilities as sovereign states and allies. A national debate over the economic and moral costs of this exchange is noteworthy for its absence. Segregated from the military and its burdens, with no reason to fear the consequences of war for themselves or their loved ones, a great majority of Americans are easily manipulated into backing a militarized response to challenges more suited to diplomacy. The purpose of hegemony is to preempt potential threats rather than respond to a clear and present danger. As voters are unlikely to support such a policy on its merits, hegemonists resort to gross exaggerations of speculative rivals, be they Russia and China or geopolitical runts such as North Korea and Iran.

The price of this deception is vast. If the Pentagon were a corporation, it would be the largest in the world as well as the most sloppily run.* Its procurement budget, at a staggering $107 billion in 2010, expands even as the number of deployable war planes, combat ships, and troops diminishes. To entice lawmakers into approving costly weapons programs, the Pentagon dangles the prospect of jobs in the states and districts of key lawmakers, a costly way of manufacturing but an astute political maneuver. Waste, inefficiency, and political patronage, no stranger to military-legislative affairs, get more lavish by the year. In April 2008, the Government Accountability Office found that ninety-five major Pentagon

---

* The Pentagon in 2010 reported $1.7 trillion in assets, $2.1 trillion in liabilities, and $676 billion in net operating costs.

projects exceeded their original budgets by a total of nearly $300 billion. A year later, it concluded that nothing had changed. In 2009, lawmakers larded the Pentagon's annual budget proposal with nearly $5 billion in programs and weapons it did not request.

With arms factories scattered like feeding troughs nationwide, America has become the equivalent of a company town with the Pentagon as primary employer. The making of war, or at least the preparation for it, has become a money center, a business line—a racket, as Marine general and Medal of Honor recipient Smedley Butler put it nearly a century ago. Despite the nation's most severe recession in eighty years, few citizens question aloud why a country capable of assassinating a suspected terrorist anywhere in the world with a few tugs on a joystick cannot provide affordable health care, quality schools, or a high-speed rail grid. Most conspicuously mute is the president himself.

Having campaigned on a promise to restore civilian authority over the nation's security apparatus, Barack Obama has matched or even outdone his predecessor in militarizing foreign policy. He has yet to liquidate the detention centers at Guantánamo, Cuba, as per his campaign pledge. The CIA's global network of "black site" chambers, where suspected terrorists are interrogated with impunity outside the United States, are still in operation. He has presided over a sharp rise in the number of targeted killings, once known as "assassinations," in Afghanistan. He clings to the Bush administration's restrictive condition that Iran's nuclear program be the sole focus of any diplomatic contact between Tehran and Washington, rather than one in a number of outstanding disputes for discussion between the two parties. Despite his claims to have "reset" U.S. relations with Russia, he offends Moscow by abetting a process that would extend NATO membership to Georgia and Ukraine. Though he has withdrawn significant numbers of troops from Iraq, some 50,000 remain as part of an ill-defined "enduring" presence there. He has rolled over an expansion of clandestine military activity, first authorized by George W. Bush, in the Middle East, Central Asia, and Africa, for the sake of intelligence gathering and reconnaissance that could enable military strikes on Iran's nuclear facilities. His Justice Department has amended a federal communications act to make it easier for the FBI to read private e-mail correspondence and Web browsing history without a judge's permission.

Most significantly, the president has doubled the number of troops in Afghanistan—in this case, at least, redeeming a key campaign promise. Possibly he believed it was the right thing to do. Most certainly he understood that failing to do so would have left him open to charges from the right of being soft on terrorism. It is a burden of proof imposed on American liberals who want to be president: to establish their credibility as a prospective commander in chief by taking a hard line on matters of national security. Having won the election by talking the talk, Obama was quickly obliged to navigate his way between a war-weary public and an emphatically hawkish troika of senior military officers: Admiral Mike Mullen, chairman of the Joint Chiefs of Staff; CENTCOM commander General David Petraeus; and General Stanley McChrystal, the commander of NATO forces in Afghanistan. From the start, they favored a dramatically enlarged, open-ended commitment, and they finessed and manipulated a presidential review of the situation to get one. In interviews, they warned that the situation in Afghanistan was serious and deteriorating and they appealed for a "fully resourced, comprehensive counterinsurgency campaign." In a written assessment of the war, duly leaked to the press, they predicted an allied "failure" absent a significant increase in troops. In October 2009, McChrystal said flatly that Vice President Joe Biden's call for a more narrowly defined mission would fail.

Here was the military's most serious challenge to presidential authority since the cashiering of Douglas MacArthur during the Korean War and President Kennedy's frequent clashes with Curtis LeMay. When a livid Obama summoned Mullen and Defense Secretary Robert Gates to the White House for a reprimand, the brass backed down, but their velvet putsch had succeeded. On November 23, the president announced he would deploy an additional 30,000 troops to Afghanistan. The president had restricted his room to maneuver with his campaign pledge, and the generals had pressed their advantage. Withdrawal was never considered as an option, despite the depravations of President Hamid Karzai's government, the patent thievery of his 2009 reelection, and the crushing burden of the war on a struggling economy at home. For Obama, there was no alternative to expanding the war, particularly if he wanted to win at least some Republican support for his domestic agenda. The only question was how many more troops to deploy, and for how long. (The president's insistence that a drawdown begin in summer 2011 was politely dismissed by his proconsuls, as well as by Robert Gates.)

Just weeks after Obama's capitulation, Richard Holbrooke, the tenacious diplomat who along with Madeleine Albright did so much to midwife the birth of Kosovo, collapsed with a torn aorta and died three days later. Holbrooke had been the president's special envoy to Afghanistan and Pakistan, and his own losing battles with the military's top brass there were remarked upon pointedly by Brian Katulis, an analyst at the Center for American Progress in Washington. "If you compare it to what he was able to do in the 1990s on Bosnia," Katulis told the *Financial Times,* "you really see that the balance of power in the interim had shifted from the State Department to the Pentagon."

Rather than expose himself to charges of appeasement, Obama convinced himself he could at least regulate the pace of militarization and eventually wind it down. Time will tell if he can evade the hard truth that bewitched so many of his predecessors: in the war counsels of Washington, militarization of policy is as difficult to resist as its consequences are hard to undo.

Though the Pentagon did not ask for empire, neither did it shirk from its calling. From 2001 to 2010, the baseline defense budget grew at an inflation-adjusted rate of 6 percent a year, to more than double its pre–September 11 size. Like interlocking threads in a great tapestry, no one really knows where the military's preserve begins and where it ends. Pentagon financial statements have been all but unauditable since 1991, the year it began submitting its accounts to Congress. In an October 2009 report, the Defense Department's Inspector General exposed more than a dozen "significant deficiencies" in Pentagon balance sheets from fiscal years 2004 to 2008. Mining opaque audit trails and murky contracting systems, the report uncovered more than $1 trillion in unsupported account entries. In September 2010, the Senate Finance Committee issued a report that slammed the Pentagon's "total lack of fiscal accountability" for "leaving huge sums of the taxpayers' money vulnerable to fraud and outright theft."

For its magnitude, opaqueness, and self-perpetuation, the Pentagon today bears a striking resemblance to the Russian VPK, the voracious defense apparatus that ultimately did in the Soviet empire. The difference between the predations of Washington's military-industrial "complex" and Moscow's industrial-military "commission" on their host economies has become one of degree, not of kind, and even that distinction seems to narrow by the day. Like the VPK, America's war machine produces weaponry almost as an end in itself, with little heed to prevailing geopolitical reality. Sadly for the United States, however, there is little prospect of a Gorbachev-like interventionist to end the outrage. Even as defense officials and war-fighters acknowledge that America's adversaries cannot be defeated with armed might alone, the Pentagon still has more lawyers than the State Department does diplomats. Washington's foreign aid budget routinely comes under assault by Congress as overly generous when in fact the United States is among the most miserly of countries when it comes to overseas assistance.* In response to a 2010 White House request for a doubling of USAID's workforce and a $5 billion funding increase over the previous year, Congress instead cut USAID's overall budget by $4 billion.

The Pentagon, meanwhile, managed to deflect pressure for fiscal discipline in 2010, and its budget grew by 3.7 percent. Faced with trillion-dollar deficits over the next decade, however, President Obama has called for $400 billion in defense spending cuts over the next twelve years. Independent analysts like Gordon Adams, a former White House policy adviser on national security outlays, describes such projections as an "opening bid" for what should be far more aggressive belt-tightening. Adams cites an array of wasteful and superfluous Pentagon programs that could lighten the nation's security burden by $1 trillion over ten years, consistent with the findings of a blue-ribbon deficit-reduction panel commissioned by the president himself. Such dramatic cuts—which as

---

* According to the OECD, as a percentage of gross national income, the United States ranked nineteen among donor countries in 2009, at 0.21 percent.

of this writing would seem to be as unlikely as serious entitlement reform—would do little to demilitarize U.S. foreign policy as the State Department can expect painful reductions of its own. Taxpayers currently spend twelve dollars on national defense for every dollar they invest in diplomacy. While the value of those two outlays may diminish in the coming Age of Austerity, their relative proportions will most likely remain unchanged.

The White House has also called for 2,200 new Foreign Service officers for the State Department and USAID—a step in the right direction, say aid workers and diplomats, but a drop in the bucket given the mismatch between the nation's resources and its commitments overseas. The number of State Department diplomats and support staff is only 10 percent greater than what it was a quarter century ago, when there were twenty-four fewer countries in the world and U.S. interests were concentrated in Europe and northeast Asia. The Pentagon, in contrast, has 1.5 million active-duty military personnel, an equal number of reservists and National Guardsmen, and 790,000 civilian employees. Moreover, unlike the U.S. military, which bases a fifth of its personnel overseas, nearly three-quarters of America's diplomatic corps are posted abroad. At any one time, a third of U.S.-based Foreign Service jobs are vacant, while 12 percent of the overseas positions, not including those in Iraq and Afghanistan, are unmanned. Nearly three-quarters of deployed officers are laboring in hardship posts, and the number of unaccompanied tours—assignments in places so dangerous that loved ones must be left behind—has risen to a fifth of the total over the past five years. Foreign language proficiency, a core competency of the service, has languished due to funding gaps. Salaries have been slashed, and stingy retirement benefits have undercut retention rates.

Beyond its paltry remuneration, the Foreign Service is poorly led, dispirited, and isolated. Its director general, who holds a position that equates roughly with the Pentagon's JCS chairman, has paled into irrelevance and makes for a weak public advocate. The State Department's dissent channel, a means through which Foreign Service officers may express constructive opposition to White House policy and air alternative views, languished under the Bush administration and shows no sign of reviving itself; in February 2010, the president of the American Foreign Service Association linked the channel's enfeeblement with "the continuing marginalization of the Foreign Service in the foreign policymaking process." American embassies loom imperiously over the skylines of the world's capital cities, barricaded against terrorist attacks and estranged from their hosts. They engender resentment from without and a siege mentality from within. In a growing number of countries, U.S. allies among them, American diplomats require armed escorts when traveling outside their gated communities.

Thanks to the gutting of State Department and foreign aid budgets by Senator Jesse Helms, followed by the disastrously militant politics of President George W. Bush, America's diplomats and aid workers are undermanned and overwhelmed. In a February 2009 article, *USA Today* reported that USAID in Afghanistan had paid private contractors hundreds of millions of dollars annually for projects that frequently fail to provide results. It quoted Secretary of State Hillary Rodham Clinton characterizing USAID as "decimated." Massive staff cuts, she said, had reduced it to "a contracting agency [rather] than an operating agency that can deliver." The secretary failed to note, however, that as president her husband was complicit in USAID's diminution by submitting to Helms's raids on overseas assistance budgets.

Absent an aggressive restructuring of America's civilian aid and diplomatic agencies, their dependence on, and submission to, the military will only intensify. An early draft of the 2010 Quadrennial Defense Review, the Pentagon's long-term threat assessment, put its civilian counterparts on notice. A key provision that demanded the Pentagon's "unprecedented say over U.S. security assistance programs" was softened to the wordy but more diplomatic: "Years of war have proven how important it is for America's civilian agencies to possess the resources and authorities needed to operate alongside the U.S. Armed Forces during complex contingencies at home and abroad." In other words, civilians must be harnessed in the service of military objectives in unstable regions or post-conflict areas, rather than focus on their core mission of nurturing U.S. diplomatic interests and reducing poverty. Or, as a source close to the QDR drafting process put it, "It is clear from the deleted parts that what DOD is saying about security assistance is: 'We want in on the whole shebang.' "

In its willingness to engage in civilian-military partnerships, USAID risks being devoured by them. In 2008 it launched with the Defense Department a so-called Focus Country Initiative to unify activity across the combatant commands, a jurisdiction that, by definition, allows the Pentagon to define the scope and character of aid programs. In 2009 the White House was forced to back away from a pledge to staff hundreds of posts in Afghanistan with civilians for lack of funding and said it would instead turn to the Pentagon. Meanwhile, efforts to stand up an expeditionary corps of some 25,000 civilians under State Department leadership have been undermined by interagency snits and congressional lethargy.

Such is the state of disequilibrium between America's civilian and military resources as it enters the post, post–Cold War world. The years that followed the end of the Soviet era were but a prelude to what will be a far more enduring shift in the topography of geopolitical affairs. For the first time in two decades, U.S. hegemony will demand a price. The transaction Washington has kept with its allies—generous subsidies in exchange for "full spectrum" control—will be subject to competing claims. In theory at least, this should bid up the value of nonmilitary methods of protecting U.S. interests overseas, and Pentagon officials are emphatic about the need to bolster civilian capacity to assert "smart" power, as diplomacy and development are known.

The aforementioned QDR, however, suggests otherwise. It makes numerous and repeated references to the centrality of "access," a catchword for the U.S. military's ability to operate unimpeded anywhere in the world. The Pentagon and other agencies, it cautions, "must be able to more comprehensively monitor the air, land, maritime, space, and cyber domains for potential threats to the United States." It identifies as a new and enduring threat "states armed with advanced anti-access capabilities and/or nuclear weapons." All of which, of course, is a veiled reference to the evolution of China as a regional power and the kind of peer competitor that Washington has made a policy of preempting. The looming rivalry between Beijing and Washington has already replaced Islamic extremism as the main preoccupation of U.S. security planners, the same way

Al Qaeda filled the void left by the departed Soviet Union on the Penta-gon's revolving rotisserie of existential threats.

Just as Washington militarized the Cold War and its response to the September 11 attacks, so too is it militarizing its relations with China. The next QDR will likely be far more explicit about the need to assert its proprietary claims to the sea, land, and sky, even if that means armed confrontation with the world's most populous country and America's largest creditor. Hawkish lawmakers will gratefully jettison talk of "win-ning hearts and minds" for manly jargon like "access denial" and "do-main awareness." The implication will be that China constitutes the first symmetrical threat the United States has faced since the Soviet era. In fact, the relationship between the United States and China is profoundly asymmetrical, and to treat it otherwise is to court disaster.

While the Pentagon insists on expanding its global network of military bases and deepwater fleets, China confines its imperial claims to a hand-ful of properties along its contiguous borders and littorals. To sustain its economy with sufficient quantities of natural resources, Beijing has struck development and exploitation deals in emerging markets worldwide while leaving it to the U.S. Navy to secure delivery of its imported crude oil and other commodities. China has kept its nuclear arsenal to a minimum and, unlike the United States, embraces a strict "no first use" policy. Should the United States blindly presume symmetry in its competition with China and budget accordingly as recommended by the QDR, it will collapse eco-nomically.

Despite a significant warming of ties between China and Taiwan, the defense of which was once the U.S. military's core mission in Asia, Washington is actively planning to "contain" China just as it did the Soviet Union. Recall the Hainan incident, the April 2001 downing of an American EP-3 spy plane by a Chinese fighter jet, recounted in the pre-vious chapter. Although the confrontation seized headlines, its origins have been largely overlooked: In late 2000, concurrent with the presi-dential election that ended with George W. Bush's bitterly contested vic-tory, a routine military review concluded that reconnaissance flights off the eastern coast of the former Soviet Union were superfluous and rec-ommended they be reduced. Loath to furlough an established mission and the aircraft and crews manning it, the Pentagon simply reassigned the flights to China, the next emerging target on its radar. As the tempo of U.S. intelligence gathering along its waters abruptly and dramatically increased, Beijing filed a démarche into the political void that exists before an outgoing administration in Washington departs and a new one finally settles in. With little in the way of a response, Chinese interceptors reacted to the stepped-up U.S. patrols with heightened aggression, making the Hainan affair the inevitable result of a reflexively intrusive Pentagon and an increasingly headstrong Beijing.

Rather than recalibrating its approach to China's rise, however, the Pentagon dug in. That same year, it produced a study called "Asia 2025," which identified China as a "persistent competitor of the United States," bent on "foreign military adventurism." A U.S. base realignment plan made public in 2004 called for a new chain of bases to be erected in Central Asia and the Middle East, in part to box in China. A 2008 deal between the United States and India that would allow New Delhi to greatly expand its nuclear weapons capability was established very much with China, their mutual rival, in mind. At the same time, the Pentagon is well into a multiyear effort to transform its military base on Guam into its primary hub for operations in the Pacific. While the QDR drily refers to "the Guam buildup" as a means to "deter and defeat" regional aggressors, John Pike of the Washington, D.C.–based Globalsecurity.org has speculated that the Pentagon wants to "run the planet from Guam and Diego Garcia by 2015."

In March 2011, *Inside the Navy* reported how the U.S. government, already involved in two Middle East wars and a NATO-led effort to oust Libyan dictator Muammar Gadhafi, was deep in the planning stages of a major military buildup in Asia. The report quoted Patrick Cronin, a senior director at the Center for a New American Security, citing the foreign intercourse Washington was engaged in for the sake of its dominion over the seas and skies of Asia. They included, according to Cronin, "access agreements, cross-servicing agreements, forward stationing agreements, partnerships, capacity building, training, [and] foreign military sales." At the very least, the Pentagon is settling in for a long cold war with China.

In response, China is expanding its fleet of diesel-powered subs at a base on Hainan Island and is developing the capacity to attack and destroy satellites as well as aircraft carriers. It has also laid a provocative marker down on a cluster of islands in the South China Sea that are the subject of a simmering territorial row between it and Vietnam, Malaysia, the Philippines, Brunei, Taiwan, and Indonesia. In 2010, Beijing identified the South China Sea as a "core interest," a term it previously applied only to Tibet and Taiwan, after several confrontations with U.S. Navy vessels that triggered memories of the EP-3 incident. The move was seized upon in Washington as a de facto declaration of sovereignty over the region and an augur of Chinese bullying to come. If a Sino-American war is inevitable, it is now generally assumed that a hotly contested South China Sea may be its epicenter.

There is nothing inevitable about an American war with China, however, and even Chinese security planners believe the U.S.-Chinese rivalry will be economic, rather than military, in character. There is, however, an emerging rhythm to Sino-U.S. affairs that readers of this book should by now recognize: the Pentagon, still clinging to the spirit, if not the letter, of the 1992 Defense Planning Guidance, reflexively interprets an emerging regional power or political movement as a strategic threat. It gathers allies and punishes neutrals in an undeclared policy to isolate it. Defense analysts exaggerate the threat's military might while discounting the historical factors that inform and motivate it. Politicians in Washington convene hearings and, briefed as to the nation's ill-preparedness, demand an immediate military buildup. Pundits condemn the commander in chief for being soft on America's adversaries even as diplomats and intelligence experts overseas assure the White House that the danger is largely in the minds of those peddling it back home. Such admonitions, however, are obscured or ignored in what is now a key election-year issue. Surveillance is met with countersurveillance. Heightened alert status provokes the same. An incident occurs, either by accident or by design.

It is war.

NOTES

INTRODUCTION

1 **News travels fast:** Excerpted from Stephen Glain, "American Leviathan," *The Nation* 289, no. 9 (September 28, 2009): 18–23.

2 **Even Robert Gates:** Ann Scott Tyson, "Gates Warns of Creeping Militarization," *Washington Post*, June 16, 2008.

4 **In 1796:** President George Washington's farewell address was originally printed in Philadelphia's *American Daily Advertiser* on September 19, 1796. **Serving President Washington:** "Thomas Jefferson: First Secretary of State, 1790–1793," http://future.state.gov/when/time_ine/1784_timeline/jefferson_first_secretary.html.

6 **"perversion of our national mission":** Frederick Merk, *Manifest Destiny and Mission in American History: A Reinterpretation* (Cambridge, MA: Harvard University Press, 1963), 263.
"cannot govern dependencies": Michael Lind, *The American Way of Strategy: U.S. Foreign Policy and the American Way of Life* (New York: Oxford University Press, 2006), 88.
Accepting his Republican: Speech on "The Duties of a Great Nation" at the opening of the gubernatorial campaign at New York City's Carnegie Music Hall on October 5, 1898, http://www.theodore-roosevelt.com/images/research/txtspeeches/604.pdf.

7 **"the American Army really is":** Harry G. Summers, Jr., *On Strategy: A Critical Analysis of the Vietnam War* (Novato, CA: Presidio Press, 1982), 11.

8 **As of 2007:** Zoltan Grossman, "Imperial Footprint: America's Foreign Military Bases," *Global Dialogue* 11 (Winter/Spring 2009), http://www.worlddialogue.org/content.php?id=450.

9 **By comparison:** For international defense budget data, see International Institute for Strategic Studies, *The Military Balance 2011: The Annual Assessment of Global Military Capabilities and Defence Economics* (London: Routledge, 2011).
In February 2011: The *Washington Post* series of articles by Dana Priest and William M. Arkin appeared under the titles "A Hidden World, Growing Beyond Control" (July 19, 2010), "National Security Inc." (July 20, 2010), and "The Secrets Next Door" (July 21, 2010).

In late 2010: "Obama Ponders Compromise Tax Plan," *Financial Times,* November 12, 2010.

Deep cuts in weapons procurement: Robert Haddick, "The Bowels/Simpson Defense Cuts Are Not 'Risk Neutral'," *Small Wars Journal* blog, November 11, 2010, http://smallwarsjournal.com/blog/2010/11/the-bowlessimpson -defense-cuts/.

10 **As the soldier-historian:** Andrew J. Bacevich, *The New American Militarism: How Americans Are Seduced by War* (Oxford; New York: Oxford University Press, 2005), 218–219.

1: ARCHETYPE

12 **George Catlett Marshall:** Forrest C. Pogue, *George C. Marshall: Statesman, 1945–1959,* vol. 4 (New York: Viking, 1987), 144.

In August, Truman ordered: Melvyn Leffler, *A Preponderance of Power: National Security, the Truman Administration, and the Cold War* (Stanford: Stanford University Press, 1992), 123–124.

13 **"clumsy lie":** "The Presidency: What I Meant to Say . . . ," *Time,* September 23, 1946.

The affair convulsed: David McCullough, *Truman* (New York: Simon & Schuster, 1992), 513–517.

A year earlier: Mark Perry, *Partners in Command: George Marshall and Dwight Eisenhower in War and Peace* (New York: Penguin, 2007), 371–373.

14 **Marshall's appointment:** Pogue, *Marshall: Statesman,* 29.

"an act of God": Dean Acheson, *Present at the Creation: My Years at the State Department* (New York: W. W. Norton & Company, 1969), 213.

"I am being explicit": Bertram Hulen, "Marshall Abjures Politics or '48 Race; Takes Up New Post," *New York Times,* January 22, 1947.

"Man of the Year": "U.S. at War: The General," *Time,* January 3, 1944.

15 **While testifying:** Forrest C. Pogue, *George C. Marshall: Ordeal and Hope, 1939–1942,* vol. 2 (New York: Viking, 1966), 150, and Pogue, *Marshall: Statesman,* 437–478.

"the presence of a great man": Forrest C. Pogue, *George C. Marshall: Organizer of Victory, 1943–1945,* vol. 3 (New York: Viking, 1973), 131.

For his refusal to support: Pogue, *Marshall: Statesman,* xiv.

"We are completely devoted": Pogue, *Marshall: Organizer of Victory,* 457–458.

16 **He graduated:** Forrest C. Pogue, *George C. Marshall: Education of a General, 1880–1939,* vol. 1 (New York: Viking, 1963), 67, 71.

17 **"the strong hand of the military":** William Manchester, *American Caesar: Douglas MacArthur, 1880–1964* (New York: Little, Brown and Company, 1978), 33.

He had studied: Pogue, *Marshall: Education,* 81–82.

While battling Philippine insurgents: Ibid., 123.

In 1918, during: Ibid., 179.

18 "Unless I hear all the arguments": Pogue, *Marshall: Ordeal and Hope*, ix.
During Marshall's first: Pogue, *Marshall: Education*, 322–323.

19 "Many Americans": Lind, *American Way of Strategy*, 94.
In the closing days: Pogue, *Marshall: Education*, 192.
In the immediate aftermath: Ibid., 205.
A year later: Ibid., 213.

20 In February 1940: *Pogue, Marshall: Ordeal and Hope*, 16–17.
As late as summer: Ibid., 144–145.

21 "I will not trouble you": Pogue, *Marshall: Education*, 349.
"Arthur MacArthur": Manchester, *American Caesar*, 30.

22 In Senate hearings: Forrest Pogue, "The Military in a Democracy: A Review: American Caesar," *International Security* 3, no. 4 (Spring 1979): 76.

23 In 1905 the two men: Manchester, *American Caesar*, 66–67.

24 So it was: Ibid., 109.

25 According to a study: Ibid., 149.
MacArthur would not listen: Ibid., 150; Douglas Porch, *The Path to Victory: The Mediterranean Theater in World War II* (New York: Farrar, Straus and Giroux, 2004), 396.
Reactions to the incident: Manchester, *American Caesar*, 149–152.

26 The president had acted: Ibid., 152.
Years after the BEF: Ibid., 150.

27 Weeks after the Bonus: Ibid., 152.
Boulanger-like: Robert Harvey, *American Shogun: General MacArthur, Emperor Hirohito and the Drama of Modern Japan* (Woodstock, NY: Overlook Press, 2006), 210. Georges Ernest Jean Marie Boulanger, the French general of the 1880s who inspired the expression "man on horseback," also liked to appear publicly in splendid fashion riding a stallion (Manchester, *American Caesar*, 355).
"a masterpiece": Manchester, *American Caesar*, 218.
By the fall of 1943: Ibid., 309–312.

28 "complete attitude of friendship": Ibid., 356.
By mid-1944: Ibid., 357.

29 MacArthur's candidacy: Ibid., 362–363.

30 The president alluded: Ibid., 152.
"He was of a very independent nature": Pogue, *Marshall: Ordeal and Hope*, 374–375.

2: THE WAGES OF FEAR

32 He returned to Washington: Walter Isaacson and Evan Thomas, *The Wise Men: Six Friends and the World They Made* (New York: Simon & Schuster, 1986), 262.

After receiving Molotov: McCullough, *Truman*, 375–376.

A month later: Isaacson and Thomas, *Wise Men*, 279.

33 **"That there were those":** Ibid., 282.

Tensions between Washington: For detailed accounts, see Ted Morgan, *Reds: McCarthyism in Twentieth-Century America* (New York: Random House, 2003), 23–69; Louis Fischer, *The Life of Lenin* (New York: Harper & Row, 1964), 297–30; and William Harlan Hale, "When the Red Storm Broke," *American Heritage Magazine* 12, no. 2 (February 1961), available at http://www.americanheritage.com/articles/magazine/ah/1961/2/1961_2_4.shtml.

Among those who recommended: Fischer, *Lenin*, 216–218.

34 **The movement was real:** Morgan, *Reds*, 80–87.

35 **"for those who would destroy":** Dean Acheson, *Present at the Creation: My Years at the State Department* (New York: W. W. Norton & Company, 1969), 358–359.

"The central fact": William Appleman Williams, *The Tragedy of American Diplomacy* (Cleveland; New York: The World Publishing Company, 1959), 188–189.

36 **Perhaps the only Truman adviser:** George F. Kennan, *Memoirs: 1925–1950* (Boston: Little, Brown and Company, 1967), 9–15; and Isaacson and Thomas, *Wise Men*, 72–78.

37 **Kennan decided to join:** Kennan, *Memoirs*, 17–23; and Tim Weiner and Barbara Crossette, "George F. Kennan Dies at 101; Leading Strategist of Cold War," *New York Times*, March 19, 2005.

38 **"The rate of construction":** George F. Kennan, "Memorandum for the Minister," *New York Review of Books* 48, no. 7 (April 26, 2001).

39 **In it, Stalin:** "Vladislav Zubok on: Stalin's 1946 Speech," Interview transcript in relation to PBS film *Race for the Superbomb*, http://www.pbs.org/wgbh/amex/bomb/filmmore/reference/interview/zubok3.html.

With his personal secretary: Kennan, *Memoirs*, 292–295; James Carroll, *House of War: The Pentagon and the Disastrous Rise of American Power* (New York: Houghton Mifflin Company, 2006), 128–131.

40 **"were of no help":** Acheson, *Present at the Creation*, 151.

Harriman and Chip Bohlen: Isaacson and Thomas, *Wise Men*, 352–356.

As he prepared to deliver: McCullough, *Truman*, 543–545.

41 **Famously known as:** Kennan, *Memoirs*, 354–367.

42 **In a series of columns:** Ronald Steele, *Walter Lippmann and the American Century* (Boston: Little, Brown and Company, 1980), 444–446.

"It had something": Kennan, *Memoirs*, 358.

43 **"shockers":** Acheson, *Present at the Creation*, 217.

"This was my crisis": Ibid., 219.

44 **A long pause:** Isaacson and Thomas, *Wise Men*, 395.

45 **In November 1946:** Daniel Yergin, *Shattered Peace: The Origins of the Cold War and the National Security State* (London: A. Deutsch, 1978), 280.

Not until it faced: David Close, *The Origins of the Greek Civil War* (London: Longman, 1995), 69, 150–182.

46 **In a speech to Congress:** Harry S. Truman, "The Truman Doctrine," http://www.americanrhetoric.com/speeches/harrystrumantrumandoctrine.html.

47 **Once, after a day:** Isaacson and Thomas, *Wise Men*, 400–401.
   "there has been no overt": Ibid., 397.
   "The notion should be dispelled:" Pogue, *Marshall: Statesman*, 205.
   George Marshall and Chip Bohlen: McCullough, *Truman*, 546.

48 **"nothing about Russia":** Isaacson and Thomas, *Wise Men*, 384.

3: SEEING REDS

52 **"McCarthy had succeeded":** Nancy Bernkopf Tucker, *China Confidential: American Diplomats and Sino-American Relations, 1945–1996* (New York: Columbia University Press, 2011), 65.
   "Three years of civil war": Barbara Tuchman, "If Mao Had Come to Washington: An Essay of Alternatives," *Foreign Affairs* 51, no. 1 (October 1972): 45.

54 **"diminish the United States":** Arthur Herman, *Joseph McCarthy: Reexamining the Life and Legacy of America's Most Hated Senator* (New York: Free Press, 1999), 189–190.
   Months earlier: Pogue, *Marshall: Statesman*, 426.

55 **John Service:** E. J. Khan Jr., *The China Hands: America's Foreign Service Officers and What Befell Them* (New York: Viking Press, 1975), 60.

56 **He joined the Foreign Service:** Ibid., 64–65.

57 **Mao Zedong and Chiang Kai-shek:** Jonathan D. Spence, "The Enigma of Chiang Kai-shek," *New York Review of Books* 56, no. 16 (October 22, 2009).
   While Chiang: Barbara Tuchman, *Stillwell and the American Experience in China, 1911–15* (New York: Macmillan Publishers, 1971), 491–494.

58 **It launched an observation group:** Khan, *China Hands*, 115–117.
   "Our policy toward China": Ibid., 130.

59 **"impotent and confounded":** Tuchman, *Stillwell and the American Experience*, 517.
   "It was easier to talk": Tucker, *China Confidential*, 27.
   "within four years": Khan, *China Hands*, 39.

60 **"whether or not [Zhou]":** Pogue, *Marshall: Statesman*, 89.
   "to the effect that the Nationalists": Tucker, *China Confidential*, 52.
   All these things: Ibid., 30–31.

61 **Ambassador Hurley:** Ibid., 122.
   With Wedemeyer's help: Ibid., 131.

62 **"bandit suppression campaigns":** Tuchman, *Stillwell and the American Experience*, 132.

63 **Prior to the war:** Henry R. Luce, "The American Century," *Life*, February 17, 1941.

64 **"Any resemblance to":** Sam Tanenhaus, *Whittaker Chambers: A Biography* (New York: Random House, 1997), 185.

65 **On April 19:** Khan, *China Hands*, 165–172.

66 **Throughout much of the 1930s:** Morgan, *Reds*, 166.
Until the Foreign: D. D. Guttenplan, "Red Harvest: The KGB in America," *The Nation*, May 25, 2009.
One of the most successful: Morgan, *Reds*, 146–147; John Earl Haynes and Harvey Klehr, *Venona: Decoding Espionage in America* (New Haven, CT: Yale University Press, 2007).

67 **On October 19:** Khan, *China Hands*, 132.
The offensive began: David Halberstam, *The Best and the Brightest* (New York: Random House, 1972), 115–116.

68 **"adequate old age":** James Chace, *Acheson: The Secretary of State Who Created the World* (New York: Simon & Schuster, 1998), 94.
"For Americans who had": Bruce Cumings, *The Origins of the Korean War*, vol. 2, *The Roaring of the Cataract, 1947–1950* (Princeton, NJ: Princeton University Press, 1990), 109.
"pompous diplomat": Chace, *Acheson*, 237.

69 **John Carter Vincent:** Gary May, *China Scapegoat: The Diplomatic Ordeal of John Carter Vincent* (Washington, DC: New Republic Books, 1979), 183.
"I say to you, gentlemen": Khan, *China Hands*, 214.

70 **On March 15:** Ibid., 217–219.
"by the natural tendency": Ibid., 221–222.

71 **Tydings, a Democrat:** Morgan, *Reds*, 403–404.
"keep talking": Chace, *Acheson*, 237.
On August 7: Ibid., 311.

72 **In later years:** Isaacson and Thomas, *Wise Men*, 612.
Resonant in his soaring appeals: Halberstam, *Best and the Brightest*, 331.
The next day: Acheson, *Present at the Creation*, 413.

73 **"a tendency to feel":** Pogue, *Marshall: Statesman*, 275.
"the attack of the primitives": Acheson, *Present at the Creation*, 354.
A Europeanist: Tucker, *China Confidential*, 78.
both he and Truman: Ibid., 56.
In August 1949: Ibid., 62.
"the intelligence and quality": Halberstam, *Best and the Brightest*, 115.
Declaring the paper: "Inquest on China," *New York Times*, August 6, 1949; and "Prospects for China," *New York Times*, August 7, 1949.

74 **"a smooth alibi":** Chace, *Acheson*, 220.
"whitewash of a wishful": Isaacson and Thomas, *Wise Men*, 476.
Even Mao Zedong: Khan, *China Hands*, 208.
"have publicly announced": Leffler, *Preponderance of Power*, 296.
In a series of articles: Steele, *Walter Lippmann*, 466.

75 **In his memoirs:** Acheson, *Present at the Creation*, 302–303.

"**They just didn't know**": Tucker, *China Confidential*, 68.

"**We got another telegram**": Ibid., 69.

Acheson, worn down: Chace, *Acheson*, 238.

76 **So great was the emotional:** Khan, *China Hands*, 17.

Two years after: Ibid., 7.

"**Tailgunner Joe**": Cumings, *Origins of the Korean War*, 116.

Vincent would be: Khan, *China Hands*, 255.

77 **The elevation of a man:** Halberstam, *Best and the Brightest*, 379.

4: INSIDE JOB

78 "**that granitic statue**": Oral History Interview with R. Gordon Arneson [22], Harry S. Truman Library, http://www.trumanlibrary.org/oralhist/arneston.htm (accessed March 5, 2009).

79 "**the least abhorrent choice**": Henry L. Stimson, "The Decision to Use the Atomic Bomb," *Harper's Magazine*, February 1947.

80 "**The chief lesson**": Henry L. Stimson and McGeorge Bundy, *On Active Service in Peace and War* (New York: Harper & Brothers Publishers, 1947), 644.

The Stimson memo: Carroll, *House of War*, 111–122.

81 **James Chace:** James Chace, "After Hiroshima: Sharing the Atom Bomb," *Foreign Affairs* 85, no. 1 (January/February 1996).

82 "**Vermont affair**": McCullough, *Truman*, 747.

"**those Asiatics**": Chace, *Acheson*, 230.

"**evidence that within**": McCullough, *Truman*, 749.

Truman's initial response: Kai Bird and Martin J. Sherwin, *American Prometheus: The Triumph and Tragedy of J. Robert Oppenheimer* (New York: Alfred A. Knopf, 2005), 417.

"**would bring about**": Carroll, *House of War*, 173.

"**blow them off**": Bird and Sherwin, *American Prometheus*, 424.

83 **General Bradley, shaken:** McCullough, *Truman*, 761.

84 "**Trojan doves**": Acheson, *Present at the Creation*, 379.

"**How do you persuade**": Chace, *Acheson*, 234–235.

In a paper dated: McCullough, *Truman*, 757.

"**one of the most important**": Kennan, *Memoirs*, 472.

On January 31: McCullough, *Truman*, 762–763.

85 "**calipers**": Carroll, *House of War*, 177.

86 "**Paul loved anything**": Ernest May, "Introduction: NSC 68: The Theory and Politics of Strategy," in *American Cold War Strategy: Interpreting NSC-68*, ed. Ernest May (Boston, New York: Bedford/St. Martin's, 1993), 13.

"**a Teutonic martinet**": Carroll, *House of War*, 178.

Nitze was indeed: Isaacson and Thomas, *Wise Men*, 482.

"**My body**": May, "Introduction: NSC 68," 10.

87 **In spring 1937:** Isaacson and Thomas, *Wise Men*, 483.

Nitze once told: Oral History Interview with Paul H. Nitze [90], Harry S. Truman Library, http://www.trumanlibrary.org/oralhist/nitzeph1.htm (accessed February 24, 2009).

Based on interviews: George Ball, *The Past Has Another Pattern: Memoirs* (New York: W. W. Norton & Co., 1982), 61–62.

The survey also concluded: Carroll, *House of War*, 62–63.

88 **"epitomized the civilian":** Ibid., 178.

The undermanned and outgunned: Isaacson and Thomas, *Wise Men*, 489.

89 **In his memoirs:** Acheson, *Present at the Creation*, 375.

The forty-seven-page: "NSC 68, United States Objectives and Programs for National Security (April 14, 1950)," in *American Cold War Strategy*, 23–82.

91 **NSC 68 landed:** Carroll, *House of War*, 186.

In the May 15 edition: May, "Introduction: NSC 68," 14.

92 **The outbreak of the Korean War:** Carroll, *House of War*, 186.

In April, having: May, "Introduction: NSC 68," 12; Isaacson and Thomas, *Wise Men*, 495.

93 **"Frustrating the Kremlin design":** "Gaddis Commentary," in *American Cold War Strategy*, 141–146.

"based on a flawed premise": Isaacson and Thomas, *Wise Men*, 503.

94 **"not only simply":** "Gaddis Commentary," in *American Cold War Strategy*, 125–128.

For all its notoriety: Isaacson and Thomas, *Wise Men*, 503. See also Strobe Talbott, *The Master of the Game: Paul Nitze and the Nuclear Peace* (New York: Alfred A. Knopf, 1988), 56.

"laid the foundation": Richard Rhodes, *Arsenals of Folly: The Making of the Nuclear Arms Race* (New York: Alfred A. Knopf, 2008), 106.

95 **Not to be outdone:** Talbott, *Master of the Game*, 59.

"Korea saved us": Isaacson and Thomas, *Wise Men*, 504.

5: ROGUE ORIENTALISTS

97 **"almost hysterical":** Cumings, *Origins of the Korean War*, 104–106.

"collect every scrap": Michael Schaller, *The American Occupation of Japan: The Origins of the Cold War in Asia* (New York: Oxford University Press, 1985), 134.

In an attempt: John W. Dower, *Embracing Defeat: Japan in the Wake of World War II* (New York: W. W. Norton & Company/New Press, 1990), 512; Cumings, *Origins of the Korean War*, 105.

"a natural-born autocrat": Manchester, *American Caesar*, 185.

"General, you don't have": Acheson, *Present at the Creation*, 424.

98 **"laggards, toadies, and fools":** Joseph P. Alsop, with Adam Platt, *I've Seen the Best of It: Memoirs* (New York: W. W. Norton, 1992), 323.

"I have absolutely no": Oral History Interview with Paul Nitze [103–104].

"the making of foreign policy": Schaller, *American Occupation of Japan*, 29.

"right-wing sycophant colonels": Oral History Interview with Paul Nitze [105].

100 **Early in the year**: Acheson, *Present at the Creation*, 355–356.

It was Rusk: McCullough, *Truman*, 777.

"no civil war in Korea": Clay Blair, *The Forgotten War: America in Korea 1950–1953* (New York: An Anchor Press Book/Doubleday, 1987), 58.

"an intense moral outrage": McCullough, *Truman*, 778.

101 **"the beginning of World War III"**: David Halberstam, *The Coldest Winter: America and the Korean War* (New York: Hyperion, 2007), 488.

Had Kim not attacked: Tucker, *China Confidential*, 78.

Stalin had no military: Bradley K. Martin, *Under the Loving Care of the Fatherly Leader: North Korea and the Kim Dynasty* (New York: St. Martin's Griffin/Thomas Dunne Books, 2006), 64.

102 **As late as fall 1949**: Kathryn Weathersby, "Korea, 1949–50: To Attack, or Not to Attack? Stalin, Kim Il Sung, and the Prelude to War," *Cold War International History Project Bulletin*, no. 5 (Spring 1995): 4–8.

103 **As the meeting was**: McCullough, *Truman*, 779.

Unbeknownst to the president: Blair, *Forgotten War*, 70–71.

104 **"Nothing . . . could be more"**: Manchester, *American Caesar*, 566–568.

105 **"The President of the United States"**: Acheson, *Present at the Creation*, 423–424.

Much later, after: Manchester, *American Caesar*, 569.

Bradley, for his part: McCullough, *Truman* 792.

"To do so did not": Acheson, *Present at the Creation*, 424.

106 **In August, while**: Pogue, *Marshall: Statesman*, 420.

"luridly close to being": Alsop, *I've Seen the Best of It*, 302.

"act as Secretary of Defense": Pogue, *Marshall: Statesman*, 422.

107 **"will not enter"**: Kathryn Weathersby, "New Russian Documents on the Korean War: Introduction and Translations," *Cold War International History Project Bulletin*, no. 6/7 (Winter 1995): 39.

"here was indeed": Kennan, *Memoirs*, 490–497.

108 **Days later, Zhou**: Khan, *China Hands*, 226.

"The theoretical alternative": Cumings, *Origins of the Korean War*, 714.

109 **"bleed us to death"**: Pogue, *Marshall: Statesman*, 465.

"little strategic interest": Clay, *Forgotten War*, 40.

Even Paul Nitze: Isaacson and Thomas, *Wise Men*, 526–527.

anything short of reunification: Ibid., 530–531.

"obliterate" the 38th: Ibid., 527.

His deputy, John: Cumings, *Origins of the Korean War*, 709–710.

110 **"the crisis in Korea"**: Carroll, *House of War*, 192.

"to restore peace there": Harry Truman, "Tough Decisions in Korean Crisis" (The Truman Memoirs: Part III), *Life* 40, no. 6 (February 6, 1956), 128.

"march up to a surveyor's": Isaacson and Thomas, *Wise Men*, 530.

The orders were heavily: Pogue, *Marshall: Statesman*, 456–457.

111 **Mao was now forced:** Chen Jian, "The Sino-Soviet Alliance and China's Entry into the Korean War," *Cold War International History Project, Working Paper No. 1* (Washington, DC: Woodrow Wilson International Center for Scholars, June 1992), 31.

On October 15: McCullough, *Truman*, 800–808.

"My views were": Douglas MacArthur, "The Old Soldier's Last Command" (Part VII: MacArthur Reminiscences), *Life* 54, no. 4 (July 24, 1964), 47.

112 **"Nothing is gained":** McCullough, *Truman*, 804.

"the most auspicious time": David Halberstam, "MacArthur's Grand Delusion," *Vanity Fair*, October 2007.

113 **Not only were the GIs:** Blair, *Forgotten War*, 375, 431.

"could for all practical": Manchester, *American Caesar*, 602–606.

On November 30: McCullough, *Truman*, 820–821.

114 **"An arrogant enemy":** Halberstam, "MacArthur's Grand Delusion."

MacArthur responded: Pogue, *Marshall: Statesman*, 472.

On March 15: Manchester, *American Caesar*, 633–640.

115 **"This looks like":** Halberstam, *Coldest Winter*, 602.

"We should have fired him": Isaacson and Thomas, *Wise Men*, 550.

In his acceptance speech: Pogue, *Marshall: Statesman*, 506–507.

It was a difficult: Ibid., 512–513.

6: TREATY-PORT YANKS

117 **speechwriter Malcolm Moos:** Charles J. Griffin "New Light on Eisenhower's Farewell Address," *Presidential Studies Quarterly* 22, no. 3 (Summer 1992): 469–479.

118 **"more and more uneasiness":** Dwight Eisenhower, *Waging Peace: The White House Years, 1956–1961* (New York: Doubleday & Company, 1965), 614–615.

119 **"the only bull":** James Mann, "Book Review of 'Churchill' by Paul Johnson," *Washington Post*, January 3, 2010.

120 **"until I thought":** Roby C. Barrett, *The Greater Middle East and the Cold War: U.S. Foreign Policy Under Eisenhower and Kennedy* (London: I. B. Tauris, 2007), 104.

"I can assure you": Patrick Seale, *The Struggle for Syria: A Study of Post-War Arab Politics, 1945–1958* (London: I. B. Tauris & Co Ltd, 1965), 285.

121 **"nothing more than":** Eisenhower, *Waging Peace*, 615.

"national security state": Daniel Yergin, *Shattered Peace: The Origins of the Cold War and the National Security State* (Boston: Houghton Mifflin Co., 1977).

"a legacy of ashes": Tim Weiner, *Legacy of Ashes: The History of the CIA* (New York: Doubleday, 2007), 167.

122 **So conclusive was:** Thomas M. Coffey, *Iron Eagle: The Turbulent Life of General Curtis LeMay* (New York: Crown Publishers, 1986), 331.

123 **"the increased destructiveness":** Gareth Porter, *Perils of Dominance: Imbalance of Power and the Road to War in Vietnam* (Berkeley, CA: University of California Press, 2005), 11.
     "must be scared as hell": John Lewis Gaddis, *We Now Know: Rethinking Cold War History* (Oxford: Clarendon Press, 1997), 110.
     "far inferior": Porter, *Perils of Dominance*, 13.
     "a very drastic resource pinch": Ibid., 19.
     In 1953: For a detailed analysis of U.S.-Soviet asymmetry, see Porter, *Perils of Dominance*, 3–13.

124 **In the late 1950s:** Dallek, *An Unfinished Life*, 374.
     On July 13: Coffey, *Iron Eagle*, 331. See also Carroll, *House of War*, 170, 195, 218, 269.

125 **As Cold War scholar:** Porter, *Perils of Dominance*, 13.
     "a great big target range": William Taubman, *Khrushchev: His Life and Times* (New York: W. W. Norton, 2003), 243.
     "I see U.S. missiles": Alex Abella, *Soldiers of Reason: The RAND Corporation and the Rise of the American Empire* (Orlando, FL: Houghton Mifflin Harcourt, 2008), 120.
     "How he quivered!": Taubman, *Khrushchev*, 332.

126 **The GOP, he wrote:** J. Peter Scoblic, *U.S. vs. Them: Conservatism in the Age of Nuclear Terror* (New York: Viking, 2008), 32.
     "wasn't especially bright": Taubman, *Khrushchev*, 335.
     In early 1953: Tyler Nottberg, "Once and Future Planning: Solarium for Today," The Eisenhower Institute, 2002, http://www.eisenhowerinstitute. org/about/living_history/solarium_for_today.dot.

127 **"We cannot defend":** Stephen Ambrose, *Eisenhower: The President* (Simon & Schuster, 1984), 224.
     He was downsizing: Ibid., 223.
     "Our most valued": Ibid., p. 171.
     In opposing Ike's: Carroll, *House of War*, 219–220.

128 **LeMay also deployed:** Coffey, *Iron Eagle*, 337–338.
     At the time of LeMay's: Porter, *Perils of Dominance*, 5–6; and Rhodes, *Arsenals of Folly*, 85–86.

129 **"A dedicated specialist":** "The Nation: Defense Under Fire," *Time*, May 14, 1956.
     Eisenhower had approved: Taubman, *Khrushchev*, 443–444; Rhodes, *Arsenals of Folly*, 71.
     Within months, the CIA: Porter, *Perils of Dominance*, 13–14; Ambrose, *Eisenhower*, 476–477.

130 **For LeMay and his allies:** Talbott, *Master of the Game*, 67–70.
     Part of the committee's: Carroll, *House of War*, 221–223.

131 **It is true:** "First Declassification of Eisenhower's Instructions to Commanders Predelegating Nuclear Weapons Use, 1959–1960," *A National Security Archive Electronic Briefing Book*, William Burr (ed.), (Washington, DC: George Washington University, May 18, 2001), Document 3, page 7, http://www.gwu.edu/~nsarchiv/NSAEBB/NSAEBB45/doc3.pdf.

132 **"a space-age raspberry":** Abella, *Soldiers of Reason*, 106–107.
Eisenhower played down: Ambrose, *Eisenhower*, 423–430.
"We have found no": Abella, *Soldiers of Reason*, 111. See also Talbott, *Master of the Game*, 66–70.
The governor of Michigan: Abella, *Soldiers of Reason*, 107.

133 **"a garrison state":** Ambrose, *Eisenhower*, 434.
"there still wouldn't be": Abella, *Soldiers of Reason*, 112.
But if Ike thought: Carroll, *House of War*, 224–226.

134 **The characters in *Dr. Strangelove*:** Christopher Coker, "Deadly Devices," *Times Literary Supplement*, July 10, 2007.

135 **"the academy of science and death":** Abella, *Soldiers of Reason*, 92.
On Thermonuclear War: Ibid., 35.

136 **Weekends were spent:** Ibid., 101–104.
"The Delicate Balance of Terror": Ibid., 117–120.

137 **Had the CIA:** Weiner, *Legacy of Ashes*, 114.

138 **"time-over-target" conflicts:** For a detailed analysis of the SIOP, including declassified documents that serve as the basis for this account, see "The Creation of SIOP-62: More Evidence on the Origins of Overkill," in *A National Security Archive Electronic Briefing Book,* no. 130, July 13, 2004, http://www.gwu.edu/~nsarchiv/NSAEBB/NSAEBB130/.

140 **"frighten[ed] the devil":** David Alan Rosenberg, "The Origins of Overkill: Nuclear Weapons and American Strategy," in *The National Security: Its Theory and Practice, 1945–1960*, edited by Norman A. Graebner (New York: Oxford University Press, 1986), 126.
"dangerously rigid": James K. Galbraith and Heather A. Purple, "Did the U.S. Military Plan a Nuclear First Strike for 1963?" Notes on National Security Council Meeting, July 20, 1961.
"horror strategy": William Burr, "The 'Horror Strategy', and the Search for Limited Nuclear Options, 1969–1972," *Journal of Cold War Studies* 7, no. 3 (Summer 2005): 34–78.
Jimmy Carter revised: Rhodes, *Arsenals of Folly*, 146.
SIOP lingered until: "Single Integrated Operational Plan," Wikipedia, last updated March 18, 2011, http://en.wikipedia.org/wiki/Single_Integrated_Operational_Plan.

141 **In response, Eisenhower:** Ambrose, *Eisenhower*, 205–206.
Calls for a nuclear strike: Ibid., 231–240.

142 **By July 1955:** Porter, *Perils of Dominance*, 27–28.

143 **"refused these overtures":** Taubman, *Khrushchev*, 399–400.

"The way to teach": Ibid., 444.

A month later: Porter, *Perils of Dominance*, 24.

144 He expected little: Taubman, *Khrushchev*, 543.

There, he would sip: Stephen Kinzer, *Overthrow: America's Century of Regime Change from Hawaii to Iraq* (New York: Henry Holt and Company, 2006), 112–117.

145 Stiff and charmless: Leonard Mosley, *Dulles: A Biography of Eleanor, Allen, and John Foster Dulles and their Family Network* (New York: The Dial Press/James Wade, 1978), 191–199.

As secretary of state: Ibid., 311.

In an effort: Ibid., 306.

Most notoriously: Alsop, *I've Seen the Best of It*, 348; Mosley, *Dulles*, 312–315.

"an outsider": Mosley, *Dulles*, 311.

146 An adventurer at heart: Ibid., 16.

Within four months: Ibid., 225.

In many ways: Mosley, *Dulles*, 104–105.

147 For Dean Acheson: Acheson, *Present at the Creation*, 214.

They were called: Weiner, *Legacy of Ashes*, 45–46.

In Asia, the CIA: James R. Lilly, *China Hands: Nine Decades of Adventure, Espionage, and Diplomacy in Asia* (New York: PublicAffairs, 2004), 80; Weiner, *Legacy of Ashes*, 58–60.

During the Truman: Weiner, *Legacy of Ashes*, 62.

148 Certainly that was: Ibid., 86–92.

Immediately after Indonesian: Ibid., 142–143.

Following his first meeting: Ibid., 94.

149 In December 1953: Ibid., 96–103.

In 1960, when: Ibid., 162–167.

7: WAR FOR PEACE

151 "Our involvement in Vietnam": Khan, *China Hands*, 294.

152 Even as the White House: H. R. McMaster, *Dereliction of Duty: Lyndon Johnson, Robert McNamara, the Joint Chiefs of Staff, and the Lies That Led to Vietnam* (New York: HarperCollins, 1997), 219.

The war was: Ibid., 72.

Truman was happy: Halberstam, *Best and the Brightest*, 104–106.

Kennedy, rattled by: Robert Dallek, *An Unfinished Life: John F. Kennedy, 1917–1963* (Boston: Little, Brown, 2003), 413.

In spring 1954: Halberstam, *Best and the Brightest*, 144.

153 When the novice: Halberstam, *Best and the Brightest*, 89.

154 Campaigning for his first term: Pogue, *Marshall: Statesman*, 497.

That same year: Dallek, *An Unfinished Life*, 162.

In reciprocation: Evan Thomas, *Robert Kennedy: His Life* (New York: Simon & Schuster, 2000), 68.

Kennedy also blamed: Christopher A. Peble, "Who Ever Believed in the 'Missile Gap'?: John F. Kennedy and the Politics of National Security," *Presidential Studies Quarterly* 33, no. 4 (December 2003): 806–807.

Within weeks: Abella, *Soldiers of Reason*, 164.

155 **"Iron Ass" LeMay:** Coffey, *Iron Eagle*, 21.

Yet he did: Ibid., 436.

LeMay knew that: Ibid., 338.

156 **According to General Frederic Smith:** Ibid., 339–340.

Throughout his political career: David Milne, *American Rasputin: Walt Rostow and the Vietnam Era* (New York: Hill and Wang, 2008), 84.

"JFK has made": Dallek, *An Unfinished Life*, 289.

Yet Kennedy: Ibid., 167, 222, 237.

157 **Once elected, Kennedy:** Ibid., 342–343.

The famously harebrained: Weiner, *Legacy of Ashes*, 164.

158 **"Nobody knew what":** Ibid., 176.

159 **The physicist-hawk:** Dallek, *An Unfinished Life*, 466.

They wanted 3,000: Halberstam, *Best and the Brightest*, 71–72.

His desire to sign: Dallek, *An Unfinished Life*, 343–344.

160 **To LeMay, first:** McMaster, *Dereliction of Duty*, 20.

The two sides clashed: Coffey, *Iron Eagle*, 369.

When McNamara refused: Ibid., 379–380.

LeMay once suggested: Abella, *Soldiers of Reason*, 140.

161 **"They had no faith":** McMaster, *Dereliction of Duty*, 20.

"every time the President": Dallek, *An Unfinished Life*, 345.

"almost as bad": McMaster, *Dereliction of Duty*, 27.

"these brass hats": Dallek, *An Unfinished Life*, 555.

162 **"was not a blockade":** McMaster, *Dereliction of Duty*, 30.

"the greatest defeat": Dallek, *An Unfinished Life*, 571.

"the first advice": McMaster, *Dereliction of Duty*, 28.

163 **"wasteland":** Halberstam, *Best and the Brightest*, 188–189.

Early in 1961: Tucker, *China Confidential*, 161–162.

164 **This was strongly opposed:** Halberstam, *Best and the Brightest*, 197.

"real Grandma Moses": Ibid., 326.

Roger Hilsman: Ibid., 392–393.

Michael Forrestal: Ibid., 376.

William Trueheart: Ibid. 371.

165 **As early as September:** "CIA and the Vietnam Policymakers: Episode 2: 1963–1965: CIA Judgments on President Johnson's Decision to 'Go Big' in Vietnam," Center for the Study of Intelligence, last updated July 7, 2008, https://www.cia.gov/library/center-for-the-study-of-intelligence/csi-publi

cations/books-and-monographs/cia-and-the-vietnam-policymakers-three
-episodes-1962-1968/epis2.html.

Kennedy interpreted Diem's: Halberstam, *Best and the Brightest*, 168; Milne, *American Rasputin*, 95.

"The inclusion of Rostow": Ball, *The Past Has Another Pattern*, 365.

166 **"indicated that the State Department":** Chester Bowles, *Promises to Keep: My Years in Public Service 1941–1969* (New York: Harper & Row Publishers, 1971), 361.

"NVN is extremely": Milne, *American Rasputin*, 98; Andrew Preston, *The War Council: McGeorge Bundy, the NSC, and Vietnam* (Cambridge, MA: Harvard University Press, 2006), 90–91.

Arriving in Saigon: Preston, *War Council*, 90–93.

167 **In a Saturday:** Ball, *The Past Has Another Pattern*, 366–367.

Chester Bowles, realizing: Preston, *War Council*, 93, 94, 96.

168 **"For many reasons":** Halberstam, *Best and the Brightest*, 177.

The additional advisers: Dallek, *An Unfinished Life*, 457–458.

169 **"He was determined":** Ted Sorensen, *Counselor: A Life at the Edge of History* (New York: HarperCollins, 2008), 359.

"we don't have a prayer": Milne, *American Rasputin*, 122.

"another Joe McCarthy": Dallek, *An Unfinished Life*, 668.

170 **It was also an act:** Sorensen, *Counselor*, 326–327.

Tellingly, Khrushchev allowed: Ibid., 327.

"start a complete": Porter, *Perils of Dominance*, 178.

8: LOOKING-GLASS WAR

172 **In 1961:** Dallek, *An Unfinished Life*, 354.

"We should make clear": Porter, *Perils of Dominance*, 181.

"was the biggest damn mess": "Tapes Show Johnson Saw Vietnam War as Pointless in 1964," *New York Times*, February 15, 1997.

He once told: Porter, *Perils of Dominance*, 183.

174 **In a July 1964 briefing:** Halberstam, *Best and the Brightest*, 465.

For Dean Rusk: McMaster, *Dereliction of Duty*, 300–302.

Arguing in a March 21: Porter, *Perils of Dominance*, 217.

"We learned from Hitler": Isaacson and Thomas, *Wise Men*, 668.

175 **A 1965 study:** Milne, *American Rasputin*, 151.

For months beginning: Abella, *Soldiers of Reason*, 173–179.

They represented a rich: Tucker, *China Confidential*, 191.

176 **"They gradually pushed":** Halberstam, *Best and the Brightest*, 130–131; Tucker, *China Confidential*, 192.

Kennedy had signaled: Halberstam, *Best and the Brightest*, 103.

So relentless were: Tucker, *China Confidential*, 91–92, 146–147, 168–169.

177 **In a May 1964:** Porter, *Perils of Dominance*, 191.
Faced with an onslaught: Halberstam, *Best and the Brightest*, 530.

178 **In a December 31 telegram:** Porter, *Perils of Dominance*, 208–209.
As Vice President Hubert: McMaster, *Dereliction of Duty*, 241–242.
"We believed in it": Interview with Leslie Gelb, July 15, 2010.

179 **Years later, Johnson:** McMaster, *Dereliction of Duty*, 213–216.
The most energized: Milne, *American Rasputin*, 144.

180 **By 1967, at the height:** Qiang Zhai, *China and the Vietnam Wars, 1950–1975* (Chapel Hill, NC: University of North Carolina Press, 2000), 132–135.
Beijing worked the Sino-American: Tucker, *China Confidential*, 138–139, 205.

181 **Under Kennedy, the rejection:** Stanley Karnow, *Vietnam: A History* (New York: Viking Press, 1983), 250.
It was a strategy inspired by: H. R. McMaster, "This Familiar Battleground," *Hoover Digest*, October 2009.
This inductive approach: Scoblic, *U.S. vs. Them*, 97.

182 **"We totally underestimated":** Robert S. McNamara, *In Retrospect: The Tragedy and Lessons of Vietnam* (New York: Vintage, 1996), 31.
"The thing that bothers": Halberstam, *Best and the Brightest*, 578.

183 **There was no evidence:** Porter, *Perils of Dominance*, 211–212.
The die was cast: McMaster, *Dereliction of Duty*, 218, 230.
In April 1967: Milne, *American Rasputin*, 190.
The conclusions of SIGMA: Milne, *American Rasputin*, 145–146.

184 **In a May 8:** McMaster, *Dereliction of Duty*, 256–257, 287.
As military historian: Ibid., 158.

185 **A decade later:** Milne, *American Rasputin*, 60–66.

187 **Undersecretary of the Air Force:** Ibid., 169
In his final memo: Ibid., 101–102.

188 **A hillbilly from Texas's:** Kevin V. Mulchahy, "Walt Rostow as National Security Adviser, 1966–69," *Presidential Studies Quarterly* 25, no. 2 (Spring, 1995): 223–236.
Rostow's growing influence: Milne, *American Rasputin*, 134.
By late 1964: Ibid., 135, 141.

189 **In 1966 a joint:** George Herring, ed., *The Pentagon Papers* (New York: McGraw Hill, 1993), 169.
With airpower alone: McMaster, *Dereliction of Duty*, 279.

190 **At one point:** Ibid., 272.
As one escalation: Halberstam, *Best and the Brightest*, 507.
In 1965, with: Milne, *American Rasputin*, 150.
Even Rostow was: Ibid., 213–214.

191 **George Ball was among:** Ball, *The Past Has Another Pattern*, 386–387.
Ten days later: Ibid., 395–396.

192 **Such arguments appealed:** Porter, *Perils of Dominance*, 224.

But the very idea: McMaster, *Dereliction of Duty*, 300–303.

McNamara, however: Herring, *The Pentagon Papers*, 129–137.

193 **McNamara, it seemed:** Porter, *Perils of Dominance*, 227.

No one, that is: Milne, *American Rasputin*, 164.

Rostow immediately extended: Ibid., 170–171, 176–177.

In December 1967: Neil Sheehan, *A Bright Shining Lie: John Paul Vann and America in Vietnam* (New York: Random House, 1988), 701.

It wasn't until 1995: William Plaff, "Mac Bundy Said He Was 'All Wrong'," *New York Review of Books*, June 10, 2010.

194 **Only a month earlier:** Sheehan, *A Bright Shining Lie*, 213–214.

On February 27: Milne, *American Rasputin*, 3–5.

"What then?": Ibid., 4–5.

195 **"Walt Rostow was a believer":** Interview with the author, July 15, 2010.

196 **One of Rostow's last:** Milne, *American Rasputin*, 235–239.

9: MADMEN

198 **"If I had to choose":** Robert Dallek, *Nixon and Kissinger: Partners in Power* (New York: HarperCollins, 2007), 197.

"Now is the time": Ibid., 46.

Both countries laid: Tucker, *China Confidential*, 227–228; Han Suyin, *Eldest Son: Zhou Enlai and the Making of Modern China, 1898–1976* (London: Pimlico, 1994), 369–371.

199 **As tensions between:** Tucker, *China Confidential*, 221–222.

In September 1969: Zhai, *China and the Vietnam Wars*, 181–182.

201 **As Ivo Daalder:** Ivo H. Daalder and I. M. Destler, *In the Shadow of the Oval Office: Profiles of the National Security Advisers and the Presidents They Served from JFK to George W. Bush* (New York: Simon & Schuster, 2009), 92.

It was a response: Steven E. Ambrose, *Nixon*, vol. 2, *The Triumph of a Politician, 1962–1972* (New York: Simon & Schuster, 1989), 38–39.

In an article: Richard Nixon, "Asia After Viet Nam," *Foreign Affairs* 46 (October 1967): 111–125.

202 **The *Foreign Affairs* article:** Ambrose, *Nixon*, 77.

Though he gives: Richard Nixon, *RN: The Memoirs of Richard Nixon* (New York: Grosset & Dunlap, 1978), 126.

"an astonishing shift": Dallek, *Nixon and Kissinger*, 267.

203 **It was 1965:** Rick Perlstein, *Nixonland: The Rise of a President and the Fracturing of America* (New York: Scribner, 2008), 132.

In his book *The Conscience*: Scoblic, *US. vs. Them*, 41.

In summer 1966: Perlstein, *Nixonland*, 130–132.

204 **Two years later:** Ambrose, *Nixon*, 150.

As it turns out: Milne, *American Rasputin*, 236.

205 **There was Nixon:** Perlstein, *Nixonland,* 22.
     Their adventures in high: Dallek, *Nixon and Kissinger,* 38–45, 47–49.
206 **It was Rockefeller's close:** Ibid., 68–78, 92–93.
     As a sophomore: Ibid., 40.
     "Napoleon's defeat in Russia": Henry A. Kissinger, *A World Restored: Metternich, Castlereagh, and the Problems of Peace, 1812–22* (Boston: Houghton Mifflin Co., 1957).
     One of its most: Scoblic, *U.S. vs. Them,* 62.
207 **Foreign Service officers:** Dallek, *Nixon and Kissinger,* 195; Duncan Clarke, "Why State Can't Lead," *Foreign Policy* 66 (Spring 1987): 130.
     Even the outreach: Dallek, *Nixon and Kissinger,* 268–269.
     Nixon, according to: Henry A. Kissinger, *White House Years* (Boston: Little, Brown and Company, 1979), 11.
208 **With the help of his:** Perlstein, *Nixonland,* 362–363.
     "Whenever there's anything": Daalder and Destler, *In the Shadow of the Oval Office,* 85.
     Chas Freeman, a Sinologist: Tucker, *China Confidential,* 269.
209 **Laird was of a different:** Dallek, *Nixon and Kissinger,* 84; Dale Van Atta, *With Honor: Melvin Laird in War, Peace and Politics* (Madison: University of Wisconsin Press, 2008), 153, 218, 481.
     His verbal jousts: Van Atta, *With Honor,* 109.
     In July 1967: Ibid., 124.
210 **Nixon demanded Laird:** Robert G. Kaufman, *Henry M. Jackson: A Life in Politics* (Seattle; London: University of Washington Press, 2000), 197–199.
     Laird agreed, but: Van Atta, *With Honor,* 4–5
     He restored trust: Ibid., 182–183.
211 **In his memoirs, Nixon:** Nixon, *RN,* 392.
     Agnew, for one: Van Atta, *With Honor,* 481.
     Immediately after his: Daalder and Destler, *In the Shadow of the Oval Office,* 57–58; see also Van Atta, *With Honor,* 156–157.
212 **Not surprisingly, Kissinger:** Kissinger, *White House Years,* 41–48.
     As Chas Freeman put it: Tucker, *China Confidential,* 240.
213 **Managing often conflicting:** Daalder and Destler, *In the Shadow of the Oval Office,* 79–80.
     Anthony Lake: Walter Isaacson, *Kissinger: A Biography* (New York: Simon & Schuster, 1992), 209.
     When William Bundy: Dallek, *Nixon and Kissinger,* 100.
     Even the frequency: Daalder and Destler, *In the Shadow of the Oval Office,* 67, 69–70.
214 **"It would be goddamn":** Dallek, *Nixon and Kissinger,* 92.
     Exasperated with his boss: Daalder and Destler, *In the Shadow of the Oval Office,* 77.
     "Why don't you get": Kissinger, *White House Years,* 109–110.

215 **"But won't it go communist?":** Halberstam, *Best and the Brightest*, 506.
     "He gave us": Tucker, *China Confidential*, 232.
216 **"We'll just slip the word":** Dallek, *Nixon and Kissinger*, 106.
     Nixon seemed to grasp: Van Atta, *With Honor*, 179.
217 **Ignoring Toon's dissent:** Dallek, *Nixon and Kissinger*, 109–110.
     "The policy behind these": William Bundy, *A Tangled Web: The Making of
     Foreign Policy in the Nixon Presidency* (New York: Hill and Wang, 1998), 498.
218 **"There should be no":** Nixon, *RN*, 889.
     Prior to assuming office: Van Atta, *With Honor*, 139–140.
     "Without Vietnamization": Ibid., 433.
219 **His promising plan:** Dallek, *Nixon and Kissinger*, 175–179, 221–222.
     "a sloppy negotiating performance": Bundy, *A Tangled Web*, 253, 324–327.
     Rogers was particularly: Daalder and Destler, *In the Shadow of the Oval
     Office*, 76.
     "a milestone in confirming": Kissinger, *White House Years*, 822.
     For Kissinger's staff: Daalder and Destler, *In the Shadow of the Oval Office*,
     76–77.
220 **Sino-American rapprochement:** Dallek, *Nixon and Kissinger*, 268. For a
     recently declassified archive of documents relating to Nixon's outreach to
     China, see the National Security Archive Electronic Briefing Book No. 145,
     http://www.gwu.edu/~nsarchiv/NSAEBB/NSAEBB145/index.htm.
     On October 1: Tucker, *China Confidential*, 240.
     On April 27: Dallek, *Nixon and Kissinger*, 288.
221 **At Zhou's insistence:** Ibid., 255–256
222 **In early February:** Zhai, *China and the Vietnam Wars*, 197–206.
     "People like me": Kissinger, *White House Years*, 1062–1063.
223 **Most historians:** Tucker, *China Confidential*, 244.
     "If we succeed": Dallek, *Nixon and Kissinger*, 268–269.
     During the Warsaw talks: Tucker, *China Confidential*, 233–234, 239–240,
     243.
     Nixon claimed that: Tucker, *China Confidential*, 238.
224 **In late April:** Isaacson, *Kissinger*, 342.
     "It was painful enough": Kissinger, *White House Years*, 728.
225 **Following the China summit:** Scoblic, *U.S. vs. Them*, 66.
226 **"There is no monolithism":** Suyin, *Eldest Son*, 383.

10: INTERREGNUM

228 **The president formally:** Nixon, "Asia After Viet Nam"; Dallek, *Nixon and
     Kissinger*, 144.
229 **In April 1965:** McMaster, *Dereliction of Duty*, 260.
     A year later: Sheehan, *A Bright Shining Lie*, 652–654.
230 **"a small tail":** Robert W. Komer, *Bureaucracy Does Its Thing: Institutional*

Constraints on U.S.-GVN Performance in Vietnam (Santa Monica, CA: RAND Corporation, 1972), xi.

"From the outset": Ibid., vi.

231 **In his hunger:** Abella, *Soldiers of Reason*, 181; Sheehan, *A Bright Shining Lie*, 733.

"the word 'Phoenix' became": Richard A. Hunt, *Pacification: The American Struggle for Vietnam's Hearts and Minds* (Boulder, CO: Westview Press, 1995), 116–118, 234.

Less than two years: Ibid., 238–240.

232 **In 1968, as part:** Nick Turse, "A My Lai a Month," *The Nation*, November 13, 2008.

Even before the Delta: Hunt, *Pacification*, 236–245.

Needless to say: Hunt, *Pacification*, 238–240.

233 **In his 1972 RAND study:** Komer, *Bureaucracy Does Its Thing*, viii.

234 **the Nixon Doctrine:** Arthur M. Schlesinger Jr., *The Imperial Presidency* (Boston: Houghton Mifflin Company, 1973), 298–299.

With the help of Anthony Russo: Abella, *Soldiers of Reason*, 214–216.

235 **Even McNamara:** Halberstam, *Best and the Brightest*, 633.

"challenged the myth": Herring, *The Pentagon Papers*, xix.

"step through the looking glass": Halberstam, *Best and the Brightest*, 409.

For Laird, the primary: Van Atta, *With Honor*, 162.

236 **Abrams was widely:** Lewis Sorley, *Thunderbolt: From the Battle of the Bulge to Vietnam and Beyond: General Creighton Abrams and the Army of His Times* (New York: Simon & Schuster, 1992), 123–124.

237 **Young officers complained:** Ibid., 333–346.

The group was named: Ibid., 347–348.

238 **Not only did Abrams:** Ibid., 361–366.

Such a reduced: Lewis Sorley, "Creighton Abrams and Active-Reserve Integration in Wartime," *Parameters* 21, no. 2 (Summer 1991): 45–46.

So trusted was Abrams: Sorley, *Thunderbolt*, 359.

239 **Inflation intensified after:** Theodore White, *America in Search of Itself: The Making of the President, 1956–1980* (New York: Harper & Row, 1982), 150–152.

241 **According to Army chief:** James Kitfield, *Prodigal Soldiers: How the Generation of Officers Born in Vietnam Revolutionized the American Style of War* (New York: Simon & Schuster, 1995), 198–200.

243 **A top-secret memo:** Steve Coll, *Ghost Wars: The Secret History of the CIA, Afghanistan, and Bin Laden, from the Soviet Invasion to September 10, 2001* (New York: Penguin Press, 2004), 48. For background and declassified documents relating to the Soviet invasion of Afghanistan and the U.S. response, see the National Security Archive, volume II, "Afghanistan: Lessons from the Last War," http://www.gwu.edu/~nsarchiv/NSAEBB/NSAEBB57/essay.html.

In 1954, CIA: David N. Gibbs, "Reassessing Soviet Motives for Invading Afghanistan: A Declassified History," *Critical Asian Studies* 38, no. 2 (June 2006): 239–263.

244 **On March 17:** "Transcript of CPSU CC Politburo Discussions on Afghani-
stan, 17–19 March, 1979," *Cold War International History Project Bulletin* 8/9
(Winter 1996): 142, http://www.wilsoncenter.org/topics/pubs/ACF193.pdf.
For much of 1979: Coll, *Ghost Wars*, 41–42; Robert M. Gates, *From the
Shadows: The Ultimate Insider's Story of Five Presidents and How They Won
the Cold War* (New York: Simon & Schuster, 1996), 145–146.

245 **The Kremlin was even:** Coll, *Ghost Wars*, 46–50.
None of this: "Personal memorandum Andropov to Brezhnev, 1 December
1979," Cold War International History Project Virtual Archive, http://www
.wilsoncenter.org; and Coll, *Ghost Wars*, 49.
The invasion transformed: Carroll, *House of War*, 371–373.

246 **Finally, Carter promulgated:** Rhodes, *Arsenals of Folly*, 146–147.
"Carter laid down": Gates, *From the Shadows*, 115.

247 **In his cover letter:** Ibid., 148.

248 **The neoconservative movement:** Benjamin Ross, "Who Named the Neo-
cons?," *Dissent*, Summer 2007.
In 1972 policymakers: Abella, *Solders of Reason*, 238–240.
In a January 1976: Talbott, *Master of the Game*, 144.

249 **Nitze formed a panel:** Ibid., 146; Rhodes, *Arsenals of Folly*, 122.
It was clear: Rhodes, *Arsenals of Folly*, 125, 130–131.

250 **Though Bush was dismissive:** Ken Silverstein, "The Trillion-Dollar Arms
Scam," *Lies of Our Times* 4, no 8 (November 1993): 13–16.

251 **Team B effectively:** Abella, *Soldiers of Reason*, 240.
it was run largely: Talbott, *Master of the Game*, 239.
Nitze would strike: Ibid., 136; Kaufmann, *Henry M. Jackson*, 257–258.

252 **"The CPD saw itself":** Scoblic, *U.S. vs. Them*, 99–100.
When Carter and Brezhnev: Kaufmann, *Henry M. Jackson*, 385.
Joining in the attack: Scoblic, *U.S. vs. Them*, 106.
SALT II allowed: Talbott, *Master of the Game*, 143.
"the president was probably": Cyrus Vance, *Hard Choices: Critical Years in
America's Foreign Policy* (New York: Simon & Schuster, 1983), 100.

11: 1983

254 **Andropov dubbed the operation:** Rhodes, *Arsenals of Folly*, 151–153.
Agents were to keep: Beth A. Fischer, *The Reagan Reversal: Foreign Policy
and the End of the Cold War* (Columbia: University of Missouri Press, 1997),
127–128.
Soviet officials with: Gates, *From the Shadows*, 270–271.

255 **In a spring 1981:** Quin Hillyer. February 6, 2011 (6:47 a.m.), "Reagan's 72nd
Birthday Party," *The American Spectator* blog, http://spectator.org/blog/2011/
02/06/reagans-72nd-birthday-party.
In fact, soon after: Rhodes, *Arsenals of Folly*, 148.

256 **In a 1980 essay:** Ibid., 146.
He would raise: Ibid., 149; Scoblic, *U.S. vs. Them*, 117–118.
Parsing through the outlays: Rhodes, *Arsenals of Folly*, 150–151.

257 **Lest anyone dare:** Charles A. Stevenson, *SECDEF: The Nearly Impossible Job of Secretary of Defense* (Washington, DC: Potomac Books, 2006), 68.
As early as September: Scoblic, *U.S. vs. Them*, 118.
Reagan hailed the book: Rhodes, *Arsenals of Folly*, 178.
The Reagan military buildup: Scoblic, *U.S. vs. Them*, 137.
In a speech delivered: Fischer, *Reagan Reversal*, 29–32.

258 **Secretary of State Alexander Haig:** Ibid., 19–25.
As it turned out: Rhodes, *Arsenals of Folly*, 152.
The Kremlin would have: James Mann, *Rise of the Vulcans: The History of Bush's War Cabinet* (New York: Viking, 2004), 74.

259 **Moscow would have seized:** Scoblic, *U.S. vs. Them*, 126–130.
To make matters more: Rhodes, *Arsenals of Folly*, 153.

260 **We now know:** Fischer, *Reagan Reversal*, 132. See also Alan F. Philips, "20 Mishaps That Might Have Started Accidental Nuclear War," Nuclearfiles .org, http://www.nuclearfiles.org/menu/key-issues/nuclear-weapons/issues/ accidents/20-mishaps-maybe-caused-nuclear-war.htm.
In another close call: Michael Dobbs, "Lost in Enemy Airspace," *Vanity Fair* (June 2008): 143–149, 181.
At least three times: Gates, *From the Shadows*, 114–115.

261 **The introduction of:** Rhodes, *Arsenals of Folly*, 135, 155–156.
Such miscues continued: Scoblic, *U.S. vs. Them*, 175.

262 **On March 8:** Ibid., 117.
For militants in the Kremlin: Rhodes, *Arsenals of Folly*, 157, 159–162.

263 **Nor did it mention:** Gates, *From the Shadows*, 266–269.

264 **Though a story:** David Shribmen, "U.S. Experts Say Soviets Didn't See Jet Was Civilian," *New York Times*, October 10, 1983. See also Michael R. Gordon, "Ex-Soviet Pilot Still Insists KAL 007 Was Spying," *New York Times*, December 9, 1996.
Finally, in early November: Gates, *From the Shadows*, 270–273.

266 **Not long after:** Rhodes, *Arsenals of Folly*, 166–167.

267 **"prisoner of necessity":** Kissinger, *White House Years*, 54.

268 **The inspiration for:** Talbott, *Master of the Game*, 188–189.

269 **His 1965 memoir:** Ronald Reagan and Richard W. Hubler, *Where's the Rest of Me? The Ronald Reagan Story* (New York: Van Rees Press, 1965), 171, 200.
During the run-up to the 1976: Mann, *Rise of the Vulcans*, 32.
By exorcising the nation: Andrew J. Bacevich, *The New American Militarism: How Americans Are Seduced by War* (New York: Oxford University Press, 2005), 106, 109–110.

270 **"What exactly is":** Irving Kristol, "The Neoconservative Persuasion," *The Weekly Standard*, August 25, 2003.

271 **Represented in the White House:** Rhodes, *Arsenals of Folly*, 147.

As Columbia University: Mark Lilla, "The Pleasures of Reaction," *New Republic*, February 27, 2008.

272 **The neoconservative movement:** Tom Gervasi, *The Myth of Soviet Military Supremacy* (New York: Harper & Row, 1986), 221.

Committee on the Present Danger: Alan Weisman, *Prince of Darkness: Richard Perle, The Kingdom, the Power and the End of Empire in America* (New York: Union Square Press, 2007), 64.

Among Wohlstetter's admirers: Abella, *Soldiers of Reason*, 130–131.

"does violence to our ability": Jeremy Stone, "Reviews" (a review of *Deadly Gambits* by Strobe Talbott), *Bulletin of the Atomic Scientists* 2, no. 5 (January 1985): 47.

273 **During the Ford administration:** Kaufman, *Henry M. Jackson*, 259.

"The Soviet record": Talbott, *Master of the Game*, 222.

"were designed to gut": Kissinger, *Years of Renewal* (New York: Simon & Schuster, 1999), 114, 849.

"You just wait and see!": Scobic, *U.S. vs. Them*, 119.

274 **Offered the Defense:** Stevenson, *SECDEF*, 59–62.

"Bear in mind": Talbott, *Master of the Game*, 199–200.

275 **"a forthright popular act":** Carroll, *House of War*, 384–385.

276 **Perle had already:** Talbott, *Master of the Game*, 167–171.

In a meeting in January: Ibid., 166, 171–181.

277 **"Well, Paul":** Rhodes, *Arsenals of Folly*, 138–140.

278 **In 1966 a report:** Ibid.

Moscow's defense industry: Stephen Brooks and William C. Wohlforth, "Power, Globalization, and the End of the Cold War: Reevaluating a Landmark Case for Ideas," *International Security* 25, no. 3 (Winter 2000/01), 22–23.

At its all-time peak: Ibid., 21, 23–24.

279 **In 1979 an English translation:** Rhodes, *Arsenals of Folly*, 140–144.

In 1980, the independent: Stephen D. Goose, "Soviet Geopolitical Momentum: Myth or Menace? Trends of Soviet Influence Around the World from 1945 to 1986," *Defense Monitor* 15, no. 5 (1986): 2–10.

281 **Such reporting became:** Silverstein, "The Trillion-Dollar Arms Scam," 15.

"Look at the difference": Scoblic, *U.S. vs. Them*, 117.

Time **magazine endorsed:** Silverstein, "The Trillion-Dollar Arms Scam," 13–16.

In *The Myth*: Gervasi, *Myth of Soviet Military Supremacy*, 121–127, 188–191.

283 **If the White House was:** Tim Weiner, "Military Accused of Lies Over Arms," *New York Times*, June 28, 1993.

The GAO findings: Eleanor Chelimsky, "The U.S. Nuclear Triad: GAO's Evaluation of the Strategic Modernization Program," Testimony Before the Committee on Governmental Affairs, United States Senate, June 10, 1993.

284 **In 2009 the Pentagon's:** John G. Hines, Ellis M. Mishulovich, and John F.

Shulle, *Soviet Intentions 1965–1985:* Vol. I, *An Analytical Comparison of U.S.-Soviet Assessments During the Cold War,* BDM Federal, Inc., September 22, 1995, 1–3, http://www2.gwu.edu/~nsarchiv/nukevault/ebb285/.

285 **This was corroborated:** "Salt II and the Growth of Mistrust," Conference #2 of the Carter-Brezhnev Project, a conference of U.S. and Russian Policymakers and Scholars held at Musgrove Plantation, St. Simons Island, Georgia, 6–9 May 1994, 26–27, http://www.gwu.edu/~nsarchiv/nukevault/ebb285/doc03.PDF.

A year earlier: Benjamin B. Fischer, *A Cold War Conundrum: The 1983 Soviet War Scare,* Center for the Study of Intelligence, last updated July 7, 2008, https://www.cia.gov/library/center-for-the-study-of-intelligence/csi-publications/books-and-monographs/a-cold-war-conundrum/source.htm.

With striking consistency: Hines et al., *Soviet Intentions 1965–1985,* vol. II, *Soviet Post–Cold War Testimonial Evidence,* 74, 100, 108.

286 **During the Carter-Brezhnev:** "Salt II and the Growth of Mistrust," 26, 33–37, 41–42, 52–53.

289 **"Because the Soviet Union":** Scoblic, *U.S. vs. Them,* 97.

12: ENDGAME

290 **En route to the 1980:** Rhodes, *Arsenals of Folly,* 172–177.

291 **On October 10:** Fischer, *Reagan Reversal,* 115–116.

292 **A short time later:** Ibid., 120–122.

293 **Was this the same:** Ronald Reagan, "A Time for Choosing " ("The Speech"), delivered on October 27, 1964, in Los Angeles, California.

Though a founding father: Joshua Green, "Reagan's Liberal Legacy: What the New Literature on the Gipper Won't Tell You," *Washington Monthly,* January/February 2003.

294 **"Those sons-of-bitches":** Scoblic, *U.S. vs. Them,* 147.

"taught me something": Fischer, *Reagan Reversal,* 136.

295 **"I believe there can":** Ibid., 135.

"So let us not be": Carroll, *House of War,* 287.

Gorbachev received: George Shultz, *Turmoil and Triumph: My Years as Secretary of State* (New York: Charles Scribner's Sons, 1993), 528–532.

296 **Weinberger in particular:** Stevenson, *SECDEF,* 60–61, 72–73.

Shultz and Weinberger: George J. Church, Bruce Van Voorst, and Johanna McGeary, "Force and Personality," *Time,* December 24, 1984.

297 **There was a convergence:** Stevenson, *SECDEF,* 69–70.

298 **The Weinberger Doctrine:** William J. Fulbright and Seth Tillman, "Weinberger Nondifferences," *New York Times,* December 9, 1984; Shultz, *Turmoil and Triumph,* 649–650.

Shultz believed: Church et al., "Force and Personality."

"If we got ourselves": Shultz, *Turmoil and Triumph,* 645.

"an erosion of control": Ibid., 725.

An ex-Marine: Church et al., "Force and Personality."

Weinberger refused appeals: Stevenson, *SECDEF*, 70.

300 **The VPK:** Brooks and Wohlforth, "Power, Globalization," 23.

The Red Army's: Hines et al., *Soviet Intentions*, vol. I, 7, 59–60.

It became the ultimate: Marshall I. Goldman, "Russia as an Economic Superpower: Fantasy or Possibility?," *Demokratizatsiya*, Winter 2003.

The VPK was also: Hines et al., *Soviet Intentions*, vol. I, 6–7.

301 **To subsidize demand:** Brooks and Wohlforth, "Power, Globalization," 19.

A CIA report: "Gorbachev's Economic Agenda: Promises, Potentials, and Pitfalls," An Intelligence Assessment, Directorate of Intelligence, Central Intelligence Agency, September 1985, 1, 3, 16, 17–18.

302 **"There is something":** Rhodes, *Arsenals of Folly*, 218.

303 **The chairman of Reagan's:** Michael Krepon and Geoffrey D. Peck, "Another Alarm on Soviet ABMs," *Bulletin of the Atomic Scientists* 41, no. 6 (June/July 1985): 34–35.

After struggling to match: Rhodes, *Arsenals of Folly*, 259.

Such a thin reed: Talbott, *Master of the Game*, 284–285.

304 **Huddling with their advisers:** Katrina Vanden Heuvel and Stephen F. Cohen, "Gorbachev on 1989," *The Nation*, November 16, 2009.

The exchanges during: For edited transcripts of the Geneva sessions as well as support documents, see "To the Geneva Summit: Perestroika and the Transformation of U.S.-Soviet Relations," National Security Archive Electronic Briefing Book No. 172, November 22, 2005, http://www.gwu.edu/~nsarchiv/NSAEBB/NSAEBB172/index.htm.

306 **It should come:** Talbott, *Master of the Game*, 190–191; Rhodes, *Arsenals of Folly*, 179–180.

In February 1983: Talbott, *Master of the Game*, 191–195; Rhodes, *Arsenals of Folly*, 158.

307 **Intoned the *New York Time*'s:** "Nuclear Facts, Science Fictions," *New York Times*, March 27, 1983.

308 **Kosta Tsipis:** Walter Isaacson, "Archive: Reagan for the Defense," *Time*, March 21, 2008; and Gregg Herken, *Cardinal Choices: Presidential Science Advising from the Atomic Bomb to SDI* (Palo Alto, CA: Stanford University Press, 2000), 214.

***Time* magazine:** "Defending Defense: Budget Battles and Star Wars" (Cover story), *Time*, April 4, 1983.

On January 15: Shultz, *Turmoil and Triumph*, 699.

309 **"a concrete program":** Rhodes, *Arsenals of Folly*, 218.

"Gorbachev surprisingly": Ibid., 221.

In mid-January: Shultz, *Turmoil and Triumph*, 700–701.

310 **Though neither man:** Rhodes, *Arsenals of Folly*, 230.

For Nitze, SDI: Talbott, *Master of the Game*, 213.

Just as he did: Ibid., 218.

311 **It was a theme:** Ibid., 235, 199–200.

That included the unreformed: Nicholas Thompson, *The Hawk and the Dove: Paul Nitze, George Kennan, and the History of the Cold War* (New York: Henry Holt, 2009), 156–157.

"more debilitating factor": Rhodes, *Arsenals of Folly*, 201.

312 **On July 18:** Ibid., 228, 231, 232–233, 235.

313 **There was a strict:** Shultz, *Turmoil and Triumph*, 756.

314 **Nitze declared it:** Ibid., 760–761

That included Japan: Martin Fackler, "Japanese Split on Exposing Secret Pacts with U.S.," *New York Times*, February 8, 2010.

At 7:10 a.m.: Shultz, *Turmoil and Triumph*, 764–765, 768.

315 **There would be no deal:** Rhodes, *Arsenals of Folly*, 261–263, 269.

316 **"You are independent":** Vanden Heuvel and Cohen, "Gorbachev on 1989."

At the Twenty-ninth Party: Rhodes, *Arsenals of Folly*, 273–274, 280, 281–282.

318 **Gorbachev's "gambit":** "The Gorbachev Challenge," *Time*, December 19, 1988.

319 **"enemy deprivation syndrome":** Interview with the author, July 14, 2010.

13: Reformation

320 **"The question is":** Christopher M. Bourne, "Unintended Consequences of the Goldwater-Nichols Act," *Joint Force Quarterly* 18 (Spring 1998): 100.

"When people came": Vanden Heuvel and Cohen, "Gorbachev on 1989."

In *Superpower Illusions*: Michael Mandelbaum, "Overpowered? Questioning the Wisdom of American Restraint," *Foreign Affairs*, May/June 2010.

322 **Though Iran had suffered:** Colin Powell, with Joseph E. Persico, *My American Journey* (New York: Random House, 1995), 459.

One could argue: James Bradley, "Diplomacy That Will Live in Infamy," *New York Times,* December 5, 2009.

323 **Later that month:** Said Aburish, *Saddam Hussein: The Politics of Revenge* (New York: Bloomsbury, 2000), 270–283.

What emboldened: Ibid., 282.

On July 31: Ibid., 278–279.

324 **The aides who advised:** Daalder and Destler, *In the Shadow of the Oval Office*, 196–197.

Yet his privileged background: Maureen Dowd, "Liberties; Fighting the Wimp Factor," *New York Times*, February 16, 2000; "George Bush: Fighting the Wimp Factor," *Newsweek,* October 19, 1987.

325 **The invasion of:** "Bush's Truman Show," *Newsweek*, February 12, 2007.

Though not given: Daalder and Destler, *In the Shadow of the Oval Office*, 199–200.

This gave him: Powell, *My American Journey*, 489.

At the urging: Gates, *From the Shadows*, 497–499.

326 **Indeed, even after:** Michael R. Gordon, "Hussein Wanted Soviets to Head Off U.S. in 1991," *New York Times*, January 20, 2011.
  "coldly implacable toward": Gates, *From the Shadows*, 499.
  "The howling in the Congress": Powell, *My American Journey*, 489.
327 **The objectives of:** Daalder and Destler, *In the Shadow of the Oval Office*, 200.
  "For a range of reasons": Powell, *My American Journey*, 529.
  "There was no war termination": Interview with Chas Freeman, July 14, 2010.
328 **Similarly, the White House:** Aburish, *Saddam Hussein*, 307–312.
329 **The decision by the Saudi:** Peter Bergen, *The Osama bin Laden I Know: An Oral History of Al Qaeda's Leader* (New York: Free Press, 2006), 112.
  According to Abu Mousab: Ibid., 116.
  In his August: "Bin Laden's Fatwa," A Newshour with Jim Lehrer Transcript, http://www.pbs.org/newshour/terrorism/international/fatwa_1996.html.
330 **"The open-ended presence":** Daalder and Destler, *In the Shadow of the Oval Office*, 203.
331 **In its March 11:** Stanley Cloud, "The Home Front: Exorcising an Old Demon," *Time*, March 11, 1991.
332 **"He sent back":** Karen DeYoung, *Soldier: The Life of Colin Powell* (New York: Alfred A. Knopf, 2006), 203.
  For an adoring press: Ibid., 194–198.
  Nor did the public linger: Alexander Simon, "The Patriot Missile: Performance in the Gulf War Reviewed," Center for Defense Information, July 15, 1996, http://www.cdi.org/issues/bmd/patriot.html.
333 **By the end of the decade:** Robin Toner, "Trust in Military Heightens Among Baby Boomers' Children," *New York Times*, May 27, 2003.
  President Bush had: Powell, *My American Journey*, 437–438.
334 **"the crazies":** Jacob Heilbrunn, *They Knew They Were Right: The Rise of the Neocons* (New York: Doubleday, 2008), 194.
335 **Perhaps Khalilzad's most:** Mann, *Rise of the Vulcans*, 209–213.
336 **The result is:** Secretary of Defense Dick Cheney, "Defense Strategy for the 1990s: The Regional Defense Strategy," January 1993, http://www.gwu.edu/~nsarchiv/nukevault/ebb245/doc15.pdf. This declassified version of January 1993 is very close to the "Defense Planning Guidance" of April 16, 1992, which remains partially classified.
338 **the Pentagon had no intention:** Author's interview with George Laudato, June 15, 2009.
  Over the years: Zoltan Grossman, "Imperial Footprint: America's Foreign Military Bases," *Global Dialogue* (Winter/Spring 2009).
339 **An April 1997:** Ron Martz, "Fewer Resources Straining Missions," *Atlanta Constitution*, April 24, 1997.
  Years later, Khalilzad: Mann, *Rise of the Vulcans*, 213.
  While neoconservatives labored: Melvin A. Goodman, "The Urgent Need

to Demilitarize the National Security State," *Truthout*, October 20, 2009, http://www.truth-out.org/1020095.

340 **Operation Eagle Claw:** Barry M. Goldwater, with Jack Casserly, *Goldwater* (New York: Doubleday, 1988), 342–350. See also Gordon Nathaniel Lederman, *Reorganizing the Joint Chiefs of Staff: The Goldwater Act of 1986* (Westport, CT: Greenwood Press, 1999), 31.

341 **It was trench warfare:** Goldwater, *Goldwater*, 341–355.
However virulent: Ibid., 357.

342 **As the president's:** Bourne, "Unintended Consequences," 103
In his memoirs: Powell, *My American Journey*, 466.

343 **"Because of Goldwater-Nichols":** Bourne, "Unintended Consequences," 103.
One of his first acts: Powell, *My American Journey*, 447.
The next day: Ibid., 439–440.

344 **The new JCS Chairman:** DeYoung, *Soldier*, 186.
Powell would always insist: Ibid., 396.
When Powell told: Ibid., 190–191.
Queried about this: Timothy Noah, "Elizabeth Cheney, Deferment Baby: How Dick Cheney Dodged the Vietnam Draft," *Slate*, March 18, 2004.

14: The Weight of Peace

348 **In 1988, with:** Author's interview with George Withers, senior fellow at the Washington Office on Latin America, Washington, D.C., May 28, 2009.
As SOUTHCOM: George Withers et al., "Ready, Aim, Foreign Policy: How the Pentagon's role in foreign policy is growing, and why Congress—and the American public—should be worried," Center for International Policy, the Latin America Working Group Education Fund, and the Washington Office on Latin America, March 2008, http://www.lawg.org/storage/documents/ready%20aim.pdf.

349 **The war on drugs:** Greg Grandin, "Muscling Latin America," *The Nation*, January 21, 2010.
"Southern Command should not": Withers et al., "Ready, Aim, Foreign Policy."

350 **According to the president's:** "President Bush's Letter of Instruction to Chiefs of Mission," Generic Letter of Instructions to Chiefs of Mission, facsimile dated October 4, 2004.
"When I was in Yemen": Interview with the author, Washington, D.C., October 3, 2008.

351 **"When we spoke":** Interview with the author, Washington, D.C., May 8, 2010.

352 **The feeble response:** Samantha Power, "Bystanders to Genocide," *Atlantic Monthly*, September 2001.

353 **When tensions erupted:** Interview with the author, Seoul, South Korea, 1994.

As a presidential candidate: George Will, "A Dog in That Fight?," *Newsweek*, June 12, 1995.

354 **At one point:** Powell, *My American Journey*, 576–577.

355 **She distinguished herself:** Walter Isaacson, "Madeleine's War," *Time*, October 10, 1999.

For the military's new: Andrew J. Bacevich, "Policing Utopia: The Military Imperatives of Globalization," *National Interest*, no 56 (Summer 1999):5.

"Business tends": Ibid., 10.

"The most obvious": Robert Jervis, "International Primacy: Is the Game Worth the Candle?" *International Security* 17, no. 4 (Spring 1993), 59.

356 **Her declaration of:** H. W. Brands, *Woodrow Wilson* (New York: Times Books, 2003), 76.

On the eve of the Kosovo: Isaacson, "Madeleine's War."

357 **Albright's peremptory expansion:** Ibid.; Dana Priest, *The Mission: Waging War and Keeping Peace with America's Military* (New York: W. W. Norton & Co., 2003), 54–55.

358 **Clark sweetened:** Peter J. Boyer, "General Clark's Battles," *The New Yorker*, November 17, 2003.

359 **"a provocation, an excuse":** Kissinger quoted in an interview with Boris Johnson, published in the *Daily Telegraph*, June 28, 1999.

With the credibility: Priest, *The Mission*, 249.

Later that month: Boyer, "General Clark's Battles.

360 **During his first:** Priest, *The Mission*, 257.

"We have to consider": Author's interview with Stefano Gatti, NATO Headquarters, Brussels, April 27, 1999.

361 **European diplomats:** Stephen Glain, "NATO May Consider New Surveillance System," *Wall Street Journal*, May 19, 1999.

Little had changed: Author's interview with Bruce Bach, NATO Headquarters, Brussels, April 29, 1999.

Indeed, precisely because: Author's interview with General Edward Looney, Washington, DC, 1995.

The Defence Capabilities: Author's interview with Paul Sauvereux, NATO Headquarters, Brussels, April 30, 1999.

"When it's all said": Author's interview with Colonel Donald Baker, NATO Headquarters, Brussels, April 27, 1999.

362 **It should be noted:** Ralph DeGennaro and William D. Hartung, "NATO Costs to U.S. Could Skyrocket," *Baltimore Sun*, March 8, 1998.

A pliant Congress: Ibid.

The Pentagon did: William Hartung, "Pentagon Welfare: The Corporate Campaign for NATO Expansion," *Multinational Monitor*, March 1998.

Pro-enlargement demagogues: Lind, *American Way of Strategy*, 134–136.

363 **Boeing's bagman:** Hartung, "Pentagon Welfare."

"Their offers have to be": Interview with the author, April 30, 1999.

364 **A UN commission:** For a summary of the Independent International Commission on Kosovo, see http://www.reliefweb.int/rw/rwb.nsf/db900SID/ACOS-64D8GD?OpenDocument.

In lieu of adequately: Priest, *The Mission*, 390–391.

In September 2010: Peter Green, "Balkans Need U.S. Troops in Kosovo, Berisha Says," *Bloomberg*, September 28, 2010.

On December 16: Doreen Carvajal and Marlise Simons, "Report Names Kosovo Leader as Crime Boss," *New York Times*, December 16, 2010.

366 **Helms served five terms:** William A. Link, *Righteous Warrior: Jesse Helms and the Rise of Modern Conservatism* (New York: St. Martin's Press, 2008), 11, 12, 15.

The other Jesse: Ibid., 75–76, 375.

367 **"'turncoat southerner'":** David Brinkley, *David Brinkley: A Memoir* (New York: Alfred A. Knopf, 1995), 89–90.

He railed against: Link, *Righteous Warrior*, 206, 247–250.

It was at the dawn: Ibid., 241.

368 **Helms wasted no time:** Ibid., 341.

As the Foreign Relations: Ibid., 426.

370 **"It was an effort":** Author's phone interview with Brian Atwood, June 24, 2010.

The dispute over: Link, *Righteous Warrior*, 426–427, 433–435.

15: DENOUEMENT

372 **"Our responsibility":** Charles Babington, "Bush: 'U.S. Must Rid the World of Evil,'" *Washington Post*, September 14, 2001.

373 **While it suited:** Thomas Friedman, "Foreign Affairs Big Mac I," *New York Times*, December 8, 1996.

Like many presidents: Weiner, *Legacy of Ashes*, 469, 474, 475; Cole, *Ghost Wars*, 526, 531.

374 **Even before the *Cole*:** Vincent J. Goulding, "From Chancellorsville to Kosovo, Forgetting the Art of War," *Parameters* 30 (Summer 2000): 4–18.

Only half of eligible: United States Elections Project, Department of Public and International Affairs, George Mason University, http://elections.gmu.edu/voter_turnout.htm.

375 **"We thought we were going":** Cullen Murphy and Todd S. Purdum, "Farewell to All That," *Vanity Fair*, February 2009, 90.

The Hainan: DeYoung, *Soldier*, 329–331.

377 **The matter of:** Daalder and Destler, *In the Shadow of the Oval Office*, 262–267.

Despite efforts from: "Bin Laden's Fatwa"; Bergen, *The Osama bin Laden I Know*, 164–166.

Bin Laden's animus: Bergen, *The Osama bin Laden I Know*, 181–183.

378 **On the night of September 20:** George W. Bush, Address to a Joint Session of
Congress Following 9/11 Attacks, delivered on September 20, 2001, http://
www.americanrhetoric.com/speeches/gwbush911jointsessionspeech.htm.
Only three weeks: Stephen Schlesinger, "Bush's Low Ratings Reflect Pre-
9/11 Views," *New York Observer*, April 23, 2006.

379 **"Rumsfeld came over":** Murphy and Purdum, "Farewell to All That," 96.
By late November: Daalder and Destler, *In the Shadow of the Oval Office*, 271.

380 **Nor were Bush:** Murphy and Purdum, "Farewell to All That," 97.
Under Bush, the Pentagon's: Winslow Wheeler, "Pentagon Reform: If Not
Now, When? If Not This Crowd, Who?" April 2009, http://pogoarchives.
org/m/ns/wheeler-presentation-20090219.pdf.

381 **For most Americans:** Murphy and Purdum, "Farewell to All That," 97.

382 **In March 2010:** Fred Kaplan, "Has Obama Turned Against Israel?" *Slate*,
March 17, 2010. See also Mark Perry, "The Petraeus briefing: Biden's embar-
rassment is not the whole story," ForeignPolicy.com, March 13, 2010.
"The neocons who wanted": Interview with the author, May 18, 2010.

383 **"the chances for a resolution":** Comments made by Richard Perle in a
debate with European Green Party leader Daniel Cohn-Bendit, "Blessed
Are the Warmakers?" ForeignPolicy.com, May 1, 2003.
On July 10: Thomas E. Ricks, "Briefing Depicted Saudis as Enemies,"
Washington Post, August 6, 2002; Akiva Eldar, "Perles of Wisdom for the
Feithful," *Ha'aretz*, October 1, 2002.

384 **Colin Powell did:** Bill Keller, "The World According to Colin Powell," *New
York Times Magazine*, November 25, 2001.
On August 5: Bob Woodward, *Plan of Attack* (New York: Simon & Schuster,
2004), 150.
The vice president: Daalder and Destler, *In the Shadow of the Oval Office*, 275.

385 **"Rice and . . . Hadley":** Ibid., 277.
"I report to": Ibid., 258.
On one occasion: Bradley Graham, "Decline and Fall: Rumsfeld's Dra-
matic End," *Washington Post Sunday Magazine*, June 14, 2009.

386 **He dismissed Cold War–era:** "Rumsfeld Kills Crusader Artillery Program,"
USA Today, May 8, 2002.

387 **Only seven months:** Stevenson, *SECDEF*, 166–167.
"skilled full-time": Kissinger, *Years of Renewal*, 175.
On September 10: Stevenson, *SECDEF*, 169.
The same group: Ibid., 170.
Relations between the two men: Priest, *The Mission*, 23–24.
In January 1998: Author's interview with Anthony Zinni.

388 **Less than a month:** Stevenson, *SECDEF*, 176.
Asked by Bush: Daalder and Destler, *In the Shadow of the Oval Office*, 274.

389 **As early as:** Murphy and Purdum, "Farewell to All That," 100, 148.

It is a measure: "Rummy and His Generals: An AFJ Routable on the State of American Civil-Military Relations," *Armed Forces Journal*, June 2006.

"Rumsfeld's continuous": Stevenson, *SECDEF*, 172.

Taking its cue: Fulton Armstrong and Thomas Powers, "The CIA and WMDs: The Damning Evidence," *New York Review of Books* 57, no. 13 (August 19, 2010), 53.

They managed to find: Lauren Johnston, "Iraqi Drones Not for WMD," *Associated Press*, August 24, 2003.

390   **Crucially, they also:** Armstrong and Powers, "The CIA and WMDs," 53.

391   **While Rumsfeld convened:** "New State Department Releases on the 'Future of Iraq' Project," National Security Archive Electronic Briefing Book No. 198, September 1, 2006, http://www.gwu.edu/~nsarchiv/NSAEBB/NSAEBB198/index.htm.

Ironically, and unknown: Author's interview with Anthony Zinni.

In addition to: Author's interview with Ryan Crocker, Washington, DC, August 17, 2004.

392   **The group of eight:** Karen DeYoung and Peter Slevin, "Pentagon, State Spar on Team to Run Iraq; Rumsfeld Rejects State Dept. Choices," *Washington Post*, April 1, 2003.

For team member: Author's interview with Kenneth Keith, Washington, DC, July 6, 2004.

393   **Prior to the invasion:** Author's interview with a former U.S. ambassador, Washington, DC, October 3, 2008.

"The plans were": Author's interview with Sandra Mitchell, Washington, DC, April 25, 2003.

When Richard Walden: Author's phone interview with Richard Walden, April 18, 2003.

394   **By late summer:** Author's interview with a senior U.S. diplomat, Washington, DC, July 23, 2004.

While operating in Iraq: Author's interview with Walden.

395   **David Kay:** "New State Department Releases on the 'Future of Iraq' Project."

397   **Such broad authority:** Department of Defense Directive No. 3000.5, November 28, 2005.

398   **Annoyed at its dependence:** Walter Pincus, "How Foreign Policy Functions Shifted to the Pentagon," *Washington Post*, August 4, 2008.

An April 2010: United States Government Accountability Office, *DOD and State Need to Improve Sustainment Planning and Monitoring and Evaluation for Section 1206 and 1207 Assistance Programs*, GAO-10-431 (Washington, DC: April 15, 2010).

In August 2009: Pincus, "How Foreign Policy Functions Shifted."

Other recipients of 1206: Editorial, "In Foreign Territory," *New York Times*, June 12, 2006.

399 **In May 2008:** Author's interview with George Withers, Washington, DC, May 28, 2009.

The Defense Security: Fawzia Sheikh, "DSCA Revamping DOD Manual's Humanitarian Assistance Guidance," *Inside the Pentagon*, April 23, 2009.

In January 2009: Sebastian Sprenger, "Joint Staff Paper Predicts Decade-Long Interagency Shortfalls," *Inside the Pentagon*, January 29, 2009.

In February 2009: Fawzia Sheikh, "DOD Official Urges Removing Hurdles to Cooperation in Stability Ops," *Inside the Pentagon*, February 5, 2009.

That April: Carlos Muñoz, "Pentagon Debates Strategy for Bolstering Future Stability Operations," *Inside the Pentagon*, April 9, 2009; Christopher J. Castelli, "Pentagon Conducts Policy Review on Foreign Assistance Authorities," *Inside the Pentagon*, April 16, 2009.

A month later: Sebastian Sprenger, "DOD Oversight of '1206' Program Moves to Special Ops Office," *Inside the Pentagon*, May 14, 2009.

400 **What began as:** Rebecca Williams, "Section 1206 and FMF: A Global View," *The Will and the Wallet* (Blog of the Stimson Center's Budgeting for Foreign Affairs and Defense Program), May 5, 2010, http://thewillandthewallet.org/2010/05/05/section-1206-and-fmf-a-global-view/.

By the end: Stewart Patrick and Kaysie Brown, *The Pentagon and Global Development: Making Sense of the DOD's Expanding Role* (Washington, DC: Center for Global Development, November 2007), 4.

"In the Dominican": Author's interview, May 22, 2009.

In a seminal June 2008 study: Reuben E. Brigety II, *Humanity as a Weapon of War: Sustainable Security and the Role of the U.S. Military* (Washington, DC: Center for American Progress, June 2008).

401 **"To the extent":** Author's interview with George Rupp, September 10, 2008.

In July 2003: Agency Coordinating Body for Afghan Relief (ACBAR), "ACBAR Policy Brief: "NGO Position Paper Concerning the Provisional Reconstruction Teams" (Kabul: ACBAR, 2003), http://www.care.org/newsroom/specialreports/afghanistan/01152003_ngorec.pdf.

In a 2003 study: Eric James, "Two Steps Back: Relearning the Humanitarian-Military Lessons Learned in Afghanistan and Iraq," *Journal of Humanitarian Assistance*, October 2003.

To be fair: Ken Dilanian, "Short-Staffed USAID Tries to Keep Pace," *USA Today*, February 2, 2009.

402 **While a senator:** Pincus, "How Foreign Policy Functions Shifted."

Lugar was concerned: "Embassies as Command Posts in the Anti-Terror Campaign," a report to members of the Committee on Foreign Relations, United States Senate, 109th Congress, December 15, 2006, 2.

403 **The report disparages:** Ibid., 2, 4.

The ambassador in Chad . . . to accommodate them: Katherine McIntire

Peters, "U.S. Counterterrorism Efforts Flounder in North Africa, GAO Says," *Government Executive*, August 5, 2008.

In 2003, then CENTCOM: Author's interview with Edward Gnehm, Washington, DC, October 3, 2008.

404 **In March 2009:** Rick Maze, "Gates Lobbies for More Funds—For State," ArmyTimes.com, March 30, 2009.

In January 2009: Fawzia Sheikh, "Joint Staff, USAID Pick Five Countries for Bid to Prevent Crisis," *Inside the Pentagon*, January 22, 2009.

CONCLUSION

407 **The founding fathers:** Alexander Hamilton, "Federalist No. 8: Consequences of Wars Between States," in *The Federalist: The Famous Papers on the Principles of American Government*, Benjamin F. Wright, ed. (New York: Barnes & Noble, 2004), 122–123.

Since the collapse of the Soviet Union: Leslie H. Gelb, *Power Rules: How Common Sense Can Rescue American Foreign Policy* (New York: HarperCollins, 2009), 161–162.

409 **Its procurement budget:** Winslow Wheeler, "The New Pentagon Budget: Paying Even More; Still Buying Less," Military.com, January 29, 2010, http://www.military.com/opinion/0,15202,209782,00.html.

The Pentagon in 2010: Inspector General of the United States Department of Defense, "Summary of DOD Office of Inspector General Audits of Financial Management," October 19, 2009.

410 **A year later:** Dana Hedgpeth, "GAO Blasts Weapons Budget," *Washington Post*, April 2, 2008.

In 2009, lawmakers: Christopher Drew, "$296 Billion in Overruns in U.S. Weapons Programs," *New York Times*, March 31, 2009.

411 **Having won:** Jonathan Alter, "Secrets from Inside the Obama War Room," *Newsweek*, May 15, 2010.

412 **Just weeks after:** Daniel Dombey and Matthew Green, "U.S. Focuses on 2014 Afghan Handover," *Financial Times*, December 16, 2010.

From 2001 to 2010: John Liang, "Defense Department IG 'Refocusing' Audit Priorities," *Inside the Pentagon*, September 16, 2010.

413 **In response to a 2010:** Josh Rogin, May 24, 2010 (6:02 p.m.), "Mullen Goes to Bat for State Department Budget," *The Cable*, http://thecable.foreignpolicy.com/posts/2010/05/24/mullen_goes_to_bat_for_state_department_budget.

414 **The number of State:** J. Anthony Holmes, "Where Are the Civilians? How to Rebuild the U.S. Foreign Service," *Foreign Affairs* 88, no. 1 (January/February 2009): 151

The State Department's: Susan R. Johnson, "Making Dissent Meaningful Again," *Foreign Service Journal*, February 2010.

415 **In a February:** Ken Dilanian, "Short-Staffed USAID Tries to Keep Pace," *USA Today*, February 2, 2009.

An early draft: John T. Bennett, "What the Pentagon's QDR Left Out," *DefenseNews*, February 22, 2010.

416 **In 2008 it launched:** Megan E. Garcia, "Driving Coordination: An Evaluation of the U.S. Agency for International Development's Office of Military Affairs," May 3, 2010, http://pdf.usaid.gov/pdf_docs/PCAAC062.pdf.

In 2009 the White House: Thom Shanker, "G.I.'s to Fill Civilian Gap to Rebuild Afghanistan," *Washington Post*, April 23, 2009.

Meanwhile, efforts: Holmes, "Where Are the Civilians?," 155.

The aforementioned QDR: United States Department of Defense, *Quadrennial Defense Review Report*, February 2010, viii, x, 15.

417 **Despite a significant:** Seymour Hersh, "The Online Threat," *The New Yorker*, November 1, 2010.

418 **That same year:** Lind, *American Way of Strategy*, 137.

A U.S. base: Ibid., 142–146.

At the same time: Koohan Paik, "Living at the 'Tip of the Spear,'" *The Nation*, May 30, 2010.

Bibliography

Books

Abella, Alex. *Soldiers of Reason: The RAND Corporation and the Rise of the American Empire*. Orlando, FL: Houghton Mifflin Harcourt, 2008.

Aburish, Said. *Saddam Hussein: The Politics of Revenge*. New York: Bloomsbury, 2000.

Acheson, Dean. *Present at the Creation: My Years at the State Department*. New York: W. W. Norton & Company, 1969.

Alsop, Joseph P., with Adam Platt. *I've Seen the Best of It: Memoirs*. New York: W. W. Norton, 1992.

Ambrose, Stephen. *Eisenhower: The President*. New York: Simon & Schuster, 1984.

———. *Nixon: The Triumph of a Politician, 1962–1972*. New York: Simon & Schuster, 1989.

Bacevich, Andrew J. *The New American Militarism: How Americans Are Seduced by War*. New York: Oxford University Press, 2005.

Ball, George. *The Past Has Another Pattern: Memoirs*. New York: W. W. Norton & Co., 1982.

Barrett, Roby C. *The Greater Middle East and the Cold War: U.S. Foreign Policy Under Eisenhower and Kennedy*. London: I. B. Tauris, 2007.

Bergen, Peter. *The Osama bin Laden I Know: An Oral History of al Qaeda's Leader*. New York: Free Press, 2006.

Bird, Kai, and Martin J. Sherwin. *American Prometheus: The Triumph and Tragedy of J. Robert Oppenheimer*. New York: Alfred A. Knopf, 2005.

Blair, Clay. *The Forgotten War: America in Korea 1950–1953*. New York: Doubleday, 1987.

Bowles, Chester. *Promises to Keep: My Years in Public Service 1941–1969*. New York: Harper & Row Publishers, 1971.

Brands, H. W. *Woodrow Wilson*. New York: Times Books, 2003.

Brinkley, David. *David Brinkley: A Memoir*. New York: Alfred A. Knopf, 1995.

Bundy, William. *A Tangled Web: The Making of Foreign Policy in the Nixon Presidency*. New York: Hill and Wang, 1998.

Carroll, James. *House of War: The Pentagon and the Disastrous Rise of American Power*. New York: Houghton Mifflin Company, 2006.

Chace, James. *Acheson: The Secretary of State Who Created the World.* New York: Simon & Schuster, 1998.

Close, David. *The Origins of the Greek Civil War.* London: Longman, 1995.

Coffey, Thomas M. *Iron Eagle: The Turbulent Life of General Curtis LeMay.* New York: Crown Publishers, 1986.

Coll, Steve. *Ghost Wars: The Secret History of the CIA, Afghanistan, and Bin Laden, from the Soviet Invasion to September 10, 2001.* New York: Penguin Press, 2004.

Cumings, Bruce. *The Origins of the Korean War: The Roaring of the Cataract, 1947–1950.* Vol. 2. Princeton, NJ: Princeton University Press, 1990.

Daalder, Ivo H., and I. M. Destler. *In the Shadow of the Oval Office: Profiles of the National Security Advisers and the Presidents They Served from JFK to George W. Bush.* New York: Simon & Schuster, 2009.

Dallek, Robert. *Nixon and Kissinger: Partners in Power.* New York: HarperCollins, 2007.

———. *An Unfinished Life: John F. Kennedy, 1917–1963.* Boston: Little, Brown, 2003.

DeYoung, Karen. *Soldier: The Life of Colin Powell.* New York: Alfred A. Knopf, 2006.

Dower, John W. *Embracing Defeat: Japan in the Wake of World War II.* New York: W. W. Norton & Company, 1990.

Eisenhower, Dwight. *The White House Years: Waging Peace, 1956–1961.* New York: Doubleday, 1965.

Fischer, Beth A. *The Reagan Reversal: Foreign Policy and the End of the Cold War.* Columbia, MO: University of Missouri Press, 1997.

Fischer, Louis. *The Life of Lenin.* New York: Harper & Row, 1964.

Gaddis, John Lewis. *We Now Know: Rethinking Cold War History.* Oxford: Clarendon Press, 1997.

Gates, Robert M. *From the Shadows: The Ultimate Insider's Story of Five Presidents and How They Won the Cold War.* New York: Simon & Schuster, 1996.

Gelb, Leslie H. *Power Rules: How Common Sense Can Rescue American Foreign Policy.* New York: HarperCollins, 2009.

Gervasi, Tom. *The Myth of Soviet Military Supremacy.* New York: Harper & Row, 1986.

Goldwater, Barry M. *Goldwater.* New York: Doubleday, 1988.

Halberstam, David. *The Best and the Brightest.* New York: Random House, 1972.

Hamilton, Alexander. "Federalist No. 8: Consequences of Wars Between States." In *The Federalist: The Famous Papers on the Principles of American Government,* edited by Benjamin F. Wright. New York: Barnes & Noble, 2004.

Han, Suyin. *Eldest Son: Zhou Enlai and the Making of Modern China, 1898–1976.* London: Pimlico, 1994.

Harvey, Robert. *Shogun: General MacArthur, Emperor Hirohito and the Drama of Modern Japan*. Woodstock, NY: Overlook Press, 2006.

Haynes, John Earl, and Harry Klehr. *Venona: Decoding Espionage in America*. New Haven, CT: Yale University Press, 2000.

Heilbrunn, Jacob. *They Knew They Were Right: The Rise of the Neocons*. New York: Doubleday, 2008.

Herman, Arthur. *Joseph McCarthy: Reexamining the Life and Legacy of America's Most Hated Senator*. New York: Free Press, 1999.

Herring, George, ed. *The Pentagon Papers*. New York: McGraw-Hill, 1993.

Hunt, Richard A. *Pacification: The American Struggle for Vietnam's Hearts and Minds*. Boulder, CO: Westview Press, 1995.

International Institute for Strategic Studies. *The Military Balance 2011: The Annual Assessment of Global Military Capabilities and Defence Economics*. London: Routledge, 2011.

Isaacson, Walter. *Kissinger: A Biography*. New York: Simon & Schuster, 1992.

Isaacson, Walter, and Evan Thomas. *The Wise Men: Six Friends and the World They Made*. New York: Simon & Schuster, 1986.

Kaplan, Robert. *Balkan Ghosts: A Journey Through History*. New York: St. Martin's Press, 1993.

Karnow, Stanley. *Vietnam: A History*. New York: Viking Press, 1983.

Kaufman, Robert G. *Henry M. Jackson: A Life in Politics*. Seattle; London: University of Washington Press, 2000.

Kennan, George F. *Memoirs: 1925–1950*. Boston: Little, Brown and Company, 1967.

Khan, E. J., Jr. *The China Hands: America's Foreign Service Officers and What Befell Them*. New York: Viking Press, 1975.

Kinzer, Stephen. *Overthrow: America's Century of Regime Change from Hawaii to Iraq*. New York: Times Books, Henry Holt and Company, 2006.

Kissinger, Henry A. *White House Years*. Boston: Little, Brown and Company, 1979.

———. *A World Restored: Metternich, Castlereagh, and the Problems of Peace, 1812–22*. Boston: Houghton Mifflin Co., 1957.

———. *Years of Renewal*. New York: Simon & Schuster, 1999.

Kitfield, James. *Prodigal Soldiers: How the Generation of Officers Born in Vietnam Revolutionized the American Style of War*. New York: Simon & Schuster, 1995.

Lederman, Gordon Nathaniel. *Reorganizing the Joint Chiefs of Staff: The Goldwater Act of 1986*. Westport, CT: Greenwood Press, 1999.

Lilly, James R. *China Hands: Nine Decades of Adventure, Espionage, and Diplomacy in Asia*. New York: PublicAffairs, 2004.

Lind, Michael. *The American Way of Strategy: U.S. Foreign Policy and the American Way of Life*. New York: Oxford University Press, 2006.

Link, William A. *Righteous Warrior: Jesse Helms and the Rise of Modern Conservatism*. New York: St. Martin's Press, 2008.

Manchester, William. *American Caesar: Douglas MacArthur, 1880–1964*. New York: Little, Brown and Company, 1978.

Mann, James. *Rise of the Vulcans: The History of Bush's War Cabinet*. New York: Viking, 2004.

Martin, Bradley K. *Under the Loving Care of the Fatherly Leader: North Korea and the Kim Dynasty*. New York: St. Martin's Griffin/Thomas Dunne Books, 2006.

Matlock, Jack, Jr. *Superpower Illusions: How Myths and False Ideologies Led America Astray – and How to Return to Reality*. New Haven, CT: Yale University Press, 2010.

May, Ernest, ed. *American Cold War Strategy: Interpreting NSC-68*. Boston, New York: Bedford/St. Martin's, 1993.

May, Gary. *China Scapegoat: The Diplomatic Ordeal of John Carter Vincent*. Washington, DC: New Republic Books, 1979.

McCullough, David. *Truman*. New York: Simon & Schuster, 1992.

McMaster, H. R. *Dereliction of Duty: Lyndon Johnson, Robert McNamara, the Joint Chiefs of Staff, and the Lies That Led to Vietnam*. New York: HarperCollins, 1997.

Merk, Frederick. *Manifest Destiny and Mission in American History: A Reinterpretation*. Cambridge, MA: Harvard University Press, 1963.

Milne, David. *American Rasputin: Walt Rostow and the Vietnam Era*. New York: Hill and Wang, 2008.

Morgan, Ted. *Reds: McCarthyism in Twentieth-Century America*. New York: Random House, 2003.

Mosley, Leonard. *Dulles: A Biography of Eleanor, Allen, and John Foster Dulles and Their Family Network*. New York: Dial Press/James Wade, 1978.

Nixon, Richard, *RN: The Memoirs of Richard Nixon*. New York: Grosset & Dunlap, 1978.

Perlstein, Rick. *Nixonland: The Rise of a President and the Fracturing of America*. New York: Scribner, 2008.

Perry, Mark. *Partners in Command: George Marshall and Dwight Eisenhower in War and Peace*. New York: Penguin Press, 2007.

Pogue, Forrest C. *George C. Marshall: Education of a General, 1880–1939*. Vol. 1. New York: Viking, 1963.

———. *George C. Marshall: Ordeal and Hope, 1939–1942*. Vol. 2. New York: Viking, 1966.

———. *George C. Marshall: Organizer of Victory, 1943–1945*. Vol. 3. New York: Viking, 1973.

———. *George C. Marshall: Statesman, 1945–1959*. Vol. 4. New York: Viking, 1987.

Porch, Douglas. *The Path to Victory: The Mediterranean Theater in World War II*. New York: Farrar, Straus and Giroux, 2004.

Porter, Gareth. *Perils of Dominance: Imbalance of Power and the Road to War in Vietnam*. Berkeley, CA: University of California Press, 2005.

Powell, Colin, with Joseph E. Persico. *My American Journey.* New York: Random House, 1995.

Preston, Andrew. *The War Council: McGeorge Bundy, the NSC, and Vietnam.* Cambridge, MA: Harvard University Press, 2006.

Priest, Dana. *The Mission: Waging War and Keeping Peace with America's Military.* W. W. Norton & Co., New York, 2003.

Reagan, Ronald, and Richard W. Hubler. *Where's the Rest of Me? The Ronald Reagan Story.* New York: Van Rees Press, 1965.

Rhodes, Richard. *Arsenals of Folly: The Making of the Nuclear Arms Race.* New York: Alfred A. Knopf, 2008.

Rosenberg, David Alan. "The Origins of Overkill: Nuclear Weapons and American Strategy." In *The National Security: Its Theory and Practice, 1945–1960,* edited by Norman A. Graebner. New York: Oxford University Press, 1986.

Schaller, Michael. *The American Occupation of Japan: The Origins of the Cold War in Asia.* New York: Oxford University Press, 1985.

Schlesinger, Arthur M., Jr. *The Imperial Presidency.* Boston: Houghton Mifflin Company, 1973.

Scoblic, J. Peter. *U.S. vs. Them: Conservatism in the Age of Nuclear Terror.* New York: Viking, 2008.

Sheehan, Neil. *A Bright Shining Lie: John Paul Vann and America in Vietnam.* New York: Random House, 1988.

Shultz, George. *Turmoil and Triumph: My Years as Secretary of State.* New York: Charles Scribner's Sons, 1993.

Sorensen, Ted. *Counselor: A Life at the Edge of History.* New York: HarperCollins, 2008.

Sorley, Lewis. *Thunderbolt: From the Battle of the Bulge to Vietnam and Beyond: General Creighton Abrams and the Army of His Times.* New York: Simon & Schuster, 1992.

Steele, Ronald. *Walter Lippmann and the American Century.* Boston: Little, Brown and Company, 1980.

Stevenson, Charles A. *SECDEF: The Nearly Impossible Job of Secretary of Defense.* Washington, DC: Potomac Books, 2006.

Stimson, Henry L., and McGeorge Bundy. *On Active Service in Peace and War.* New York: Harper & Brothers Publishers, 1947.

Summers, Harry G., Jr. *On Strategy: A Critical Analysis of the Vietnam War.* Novato, CA: Presidio Press, 1982.

Talbott, Strobe. *The Master of the Game: Paul Nitze and the Nuclear Peace.* New York: Alfred A. Knopf, 1988.

Tanenhaus, Sam. *Whittaker Chambers: A Biography.* New York: Random House, 1997.

Taubman, William. *Khrushchev: His Life and Times.* New York: W. W. Norton, 2003.

Thomas, Evan. *Robert Kennedy: His Life.* New York: Simon & Schuster, 2000.

Thompson, Nicholas. *The Hawk and the Dove: Paul Nitze, George Kennan, and the History of the Cold War.* New York: Henry Holt, 2009.

Tuchman, Barbara. *Stillwell and the American Experience in China, 1911–15.* New York: Macmillan Publishers, 1971.

Tucker, Nancy Bernkopf. *China Confidential: American Diplomats and Sino-American Relations, 1945–1996.* New York: Columbia University Press, 2011.

Van Atta, Dale. *With Honor: Melvin Laird in War, Peace and Politics.* Madison, WI: University of Wisconsin Press, 2008.

Vance, Cyrus. *Hard Choices: Critical Years in America's Foreign Policy.* New York: Simon & Schuster, 1983.

Weiner, Tim. *Legacy of Ashes: The History of the CIA.* New York: Doubleday, 2007.

Weisman, Alan. *Prince of Darkness: Richard Perle, the Kingdom, the Power and the End of Empire in America.* New York: Union Square Press, 2007.

White, Theodore. *America in Search of Itself: The Making of the President, 1956–1980.* New York: Harper & Row, 1982.

Williams, William Appleman. *The Tragedy of American Diplomacy.* Cleveland; New York: World Publishing Company, 1959.

Yergin, Daniel. *Shattered Peace: The Origins of the Cold War and the National Security State.* London: A. Deutsch, 1978.

Zhai, Qiang. *China and the Vietnam Wars, 1950–1975.* Chapel Hill, NC: University of North Carolina Press, 2000.

Articles and Other Materials

Agency Coordinating Body for Afghan Relief. "NGO Position Paper Concerning the Provisional Reconstruction Teams." ACBAR Policy Brief, 2009, http://www.care.org/newsroom/specialreports/afghanistan/01152003_ngorec.pdf.

Alter, Jonathan. "Secrets from Inside the Obama War Room." *Newsweek*, May 15, 2010.

Armstrong, Fulton, and Thomas Powers. "The CIA and WMDs: The Damning Evidence." *New York Review of Books*, August 19, 2010.

Arneston, R. Gordon. Oral History Interview [22]. Harry S. Truman Library. http://www.trumanlibrary.org/oralhist/arneston.htm (accessed March 5, 2009).

Babington, Charles. "Bush: 'U.S. Must Rid the World of Evil.'" *Washington Post*, September 14, 2001.

Bacevich, Andrew J. "Policing Utopia: The Military Imperatives of Globalization." *The National Interest*, no. 56 (Summer 1999): 5–13.

Bennett, John T. "What the Pentagon's QDR Left Out." *DefenseNews*, February 22, 2010.

"Bin Laden's Fatwa." *Newshour with Jim Lehrer* transcript, http://www.pbs.org/newshour/terrorism/international/fatwa_1996.html.

Bourne, Christopher. "Unintended Consequences of the Goldwater-Nicholas Act." *Joint Force Quarterly* 18 (Spring 1998): 99–108.

Boyer, Peter J. "General Clark's Battles." *The New Yorker*, November 17, 2003.

Brigety, Reuben E., II. *Humanity as a Weapon of War: Sustainable Security and the Role of the U.S. Military.* Washington, DC: Center for American Progress, June 2008.

Brooks, Stephen, and William C. Wohlforth. "Power, Globalization, and the End of the Cold War: Reevaluating a Landmark Case for Ideas." *International Security* 25, no. 3 (Winter 2000/01): 5–53.

Burr, William. "The 'Horror Strategy', and the Search for Limited Nuclear Options, 1969–1972." *Journal of Cold War Studies* 7, no. 3 (Summer 2005): 34–78.

"Bush's Truman Show." *Newsweek*, February 12, 2007.

Carvajal, Doreen, and Marlise Simons. "Report Names Kosovo Leader as Crime Boss." *New York Times*, December 16, 2010.

Castelli, Christopher J. "Pentagon Conducts Policy Review on Foreign Assistance Authorities." *Inside the Pentagon*, April 16, 2009.

Chace, James. "After Hiroshima: Sharing the Atom Bomb." *Foreign Affairs* 85, no. 1 (January/February 1996).

Chelimsky, Eleanor. "The U.S. Nuclear Triad: GAO's Evaluation of the Strategic Modernization Program." *Testimony Before the Committee on Governmental Affairs*, United States Senate, June 10, 1993.

Cheney, Secretary of Defense Dick. "Defense Strategy for the 1990s: The Regional Defense Strategy." January 1993, http://www.gwu.edu/~nsarchiv/nuke vault/ebb245/doc15.pdf.

Church, George J., Bruce Van Voorst, and Johanna McGeary. "Force and Personality." *Time*, December 24, 1984.

"CIA and the Vietnam Policymakers: Episode 2: 1963–1965: CIA Judgments on President Johnson's Decision to 'Go Big' in Vietnam." Center for the Study of Intelligence. Last updated July 7, 2008, https://www.cia.gov/library/ center-for-the-study-of-intelligence/csi-publications/books-and-mono graphs/cia-and-the-vietnam-policymakers-three-episodes-1962-1968/ epis2.html.

Clarke, Duncan. "Why State Can't Lead." *Foreign Policy* 66 (Spring 1987): 128–142.

Cloud, Stanley. "The Home Front: Exorcising an Old Demon." *Time*, March 11, 1991.

Cohn-Bendit, Daniel, and Richard Perle. "Blessed Are the Warmakers?" Foreign Policy.com, May 1, 2003.

Coker, Christopher. "Deadly Devices." *Times Literary Supplement*, July 10, 2007.

"The Creation of SIOP-62: More Evidence on the Origins of Overkill." In *A National Security Archive Electronic Briefing Book No. 130*, edited by William Burr. Washington, DC: George Washington University, July 13, 2004, http://www.gwu.edu/~nsarchiv/NSAEBB/NSAEBB130.

"Defending Defense: Budget Battles and Star Wars." *Time*, April 4, 1983.

DeGennaro, Ralph, and William D. Hartung. "NATO Costs to U.S. Could Skyrocket." *Baltimore Sun*, March 8, 1998.

Department of Defense Directive No. 3000.5. *Military Support for Stability, Security, Transition, and Reconstruction (SSTR) Operations*. November 28, 2005.

DeYoung, Karen, and Peter Slevin. "Pentagon, State Spar on Team to Run Iraq; Rumsfeld Rejects State Dept. Choices." *Washington Post*, April 1, 2003.

Dilanian, Ken. "Short-Staffed USAID Tries to Keep Pace." *USA Today*, February 2, 2009.

Directorate of Intelligence. "Gorbachev's Economic Agenda: Promises, Potentials, and Pitfalls." Central Intelligence Agency, September 1985.

Dobbs, Michael. "Lost in Enemy Airspace." *Vanity Fair* (June 2008): 142–149, 177–181.

Dombey, Daniel, and Matthew Green. "U.S. Focuses on 2014 Afghan Handover." *Financial Times*, December 16, 2010.

Dowd, Maureen. "Liberties; Fighting the Wimp Factor." *New York Times*, February 16, 2000.

Drew, Christopher. "$296 Billion in Overruns in U.S. Weapons Programs." *New York Times*, March 31, 2009.

Eldar, Akiva. "Perles of Wisdom for the Faithful." *Ha'aretz*, October 1, 2002.

Fackler, Martin. "Japanese Split on Exposing Secret Pacts with U.S." *New York Times*, February 8, 2010.

"First Declassification of Eisenhower's Instructions to Commanders Predelegating Nuclear Weapons Use, 1959–1960." In *A National Security Archive Electronic Briefing Book*, edited by William Burr. Washington, DC: George Washington University, May 18, 2001. Document 3, page 7, http://www.gwu.edu/~nsarchiv/NSAEBB/NSAEBB45/doc3.pdf.

Fischer, Benjamin B. *A Cold War Conundrum: The 1983 Soviet War Scare*. Washington, DC: Center for the Study of Intelligence, last updated July 7, 2008, https://www.cia.gov/library/center-for-the-study-of-intelligence/csi-publications/books-and-monographs/a-cold-war-conundrum/source.htm.

Friedman, Thomas. "Foreign Affairs Big Mac I." *New York Times*, December 8, 1996.

Fulbright, William J., and Seth Tillman. "Weinberger Nondifferences." *New York Times*, December 9, 1984.

Galbraith, James K., and Heather A. Purple. "Did the U.S. Military Plan a Nuclear First Strike for 1963?" *Notes on National Security Council Meeting*, July 20, 1961.

Garcia, Megan E. "Driving Coordination: An Evaluation of the U.S. Agency for International Development's Office of Military Affairs." Goldman School of Public Policy, University of California at Berkeley, May 3, 2010, http://pdf.usaid.gov/pdf_docs/PCAAC062.pdf.

Gibbs, David N. "Reassessing Soviet Motives for Invading Afghanistan: A Declassified History." *Critical Asian Studies* 38, no. 2 (June 2006): 239–263.

Glain, Stephen. "American Leviathan." *The Nation,* September 28, 2009.

———. "NATO May Consider New Surveillance System." *Wall Street Journal,* May 19, 1999.

Goodman, Melvin A. "The Urgent Need to Demilitarize the National Security State." Truthout, October 20, 2009, http://www.truth-out.org/1020095.

Goose, Stephen D. "Soviet Geopolitical Momentum: Myth or Menace? Trends of Soviet Influence Around the World from 1945 to 1986." *Defense Monitor* 15, no. 5 (1986): 1–32.

"The Gorbachev Challenge." *Time,* December 12, 1988.

Gordon, Michael R. "Ex-Soviet Pilot Still Insists KAL 007 Was Spying." *New York Times,* December 9, 1996.

———. "Hussein Wanted Soviets to Head Off U.S. in 1991." *New York Times,* January 20, 2011.

Goulding, David Vincent J. "From Chancellorsville to Kosovo, Forgetting the Art of War." *Parameters* 30 (Summer 2000): 4–18.

Graham, Bradley. "Decline and Fall: Rumsfeld's Dramatic End." *Washington Post Sunday Magazine,* June 14, 2009.

Grandin, Greg. "Muscling Latin America." *The Nation,* January 21, 2010.

Green, Joshua. "Reagan's Liberal Legacy: What the New Literature on the Gipper Won't Tell You." *Washington Monthly,* January/February 2003.

Green, Peter. "Balkans Need U.S. Troops in Kosovo, Berisha Says." *Bloomberg,* September 28, 2010.

Griffin, Charles J. "New Light on Eisenhower's Farewell Address." *Presidential Studies Quarterly* 22, no. 3 (Summer 1992): 469–479.

Grossman, Zoltan. "Imperial Footprint: America's Foreign Military Bases." *Global Dialogue* 11 (Winter/Spring 2009), http://www.worlddialogue.org/content.php?id=450.

Guttenplan, D. D. "Red Harvest: The KGB in America." *The Nation,* May 25, 2009.

Haddick, Robert. "The Bowles/Simpson Defense Cuts Are Not 'Risk Neutral'," *Small Wars Journal Blog,* November 11, 2010, http://smallwarsjournal.com/blog/2010/11/the-bowlessimpson-defense-cuts/ (accessed November 11, 2010, 11:47 a.m.).

Hale, William Harlan. "When the Red Storm Broke." *American Heritage Magazine* 12, no. 2 (February 1961), http://www.americanheritage.com/articles/magazine/ah/1961/2/1961_2_4.shtml.

Hartung, William. "Pentagon Welfare: The Corporate Campaign for NATO Expansion." *Multinational Monitor,* March 1998.

Hedgpeth, Dana. "GAO Blasts Weapons Budget." *Washington Post,* April 2, 2008.

Herken, Gregg. *Cardinal Choices: Presidential Science Advising from the Atomic Bomb to SDI.* Palo Alto, CA: Stanford University Press, 2000.

Hersh, Seymour. "The Online Threat." *The New Yorker,* November 1, 2010.

Hillyer. Quin. "Reagan's 72nd Birthday Party." *The American Spectator Blog*, http://spectator.org/blog/2011/02/06/reagans-72nd-birthday-party (accessed February 6, 2011, 6:47 a.m.).

Hines, John G., Ellis M. Mishulovich, and John F. Shulle. *Soviet Intentions 1965– 1985*. Vol. I. *An Analytical Comparison of U.S.-Soviet Assessments During the Cold War*. Vol. II. *Soviet Post–Cold War Testimonial Evidence*. BDM Federal, Inc., September 22, 1995, http://www2.gwu.edu/~nsarchiv/nukevault/ebb285/.

Holmes, Anthony J. "Where Are the Civilians? How to Rebuild the U.S. Foreign Service." *Foreign Affairs* 88, no. 1 (January/February 2009): 148–160.

Hulen, Bertram. "Marshall Abjures Politics or '48 Race; Takes Up New Post." *New York Times*, January 22, 1947.

"In Foreign Territory." *New York Times*, June 12, 2006.

"Inquest on China." *New York Times*, August 6, 1949.

Isaacson, Walter. "Archive: Reagan for the Defense." *Time*, March 21, 2008.

———. "Madeleine's War." *Time*, October 10, 1999.

James, Eric. "Two Steps Back: Relearning the Humanitarian-Military Lessons Learned in Afghanistan and Iraq." *Journal of Humanitarian Assistance*, October 2003.

Jervis, Robert. "International Primacy: Is the Game Worth the Candle?" *International Security* 17, no. 4 (Spring 1993): 52–67.

Jian, Chen. "The Sino-Soviet Alliance and China's Entry into the Korean War." Cold War International History Project, Working Paper No. 1. Washington, DC: Woodrow Wilson International Center for Scholars, June 1992.

Johnson, Susan R. "Making Dissent Meaningful Again." *Foreign Service Journal*, February 2010.

Johnston, Lauren. "Iraqi Drones Not for WMD." Associated Press, August 24, 2003.

Kaplan, Fred. "Has Obama Turned Against Israel?" *Slate*, March 17, 2010.

Keller, Bill. "The World According to Colin Powell." *New York Times Magazine*, November 25, 2001.

Kennan, George F. "Memorandum for the Minister." *New York Review of Books* 48, no. 7 (April 26, 2001).

Komer, Robert W. *Bureaucracy Does Its Thing: Institutional Constraints on U.S.-GVN Performance in Vietnam*. Santa Monica, CA: RAND Corporation, 1972.

Krepon, Michael, and Geoffrey D. Peck. "Another Alarm on Soviet ABMs." *Bulletin of the Atomic Scientists* 41, no. 6 (June/July 1985): 34–36.

Kristol, Irving. "The Neoconservative Persuasion." *The Weekly Standard*, August 25, 2003.

Liang, John. "Defense Department IG 'Refocusing' Audit Priorities." *Inside the Pentagon*, September 16, 2010.

Lilla, Mark. "The Pleasures of Reaction." *New Republic*, February 27, 2008.

Luce, Henry R. "The American Century." *Life*, February 17, 1941.

MacArthur, Douglas. "The Old Soldier's Last Command" (Part VII: MacArthur Reminiscences). *Life* 54, no. 4 (July 24, 1964): 36–53.

Mandelbaum, Michael. "Overpowered? Questioning the Wisdom of American Restraint." *Foreign Affairs*, May/June 2010.

Mann, James. "Book Review of 'Churchill' by Paul Johnson." *Washington Post*, January 3, 2010.

Martz, Ron. "Fewer Resources Straining Missions." *Atlanta Constitution*, April 24, 1997.

Maze, Rick. "Gates Lobbies for More Funds—For State." ArmyTimes.com, March 30, 2009.

McMaster, H. R. "This Familiar Battleground." *Hoover Digest*, October 2009.

Mulchahy, Kevin V. "Walt Rostow as National Security Adviser, 1966–69." *Presidential Studies Quarterly* 25, no. 2 (Spring, 1995): 223–236.

Muñoz, Carlos. "Pentagon Debates Strategy for Bolstering Future Stability Operations." *Inside the Pentagon*, April 9, 2009.

Murphy, Cullen, and Todd S. Purdum. "Farewell to All That," *Vanity Fair*, February 2009.

"The Nation: Defense Under Fire." *Time*, May 14, 1956.

"New State Department Releases on the 'Future of Iraq' Project." National Security Archive Electronic Briefing Book No. 198. September 1, 2006, http://www.gwu.edu/~nsarchiv/NSAEBB/NSAEBB198/index.htm.

Nitze, Paul H., Oral History Interview [90], Harry S. Truman Library, http://www.trumanlibrary.org/oralhist/nitzeph1.htm (accessed on February 24, 2009).

Nixon, Richard. "Asia After Viet Nam." *Foreign Affairs* 46 (October 1967): 111–125.

Noah, Timothy. "Elizabeth Cheney, Deferment Baby: How Dick Cheney Dodged the Vietnam Draft." *Slate*, March 18, 2004.

Nottberg, Tyler. "Once and Future Planning: Solarium for Today." The Eisenhower Institute, 2002, http://www.eisenhowerinstitute.org/about/living_history/solarium_for_today.dot.

"Nuclear Facts, Science Fictions." *New York Times*, March 27, 1983.

"Obama Ponders Compromise Tax Plan." *Financial Times*, November 12, 2010.

Paik, Koohan. "Living at the 'Tip of the Spear.'" *The Nation*, May 30, 2010.

Patrick, Stewart, and Kaysie Brown. *The Pentagon and Global Development: Making Sense of the DOD's Expanding Role.* Washington, DC: Center for Global Development, November 2007.

Perry, Mark. "The Petraeus Briefing: Biden's Embarrassment Is Not the Whole Story." ForeignPolicy.com, March 13, 2010.

"Personal Memorandum Andropov to Brezhnev, 1 December 1979." Cold War International History Project, http://www.wilsoncenter.org.

Peters, Katherine McIntire. "U.S. Counterterrorism Efforts Flounder in North Africa, GAO Says." *Government Executive*, August 5, 2008.

Pfaff, William. "Mac Bundy Said He Was 'All Wrong.'" *New York Review of Books*, June 10, 2010.

Philips, Alan F. "20 Mishaps That Might Have Started Accidental Nuclear War." Nuclearfiles.org, http://www.nuclearfiles.org/menu/key-issues/nuclear-weapons/issues/accidents/20-mishaps-maybe-caused-nuclear-war.htm.

Pincus, Walter. "How Foreign Policy Functions Shifted to the Pentagon." *Washington Post*, August 4, 2008.

Pogue, Forrest. "The Military in a Democracy: A Review: American Caesar." *International Security* 3, no. 4 (Spring 1979): 58–80.

Power, Samantha. "Bystanders to Genocide." *Atlantic Monthly*, September 2001.

"The Presidency: What I Meant to Say . . ." *Time*, September 23, 1946.

"President Bush's Letter of Instruction to Chiefs of Mission," Generic Letter of Instructions to Chiefs of Mission, facsimile dated October 4, 2004.

Priest, Dana, and William M. Arkin. "A Hidden World, Growing Beyond Control." *Washington Post*, July 19, 2010.

———. "National Security Inc." *Washington Post*, July 20, 2010.

———. "The Secrets Next Door." *Washington Post*, July 21, 2010.

"Prospects for China." *New York Times*, August 7, 1949.

Ricks, Thomas E. "Briefing Depicted Saudis as Enemies." *Washington Post*, August 6, 2002.

Rogin, Josh. "Mullen Goes to Bat for State Department Budget." *The Cable*, http://thecable.foreignpolicy.com/posts/2010/05/24/mullen_goes_to_bat_for_state_department_budget (accessed May 24, 2010, 6:02 p.m.).

Rosenau, William, and Austin Long. *The Phoenix Program and Contemporary Counterinsurgency*. Santa Monica, CA: RAND Corporation, 2009.

Ross, Benjamin. "Who Named the Neocons?" *Dissent*, Summer 2007.

"Rummy and His Generals: An AFJ Roundtable on the State of American Civil-Military Relations." *Armed Forces Journal*, June 2006.

"Rumsfeld Kills Crusader Artillery Program." *USA Today*, May 8, 2002.

"SALT II and the Growth of Mistrust," Conference #2 of the Carter-Brezhnev Project, A Conference of U.S. and Russian Policymakers and Scholars Held at Musgrove Plantation, St. Simons Island, Georgia, May 6–9, 1994, 26–27, http://www.gwu.edu/~nsarchiv/nukevault/ebb285/doc03.PDF.

Schlesinger, Stephen. "Bush's Low Ratings Reflect Pre-9/11 Views." *New York Observer*, April 23, 2006.

Scott Tyson, Ann. "Gates Warns of Creeping Militarization." *Washington Post*, July 16, 2008.

Shanker, Thom. "G.I.'s to Fill Civilian Gap to Rebuild Afghanistan." *Washington Post*, April 23, 2009.

Sheikh, Fawzia, "DOD Official Urges Removing Hurdles to Cooperation in Stability Ops." *Inside the Pentagon*, February 5, 2009.

———. "DSCA Revamping DOD Manual's Humanitarian Assistance Guidance." *Inside the Pentagon*, April 23, 2009.

———. "Joint Staff, USAID Pick Five Countries for Bid to Prevent Crisis." *Inside the Pentagon*, January 22, 2009.

Shribmen, David. "U.S. Experts Say Soviets Didn't See Jet Was Civilian." *New York Times*, October 10, 1983.

Silverstein, Ken. "The Trillion-Dollar Arms Scam." *Lies of Our Times* 4, no. 8 (November 1993): 13–16.

Simon, Alexander. "The Patriot Missile: Performance in the Gulf War Reviewed." Washington, DC: Center for Defense Information, July 15, 1996, http://www.cdi.org/issues/bmd/patriot.html.

Sorley, Lewis. "Creighton Abrams and Active-Reserve Integration in Wartime." *Parameters* 21, no. 2 (Summer 1991): 35–50.

Spence, Jonathan D. "The Enigma of Chiang Kai-shek." *New York Review of Books* 56, no. 16 (October 22, 2009).

Sprenger, Sebastian. "DOD Oversight of '1206' Program Moves to Special Ops Office." *Inside the Pentagon*, May 14, 2009.

———. "Joint Staff Paper Predicts Decade-Long Interagency Shortfalls." *Inside the Pentagon*, January 29, 2009.

Stimson, Henry L. "The Decision to Use the Atomic Bomb." *Harper's Magazine*, February 1947.

Stone, Jeremy. "Reviews." *Bulletin of the Atomic Scientists,* January 1985.

"Tapes Show Johnson Saw Vietnam War as Pointless in 1964." *New York Times*, February 15, 1997.

"To the Geneva Summit: Perestroika and the Transformation of U.S.-Soviet Relations." National Security Electronic Briefing Book No. 172. November 22, 2005, http://www.gwu.edu/~nsarchiv/NSAEBB/NSAEBB172/index.htm.

Toner, Robin. "Trust in Military Heightens Among Baby Boomers' Children." *New York Times*, May 27, 2003.

"Transcript of CPSU CC Politburo Discussions on Afghanistan, 17–19 March, 1979." *Cold War International History Project Bulletin*, no. 8/9, http://www.wilsoncenter.org/topics/pubs/ACF193.pdf.

Tuchman, Barbara. "If Mao Had Come to Washington: An Essay of Alternatives." *Foreign Affairs* 51, no. 1 (October 1972): 44–64.

Turse, Nick. "A My Lai a Month." *The Nation*, November 13, 2008.

United States Department of Defense. *Quadrennial Defense Review Report*, February 2010.

United States Elections Project, Department of Public and International Affairs, George Mason University, http://elections.gmu.edu/voter_turnout.htm.

United States Government Accountability Office. "DOD and State Need to Improve Sustainment Planning and Monitoring and Evaluation for Section 1206 and 1207 Assistance Programs." GAO-10-431, April 15, 2010.

United States Senate. "Embassies as Command Posts in the Anti-Terror Campaign. A Report to Members of the Committee on Foreign Relations, 109th Congress, Second Session." Washington, D.C.: U.S. Government Printing Office, December 15, 2006.

Vanden Heuvel, Katrina, and Stephen F. Cohen. "Gorbachev on 1989." *The Nation,* November 16, 2009.

Weathersby, Kathryn. "Korea, 1949–50: To Attack, or Not to Attack? Stalin, Kim Il Sung, and the Prelude to War." *Cold War International History Project Bulletin,* no. 5 (Spring 1995): 1–9.

———. "New Russian Documents on the Korean War: Introduction and Translations." *Cold War International History Project Bulletin,* no. 6/7 (Winter 1995): 30–84.

Weiner, Tim. "Military Accused of Lies Over Arms." *New York Times,* June 28, 1993.

Wheeler, Winslow. "The New Pentagon Budget: Paying Even More; Still Buying Less." Military.com, January 29, 2010, http://www.military.com/opinion/ 0,15202,209782,00.html.

———. "Pentagon Reform: If Not Now, When? If Not This Crowd, Who?" April 2009, http://pogoarchives.org/m/ns/wheeler-presentation-20090219 .pdf.

Will, George. "A Dog in That Fight?" *Newsweek,* June 12, 1995.

Williams, Rebecca. *Section 1206 and FMF: A Global View.* May 5, 2010, http:// thewillandthewallet.org/2010/05/05/section-1206-and-fmf-a-global-view/.

Withers, George, et al. "Ready, Aim, Foreign Policy: How the Pentagon's Role in Foreign Policy Is Growing, and Why Congress—and the American Public—Should Be Worried." Center for International Policy, the Latin America Working Group Education Fund, and the Washington Office on Latin America, March 2008, http://www.lawg.org/storage/documents/ ready%20aim.pdf.

Interviews

Adams, Gordon. Washington, D.C., July 19, 2008, and September, 24, 2008.

Adams, Gregory Elias. Washington, D.C., August 4, 2008, and May 21, 2009.

Alterman, John. Washington, D.C., August 17, 2004.

Atwood, Brian. Phone interview, June 24, 2010.

Bach, Bruce. NATO Headquarters, Brussels, April 29, 1999.

Baker, Colonel Donald. NATO Headquarters, Brussels, April 27, 1999.

Baltazar, Thomas P. Washington, D.C., September 26, 2008.

Barber, Ben. Washington, D.C., October 28, 2008.

Bourne, Christopher M. Washington, D.C., May 14, 2010.

Clad, James. Washington, D.C., July 6, 2010.

Clayman, Paul. Washington, D.C., September 6, 2008.

Cole, Beth. Phone interview, May 15, 2009.

Crocker, Ryan. Washington, D.C., August 17, 2004.

Freeman, Chas. Washington, D.C., July 14, 2010.

Funk, Stephanie. Djibouti City, November 25, 2008.

Ganyard, Steve. Washington, D.C., August 22, 2010.

Gatti, Stefano. NATO Headquarters, Brussels, April 27, 1999.

Gelb, Leslie, New York City, July 15, 2010.

Gnehm, Edward. Washington, D.C., October 3, 2008.

Hughes, Paul. Washington, D.C., February 17, 2009.

Keith, Kenneth. Washington, D.C., July 6, 2004.

Laney, James. Seoul, Summer, 1994.

Laudato, George. Washington, D.C., June 15, 2009.

Looney, General Edward. Washington, D.C., Summer, 1995.

Lumpe, Lora. Washington, D.C., July 22, 2008.

Madden, Dan. Washington, D.C., August 31, 2008.

Mallory, C. King. Phone interview, August 7, 2008.

Mitchell, Sandra. Washington, D.C., April 25, 2003.

Monahan, William. Washington, D.C., May 22, 2009.

Rumbaugh, R. Russell. Washington, D.C., July 25, 2008.

Rupp, George. Phone interview, September 10, 2008.

Sauvereux, Paul. NATO Headquarters, Brussels, April 30, 1999.

Scowcroft, Brent. Washington, D.C., October 2, 2009.

Simonyi, Andras. NATO headquarters, Brussels, April 30, 1999.

Walden, Richard. Phone interview, April 18, 2003.

Whelan, Theresa M. Washington, D.C., November 11, 2008.

Wilson, Joseph. Santa Fe, July 26, 2010.

Withers, George. Washington, D.C., May, 28, 2009.

Zinni, Anthony. Reston, VA. May 8, 2010.

ACKNOWLEDGMENTS

I am grateful to Crown Publishers editor Sean Desmond, who, after my failure to woo the publishing world with the concept of a "biography" of the U.S. State Department, urged me to recast it as a history of modern American militarism and its consequences. Though responsible for a stable of Thoroughbred A-listers, Sean still found time to groom my unruly drafts into something worthy of Crown's readership. I was also privileged enough to have in my corner Sean's colleagues, publicity and marketing experts Seth Morris, Patty Berg, and Dannelle Catlett.

During my research for the book, Anthony Zinni and Brent Scowcroft were exceedingly generous with their time given the pressing demands for their wise counsel on national security and global affairs. It was an interview with Ambassador Joe Wilson in 2004 that convinced me this was a project worth pursuing. Chas Freeman readily shared with me his many firsthand accounts of key Cold War inflection points, as did the inimitable and tireless Leslie Gelb. Christopher Bourne graciously offered me his time and insights into the state of civilian-military relations in America today.

Esther Kaplan at the Nation Institute invested in me the resources to report firsthand how American troops are assuming the burden of our depleted civilian aid and diplomatic agencies. Andrew Maxwell-Hyslop, who years ago beat my first book into shape and who remains a dear friend and shadow editor, went through draft chapters and came back with smart suggestions for improving them. Hugh Pope, my former colleague and most elegant houseguest, as well as renowned writer, adventurer, and Orientalist, is an inspiration in more ways than he'll ever know.

My wife, Christina Balis, edited the first draft of the book as well as the next seven versions that followed over a two-year period. She also spent dozens of man hours making sense of my source notes. The scope of her contribution is inestimable, particularly as it coincided with the arrival of another full-time job, our son, Atticus. My parents, John and Josephine Glain, and my sister, Sandy, faithfully acquitted themselves as a full-service support group when I desperately needed one, as they have for as long as I can remember.

Finally, I am indebted to the legions of men and women who serve in our nation's military and diplomatic corps—particularly those among the harried junior ranks—who have helped guide me through complex and at times hostile corners of the empire in the quarter century I've lived and worked abroad. Theirs is an authentic and valuable understanding of a world that has too often paid the price of Washington's queered impressions of it. While they don't make U.S. foreign policy, the world might well be a better place if they did.

Index

About the Author

STEPHEN GLAIN is an author and journalist with twenty-five years of experience working in the United States and abroad. In 1987 he set out for Hong Kong, where he worked with the local *South China Morning Post* and the *International Herald Tribune* before settling three years later at the *Wall Street Journal*. For the next ten years, as a *Journal* correspondent, he covered Asia and the Middle East from bureaus in Seoul, Tokyo, Tel Aviv, and Amman. His first book, *Mullahs, Merchants, and Militants: The Economic Collapse of the Arab World*, was published in 2004. From his base in Washington, D.C., he has spent the last decade covering and interpreting global and U.S. domestic news for *Newsweek International*, *The New Republic*, *The Atlantic Monthly*, *The Nation*, the *Washington Post*, *The Progressive*, the *Financial Times*, *Institutional Investor*, *Gourmet*, *Smithsonian*, and other publications.